The Legal, Real and Converged Interest in Declaratory Relief

International Arbitration Law Library

VOLUME 48

Editors

Professor Julian D.M. Lew QC has been involved with international arbitration for more than forty years as counsel, as arbitrator and as an academic. He is the founder and has been the Head of the School of International Arbitration, Centre for Commercial Law Studies, Queen Mary University of London since its creation in 1985. He is now an independent international arbitrator at 20 Essex Street, London.

Stavros Brekoulakis is Professor at Queen Mary University of London and an associate member of 3 Verulam Buildings (Gray's Inn). He is a leading academic in international arbitration and has led, or been involved in, several projects with ICCA, ICC Commission and ILA. He also acts as an independent arbitrator and has been appointed as chairman, sole arbitrator, co-arbitrator and emergency arbitrator under the rules of all the major arbitration rules.

Introduction

Since its first volume published in 1993, this authoritative practitioner-oriented series has published in-depth and analytical works on niche aspects of international arbitration, authored by specialists in the field.

Objective

This authoritative and established series covering in-depth analyses of niche areas appeals to both practitioners and academics. The series includes specific monographs and PhD dissertations of high quality, which are practical and cover issues not fully explored in general texts.

Frequency

A volume is published whenever an interesting topic presents itself.

The titles published in this series are listed at the end of this volume.

The Legal, Real and Converged Interest in Declaratory Relief

Beata Gessel-Kalinowska vel Kalisz

Wolters Kluwer

Published by:
Kluwer Law International B.V.
PO Box 316
2400 AH Alphen aan den Rijn
The Netherlands
E-mail: international-sales@wolterskluwer.com
Website: lrus.wolterskluwer.com

Sold and distributed in North, Central and South America by:
Wolters Kluwer Legal & Regulatory U.S.
7201 McKinney Circle
Frederick, MD 21704
United States of America
Email: customer.service@wolterskluwer.com

Sold and distributed in all other countries by:
Air Business Subscriptions
Rockwood House
Haywards Heath
West Sussex
RH16 3DH
United Kingdom
Email: international-customerservice@wolterskluwer.com

ISBN 978-94-035-1244-0

e-Book: ISBN 978-94-035-1245-7
web-PDF: ISBN 978-94-035-1250-1

To Grzegorz, Józef and Klemens

[A declaration is] one of the most valuable contributions that the courts have made to the commercial life of this country

Lord Atkin, 1919
Spettabile consortio Consortio Veneziano di Armamento e Navigazione v Northumberland Shipbuilding Co., Ltd (1919) 121L.T. 628 at 635

Table of Contents

Preface and Acknowledgements

Finally, I would like to thank Bartek Swietlik and Izabela Bukowińska for their efforts in editing the text of this book and to editorial and production teams of Wolters Kluwer for their help and support in bringing this book to publication.The idea of this book arose at the juncture of my three main areas of professional interest. Firstly, as a result of my great attention to comparative law which, in my conviction, enables a better and wider look at the system of law within which we practise. This intellectual habit was inculcated in me by my great Professor Jerzy Rajski back in my student days. Secondly, studies on remedies for breach of representations and warranties in M&A transactions have shown what peculiarities of declaratory relief and remoteness of its prerequisites may be encountered in Germanic systems of law, including my, as it were, native Polish law. Finally, my international arbitration practice and academic research have demonstrated how a different approach might be adopted if cases are considered outside the strict confines of national legal orders and decided on the basis of legal intuition. Pushed on from this juncture by these basic considerations, I set out to analyse the legal interest in its comparative law dimension and from the perspective of the access to justice principle, arriving at the conclusion that a change in perception is necessary.

My great debt of gratitude is owed to Professor Marek Michalski for his inspiration and guidance.

My studies as a visiting academic at the Law Faculty of Oxford University and, later on, at Cambridge University within the Herbert Smith Visiting Professors Programme have been very helpful. I would like to express my special thanks to Wolfson College, Oxford University and, in particular, to Professor Bettina Lange and Dr Tomasz Gromelski for all their support.

Chapter 4 would not have been written without the support of the ICC International Court of Arbitration, and especially its President, Alexis Mourre and Alexander Fessas, Secretary General, for which I am very greatful.

As I was writing this book, I had the privilege of meeting many people who shared their knowledge and time in discussing questions of concern to me at the given point of my work and who helped me in all and sundry ways. I am grateful to all of them. My special thanks go to Dr Artur Kotowski, Professor Marcin Matczak, Christian Schmidt – my partner at GESSEL, Jeremy Woolf, Dr Rafał Zakrzewski and to all the contributors of reports to this book – Ulrich Kopetzki, Alicja Zielińska-Eisen, Tobias Strecker, Joanna Kisielińska-Garncarek, Dr Nino Sievi - for their valuable comments.

Finally, I would like to thank Bartek Świetlik and Izabela Bukowińska for their efforts in editing the text of this book and to editorial and production teams of Wolters Kluwer for their help and support in bringing this book to publication.

List of Abbreviations

AAA	American Arbitration Association
ABGB	Austrian Civil Code
AGO	*Allgemeine Gerichtsordnung für die Preußischen Staaten*, Prussia General Court Rules
AktG	*Aktiengesetz*, German Stock Corporation Act
ASGG	Austrian Labour and Social Courts Act
Austrian CCP	Austrian Code of Civil Procedure
BAG	*Bundesarbeitsgerich*, German Federal Labour Court
BGE	Official collection of decisions of the Swiss Federal Tribunal
BGH	*Bundesgerichtshof*, German Federal Supreme Court
CHF	Swiss Franc(s)
DIS	*Deutsche Institution für Schiedsgerichtsbarkeit*, German Arbitration Institute
ECHR	European Court of Human Rights
FGO	*Finanzgerichtsordnung*, German Fiscal Procedure Code
Former German CCP	*Civilprozessordnung*, German Civil Procedure Code of 30 January 1877
German CCP	*Zivilprozessordnung*, German Civil Procedure Code
GKG	*Gerichtskostengesetz*, German Courts' Fees Act
ICC	International Chamber of Commerce
InsO	*Insolvenzordnung*, German Insolvency Code
KG	*Kammergericht*, German Higher Regional Court of Appeal
KSchG	*Kündigungsschutzgesetz*, German Dismissal Protection Act
LAG	*Landesarbeitsgericht*, German Regional Labor Court
LCIA	The London Court of International Arbitration

LG	*Landgericht*, German District Court(s)
M&A	Merges and Aquisitions
NDA	Non-disclosure Agreement
OLG	*Oberlandesgericht*, German Higher Regional Court
Polish CCP	Polish Code of Civil Procedure
RG	*Reichsgericht*, Supreme Court of the German Reich
RVG	*Rechtsanwaltsvergütungsgesetz*, German Attorneys' Fees Act
SIAC	Singapore International Arbitration Centre
SGG	*Sozialgerichtsgesetz*, German Social Courts Act
SHA	Shareholders Agreement
SPA	Share Purchase Agreement
Swiss CC	Swiss Civil Code
Swiss CCP	Federal Code of Civil Procedure
Swiss FDEB	Federal Act on Debt Enforcement and Bankruptcy
Swiss Patents Act	Federal Act on Patents for Inventions
VIAC	Vienna International Arbitration Center
VwGO	*Verwaltungsgerichtsordnung*, German Administrative Procedure Code

Definitions

Declaratory Relief Norm	as defined in Chapter 5 section §5.06 *infra*
Model Legal Interest	as defined in Chapter 5 section §5.01 *infra*
Sample Case or Sample Judgement	Judgement of 30 October 1990, I CR 649/90, Lex 158145 (Polish Supreme Court)

CHAPTER 1
Declarations in General

§1.01 PRELIMINARY REMARKS

Declarations are encountered in dispute resolution, both in litigation and arbitration. Declarations are a part of every judicial decision, but they do not always appear in the dispositive section of the award or the order. As a rule, they are an element of the reasoning or *obiter dictum* of the award/judgement. As an example, we have statements which pronounce a given contract to be breached, as claimed by the claimant, and therefore the tribunal or the judge, in the dispositive section, orders respondent to pay a certain amount of money as compensation. The declaration relates, then, purely to the reasoning for the award/judgement.

Each court decision which, for any reason, dismisses the claim for performance or constitutive claim is by its nature a negative declaration, stating absence of the entitlement sought.

There can be pure declarations which constitute the main and only relief claimed, envisaged in the dispositive part of the judgement, as is typical for the Continental jurisdictions. Taking a breach of contract as an example, there is the declaration stating invalidity of a given contract and nothing more.

There can be a declaration and subsequent coercive measure sought, like in situations in which the claimant asks the court or tribunal to declare the breach of contract and to award appropriate damages. Both the declaration and order to pay a particular sum as damages is provided in the dispositive. This is more typical to common law jurisdictions. In the Continental view, the declaration sought in such a context will most probably be dismissed and will form a part of the reasoning of the judgement rather than of its dispositive part.

The court may give a declaration as an interim measure, similar to the one provided in Rule 25 of CPR,[1] which is a final decision in the sense that it is not necessarily followed by a coercive measure.

What is a matter of interest in this book is a declaration which is, on the one hand, a remedy sought and, on the other, is granted or denied by the judicial authority in the dispositive section of the judgement. The main focus is on the declarations which relate to the private law realm, with especial emphasis on commercial relationships, resolved within the framework of commercial arbitration.

§1.02 DECLARATORY RELIEF IN LITIGATION

Declarations as a remedy, even if differently shaped, appear in the body of positive law of basically all national legislative systems other than those of France and the jurisdictions following the French model. Interestingly enough, this phenomenon includes also common law jurisdictions. Declarations appeared in English law in the nineteenth century by way of a statutory instrument, namely the Chancery Act of 1850, which broke the judges' reluctance to issue mere declarations. The present procedural rule is CPR 40.20 states that *'[t]he court may make binding declarations whether or not any other remedy is claimed'*. In United States, meanwhile, there is the Declaratory Judgement Act,[2] which provides in § 2201: 'In a case of actual controversy within its jurisdiction [...] upon the filing of an appropriate pleading, may declare the rights and other legal relations of any interested party seeking such declaration, whether or not further relief is or could be sought. Any such declaration shall have the force and effect of a final judgment or decree and shall be reviewable as such.' § 2202 continues: 'Further necessary or proper relief based on a declaratory judgment or decree may be granted, after reasonable notice and hearing, against any adverse party whose rights have been determined by such judgment.'

In Germanic jurisdictions, the norm is more or less similar. Under § 256 of the German CCP, a complaint may be filed to establish the existence or non-existence of a legal relationship or to recognize a deed or to establish that it is false, provided that the plaintiff has a legal interest[3] in having the legal relationship, or the authenticity or the falsity of the deed, established by a judicial ruling. Similar norms may be found in § 228 of the Austrian Code of Civil Procedure (Austrian CCP), Article 88 in connection with Article 59(2)(a) of the Federal Code of Civil Procedure (Swiss CCP) and Article 189 of the Polish Code of Civil Procedure (Polish CCP).

1. English Civil Procedure Rules 1998 (SI 1998/3132) as amended by Rule 13 of the Civil Procedure (Amendment) Rules 2001 (SI 2001/256).
2. 28 U.S. Code Chapter 151 – Declaratory Judgments, https://www.gpo.gov/fdsys/pkg/USCODE-2009-title28/pdf/USCODE-2009-title28-partVI-chap151-sec2201.pdf (accessed 31 January 2019).
3. In the translation at https://www.gesetze-im-internet.de/englisch_zpo/englisch_zpo.html (accessed 24 January 2019) the term 'legitimate interest' is used, however 'legal interest' is more proper.

French civil procedure does not expressly provide for, or separately regulate, declaratory relief. Article 31 of French Code of Civil Procedure (French CCP)[4] provides in general that the right of action is available to all those who have a legitimate interest (actual interest) in the success or dismissal of a claim. Due to the fact that French law provides no specific regulation of the declaratory relief, the popularity of this remedy is limited. Thus, the opinion that judicial practice should evolve towards broader use of declarations has been voiced; such a development would be welcomed, in particular, in contractual matters, where interpretation of contractual stipulations is necessary.[5]

Israel, as a representative of the mixed jurisdictions group, provides in section 75 of the Israeli Courts Act of 1984[6] that 'any court hearing a civil case has jurisdiction to grant a declaratory judgement, an order to do or not to do, an order to perform, and any other remedy as the court sees appropriate in the circumstances at hand'. This provision, broadly drafted, vests the court with wide powers similar to the solutions adopted in English law.

Comparing briefly the above examples, some preliminary remarks may be ventured. First, the regulatory method – again, with the exception of France and French adopters – has been followed the world over in broadly the same way: short and economic in words, leaving it to the doctrine and to practise, as the case maybe, to develop the detailed applications. Second, in Germanic jurisdictions, the concept of legal interest is introduced as a prerequisite to granting a declaration, while in the common law tradition no such limitation exists. Third, in the common law tradition it is emphasized that a declaration can be granted in addition to a coercive measure or independently, what is *prima facie* not allowed under Continental legal regimes. Fourth, in common law jurisdictions there is no limitation as to the subject matter of the declaration, while in the Germanic regulations it is limited to legal relationships or rights.

Declarations are identified in legal writing as a distinct remedy in all jurisdictions, regardless of whether they belong to the common law or Continental law tradition. In Germanic jurisdictions, there are three principal categories of remedies: claims for performance (*Leinstungklagen)*, which are aimed at seeking performance, including orders to perform or to abstain from performance or to tolerate performance; constitutive claims (*Gestaltungsklagen)*, which are aimed at seeking creation or modification or extinction of a right or legal relationship; and, finally, declaratory claims (*Feststellungsklagen*), aimed at seeking declaration of existence of a certain right or legal relationship, defined in English language as constitutive claim.[7]

4. https://www.legifrance.gouv.fr/content/download/1962/13735/version/3/.../Code_39.pdf (accessed 31 January 2019).
5. Patrick Dunand & Maria Kostytska, *Declaratory Relief in International Arbitration*, 29(1) J. Intl. Arb. 1, 9 at fn. 42 (2012).
6. https://wipolex.wipo.int/en/legislation/details/15289 (accessed 24 February 2019).
7. Michael Schneider, *Non-Monetary Relief* in *International Arbitration: Principles and Arbitration Practice,* in *Performance as a Remedy: Non-Monetary Relief in International Arbitration* 3, 8 (Michael Schneider & Joachim Knoll eds., ASA Special Series 24–25, 2011).

In common law jurisdictions, there is more variety in taxonomies.[8] For example, A. Burrows[9] based his taxonomy on functional criteria identifying the following primary functions that remedies may serve: compensation, restitution, punishment, compelling performance of positive obligations, preventing a wrong, compelling the undoing of a wrong and declaring rights. Within the latter category, there are three types of remedies: nominal damages, contemptuous damages and declarations. Nominal damages, in the trivial sum of 2 to 10 pounds, can be awarded in the case of certain torts and of breach of contract, where proof of damage is not necessary. Nominal damages, then, are not in any sense compensatory in their function. They serve only to declare that the defendant has perpetrated a wrong against the claimant and, hence, that the claimant's rights have been infringed.[10] Contemptuous damages likewise serve as nominal damages, but in the context of some defamation cases. Declaration is a remedy, generally regarded as statutory, but of equitable origin, by which a court simply pronounces on the rights or the remedies of the parties.

N. Andrews provides a simpler taxonomy, dealing with damages, debt, specific performance injunctions or declarations.[11]

M. J. Tilbury,[12] referring to Australian law, finds that a claimant may obtain three basic reliefs in civil proceedings: declaratory, where the plaintiff seeks an authoritative judicial statement of the legal relationship; substitutionary, which consists of a judgement in money as a substitute; and a specific relief, where the plaintiff seeks by way of the judgement to coerce the defendant in some particular way.

In F.H. Lawson's[13] taxonomy, declarations coexist with action for performance leading to coercive judgements and constitutive judgements which automatically change the legal position of the parties. The starting point, quite surprisingly, for this taxonomy was the German division of claims into *Leistungsklagen*, *Feststellungsklagen* and *Gestaltungsklagen*.

In French doctrine, the classic taxonomies divide remedies into personal, real and mixed, or those relating to movables/chattels and to immovables/real property, although the classic distinction into claims for performance, claims for declaration and constitutive claims is also present in the modern doctrine.[14]

8. Rafał Zakrzewski, *Remedies Reclassified* 23–42 (2005). Provided a summary of various taxonomies, proposed by Andrew Burrows, Roderick P. Meagher, Michael J Tilbury, David M. Walker, Neil Andrews and his own. In all these taxonomies, declaration appears as a distinct remedy.
9. Andrew Burrows, *Remedies for Torts and Breaches of Contract* 9–11 (3rd ed., 2004).
10. *Ibid.*, at 589. The author refers as an example to *C and P Haulage v Middleton* [1983] 1 WLR 1461.
11. Neil Andrews, *English Civil Procedure* para. 34.48 (2003); more andvanced taxonomies *see ibid.*, at 34.53 et seq.
12. Michael J. Tilbury, *Civil Remedies, Vol I Principle of Civil Remedies* 1028 (1990). *See also* Zakrzewski, *supra* n. 8, at 36.
13. Frederick H. Lawson, *Remedies of English Law* 12 (2nd ed., 1980).
14. Schneider, *supra* n. 7, at 9.

§1.03 DECLARATORY RELIEF IN ARBITRATION

Following N. Blackaby et al.,[15] the arbitral tribunal's power to grant appropriate relief is based on the arbitration agreement and the applicable arbitration law. The basis on which an arbitral tribunal orders a remedial measure flows from the arbitration agreement of the parties. While an arbitration agreement could specify the remedial measures to be conferred upon the tribunal, the common practice is that it will be silent on that point. In such circumstances, the tribunal must look to the relevant arbitration rules or applicable national law on arbitration to determine the types of relief available to it.

Domestic regulations, as a rule, do not provide particular guidelines in this respect, save for Article 48 of the English Arbitration Act 1996,[16] which explicitly provides that, unless otherwise agreed by the parties, the tribunal has the power to make a declaration as to any matter to be determined in the proceedings and to order payment of a sum of money in any currency. Also, it is sometimes stated that the tribunal has the same powers as the court to order a party to do, or refrain from doing, anything to order specific performance of a contract (other than a contract relating to land) and to order the rectification, setting aside or cancellation of a deed or other document.[17]

The arbitration rules also do not provide any specific regulations concerning available remedies. The ICSID Convention, under Article 48, requires arbitrators to deal with every question submitted to them,[18] which should include also declarations. Article 43(a) of the American Arbitration Association (AAA) Arbitration Rules[19] empowers the tribunal to grant any remedy or relief that the arbitrators deem just and equitable and within the scope of the agreement of the parties. The Uncitral Model Rules do not address the issue at all, and neither do other arbitration rules.

It is generally admitted that the arbitral tribunal has at its disposal any remedy which is available to the state courts.[20] Moreover, some authors emphasize that arbitral tribunals are not restricted to the remedies which are available to the courts at the seat.[21] The power to grant any remedy which, in the opinion of the arbitrators, is

15. Nigel Blackaby et al., *Redfern and Hunter on International Arbitration* 315 para. 5.08 (5th ed., 2009).
16. https://www.legislation.gov.uk/ukpga/1996/23/contents (accessed 31 January 2019).
17. Previously, Art. 26 of Irish Arbitration Act provided for similar enumeration, but the version from 2010 adopts in general the Model Law with the only reference to specific performance in section 2020: 'Without prejudice to the generality of the Model Law, an arbitral tribunal shall, unless otherwise agreed by the parties, have the power to make an award requiring specific performance of a contract (other than a contract for the sale of land).' *See* also Singapore International Arbitration Act s. 12(5) (2012)
18. Christoph Schreuer, *Non-Pecuniary Remedies in ICSID Arbitration*, 20 Arbitration International 325, 325 (2004).
19. AAA Commercial Arbitration Rules, https://www.adr.org/sites/default/files/CommercialRules_Web.pdf (accessed 31 January 2019).
20. Julian D.M. Lew & Loukas A. Mistelis, et al., *Comparative International Commercial Arbitration* 649 (2003).
21. Klaus Peter Berger, *International Economic Arbitration* 339 (1993); this opinion was voiced in the context of interim meaures.

feasible may be derived even from the standard wording of arbitration clauses proffered by the arbitration institutions. The usual wording typically includes language to the effect that all disputes arising out of or in connection with the contract shall be finally settled under the relevant rules by the arbitral tribunal. Unless the parties choose to make some caveat, the term 'any dispute' must mean full liberty to file claims for resolution, including declaratory claims.[22]

The taxonomies of remedies at the arbitrators' disposal presented in legal writings are similar to those of courts remedies[23] and always include declarations. N. Blackaby et al.[24] posit the following detailed and casuistic classification: monetary compensation; punitive damages and other penalties; specific performance and restitution; injunctions; declaratory relief; rectification; adaptation of contracts and filling gaps; interest and costs. Lew, Mistelis, Kroll propose: specific performance, damages /monetary compensation, declaratory relief, gap-filling and contract adaptation, punitive damages and exemplary damages, restitution, rectification and injunctive relief.[25]

§1.04 LEGAL, REAL AND CONVERGED INTEREST IN DECLARATORY RELIEF: THE CONCEPT OF THE BOOK

The discussion set out in this book is focused on the notion of 'legal interest', a term introduced into the body of civil procedure law in Germanic jurisdictions as a prerequisite to granting the declaration. As could be observed from the earlier description, Germanic systems enable a claimant to seek declaratory relief only if he can demonstrate a sufficient legal interest before the court examines his case on the merits. This is a serious limitation of access to justice. The law does not give precise guidelines how this term could be interpreted. All features of the legal interest are a product of established jurisprudence and doctrine. Analysing this problem more thoroughly affirms the conviction that the understanding of the term is not clear on one hand, and too restrictive on the other. This, in turn, brought the reflection that the concept of legal interest as a prerequisite to declaratory relief requires more attention and a certain redefinition in order to respond to the needs of modern legal dealing. Seeing as this problem is not exactly predominant on the agenda of academic discourse, this book is meant to fill this gap. Its purpose is not to present pure, dogmatic analysis of the doctrine in the Germanic family of law, even if such an analysis is contained herein. The intention was to capture the perceived spirit of the law reflected in its normative mirrored picture. This is why the opinions of judges and scholars are confronted with statistical data and intuitions of non-judges, meaning users and clients of the system, parties to arbitration and litigation proceedings and arbitrators. The current perception of the legal interest was filtered through the concepts of the theory

22. *See* more: Chapter 4, section §4.01[B] *infra*.
23. M.E. Schneider rightly points out that the taxonomy of remedies available in arbitration, as proposed by numerous authors, is very similar to those adopted by the general courts, Schneider *supra* n. 7, at 13.
24. N. Blackaby et al., *supra* n. 15, at para. 9.39.
25. Lew, Mistelis, et al., *supra* n. 20, at 649.

of justice and juxtaposed with English practice and law, providing a new dimension for analysis. This comparative approach is based on the assumption that the legal system of every society faces essentially the same problems, but goes about solving these problems by quite different means, though very often with similar results. Comparative law does not simply criticize what it finds, but can claim to show the way to a better mastery of the legal material, to deeper insights and thus, in the end, to better law.[26] All these methods were adopted to formulate final conclusions for perfection of the legal interest concept both in *de lege lata* and *de lege ferenda* dimension.

The book is constructed in the following way. Chapter 2 contains a comparative study of the legal interest concepts in the four jurisdictions belonging to Germanic family of law. In Germany, the concept of legal interest was created as a master pattern transplanted later on to other Germanic jurisdictions. Austria appears to be the closest heir of the German idea. Switzerland is an example of very interesting evolution of the German concept in a more liberal and pragmatic direction. The fourth representative is Poland, where the German concept of legal interest was adopted through both the German and Austrian traditions, then survived the rough ride of socialistic reforms, and which might be assessed as the most conservative system. Based on these four examples, Chapter 2 adopts a synthetic approach, showing the common features of legal interest in the Germanic system and presenting this as a certain model, further analysed in Chapter 5.

The comparative study contained in Chapter 2 is not aimed at full presentation of particular legal systems and readers are directed in this respect to the reports, contributed by my colleagues from the respective jurisdictions, namely Ulrich Kopetzki (Austria), Alicja Zielińska-Eisen, Tobias Strecker (Germany), Joanna Kisielińska-Garncarek (Poland) and Nino Sievi (Switzerland) and to make reference easy are annexed to this book. The reports present short characteristics of the relevant systems of law.

Then, in Chapter 3, the Germanic concept is juxtaposed with a system which is on the other extreme, i.e., the English system as an example of a common law system. English law provided a convenient example, being as it is a common law jurisdiction which was also part of the European Union. Both English and Germanic law provide for declaratory relief by statutory instrument, granting judges much discretion. The legal interest was so general that the courts had much room to interpret it. English law did not recognize any legal interest in the context of declaratory relief. There is, however, a complex of premises limiting the judges' discretion, which I have called 'real interest' for the purpose of juxtaposition. Such juxtaposition brings an interesting perspective for observing what results could be achieved if no limitations in the form of strict prerequisites are introduced into the law and how such a situation can be assessed from the perspective of the user.

Chapter 4 is devoted to analysis of arbitration practice and the approach of arbitrators to the strict notion of legal interest contained in domestic law, in terms of being national or a-national. The latter situation was important for showing how

26. Konrad Zweigert & Hein Kötz, *Introduction to Comparative Law* 34 (2011).

arbitration can neutralize the strict notion of the legal interest if based on certain intuitions of arbitrators only. The findings of this chapter are illustrated by a significant number of arbitration awards. The research encompassed two sorts of arbitration awards. First, it was examined how the problem of declarations was approached by arbitrators in one business sector, namely disputes relating to merges & aquisitions (M&A) transactions. Seeing that, as it turns out, not many of them took the issue of legal interest into consideration, the declaratory awards dealing with legal interest were analysed, regardless of the business sector in question.

The final Chapter 5 includes a critical approach to legal interest in light of procedural justice principles, which were proposed as a new cognitive perspective where both English law and arbitration practice contribute a number of arguments. The analysis in this part, conducted from the perspective of the principles of access to justice perspective, is based on dogmatic review of the system of law, encompassing civil substantive and procedural law enriched by theory of justice, comparative analysis and statistical analysis.

Terminology. Discussion of issues relating to declaratory relief inevitably revolves around three basic terms: claim, relief and remedy. These notions may diverge and/or overlap, depending on the adopted taxonomy, local jurisdictional context, the translation and the procedural or substantive approach. For example, the term 'remedy' may have different meanings even within the English language. R. Zakrzewski defines a remedy as the rights that arise from a particular class of events, i.e., the making of certain judicial commands or statements. He points out, however, that it is also used in other meanings, like only primary rights, or only secondary rights, an action or cause of action or means of enforcement of a court order.[27]

For purposes of this book, I will use the term declaratory remedy/declaratory relief interchangeably in both meanings: as a declaration sought by the parties and a declaration granted by the judicial authority. In the context of comments referring to both I will use the generic term 'declarations'. There will also be a need to use the phrase 'declaratory judgements' or 'declaratory awards', which will mean judicial or arbitral pronouncements whereupon the declaratory remedies shall arise. 'Declaratory claim' or 'declaratory action' will be used, as a rule, in the context of the tripartite system of claims: for performance, for declaration and for reshaping the legal relationship (constitutive claim).

27. Zakrzewski, *supra* n. 8, at 7–22.

CHAPTER 2

The Concept of 'Legal' Interest in Germanic Systems of Law

§2.01 GENESIS OF THE CONCEPT OF DECLARATORY RELIEF

Introduction. In contemporary Europe, it is not an easy task to trace the pedigree of various legal institutions. There are three substantial factors which contribute to this state of affairs. First, there is the series of historical and political changes, especially those occurring after WWI. Second, the European Union has driven unification and harmonization processes in contemporary Europe, resulting in juridical amalgamations. Third and finally, after WWII there has been considerable Anglo-Americanization of law through legislative processes and through legal transplants into practice. All the above have resulted in some interesting mixtures, so that even the classical division of Continental jurisdictions into the Romanistic and Germanic family of law has blurred to some extent.[1]

This, however, cannot be said about the concept of declaratory relief as adopted in the Germanic family of law, in countries such as Germany itself, Austria, Switzerland or Poland. Legal interest is clearly a German concept, formulated in the nineteenth century, in the spirit of historical pandectists. The pandectist school of the nineteenth century, starting with Carl Friedrich von Savigny, aimed at dogmatic and systemic study of Roman material. Their approach was marked by exaggerated dogmatism. As tackled by the pandectists, application of law became a merely 'technical' process, based on 'logical necessity' of abstract concepts and completely detached from practical reasons, societal value judgements and ethical or economic considerations. The pandectist method puts conceptual calculations before societal needs, and social, ethical or practical problems were not explored to work out the most ergonomic

1. Beata Gessel-Kalinowska vel Kalisz, *Mixing Legal Systems in Europe; the Role of Common Law Transplants (Polish Law Example)*, 25(4) ERPL 789, 789 et seq. (2017).

solutions.[2] In such an intellectual climate, the institution of declaratory relief, equipped with the abstract concept of legal interest as a prerequisite, was introduced to the legal order of German law and consequently copied by other legislatures hailing from the Germanic family.[3] This observation is important for understanding the rationale informing the regulation and starting point for deliberation on eventual necessity of redefinition of the whole concept.

The present analysis covers four jurisdictions belonging to the Germanic family of law. German and Austrian laws are the most obvious representatives of the family, German law being the predecessor of other regulations, and Austrian law – a direct heir of the German concept. Swiss law is an interesting example of departure from the classic conservative concept towards a more pragmatic approach, however not entirely cutting ties with it. Polish law consciously inherited the entire Germanic concept together with the doctrinal baggage coming from both Germany and Austria, retaining it through the socialistic era. From today's vantage point, the Polish approach can probably be qualified as the most conservative one if jurisprudence as well as doctrine are considered. The need for liberalization in this respect was not found compelling by the Polish judicature or by doctrine.

This chapter is not aimed at detailed description of specific jurisdictions – such analysis is endeavoured further below, in Annex. At this point, I would just like to present the overall model representative of Germanic jurisdictions which can be constructed based on the demonstrated similarities and to highlight certain departures, in particular jurisdictions which can be discussed in the context of possible developments as guidelines for other members of the Germanic legal family. Such transplants are the natural way of growth in the legal field. In this chapter, I will first discuss the genesis of declaratory relief and then proceed to the current status and features of the common Germanic model of legal interest as a prerequisite to granting declarations.

§2.02 HISTORY OF THE GERMAN CONCEPT

The history which led to the current regulation of declaratory relief has been competently presented by M. Jacobs.[4] Here is a brief summary, which shows that, contrary to the common law system, in the Germanic tradition declarations were a regular tool often used in civil proceedings long before the current concept was adopted in the nineteenth century. Due to this long history, it is not possible to designate a single institution from which declaratory reliefs directly derive – Roman law, medieval German law as well as canon and Italian laws have all had certain impact on the legal concept of *Feststellungklage* in the German legal system.

Roman law recognized, among others, the so-called *actiones praeiudiciales*, which had a declaratory essence and are frequently considered as an ancient basis for contemporary declaratory reliefs. Their field of application was relatively narrow and

2. Konrad Zweigert & Hein Kötz, *Introduction to Comparative Law* 140–141 (2011).
3. In Romanistic legal family members, like France or Belgium, declarations as a distinct type of claim do not appear at the normative level of the code of civil procedure.
4. Matthias Jacobs, *Der Gegenstand des Feststellungsverfahrens*, 103–104 at paras 5–6 (2005).

limited to declaration of existence of marital status or class status. It is disputed whether *actiones praeiudiciales* might have been used for declaration of existence of contractual relationships or rights. Although it was possible to bring *actiones praeiudiciales* as independent claims, they often served as the first stage of more far-reaching proceedings for performance. Roman law also recognized what the German nomenclature refers to as *Kautions-* and *Liberationsklagen* of declaratory nature; *Kautionsklage* served mainly as security for future claims which were not due yet. The function of the *Liberationsklage* served as an instrument of the defendant, who had a *defence* against a claim. By raising this kind of action, the 'defendant' could obtain a judgement declaring formally the alleged claim/legal relation as not existent/valid. Therefore, the *Liberationsklage* can be considered as comparable to the negative declaratory relief (*negative Feststellungsklage*).

The concept of declaratory reliefs was developed in canon and Italian laws within the so-called *Extraiudicialappellation*. The claimant could seek judicial protection by bringing a declaratory claim to be resolved by the Pope (or an appellate judge nominated by the Pope) if this was necessary to prevent violation of claimant's rights in the future. Such threat of violation must have been considered as justified and serious. Even more important for the historical development of declaratory reliefs in Germany were two specific institutions: *remedium ex lege diffamari* and *remedium ex lege Si condendat,* known later to German lawyers (since the seventeenth century) as *Provokationen.* This specific legal construct assumed that if the claimant was able to prove the existence of risk of violation of his rights, he could 'provoke' the counterparty to enter into the proceedings with the purpose of settling the matter conclusively and prevent future disputes regarding the issue at stake. In other words, the claimant could request the court to order the respondent to bring his own claim or, otherwise, be precluded from initiating such proceedings in the future. In this way, the declaratory claimant could remove the state of his legal uncertainty and force the counterparty to engage in the proceedings. If the respondent had initiated the proceedings for performance, the 'provocation' (merely declaratory) proceedings must have been brought to an end. The purpose of *remedium ex lege diffamari* was to obtain a declaration on non-existence of respondent's right, whereas *remedium ex lege Si condendat* was an instrument to protect the debtor against loss of a defence. The effect of such action would be that the action for performance was precluded. If the claim for performance was not raised in time, the defence was considered as practically established.

Although the above-mentioned did not constitute declaratory claims per se, to some extent they had the same purpose as *Festellungsklage* under ZPO – to prevent infringement of rights and to achieve legal certainty. *Remedium ex lege diffamari* is currently considered to be the most important remedy of declaratory purpose until the codification of civil procedure in Germany.

The remedies of Roman and canon origins gave rise to more modern versions of *Feststellungsklage* (earlier referred to as *Annerkennungsklage* – claims for acknowledgement). For instance, Roman actiones praeiudiciales were refined to apply to a broader scope of legal relationships. Also, the prerequisites of declaratory reliefs evolved over time. In this aspect, two notions recognized under German law must be distinguished: *Rechtsverletzung* (violation of rights) and *Rechtsinteresse* (legal interest).

Specific declaratory actions served as precautionary measures applicable in the event of violation of claimant's rights. In other words, the right to bring declaratory action constituted a simple reflection of infringement of claimant's subjective rights. Mere risk of infringement was not enough. What is more, claimant's rights could have been subject to civil proceedings solely if they were due at the moment of bringing the claim.

The above-mentioned prerequisite was subject to mitigation, evolving from 'violated right' (*verletztes Recht*) towards 'right requiring protection' (*schutzbedürftiges Recht*). It was particularly prevalent in the case of continuing obligations (*Dauerschuldverhältnisse*), in which the creditor usually demonstrated the need for protection of his future claims. It was generally deemed reasonable to grant the claimant a certain right to establish the existence or non-existence of a legal relationship instead of initiating the proceedings every time some part of the claim became due. In the beginning, such modern declaratory action was permissible solely if the declaration sought was 'ancillary, in connection with claim for performance of due receivables'. It is interesting to note that such hesitance to grant a mere, or 'naked', declaration was also typical in England.[5] Then, autonomous declaratory actions became permissible – subject to respondent's consent and, subsequently, solely on the basis of the prerequisite of legal interest on the side of the claimant (*Rechtsinteresse*), replacing the prerequisite of violation of rights.

The diversity of legal remedies aiming at declaration at different levels led to gradual codification of this legal concept and harmonization thereof.

Already in 1793, a simplified version of *remedium ex lege diffamari* was incorporated into § 2 of General Court Laws for the Prussian States, thirty-second title (*Allgemeine Gerichtsordnung für die Preußischen Staaten–Prussia General Court Rules* (AGO)). In accordance with the aforementioned provision, if the claimant knew that his counterparty might assert a right to be invoked against the claimant, he was able to initiate the proceedings himself in order to prove that this right is inaccurate or invalid. A specific kind of declaratory relief was also introduced with reference to inheritance law.

The second half of the nineteenth century brought several codifications of claims for declaratory/acknowledgment reliefs (*Feststellungs-* and *Anerkennungsklage*), although their application was limited to particular territories of Germany. The first codification was introduced to the Procedural Code of Baden dated 1851 (*Badische Prozessordnung*). In accordance with its § 278, the claimant was entitled to seek a declaration on a legal relationship and rights connected therewith (even if the violation of his rights had not taken place) if the respondent expressly or tacitly consented thereto or if the claimant had a legal interest (*rechtliches Interesse*) in bringing such claim. At the same time, the drafts of civil procedural codes in the Grand Duchy of Hessen dated 1856 (*Großherzoglicher Zivilprozeßentwurf*) abandoned the prerequisite of legal interest, making declaratory relief possible solely upon the respondent's consent. The prerequisite of legal interest was also reflected in the laws of Kurhessen (1863).

5. *See* Chapter 3 *infra*.

As can be seen from the above, the legal prerequisites and the potential object of declarations varied. The legal interest prerequisite was established for good with the first general procedural regulation of declaratory relief introduced by § 231 of the German Code of Civil Procedure of 30 January 1877, which came into force on 1 October 1879 (German FCCP). Its adoption was preceded by lively disputes regarding the character and content of the *Feststellungsklage* legal concept. Certain doubts were expressed as to the prerequisite of legal interest in obtaining a declaration which might be too imprecise. On the contrary, the legal interest was necessary to protect the courts against a flood of unnecessary claims.[6] At a certain point, the codification committee even toyed with the notion of not introducing declaratory reliefs into procedural law at all.

Under § 231 German FCCP, one could claim for a declaration of the existence or non-existence of a legal relationship if one had a legal interest in the judicial declaration. The legislature expressly acknowledged that there might be a legitimate interest in obtaining a declaration that a legal relationship exists even before a specific claim becomes due, as it affords legal certainty to the parties. The prerequisite of legal interest was introduced in order to prevent abuse of declaratory reliefs and to lay down certain boundaries for such actions on the side of the claimant. Following amendments in 1898, § 231 German FCCP became § 256 (1) German CCP, but the content of the norm remained unchanged.

§2.03 IMPACT OF THE GERMAN CONCEPT ON OTHER GERMANIC JURISDICTIONS

The German declaratory relief norm, unchanged in its wording since 1877, provides:

> [t]o declare the existence or non-existence of a legal relationship, to recognize a document or to establish that it is false, an action may be filed, if the claimant has a legal interest in having the legal relationship or the authenticity or falsity of the document established soon by a judicial ruling.[7]

This wording has inspired, whether directly or indirectly, a number of other Germanic jurisdictions. The framers of the Austrian Code of Civil Procedure (Austrian CCP) of 1879 adopted large parts of the German FCCP almost verbatim, including those on declaratory relief. And thus, § 228 of the Austrian CCP, unchanged since its initial enactment,[8] provides that:

6. Carl Hahn, *Die gesammten Materialien zu den Reichs-Justizgesetzen, Zweiter Band: Die gesammten Materialien zur Zivilprozeßordnung und dem Einführungsgesetz zu derselben vom 30. Januar 1877. Zweite Abtheilung*, 255 (1881).
7. Translation by Tobias Strecker, Alicja Zielińska-Eisen: Auf Feststellung des Bestehens oder Nichtbestehens eines Rechtsverhältnisses, auf Anerkennung einer Urkunde oder auf Feststellung ihrer Unechtheit kann Klage erhoben werden, wenn der Kläger ein rechtliches Interesse daran hat, dass das Rechtsverhältnis oder die Echtheit oder Unechtheit der Urkunde durch richterliche Entscheidung alsbald festgestellt werde.
8. Annex I.I by Ulrich Kopetzki *infra*.

> [o]ne can bring an action for the determination of the existence or non-existence of a legal relation or a right, on the recognition of the authenticity of a document or the determination of its inauthenticity, if the claimant has a legal interest that said legal relation or right or authenticity of a document shall be determined shortly by a judicial decision.[9]

There is, however, one difference which becomes apparent when comparing the Austrian statute and the German one: the object of the claim encompasses not only declaring a legal relationship, but also a legal right, yet in practice this does not amount to a major change, assuming that subjective rights are being established based on the legal relationship.

In Switzerland,[10] most of the old cantonal codes of civil procedure contained a specific provision dealing with declaratory actions providing that declaration of existence or non-existence of a legal relationship or the authenticity or inauthenticity of a document is only possible if a specific legal interest is proved. These provisions were evidently inspired by § 256 of the German FCCP. Later on, the Swiss Federal Tribunal held that, also outside of these cantonal acts, Swiss federal law envisages a general declaratory action.[11] The Swiss Federal Tribunal reasoned that federal private law had to ensure its uniform enforcement.[12] In line with this decision, a specific provision on declaratory actions was included in the Swiss CCP,[13] which replaced all cantonal codes of civil procedure in 2011. Article 88 of the Swiss CCP currently provides that '[b]y filing an action for a declaratory judgement, the plaintiff demands that the court establish that a right or legal relationship exists or does not exist'.[14]

Admissibility of such actions depends, as in other Germanic jurisdictions, on the claimant having an interest in its claim. The approach taken in regulating it, however, is different. Under Article 59(2)(a) of the Swiss CCP, similar to the French style of regulation,[15] in each type of claim (not only in the case of declaration) it is examined *ex officio* whether the claimant has sufficiently demonstrated a legitimate interest in the requested relief (*Rechtsschutzinteresse*). In practice, however, it does not differ from the German approach in this respect, as existence of such legitimate interest for actions of performance or money is generally presumed.[16] An interesting change could be observed at the level of textual formation of the respective law, as the term *rechtliches*

9. Translation by Ulrich Kopetzki: Es kann auf Feststellung des Bestehens oder Nichtbestehens eines Rechtsverhältnisses oder Rechtes, auf Anerkennung der Echtheit einer Urkunde oder Feststellung der Unechtheit derselben Klage erhoben werden, wenn der Kläger ein rechtliches Interesse daran hat, dass jenes Rechtsverhältnis oder Recht oder die Urkundenechtheit durch eine gerichtliche Entscheidung alsbald festgestellt werde.
10. Annex IV.I by Nino Sievi *infra*.
11. Decision of the Swiss Federal Tribunal dated 30 October 1984, published in BGE 110 II 352.
12. Decision of the Swiss Federal Tribunal dated 30 October 1984, published in BGE 110 II 352, consideration no. 1: Cf. also decision of the Swiss Federal Tribunal dated 1 July 1993, published in BGE 119 II 368, consideration no. 2.a.
13. (19 December 2008), SR 272, https://www.admin.ch/opc/en/classified-compilation/20061121/index.html (accessed 4 December 2018).
14. Article 88 Mit der Feststellungsklage verlangt die klagende Partei die gerichtliche Feststellung, dass ein Recht oder Rechtsverhältnis besteht oder nicht besteht.
15. *See* Art. 31 of French CCP.
16. Annex IV.II by Nino Sievi *infra*.

Interesse (legal interest) as used in § 92[17] of the Zurich CCP of 1913 and § 59 of the Zurich CCP of 1976[18] has been changed into *schutzwürdiges Interesse* (legitimate interest) in the current Swiss CCP. This is a meaningful alteration, as it has been observed that the perception of legal interest has evolved in a more liberal direction so as to include not only strict legal, but also factual interest.[19]

The situation in Poland[20] was different than in the two countries just discussed. Until 1918, parts of Poland were incorporated into Germany and Austria, so the German FCCP and CCP were directly applicable in large parts of the Polish-speaking realm for over 100 years. German inspirations were inevitable. After 1918, there were two stages of legislative creation in the newly independent Polish state. The first one occurred directly after 1918 within the framework of a special codification commission employing the comparative method and drawing certain inspirations from modern European legal systems in order to create the former Polish Code of Civil Procedure (Polish FCCP). In the case of declaratory reliefs, the codification commission chose to refer mainly to the German institution of *Feststellungsklage*. Article 3 of the Polish FCCP stated that anyone may seek judicial protection while preventing violation of his right and, at the same time, while having legal interest in establishment of a legal relationship or right. At that point in time, declaratory relief was deemed mainly a precautionary procedural measure, aimed purely at prevention. The legislature opted not to include here declarations as to authenticity of documents, in which case the French regulation was followed.[21] The authors of the Polish FCCP also did not employ the urgency element (*alsbald*), assuming that this is implied in the notion of the very term of 'legal interest'. The second transformation took place after WWII, when Poland found itself under the political influence of the Union of Soviet Socialist Republics. The new Code of Civil Procedure of 1964, remaining in force until today (Polish CCP), included Article 189 of the Polish CCP,[22] providing that the claimant may apply to the court for establishment of the existence or non-existence of a legal relationship or a right if he has legal interest in doing so. Therefore, the possibilities for obtaining a declaration were, *prima facie*, considerably extended and came to more closely approximate the German original.

17. § 92 Zurich CCP 1913: 'Auf Feststellung des Bestehens oder Nichtbestehens eines Rechtsverhältnisses, auf Anerkennung einer Urkunde oder auf Feststellung ihrer Unechtheit kann Klage erhoben werden, wenn der Kläger ein **rechtliches Interesse** [legal interest] daran hat, dass das Rechtsverhältnis oder die Echtheit oder Unechtheit der Urkunde alsbald durch richterliche Entscheidung hergestellt werde.'
18. § 59 Zurich CCP 1976 'Auf Klagen betreffend Feststellung des Bestehens oder Nichtbestehens eines Rechtsverhältnisses oder der Echtheit oder Unechtheit einer Urkunde wird nur eingetreten, wenn ein **rechtliches Interesse** an der Feststellung besteht.'
19. Annex IV.II by Nino Sievi *infra*.
20. Annex III.I. by Beata Gessel-Kalinowska vel Kalisz & Joanna Kisielinska-Garncarek *infra*.
21. Franciszek Ksawery Fierich, *Postępowanie przed sądami okręgowemi* in *Polska procedura cywilna. Projekty referentów z uzasadnieniem. Komisja Kodyfikacyjna R.P., Sekcja postępowania cywilnego*, 328 (1928).
22. Article 189 *Powód może żądać ustalenia przez sąd istnienia lub nieistnienia stosunku prawnego lub prawa, gdy ma w tym interes prawny.*

§2.04 THE NOTION OF LEGAL INTEREST AS A PREREQUISITE

Germanic jurisdictions generally accept classification of remedies accounting for three types: claim for performance (*Leistungsklagen*); constitutive claims shaping legal relationship for future (*Gestaltungsklagen*); and claim for declaratory relief (*Feststellungsklagen*).[23] It is also generally accepted that any court action requires existence of legal interest.[24] In the first two types of claims, such interest is assumed to exist, and is deemed missing only in exceptional circumstances.[25] The claimant has nothing to prove in this respect. In the latter case, the situation is opposite. The requirement to prove an existing interest is regulated by the positive provisions of the relevant codes of civil procedure and is incumbent on the claimant at the outset of the proceedings. Only the Swiss legislative solutions *prima facie* equalize the position of the claimant in all three claims following Article 59(2)(a) of the Swiss CCP; that said, in the practice of the Swiss courts, the situation is the same as in other Germanic jurisdictions.

The legal interest is not a legally defined term. There are a number of features worked out by the jurisprudence and doctrine which, when considered together, may be seen as adumbrating the essence of the term. There is controversy among legal scholars and judges as to the list of these features. The above notwithstanding, each of these features - certainly if taken on its own - is rather vague, leaving the entire concept a bit elusive. On the one hand, it should not be dismissed altogether, as general principles of law allow for the system to be flexible enough to adjust to the changing needs of day-to-day legal practice. On the other hand, if such a general clause is a precondition for the claimant to having his case heard, there arises the legitimate question whether such a decisive limitation of a party's rights does not merit more precise formulation.

Swiss law is again a pragmatic exception. Swiss jurisprudence approached the problem in a more methodical way and produced the test used not only in litigation, but also as a benchmark in arbitration,[26] one which unites all the necessary components of legal interest. The list of these components resembles those named in other jurisdictions.

Legal nature of interest. The interest which must be demonstrated as a prerequisite to granting a declaration must be of a legal nature (*rechtliches Interesse*). This is not, however, a question of being legal or illegal. The notion of legal interest is contrasted with other interests which might constitute a basis for a declaration to claimant's benefit, which could include practical needs of the civil law subjects - economic, scientific or others. Swiss law took a more liberal path, foregoing the adjective 'legal' and introducing the 'legitimate interest' (*schutzwürdiges Interesse)*.

23. Annex I.II by Ulrich Kopetzki *infra*. *See* Jan Grundz in Adolf Baumbach & Wolfgang Laterbach, et al., *Zivilprozessordung mit FamFG, GVG und anderen Nebengesetzen*, § 253, nn. 8–10 (2017).
24. Annex I.II by Ulrich Kopetzki, II.3.A. by Alicja Zielińska-Eisen & Tobias Strecker, III.2.3 by Beata Gessel-Kalinowska vel Kalisz, Joanna Kisielinska-Garncarek, IV.3.1. by Nino Sievi *infra*.
25. Annex II.III[A] by Alicja Zielińska-Eisen & Tobias Strecker *infra*. In Austria, there is a debate whether the claimant's need for legal protection is a general prerequisite or arises only in cases where it is required by specific provision of law, Annex I.III[D] by Ulrich Kopetzki *infra*.
26. *See* Chapter 4, section §4.01 *infra*.

This is not only a mere textual difference. It is generally stated that the interest as a prerequisite may be of a factual nature as well.[27]

Legality of the interest of the claimant derives on the one hand from the object of the declaration, which is a legal right or legal relationship.[28] In other words, legal interest stems from the claimant's uncertainty as to his legal position and/or law.[29] On the other hand, the claimant's legal position must be rooted in the legal order in general.[30] As practice shows, there is no clear-cut division as to what is and what is not a patently 'legal' interest. A desire to gain a mere procedural interest, i.e., the desire to gain a procedural advantage, is not sufficient to establish legal interest (in a case where the problem of definition of jurisdiction was considered) in Austria, but may qualify in Switzerland.[31] Avoiding future difficulties in production of evidence is sometimes qualified as a legal,[32] and sometimes as non-legal interest.[33]

Especial attention is warranted as regards the relation between the legal and economic interest. It is correct that the legal doctrine in Germany in the nineteenth century was dominated by the idealist philosophy. However, starting in particular with Rudolf Jhering this approach came to be increasingly criticized as jurisprudence of concepts (*'Begriffsjurisprudenz'*),[34] which demanded a more pragmatic methodology.[35] The jurisprudence of concepts was replaced by the jurisprudence of interests (*'Interessenjurisprudenz'*),[36] which insisted that interpretation of law should be focused on the interests which the legislature wanted to regulate. Thus, legal doctrine was opened also for commercial considerations. This shift of perspective was not reflected in the wording of the German CCP.[37] But it had a certain influence on interpretation of the relevant statutory provision and its application in court practice. Thus, *the Supreme Court of the German Reich – Reichsgericht (RG)* (Imperial Court of Justice) originally refused to determine the legal interest taking into account the potential effects of the alleged right on the economic and financial status of the plaintiff and to replace the legal interest by an economic or a financial interest.[38] Later judgements, however, acknowledged that the legal interest could be constituted by other interest which could in any way be related to the plaintiff's legal relations, including his economic interest.[39] Therefore, 'practical difficulties with the conceptual delimitation between legal and economic interest'[40] were already observed in the

27. Annex IV.II. by Nino Sievi *infra.*
28. Annex I.III[C] by Ulrich Kopetzki *infra.*
29. Annex III. III Beata Gessel-Kalinowska vel Kalisz & Joanna Kisielinska-Garncarek *infra.*
30. Annex I.VII by Ulrich Kopetzki *infra.*
31. Annex I.III[C] by Ulrich Kopetzki, IV.3.D.b. *infra.*
32. Annex I.III[C] by Ulrich Kopetzki *infra.*
33. *Ibid.*
34. Rudolf von Jhering, *Scherz und Ernst in der Jurisprudenz* 337 (1884).
35. Cf. Karl Larenz, *Methodenlehre der Rechtswissenschaft* 49 (6th ed.,1991).
36. *See* in particular Philipp Heck, *Gesetzesauslegung und Interessenjurisprudenz*, in 112 *Archiv für die zivilistische Praxis*, 6, 8 et seq., 230 et seq. (AcP) (1914).
37. Originally § 231 German FCCP, currently § 256 subpara. 1 German CCP.
38. *See*, e.g., Reichsgericht, judgement of 27 September 1883, Case no. IV 229/83, published in RGZ 10, 368.
39. *See* Jacobs, *supra* n. 4, at 56.
40. *Ibid.*, at 118.

jurisprudence and, to some extent, taken into consideration in drafting other German statutes by replacing the term 'legal interest' (*rechtliches Interesse*) with the notion of legitimate interest (*berechtigtes Interesse*).[41] In the current jurisprudence in Germany, cases where mere economic interest is noted without legal interest are rather rare, but the basic distinction remains valid.[42]

In the cases discussed below, the *prima facie* object of the declarations encompassed legal actions and contracts, however the interest of the claimant was not deemed to be legal. In Poland, a claim aimed at obtaining a declaration of non-existence of a shareholders' resolution referring to appointment of the management board of a company was dismissed in that claimants' interest was not deemed legal. Questioning proper representation of a company aimed at clarification (despite relevant entries in the National Court Register) whether the company is represented by duly authorized persons was assessed solely as a factual interest.[43] A Polish court discerned merely economic, and not legal, interest in a case[44] in which a company sought a declaration of invalidity of a framework contract regarding currency transactions, since it had been already terminated in the past and did not cause any legal effects for the future. Even if the claimant did have certain pecuniary claims arising out of transactions conducted on the basis of the contract in the past, it could demonstrate only an economic (and not legal) interest in obtaining a declaration. At the same time, the court explained that the contract's termination implies effects for the future but does not eliminate the consequences of actions undertaken before service of the termination notice.

The purely economic interest of the claimant was the reason for dismissing the declaration of invalidity of a sale contract executed with respect to real estate between two companies while the claimant was the creditor of one of them.[45] The agreement made to the creditor's detriment should be declared invalid. The Court of Appeal decided that the sale agreement did not have a direct impact on the claimant's legal sphere but could be perceived solely in the context of securing debtor's assets and possible satisfaction of the claim in the future.

A telling difference becomes apparent when reviewing the Swiss approach, which has jettisoned, at the literal as well as practical levels, the word 'legal' as characterizing the requisite interest on claimant's part. Legitimate interest, as a prerequisite for declaratory relief, may be based on purely economic considerations, in particular where uncertainty of a legal relationship inhibits a party's economic freedom.[46] Exemplification of this difference is visible in the approach to the issues of

41. § 55 I Sozialgerichtsgesetz (SGG – Social Courts Act) of 3 September 1953; § 43 I Verwaltungsgerichtsordnung (VwGO – Code of Administrative Court Procedure) of 21 January 1960; § 41 I Finanzgerichtsordnung (FGO – Code of Finance Court Procedure) of 6 October 1965.
42. Annex II.III[G] – 3.21. by Alicja Zielińska-Eisen & Tobias Strecker *infra*.
43. Annex III.III[A] Beata Gessel-Kalinowska vel Kalisz & Joanna Kisielinska-Garncarek *infra* and judgement cited previously, where the claimant intended to collect his debts from the company and wanted to ensure that his future dealings will be conducted with lawfully appointed persons.
44. Annex III.III[C] Beata Gessel-Kalinowska vel Kalisz & Joanna Kisielinska-Garncarek *infra*.
45. Annex III.III[D] Beata Gessel-Kalinowska vel Kalisz & Joanna Kisielinska-Garncarek *infra*.
46. Annex IV.II by Nino Sievi *infra*.

procedural advantages and, in particular, in ascertainment of jurisdiction of the given court. In the aforementioned Austrian case, the question of clarifying jurisdictional matters was not deemed to amount to a legal interest. In a recent Swiss case, after a long discussion in the literature and in the doctrine, the court finally discerned legitimate interest in a situation in which the claimant had initiated a negative declaratory action in Switzerland with the purpose of preventing the counterparty from bringing proceedings in England[47]. The Swiss Federal Tribunal held that, in an international case, a party's interest in having the case considered in a certain forum was sufficient to deem a (negative) declaratory action admissible.

§2.05 THE COMPONENTS CONSTITUTING LEGAL INTEREST

It has been stated above that the basic feature of the interest to be proved by the claimant seeking declaration is an interest which is legal, rather than factual or economic. The Swiss jurisdiction is an exception in requiring a minimum of legitimate interest. As regards other features, the four jurisdictions discussed here do not differ much.

The Swiss Federal Tribunal generally follows a standard test in order to determine whether a claimant has sufficient interest in a requested declaratory relief. However, sufficient interest can also exist outside of this standard test.[48]

Pursuant to the standard test,[49] a declaratory action is admissible if (i) there is an uncertainty (ii) whose continuation is no longer bearable to the claimant and (iii) provided that there is no other relief available to the claimant (hereinafter referred to as the subsidiarity principle). Additionally, (iv) in the case of a negative declaratory action, the claimant's interest must further be balanced against the defendant's interest in not having to conduct the proceedings at that point in time. This test has been adopted so broadly that even in arbitrations where the procedural requirement in the form of classic legal interest does not survive, it is referred to in Swiss cases as a certain benchmark.[50]

Based on the practice and doctrine of all the Germanic jurisdictions discussed here, this list of features should be augmented with the following: (i) the dispute will be definitively settled by the granted declaration, (ii) the uncertainty relates to the particular right or legal relationship rather than to the facts and (iii) the claimant's interest in receiving a declaration is of objective, not only subjective, character. It does not matter anymore whether the legal interest derives from threatened breach or from actual breach, although the latter may have consequences in application of the subsidiarity principle. All the features will be discussed below.

47. Annex IV.III[D][2] by Nino Sievi *infra*.
48. Annex IV.III[C] by Nino Sievi *infra*.
49. *Ibid.*
50. Chapter 4 *infra*.

§2.06 UNCERTAINTY

Uncertainty assumes that there are at least two opposite standpoints of the parties in relation to existence or non-existence of a certain right or relationship. In other words, legal interest stems from the claimant's uncertainty as to his legal position and/or law.[51] Such disagreement is usually evidenced by the parties' assertions or protests.[52] There might be a different approach to the problem of uncertainty regarding how strongly such disagreement should be evidenced and whether it is enough if such uncertainty is perceived by the party subjectively or must be of objective character. Outlooks on the degree of subjective perception differ in various jurisdictions. In Germany, it is sufficient if the parties are in doubt as to their legal relationship, even if the court discerns little justification for such doubt,[53] as long as the uncertainty is rooted in the legal relationship of the parties, not their doubt as to applicability and scope of a general legal norm.[54] The resulting uncertainty must objectively impair or endanger the claimant's position. Therefore, the respondent's mere initiative to examine a legal relationship does not create a legal interest for the claimant[55] - claimant must clearly deny or claim existence of a certain relationship. In this vein, filing of independent proceedings for the taking of evidence is not sufficient to constitute a legal interest of the claimant in the declaration. For legal interest to exist, the respondent would have to expressly allege to have a claim against the claimant.[56] It appears that the degree of disagreement between the parties is treated more seriously in Austria. In cases of so-called 'positive' declaratory relief, legal interest is considered to arise when existence of the disputed legal relation is flatly denied by the respondent, leading to insecurity and uncertainty.[57] Mere factual infringement of the claimant's rights without claiming the existence of a right does not constitute a legal interest in negative declaratory relief. In such a case, where there is no disputed legal situation requiring clarification beyond the incident in question, the claimant may bring an action for an injunction which provides greater legal protection than the requested declaration.[58]

In Poland, it is very clearly stated that claimant's subjective conviction of prevailing uncertainty cannot be sufficient. The court must establish objectively existing uncertainty or endangerment connected with respondent's activities.[59]

---

51. Annex III.III. by Beata Gessel-Kalinowska vel Kalisz & Joanna Kisielinska-Garncarek *infra*.
52. Annex IV.III[C][4] by Nino Sievi *infra*.
53. Annex II.III[E] by Alicja Zielińska-Eisen & Tobias Strecker *infra*.
54. *Ibid.*
55. *Ibid.*
56. *Ibid.*
57. Annex I.III[C] by Ulrich Kopetzki *infra*.
58. *Ibid.*
59. Judgement of 7 March 2013, I ACa 1053/12 (Polish Court of Appeal in Warsaw); Judgement of 2 February 2017, I CSK 137/16 (Polish Supreme Court).

§2.07 UNCERTAINTY UNBEARABLE FOR THE CLAIMANT

In the Swiss test, continuation of the uncertainty must be unbearable to the claimant. This feature is quite specifically designed in Swiss law. The requirement is composed of two elements. On the one hand, the uncertainty must have such an effect on the claimant that it inhibits his economic freedom of decision (*wirtschaftliche Bewegungs- und Entscheidungsfreiheit*).[60] Causing the claimant to make provisions in its balance sheet,[61] hindering a party's investment activities due to uncertainty as to the available funds,[62] influencing a party's credit rating as well as trustworthiness could serve as examples.[63]

However, a party's economic freedom of decision is not considered inhibited if the dispute only concerns a moderate amount.[64] In doctrine, it is argued that the threshold should be set at a low level in order to ensure that access to justice is not denied.[65] This is contradictory to the notion of interest, which, while being 'legal', always deserves protection, independently of its economic value.[66]

The second element of the unbearableness requirement relates to the foreseeable duration of the uncertainty. If the uncertainty will be resolved in the near future anyway, a claimant does not have sufficient interest in a declaratory relief.[67]

This is of particular relevance for negative declaratory actions. If the creditor is about to initiate legal proceedings, the uncertainty is bound to be resolved soon. Accordingly, the Swiss Federal Tribunal has held that a negative declaratory action is not admissible if the initiation of a claim for performance or money is imminent, what by itself is not clear from the Swiss Federal Tribunal's jurisprudence.[68]

The above test is quite unique. First, it relates to the economic interest of the parties, which in principle is not recognized in other Germanic systems. Second, in all other situations no monetary threshold to limit the claims has been instituted. Nevertheless, this approach should be appreciated for its attempt to make the definition of legal interest more predictable.

In other jurisdictions, the unbearable character is related more to the results of the uncertainty for the state of the claimant's affairs. The uncertainty must objectively impair or endanger the claimant's position.[69] Similarly, in Austria,[70] it is crucial that the claimant's interest can be justified by objective factors. There must be a specific and

60. Annex IV.III[C][2] by Nino Sievi *infra*.
61. *Ibid.*
62. *Ibid.*
63. Annex IV.III[A] by Nino Sievi *infra*. Also cf. Annex IV.4.[D][1] by Nino Sievi *infra*.
64. Annex IV.III[C][2] by Nino Sievi *infra*.
65. *Ibid.*
66. Tadeusz Rowiński, *Interes prawny w procesie cywilnym i w postępowaniu nieprocesowym*, 102–103 (1971).
67. Annex IV.III[C][2] by Nino Sievi *infra*.
68. Annex IV.III[D][[2] by Nino Sievi *infra*. The rationale of this requirement is clearly to prevent the courts from being overburdened with unnecessary/frivolous proceedings. When a claim is imminent, it is already evident that the courts will have to address the dispute between the parties anyway. This is a premise also for the next requirement, viz the subsidiarity principle.
69. Annex II.III[E] Alicja Zielińska-Eisen & Tobias Strecker *infra*.
70. Annex I.III[C] by Ulrich Kopetzki *infra*.

current (insofar as objective circumstances seem to seriously and concretely – not only presumably – endanger the claimant's legal position) reason which requires a swift court decision to prevent an actual and serious threat to the claimant's legal position.

§2.08 FINAL SETTLEMENT: SUBSIDIARITY PRINCIPLE

The subsidiarity principle is the product of the three elements derived from the notion of the term legal interest. First, it is raised that the claimant may have a legal interest in a declaration if such granted declaration will settle the dispute once and for all. Second, there is no legal interest where the declaration is to serve as a premise in the other dispute because the claimant has legal interest in these second proceedings and not in the first proceedings. Third, it is the judge who will decide whether objectively, to larger or lesser degree, the chosen path to resolve a controversy is the most proper one, or at least comparable. Therefore, the claimant will be able to demonstrate a proper legal interest only if there is no other relief available to the claimant in the given respect. The subsidiarity principle causes the declaratory relief to be a remedy less valued than others, and one which is not allowed in cases where a more comprehensive remedy is available.

Polish court practice in applying the subsidiarity principle seems to be the most consistent and conservative of the four jurisdictions under consideration. The Polish Supreme Court has confirmed that legal interest shall be perceived as an objective need either to protect the rights of the claimant or to eliminate the uncertainty as to the existence of a legal relationship or right. In the case of a claim for performance, a lack of legal interest is connected with the fact that a declaration would constitute solely one of the prerequisites to grant a claim for performance, e.g., claim for payment.[71] In other words, in such a situation, a claim for declaration loses its autonomous and independent character[72] in that the claimant is able to obtain fuller protection by means of other remedies.[73] As a rule, however, not only a possibility to initiate court action based on a more far-reaching claim disqualifies declaratory relief. The mere possibility of any other remedy, not better but equivalent, likewise excludes existence of legal interest in seeking a declaration of right or legal relationship. There is no room for any discretionary choice between the remedies open to the claimant.[74] Such other, equivalent remedy may be offered not only by civil law, but may also derive from quarters such as the Land and Mortgage Register law or administrative remedies.[75] Only in exceptional situations, usually in cases involving a long-term contract which generates a number of rights and duties of the parties, the court may find an excuse to grant a declaration on validity of the entire contract even if a claim for performance would

71. Annex III.III by Beata Gessel-Kalinowska vel Kalisz & Joanna Kisielinska-Garncarek *infra*.
72. Annex III.II by Beata Gessel-Kalinowska vel Kalisz & Joanna Kisielinska-Garncarek *infra*.
73. Annex III.III[B], III.III[B] by Beata Gessel-Kalinowska vel Kalisz & Joanna Kisielinska-Garncarek *infra*.
74. Annex III.I., III.V[A] by Beata Gessel-Kalinowska vel Kalisz & Joanna Kisielinska-Garncarek *infra*.
75. *See* Annex III.III[B] by Beata Gessel-Kalinowska vel Kalisz & Joanna Kisielinska-Garncarek *infra*.

resolve the given controversy.[76] It depends on the individual perception of the judge deciding the case and on how deeply he delves into examination of the possible consequences of the declaration to be granted.

In Switzerland, the subsidiarity principle is applied in a similar way, but the main focus is on the problem of declaratory versus performance or constructive remedy.[77] The Swiss courts draw the line depending on whether the declaratory action is devised purely as a preparation for a later claim for money or performance because of lacking sufficient interest or because the interest of pursuing procedurally inefficient routes simply is not worthy of protection. The issue of potential alternative administrative or other non-judicial measures was not discussed. It is important to note that a discussion has been initiated in Swiss legal literature concerning the viability of insisting on the subsidiarity principle in the future; in Polish literature, this problem does not raise any reflection.

As A. Zielińska-Eisen and T. Stracker maintain, in Germany there is no expressed principle of subsidiarity stating that a claim for declaratory relief is always inadmissible if other claim is available.[78] Rather, the relationship between the two types of claims is framed in terms of the requirement of legal interest.[79] Nevertheless, in general, the claimant lacks legal interest in the declaratory relief if it is possible for it to obtain an enforceable judgement. This, however, does not always make declaratory relief subsidiary to actions for performance. Despite the possibility to claim for performance, a claim for declaratory relief could be admissible due to reasons of procedural economy if the declaration suffices to resolve the dispute sensibly and appropriately,[80] with long-term and complex contracts providing a good example. There are also more examples from the realm of competition law.[81]

The status in Austria is similar.[82] In accordance with broadly accepted lines of judicial authority and unanimous legal doctrine, the requisite legal interest for obtaining declaratory relief is missing if the claimant could reach its aim in a simpler way or if there is an option available that grants more extensive legal protection. Conversely, if the court finds that all other legal remedies available would lead to greater procedural efforts or to less legal protection, it will affirm legal interest. As noted, it is not always the case that an action for performance will provide greater legal protection than an action for declaratory relief. Contrary to the Polish approach, declaring a premise to other proceedings, which will be of *res judicata* character, may amount to a valid legal interest. The courts presiding over future proceedings will be bound by the previous determination of the preliminary question.

Similarly, if not all claims are already due - especially in cases of continuing obligations - a declaratory relief clarifying the entire underlying legal relation is

76. *Ibid.*
77. Annex IV.[III][C][3] by Nino Sievi *infra.*
78. Annex II.III[G] by Alicja Zielińska-Eisen & Tobias Strecker *infra.* Certain exceptions however may apply, *see* Chapter 5, section §5.07 *infra.*
79. Annex II.III[G] by Alicja Zielińska-Eisen & Tobias Strecker *infra.*
80. *Ibid.*
81. *Ibid.*
82. Annex I.III[D] by Ulrich Kopetzki *infra.*

possible,[83] irrespective of whether an action for performance would be possible for some claims arising out of the contractual relationship that have already become due.[84] The same principle applies if claimant merely requests a declaration on liability for future damage even though some damage has already occurred. In such cases, the courts have allowed actions for declaratory relief for possible future damage even though claimant could already have brought an action for performance with respect to the harm already sustained from the same incident.[85]

§2.09 THE OBJECT OF THE DECLARATION

There is a strong correlation between the object of the declaration and the legal interest itself. The interest of the claimant in clarifying the uncertainty must relate to the legal relationship or to a subjective right. In all the jurisdictions examined - Switzerland included, which appears to be logically inconsistent - uncertainty as to the facts cannot constitute a legal interest. The only facts which can be subject to declaration under the normative Austrian and German provisions is the authenticity of documents, which on the contrary is not possible in Poland and Switzerland.

The distinction between the facts and the subjective rights may appear clear enough in theory, in practice it gives rise to further problems. For example, in Austria, ascertaining termination of the contract as invalid is qualified as a statement of fact,[86] however if rephrased into a declaration that the contract still exists because its termination was improper changes the qualification into statement of legal right.[87] The need for a more flexible approach to such facts drove the development of the concept of legally relevant facts and law-creating facts by the judiciary in Poland.[88] For instance, it is generally admissible for the court to declare the fact of a contract's execution, tortious behaviour or contribution to incurred loss.[89] All these factual circumstances imply per se an impact on the respective legal positions of the parties. The mere fact that a contract was effectively made entitles the parties to bring claims in the event of improper performance or non-performance thereof. Similarly, a partner has a legal interest in requesting the declaration that a civil partnership agreement has been effectively terminated on a specific date - such declaration aims de facto at establishment of existence or non-existence of a legal relationship or right.[90] This concept is clearly denied in Germany.

83. Annex I.III[B] by Ulrich Kopetzki *infra*.
84. *Ibid*.
85. *Ibid*.
86. It must be emphasized that the will of the civil law subjects as such is a fact rather than a right, therefore prima facie validity of the declaration of intent is, as a rule, qualified as a statement of fact, cf. Rowiński, *supra* n. 66, at 94.
87. Annex I.IV[D] by Ulrich Kopetzki *infra*.
88. Annex III.IV[A] by Beata Gessel-Kalinowska vel Kalisz & Joanna Kisielinska-Garncarek *infra*.
89. Annex III.III by Beata Gessel-Kalinowska vel Kalisz & Joanna Kisielinska-Garncarek *infra*.
90. *See* Annex III.IV[A] by Beata Gessel-Kalinowska vel Kalisz & Joanna Kisielinska-Garncarek *infra* and specifically the judgement of 15 November 2000, I ACa 947/00 (Court of Appeal in Katowice) cited, which is contrary to the findings of the above-mentioned Austrian case.

The following may, as a rule, be an object of a declaration: validity of the relevant provisions of the contract[91] (but not validity of certain legal acts like statements, declarations or notices),[92] interpretation of the relevant provisions of the contract[93] and legal qualification of the contract.[94] Future relationships or abstract questions of law cannot be declared.

There is an important difference as regards declaration of liability for future damages. Logically, if the subsidiarity principle is followed as logic suggests, where the damage did not materialize yet but all other elements of the cause of action are already actualized, the claim for declaration would be a logical option because the claim for performance is not yet available to the aggrieved party. But this is not unanimously accepted.[95] This rationale informs Swiss court verdicts. If the harm has not yet occurred or is still increasing, a claim for money is simply not possible yet, and an application for declaration that a defendant is liable for future damages stemming from its unlawful actions is considered admissible.[96]

Also in Austria, according to established jurisprudence, declaratory relief can be granted if no damage has yet occurred.[97] As indicated above, Austrian judgements used to be inconsistent, and there has been considerable evolution on this matter. While, in some cases, declaratory relief of liability for future damages was allowed if at least some damage had already occurred,[98] it has by now become established that this is not a mandatory requirement. The OGH has decided that, under certain circumstances, no damage must have occurred in order to allow a declaration of liability for future damages. The courts consider, *inter alia*, that by granting the requested declaration, they facilitate avoidance of future disputes. In fact, such future dispute may be avoided altogether because respondent may now plan his activities so as not to actually be held liable for any damage. Furthermore, if the damage eventually did occur, the dispute would be limited since the question of liability will already have been determined.[99]

Similarly in Germany, motions for a declaration that the respondent is liable for certain future damages when their amount cannot be calculated yet or if harm has not occurred yet but will likely – or at least possibly[100] – occur under normal circumstances is regularly admitted by the courts.[101] The Polish judiciary, meanwhile, has arrived at completely opposite results. Only future harm resulting from personal injury, as a matter of exception, may become the object of a declaration of liability, and such a declaration will be barred in any other circumstances.[102]

---

91. Annex I.IV[A] by Ulrich Kopetzki *infra*.
92. Annex I.IV[D] by Ulrich Kopetzki *infra*.
93. Annex I.IV[A] by Ulrich Kopetzki *infra*.
94. Annex II.IV[A][2] by Alicja Zielińska-Eisen & Tobias Strecker *infra*.
95. *See also* Chapter 4 *infra*.
96. Annex IV.III[C][3] by Nino Sievi *infra*.
97. Annex I.IV[B] by Ulrich Kopetzki *infra*.
98. *Ibid.*
99. *Ibid.* This stance is however further inconsistent with general position of Austrian courts, that only entire legal relationship can be declared and not particular elements of the legal relationship.
100. Annex II.IV[A][3] by Alicja Zielińska-Eisen & Tobias Strecker *infra*.
101. *Ibid.*
102. Annex III.IV[B] by Beata Gessel-Kalinowska vel Kalisz & Joanna Kisielinska-Garncarek *infra*.

In all the jurisdictions discussed here, recent developments have allowed for declaration of the legal relationship not only when the claimant is a party, but also when the claimant is not a party to the declared relationship, but such relationship is interfering with his legal sphere.[103]

§2.10 BALANCING THE INTERESTS OF THE PARTIES IN NEGATIVE DECLARATIONS

In English law the issue of fairness to both parties is one of the major concerns in granting the declaration. It is striking, how little of the attention is given to this problem in discussions on Germanic laws. The justification of the draft German FCCP, does not provide any specific evidence that fairness to the parties in the proceedings was any special concern in the process of constructing the new remedy. In certain subsequent writings, the point is raised that legal interest as a prerequisite is also important for protecting the respondents against excessive and unnecessary claims.[104] Not much reflection is devoted to balancing the interests of both parties, although some thought has been spared to the problems relating to the negative declarations. Swiss law has gone through a very interesting change in this respect. The main concern was how to properly balance the claimant's interest against the respondent's (i.e., creditor's) interest in not having to conduct the proceedings at that point in time. This problem relates to evidentiary issues. The claim for a negative declaration pulls the creditor into the proceedings at a moment when he is not ready yet with his evidence. The issue was important enough to be subsumed within a general test of sufficient interest. The ongoing discussion in the Swiss literature points out that this line of argument results in unequal treatment of the parties - the overriding principle being, of course, that the burden of proof should apply equally to both parties. Recent jurisprudence of the Supreme Court in Switzerland shows that the interests of merely a creditor might no longer be relevant in the test of sufficient interest.[105] The court decision related to another problem known as forum running, where the creditor (through a claim for performance) and the debtor (through a claim for negative declaration) try to secure what they consider a more advantageous venue by filing their claim before the other party files its claim elsewhere. Previously, the Swiss courts found that debtor does not have an interest in seeking a negative declaration because the uncertainty could not be recognized as unbearable in that it was soon to be resolved by the performance claim. This stance has been criticized in doctrine on the point that leaving the choice of the forum to one party only breaches the equality of arms principle, which led the courts to change its traditional line of judgement.[106] This is a very important debate, and its

103. Annex I.IV[C] by Ulrich Kopetzki, II.IV[B] by Alicja Zielińska-Eisen & Tobias Strecker, III.IV[C]. by Beata Gessel-Kalinowska vel Kalisz & Joanna Kisielinska-Garncarek *infra.*
104. Annex I.III[B] by Ulrich Kopetzki, II.III[B] by Alicja Zielińska-Eisen & Tobias Strecker, III.III[C] by Beata Gessel-Kalinowska vel Kalisz & Joanna Kisielinska-Garncarek, IV.III[C] by Nino Sievi *infra.*
105. Annex IV.III[D][2] by Nino Sievi *infra.*
106. Annex IV.III[D][2] by Nino Sievi *infra.*

results put the concept of interest as a protection of the respondent in a very different light.

§2.11 THE DEGREE OF SUBJECTIVITY IN LEGAL INTEREST ASSESSMENT

The legal interest as a dam against massive inflow of claims to the courts may be assessed as more or less severe depending on the degree to which we perceive it as subjective. In Germany it appears that assessment whether there is an uncertainty entitling a party to seek declaration proceeds in reference to legal interest viewed as more subjective. It could be sufficient if the parties are in doubt about their legal relationship, even if the court discerns little justification for such doubt.[107] The resulting uncertainty must, however, objectively impair or endanger the claimant's position.

In Austria, the degree of objectivity is higher. While the subjective interest in the requested declaration is indicated by the claimant taking legal action, it is crucial that this subjective interest can be justified by objective factors. Accordingly, there must be a specific and current reason which requires a swift court decision to prevent an actual and serious threat to the claimant's legal position.[108] The legal interest in the judicial decision must be current meaning that objective circumstances seriously, concretely (not only presumably) endanger the claimant's legal position.[109]

In Poland, an even higher degree of objectivity is observed while evaluating the claimant's legal interest. The mere fact that an interest in obtaining declaratory relief is described as 'legal' appears to indirectly imply such objectivity.[110] Objectivity of legal interest in obtaining a declaration means that this prerequisite may not be assessed from the perspective of the claimant's subjective beliefs and needs.[111] It is an interest perceived as deserving protection by the legislature and objectively justified in light of the law. The objective element, in the context of declaratory reliefs, refers to the necessity of securing an award settling the uncertainty of a legal relationship or a right.[112] In this context, judges often refer to 'reasonable assessment of the situation', separated from the claimant's personal perception of the need for a declaratory award.[113] In other words, it is not the claimant's but the average person's sense of reasonableness that shall be taken into account, and not the position of the particular claimant. It is tempting to see such a marked departure from the subjective needs of the

107. Annex II.III[E] by Alicja Zielińska-Eisen & Tobias Strecker *infra.*
108. Annex I.III[C] by Ulrich Kopetzki *infra.*
109. *Ibid.*
110. Rowiński, *supra* n. 66, at 20–22; Annex III.III[A] by Beata Gessel-Kalinowska vel Kalisz & Joanna Kisielinska-Garncarek *infra.*
111. Annex III.III[A] by Beata Gessel-Kalinowska vel Kalisz & Joanna Kisielinska-Garncarek *infra.*
112. *Ibid.*
113. Zygmunt Hahn, *Interes prawny w skardze o ustalenie,* 23 PPC, 705, 708 (1935); Annex III.III[A] by Beata Gessel-Kalinowska vel Kalisz & Joanna Kisielinska-Garncarek *infra.*

party as a reflection of the socialistic legacy, where 'subjective' meant egoistic needs of a single human being and, as such, was frowned upon.[114]

One of the consequences of objectivization of the criteria qualifying certain manifestations as legal interest could be enhancement of predictability of the process. In this vein, Swiss court practice made attempts to quantify the legal interest in relation to the total assets of the claimant. In order to have sufficient interest, the value of the problem to be declared must weigh financially. As an example, courts have held amounts of CHF 14,000,[115] CHF 37,900[116] or CHF 77,000[117] to be sufficient for private individuals, but not CHF 2,000[118] or CHF 376.30.[119] In like spirit, a claim for CHF 10.6 million brought by a bank with a balance sheet total of CHF 1 billion was dismissed.[120]

Objectivization of the legal interest created a basis for the adoption of the subsidiarity principle. While the claimant could seek remedies other than declaration, objectively he had no legal interest in seeking declaratory relief.

§2.12 PROCEDURAL OR SUBSTANTIVE NATURE OF THE LEGAL INTEREST

Review of the opinions relating to the nature of the legal interest as a prerequisite to granting a declaration demonstrates the change in the approach in Germanic jurisdictions.

In Germany, originally in the nineteenth century, under the FCCP the nature of the declaratory relief, including the legal interest, was not so clear. With time, however, the processualist stance prevailed. It was argued that the declaration sought was not one by the debtor, but one by the court, and that the substantive theory could not explain negative declaratory relief which was not based on a subjective right.[121] Wach developed a theory to the effect that entitlement to legal protection was not the expression of a subjective right, but of a public one and primarily directed against the state in order to protect the claimant's rights. Currently, German courts as well as doctrine tend to regard legal interest in terms of its procedural nature.

In Austria, a dissonance prevails between the doctrine and the jurisprudence. According to prevailing doctrine, legal interest in declaratory relief is deemed to be

114. Rowiński's exact point was that, in the realm of socialistic legal procedure, the claimant's interest cannot be narrowed down to his subjective and egoistic interests as a single human unit. *See* Rowiński, *supra* n. 66, at 21. It seems that such a strong declaration on necessary objectivization of the legal interest criterion had a strong impact on Polish jurisprudence which, even when stripped of its political context, is unconsciously echoed in reasonings.
115. Annex IV.III[C][2] by Nino Sievi *infra.*
116. *Ibid.*
117. *Ibid.*
118. *Ibid.*
119. *Ibid.*
120. *Ibid.*
121. Annex II.III[D] by Alicja Zielińska-Eisen & Tobias Strecker *infra*; *see also* Jacobs, *supra* n. 4, at 127.

procedural requirements.[122] However, according to jurisprudence, Austrian courts treat the prerequisites as substantive requirements.[123]

Polish doctrine and court practice almost unanimously treat the legal interest as a substantive law issue.[124] The first dissenting opinion was expressed by a prominent Polish scholar and judge, K. Weitz, commenting on the processual character of legal interest in 2016.[125] He rightly pointed out that the issue is whether we can hear the case (admissibility), and not how we can decide the case (decision on merits).[126] K. Weitz also posited that legal interest, as a prerequisite to declaratory relief, does not belong to the object of the proceedings aimed at declaration, evaluation of the legal interest does not belong to the course of examination of the object of the proceedings, and that the decision on existence of the legal interest is not a decision on the object of the proceedings. The object of the proceedings is the declaration of existence of a right or legal relationship, together with examination of underlying facts adduced by the parties to prove existence of such right or legal relationship (and not existence of the legal interest). Normative regulation of the legal interest belongs to the procedural realm as it applies to the relations between the court and a claimant rather than to substantive relations between the parties. Further arguments may be added. First, that also the procedural nature of the legal interest is visible from the perspective of the goal to be achieved by introduction of the legal interest, namely protection of the courts against frivolous claims. Second, the subsidiarity principle guiding the claimant's choice between numerous procedural paths is the argument *per se* supporting procedural character of the legal interest. Legal interest cannot be a substantive source of a declaration. Particular regulations of a given right and legal relationship included in the civil code and other substantive regulations constitute a substantive source. Third, ontologically speaking, a similar status may be observed in the case of preliminary rulings in bifurcated proceedings, and the possibility of issuing such an award does not raise doubts as to its procedural nature.

Swiss law is an example of the rapid switch from substantive to procedural theory. Before entry into force of the Swiss CCP, the Swiss Federal Tribunal had consistently held that the interest in a declaratory relief was of substantive nature.[127] This stance could be explained largely by the Swiss Federal Tribunal's objective of ensuring that access to a declaratory action was regulated on a federal level.[128] At the time, civil procedure still remained within the ambit of individual cantons so, for the Swiss Federal Tribunal to attain its objective, it had to qualify the interest in a

122. Annex I.II by Ulrich Kopetzki *infra*.
123. *Ibid*.
124. Examples: judgement of 19 March 2015, IV CSK 362/14 (Polish Supreme Court); judgement of 24 April 2014, III CSK 182/13 (Polish Supreme Court). Judgement of 3 April 2000, I CKN 582/98 (Polish Supreme Court); judgement of 6 August 2014, I CSK 559/13 (Polish Supreme Court); judgement of 19 March 2015, IV CSK 362/14 (Polish Supreme Court); Annex III.II by Beata Gessel-Kalinowska vel Kalisz & Joanna Kisielinska-Garncarek *infra*.
125. Annex III.II by Beata Gessel-Kalinowska vel Kalisz & Joanna Kisielinska-Garncarek *infra*.
126. Similarly, Stefan Leimgruber, *Declaratory Relief in International Commercial Arbitration*, 32 ASA Bulletin 467, 479 (2014).
127. Annex IV.III[A] by Nino Sievi *infra*.
128. *Ibid*.

declaratory relief as a matter of substantive law, which was governed on a federal level. In doctrine, the prevailing opinion was that interest in declaratory relief belongs to procedural law due to dogmatic arguments as well as pragmatic requirements. In 2018, the Swiss Federal Tribunal finally confirmed the doctrine's position and classified the interest in a declaratory relief as being of procedural nature, emphasizing that, as a condition of admissibility, it formed part of procedural law.[129]

The current picture shows the preponderance of the proceduralists in assessing the legal interest expanding at speed. The discourse is not only a theoretical one. The most critical application can be seen in arbitration. As long as legal interest is qualified as a substantive feature, this prerequisite will find its application directly in the realm of applicable substantive law. If qualified as procedural, such application is not required, as M. Schneider rightly points out.[130] There are also representatives of the doctrine who try to strike a right balance, which would mean introduction of the legal interest into arbitration on a more relaxed basis.[131] Qualification of legal interest as a substantive factor may enable evading the question whether functioning of this prerequisite is in fact a serious limitation of access to justice. In Polish jurisprudence, this problem is touched upon on the margins of a few judgements. If the legal interest constitutes a substantive rather than procedural premise, the decision of the court is not deemed to be evaluation of formal prerequisites, therefore it cannot be claimed that the case was not examined on merits.[132] The issue of relation between legal interest and procedural justice requires deeper analysis.[133]

§2.13 EX OFFICIO

As a final feature of the legal interest, it is important to emphasize that this prerequisite, being by its nature imprecise, can be applied by the court at any stage of the proceedings without any motion or objection of a party. Even a court of second instance can address this question *ex officio*.[134] Thus, a court of second instance could find that a claimant lacks the requisite interest in the requested relief, although neither the opposing party nor the court at first instance have brought up this issue. Save for Switzerland, where it is rather unlikely in practice that a court of second instance would do so, as the Swiss courts have already declared that it is generally incumbent upon the appellant to address any flaws at first instance[135], in all other jurisdictions in question such a surprising step can be taken at any stage of the proceedings.

The German Federal Supreme Court (*Bundesgerichtshof*, BGH) has adopted the position that the purpose of ensuring effective administration of justice allows the

129. *Ibid.*
130. Michael Schneider, *Non-Monetary Relief* in *International Arbitration: Principles and Arbitration Practice*, in *Performance as a Remedy: Non-Monetary Relief in International Arbitration* 3, 30 (Michael Schneider & Joachim Knoll eds., ASA Special Series 24–25, 2011).
131. *See* Annex II.XI by Alicja Zielińska-Eisen & Tobias Strecker *infra*.
132. Annex III.II by Beata Gessel-Kalinowska vel Kalisz & Joanna Kisielinska-Garncarek *infra*.
133. *See* Chapter 5 *supra*.
134. Annex IV.III[E] by Nino Sievi *infra*.
135. *Ibid.*

courts to omit examination of legal interest and to leave this question open if it is faster or more efficient to dismiss the case on substantive grounds.[136] However, if the court does rule on the question and finds that the claimant lacks legal interest, it has to dismiss the action on procedural grounds.[137]

In Poland, as Article 189 of the Polish CCP constitutes a substantive source of the right to apply for a declaration,[138] existence of legal interest shall be deemed as a substantive condition of declaratory relief.[139] Therefore, it cannot be treated solely as a formal aspect of the declaratory claim which would lead to rejection of a statement of claim. Quite on the contrary, lack of legal interest leads, as a rule, to dismissal of the claim.[140]

§2.14 PURPOSE OF THE DECLARATION AND LEGAL INTEREST PREREQUISITE

In the tripartite system of claims, each claim category has its function to fulfil within a system of justice in the civil procedure area. Each of them responds differently to the needs of the subjects of civil law. The performance claim is a coercive type of remedy by which a claimant may ascertain its rights without their alteration and enforce them. The constitutive claim allows the court to reshape the legal relationship and to enforce such reshaped legal relationship. Basing upon a declaratory claim, the claimant may confirm existing rights - but without enforcement. As a non-coercive measure, the declaratory relief was qualified as being subsidiary to others in a solution resembling the subsidiarity principle. At the very outset, the aim of this relief was defined as creating legal certainty about the current status of rights and legal relationships. Resolving disputes about the existence of rights and legal relationships preventively ensures legal peace and, thus, ultimately serves enforcement of substantive private law.[141] The practical application of this function is widely described in the arbitration area,[142] what could be applied also in litigation.

Declarations may have a preventive function and help to prevent future violation of rights (thus avoiding future court proceedings[143]). This is not to say that declaratory relief may only be sought before a right has been violated - declaratory relief may clarify the legal relationship and thereby prevent further infringements also in cases where a violation has already taken place.

Declaratory relief also serves the purpose of procedural efficiency by clarifying the legal situation in cases where the legal order recognizes a legitimate need to clarify

136. Annex II.III[B] by Alicja Zielińska-Eisen & Tobias Strecker *infra.*
137. *Ibid.*
138. Annex III.II by Beata Gessel-Kalinowska vel Kalisz & Joanna Kisielinska-Garncarek *infra.*
139. *Ibid.*
140. *Ibid.*
141. Annex IV.IV by Nino Sievi, I.III[B], II.II by Alicja Zielińska-Eisen & Tobias Strecker, III.II by Beata Gessel-Kalinowska vel Kalisz & Joanna Kisielinska-Garncarek *infra.* Annex IV.IV by Nino Sievi *infra.*
142. Chapter 4, section §4.01[B] *infra.*
143. Annex I.III[B] by Ulrich Kopetzki *infra.*

disputed legal relations, not only in order to avoid future disputes but also to create a basis for future court decisions.[144] It binds the judge of a later trial. If the subject matter comes up as a preliminary question in a later trial, the judge is obliged to base her decision on this existing ruling, without further examination or taking of evidence. By creating a basis for future decisions, declaratory judgements may also reduce the complexity of future proceedings. Furthermore, declaratory judgements may increase procedural efficiency by avoiding future problems relating to the taking of evidence in cases where a period of time has elapsed between the damaging incident and the occurrence of the damage.

In addition, some scholars ascribe to declaratory actions a compensatory nature where a claimant seeks the declaration that certain behaviour of the defendant was unlawful. The judicial declaration shall ease the non-material suffering of the claimant.[145] For example, a violation of honour is usually responded to by a declaration of the relevant act's unlawfulness, rather than awarding a certain amount of money as compensation.[146] This function is further increased if such action is combined with a request for publication of the judgement, as it seeks to liberate the claimant from the negative effects of the defendant's behaviour also on a public level.

In addition, a negative declaratory action also serves the anticipated defence against an asserted claim. The debtor is not required to await the initiation of the claim by the creditor but can start proceedings itself. In this regard, declaratory actions contribute to procedural equality of parties.[147]

Given that a judgement granting declaratory relief does not directly alter a specific right or legal relation, and given that it does not enjoin any performance, the legislature found it necessary to limit a claimant's entitlement to such judgements for reasons of efficiency by introducing the legal interest as a prerequisite. In particular, the legal interest and subsidiarity principle subordinated the declaratory claim under two other types of claim. While there is a potentially unlimited number of abstract conflicts, specifically between a person's absolute rights and other legal subjects, legal protection shall only be afforded in case an abstract conflict specifically materializes.[148] It is undisputed in all four Germanic jurisdictions that the purpose of the legitimate interest is to ensure that the courts are not burdened with unnecessary claims.[149] This background has important further implications for interpretation of the legal interest, what is the subject of Chapter 5. The second reason for introduction of a legal interest, the protection of respondent against unnecessary claims, only arose with the passage of time – no such concern is mentioned in the justification for the original German FCCP.[150]

144. *Ibid.*
145. Annex IV.IV by Nino Sievi *infra.*
146. *Ibid.*
147. *Ibid.*
148. Annex I.III[B] by Ulrich Kopetzki *infra.*
149. Annex IV.III[B] by Nino Sievi *infra.*
150. *See* fn. 6 *supra.*

§2.15 CONCLUSION: THE GERMANIC CONCEPT OF LEGAL INTEREST

Declaratory relief has been present in Continental Europe since Roman times. This distinguishes the continent from England, where declarations were not in use until the second half of the nineteenth century. It was subject to many changes as regards its scope and prerequisites until, in the late nineteenth century, it achieved its final shape in Germanic jurisdiction as a product of the pandectist approach. It must be emphasized that the legal doctrine in nineteenth century Germany was dominated by efforts to construct from the sources of Roman law ('pandects'), with inspiration from idealist philosophy, an integrated system of law,[151] and this development can be seen as a great achievement of the pandectist school of legal doctrine in Germany in this era.[152] This school also had considerable influence on the important codifications of civil law[153] and civil procedural law[154] in the second half of the nineteenth century.

At that time, allowing for declarations in such a general shape was a modern solution but, regarding the question from today's perspective, one must be aware that conceptual correctness was accorded precedence over the practical needs of the parties. The biggest fear was that the courts will be inundated with frivolous and unnecessary claims. It must be borne in mind that certain former local laws were designed to allow for declarations only in a limited scope of matters or upon the acceptance of the other party. As it appears from the justification to the draft German code, the sole concern motivating introduction of the concept of legal interest lay in the protection of the courts; it was hoped that, together with the cost factor, it would amount to a barrier against potential hyperactivity of claimants. Protection of the respondents was not the driving factor in this respect. The approach to the users was quite different, and the position of the courts in the system of justice was not defined as that of a service provider; concepts such as human rights in the legal realm or the right to a fair trial did not weigh too heavily,[155] and the level of legal awareness of society was quite low.

151. Cf. in particular Friedrich Carl von Savigny, *System des heutigen Römischen Rechts, I – VIII* (1840–1849).
152. Cf. Larenz, *supra* n. 35, at 19.
153. Bürgerliches Gesetzbuch (BGB – Civil Code) of 18 August 1896.
154. Zivilprozeßordnung (CPO – Civil Procedure Code) of 30 January 1877.
155. Ian Langford, *Fair Trial: The History of an Idea*, 8(1) Journal of Human Rights 37–52 (2009), DOI:

https://doi.org/10.1080/14754830902765857 (accessed 30 January 2019).

For several hundred years, 'fair trial' meant a trial that was conducted according to correct procedure. It was a very rare expression. This meaning shifted at the turn of the twentieth century to imply a trial where the rights of a party were observed. Rights such as the right to a public hearing within a reasonable time, to an impartial tribunal, to knowledge of the charge and to examine witnesses. This new meaning turned invocations of 'fair trial' from a rarity to a commonplace device. The Universal Declaration of Human Rights (UDHR) was the first international document that spelled out the 'basic civil, political, economic, social and cultural rights that all human beings should enjoy'. The UN General Assembly ratified the declaration unanimously on 10 December 1948, https://www.ohchr.org/EN/UDHR/Documents/UDHR_Translations/eng.pdf (accessed 30 January 2019).

Due to the impact exerted by German law on other members of the Germanic legal family, declaratory relief is regulated quite similarly in all four national systems discussed here – at least on the statutory level, even if consequent court practice and doctrine could, and did, lead to diversified developments. The main concept was founded on the legal interest as a prerequisite to the declaration, which had only legal relationship and/or legal right as its object. The only fact to be declared, mentioned in certain regulations, was the authenticity of a document. The model legal interest assumed the following components:

(1) the nature of the interest is legal, as opposed to economic or factual;
(2) there is a dispute or controversy between the parties;
(3) the uncertainty relates to the particular right or legal relationship, and not to the facts;
(4) the uncertainty is no longer acceptable to the parties;
(5) the claimant's interest in receiving a declaration is of an objective, and not subjective, character;
(6) the declaration will finally settle the dispute;
(7) there are no other means to resolve said uncertainty, in particular by means of claim for performance;
(8) in the case of a negative declaratory action, the claimant's interest must further be balanced against the defendant's interest in not having to conduct the proceedings at that point in time.

The last point (8) requires more comment. In general, it should be noted that – save for Switzerland as concerns negative declarations – not much reflection was devoted to balancing the interests of the parties, and it was only with time that the legal interest came to be understood as not only protection of the courts, but also as protection of the respondents. A certain unconscious bias in protecting respondent without due respect for the interests of the claimants could be observed. The Swiss debate on forum running opened a new dimension in the discourse, and this is why this feature was left on the list.

Analysis of the law in the four representative jurisdictions proves that the concept evolved in Germany, Austria and Poland in more or less the same way, meaning that evolution was quite slow, leaving the foundations of the conservative concept almost untouched, albeit with a discernible liberalizing tilt. Manifest examples of such liberalization include the new approach to declarations aimed at ascertaining a legal relationship to which claimant is not a party, but which might impact the legal status of the claimant; the Austrian opening towards broader application of declaring liability for future damage; the German possibility to avoid examining the legal interest in specific situations and observed difficulties in distinction between legal and economic interests; and the Polish concept of facts legally relevant to be declared.

I would assess Polish law as being the most conservative. It can be seen as excessively emphasizing objectivity, causing the subsidiarity principle to be adopted very mechanically, without due regard for what is the most expedient solution from the perspective of the parties. Also, declarations concerning liability for future damage are not possible, and Polish legal authorities provided no persuasive reasoning in this respect.

In Switzerland, development of declarations was characterized by the most liberal and pragmatic approach. This includes foregoing legal interest and accepting legitimate interest as sufficient, practically abandoning the *ex officio* regime in dismissing the claim for lacking legal interest; attempts to provide more predictability by introducing claim value as a decisive factor; and the debate on new understanding of the principle of equality as between claimant and respondent.

In all four jurisdictions, the subsidiarity principle remains the most striking phenomenon, especially in connection with the ability of the courts to dismiss the claims based on the legal prerequisite *sua sponte* at any stage of the proceedings. That said, feasibility of this component is already being debated, at least in Switzerland.

The manifestations of liberal evolution, slow though it is, provide food for thought in that they help to understand that the need for further steps in redefinition of legal interest in the Germanic jurisdictions is nothing unusual, but simply a normal step in the evolution of this institution. The problem of redefinition is further discussed in Chapter 5 *infra*.

CHAPTER 3

The Concept of 'Real' Interest in English Law

§3.01 THE GENESIS OF DECLARATIONS IN ENGLISH LAW

The history of declarations on continent derives from the Roman law, which through canon and local regulations culminated in the regulation of the German FCCP, giving rise to current solution in Germanic family of law. The history of declarations is much shorter in English law.[1] Before nineteenth century, judges were reluctant to issue mere declarations, and did not appreciate that it might be beneficial to clarify the party's alleged rights before they were infringed. In order to break this practice, and inspired by the law of Scotland, where declarations had been recognized since sixteenth century, the Chancery Act of 1850 was adopted. The act related to the interpretation of Acts of Parliament, written instruments and opining on title or legal evidence of a title to any real or personal property. Since that time, a number of further acts were issued, up until the adoption of Pt.40.20 of the Civil Procedure Rules (CPR).[2] The present procedural rule CPR 40.20 states that '[t]he court may make binding declarations whether or not any other remedy is claimed'. There are two important problems resolved in this quite short passage. First, the final part, being a significant advance in comparison with earlier regulations, emphasized that declarations can be granted both together with any other relief or as a sole remedy. The courts used to interpret in the past its own competence narrowly, to be exercised only in situations that any consequential relief could be granted.[3] As Knight Bruce V.C. said, 'Nakedly to declare a right, without doing or directing anything else relating to the right, does not, I

1. Lord Woolf & Jeremy Woolf, *Zamir & Woolf: The Declaratory Judgment* 9-36 (4th ed., 2011).
2. English Civil Procedure Rules 1998 (SI 1998/3132) as amended by Rule 13 of the Civil Procedure (Amendment) Rules 2001 (SI 2001/256).
3. Woolf, *supra* n. 1, at 11.

conceive, belong to the functions of this Court.'[4] The second novelty was to omit the word 'right'. Earlier regulations, namely Ord. 25 r. 5 of the 1965 Rules empowered the courts to 'make binding declarations of right'. The leading case of *Guaranty Trust Co of New York v Hannay &Co*[5] demonstrated that such language may cause interpretation problems. In his dissenting opinion, Buckley LJ said that what the claimant seeks, namely a declaration that he is not bound by certain contractual obligations, is not allowed, because the competence of the courts is focused on declaring rights and not obligations. The opinion expressed by Bankes LJ, namely that the 'rule should receive as liberal construction as possible',[6] prevailed not only in this case but also in the final wording of the statutory norm of CPR 40.20.[7]

Rule 25.1.(b) provides further that the court may grant declarations as an interim measure, which had also previously been problematic.[8]

Gradually, declarations became more and more popular, assumed new functions and became a remedy of a very wild scope. Judges grew to be less reluctant to give a declaratory judgement, due to the greater appreciation of its advantages.[9] It is important to notice that declarations as a form of relief to be obtained against the Crown in civil proceedings played an important role in the development of administrative law in England and Wales. This experience, on the contrary, contributed to the development of declarations in private law matters.[10] Once started, the development went visibly towards supporting business relations. SJ Banks in the aforementioned case of *Guaranty Trust*[11] quite clearly stated:

> Subject to this limitation, I see nothing to fetter the discretion of the court in exercising a jurisdiction under the rule to grant relief and having regard to general business convenience and the importance of adapting the machinery of the courts to the needs of suitors.

In *Eli Lilly & Co v Human Genome Sciences Inc*,[12] it was underlined that a business needs to know where it stands, and that the court should assist in providing that certainty through appropriate declarations. While analysing the application of legal prerequisites necessary for a declaration to be granted, it is important to bear in mind this axiology, which in English law is not new. It continues the tradition of pragmatic approach to the development of commercial law, based on real knowledge of business practice and usages, started as early as in XIX c by Lord Mansfield.[13]

4. *Clough v Ratcliffe* (1847) 1 De G. & S.M.164, 178 (63 E.R. 1016), cited in Woolf, *supra* n. 1, at 9–12.
5. *Guaranty Trust Co of New York v Hannay & Co* [1915] 2 K.B.536, affirmed [1915] W.N. 38 (English Court of Appeal).
6. *Guaranty Trust Co of New York v Hannay & Co* [1915] 2 K.B.536, 572 (English Court of Appeal).
7. Woolf, *supra* n. 1, at 17–19.
8. *Ibid.*, 90 et seq.
9. *Ibid.*, 129 et seq.
10. *Ibid.*, 27 et seq.
11. *Guaranty Trust Co of New York v Hannay & Co* [1915] 2 K.B.536, 572 (English Court of Appeal).
12. *Eli Lilly & Co v Human Genome Sciences Inc* [2012] EWHC 2290 (Pat), 83 (English High Court).
13. Nicholas HD. Foster, *Comparative Commercial Law: Rules or Context?* in *Comparative Law. A Handbook* 263, 271 (Esin Örücü & David Nelken eds., 2007).

§3.02 WHAT 'INTEREST' ALLOWS ENGLISH COURTS TO GRANT A DECLARATION

As previously stated, CPR 40.20 does not provide for any specific prerequisites for a declaration to be granted. The court may simply grant declarations. This broad discretion has, however, been limited by the jurisprudence, whereby a claimant needs to persuade the court to grant a declaration even though he had already proven his case. A concept of certain interest to be demonstrated by the claimant was worked out. Clear associations with the continental concept of legal interest appear immediately on the minds of continental lawyers, though this way of thinking seems to be misleading when taking a closer look at number of examples.

The concept of 'legal interest' as a prerequisite for granting a declaration is unknown to the English legal culture. Reviewing more than eighty of the court decisions that can be found in the Westlaw database with reference to CPR 40.20, there has been no single use of the term 'legal interest'. Probably it would be confusing for an English recipient, as the term 'legal interest' has established the connotation of a legally enforceable right to possess or use property.[14] This potential semantic confusion does not seem to be the only reason why the legal interest is not in use in terms of declaratory relief. As it will be clear below, there is also a different axiology that stands behind the formation of limitation criteria to a declaration in English law. There are other 'interests' referred to by the parties to a dispute or the court with certain frequency, while discussing the borders of discretion of the court. Therefore, in order to be granted a declaratory relief, claimants must demonstrate, as the case may be, '**real interest**', like in *Greenwich Healthcare NHS Trust v London* and *Quadrant Housing Trust*;[15] '**commercial interest**', like in *InterDigital Technology Corp v Nokia Corp*;[16] '**real commercial interest**' like in *Nokia Corp v InterDigital Technology Corp*;[17] '**legitimate interest**' like in *Milebush Properties Limited v Tameside Metropolitan Borough Council*;[18] '**proprietary interest**', like in *CPC Group Limited v Quatari Diar Real Estate Investment Company*;[19] '**public interest**', like in *Rolls-Royce plc v Unite the*

14. To be honest, the term legal interest was used once, but in the context of legal interest versus beneficial interest, *See Fujifilm Kyowa Kirin Biologics Company Limited, Samsung Bioepsis UK Limited and Biogen IDEC Limited v AbbVie Biotechnology Limited* [2017] EWHC 395 (Pat) (English High Court).
15. *Greenwich Healthcare NHS Trust v London and Quadrant Housing Trust* [1998] 1 WLR 1749,1756 A-B (Chancery Division), citing Lord Goff in *In re F* [1990] 2 AC 1, 82 (House of Lords); *Toropdar v D* [2009] EWHC 567 (QB); [2010] Lloyd's Rep. I.R. 358 (English High Court); *Point Solutions Ltd v Focus Business Solutions Ltd* [2007] EWCA Civ 14 (English Court of Appeal).
16. *InterDigital Technology Corp v Nokia Corp* [2008] EWHC 504 (Pat) (Chancery Division).
17. *Nokia Corp v InterDigital Technology Corp (Application to Set Aside)* [2006] EWCA Civ 1618, 571 (English Court of Appeal).
18. *Milebush Properties Ltd v Tameside MBC* [2011] EWCA Civ 270, 88 (English Court of Appeal); also *Football Association Premier League Ltd v QC Leisure* [2012] EWCA Civ 1708 (English Court of Appeal); *Re Trident Fashions Plc Re The Insolvency Act 1986 Exeter City Council v Bairstow and Others* [2006] EWCA Civ 203 (English Court of Appeal).
19. *CPC Group Limited v Qatari Diar Real Estate Investment Company* [2009] EWHC 3204 (Ch), 62 (English High Court).

Union;[20] or simply '**sufficient financial interest**', like in *Toneylogo Limited v Totem Communications Limited, British Telecommunications Group Plc.*[21]

In Continental law, there is a tendency to qualify, quantify, make generalizations and classifications of things. In English law, it appears there is no such need. This lack of inherent need to pursue such academic exercises was deep-rooted in English legal culture.[22] Some generalization and classification as to the meaning of such 'interests', however, is required to test the compatibility, or contrarily the lack of compatibility in whatever scope, to the notion of legal interest in Germanic systems of law.

First, it is interesting to find out whether those terms listed above refer to different interests, or whether they in fact overlap, and what do they mean? Second, how do such terms relate to the continental concept of legal interest and their designates? In order to explain these things, I will analyse various manifestations of 'interest' in English law, juxtaposing them with components of continental legal interest. Third, I will seek to discover whether those concepts of interest fulfil the same function in the process of adjudication in Germanic systems and English law respectively, where the discussion on the issue of jurisdiction versus discretion might contribute.

Below, I will examine in what contexts all these 'interests' appear, based on a number of cases. '**Real interest**' appears in many decisions as a basic footing for granting the declaration. The basic case, which is referred to in many subsequent decisions, is *F v West Berkshire HA.*[23] Although this does not relate to commercial matters, it laid the foundations for solutions used in commercial cases. In this case, the relief claimed by the claimant was a declaration that a planned sterilization would not amount to an unlawful act. The argument was that a declaration was not an appropriate procedure in this case, because it changed nothing, contrary to granting an appropriate permit issued before the treatment is carried out. Lord Goff found no jurisdictional basis upon which such approval could be granted, so found that a declaration was a suitable relief. Based on the then current content of the Rule of the Supreme Court, Ord. 15, r. 16. Rule 16 which provided:

> No action or other proceeding shall be open to objection on the ground that a merely declaratory judgment or order is sought thereby, and the court may make binding declarations of right whether or not any consequential relief is or could be claimed.

He could see no procedural objection to the declaration having been granted, either as a matter of jurisdiction or as a matter of exercise of discretion conferred by the

20. *Rolls-Royce Plc v Unite the Union* [2010] 1 WLR 318, 120 (English Court of Appeal); *also Eli Lilly & Co v Human Genome Sciences Inc* [2012] EWHC 2290 (Pat) (English High Court); *David Emmanuel Merton Mond, ClearDebt Limited v MBNA Europe Bank Ltd* [2010] EWHC 1710 (Ch) (English High Court); **487 Arrow Generics Ltd and Another v Merck & Co Inc* [2007] EWHC 1900 (Pat); *Financial Services Authority v Rourke* [2002] C.P. Rep.14 (English High Court).
21. Judgement of 28 February 2005 *Toneylogo Limited v Totem Communications Limited, British Telecommunications Group Plc*, unreported, Westlaw UK, (2005) (English High Court).
22. John Cartwright, *Contract Law. An Introduction to the English Law of Contract for the Civil Lawyer* 12–13 (2nd ed., 2013).
23. *In re F* [1990] 2 AC 1, 82 (House of Lords).

relevant provision. This gave a general power to make a declaration, which on the other side was not unlimited.[24]

Referring to the Scottish action of declarator,[25] Lord Goff saw those limits in the concept of the reality of the question raised and the interest of the claimant. He said that:

> a declaration will not be granted where the question under consideration is not a **real question**, nor where the person seeking the declaration has no **real interest** in it, nor where the declaration is sought without proper argument, e.g. in default of defence or on admissions or by consent. [...] Here the declaration sought does indeed raise a real question; it is far from being hypothetical or academic. (emphasis added)

As follows from the reasoning, that the reality of the question and of the claimant's interest was understood as the limits of the court's discretion and was opposed to an academic or hypothetical question. In the case at hand, Lord Goff found that the question and the claimant's interest were both real.

The concept of **real interest**, as shaped by Lord Goff in *F v West Berkshire HA*, was applied to a commercial case in *Greenwich Healthcare NHS Trust v London and Quadrant Housing trust*[26] by Lightman J. This is one of the key cases cited in subsequent declaratory decisions. In this case, the claimant, who was in the process of building a hospital, needed to realign the road, over which all but one of the defendants had rights of way. The land was also subject to a restrictive covenant limiting its use, to the benefit of which all the defendants were or might be entitled. The defendants had been given notice of the proposed development, but none had objected to it. Furthermore, the realignment of the right of way would improve the safety and convenience of access to the public highway, such that no reasonable objection could be made to it. Because of concern that, at some future date, the defendants might object to the realignment of their right of way or to the changed use of the land, the claimant applied for declarations that it was entitled to realign the right of way, and that the defendants were not entitled to an injunction to restrain the proposed realignment, but that their rights, if any, were limited to an award of damages or compensation, as the case may be. Lightman J. found, that:

> [in] this case there is **a real question** whether the defendants have a right to an injunction or damages in respect of the restrictive covenant and to an injunction in respect of the easement; the plaintiff has a very **real interest** in obtaining the declarations sought; and I have heard full argument.[27] (emphasis added)

24. *Ibid.*
25. *Russian Commercial and Industrial Bank v British Bank for Foreign Trade Ltd.* [1921] 2 A.C. 438, 448 (House of Lords); *Vine v National Dock Labour Board* [1957] A.C. 488, 500 (House of Lords).
26. *Greenwich Healthcare NHS Trust v London and Quadrant Housing Trust* [1998] 1 WLR 1749 (Chancery Division).
27. *Greenwich Healthcare NHS Trust v London and Quadrant Housing Trust* [1998] 1 WLR 1749, 1757 A-B (Chancery Division).

In *Rolls-Royce*,[28] the **public interest** is raised and referred to in the context of declarations that can somehow be qualified as resolving an academic issue. It appears that, if public interest requires, there is no bar to declaring academic or test questions. Public interest secures the reality of the question and interest of the parties. In this case collective redundancy agreements, which contained provisions for the length of service as a selection criterion within the redundancy matrix, were concluded between the claimant and the trade unions, being the defendant in these proceedings, but not with particular employees. The company claimed a declaration as to the validity of this criterion and conformity with the relevant legislation and asked for a declaration of the proper construction of the legislation.

The reality of the interest was linked by Aikens LJ to the following factors:[29]

> (2) There must, in general, be a **real and present dispute** between the parties before the court as to the existence or extent of a legal right between them. However, the claimant does not need to have a present cause of action against the defendant. (3) Each party must, in general, be affected by the court's determination of the issues concerning the legal right in question. (4) The fact that the claimant is not a party to the relevant contract in respect of which a declaration is sought is not fatal to an application for a declaration, provided that it is directly affected by the issue. (5) The court will be prepared to give declaratory relief in respect of a 'friendly action' or where there is an 'academic question' if all parties so wish, even on 'private law' issues. This may particularly be so if it is a 'test case', or it may affect a significant number of other cases, and it is in the public interest to decide the issue concerned. (emphasis added)

What was important, contrary to the cases cited earlier, was that the academic question or a test case might be the subject of a declaration if it is in the **public interest.**[30] Providing a construction of a Statutory Instrument deriving from the European Directive on Age Discrimination was both a matter of public importance, and one of that court's proper functions, as stated by Wall LJ. Bearing in mind that the court would have to declare on the construction of the relevant piece of legislation, the case was to be qualified as academic. Wall LJ, however, found that it was not an academic case and that, although there was no immediate *lis*[31]between the parties, if not resolved by this court it would have led to a dispute between the company and the union, who did not agree on it.[32]

28. *Rolls-Royce Plc v Unite the Union* [2010] 1 WLR 318 (English Court of Appeal).
29. *Rolls-Royce Plc v Unite the Union* [2010] 1 WLR 318, 120 (English Court of Appeal).
30. As pointed in a note to section 19 of the Supreme Court Act 1981, para. A – 77, White Book 2017, the law is not settled. In modern times, the appellate courts have indicated a greater willingness to entertain proceedings which raise points of law which, although 'academic' or 'hypothetical', are points of general public interest (*See* cases cited arguendo in *R. v Canons Park Mental Health Review Tribunal Ex p. A* [1995] Q.B. 60) but no general principle to this effect has emerged.
31. One of the main concerns in this case was that it really concerned a potential dispute between a particular employee (made redundant in the future by the company) and the company, and not the Union and the company; the outcome of this dispute could directly affect a large number of such employees, without any of those people having an opportunity to present their stance. Wall LJ, however, accepted that the present decisions would not prejudice any employee's rights to claim their own arguments in an Employment Tribunal.
32. *Rolls-Royce Plc v Unite the Union* [2010] 1 WLR 318, 55 (English Court of Appeal).

Public interest was taken into consideration in *FSA v Rourke*.[33] The FSA sought declaratory relief against the defendant in relation to his acceptance of unauthorized deposits contrary to the banking law and, for the purpose of inducing others to make the deposits, his making false statements. Neuberger J found that it was in the public interest that declarations should be granted, as it might assist members of the public from whom unauthorized deposits had been taken by Mr Rourke. The declaration would clarify what could be publicized to help the FSA investigate the extent of the defendant's deposit-taking. In order to give full effect, the FSA had to identify as many depositors as possible. The declarations would clearly indicate what FSA could publicize, and what answers to a particular problem arose from the confidentiality regime under the banking law.

In *Nokia v InterDigital*[34] both terms appear: real and commercial interests as a basis for the court's discretion. The problem of the reality of the interest was connected with, among other things, the issue of negative declarations and special caution to be ensured while giving this kind of declaration. Here the respondent had licensed its patents to the claimant, who had commenced proceedings seeking declarations to the effect that a number of the respondent's patents were not essential for compliance with the internationally agreed 3G standard for mobile phones. InterDigital did not commence any proceedings against Nokia, so in the opinion of the respondent, there was no sufficient claim of the right to give rise to a declaratory judgement. In any event, the declaration sought was to confirm whether or not Nokia was infringing the rights of the Respondent. Jacob LJ concluded[35] that:

> 15. (...) Normally, before the Court will exercise its discretion to grant a declaration, there must be some **real reason** for doing so. Normally it will decline to grant a declaration in favour of a party against whom no claim has been formulated for the obvious reason that there is no **real point** in doing so. (emphasis added)

In this case, the feature of reality was combined with **a real threat** that legal action will be commenced against the claimant.

On the other hand, however, it was further stated[36] that the argument relating to the lack of legal action, or the threat thereof, was commercially unrealistic, as Nokia had a manifest and **real commercial interest** in a decision of the kind being sought. Nokia would be 'technically infringing' the respondent's rights if they were wrong. An interest in making 3G telephones, which had to comply with certain standards, was clearly sufficient.

InterDigital and Nokia had quite an interesting series of disputes, contributing to the development of legal interpretations. In *InterDigital Technology Corp v Nokia Corp*[37] the term **real commercial** interest is used in the context, **as opposed to tactical**

33. *Financial Services Authority v Rourke* [2002] C.P. Rep.14 (English High Court); (2001) 98(46) L.S.G. 36.
34. *Nokia Corp v InterDigital Technology Corp* [2006] EWCA 1618 Civ (English Court of Appeal).
35. *Nokia Corp v InterDigital Technology Corp* [2006] EWCA 1618 Civ, 15 (English Court of Appeal).
36. *Nokia Corp v InterDigital Technology Corp* [2006] EWCA 1618 Civ, 19–20 (English Court of Appeal).
37. *InterDigital Technology Corp v Nokia Corp* [2008] EWHC 504 (Pat) (Chancery Division).

reasons relating to other ongoing litigations between the parties. It appears that tactical reasons, even in the opinion of the claimant itself, do not qualify as a real commercial interest. The claimant clearly divided those two issues, submitting[38] that, once a real commercial reason for commencing the litigation is shown, then the existence of tactical considerations is irrelevant. It further said that no amount of tactical benefit would cause the commercial interest in having the declaration, and therefore its practical utility, to cease to exist.

Floyd J observed[39] in this context that it could be material, in deciding whether there was **sufficient interest**, for the judge to see all the motivations of the claimant. The tactical reasons raised by the respondent must be balanced against whatever commercial interest is finally proven. Therefore:

> it is not a question of whether those factors will cause a commercial interest to cease to exist, but whether such commercial interest which is proved **is sufficient**, when viewed against the other matters on which Nokia seek to rely, to justify the exercise of the declaratory jurisdiction. (emphasis added)

Concerning **commercial** interest itself, it was found that it, it should be 'manifest and real', as required by the authorities.

The issue of tactical reasons is raised from time to time, with no particular negative connotation. In *CPC Group v QD,* Warren J precisely stated[40] that:

> For QD to accuse CPC of attempting to obtain a tactical advantage by dressing up its claim as one for declaratory relief and thus providing a hook on which to hang an application for and expedited trial, is not a fair criticism. There is nothing unfair in a party to a contract wishing to know, in a case of dispute, what it means and what its effect is in order that he may then proceed on the basis of certainty rather than uncertainty.

If it is obvious that the claimant's negotiating position with the defendant would be stronger if a declaration is granted, while the use of tactical reasons do not create a real interest, they do not, by themselves, jeopardize it.

A legitimate interest as a proper footing for granting a declaration is referred to, among others, by the judge in *Football Association Premier League Ltd v QC:*[41]

> These are powerful points but, once again, I have been persuaded by Mr Howe that the defendants do have a **legitimate interest** in securing, in the form of a formal declaration, a clear statement of the findings of this court in the light of the judgement of the Court of Justice.
>
> (...) I believe justice would be achieved by the grant of a declaration that the relevant obligations in the agreements in issue constituted a restriction on competition prohibited by Article 81 EC and were void under Article 81(2) EC to the extent that such obligations prohibited Netmed from supplying for use in the

38. *InterDigital Technology Corp v Nokia Corp* [2008] EWHC 504 (Pat), 23 (Chancery Division).
39. *InterDigital Technology Corp v Nokia Corp* [2008] EWHC 504 (Pat), 33–37 (Chancery Division).
40. *CPC Group Limited v Qatari Diar Real Estate Investment Company* [2009] EWHC 3204 (Ch), 66–68 (English High Court).
41. *Football Association Premier League Ltd v QC Leisure* [2012] EWHC 108 (Ch), 97–99 (English High Court).

> UK satellite decoder cards which were capable of permitting any person to view the relevant transmissions in an intelligible form. (emphasis added)

In this case, the publicans, who were the defendants, were claimed to have communicated to the public, in breach of the claimants' copyrights, by transmitting the claimants' broadcasts, via their television screens and speakers, to the customers present in their public houses. The defendants were concerned that the contractual terms in question were alleged to have made their activities wrongful in a serious, indeed quasi-criminal, way, thereby giving rise to liability for penalties as well as civil liabilities, and that the claimants, or others, may seek to put pressure on their licensees not to supply cards in response to orders which they place.

In the context of this case, it appears that legitimate interest is similar to the notion of real interest – there was a real need to clarify the situation on the side of the defendants, in order to be able to run their business soundly.

The parties in *CPC Group Limited* referred to a missing '**proprietary interest**' in a certain project, which was to be adequately protected by an award of damages.[42] The notion of this term was not only left unexplained, but annotated by the judge with the words 'whatever it means', though it is difficult to comment on this either,[43] save for the remark that such a qualification is more likely to be used in a continental discourse on declarations than in English law.

The concept of **financial interest** as grounds for declarations was used in *Toneylogo Ltd v Totem Communications Group Plc* (Costs).[44] Under an agreement, Toneylogo was appointed as a reseller of the relevant products, which included the premium numbers at issue in these proceedings.

According to the agreement, Totem was responsible for collecting from its carriers any monthly call revenue generated by call traffic to the telephone numbers supplied by the reseller, and undertook to use all reasonable endeavours to collect this. The claimant sought a declaration that Totem had failed to commence and to carry out legal proceedings against BT, one of the carriers, and that BT's retention of the monthly call revenue was unlawful. The defendant submitted that the claimant could claim the relevant declaration directly from BT, on the basis that it had a sufficient **financial interest** in the outcome to warrant such a course, and relied upon cases such as *In Re S Hospital Patient* which demonstrated that the jurisdiction under CPR Part 40.20 is broad enough. This stance was basically accepted by Alton J, who said that the point had, at least, a real prospect of success.

Summing up the above examples, preliminary conclusions may be drawn. First, there are a wide range of interests that may trigger granting a declaration, but no clear-cut classification can be derived from them. The term 'real interest' seems to be the most universal and overwhelming one. The interest that triggers the grant of a

42. *CPC Group Limited v Qatari Diar Real Estate Investment Company* [2009] EWHC 3204 (Ch), 62 (English High Court).
43. It appears that proprietary interest did not refer to the basis of the discretion of the judge, but shareholding in the target company, which resulted in a situation whereby the Claimant lost its 'proprietary interest', meaning shares in the project.
44. *English High Court Judgement of 28 February 2005* in *Toneylogo Ltd v Totem Communications Group Plc*, unreported, Westlaw UK (2005) (English High Court).

declaration may be commercial, including purely financial, or may not have a commercial nature, private or public, but must still be real. This reality is often associated with utility, which calls for further exploration.

Legitimate and real interests are used interchangeably without any special meaning attached to the dispute. Legitimate interest should be treated as a synonym of the term real interest. The appearance of public interest is recognized in specific circumstances, namely when the question is of a more general nature, usually an academic one. The appearance of public interest makes the question to be analysed, and the interest of the claimant, more real. This will be examined further, together with the problem of utility.

§3.03 THE REAL INTEREST SETTING

Real interest in the context of judicial tests. Reviewing the examples cited in Chapter 2 above, one may find that certain manifestations of the real, commercial or whatever other term is used, interest are very similar to the continental concept of legal interest: no academic issues are to be declared, or at least declared but with special caution, the same caution in the event that there is no threat of legal action on the side of the defendant. Each party must, in general, be affected by the court's determination of the issues concerning the legal right in question. *Prima facie* it could be a correct finding, however having this issue further analysed, one may find it misleading.

First, it has to be explained that it is a useless exercise to analyse the term 'real interest' alone, without all the accompanying tests worked out by the judicature. A simple comparison of 'real interest' and 'legal interest' would also be a misunderstanding. The concept of legal interest, as it is interpreted by jurisprudence in the Germanic legal tradition, is categorically much broader than the concept of real interest alone. The concept of 'real interest' as a factor denominating the court's discretion is also a part of a larger picture. It cannot be fully understood without the whole context of other factors limiting that discretion, which construct tests that are usually called upon in various cases. Woolf LJ provides that there is no limit to the number of considerations that may be taken into account by the courts in the exercise of their discretion,[45] though certain tests are repeatedly considered in the courts' practice.

In *In re F. (Mental Patient: Sterilisation)* Lord Goff of Chieveley pointed to three conditions that need to be satisfied if that jurisdiction is to be exercised. These conditions are that:

(1) the question under consideration is a real question;
(2) the person seeking the declaration has a real interest; and
(3) there has been a proper argument.

45. Woolf, *supra* n. 1 at 127.

Later, the test was transformed and extended by Neuberger LJ in *FSA v Rourke*,[46] who placed emphasis on what 'justice' required, after citing the earlier cases of *Patten v Burke*[47] and *Messier – Dowty v Sabena*.[48] He concluded that, when considering whether or not to grant a declaration, the court should take into account:

(1) justice to the claimant,
(2) justice to the defendant,
(2) whether the declaration would serve a useful purpose, and
(3) whether there are any other special reasons why or why not the court should grant the declaration.

This was a very important change in the application of Article 40.20 of CPR. Neuberger LJ does not cite *Re F nor Greenwich*, and in my view the test is not contradictory to the earlier one, but rather shifts the accents within it. Where, then, does the reality of the question, or the interest of the claimant come into play? It is included in the notion of justice as such. If no real question is to be decided, or no real interest can be attributed to the claimant, then it will be an injustice to the defendant to deal with such a declaration, and to subject him to the stress as well as the time and expense involved. So what Neuberger LJ requires is even more than the reality of the question and the claimant's interest. This is especially apparent in the case of negative declarations, where the alleged aggrieved party and the potential claimant is faced with a claim for a declaration on the non-existence of a breach or fraudulent action before he is ready[49] with its own action.

Other elements of the test include:[50]

(1) the power to make declarations appears to be unfettered;
(2) the court can grant a declaration as to the parties' rights, or as to the existence of facts, or as to a principle of law, where those rights, facts, or principles have been established to the court's satisfaction;

46. *Financial Services Authority v Rourke* [2002] C.P. Rep.14 (English High Court).
47. *Patten v Burke Publishing Co Ltd* [1991] 1 WLR 541 (Ch).
48. *Messier-Dowty v Sabena* [2001] 1 All ER 275 (English Court of Appeal).
49. *See Messier Dowty Ltd v Sabena SA* [2000] 1 W.L.R. 2040 (English Court of Appeal) in this respect.
50. *See* the full citation:

> The court's power to grant a declaration is to be found in CPR Part 40.20, which in these terms: 'The court may make binding declarations whether or not any other remedy is claimed.
>
> Accordingly, so far as the CPR are concerned, the power to make declarations appears to be unfettered. As between the parties in the section, it seems to me that the court can grant a declaration as to their rights, or as to the existence of facts, or as to a principle of law, where those rights, facts, or principles have been established to the court's satisfaction. The court should not, however, grant any declarations merely because the rights, facts or principles have been established and one party asks for a declaration. The court has to consider whether, in all the circumstances, it is appropriate to make such an order. (...)
>
> It seems to me that, when considering whether to grant a declaration or not, the court should take into account justice to the claimant, justice to the defendant, whether the declaration would serve a useful purpose and whether there are any other special reasons why or why not the court should grant the declaration'.

(3) establishing the rights, facts or principles to the court's satisfaction is not enough to ask for a declaration;
(4) all the circumstances of the case show that it is appropriate to make such an order.[51]

Later, Aikens LJ, for the purposes of the *Rolls-Royce* case, summarized the following principles:[52]

(1) The power of the court to grant declaratory relief is discretionary.
(2) There must, in general, be a real and present dispute between the parties before the court as to the existence or the extent of a legal right between them. However, the claimant does not need to have a present cause of action against the defendant.
(3) Each party must, in general, be affected by the court's determination of the issues concerning the legal right in question.
(4) The fact that the claimant is not a party to the relevant contract in respect of which a declaration is sought is not fatal to an application for a declaration, provided that it is directly affected by the issue.
(5) The court will be prepared to give declaratory relief in respect of a 'friendly action' or where there is an 'academic question', as long as all the parties so wish, even on 'private law' issues. This may particularly be so if it is a 'test case', or where it may affect a significant number of other cases, and it is in the public interest to decide the issue concerned.
(6) However, the court must be satisfied that all sides of the argument will be fully and properly put. It must therefore ensure that all those affected are either before it or will have their arguments put before the court.
(7) In all cases, assuming that the other tests are satisfied, the court must ask: is this the most effective way of resolving the issues raised? In answering that question, it must consider the other options of resolving this issue.[53]

Pumfrey J, in *Nokia Corporation v InterDigital Technology Corp*[54] followed a line of authority running from *Guaranty Trust Company of New York v Hannay & Co [1915] 2 KB 536* through *Messier-Dowty Ltd v Sabena SA* [2001] 1 All ER 275, culminating in the judgement of Neuberger J in *Financial Services Authority v Rourke (unreported) 19 October 2001*, which established three relevant principles:

51. Reference to this test can be seen in, for example: *Football Association Premier League Ltd v QC; Day (t/a Appledore Clinical Services) v Barclays Bank Plc* [2018] EWHC 394 (QB); *Fujifilm Kyowa Kirin Biologics Company Limited, Samsung Bioepsis UK Limited and Biogen IDEC Limited v AbbVie Biotechnology Limited* [2017] EWHC 395 (Pat) (English High Court); *Bronze Monkey LLC v Simmons and Simmons LLP* [2017] EWHC 3097 (Comm) (English Commercial Court).
52. *Rolls-Royce Plc v Unite the Union* [2009] EWCA Civ 387 (English High Court), *Rolls-Royce Plc v Unite the Union* [2010] 1 WLR 318, 120 (English Court of Appeal).
53. Cited in *Bronze Monkey LLC v Simmons and Simmons LLP* [2017] EWHC 3097 (Comm) (Commercial Court).
54. *Nokia Corp v InterDigital Technology Corp* [2006] EWHC 802 (Pat), 20 (English High Court).

(1) The correct approach to the question of whether to grant negative declarations was one of discretion rather than jurisdiction.
(2) The use of negative declarations should be scrutinized, and their use rejected where it would serve no useful purpose, but where such a declaration would help ensure that the aims of justice were achieved, the court should not be reluctant to grant a negative declaration.
(3) Before a court can properly make a negative declaration, the underlying issue must be sufficiently clearly defined to render it properly justiciable.

The test adopted for the purposes of the decision in *CIP Property (AIPT) Ltd v Transport* for London[55] contained three questions:

(1) is the claim premature;
(2) would the declaration sought serve a useful purpose; and
(3) are the issues sufficiently clearly defined to be properly justiciable?

The court stated, however, that, though properly formulated as separate considerations, they overlap: the propositions summarized in points (2) and (3) are in fact just tests for prematurity under (1).[56]

If taken together, the above tests form a setting that I would call in aggregate a real interest, as opposed to the continental setting of legal interest. While reviewing the above tests, two main features of real interest, as a limitation of the court's discretion, are predominant: justice to the parties and the utility of the adopted measure. These will be presented in more detail in subsequent paragraphs. The potential adoption of the subsidiarity principle, which is one of the main threads in the discussion on the continental concept of legal interest in this book, is clearly a derivative of the concept of useful purpose and will be analysed separately.

While reviewing the cases, another phenomenon arose that is worthy of attention, namely the adaptability and evolution of this measure, especially in relation to the rather petrified notion of legal concept. I would like to devote more attention to this issue at the end of this chapter.

Justice to the parties: While we compare those two settings, namely what can be called a real interest and that of legal interest, we see immediately one very strong difference: justice as an optimal feature of the judges' discretion. In the continental discourse this is problem was raised mainly in relation to the negative declarations and

55. *CIP Property (AIPT) Ltd v Transport for London* [2012] EWHC 259 (Ch) (English High Court); here the claimant raised claims for a negative declaration and mandatory injunction, arising from the alleged infringement of his right to light for property overlooking a site on which development was proposed, had no prospect of success. The action was premature and served no useful purpose, since the proposed development lacked planning permission and could not take place for at least five years. Followed, among others, in *San Juan v Allen* [2016] EWHC 1502 (Ch) (English High Court).
56. The test for its prematurity issue was later cited, *See San Juan v Allen* [2016] EWHC 1502 (Ch) (English High Court), *Pavledes v Hadjisavva* [2013] EWHC 124 (Ch) (English High Court). The summary of various tests was presented by the party representative, Mr Gore in *Toropdar v D* [2009] EWHC 567 (QB); [2010] Lloyd's Rep. I.R. 358 (House of Lords).

not as distinct component. In *Patten v Burke Publishing Co. Ltd.* [1991] 1 W.L.R. 541, 544,[57] Millett J emphasized the importance of the consideration whether the paramount duty of the court *to do the fullest justice* to the claimant, to which he is entitled, can be fulfilled without granting such a declaration. In this case, the declaration that the agreement with a former publisher had been determined by the defendants' breach and that the claimant was no longer bound by its terms, which could allow the claimant to publish his book by offering it to a new publisher. The omission of any declaration to that effect from the judgement could seriously inhibit the claimant in any attempt to negotiate terms for the publication of the work, or any similar book he may write in the future. In this case, there was an argument that other means, such as damages or an injunction, should be sufficient. However, Millet J concluded his decision as follows: 'In my judgment, this is a case of such a character that the normal practice must give way to the paramount duty of the court to do the fullest justice to the plaintiff, to which he is entitled.'

Neuberger LJ, while setting the foundations to his discretion, stated that:

> It seems to me that, when considering whether to grant a declaration or not, the court should take into account **justice to the claimant, justice to the defendant**, whether the declaration would serve a useful purpose, and whether there are any other special reasons why or why not the court should grant the declaration. (emphasis added)

He cited in this respect Lord Woolf in *Messier-Dowty v Sabena* [2001] 1 All ER 275, where he said, in relation to the issue of negative declarations:

> the issue was whether a negative injunction should be granted. Lord Woolf said this: 'The deployment of negative declarations should be scrutinised and their use rejected where it would serve no useful purpose. However, where a negative declaration would help to ensure that the aims of justice are achieved, the courts should not be reluctant to grant such declarations. They can and do assist in achieving justice.'

In *Pathfinder Minerals,*[58] Field J ultimately states that he will grant the declaration, because to do so would be to serve a useful purpose and because justice requires it.

Justice is a clearly overriding principle, even overriding the principle of useful purpose. We can see this in the above cases, followed by many others. In all those cases, the principles of justice constitute a principal qualifier of other features. Such qualifier does not appear directly in the interpretations of legal interest in Germanic legal tradition.

Making justice to the parties also includes a consideration as to whether refusing the declaration would not constitute a denial of justice. This issue was considered in *Ms L v Ms C.*[59] Ms L sought a declaration that, at the point of G's departure from England, Ms L was acting as her 'psychological parent' and that they shared family life within the

57. *Patten v Burke Publishing Co Ltd* [1991] 1 WLR 541 (Ch), 544.
58. *Pathfinder Minerals Plc v Veloso & Ors* [2012] EWHC 2856 (Comm), 170 (English High Court).
59. *L v C (Applications by Non-Biological Mother)* [2014] EWFC 1 (English Family Court).

meaning of Article 8 of the European Convention on Human Rights. The judge concluded that, if this court is impotent to make human rights declarations arising from past events occurring within its territorial jurisdiction, then this would, to his mind, be capable of leading to a denial of justice. He found that the international element is undoubtedly a special feature of the case but did not find that it provided a reason for declining a declaration, and there were no existing proceedings in Ireland. The limited nature of the declaration in question would therefore not trespass on any potential Irish proceedings and might even assist if there were any. The availability of an alternative legal remedy in the Irish courts, as suggested by the defendant, rested, in the opinion of the judge, on the doubtful assumption that the claimant had emotional and financial resources to pursue that course in practice.[60]

It appears that the principle of justice and useful purpose are not completely separate and may easily overlap. In *JPMorgan Europe v Primacom Management GmbH*,[61] the dispute arose on the basis of the complex of financing agreements. There were a number of proceedings initiated before English and German courts. A declaration was sought in relation to the validity and enforceability of an agreement in writing (referred to as the 'Senior Facility') and made between the claimant, various other financial institutions named in the Senior Facility and the various defendants. Cooke J found that, in the absence of a final judgement of the English court declaring the validity and enforceability of the Senior Facility, the senior lenders would remain at risk of tactical proceedings being commenced by the Primacom group in Germany, in breach of the English jurisdiction clause, for the purpose of frustrating or delaying the enforcement of the Senior Lenders' rights under the Senior Facility. In his judgement, it would be unjust not to grant the declarations sought, though it could also be qualified as useful purpose as well.

§3.04 UTILITY

Scope of declarations. The scope of possible declarations affects the scope of utility and interrelates with the legal interest components on the continent as well. There is no doubt, that an English court may declare rights, facts and principles of law, as confirmed by Neuberger LJ in *FSA v Rourke*.[62] Earlier it was discussed whether negative declarations are included in the court's jurisdiction. The new content of CPR 40.20 cut off such doubts, which is confirmed also by the case cited above. This makes a huge difference in confrontation with Germanic concept. Here the court may only declare a legal relationship,[63] or a legal relationship and rights.[64] Under German and Austrian laws, as an exception, the court may declare the authenticity or falsity of a deed that is a statement of fact. In Poland, the interpretation of the law, however, goes

60. *L v C (Applications by Non-Biological Mother)* [2014] EWFC 1, 50, 58 (English Family Court).
61. *JP Morgan Europe Ltd v Primacom Management GmbH* [2005] EWHC 2426 (Comm), 25–26 (English High Court).
62. *Financial Services Authority v Rourke* [2002] C.P. Rep.14 (English High Court).
63. Article 256 of the German CPC.
64. Article 88 of the Swiss CPC, Art. 189 of the Polish CPC:

into the direction that facts triggering the right or otherwise having an impact on the right or the legal relationship, may be also established as a matter of a declaration.[65] This interpretation converges both systems to some extent, especially if we consider that facts in English practice will be established not for themselves, but only if such a declaration will serve a useful purpose. This useful purpose might be focused on establishing a legal relationship or a right.

Another difference relates to the possibility of decoding the positive law. This applies to hypothetical, academic or test cases. In continental law, the independent action aimed at ascertaining issues of a hypothetical nature, including the content of positive law, is not possible in the form of a declaration. The positive law will be interpreted in the process of analysing the footing of a particular case aimed at deciding a claim for performance or shaping the obligation of the defendant. The same stance used to be taken by English courts in the past. The primary role of the courts was to resolve the disputes existing between the parties, where the courts' decision would have immediate and practical consequences for at least one of the parties.[66] However, the rules concerning the authority to grant declarations in the case of hypothetical questions and test cases developed. Public interest, as mentioned earlier, may be a reason to establish an interpretation of the law in force.[67] In England, this approach led to further developments. The Financial Markets Test Case Scheme is an innovative mechanism that allowed declaratory relief on a point of English law that is contested by parties with 'opposing interests'. Such a claim, introduced into the Financial List, must raise issues of general importance to the financial markets in relation to which immediately relevant authoritative English law guidance is required. Such a claim is assigned to judges with an exceptional knowledge of financial markets.[68]

The English courts' jurisdiction is also broad enough to grant declarations on hypothetical issues. It can only be limited by exercising the court's discretion. Nevertheless, the hypothetical nature of a claim will be still a compelling argument why a declaration should not be granted.[69] In this vein, Lord Phillips MR underlined that the courts were not intended to be 'general advice centres', as there are 'dangers that the court will enunciate propositions of principle without fully appreciating the implications that these will have in practice'.[70] In Continental courts, the hypothetical nature of a case is deemed to be evidence of the lack of legal interest of the claimant. There is no legal interest if the court decision does not affect a particular and defined legal right of the claimant, relating to a particular and defined factual situation.

There is a difference between hypothetical and future rights.[71] Hypothetical rights come into existence upon a certain contingency, while future rights upon the

65. *See* Chapter 2 *infra*.
66. Woolf, *supra* n. 1, at 140.
67. *See Rolls-Royce Plc v Unite the Union* [2010] 1 WLR 318 (English Court of Appeal).
68. Financial List Guide, http://www.gov.uk/government/uploads/system/uploads/attachment_data/file/465590/financial-list-guide.pdf (accessed 31 January 2019).
69. Woolf, *supra* n. 1, at 145.
70. *R. (on the Application of Burke) v General Medical Council* [2006] QB 273, 293 at para. 21 (English High Court).
71. Woolf, *supra* n. 1, at 184–191.

occurrence of a date or specific condition. Until the introduction of Ord. 25. r.[72] the court did not have jurisdiction to declare future rights, because a declaration could only be granted if a consequential relief could have been claimed as well. The amendment of law allowed declarations to be made on future rights, by making it clear that declarations can be granted in addition to other remedies, or not.[73] In deciding how to exercise discretion, the fact that a declaration of future rights will serve the present interest of the claimant is an important consideration. A good example of this situation is where the current price for a piece of real estate is dependent on the validity of the option to continue the actual lease contract in the defined future. The validity of a future right embodied in an option could well be the subject of a declaration.

The courts are more ready to pronounce upon future rights that are to be based on the construction of the contract purely, rather than on the facts. In *Sarah v Legg*,[74] the defendant in a counterclaim sought a declaration as to his rights upon the expiry of the notice to quit on the claimant being a user of a piece of real estate. The judge found that the claim is, in essence, a future claim, because the date of expiry had not arrived yet, but it did not deal with a hypothetical question. It dealt with a real question, because litigation had been already on foot between parties as to their rights, and the defendant served a notice during the proceedings that (if valid) would affect those rights, and a real question between the parties was clearly going to arise on its expiry. Given this situation, it made no sense to insist on the defendant waiting for the expiry of the notice before starting a counterclaim, if all that was being sought was a declaration as to the position on the expiry of the notice.

When speaking about future rights, this raises the question of prematurity. As already mentioned, while discussing the test adopted in CIP Property,[75] no declaration can be granted if the claim is premature based on hypothetical facts, because it is not possible for the issues to be sufficiently clearly defined to be properly justiciable. It would not simply serve a useful purpose. In the given case, the property where the development was planned had not been finally purchased yet, subject to certain conditions, and no final plans were adopted, or a final construction permit received. Therefore, a claim for a declaration that the respondent was not entitled to erect any structure that would diminish or obstruct its ancient right to light, and a mandatory injunction restraining any development interfering with that right, was deemed to be premature.

Useful purpose. In the Continental tradition, legal interest is often explained as an objective needed to receive a given court decision in order to finally settle the uncertainty of a right or legal relationship in case that right or legal relationship is breached or threatened to be breached. There is a utility feature built into this definition, though the utility refers only to legal matters. In England, useful purpose is also a component of the term real interest, though this utility strongly relates to

---

72. The Supreme Court of Judicature Act of 1875.
73. Woolf, *supra* n. 1, at 185.
74. *Gilpin v Legg* [2017] EWHC 3220, 114–115 (Ch).
75. *CIP Property (AIPT) Ltd v Transport for London* [2012] EWHC 259 (Ch), 26 (English High Court), *See also San Juan v Allen* [2016] EWHC 1502 (Ch) (English High Court).

practical matters. While legal interest, by definition, relates to legality; real interest relates to practicality. It does not mean that these sets of denominations are separate. There are a number of manifestations that are joint for both of them.

If useful purpose cannot be demonstrated to the court, 'it will weigh heavily on the scales against the grant of declaratory relief'. Useful purpose allows a declaration, even in cases that are to be *prima facie* qualified as hypothetical or academic.[76] Pumfrey J paraphrased useful purpose in a picturesque way: 'Would the declaration, if granted, be the legal equivalent of shouting in an empty room, or is there some point to it?'[77]

While reviewing various tests, quoted earlier in, the term useful purpose is *expressis verbis* named by Neuberger LJ,[78] but utility, as a main principle guiding judges in the process of granting a declaration, is present elsewhere as well. Lord Goff[79] speaks about real questions and real interest. Therefore, in cases where there is no real question to be answered, where there is no disagreement, there is also no useful purpose for a declaration to be granted.[80] Aikens LJ[81] states that there must be a present dispute and that the declaration must somehow affect the parties.

The general guideline in commercial matters was expressed by Kitchen J, who simply said that '[b]usiness needs to know where it stands,' finding that **commercial certainty** is in the public interest.[82] Commercial certainty is a recurring principle in a number of cases. It is important not only in relations as between the parties to the case, but also in relations to potential third parties. In *Fujifilm*,[83] where there was a case of declaring a lack of novelty of a certain patented solution, the court granted declaratory relief confirming that the declarations would serve a useful purpose by:

> (a) providing commercial certainty for the claimants regarding the intended launch of their biosimilar adalimumab products; (b) dispelling commercial uncertainty in the UK (and European) market created by the defendant's threats to enforce its patents against biosimilar competition anywhere in the world; (c) providing clarity to third parties in the UK (...).

Commercial certainty is important in declaring the proper construction of the contracts. This is even more important in the case of long-term contracts, where the

76. Woolf, *supra* n. 1, at 168.
77. *Nokia Corporation v Interdigital Technology Corporation* [2007] EWHC 3077 (Pat) (English High Court).
78. *Financial Services Authority v Rourke* [2002] C.P. Rep.14, 3 (English High Court).
79. *In re F* [1990] 2 AC 1, 82 (House of Lords).
80. *Thomas Brown Estates Ltd v Hunters Partners Ltd* [2012] EWHC 21 (QB), 16 (English High Court); *See also Brown v Innovatorone Plc (In Liquidation)* [2010] EWHC 2281 (Comm), 38 (English High Court).
81. *Rolls-Royce Plc v Unite the Union* [2009] EWCA Civ 387 (English Court of Appeal).
82. In *Eli Lilly & Co v Human Genome Sciences Inc* [2012] EWHC 2290 (Pat), 83 (English High Court), Kitchin J said that there is 'a public interest in commercial certainty in patent matters as in any others. Business needs to know where it stands. I believe this court should assist in providing that certainty where it properly can'.
83. *Fujifilm Kyowa Kirin Biologies, Co. Limited (a Company Incorporated under the Laws of Japan) v AbbVie Biotechnology Limited, AbbVie Limited* [2016] EWHC 1584 (Pat), 7 (English High Court).

term of the contract has a number of years remaining.[84] In Greenwich, the court decided that, in order to avoid 'damaging uncertainty', granted a declaration that the defendants even if they had a cause of action, would not have the right to an injunction, as the purpose of the certain realignment was to make a dangerous road junction safe.[85]

It was earlier mentioned that **public interest** could be qualified *per se* as a useful purpose. In addition to providing clarity, declarations may warn members of society against unlawful actions that could be detrimental to the public. The *FSA v Stephen Ronald Watkins* is one such example.[86] In this case, the FSA stated that the defendant's business was an unauthorized collective investment scheme pursuant to the *Financial Services and Markets Act 2000, 235*, which was a regulated activity, and sought a declaration in this respect. Proudman J found five categories of useful purpose that allowed her to grant a declaration in the case. The first purpose was to make general public more aware of the risk of investing money in unauthorized schemes organized in breach of law, not only by the defendant in the proceedings in question, but also others operating similar land banking schemes. Second, to make it clear to the investors of this particular scheme that they have a right to the return of invested funds. Third, this declaration would assist the regulator in determination whether this particular person is proper to run regulated activities. Fourth, it may be useful to inform overseas regulators in order to allow them to properly evaluate the granting of authorizations, if any, to the defendant, Finally, the declarations would assist the FSA in potential future claims against third parties who may have been involved in the scheme.

An imminent threat of a breach of the claimant's right is a very important factor in ascertaining legal interest. In English law, this is not necessary. An imminent threat, as a factor that defines the court's discretion in granting a declaration, was analysed in the context of *quia timet* (because he fears), which is used to prevent a threatened wrong. It was clearly stated that there was provided a clear division between a *quia timet* injunction and declarations, and stated that, applying the test of an imminent threat is possible to the claim for an injunction, but not to the claim for a declaration.[87] There is no principle providing that, before the court will grant a declaration as to the claimant's rights, there must be shown to be either an actual infringement, or the threat of an imminent infringement.[88] They do not constitute a *sine qua non* condition for a declaration to be granted. The court may, however, refuse a declaration on the grounds of prematurity, or because it would not serve a useful purpose anyway, or not being justice to the parties.

84. Judgement of 17 August 2016, *In International Air Transport Association v Accelya World SLU*, unreported, Westlaw UK (2016) (English High Court).
85. *Greenwich Healthcare NHS Trust v London and Quadrant Housing Trust* [1998] 1 WLR 1749 (Chancery Division).
86. *Financial Services Authority v Watkins (t/a Consolidated Land UK)* [2011] EWHC 1976 (Ch), 25–30 (English High Court).
87. *Pavledes v Hadjisavva*, [2013] EWHC 124 (Ch) (English High Court); [2013] 2 E.G.L.R. 123 at 38–40.
88. In earlier decisions, the opposite opinions could be found, *See In New Hampshire Insurance Co v Phillips Electronics North America Corp* [1998] C.L.C. 1062 (English Court of Appeal).

The cases below show that making declarations regarding actions that **impact good standing** in general, **or the commercial value** of the given asset, serves a useful purpose, what differs from the notion of legal interest. In *Pavledes v Hadjisavva* the judge explained that useful purpose may mean an **impact on the commercial value** of the property at hand in the case of sale.[89] The defendant raised here that if the claimants had plans to sell their property, there would be justification for the grant of a declaration at that stage, but not in circumstances where a sale was no more than a possibility in the future. The court opposed this stance, saying that the declaration would bring finality to the dispute, enabling all parties to know where they stood. He found no reason to wait until the claimants wished to sell the property. The court therefore granted a declaration concerning the claimant's right of light where the defendant had not infringed that right yet, but had failed to acknowledge the claimant's right while obtaining planning permission to build a two-storey extension of the house. The bad **impact on a business** was also used in *Point Solutions v Focus Business Solutions*.[90] Here the claimant sought a declaration that the computer software he produced was not a copy of the software produced by the defendant, and therefore it did not infringe the defendant's rights. The claimant raised that the defendant's 'bad mouthing' had led to the situation where the company had started losing customers and was not able to secure venture capital financing. The court found those arguments legitimate, though not sufficiently proved, which was the reason for denying the claim.

A bad impact on the good standing of the creditor was dealt with in *Monks v National Westminster Bank PLC*.[91] The claimant sought a declaration and an injunction aimed at establishing that he had been subjected to double charging on his mortgage accounts, that he had not been in arrears in respect of those accounts, and that the defendant bank should delete adverse erroneous records. The court found useful purpose in the formal correction of the record, including towards a third-party regulator, which would allow the claimant to restore his financial good standing.

Useful purpose can be connected with the issue of **time and cost**. First, it must be stressed that utility is not a function of the value of the claim, where low value could exclude the useful purpose of the whole proceedings aimed at granting a declaration.[92]

As on the continent, the English court might not find, in this vein, sufficient utility in cases where a declaration **will not finally settle the dispute.**[93] Ascertaining the useful purpose engages the court in balancing the usefulness of the declaration against any inconvenience it may cause to the defendant. This balancing exercise is also reflected in the continental principle of subsidiarity (*see* Chapter 2 *supra*). One of the arguments in favour of striking out declarations in the case where a claim for

89. *Pavledes v Hadjisavva* [2013] EWHC 124 (Ch), 50 (English High Court).
90. *Point Solutions Ltd v Focus Business Solutions Ltd* [2005] EWHC 3096, 115–120 (English High Court).
91. *Monks v National Westminster Bank Plc* [2015] EWHC 2310 (Ch), 72 (English High Court).
92. This reservation is not groundless; in the past there was a threshold of 10 pounds for declaratory relief to be brought before Court of Chancery; now this is no longer valid, *See* Woolf, *supra* n. 1, at 174. Opposite trend can be observed in the Swiss law, *see* Annex IV.III.[C][2] by Nino Sievi *infra*.
93. Woolf, *supra* n. 1, at 178; This question is closely related to the continental principle of subsidiarity and will be dealt with separately below.

performance as a more far-reaching claim is available, is that the defendant should not incur more time and costs by being in two proceedings instead of one. As an example, in damages case, where two proceedings, one seeking the merit and one seeking quantum, could be run, the first one without the second one would not be allowed.

The cost and time issue was raised in *AXA Insurance UK Plc v Thermonex Ltd (in liquidation)*.[94] Here, while discussing the court's discretion, it was said that granting a declaration by an English court would avoid the need for lengthy and costly proceedings abroad.

One of the utility goals of declarations is to **ease settlement** between the parties, or otherwise facilitate **avoiding litigation**. In the *Fujifilm* case mentioned above,[95] where there was a case for declaring a lack of novelty of a certain patented solution, the court granted declaratory relief, confirming that declarations would serve a useful purpose, namely by promoting the likelihood of a settlement on a European or even global basis. In *Mitsui Osk Ltd v Salgaocar Mining Industries Private Ltd*,[96] the claimant sought a declaration on the jurisdiction of the English courts in a case involving a guarantee issued by the defendant. The court found that the purpose of this declaration was to avoid any possible disputes that might arise hereafter.

From the perspective of the continental lawyer, the case *Lloyd v Svenby* is especially interesting.[97] Burnton J used the criteria, typical to those of the legal interest, while denying a declaration in a dispute relating to the genealogy of old automobiles. He said,[98] save for the issue of jurisdiction, which should have been left with the Secretary of State for Transport, who decides about particular registration numbers, the genealogy of motor cars is not of itself a proper subject for the court to investigate, unless the investigation is for the purpose of deciding on the **justiciable rights** of the parties, and registration marks neither constitute a right of property nor a tortious cause of action. These criteria, however, were deduced from the useful purpose necessary for the declaration to be granted, and not from the legal interest itself. The case dealt with valuable old automobiles, which had been subject to a number of

94. *AXA Insurance UK Plc v Thermonex Ltd* [2013] T.C.L.R. 3; [2013] Lloyd's Rep. I.R. 323, 41 (English High Court).
95. *Fujifilm Kyowa Kirin Biologics Co., Ltd v AbbVie Biotechnology Ltd (No. 4)* [2017] EWHC 395 (Pat), 409 (Patents Court).
96. *Mitsui OSK Lines Ltd v Salgaocar Mining Ltd* [2015] EWHC 565 (Comm); [2015] 2 Lloyd's Rep. 518, 61 (English High Court). The claimant, sought the following declaration, *ibid.*, 8:

> The English court has jurisdiction to determine the claimant's claim against the defendant under the guarantee because England is an appropriate forum in which to determine the claim because the claim has been properly served on the defendant in India and because each of the following grounds for exercising jurisdiction are satisfied -
>
> (a) the guarantee contains a term conferring jurisdiction on the English court, and
> (b) the guarantee is subject to English law, and
> (c) the guarantee was concluded in England and through agents of the defendant operating in England.

97. *Lloyd v Svenby* [2006] 315 (QB) (English High Court).
98. *Ibid.*, 77–78, 85. Justiciable issues between the parties could be in this case, for example, a dispute as to whether a car sold by description complies with that description.

crashes and reconstructions. There was a dispute as to how much of the original cars were left in particular two ones. The declarations sought in these proceedings were very atypical, including one whereby Mr Lloyd's car had a better claim than Mr Svenby's car to be the car that William Frank ('Bill') Moss had registered with Bedford District Council on 23 March 1959 with registration mark WTM 446.

There are cases in which the courts are willing to grant declarations **despite them finding a low degree of utility** concerning the parties involved. The existence of a public interest might be such an occasion. We saw this in the case of Rolls-Royce, where providing a construction of a Statutory Instrument deriving from the European Directive on Age Discrimination was a matter of public importance.

Utility does not necessarily mean that a declaration is the only remedy that will relieve the claimant of his problems. It may be sufficient if the declaration, despite not being absolutely necessary, will be **convenient and useful**. In *Gunton v Richmond,*[99] the claimant was appointed by the defendant council under a contract of service, terminable by one month's notice. The relevant regulations setting out the procedure for the dismissal of employees on disciplinary grounds were subsequently adopted by the council and formed part or the claimant's contract. Although the reason for the claimant's dismissal was disciplinary, the procedure prescribed by the regulations was not fully complied with. Accordingly, the claimant brought an action for a declaration that the council's purported termination of his appointment was invalid. The judge granted the claimant a declaration that the notice of dismissal was ineffective and, on the claimant electing to claim damages under common law, ordered an inquiry as to damages on the basis that the claimant was entitled to remain in the council's employment until retirement age, unless in the meantime he was liable to redundancy or dismissal under the disciplinary procedure. Buckley LJ stated that this is not a case in which any declaratory relief is really necessary, but that the declaration contained in the judge's order, namely that the notice was ineffective lawfully in order to determine the contract of service of the claimant with the council, was, in his view, correct in law and inoffensive in its effect, so he saw no particular reason for interfering with that part of the order.[100]

Forum shopping as a rule, does not qualify as a useful purpose. 'The court must be particularly careful to ensure that a negative declaration is sought for a valid and valuable purpose, and not an illegitimate attempt to pre-empt the jurisdiction in which the dispute between the parties is to be resolved.'[101] Achieving **tactical advantages,** as happened in *InterDigital Technology Corp v Nokia Corp*[102] and *CPC Group v QD,*[103] in

99. *Gunton v Richmond-upon-Thames London Borough Council,* [1981] Ch. 448 (English Court of Appeal).
100. *Ibid.,* 471.
101. *Howden North America Inc & Anor v ACE European Group Ltd & Ors.*, [2012] EWCA Civ 1624, 23 (English Court of Appeal), citing Phillips LJ in *New Hampshire Insurance Co & Ors v Philips Electronics North America Corp.* [1998] CLC 1062 (English Court of Appeal). Different approach has been recently worked out in Swiss law, *see* Annex IV.III.[D][2] by Nino Sievi *infra.*
102. *InterDigital Technology Corp v Nokia Corp* [2008] EWHC 504 (Pat) (Chancery Division).
103. *CPC Group Limited v Qatari Diar Real Estate Investment Company* [2009] EWHC 3204 (Ch), 66–68 (English High Court).

general are not criticized, but are balanced against the features of justice and useful purpose.

If the issues to be declared cannot be **sufficiently clearly defined** to be properly justiciable, then there is no useful purpose *and* no declaration may be granted. The reason may be that a claim is premature and based on hypothetical facts. In *Mac Manus v European Insurance*[104] the court held that partners in a firm of solicitors had validly notified their personal indemnity insurer of possible claims against them, even though they had not identified particular defects in specific files. Their firm was a successor firm to one whose entire caseload, they suspected, was tainted with shortcomings that could give rise to claims. However, in the case at hand, any declaratory relief would almost inevitably be too narrow or too broad, and would risk creating more problems than it solved. A declaration would not serve any useful purpose.[105] The content of the declaration sought itself may not be eligible to be properly formulated despite being properly proved. In *Force India Formula One Team Ltd v Malaysia Racing Team SDN BHD,*[106] Arnold J found that properly reflected the court's findings would result in a declaration of such complexity that he did not believe it would serve any useful purpose. In such situations, however, courts are sometimes ready to give guidelines or conclusions that may direct parties in their dealings, but do not have a *res judicata* effect.[107]

§3.05 SUBSIDIARITY PRINCIPLE

The subsidiarity principle is derived from the general concept of legal interest as interpreted in the Germanic tradition. The possibility to seek performance based on a given cause of action excludes the occurrence of legal interest to seek only a declaration of rights or legal relationship. A lack of legal interest is demonstrated here because the declaration's function is merely to give a premise in the prospective proceedings in which ultimate performance will be sought. Therefore, a claim for performance gives fuller protection than a mere claim for a declaration. Usually separate declarations may be obtained in situations where further consequences, not embodied in the potential decision ordering performance or shaping the legal relationship, may occur. In certain situations, the subsidiarity principle goes even further, providing that there is no legal interest whatsoever in case the claimant has at his disposal any other relevant alternative way to protect its rights, even if it is not better but merely equally protective in the eyes of the court. Along with this principle, the courts will not grant declarations

104. *McManus v European Risk Insurance Co hf* [2013] EWHC 18 (Ch) (English High Court).
105. *CIP Property (AIPT) Ltd v Transport for London* [2012] EWHC 259 (Ch), 40 (English High Court); *See also San Juan v Allen* [2016] EWHC 1502 (Ch) (English High Court).
106. *Force India Formula One Team Ltd v 1 Malaysia Racing Team SDN BHD* [2012] EWHC 1621 (Ch), 5 (English High Court).
107. *McManus v European Risk Insurance Co hf* [2013] EWHC 18 (Ch) (English High Court).

in addition to other relief. Statements declaring rights or a legal relationship constituting premises of the final outcome, such as damages or an injunction, will be included in the grounds of the court's decision, but not in the decision itself.[108]

English law is principally different from the above. First, the very content of CPR 40.20 says that a declaration can be granted in addition to any other remedy. What is even more interesting, claims for declarations alone are unusual. Generally, declarations are sought and granted together with other forms of relief (often in the form of injunctions),[109] being a step in the process of claiming substantial relief.[110] It has been observed that, where a claimant seeks declaratory relief only, then the court applies careful scrutiny to the claim and asks whether the grant of such a declaration would be useful. This requirement has been developed in cases in which 'negative declarations' have been sought, but it is also valid where 'positive declarations' are concerned as well.[111]

In English law, certain threads present in the continental discourse have been sometimes also subject to the courts' consideration, though with various outcomes. In *Patten v Burke*,[112] the author and owner of the copyright in a book gave a publishing company the sole and exclusive right to print and publish the book in return for royalties. The company later went into receivership, having failed for some time to pay the royalties due. The author brought an action against the company seeking damages for a breach of contract and a declaration that the contract between the parties had been determined by the company's breach of contract, so that he was no longer bound by its terms. Millet J, as a matter of justice, stated that:

> Where the claim is for breach of contract and the plaintiff alleges that the contract is still subsisting, **the grant of an injunction restraining further breaches will sufficiently show the basis on which the judgment is given. It will in the normal case be unnecessary to grant a declaration that the contract still subsists**. Where the contract has been broken and the plaintiff's case is that it has been repudiated, however, it may not be at all clear, in the absence of a declaration to that effect, that the court is proceeding on the basis that the contract is at an end and that the plaintiff is no longer bound thereby. (emphasis added)

In this case, the court granted the declaration in order to set a clear finding on the contract ending, though it did not finally point to any specific consequences that, while not covered by the decision on damages, are achieved by that.

At various aspects however, the arguments used in relation to the subsidiarity principle are mirrored also in English law, though doubts appear while taking a closer look.

First, similar arguments will be found while analysing the problem of utility. Zamir and Woolf say:

108. *See* more in Chapter 2 and Chapter 5 *infra*.
109. White Book 2018, item 40.20.2; Westlaw UK, Commentary last updated 27 November 2017.
110. *Re Trident Fashions Plc Re The Insolvency Act 1986 Exeter City Council v Bairstow and Others* [2006] EWCA Civ 203, 11 (English Court of Appeal).
111. *Howden North America Inc & Anor v ACE European Group Ltd & Ors.*, [2012] EWCA Civ 1624, 21 (English Court of Appeal).
112. *Patten v Burke Publishing Co Ltd* [1991] 1 WLR 541 (Ch).

> The court may not regard a declaration to serve a useful purpose if it may not **settle the dispute** between the parties.[113] (emphasis added)

Saying that, however, the examples used to illustrate this problem do not fit exactly into what on the continent would constitute a legal interest. In *Lewis v Green*,[114] the claimant sought a declaration as to whether, on the true construction of certain deeds, the respondent owed him a given amount of money. The respondent argued that, even if the court made the declaration asked for, he would not be liable under these deeds, as he had some defences to the applicant's claim that were independent of the construction of the deeds, and which he might raise in further proceedings. Here in this case, the court did not reject the declaration on the basis that the claimant's proper claim was a claim for debt, and not merely for a declaration of debt, which is only half way. The reason for the rejection was the situation that, in the proceedings in question, not all the arguments of the defendant could be raised, and only in this context the court held that the entire dispute could not be settled by a mere declaration.

In *Bank of Petersburg v Arkhangelsky*,[115] the application for a declaration that the parties had acted in breach of a worldwide freezing order was refused. The judge saw no real utility in making a declaration, even if the alleged breaches could have been established, and a possible injustice to the defendants if there was possibility that granting a declaration would be treated as if it were a finding of contempt. It was open to the claimants to establish contempt and seek committal, but he found no reason for or utility in the half-way they proposed.

In both cases, the declarations sought were connected with other proceedings: to order damages and, in the second case, to establish contempt. In both cases the footing of the decision denying the declaration was based on the principles of justice, and or the lack of useful purpose in these particular cases, rather than on the objective possibility of achieving the same goal in other proceedings.

Interesting situations are referred to while discussing declarations of future rights. In the case of *quia timet* action (because he fears), which is used to prevent a threatened wrong, both a declaration and an injunction can be granted. There will be a declaration if, in the opinion of the judge, it is unlikely that the defendant will continue to pursue his intention to commit a wrongful act once the court has ruled on the legal position. This will enable the claimant to be granted injunctive relief in the future, should that become necessary, without commencing separate proceedings or relitigating the question already determined in the proceedings.[116] This situation is quite contrary to the subsidiarity principle, which always gives priority to other actions rather than declarations. In the continental tradition, where a case enables an injunction, the claimant has no legal interest in claiming merely a declaration. It should also be underlined that the court admitted that a declaration would serve perfectly well as the premises for any subsequent claim for an injunction, contrary to what was said

113. Woolf, *supra* n. 1, at 178
114. *Lewis v Green* [1905] 2 Ch. 340.
115. *Bank St Petersburg v Arkhangelsky* [2014] EWHC 574 (Ch), 13 (English High Court).
116. Woolf, *supra* n. 1, at 190–191.

about the Germanic concept of legal interest, which does not recognize this need as its component.

In *Monks v National Westminster Bank PLC*,[117] the claimant sought a declaration and an injunction aimed at establishing that he had been subjected to double charging on his mortgage accounts, that he had not been in arrears in respect of those accounts, and that the defendant bank should both delete the adverse credit data in its own records and inform the credit reference agencies of the correct position. In this case, the judge found that the criteria engaging the power to make a declaration were made. The court made a declaration that, for a period of approximately a year, the bank had wrongly maintained that the claimant owed unpaid arrears of interest on his mortgage accounts, in addition to the balances on his mortgage accounts already including the corresponding interest charges, and, in so doing, overstated the claimant's liability under his mortgages both internally and to one or more third parties. On the contrary, he withheld the injunction on the evidence that the bank had agreed to make the necessary corrections and notifications by itself.

The possibility of alternative proceedings as a matter blocking the discretion of the court is not excluded in the discourse of English jurisprudence and legal literature. Aitken LJ, as a seventh point of his test, asks the question whether granting a declaration is the most effective way of resolving the issues raised in the proceedings. Additionally, in answering that question, the court must consider the other options of resolving the issue. This could look very similar to the legal interest argument. This conclusion is, however, very strongly opposed while reviewing the issue more in depth.

As stated by Zamir and Woolf:

> [T]he general principle is that where there are two procedures available, it is for the litigant to decide which he wishes to adopt.[118]

As long as a declaration serves a useful purpose, it will be granted. The court may react, however, in terms of cost apportionment. In the event that the most expensive procedure is chosen by the party, the court may not award him all costs, as sought. In civil law cases there are some reservations. The court may not grant a declaration, for example, if the claimant's pleading is shaped in a way that would prevent the respondent's defences.[119]

It is claimed that the court may decide not to grant a declaration in a situation where there is an alternative procedure that is more convenient or more appropriate. This rule is mainly appropriate in the public law domain. If there are special remedies in statutory law, it will usually be found that this is the most appropriate remedy, even if judicial review is not expressly excluded. However, the courts will exercise its jurisdiction if statutory remedy is either ineffective or incapable of doing justice to the claimant. For example, the merits of the case may be so obvious that they can be immediately determined without remitting the case to the proper tribunal or authority,

117. *Monks v National Westminster Bank Plc* [2015] EWHC 2310 (Ch) (English High Court).
118. Woolf, *supra* n. 1, at 219.
119. *See Lewis v Green* [1905] 2 Ch. 340.

or because statutory proceedings are lengthier and therefore less satisfactory to the claimant, or because the legal issues are so complex that it is better to have the case resolved in court.[120] Such criteria were adopted by the court in *HC Trading Malta v Tradeland Commodities SL,*[121] in order not to grant a declaration while the debated issue could have been decided by the arbitration panel. The court stated that it was impossible to say whether it would necessarily be quicker and/or cheaper to use the court process rather than the arbitrators, while there was no practical impediment to the claimant commencing the arbitration right away.

Similarly, in *Football Association Premier League v QC Leisure,*[122] Kitchen J decided to transfer the case relating to the infringements of IP rights to the Patents County Court because the large scale of the infringements made it more appropriate to be heard by this court. The judge hearing this matter in the Patents County Court will be in a much better position to assess what, if any, further orders for disclosure are necessary and proportionate to enable any outstanding issues to be disposed of.

§3.06 THE EVOLUTIONARY NATURE OF THE ENGLISH LAW ON DECLARATIONS

For a better understanding of the very nature of declarations in a juridical sense, it is helpful to observe how it has been evolving through all this time. In Germanic countries, declarations were quite common in local laws and were granted in various types of proceedings. The modern concept of this institution, *Feststellungsklage,* aimed to put things into order and limited access to this relief. It was drafted in the spirit of pandectism, while codifying German laws in the form of German FCCP (*Zivilprozessordnung*) of 1879. The wording has not been changed basically until now.

English law, on the contrary, started from an absence of declaratory relief in legal proceedings up until 1850, when the Chancery Act of 1850 was adopted. Since then it seems that the English law on declaratory relief has been a law in transition, vibrantly changing over the decades, contrary to Germanic jurisdictions. It is a very important feature that is striking while analysing the court decisions. I see a number of areas that have evolved towards subsequent liberalization, since the declaration as a permitted relief was recognized. Subsequent amendments of law allowed for declarations of future rights, and then the scope of matters to be declared was extended by the inclusion of facts and legal principles in addition to rights. It is quite significant that those changes, unlike the traditional English instrument of precedent, were introduced by the statutory law. That means that certain barriers to the development were really laid down in the past by jurisprudence, and that a statutory instrument was used to break the then current attitude. The final wording of CPR 40.20 gives the courts the full discretion in granting a declaration. Further developments were left to jurisprudence,

120. Woolf, *supra* n. 1, at 219–223.
121. [2016] EWHC 1279 (Comm); [2016] 1 W.L.R. 3120; [2017] 2 All E.R. (Comm) 259; [2016] 2 Lloyd's Rep. 130; [2016] 2 C.L.C. 27; 166 Con. L.R. 94.
122. *Football Association Premier League Ltd v QC Leisure* [2012] EWHC 108 (Ch) (English High Court); [2012] 2 C.M.L.R. 16; [2012] F.S.R. 12; [2012] L.L.R. 375 at 102.

which dealt mainly with working out the limitations of the court's discretion, earlier combined with the limits of the court's jurisdiction, dealing with various aspects of the principles of justice and utility. The very recent Financial List Scheme shows how judiciary in a pragmatic way responds to the changing needs of users.

It is quite often noticed that the possibilities of obtaining declarations is widening. Confirmation of this can be found in the White Book,[123] in the leading court decisions on various occasions; Aikens LJ, to give an example, made the following statement:

> The grant of a declaration is discretionary. The law has developed since the statement of principle by Lord Diplock in the leading case of Gouriet v Union of Post Office Workers.[124] I have looked again at Gouriet's case, the decisions of this court in Meadows Indemnity Co Ltd v Insurance Corporation of Ireland Pld and the International Commercial Bank Plc,[125] In Re S,[126] Feetum v Levy,[127] and most recently, The Office of Fair Trading v Foxtons Ltd,[128] as well as the decisions referred to in Wall LJ's judgement. There is no doubt that the circumstances in which the court will be prepared to grant declaratory relief are now considerably wider than they were thought to be after Gouriet's case and the Meadows case. In the words of Jonathan Parker LJ in Feetum v Levy, (...) things have indeed moved on since the Meadows case was decided; and the courts should not nowadays apply such a restrictive meaning to the passage in Lord Diplock's speech in Gouriet's case.[129]

The question concerned the possibility of making declarations relating a contract, to which the parties were not the parties to the proceedings. In *Feetum v Levy* [2006] Ch 585, it was observed that things had 'moved on' and that declaratory relief should not be refused on the grounds that the claimants are seeking declaratory relief as to the effect of a contract to which they are not parties, as long as they are not merely directly *interested* in the issue as to the validity of the appointment, but are directly *affected* by it. The declaration stated that the appointment of administrative receivers of a limited liability partnership was prohibited by the Insolvency Act 1986 section 72A, and was therefore invalid. It was sought by the partners of the partnership as a party to the debenture, which provided the authority to the defendant to appoint receivers.[130] In *Millebush Properties Limited v Tameside Metropolitan Borough Council,*[131] the claimant

123. White Book 2018, 1318, Westlaw UK, Commentary last updated 27 November 2017.
124. In *Gouriet's case* [1978] AC 435, 501 (House of Lords), Lord Diplock stated:

> for the court to have jurisdiction to declare any legal right, it must be one which is claimed by one of the parties as enforceable against an adverse party to the litigation, either as a subsisting right or as one which may come into existence in the future conditionally on the happening of an event.

125. *Meadows Indemnity Co Ltd v Insurance Corporation of Ireland Pld and the International Commercial Bank Plc* [1989] 2 Lloyd's Rept 298 (English Supreme Court of Judicature Court of Appeal).
126. *In Re S* [1996] Fam 1 (House of Lords).
127. *Feetum and Others v Levy and Others* [2006] Ch 585 (English Court of Apeal).
128. *The Office of Fair Trading v Foxtons Ltd* [2009] EWCA Civ 288 ((English Supreme Court of Judicature Court of Appeal)
129. *Rolls-Royce Plc v Unite the Union* [2010] 1 WLR 318, 119 (English Court of Appeal).
130. *Feetum and Others v Levy and Others* [2006] Ch 585, 81–82 (English Court of Apeal).
131. *Milebush Properties Ltd v Tameside MBC* [2011] EWCA Civ 270 (English Court of Appeal).

claimed for declarations in respect of the rights of way, to be granted to him, as referred to in an agreement under the Town and Country Planning Act 1990 section 106, to which he was not a party. The agreement was concluded between the borough authorities and a developer, respondent in these proceedings. This case raised a point of interest on the availability, in private law proceedings between non-contracting parties, of a declaration on the meaning and effect of a planning obligation contained in a deed made pursuant to provisions in the planning legislation. Based on authorities cited in the *Rolls-Royce* case, he confirmed[132] that the general tenor of later cases is that this passage in Lord Diplock's speech should not been treated literally as precluding the grant of a declaration on the construction of a contract to which the claimant is not a party.[133]

In this area, similar developments are to be observed also in Germanic laws. In Poland, the starting point for such an interpretation was, however, different and concerned the right to justice as set out in Article 45 of the Polish Constitution and Article 14 of the International Covenant on Civil and Political Rights, as referred to in the decision of the Polish Supreme Court.[134] Based on that argument, it was stated that procedural standing in declaratory proceedings can be attributed to everyone who pursues his legal interest to declare his right or legal relationship, and not only to parties to the contract in question. It was underlined that legal protection can always be sought when there is a need to achieve a better legal position through its relevant clarification.

Negative declarations were allowed once Ord. 25 r. 5 was introduced in 1883, when it ceased to be necessary to prove entitlement to consequential relief in order to obtain a declaration.[135] As case law shows, the judges still had reservations about granting negative declarations, which in fact declare neither right nor liability. The evolution of negative declarations has been noted in a number of cases. In *Messier Dowty v Sabena,*[136] Sabena claimed lack of jurisdiction of the court to grant negative declarations, based on the *Re Clay*[137] case, followed by *Midland Bank Plc v Laker Airways Limited.*[138]

Lord Woolf MR[139] recalled the history of negative declarations, concluding that the level of acceptance of negative declarations had changed. He underlined that the approach was more pragmatic, being not a matter of jurisdiction, but one of discretion. The deployment of negative declarations should be scrutinized and their use rejected

132. *Rolls-Royce Plc v Unite the Union* [2010] 1 WLR 318, 38 (English Court of Appeal).
133. It appears that this line of jurisprudence coincides anyway with the works of the law commission on reforming the privity rules by granting rights to third parties to the contract, enforceable directly, what finally resulted in the passing of the Contracts (Rights of Third Parties) Act 1999, *See* John Cartwright, *Contract Law, An Introduction to the English Law of Contract for Civil Lawyers*, 234 et seq. (2nd. ed., 2013).
134. Judgement of 2 February 2006, II CK 395 /05 (Polish Supreme Court), Judgement of 14 July 2016, I ACa 49/16 (Appellate Court in Białystok).
135. Woolf, *supra* n. 1, at 192.
136. *Messier Dowty Ltd v Sabena SA* [2000] 1 W.L.R. 2040 (English Court of Appeal).
137. *Re Clay* [1919] 1 Ch. 66 (English Court of Appeal).
138. *Midland Bank Plc v Laker Airways Limited* [1986] QB 689.
139. Woolf, *supra* n. 1, at 41–42.

where it would serve no useful purpose. However, where a negative declaration would help to ensure that the aims of justice are achieved, the courts should not be reluctant to grant such declarations.

Meanwhile he stated that negative declarations are an unusual remedy in so far as they reverse the more usual roles of the parties. The natural defendant becomes the claimant and vice versa, which can result in procedural complications and possible injustice to an unwilling 'defendant'. This in itself justifies caution, but, subject to the exercise of appropriate circumspection, there should be no reluctance to their being granted when it is useful to do so. Negative declarations can and do assist in achieving justice. A pragmatic approach should be adopted.[140]

This shows how the approach to negative declarations has come a long way. The current trend is envisaged in *Toropdar v D*[141]by Clarke J, who simply said that, with regard to history, the availability to both sides of the evidence and material necessary to address the issue of the claimant's alleged negligence, and the fact that each side was represented, it would 'have bordered on the perverse if, having decided that the claimant was no liable, he had declined, as a matter of discretion, to declare that to be so'.

Jurisdiction versus discretion. Finally the question of requalification of the courts authority from jurisdiction to the discretion, seems to be an exercise in liberalization by itself. For the continental lawyer, the discussion on whether the authority to grant a declaration is a matter of the court's discretion or jurisdiction, is rather odd. The jurisdiction of the given court is derived from particular provisions of the statutory law. The civil law, just as private law, is separate from the administration law, with a separate jurisdiction of civil law courts from the court dealing with administration matters. In English law, this matter is not so clear. In many courts' decisions on declarations, it is underlined that the authority in question is a matter of discretion and not of jurisdiction, suggesting that in each case this dilemma is raised and again decided in favour of discretion. The meaning of this confusion is sometimes disregarded for practical reasons. *In Michael Toth v Emirates,*[142] Mann J, refused to grant a declaration in internet domain case because of the powers granted to the DRS,[143] said directly:

> This argument only works for Mr Turner if the contract constituted by the DRS leaves it open to the court to grant a declaration. If it is a contract that leaves the question of abusive registration to the expert (and appeal panel) then the court must decline to grant a declaration, either as a matter of jurisdiction, or as a matter of discretion (it does not matter which). (emphasis added)

140. This development was confirmed by *InterDigital Technology Corp v Nokia Corp* [2008] EWHC 504 (Pat), 13 (Chancery Division); *Financial Services Authority v Rourke* [2002] C.P. Rep.14 (English High Court); *Nokia Corp v InterDigital Technology Corp (Application to Set Aside)* [2006] EWHC 802 (Pat), 22 et seq. (English High Court).
141. *Toropdar v D* [2009] EWHC 567 (QB) (English High Court).
142. *Toth v Emirates* [2012] EWHC 517 (Ch), 65.
143. DRS is a dispute resolution procedure created by Nominet UK, a non-profit organization that registers national internet domain names such as those ending '.co.uk'.

He further states that it was the effect of a contract, so the declaration route is not open and the DRS did not permit the court a role. This statement, however, gives the impression that the court does not have jurisdiction. He could not grant a declaration, even if he wanted to, because 'the declaration route is not open'.[144] The jurisdiction would mean the power of the court to make a judgement, though as a matter of discretion only such a declaration is denied.

In earlier cases, the limitations of the court's powers were deemed to be a matter of jurisdiction. Lord Diplock described the power to grant declarations as jurisdiction, though discretionary.[145] He stated that:

> It is when an infringement of the plaintiff's rights in the future is threatened or when, unaccompanied by threats, there is a dispute between parties as to what their respective rights will be if something happens in the future, that the **jurisdiction** to make declarations of right can be most usefully invoked. But the **jurisdiction** of the court is not to declare the law generally or to give advisory opinions; it is confined to declaring contested legal rights, subsisting or future, of the parties represented in the litigation before it and not those of anyone else.

In later decisions, the term discretion becomes more congruent and replaces usage of the term jurisdiction.

The courts derive the jurisdiction to grant declarations from the content of section 19 of the Senior Courts Act 1981[146] which is reiterated in CPR rule 40.20.[147] From the wording of CPR 40.20, namely that 'The court may make binding declarations whether or not any other remedy is claimed', it was found that the jurisdiction of the courts to grant declarations is unlimited.[148] The basic quotation in this respect is of Neuberger LJ, who said:

---

144. This finding stands against what other authorities provide. Woolf, *supra* n. 1, at 86, underline that a provision in the contract that purports entirely to oust the jurisdiction of the courts will be regarded as contrary to public policy. The parties can agree, as a condition precedent to commencing proceedings, that a point be referred first to a particular person or body, including arbitration.
145. *Gouriet's case* [1978] AC 435, 501 (House of Lords).
146. 19.– General jurisdiction of High Court.
    (1) The High Court shall be a superior court of record.
    (2) Subject to the provisions of this Act, there shall be exercisable by the High Court–
        (a) all such jurisdiction (whether civil or criminal) as is conferred on it by this or any other Act; and
        (b) all such other jurisdiction (whether civil or criminal) as was exercisable by it immediately before the commencement of this Act (including jurisdiction conferred on a judge of the High Court by any statutory provision)(...).
147. *Mitsui OSK Lines Ltd v Salgaocar Mining Ltd* [2015] EWHC 565 (Comm); [2015] 2 Lloyd's Rep. 518, 6 (English High Court).
148. In *Guaranty Trust Co. of New York v Hannay & Co.* [1915] 2 K.B.536, affirmed [1915] W.N. 38 (English Court of Appeal), Pickford L.J. said, at p. 562: 'I think therefore that the effect of the rule is to give a general power to make a declaration whether there be a cause of action or not, and at the instance of any party who is interested in the subject matter of the declaration.' *See also* Kennedy LJ in *Padden v Arbuthnot Pensions & Investments Ltd*, [2004] EWCA Civ 582, 19 (English Court of Appeal).

> Accordingly, so far as the CPR is concerned, the power to make declarations appears to be unfettered. As between the parties in the section, it seems to me that the court can grant a declaration as to their rights, or as to the existence of facts, or as to a principle of law, where those rights, facts, or principles have been established to the court's satisfaction.[149]

In this vein, it is declined to use the term jurisdiction, as the powers of the court are not limited by statutory law. Judges apply their discretion, which is however subject to certain limitations worked out by the judicature. In *Messier-Dowty v Sabena* [2001] 1 All ER 275 Lord Woolf said this:

> However, if it would, that it would then be appropriate to grant a declaration was agreed. The approach is pragmatic. It is not a matter of jurisdiction. It is a matter of discretion.(...) So in my judgement the development of the use of declaratory relief in relation to commercial disputes should not be constrained by artificial limits wrongly related to jurisdiction. It should instead be kept within proper bounds by the exercise of the court's discretion. A similar tenor sounds in other judgements. Pumfrey J said: 'So in my judgment, the development of the use of declaratory relief in relation to commercial disputes should not be constrained by artificial limits wrongly related to jurisdiction. It should, instead, be kept within proper bounds by the exercise of the courts' discretion.[150]

In cases where specific remedy is provided by legislation, it will usually be presumed that, even though the legislature has not expressly excluded the power of the courts to grant the declaration, the courts will be hesitant to pursue its remedies instead remedies provided by the law.[151] In *HC Trading Malta v Tradeland Commodities SL*,[152] the claimant had entered into a contract containing a London arbitration clause. The claimant intended to make a contractual claim against the defendant in a London arbitration. The defendant did not intend to take proceedings anywhere, since it denied that there was any contract. Its position was that, when the claimant commenced arbitration in London, it would contest the arbitrator's jurisdiction. The claimant then sought a declaration that there was a binding arbitration agreement before starting the arbitration proceedings. In this case, the declaration was refused. It was held, that, 'on the application of a party to arbitral proceedings, the court could rule on the substantive jurisdiction of the tribunal either with the parties' agreement in writing, or the tribunal's permission; it would be wrong, therefore, in principle for a court to grant a declaration as to the existence of a binding arbitration agreement'. This argument is very close to jurisdiction again. The judge said that it was wrong in principle to grant declaratory relief due to the content of section 30 of the Arbitration Act, which grants this power to the arbitration panel.

Finally he said, however, that even if there had not been any principled argument against the granting of declaratory relief, the declaration would not have been granted based on discretional power. The reasons for refusing the declaration constituted a mix

149. *Financial Services Authority v Rourke* [2002] C.P. Rep.14, (3) (English High Court).
150. *See Nokia Corporation v Interdigital Technology Corporation* [2007] EWHC 3077 (Pat) (English High Court).
151. Woolf, *supra* n. 1, at 220.
152. *HC Trading Malta Ltd v Tradeland Commodities SL* [2016] EWHC 1279 (Comm).

of the aforementioned hesitation to take over other tribunal, as well as a lack of utility:[153]

> The question of jurisdiction are still relevant, however they appear in specific situations, like where competition law proceedings under EU law were raised as a bar to the court's declaration,[154] or an overlapping jurisdiction of two or more states,[155] or in the case of a declaration involving fraudulent conduct.[156]

The practical consequences broadening the scope of jurisdiction and putting emphasis of the problem of discretion are clearly aimed at liberalizing the criteria, adopted to the set limits of judicial powers due to the change in legal statutory infrastructure. The interference of the upper courts into the judge's discretion may appear only if the decision is based on an incorrect legal principle, or if, for some other reason, his decision was plain wrong.[157]This shows how English law went quite a long way from a total prohibition of granting declarations, to full freedom-termed discretion. The limits of this discretion are being now worked by subsequent precedents that address the questions of justice and utility. It is claimed that discretion allowed declarations to be a flexible instrument, which in turn leads to its increasing popularity.[158]

---

153. At 41–42:

> Finally, even if there is no principled argument against the granting of declaratory relief here and it is all a matter of discretion, I would unhesitatingly refuse to exercise it in favour of granting relief here for the following reasons.
>
> (1) It is a needless invocation of the court's powers where there is another body particularly suited to declaring the validity or otherwise of the arbitration agreement, namely the arbitral tribunal itself. (2) It is impossible to say now (for the reasons given in para. 20 above) that it would necessarily be quicker and/or cheaper to use the court process rather than the arbitrators. (3) In a case such as this, there is a very real risk that in deciding the issue as to the existence or otherwise of the arbitration agreement, the court will probably be deciding the central issue between the parties which is whether there was a binding contract of sale at all – that is, on any view, the province of the arbitrators. (4) There is no practical impediment to HCT commencing the arbitration right away here and none has been suggested. (5) It is said that to grant a declaration here would not usurp the function of the arbitrators. In fact it might – if the court was to decide a central issue between the parties, as noted above. But putting that to one side, I agree in a narrow sense that there would be no usurpation for reasons given in para. 18 above. But in a wider sense there would be, because simply allowing the court to decide the matter would be failing to give any weight to the scheme established by the Act and in particular s. 30. Even if the scheme and principles of the Act are not such as to 'trump' other matters so as to make it wrong in principle to exercise the discretion in a case like this, they still have force as a discretionary factor. (6) Finally, it is said that a negative determination would ensure that Tradeland will not become subject to the process to which it did not agree. That is true, but on the other hand, the arbitrators can do the same under s. 30.

154. *See Nokia Corp v InterDigital Technology Corp (Application to Set Aside)* [2006] EWCA Civ 1618, 21–22 (English Court of Appeal). What is interesting here is that the defendant asked the court to decline jurisdiction as a matter of discretion; *ibid.*, at 11.
155. *L v C (Applications by Non-Biological Mother)* [2014] EWFC 1 (English Family Court).
156. In *Patten v Burke Publishing Co Ltd* [1991] 1 WLR 541 (Ch), Millett LJ stated that, in effect, it was the court's duty 'to do the fullest justice to the plaintiff to which he is entitled,' and he went on to hold that there was no rule of law that prevented a declaration of fraudulent conduct.
157. *Milebush Properties Ltd v Tameside MBC* [2011] EWCA Civ 270, 29 (English Court of Appeal).
158. Woolf, *supra* n. 1, at 125.

§3.07 SUMMARY

What binds both, Germanic and English law systems is that they are grounded in statutory law, both are of a general nature, and in both systems, it is the judges who developed the legal infrastructure on how to use this mechanism, with the reservation that the Germanic system was originally rooted in academia.

In Germanic laws the approach to declarations is based on the academic concept of legal interest, protecting the courts from being overloaded with an excessive number of claims. The English approach is more pragmatic, not to be unduly purist, because the 'thrust of modern authority favours engagement rather than abstention' is a postulate confirmed by judicial practice,[159] and this direction will most probably survive. Zamir and Woolf criticized statements that declarations should be treated with special caution, as the same can be said of other remedies:

> [t]here is nothing particular about the nature or the consequences of declaratory relief which calls for extraordinary caution. On the contrary, not being coercive relief, it is less harmful, potentially, than other remedies, notably injunctions and specific performance. Extreme caution is both unnecessary and undesirable. On the other hand, care is needed, not only to avoid indiscriminate an unjustified use of declaratory power, but also to prevent declaratory actions from being dismissed and the scope of the remedy being unduly restricted our of extreme caution.[160]

In both systems, the claimant must demonstrate an interest in obtaining a declaration; he cannot be just a common 'busybody'. The notion of the term 'interest' is, however, quite different in the two systems, and starts from different axiological assumptions.

In English law, performing justice and utility were the goals to be achieved while evaluating the interest of the claimant. This entire setting combined of principles of justice and utility has been qualified for the purposes of this publication as real interest. Germanic law seems anxious about exceeding the formal legitimacy of the party seeking the declaration, namely exceeding the borders of legality embodied in the term 'legal interest', used in all statutes. This is the fundamental difference that divides both systems.

This has resulted in a different perspective of the judge as to the function of respective interests. Legal interest is a prerequisite, a prior condition to granting the

---

159. *Rolls-Royce Plc v Unite the Union* [2009] EWCA Civ 387, 57–58 (English High Court) LJ Wall exactly said:

> Finally, and I accept that this is a **pragmatic point**, we are being asked (by both parties) to hear the appeal, and it has been fully argued both before the judge and before us. Both we and counsel have invested a substantial amount of time in it. In general terms, therefore, I have come to the conclusion that it would be **unduly purist** for this court to decline to adjudicate on a point which has been brought before us by means of a procedure which has been deemed by the parties and by the court below to be appropriate. It seems to me further that the **thrust of modern authority favours engagement rather than abstention.** (emphasis added)

160. Woolf, *supra* n. 1, at 130.

declaration. The existence of real interest indicates the borders of the judge's freedom to grant declarations, and to some extent plays a role of 'post-requisites'. Continental judges grant declarations 'only if' legal interest is proven; English judges grant declarations 'unless' there is no real interest in doing so. In other words, a Continental judge asks the question 'can I grant a declaration?' before it starts analysing whether the content of the declaration is proven. The English judge analyses the content of the declaration with the view that it can grant it, and then asks the question 'are any limitations on my discretion?' In practice, those layers of interpretations and valuations are interrelated and do not appear in such an academic order. In *Interdigital v Nokia*[161] it was material for the judge to see the whole picture of what motivated InterDigital to bring the proceedings in deciding whether there was sufficient interest in granting a declaration. In *Trimast Holding Sarl v Telecolumbus GMBH,*[162] however, a different order was adopted, and the judge found that, before answering certain questions relating to the nature of rights under the relevant inter-creditors agreement, first he had to decide whether the questions should be decided. In general, however, it may be observed that limitations of discretion are examined on top of the entire case analysis.

The principle of justice and useful purpose allows English law to have a broad spectrum of matters being declared, including rights, legal relationships, remedies, facts and principles of law. Germanic declarations are granted in relation only to rights and legal relationships.

The different axiology of the respective interests leads to the conclusion that legal interest should be objective by nature, neglecting the real needs of the claimant. This evolved into the subsidiarity principle, which does not allow for a choice among the remedies open to him. Declaratory relief appears to be, by definition, a remedy less valued than other remedies, and not allowed in case there is a remedy more far-reaching than a declaration. As discussed in this chapter, the evaluation of possible remedies is also practised in English courts, but in each case from the perspective of justice and utility, including the factors of time and cost, rather than as a strict rule to follow. In the event that more than one avenue is possible, the choice will more frequently lie with the claimant, with any possible financial consequences also falling on the claimant.[163]

Although in continental thinking there is a reflection of utility - not to put too much burden on the defendant, as can be found in some textbooks, and not put too much unnecessary burden on the court, in reality it is the dogmatic argument that prevails, and individual approach is rather not undertaken.[164]

It is interesting to see also how large a role is played by public interest in the process of exercising the judges' discretion, which leads to interesting developments of importance to the public. An example of this can be found in all the declarations sought by the FSA or appearing on the Financial List.[165] This particular goal is not reflected in

161. *InterDigital Technology Corp v Nokia Corp* [2008] EWHC 504 (Pat), 32–33 (Chancery Division).
162. *Trimast Holding Sarl v Tele Columbus GmbH* [2010] EWHC 1944 (Ch) (English High Court).
163. Woolf, *supra* n. 1, at 219 n. 4.223.
164. In Hungary, the subsidiarity principle has recently been transformed into a principle of law.
165. Such a result is more naturally achieved, as English law does not provide for the strict segregation of administration and civil procedures. It should not be forgotten that the

the notion of the legal interest. Interestingly enough, in order to secure a public interest in declarations sought in class actions in Poland, the legislator had to do away with this prerequisite otherwise it was too risky for the claimant.[166]

development of declaratory remedy originated precisely in administrative proceedings, and only later expanding into civil and commercial relations; *See* Woolf, *supra* n. 1, at. 27.

166. *See* The Law on Class Actions as of 17 December 2009, as amended (Journal of Laws of 2010, No. 7, item 44), Art. 2.3.

CHAPTER 4

The Concept of 'Converged' Interest in International Arbitration Awards*

§4.01 INTRODUCTION

[A] The Practical Value of Declarations

Declarations are valued and frequently used in arbitration. The utility of this measure is underlined much more often in the context of arbitration then in litigation, possibly due to the specific needs of commercial dealing. As emphasized by Dunand and Kostsyska,[1] the parties seek declaratory relief to ascertain their legal positions, clarify their rights and obligations, and to determine whether they are bound by contracts or other legal instruments. Declaratory awards are meant to enable the parties to settle their disputes early on, quickly and cost-effectively, before they suffer more extensive damage. By clarifying the strengths and weaknesses of the parties' legal positions and establishing legal certainty, declaratory awards may facilitate the settlement. In some cases, a declaration of rights and liabilities alone can be a sufficient measure of satisfaction. In cases where purely declaratory relief proves to be insufficient, the winning party may later rely on the declaratory award in seeking monetary or injunctive relief. Weincymer[2] points out that, in some cases such as distribution, franchise and joint venture agreements, in the event of disagreement about proper prices or profit-sharing arrangements, an arbitral decision may specify the prices for a particular period of time. A declaratory award 'may be useful for further negotiations or adaptation of contracts in long-term or relational contracts'. Formal declarations of

* The author would like to thank the ICC Court and, in particular, Alexis Mourre and Alex Fessas for their support in pursuing this project, as well as Sylvie Picard Renault for her invaluable guidance in the realm of court practice.

1. Patrick Dunand & Maria Kostytska, *Declaratory Relief in International Arbitration*, 29(1) J. Intl. Arb. 1, 2 (2012).
2. Jeffrey Waincymer, *Procedure and Evidence in International Arbitration* 1113 (2012).

an arbitral tribunal may also constitute steps along the tribunal's progress towards a final award. They are a useful device, particularly where the parties have a continuing relationship and want to resolve what is, in the greater scheme of things, a minor dispute without risking the relationship as a whole by demands for monetary compensation. Of course, the above utility features are attributable not only to arbitration awards, but to declarations granted by the state courts as well, however this layer of analysis is more frequently presented as concerning declaratory activity in arbitration.

Declarations embodied in the award establish the legal position definitively, may have the *res judicata* effect and may, therefore, be binding on the parties, on other arbitral tribunals and on courts in subsequent proceedings.[3] Declarations, being as they are a non-coercive measure, are not subject to enforcement, but they may be the subject of recognition.[4]

The London Court of International Arbitration (LCIA) has reported that 29% of arbitrations in 2012 and 31% of arbitrations in 2011 sought declaratory relief or specific performance.[5] Recent 2017 LCIA[6] statistics are not exactly comparable: they show that, in 8% of the cases, non-monetary relief, i.e., declaration and specific performance, was sought; in the next 28% of cases, non-monetary relief was sought together with monetary relief, making for a total of 36%. As will be demonstrated below, experience of the International Chamber of Commerce (ICC) likewise shows that declarations are an important measure in arbitration practice.

[B] The Arbitrators Authority to Grant Declarations

The question of declaratory relief in arbitral awards has been raised in a number of writings. As noted by G. Born,[7] the most critical aspect of any arbitral award is the relief that it grants. In many cases, this is a straightforward matter, like amounts due in payment for goods or services, or satisfaction of a debt or guarantee. In other cases, including declaratory orders, some forms of monetary damages (e.g., punitive damages or interim measures), disputes may arise as to the tribunal's actual power to award such relief and the appropriate standards for doing so.

The remedial powers of an international arbitral tribunal may be defined, in the first instance, by the parties' arbitration agreement.[8] Alas, as practice shows, this happens very rarely, even if taking into consideration different sets of arbitration

3. Stefan Leimgruber, *Declaratory Relief in International Commercial Arbitration*, 32(3) ASA Bulletin 467, 467 (2014); Dunand & Kostytska, *supra* n. 1, at 2.
4. Sigvard Jarvin, *Non-Pecuniary Remedies: The Practice Of Declaratory Relief and Specific Performance in International Commercial Arbitration* in *Contemporary Issues in International Arbitration and Mediation – The Fordham Papers* 167, 178 (Arthur W. Rovine ed., Fordham Papers 2007).
5. LCIA, *Registrar's Report* (2012), 3, http://www.lcia.org/lcia/reports.aspx (accessed 25 September 2018).
6. LCIA, *Facts and Figures – 2017 Casework Report*, 8, http://www.lcia.org/lcia/reports.aspx (accessed 25 September 2018).
7. Gary Born, *International Commercial Arbitration* 2478 (2d ed., Kluwer Law International 2014).
8. Alan Redfern & Martin Hunter, *Law and Practice of International Commercial Arbitration* 515 para. 9.40 (3rd ed., 1999).

rules.[9] Aramco is the usual case on call for declaratory relief.[10] In this dispute, Aramco claimed that its exclusive right to transport oil from its concession area in Saudi Arabia had been infringed by the agreement made between the Saudi Arabian government and the late Aristotle Onassis and his company. The dispute was significant enough, but neither party wished it to jeopardize their trading relationship as a whole, first established in the 1930s. Accordingly, it was agreed that the award should be of declaratory effect only, with neither party claiming damages for any alleged injury. The issue in this case was to limit the competence of the tribunal down to mere declaration and the arbitral tribunal confirmed that its competence may be limited in such a way.[11] This case confirms, then, that declaratory relief is an inherent competence of the arbitration tribunal and can be dealt with by the parties in the arbitration agreement. P. Schlosser said in the context of arbitration that 'to a German, the declaratory function of the judiciary is the most natural thing in the world'.[12]

In a few jurisdictions, like English or Singapore law, arbitration legislation affirmatively vests arbitral tribunals with the authority to grant declarations.[13] Most, however, are silent as regards remedies within the arbitrators' toolbox. It is enough to say that arbitral tribunals are at least equipped with the same prerogatives as state courts.[14] Some authors go further and observe that they are not restricted to the remedies available to the court of the seat of the arbitration. In general, the arbitrators are granted freedom in selecting the appropriate remedy with the aim to fully and satisfactorily resolve the dispute in a practical manner. That said, there have been occasional decisions to the contrary, suggesting that the arbitrators' remedial authority is inherently narrow and limited, but these are in the minority.[15]

It is uncontroversial, that the authorization is to be sought firstly in the very arbitration agreement itself. The wording used in most of the arbitration agreements is similar in this respect. In the ICC standard clause, the language is the following: '[a]ny dispute arising out of or in connection with the present contract shall be finally settled under the Rules of Arbitration of the International Chamber of Commerce [...]'.[16] In some cases the parties add 'any dispute or controversy', which does not change the overall meaning that the arbitral tribunal is called upon to resolve the dispute. This language is broad enough to give the arbitrators authority to rule on all kind of

9. *See* section §1.03 *supra*.
10. Nigel Blackaby & Constantine Partasides, et al., *Redfern and Hunter on International Arbitration* 534–535 (5th ed., Oxford University Press 2009).
11. *Saudi Arabia v Arab Am. Oil Co.* ('Aramco') 27 ILR 117, 117–118 (1963).
12. Peter Schlosser, *Right and Remedy in Common Law Arbitration and in German Arbitration Law*, 4 Journal of International Arbitration, 27 (1987).
13. English Arbitration Act s. 48 (1996); Singapore International Arbitration Act s. 12(5) (2012) (granting arbitrators the power to award any remedy or relief that could be ordered by a Singapore court if the dispute had been subject of civil proceedings in such court and power to award interest)?
14. Julian D.M. Lew & Loukas A. Mistelis, et al., *Comparative International Commercial Arbitration* 649 at 24–70 (2003).
15. Born, *supra* n. 7, at 2487–2479.
16. *See also* SIAC, China International Economic and Trade Arbitration Commission (CIETAC), LCIA, DIS.

remedies claimed by the parties, unless such authority is explicitly excluded by the relevant law or arbitration rules.

Presumably, this language, however, may raise questions in the context of legal interest and *competenz-competenz* authority of the tribunal. Berger & Kellerhals tend to suggest, that legal interests have some indirect impact on the jurisdiction of the tribunal in case of declaratory relief is sought.[17] One of the components of the legal interest is whether there is a dispute or controversy between the parties (the attendant one being that this dispute is no longer bearable to the parties). According to *expressis verbis* content of the arbitration clause, the tribunal is empowered to settle the disputes only. One could say, that if there is no dispute, there is no authority flowing from the arbitration agreement for the tribunal's activity, what in fact is a manifestation of lack of legal interest. There is then the question of whether the tribunal is authorized to examine whether the parties are in a genuine dispute or whether the formal aspect is decisive, viz. the mere fact that claimant submitted its claim and paid for its settlement. What if respondent admits the claim, demonstrating that in fact there is no dispute as between the parties. The short answer is that legal interest does not apply in arbitration due to the prevailing opinion on its procedural nature.[18]

In general, it must be emphasized, that formal initiation of arbitration is enough for the arbitrators to define the matter as being in dispute, despite the fact of admission or other similar actions of the other party. Any hesitation of the other party as to the fact of appearance of the dispute will constitute a dispute anyway.

Every claim in arbitration initiates a dispute which must be resolved by the arbitrators, unless it is properly withdrawn. The only limitation flowing from the arbitration agreement is its connection with the main agreement. This is valid and unquestionable for disputes based on the claims for performance and constitutive claims, and must be valid also for the declaratory claims in the absence of any particular reservation. Further, the claimant's subjective conviction of existing controversy is enough to define a dispute. The general language of the clause allows to accept for settlement all disputes, also those defined as such in the individual account of the given party. There are no grounds to analyse the genuineness of the dispute itself in objective terms as dictated by the concept of legal interest. After initiation of the proceedings and based on the gathered materials, the tribunal must decide on the merits of the declaration.

17. Bernhard Berger & Franz Kellerhals, *International and Domestic Arbitration in Switzerland* n. 678 (2d ed., 2010)
18. The competence of the arbitrators may be impacted by the classification of the remedy as procedural or substantive. This classification might determine whether the relevant applicable law is the law governing the arbitration or the law applicable to the merits. In any event arbitrators should be careful not to exceed their mandate. *See* Julian D.M. Lew & Loukas A. Mistelis, et al., *supra* n. 14, at 649 ss. 24-70; As noticed Born, *supra* n. 7, at p. 2479 what is however not clear enough, a possible challenge would be most probably unsuccessful, being treated as groundless substantive objections as to the merits.

[C] The Legal Interest in Case of Declarations in Arbitration

It has been very strongly voiced that legal interest as defined in Germanic jurisdictions does not apply in arbitration due to its procedural character.

In modern arbitration, the domestic procedural norms, contrary to substantive norms, do not apply in arbitration either by analogy or subsidiarily,[19] hence classification of declarations as belonging to the substantive or procedural realm is important. In Germanic countries, the trend is to assume procedural nature of declarations. In Austria, according to prevailing doctrine, legal interest in declaratory relief is deemed to be a procedural requirement.[20] However, according to jurisprudence, Austrian courts treat the prerequisites as substantive requirements.[21] Swiss law is an example of the rapid switch from substantive to procedural theory. Before entry into force of the Swiss CCP, the Swiss Federal Tribunal has consistently held that the interest in a declaratory relief was of substantive nature.[22] In 2018, the Swiss Federal Tribunal finally confirmed the doctrine's position and classified the interest in a declaratory relief as being of procedural nature, emphasizing that, as a condition of admissibility, it formed part of procedural law.[23] The Polish jurisdiction is an example of the most conservative approach in this respect, as both doctrine and court practice almost unanimously treat the legal interest as a substantive law issue.[24] Recently, however, the first dissenting opinion was expressed by a prominent Polish scholar and judge, K. Weitz, what may be a starting point of a new line of judgements. Anyway, it was admitted in literature, that economic interest is enough to be proved in arbitration.[25]

Older authorities have claimed that standards applied in state courts, including proving the legal interest, must be followed by arbitral tribunals given the substantive content.[26]

The modern status is different. As noted by M. Schneider[27], S. Leimgruber and others,[28] this view has often been criticized for neglecting the fact that, historically, the

19. *See* Michael E. Schneider, *Non-Monetary Relief* in *International Arbitration: Principles and Arbitration Practice* in *Performance as a Remedy: Non-Monetary Relief in International Arbitration* 3, 30 (Michael E. Schneider & Joachim Knoll eds., ASA Special Series no. 30, 2011), *see also* Annex II.XI by Alicja Zielińska-Eisen & Tobias Strecker for Germany. In the Uncitral Model Law jurisdictions it is a consequence of Art. 19, constituting the principle of procedural freedom.
20. Annex I.II by Ulrich Kopetzki *infra*.
21. Annex.I.III. by Ulrich Kopetzki *infra*.
22. Annex IV.III[A] by Nino Sievi *infra*.
23. *Ibid.*
24. Examples: judgement of 19 March 2015, IV CSK 362/14 (Polish Supreme Court); judgement of 24 April 2014, III CSK 182/13 (Polish Supreme Court). Judgement of 3 April 2000, I CKN 582/98 (Polish Supreme Court); judgement of 6 August 2014, I CSK 559/13 (Polish Supreme Court); judgement of 19 March 2015, IV CSK 362/14 (Polish Supreme Court); Annex III.II by Beata Gessel-Kalinowska vel Kalisz & Joanna Kisielińska-Garncarek *infra*.
25. Tadeusz Ereciński, *Sąd arbitrażowy* 301 (2008).
26. *See* Bernhard Berger & Franz Kellerhals, *International and Domestic Arbitration in Switzerland* n. 617 (2d ed., 2010); Günter Henn, *Schiedsverfahrensrecht: Handbuch für die Praxis* nn. 330 et seq (3d ed., 2000).
27. Schneider, *supra* n. 19.
28. Leimgruber, *supra* n. 3, at 474 and literature cited in nn. 44 and 45; from a German perspective Rolf A. Schütze, Dieter Tscherning & Walter Wais, *Handbuch des Schiedsverfahrens: Praxis der deutschen und internationalen Schiedsgerichtsbarkeit* n. 377 (2d ed., 1990) ('bei weitem nicht so

restrictions to declaratory actions in state court proceedings were implemented to prevent unnecessary recourse to, and burdening of, the state judiciary. Seeing as, in arbitration, the strain on the state judiciary and on public funds is negligible, as the costs are borne by the parties, other scholars suggest that the requirements for declaratory relief should be much more lenient in the case of arbitral tribunals, or abandoned altogether. This means that, even if declarations would be qualified as a substantive law measure, the legal interest as defined by jurisprudence is not applicable to arbitration due to the rationale standing behind this concept in litigation and which is not valid for arbitration. In this vein, the above authorities contend that, as the adoption of national litigation standards in international arbitration has no legal basis, a tribunal may reject abusive or pointless claims on the basis of its own opinion that they violate the principle of good faith. The principle of good faith as a general prerequisite in arbitration was proposed in legal writings such as those of S. Leimgruber, who defines the principle of good faith in seeking declaratory relief as follows: (i) the legal position of (one of) the parties to the arbitration was in dispute; (ii) the requested declaration was suitable to resolve the dispute; and (iii) the declaratory award would serve a practical purpose.[29] This proposal is escaping the national Swiss test of legitimate interest and constitutes and interesting a-national approach, however some redundancy could be observed in comparing points (ii) and (iii). Basically, point (iii) should be omitted or rewritten. If rewritten, it should be added in point (iii) that the declaratory award would serve *any other* practical purpose, because resolving the dispute mentioned in point (ii) is, *ipso facto*, a practical purpose by itself. Depending on the intention of the author, if no other practical purpose is considered, point (iii) should be omitted altogether. It is hard to imagine that resolving a dispute does not serve a practical purpose.

It must be stressed very clearly, that there is no *ratio legis* standing behind the stance, that legal interest should be adopted as a prerequisite in arbitration in classic Germanic form or even a moderate one. The arbitrators have a duty to address all declaratory claims on the merits. It cannot be excluded, that the liberal approach of arbitration, which is inevitable considering that arbitration is a private system of settlement, may lead sometimes to abuse of rights by the claimant if, for example respondent did not give legitimate reason for raising such a claim. This situation is possible not only in the case of declarations and should be addressed as in other types of claims, namely by the appropriate cost apportionment in the final ruling.

The question of how the arbitral tribunals in fact approach this problem will be examined below, basing on research of arbitral declaratory awards issued by ICC tribunals as well as awards currently available in public domain (*see* section §4.03[B]

streng'); Karl Heinz Schwab & Gerhard Walter, *Schiedsgerichtsbarkeit: Kommentar* Ch. 16 n. 1 (7th ed., 2005); *see also* Jens-Peter Lachmann, *Handbuch für die Schiedsgerichtspraxis* n. 1448 (3d ed., 2008); Schneider, *supra* n. 19, at 30 n. 1; Marco Stacher, *Das Rechtsschutzinteresse im internationalen Verhältnis*, 9 AJP/JPA 1124, 1132 et seq. (2007); Richard H. Kreindler, Jan K. Schäfer & Reinmar Wolf, *Schiedsgerichtsbarkeit Kompendium für die Praxis* nn. 757 et seq. (2006); *see also* Diana Akikol, *Die bundesgerichtliche Rechtsprechung zur Schiedsgerichtsbarkeit im Jahr 2010*, 8 Jusletter 1, 23 n. 117 (August 2011).

29. Leimgruber, *supra* n. 3, at 482–483.

infra, autonomous definition). There are basic questions to be addressed and answered in this chapter: is legal interest recognised in arbitration and if so, do arbitrators depart from domestic regulations in their practice and, what is their approach to the criteria of admissibility? What guidelines are more persuasive -- those stemming from common law or from Germanic principles? Are common law and civil law components mixed in creating admissibility tests for declaratory relief? Or do tribunals work out new tests of their own? The awards analysed below support the thesis that, in the realm of arbitration, the elements typical to common law and Continental law are blurred and converged, forming a new autonomous quality.

[D] The Scope of Research

Confidentiality of the arbitral awards inevitably makes for a certain dissatisfaction in accessing relevant information resources exemplifying arbitrators' approach when dealing with the problems of applying various standards in admitting declarations in the proceedings. Lack of transparency of arbitral awards in this sense and the resulting negative impact on development of business law have been discussed in depth recently and has been addressed by the ICC initiative to publish the awards more intensively. The purpose of the research into ICC awards in this area was to enhance knowledge and to afford an additional perspective in examining how the notion of 'interest' as a prerequisite to the granting of declaration in the cosmopolitan environment of international arbitration is understood and which line of axiology, Germanic or common law, prevails in the arbitrators' practice. Arbitration also provides another, more intuitive perspective, considering that arbitrators are not professional judges – while by no means laymen, in some instances they are no't even trained lawyers.

In the interests of a reasonably full picture, the problem has been approached in a twofold way. First, the problem was examined in a certain segment of legal relations, regardless of the national law applicable to the merits of the case or the lex arbitri. Such a methodology yielded a cross-section overview of the functioning of declarations, showing how often, and to what extent, the problem of their admissibility appears. For this purpose, I have chosen to focus on M&A arbitration awards because, from observations made in my academic work as well as my professional practice, I have noticed that declarations as a non-coercive relief play a significant role in resolution of such disputes. I dealt mainly with share purchase transactions, less often with transfer of the business enterprise or with mergers *sensu stricte*. Examining the period of 2010–2012, I have identified seventy-nine English language awards.[30] Among those, thirteen dealt with a declaration in their dispositive part, if not always using the express term 'declaratory relief'; this accounts for 16% of the total number of awards. For the purposes of full anonymization, the awards are only numbered by their consecutive numbers, ICC 1.1 through ICC 1.13.

30. It is not guaranteed – for various reasons, including the way that the awards are digitalised and the ambiguity of the presentation of the relief sought in the awards – that these are all awards dealing with M&A in the given period of time. Be that as it may, my research has produced a sufficient number of awards based on which representative conclusions could be drawn.

Second, departing from the sectoral approach, the problem of admissibility was analysed in general research. As will be clarified further on, the tribunals did not deal with the issue of admissibility of the declaratory relief sought very often, embarking from the outset on direct analysis of the merits of the case. Therefore, it was necessary to establish more precisely how the arbitrators approach this problem if they see the question of legal interest as a condition for admissibility of the declaratory relief. Hence, twenty awards issued in the relevant years of 2010–2014 were identified by the key words 'declaratory' and 'legal interest'; they are numbered ICC 2.1. through ICC 2.20 and analysed in section §4.03 *infra*.

Four ICC awards issued at a later time, i.e., after 2014, were added to enhance the illustration of certain problems by virtue of the interesting findings of the tribunals which, I hope, will be useful from the perspective of the goals of this chapter. These are numbered ICC 3.1 through ICC 3.4.

The legal literature and jurisprudence upon which the arbitral tribunals respectively relied is also cited herein (in the footnotes).

Bearing in mind that arbitration awards have not been made accessible to the broader public, they are described in greater detail compared with court judgements.

[E] Declaratory Relief in Arbitration

As a general introduction, it has been emphasized earlier that the authority of the arbitrators to grant declaratory relief should not be questioned in modern jurisprudence or in doctrine. The same can be said about analysed arbitration awards. The authority of the arbitrators to grant declaratory relief has been confirmed in all of them, despite the fact that the ICC rules do not specifically refer to this issue. That said, on several occasions the respondents raised defences in these areas, citing lack of special authorization in the applicable law or in the ICC rules or in the agreement. The tribunals, for the most part, did not deal specifically with the question of authority. Of the exceptions, in ICC case ICC 2.3, the arbitrators expressly confirmed their authority to grant declaratory relief which is not derived from particular authorization in the applicable arbitration law or in procedural rules,[31] and likewise their authority to grant other remedies, including injunctions and specific performance. In ICC case ICC 2.6, the tribunal clearly stated that tribunals hearing international disputes under the rules of a number of organizations, among them the ICC, not infrequently do grant declaratory relief and that no particular authorization is necessary in this respect. An interesting point was raised in case ICC 2.16, where the claimant alleged that the contract which regulated the possibility to raise certain claims only related to claims for loss of profit, but not to claims for liability in general and, notably, not to a claim for declaratory relief. The arbitrator disagreed because the relevant article of the contract spoke of the buyer losing 'his right for loss compensation' only, so the proper position

31. Arbitrators referred to: Menno Aden, *Internationale Handelsschiedsgerichtsbarkeit* 130 (2nd ed., C.H.Beck 2003); David R. Muñoz, *The Power of Arbitrators to Make Pro-Futuro Orders* in *Performance as a Remedy: Non-Monetary Relief in International Arbitration* 87, 30 (Michael E. Schneider & Joachim Knoll eds., ASA Special Series no. 30, 2011).

must be that the parties intended not to forfeit any warranty claims, claims for declaratory relief included.

[F] Declarations upon Jurisdiction

The analysis of the awards is focused on declarations referring to the merits of the case – declarations on rights and duties of the parties, interpretation of contracts, etc. – irrespectively whether or not they are granted together with other relief. Undoubtedly, arbitration tribunals are also asked to grant a lot more declarations which concern their jurisdiction, including validity of the arbitration agreement, the scope of the arbitration agreement or arbitrability of the matters referred to the tribunal for resolution. The jurisdictional declarations are not barred by any specific prerequisites, as the capacity to issue such declarations is normally rooted in positive statutory norms and in specific arbitration rules. Therefore, the problem of demonstration of any legal or other legitimate interest is not applicable; the interest in having the jurisdiction confirmed in case of doubt is inherently implied in the very request for arbitration. The jurisdictional declarations will not be a matter of interest here, because they constitute a distinct type of declarations with a very specific range of qualities and legal problems, having a special place in legal arbitration literature. Jurisdiction and arbitrability issues belong to the basic subjects in this respect. Based on the analysed awards, however, a problem of clear identification deserves to be highlighted in this part.[32]

Similarly to the dilemma of juridical classification of declaration between procedural and substantive realm, it is not always clear to the tribunals which declarations belong to the jurisdiction sphere, and which ones to the merits. This problem appeared in case ICC 3.2 in relation to legal qualification of declaring the *res judicata* effect of a state court decision. As regards the object of the dispute, the respondents proposed to claimants an investment in construction of two new vessels. The claimants were intended to be the principal within the construction project and to conclude the construction agreement with the shipyard, and the respondents' side was to provide financing for the project. The structure of the investment was complicated and the parties entered into several contractual relationships, including an assortment of letters of intent, loan agreements and guarantees. At a certain point of the entire project, the claimants took the view that respondents had been contractually obligated to accept the transfer of one of the vessels and to make an additional payment in this regard and that, in failing to do so, the respondents had violated various obligations leading to liability for any damages suffered by claimants as a result of such conduct. Respondents, on the contrary, adopted the position that, based on the scheme as initially agreed upon by the parties, claimants had failed to fulfil their contractual duty to transfer, by the agreed delivery date, the ownership of the two vessels as repayment of the loans granted by respondents for the financing of the vessels, which entitled

32. P. Dunand and M. Kotsyska also make a distinction between declarations sensu largo, which include all kinds of declarations, and declarations sensu stricte, where the arbitral tribunal declares rights and obligations of the parties or interprets a contract or treaty but does not award damages or injunctions, *see* Dunand & Kostytska,*supra* n. 1 at fn. 1.

respondents to claim for repayment of the loans in pecuniary form. To obtain such repayment, respondents initiated legal proceedings before the state commercial courts in the relevant jurisdiction and obtained a final decision which vindicated the respondents' claim. The arbitral tribunal dealt in these proceedings with a number of jurisdictional issues and found itself to have jurisdiction over the dispute. It also held that, albeit raised in the context of respondents' jurisdictional objection, the issue of *res judicata* of the court decision already issued was not a jurisdictional one but, rather, dealt with the merits of the claims. In the dispositive section, the arbitral tribunal stated that:

> it is confirmed that the judgement of the [...] Supreme Court does not have *res judicata* effect, and thus the claims raised by [Claimants] against [Respondents] and vice versa are admissible.

This conclusion was based, in particular, on the consideration that it would have been up to the respondents to demonstrate that a judgement issued in the parallel proceedings could be recognized in Switzerland, and that this burden of proof has not been met by the respondents. The tribunal, citing Berger and Kellerhals,[33] stated that a defence of *res judicata* raised against specific claims (which are covered by an arbitration clause) 'would still fall within the jurisdiction of an arbitral tribunal under the terms agreed upon in the arbitration agreement'. Moreover:

> if a party seizes an arbitral tribunal with its seat in Switzerland with an identical claim between the same parties that has already been the subject of court judgment made in a country other than Switzerland, the Swiss arbitral tribunal shall declare such claim inadmissible, provided that the foreign court judgment can be recognized in Switzerland.

The arbitral tribunal did not engage in any further explanations as to the admissibility of this claim.

This problem requires a comment. It is important to note the distinction that the tribunal made in the dispositive section of the award: it used both the verbs 'to declare' and 'to confirm'. The former expression is used to declare that the respondents have violated the arbitration agreement by going before the state court and obtaining relief there, and the latter is used to confirm lack of *res judicata* effect. The meaning of both verbs, however, is similar, and both of them are declarations. They definitely do not constitute an order to perform or to shape the legal relationship. Also, the tribunal clearly stated that the analysed issue is not a jurisdictional one, but that it belongs to the merits. Therefore, there is some ambiguity in the fact that arbitrators did not adopt the same prerequisite to grant the confirmation of *res judicata* issue as was adopted to grant the other declarations. The tribunal conducted in-depth analysis whether the admissibility issue could be approached as a procedural matter and/or as a substantive one and found that, in both scenarios, i.e., regardless of whether admissibility is qualified as a substantive or procedural issue (and, consequently, irrespectively of

33. Berger & Kellerhals, *supra* n. 26, at n. 625.

whether the matter is assessed under Swiss substantive law or the governing procedural rules), the principle of good faith was applicable and established a minimum standard which any declaratory relief must meet. This test, however, was not applied to the *res judicata* declaration, despite the fact that this declaration was qualified as substantive.

Surprisingly, here all criteria relate to the useful purpose and remain silent about fairness as such, mention of which might reasonably be expected in a discussion of good faith.

§4.02 DECLARATORY RELIEF AND ITS ADMISSIBILITY IN SECTORAL RESEARCH OF M&A ARBITRATIONS

[A] General Remarks

As has been said earlier, generally 16% of requests for arbitration in M&A cases include declaratory relief. In other words, declaratory relief is, at least in the context of M&A disputes, an important part of the examined area, and has not only theoretical relevance, but practical import as well.

The arbitral tribunals and the parties do not always use the exact term 'declaratory relief'. The tribunals may, in their awards, 'declare' a certain status, or 'confirm' it, or 'order' that a certain status be brought about, or simply 'determine'. This is why it is not easy to identify cases for analysis by a mere keyword search for 'declaratory relief' or simply for 'declarations' – more in-depth research of all arbitration awards, as discussed below, was required.

There is a wide range of very different declarations as regards their content. And thus, the subject matter of the declarations sought by the parties included: declaring validity of contracts such as share purchase agreements (SPAs), shareholders agreements (SHAs) and of various share option instruments, declaring construction – or, as Continental usage terms it, interpretation – of contracts, qualification of certain actions as an indirect expropriation, declaring commission of a breach of contract (where, oftentimes, breaches relate to representations and warranties and confidentiality or non-compete obligations), declaring validity of certain legal actions (including termination of contracts and enforcement of certain rights like exercising put options, confirmation of results of various price formulas and their adjustments), declaring liability for breach of contract including future liability and finally declaring remedies (such as in case ICC 3.1, where the tribunal declared whether the claimant was entitled to the claim). The way how relevant dispositive parts of the awards are structured are very different, from very concise forms, simply declaring breach or validity up to complicated statements and answers to multiple questions, as provided in case ICC 1.3 (*see* below). The way in which the declaration sought is formulated impacts the content of the arbitral tribunal's decision or even whether or not to grant the declaration in question. As Leimgruber puts it, the declaration is useless and does not meet the test of good faith if it is too vague or too broad to provide guidance regarding the parties' rights or conduct under a contract.[34]

[B] Lack of Legal Interest

Of the thirteen ICC M&A cases analysed, only in one did the tribunal dismiss the claim due to lack of legal interest. In case ICC 1.1 (Austrian *lex arbitri* and *lex contractus*), claimant sought a declaration on breach of the contract and, in particular, misrepresentation of tax obligations in the financial statements.[35] In addition to its claim for monetary relief, the claimant requested that the arbitral tribunal declare that respondents are in breach of their contractual obligations and are jointly liable to indemnify claimant. The tribunal found, under established principles of Austrian law and within the tribunal's procedural discretion under Austrian arbitration law and the ICC Rules that, to the extent that monetary relief is ordered based upon the same facts in respect of which a declaratory award is requested, the declaration is encompassed by the award of monetary relief and is not to be declared separately. It simply followed the subsidiarity rules, however not explicitly using the term 'legal interest'. In this case, it is important to note, however, that the claims also encompassed other monetary relief in a certain minimum and were accompanied by a further request to declare the general rule of liability for any damages to be incurred in the future. Such a declaration was also denied, however based on the the merits. The reason was that, in the opinion of the tribunal, claimant had not substantiated its claim for future losses, and the arbitral tribunal found that it cannot - and, indeed, should not under Austrian law - award on premises of its own creation. The uncertainty attaching to any future tax liability for the target company's past operations also led the tribunal to conclude that it did not have the tools to effectively decide on any potential future liability in this respect.[36]

[C] No Admissibility Issue Raised

In the other twelve cases,[37] the tribunals were dealing with declarations without focusing on the prerequisites to their admissibility. This is hardly surprising in cases which were subject to common law. It has been clearly proved earlier (Chapter 3 *supra*) that the concept of a necessary prerequisite for granting a declaration is not typical of common law. Matters become interesting, however, in cases subject to civil / Continental law, where the specific prerequisite of legal interest is recognized (Chapter 2 *supra*). Below, common law cases will be presented separately from the civil law cases.

34. Leimgruber, *supra* n. 3, at 484. *See* more in section §4.04[D] *infra*.
35. *See* case ICC 1.8 for the decision to the contrary.
36. *See* opposite findings below, in section §4.04[B] *infra*.
37. Two outstanding cases were terminated due to settlement reached by the parties; in order to present the complete view of the results of the research, the relief sought is referred to below in section §4.02[G] *infra*.

The distinction is drawn based on the *lex arbitri* because, in the majority of arbitrations, the problem of legal prerequisites to the declaratory relief, if discussed by arbitral tribunals, is classified as a matter of procedural law (*see* Chapter 2 *supra*).

[D] Common Law as *Lex Arbitri*

ICC case ICC 1.2 revolved around a post-merger dispute related to the effect of 'Non-competition Clause by Claimant' in the shareholders agreement (the disputed restraint). In this case, an interesting problem of admissibility of the declaration on interpretation of the contract versus inadmissibility of the claim for rewriting of a contract was raised.

The respondents asserted that the claimants' conduct was in breach of the disputed restraint and resulted in business that belonged to respondent being wrongfully appropriated by the claimants in respect of the entitlement to the profits. That business consisted of agreements allegedly entered into by claimant's group entities in breach of the disputed restraint. The main problem was related to the phrase 'or to elsewhere in the world', which was ambiguous as to the location of the restrained business. The requested declaration related to construction of the non-competition clause of the SPA. The award included very exhaustive arguments by both parties and by the tribunal on the legal admissibility of such a declaration versus inadmissibility of rewriting the contract. I will not endeavour here to classify this problem to be more of a substantive or a formal character, especially given that, in common law, this does not really matter anyway. The overall impression was that the problem dealt with fairness of the expected result to the parties, and not admissibility as a procedural prerequisite.

The claimants submitted that there were three alternative means by which they could succeed on construction. The first two of these were founded on the premise that the interpretative route was essentially one of resolving an ambiguity. The third invited the tribunal to correct a drafting or linguistic mistake by construction, to use Lord Hoffman's expression in *Chartbrook*.[38]

The respondents, for their part, submitted that the claimants had overstated the willingness of common law courts to rewrite contracts in commercial disputes. They argued that, to the extent that the claimants sought to invoke *Chartbrook* as an authority permitting the tribunal to ignore paragraph (a) of the definition of restrained businesses or the natural meaning of 'elsewhere in the world' in the contested non-competition clause, they misstated the effect of that case. By reference to Lord Hoffman's speech in *Chartbrook*, the respondents submitted that it must be clear (a) that 'something has gone wrong with the language' and (b) 'what a reasonable person would have understood the parties to have meant' before one can ignore that language.

The tribunal accepted, following Lord Hoffman in *Chartbrook*, that if it concludes from the context and background that something must indeed have gone wrong with the language of the disputed restraint, the law does not require it to attribute to the parties an intention which they plainly could not have had. This case makes it clear

38. *Chartbrook Limited v Persimmon Homes Limited*, [2009] UKHL 38.

that, before the tribunal can correct a mistake by construction, not only must it be obvious that, in Lord Hoffman's words, 'something has gone wrong with the language' but it must also be clear what a reasonable person would have understood the parties to have meant.

Ultimately, the relevance of business common sense to the task of interpretation was an aspect of the objective approach to contractual construction. In the context of ambiguity, it may have meant no more than preferring the construction which would avoid consequences which appeared to be capricious, unreasonable, inconvenient or unjust because such an approach was likely to best give effect to the intent of the parties.

Here, the tribunal concluded from the context and background that the problem in fact did lay with the language of the disputed restraint. In particular, the tribunal was satisfied that no reasonable party in the claimants' position would had been willing to enter into a restraint the result of which would had involved such a fundamental departure from the successful business model that the claimant group operated under, not only for respondent but also for other claimant group companies worldwide.

As a result, the tribunal gave in the dispositive part the correct construction of the disputed no-competition clause.

In case ICC 1.3, where arbitration was seated in London and UAE was the law applicable, claimant purchased shares in a company and executed the shareholders agreement which imposed certain duties on the parties. Claimant averred that respondents' contractual breaches gave the claimant the right to call for respondents' shares in target under the SHA. The respondents, meanwhile, denied the claimant's assertions and submitted that, in any case, claimant had not served the breach notice, default notice and default call option notice in accordance with the requirements of the SHA. The respondents also raised counterclaims and alleged that claimant was in breach of its contractual obligations. The claimant sought a number of reliefs, including the declarations:

(1) That the respondents are in material breach of the agreements.
(2) That the respondents are parties in default.
(3) That the respondents had been served with a valid default call option notice.

Apart from that, claimant also sought specific performance, *viz.* that the respondents shall transfer all their shares onto the claimant pursuant to the default call option notice in accordance with the SHA upon the claimant paying the fair market value, as determined by the valuator, less the default discount. In alternative, the claimant sought damages.

The respondents requested, in addition to monetary compensation, a number of declarations, *inter alia* on:

- claimant's notices of breach and default and default call option to be invalid and unfounded;
- claimant to be in default under the SHA and the SPA;

- the respondents' notice of default to be valid and declaring the respondents' entitlement to rights of default under the SHA and the SPA.

The parties' positions were quite complex. Based on all the material gathered in the proceedings, the arbitral tribunal identified twelve issues raised in the submissions to be decided and, following this classification, it structured the declarations granted in the dispositive section.[39] It did not examine whether the declaratory claims were admissible; all were admitted without discussion.

In case ICC 1.4 (*lex contractus* New York, *lex arbitri* UK), the dispute concerned exercise of a put option pursuant to an agreement made between the respondent and claimant (option agreement). The claimant was a joint-stock company. The respondent was the largest shareholder of a company. The company entered into a consulting services agreement (CSA) with the claimant pursuant to which the claimant agreed to provide certain services. The payment was agreed to be partly in cash and partly (over 50%) in equity. The claimant also entered into a put and call option agreement. In essence, this was a dispute about whether the claimant was entitled to put its company shares, which he had acquired as remuneration for the consulting services, to the respondent in accordance with the option agreement. The claimant sought a declaration that the respondent had materially breached its obligation under the option agreement to purchase the shares from the claimant, and an order that the respondent pay the amount of the put price as required under the option agreement, and also an order, upon receipt by the claimant of the put price, that the claimant transfer the

39. The structuring of the dispositive part was interesting from the perspective of a Continental lawyer – so much, in fact, that it is cited here *in extenso*. The Sole Arbitrator determined and ordered as follows:

> The answer to Issue No. 1 (Notices) is as follows:
> The various Breach Notices and Default Call Options Notices exchanged between the parties are invalid, and accordingly, neither Party is entitled to purchase the other Party's Shares.
> The answer to Issue No.2: the Claimant is entitled to rescind the SPA.
> The answer to Issue No. 3 [Project 1] is as follows:
> The Respondents are in breach of their representations and warranties, acknowledgments, confirmations, disclosures and undertakings under [] of the SPA, and accordingly, the Claimant is entitled to rescind the SPA. With the rescission of the SPA, the SHA is automatically rescinded and the parties' are restored to their status quo ante. The Claimant's (...) holding of the Company's Shares are hereby reassigned to the Respondents. The Claimant's compensation for the rescission of the SPA appears in the table below under item '1-Termination (Purchase Price)' and item '2-Termination (Damages)'.
> [...]
> The answer to Issue No. 5 [Project 3] is as follows:
> The Claimant's claim is dismissed.
> 2242. The answer to Issue No. 6 (Finances of [Target]) is as follows:
> The Claimant's claim is dismissed.
> [...]
> 2249. The answer to Issue No. 13 (The Counterclaim) is as follows:
> The Respondents' Counterclaims, to the extent they were admitted, are dismissed in their entirety.
> 2250. Quantum is as follows:
> (...)
> 2252. All other requests for relief, claims and counterclaims are hereby rejected.

shares to respondent or disposes of such shares as the respondent may direct. In addition, the claimant sought interest and such other relief as the tribunal deems to be appropriate under the circumstances, including specific performance and other equitable remedies to the extent necessary to effectuate the foregoing relief.

The arbitral tribunal did not make any findings on the admissibility of the declaratory relief and on whether it is useful or justified to grant it. The major problem in this case was posed by the authority to grant specific performance, which in English law is subject to certain limitations. Therefore, it was stated that the claimant's principal claim was for payment of a sum of money representing the value of the shares as calculated according to a formula in the option agreement. No action was required on the part of the respondent other than to pay this money. The obligation to transfer the shares rested upon the claimant, therefore the arbitral tribunal considered that this was not a claim for specific performance in the normal sense of the term.

Accordingly, for the above reasons the arbitral tribunal considered that the appropriate remedy here was to order the respondent to pay the put price to the claimant.

The tribunal did not engage in any deliberations on the issue of declaratory relief sought by the claimant. It straightforwardly declared in the dispositive section that the respondent had breached the option agreement in failing to comply with the notice of exercise of the put option and, accordingly, ordered payment of the sum representing the put price.

[E] No Admissibility Issue Raised: French Law as *Lex Arbitri*

In French law, declaratory relief is not very popular, and the French Civil Procedure Code does not establish any regulation in this respect. Traditionally, declaratory claims were not identified as a distinct kind of claim.[40] An actual interest (*un interet ne et actuel*) is a prerequisite, and must be demonstrated, in every claim raised before the French general courts.[41] Some interpretations narrow down the possibility to issue declarations under French law, as clearly formulated by the respondent in the case ICC 2.8. In the two decisions discussed next, parties did not raise this issue, and the tribunal likewise did not focus on it.

In the collection of M&A awards, the case ICC 1.5 appeared to be an investment arbitration case which was instituted against the state, being of French law tradition, which however incorporated the Germanic rule, that interested party may request confirmation of the existence of absence of a right, subject to the principle of subsidiarity. The subject matter of this case exceeds the scope of the present analysis, as investment arbitration is driven by different criteria than commercial disputes. Basically, arbitral tribunals are open to granting declaratory relief where it facilitates

40. M.E. Schneider, *supra* n. 19, at 9.
41. Article 31 of the French Civil Procedure Code. For more on the requirement of *un intérêt né et actuel* under French law, *See* Dunand & Kostytska, *supra* n. 1, at 8.

settlement,[42] where other forms of relief are unavailable,[43] and provided that declaratory relief does not interfere with state sovereignty.[44] In the below case, the situation was simpler, as the claimant sought both monetary and non-monetary relief.

According to the request for arbitration, claimant and respondent's subsidiary, wholly owned by respondent, agreed to set up the target - corporation. Claimant agreed to transfer to the target its know-how for the production of a certain product and the use of its trademarks and patents. Due to the shareholder deadlock existing in target, respondent's subsidiary agreed to buy claimant's shares in target ('the agreements').

Claimant alleged that respondent's subsidiary subsequently breached the agreements by leading target to a deadlock, changing the components of the product without claimant's authorization and failing to buy claimant's shares. Claimant further alleged that the agreements, considered together, constituted an 'investment' and that, as such, they fell within the ambit of the Bilateral Investment Treaty between the relevant states ('BIT'), with the implication that the respondent should be held liable for failing to protect claimant's investments. The arbitral tribunal, in the dispositive section, declared that certain actions constituted an indirect expropriation and awarded damages.[45] As concerns admissibility issues, the arbitral tribunal only focused on prerequisites typical to investment arbitration, relating to steps to be undertaken prior to invoking the BIT.

In case ICC 1.6, in which French law was applicable, claimant and respondent had executed a share purchase agreement by which claimant acquired from Respondent a group of companies ('target group') engaged in the development, manufacturing and commercialization of certain products. Claimant alleged that its main interest in acquiring the target group was that it held the rights to certain product protected by a European Patent, which generated most of the group's turnover. Claimant alleged that, following the acquisition, several nullity actions were brought against the European Patent by third parties. Claimant asserted that, during the due diligence process, respondent had not disclosed information concerning the potential risks facing the business of the target group.

Claimant requested that the arbitral tribunal make the following two declarations: finding that respondent is liable for a breach of its contractual obligations under the SPA, in particular the representations, warranties and covenants granted under its terms and Articles 1134 and 1147 of the French Civil Code, and finding that respondent's breach of its representations, warranties and covenants constitutes a fraud

42. *Saudi Arabia v Arab Am. Oil Co.* ('Aramco') 27 ILR 117, 117–118 (1963).
43. *Biwater v Tanzania*, ICSID Case no. ARB/05/22, Final Award of 24 July 2008; here the tribunal found that a declaratory was granted in lieu of a monetary award due to the fact that claimant suffered no loss.
44. *Libyan Am. Oil Co. ('Liamco') v Gov't of the Libyan Arab Republic*, Award of 12 April 1977, 6 Y.B. Com. Arb. 89, 90–91 (P. Sanders ed., 1981). For more on the subject *see* Dunand & Kostytska, *supra* n. 1, at 9–16.
45. The concept of common law real interest described in Chapter 3 *supra*, which allows for simultaneous granting of a declaration and coercive measure, is nothing extraordinary in investment arbitration. In *Enron v Argentina*, ICSID Case no. ARB/01/3 (14 January 2004). The Tribunal held that 'in addition to declaratory powers, it has the power to order measures involving performance of injunction of certain acts'.

under Article 9.7.1 of the SPA and an intentional breach under Article 1150 of the French Civil Code. In addition, it sought a compensation for the loss incurred as a result of such breach. Claimant also presented a number of alternative reliefs sought.

The arbitral tribunal found that respondent had breached the representations and warranties clause in the agreement which required that any 'threat' of claim from third parties shall be disclosed to the potential buyer during the due diligence phase. The arbitral tribunal found that this threat had been sufficiently manifested prior to the acquisition of the shares so as to fall under the scope of the clause, irrespective of whether claimant could have independently obtained information regarding such threat. The arbitral tribunal rendered an award in which it granted both a declaration and relevant compensation.[46] No deliberation on admissibility was included.

[F] No Admissibility Issue Raised: Germanic (Swiss and German) Law as *Lex Arbitri*

In the following cases, where admissibility of declaration was not a matter of concern, the tribunals were seated in Germanic jurisdictions.

In case ICC 1.7 (Spanish law, Geneva as a seat of the arbitration), claimant and respondent were shareholders in the target company. The claimant was a producer of certain equipment, and the respondent was in the business of its commercialization. Respondent breached the non-competition obligations (allegedly comprised in the SPA and the shareholders' agreement) by executing new agreements for supply of services with target's direct competitors. In its statement of claim, the claimant first asked the tribunal to rule that respondent had breached the non-competition obligations which it assumed under the contract of sale of shares in target and in the shareholders' agreement and, second, to order that respondent must compensate claimants for the damages and losses it has suffered as a result of this breach. In the dispositive section of its decision, the arbitral tribunal ruled that respondent has in fact breached the contracts and, accordingly, ordered the claimant to pay a sum equal to the lost profits and, by way of damages, for the operating costs and expenses of marketing and acquiring customers during the given period.

In case ICC 1.8 (*lex arbitri* and *lex contractus* both German), the dispute between the claimants and the respondents concerned a series of interrelated agreements, including a share purchase agreement and an escrow agreement. Claimants alleged that the accounts of target had been manipulated and, accordingly, that several warranties in the SPA had been breached. In particular, claimants alleged that the accounts of target contained a deferred tax asset for acquisition by target of shares in a certain other company, which was in fact not tax deductible under the applicable law.

46. The literal wording of this part of the award was as follows:

> (1). Respondent is liable for a breach of its contractual obligations under the SSPA, in particular the Representations, Warranties and Covenants granted under the SSPA.(2.) As of the date of this Award, claimant shall pay to Respondent the amount of EUR [], plus interest at a rate of EURIBOR 3 months +3% per annum starting from [] until payment.

At the time the dispute was taken to arbitration, no tax decision had been issued yet. The arbitrators relied on tax experts, interrogated in the proceedings.

The claimants sought that respondent 2 be ordered to agree on, and respondent 1 be ordered not to interfere with, a release to claimant from the escrow account of an amount corresponding to the amount of damages to be paid due to breach of representations and warranties. In case the arbitral tribunal found that the claim is premature, the claimants sought, alternatively, that respondent 2 be ordered to agree on, and respondent 1 be ordered not to interfere, with a release to claimant 1 from the escrow account of an amount corresponding to all the costs and fees relating to this arbitration as well as a declaratory final award that respondents are jointly and severally liable to compensate claimants as joint and several creditors to the extent a tax loss, as mentioned above, is not acknowledged by the competent tax authorities, and such other relief as the arbitral tribunal shall deem just and appropriate. The arbitral tribunal found that respondents had indeed breached the warranties under the SPA since the purchase price paid by target for the shares was not at arm's length and was not aimed at generating revenue. Consequently, the findings continued, target's accounts had not been prepared in accordance with the applicable law with respect to the deferred tax asset for the questioned transaction capitalized therein and, thus, did not fairly represent target's state of affairs as at the accounting date. While the arbitral tribunal granted the relief[47] requested by the claimant in the first place, alternative prayer for declaratory relief was denied as no longer needed.

In case ICC 1.9 (French law as *lex contractus*, Swiss law as *lex arbitri*), claimant and respondent had executed a joint venture agreement (JVA) pursuant to which they would incorporate a company for the production of accessories on an exclusive basis. Claimant alleged that respondent, in pursuing business relations with another entity, had breached the exclusivity obligations, and also transferred development work, goodwill, commercial and industrial secrets developed by the joint venture company. Claimant contended that such unlawful transfer had caused a loss of income to the joint venture company. Claimant also argued that respondent had been deliberately undermining the joint venture company by other actions, committing multiple violations of the JVA and of applicable law in the process. Moreover, claimant alleged that respondent had failed to honour a promise agreement to purchase claimant's shares in the joint venture company included in the term sheets.

Claimant sought a number of declarations, including:

(1) that respondent was liable for payment to claimant of damages and loss of income arising out of its unlawful conduct in violation of the JVA and of applicable law;
(2) that the liability of respondent to pay damages and loss of income to claimant applied also to any future project, without prejudice to the determination of the 'quantum' of such damages and loss of income;

47. The Tribunal expressly stated: 'Respondent 2 is ordered to agree on, and Respondent 1 is ordered not to interfere with, the release to Claimant 1 from the Escrow Account of an amount of EUR []'.

(3) that the share price agreed by respondent and claimant in the term sheet constituted irrefutable evidence of the damage caused by respondent to claimant due to the total loss of the value of joint venture company at the moment of breach of the JVA by respondent;
(4) that the trademarks granted by respondent to joint venture company under the trademark licensing agreement had been granted exclusively according to the JVA.

Claimant also requested that the arbitral tribunal order specific performance and damages for various losses incurred by the claimant in result of the breach of obligations by the respondent, including loss of value of the joint venture company, loss of certain lease income, loss of administration and management fees and loss of income due to awarding of the orders to a third-party company.

In its award, the tribunal grouped all the declarations sought into a single one in which it stated that respondent had violated the JVA by constituting the joint venture company with a third party and, accordingly, ordered respondent to pay to the claimant damages as well as specific performance aimed at respondent complying with the joint venture agreement.

[G] No Admissibility Issue Raised: Other Jurisdictions

In case ICC 1.10 (Turkish law[48] as *lex contractus* and *lex arbitri*), the parties executed a share purchase agreement pursuant to which respondent agreed to purchase stakes in claimant's certain companies. The purchase price was to be paid in two instalments, the second part being payable on the date of the transaction's closing. Claimant alleged that respondent did not complete the transaction in that it failed to take the necessary actions and to pay on the agreed date in breach of the SPA. Claimant alleged to have validly terminated the SPA. More particularly, claimant submitted that respondent 1 had breached the SPA by failing to provide due diligence documents and to complete the final version of documents required for closing. Claimant asserted that, as a consequence of respondents' failure to complete the transaction pursuant to the agreement, it had suffered loss and harm, including (a) the time and money cost of negotiating with respondent within the public tender, (b) the lost opportunity to negotiate with a bidder who could have proceeded to closing and (c) various damages as a result of respondents' failure to pay. Claimant sought *inter alia* a declaration that claimant validly terminated the agreement and that it was therefore entitled to retain the first instalment paid by respondents and compensation for loss and damages claimant suffered as a consequence of respondents' failure to complete the transaction.

48. The prerequisites for an action for declaratory judgement are stipulated in section 106 of the Turkish Code of Civil Procedure. A declaratory judgement may be requested from a court to determine the existence of a right or a legal relationship or to determine whether a document is forged. The person bringing the action, with some certain exceptions defined in various statutes, must have a current interest that needs legal protection related to the action. Material facts cannot constitute the subject of a declaratory judgement on their own.

The arbitral tribunal ruled in the dispositive section, after reviewing the merits of the case, that the SPA was valid and binding and refused to order claimant to return the initial payment amount to respondents. The arbitral tribunal found that claimant had not breached the SPA. Also, the arbitral tribunal declared that the claimant properly exercised its right to terminate the SPA and that the termination was valid. Claimant had not abused its right to terminate the SPA. The arbitral tribunal rejected respondent 1's request that claimant return the initial payment amount. There was no analysis as to admissibility of the case.

In case ICC 1.11 (Spanish law,[49] arbitration seat Madrid), there was a preclosing dispute based on a letter of intent signed with the purpose of defining the basis on which claimant would acquire 100% of the fully diluted equity of target from respondent once certain conditions precedent were met. Claimant contended that, despite the fact that it was well prepared to execute the share purchase agreement, respondent began to obstruct the transaction by 'sabotaging' the claimant's due diligence efforts. Claimant contended that, ultimately, respondent walked away from the transaction in breach of the terms of the letter of intent, with these breaches comprising, in particular, (1) not allowing claimant to conduct the due diligence in accordance with the agreed terms, (2) failing to notify claimant of any competing offer made by another company and (3) refusing to execute a share purchase agreement.

Claimant sought a declaration that respondent had breached the letter of intent and that claimant would be entitled to specific performance of respondent's obligations under the letter of intent to consummate the transaction but in the situation of obstacles envisaged by the tribunal to enforcement of a specific performance award and an order directing respondent to pay to damages to the claimant. The claimant also sought monetary relief and injunctions and, finally, such other relief as the tribunal might deem just and proper.

The arbitral tribunal first found that the letter of intent amounted to a binding contract under Spanish law, although it was not a sale agreement and did not contain an obligation to sell. Rather, it was an agreement to endeavour to execute a purchase agreement. Respondent did not breach its obligations in connection with due diligence, but it did breach the confidentiality and exclusivity obligations as well as the obligation to endeavour to execute a purchase agreement. Instead of the general declaration on breach of the letter of intent sought by the claimant, the tribunal specified in its ruling in what respect the letter of intent had been breached. Thus, the tribunal declared, in the dispositive section, that respondent breached the confidentiality obligation, the exclusivity obligation, as well as the obligation to endeavour to execute a purchase

49. In Spanish law, like in other legislations qualified to be a member of French family of law, declaratory relief is not specifically regulated in the civil procedure norms. As provided by the case law, however, certain legal interest must be demonstrated by the party. The concept of legal interest is not understood in such a strict manner as in Germanic system and a mere declaration can be granted even if full claim for performance is exercisable. In particular, a party seeking declaratory relief must prove that the legal positions of the parties are in dispute. *See* Art. 5 of Spanish Civil Procedure Code (Law 1/2000, of 7 February, of Civil Procedure) and judgement of 8 April 1991, 71/1991 (Spanish Constitutional Court; judgement of 30 November 1992, 210/1992 (Spanish Constitutional Court).

agreement in accordance with the letter of intent and ordered payment of relevant compensation.[50]

[H] Cases Settled

Two of the cases under discussion were not ruled upon by the arbitral tribunals because the parties reached settlements, but they merit mentioning in this context on account of how the declaratory relief was formulated. In case ICC 1.12 (Turkish law,[51] Vienna), one of the respondents sold a business enterprise to the claimant. He committed to transfer to the claimant employees, certain fixed assets, all rights and obligations arising from the contracts of business division and entire shareholdings in three different companies. The claimant, on the basis of the cooperation agreement, was to be paid 'all current and future benefits arising from one excluded from the transaction division'.

Claimant alleged that respondents had breached their obligations under the purchase contract and the cooperation agreement mainly by failing to transfer to it certain shares and assets, by breaching the non-competition obligations and by failing to pay the fees due. Claimant requested that the arbitrators declare that respondents 1&2 had breached both of the agreements and are therefore liable for all of the breaches and that respondent 3 and respondent 2, standing as guarantors, are jointly and severally liable with respondent 1 to pay the compensation and penalty amounts to be determined by the tribunal.

The request for declarations was accompanied by claims for damages, including penalty fees for the breaches declared as above, compensation for losses and harm and an injunction preventing use of certain intellectual property assets by the respondents.

In the other case settled, case ICC 1.13 (Austrian law as *lex contractus* and *lex fori*), the dispute arose as a result of the parties' different readings of the purchase price provisions of an agreement concerning sale by the respondent to the claimant of all the shares in the target. The purchase price was calculated using a specific yield which was expressed as a multiplier of the net rental income of the real property, the sole asset of the target. The agreement did specify which operating costs are to be taken into account as impossible to be passed on to the tenants. Accordingly, claimant sought payment of an appropriate amount as price adjustment from respondent. Further, claimant sought a declaration that it was entitled to request recalculation of any further uncovered maintenance costs if not covered by the amount awarded by the tribunal in this proceedings.

The arbitral tribunal dismissed all of claimant's claims. It found that the document entitled 'Protocol' by which respondent was obligated to pay certain sums constituted a valid and binding settlement agreement, encompassing also the claims in question. Therefore, it did not elaborate on the nature of the declaration sought by

50. It is important ruling in the context of analysis to what extent formulation of the declaration sought impacts the arbitration authority to amend such formulation. *See* §4.04[D] below.
51. As concerning Turkish regulation of declaratory relief, *See supra* n. 41.

claimant – a potentially interesting point for debate on declaring liability for future harm (*see* section §4.04[B] *infra*).

[I] Conclusions

The sectoral research summarized above provides grounds for the following observation. Arbitration tribunals do not pay much attention to questions of admissibility of the declaratory relief. In these eleven decided cases, based in civil as well as common law roots, admissibility was in fact analysed by the tribunal only once, in case ICC 1.1, and with a negative effect. In this case the court dismissed two sorts of declarations. In the first instance, the problem concerned two joint claims relating to the same cause of action. The claimant simultaneously sought declarations of a breach of contract and damages arising therefrom. This dismissal qualifies as a softer one. The claimant received confirmation of the breach, albeit not in dispositive form (in which situation such a declaration would benefit from *res judicata* effect), but in the body of the justification. The second dismissal was based on the finding that, due to lack of sufficient substantiation, the claim for future damages is not allowed. The problem of liability for future harm is not uniformly addressed by the arbitrators and was the subject of other awards, as presented below.

The remaining ten awards did not deal with the problem of admissibility at all. This justifies the view that, based on the legal intuitions of the arbitrators considering these various cases, this problem does not come into play. It is very important to underline, that this is the merits of the case that are decisive; the problem of admissibility is seen as somehow artificial and not intrinsically built into the intuitive legal perception of declaratory relief.

The above case study did not answer the question of how procedural prerequisites are interpreted in a situation where the tribunal finds the admissibility issue important. For these reasons, more research of a non-sectoral, general basis is presented below.

In majority of cases, including those based on Germanic tradition, the arbitral tribunal found no problem in granting declarations together with a subsequent coercive measure, following quite intuitively the common law fashion (*see*: ICC 1.4, ICC 1.5, ICC 1.6, ICC 1.7, ICC 1.9, ICC 1.11).

§4.03 THE CONCEPT OF LEGAL INTEREST IN GENERAL ARBITRATION RESEARCH

[A] Introduction

As discussed in the preceding section, the problem of admissibility of declarations is not foremost on the minds of the parties to arbitration, or of the arbitrators themselves. Of thirteen M&A cases, only one addressed the question of legal interest. My research answered the question of how much of the attention of participants of the arbitrations proceedings is devoted to the problem of admissibility as such, but it did not address the question of how legal interest is defined in those cases where the arbitrators find this problem to be worthy of attention in the first place. Accordingly, in this part of my analysis, I propose to focus on the perception of legal interest, insofar as deemed applicable, to be demonstrated by the claimant to seek declaration in arbitration, as well as the issue of whether this interest should be treated more as 'legal' (in the Continental tradition) or as 'real' (in accordance with the common law approach). In this context, I am working on the basis of a selection of ICC awards, identified for this purpose in the three consecutive years of 2011–2014.

At the outset, it might be ventured that, in international arbitration, considering that arbitral tribunals are often composed of lawyers steeped in common as well as Continental law traditions, an amalgam of the Germanic and common law approaches should be in evidence. Mixing and converging both systems and/or totally departing from domestic normative sources is expected to be a frequent result. Therefore, the first part of my analysis in section §4.03[B] *infra* will comprise awards which depart from the national understanding of the legal/legitimate interest. The next part, section §4.03[C], will focus on the minority of cases where a tendency to strictly follow one or the other national tradition is clearly in evidence.

[B] The Autonomous Approach

While the autonomous approach has a certain tradition in ICC court cases, it has not been an established practice in the past. In ICC case 9617, based on French procedural law found that the claimant must demonstrate legal interest in accordance with the formula *pas d'intérêt, pas d'action* to be granted a declaration. The claimant had to prove serious threat and useful, and not merely theoretical purpose of the declaration sought.[52] One of the later cases, published in 2009,[53] shows a tribunal sitting in Paris and applying French substantive law granting declaratory relief despite its alleged inadmissibility under the French procedural law. The tribunal concluded that the French rules of civil procedure were 'not applicable to international arbitrations' and that 'nothing prevents a party from seeking a declaratory award under the French rules on arbitration or under the ICC Rules'. In the case delivered by F. Mazza[54] in 2011, the opposite approach was taken by the tribunal, which adopted the Germanic principle of subsidiarity. The arbitral tribunal explicitly referred to Swiss law and the concept of legal interest, which bars obtaining declaratory relief where performance can be requested.

The cases described below can shed more light on the arbitrators' practice, helping to identify the predominant perception.

52. ICC Award in Case no. 9617, Clunet 2005, also in Collection of ICC Awards 2001–2007, 711.
53. Final Award in ICC Case no. 12502, paras 85–86, in 34 Y.B. Com. Arb., 130 (van den Berg ed., 2009).
54. Arbitrators referred to: 'F. Mazza, in *ASA. Performance* ... (M. Schneider, J. Knoll eds.), p. 144 (point 4)'; here, the tribunal followed Swiss law in dismissing the respondent's request for declaratory relief that it was entitled to exercise the call option. After changing its prayer for relief, it was decided to grant him a specific performance, ordering the claimant to transfer the specified number of shares.

It appears that the autonomous approach has recently made inroads as an established practice observed in the vast majority of awards, no matter whether more or less restrictive or whether more or less inspired by regulations at domestic/national level. The term 'autonomous approach' is taken as meaning that the tribunal does not deem itself bound by any domestic regulations, considering them only as certain guidelines which may or may not be followed by the arbitrators in their process of adjudication. Only in two awards did the arbitrators follow the domestic rules as binding rules providing for a restrictive approach towards declarations.

Among the analysed cases, the broadest reasoning is found in the award issued in case ICC 2.1, which was based on extensive analysis of various authorities. In this case, claimant was seeking a declaration concerning liability for breach of a sale contract. The goods subject to this original sale were resold further by the claimant, and the final buyer claimed damages in separate litigation, alleging that the product did not fit the intended use - for which the respondent, in his capacity as producer, was allegedly liable. The litigation in question was suspended, and claimant was seeking an *in eventu* declaration on respondent's liability for damages to be paid by the claimant to the final buyer as a result of the separate litigation.

Irrespective of the fact that both the applicable law and the seat of the arbitration were in countries squarely within the Germanic legal system (Swiss law, Vienna as a seat) the arbitral tribunal does not use the term 'legal interest', preferring not only 'legitimate interest' - what is closer to the Swiss culture but also 'actual and economic interest' instead,.

The arbitral tribunal started by explaining lack of impact of the legal interest standards as a condition for the admissibility of a claim for declaratory relief, as worked out by the state courts,[55] on the arbitration. Claims for declaratory relief, the tribunal expounded, should be admissible in arbitration based on claimant's legitimate interest to legal protection[56] - a claimant should be required to show that legal protection is indeed called for. The point that tipped the scales against claimant's interest in its claim for declaratory relief in civil proceedings was the state's interest that courts are not unduly burdened. The admissibility of claims - and, more specifically, the question of a legitimate interest as a condition precedent for a given claim - concerns the administration of justice: every state has a paramount interest that its courts are not unduly clogged up with 'hypothetical' questions - the judicial system's resources

55. The arbitrator relied here on: 'SFCD 4C.7/2003 of May 23,2003, pt. 5: "Pas d'intérêts, pas d'action"; O. Vogel and K. Spühler, Ch. 7 n. 23 ss.; A. Staehelin, D. Staehelin and P. Grolimund, 14 n 25; W.H. Rechberger and D.A. Simotta, *Zivilprozessrecht*, 7th ed., Vienna 2009; n 550; H. W. Faschin, A. Konezny, *Kommentar zu den Zivilprozessgesetzen*, vol. 3, 2nd ed., Vienna 2004, 226 ACCP n 7; A. Baumbach, W. Lauterbach, J. Albers and P. Hartmann, *Zivilprozessordnung*, 68th ed., Munich, 256 German Code of Civil Procedure, n 21; R. Zöller and R. Greger, *Zivilprozessordnung*, 28th ed., Cologne 2010, n 256. German Code of Civil Procedure, n 7; Guinachrd/Ferran, *Procédure civile*, 28th ed., Paris 2006; n 122; G. Couchez, *Procédure civile*, 14th ed., Paris 2006, n 152.'
56. The arbitrator cited 'ICC No. 9617 [1999], published in J.J. Arnaldez, Y. Derains and D. Hascher, *Collection of ICC Awards 2001 to 2007*, Kluwer Law International 2009, p. 711.'

should be conserved to deal with actual and real matters.[57] Each state must refer to its *lex fori* to weigh this interest against the claimant's interest in fair access to justice.

The above should be irrelevant in arbitration, where it is the parties concerned who provide the resources for the arbitration and bear its costs,[58] which should result in the situation that the standards of domestic civil procedures are not applied or, at the very least, should be lowered significantly.[59] In any case, the opposing view, which has it that the limitations on admissibility of claims for declaratory relief are the same in civil procedure and in arbitration,[60] is outdated and untenable, as confirmed also by Swiss jurisprudence.[61] International commercial arbitration:

> 'aims at providing for plain and efficient proceedings with an easy and possibly unified access to justice', where 'claimant's legitimate interest as condition precedent to its claim for declaratory judgment must not be ambitious but should be modest'.[62]

On the contrary, it is not acceptable that claims for declaratory relief should be admitted without limitation and barred only if they amount to a manifest abuse of rights.[63] In this respect, it is common both in civil procedure and in arbitration that respondents are to be protected against unnecessary or frivolous claims.[64] It seems unfair that it should be respondent's burden to prove claimant's manifest abuse of rights, rather than the claimant having to show a legitimate interest to its claim for declaratory relief, even though claimant has initiated on arbitration asking for a declaration against respondent. In practice, a respondent would hardly ever be able to meet such a burden[65] explaining that a party to an arbitral agreement, by executing such an agreement, has not consented to unnecessary claims.

The arbitrator supported his stance with comparative observations, noting that common law jurisdictions such as the USA or Australia also adopt the straightforward

57. The arbitrator referred to: 'Dasser, n 17 and 21; M. Stacher, *Das Rechtsschutzinteresse im internationalen Verhältnis*, AJP/PJA 9/2007, n 32, p. 1131.'
58. Arbitrators relied here on: 'K.H. Schwab and G. Walter, *Schiedsgerichtsbarkeit*, 7th ed., 2005, Ch. 16 n. 1; M. Stacher, *Das Rechtsschutzinteresse*, n. 38, p. 1132.'
59. Arbitrators referred to: 'R.A. Schütze, D. Tscherning and W. Wais, *Handbuch des Schiedsverfahres*, 2nd ed., Berlin 1990, n 377; K.H. Schwab and G. Walter, *Schiedsgerichtsbarkeit*, Ch. 16 n. 1, p. 135; J.F. Poudret and S. Besson, *Comparative Law of International Arbitration*, 2nd ed., London 2007, n 572.'
60. *See*, e.g., 'T. Rüede and R. Hadenfeldt, *Schweizerisches* ..., fn 10, p. 48' (as cited in the award).
61. The Sole Arbitrator stated that the SFC itself seriously questioned whether the principles re admissibility of claims for declaratory relief developed for courts have any bearing on arbitral proceedings at all (*see* SFCD 4A_444/2009 of February 11, 2010, pt. 4.2.1).
62. 'J.F. Poudret and S. Besson, *Comparative*..., n 572' (as cited in the award, ICC case ICC 2.1).
63. 'M. Stacher, *Das Rechtsschutzinteresse*..., n 41 ss., p. 1133' (as cited in the award, ICC case ICC 2.1).
64. 'K.H. Schwab and G. Walter, *Schiedsgerichtsbarkeit*..., Ch. 16 n 1, p. 135' (as cited in the award, ICC case ICC 2.1).
65. 'M. Stacher, *Das Rechtsschutzinteresse*..., n 38 and 40, p. 1132' (as cited in the award, case ICC 2.1).

approach. Under the United States Code 2201, the existence of an actual controversy between two parties suffices to grant declaration.[66]

In this particular case, the arbitrator found that claimant has a legitimate interest in granting a declaration.

First, respondent contested that it had been foreseeable that claimant would resell the product and that respondent had to bear the responsibility of a (contested) defect vis a vis a third-party customer - what creates controversy and what results in turn in creation for the claimant an actual and economic interest, sufficient as a prerequisite to admit the declaratory relief.

Second, in this context, the arbitrator also considered the argument of prematurity. The respondent argued that claimant had suffered no actual harm yet and that, accordingly, any claim for damages is premature and the claim for declaration is simply a circumvention. The arbitrator found that, quite on the contrary, declaratory relief cannot be considered unnecessary especially in a situation where claim for damages is not possible under the circumstances.[67] Claims for declaratory relief, the arbitrator held, are useful tools[68] especially in cases such as this one, involving a chain of distribution with damage occurring in the first order of sequence at the very end of the chain with unknown responsibilities and various contractual liability regimes along the distribution chain.[69]

Summing up, a claimant, in order to obtain declaratory relief, must demonstrate his legitimate interest, i.e., that he is indeed in real need of receiving the declaration, although this is balanced by the requirement to protect the other party against unnecessary claims. What is important, the arbitrator does not limit his analysis to the 'legal' interest, stating precisely that legitimate interest in this case is equal to 'actual and economic' interest. These two factors are very close to the ones adopted in English law, as described earlier in Chapter 3 *supra*, namely utility and justice to the parties.

The arbitrator did not verbalize his attitude to the subsidiarity principle, as in this case a more far-reaching claim, i.e., for damages, could not have been submitted. In fact, this deficiency was raised by respondent as a defence against the claim for declaration. If, however, one continues the line of argument presented here in cases were a claim for performance is sufficiently mature to be raised, the relevant declaratory relief would most probably again be analysed from the two perspectives of utility and justice, and not from the formalistic subsidiarity principle.

The problem of prematurity in the context of declaratory relief was also raised in case ICC 2.2 (*lex contractus* and *lex arbitri* - Swiss). The claimant sought a declaration that it has the right to terminate a supply agreement in accordance with its terms as a

66. The arbitrators relied here on: 'W. Tabb and R. Shoben, *Remedies in a Nutshell*, St. Paul 2005, p. 248 s.', referring to; the situation in Australia is similar: 'W. Covell and K. Lupton, *Principles of Remedies*, 4th ed., 2008, n 13.4'.
67. *See* section §4.04[B] *infra*.
68. The arbitrators referred to: 'A. Redfern and M. Hunter, *Law and Practice of International Commercial Arbitration*, 3rd ed., London 1999, 8-22; M.J. Mustill and S.C. Boyd, *Commercial Arbitration*, London 1982, p. 344.'
69. 'OGH of Feb. 6, 1996, CISG-online 224, in fine' (as cited in the award, case ICC 2.1).

result of respondent's material breach of both the supply agreement and the related licence agreement.

The arbitral tribunal found that, by this prayer for relief, claimant was not asking the arbitral tribunal to simply declare that a theoretical right to terminate exists under the referenced provisions of the agreement (in fact, if it had been asking for such relief, the request would have been deemed inadmissible for lack of legal interest, since a declaration by the arbitral tribunal to that effect would have been redundant given the contractual existence and definition of the remedy). Also claimant was not asking the arbitral tribunal to declare that an existing act of termination by claimant was rightfully and validly made, i.e., that claimant had properly exercised his right – otherwise the prayer for relief would have sought a declaration that claimant has rightfully terminated the agreements, and the prayer would have been linked to an underlying claim alleging and substantiating the existence of an act of termination. Instead, this prayer for relief was deemed to amount to asking the arbitral tribunal to declare that claimant has the right to terminate the agreements in the future on the basis of acts that occurred in the past. The arbitral tribunal found that such prayer for relief was not admissible because entertaining it would have required the arbitral tribunal to make its decision on the basis of assumptions, obliging it to speculate about future fulfilment of contractual and legal conditions of termination. If the arbitral tribunal had been asked to declare that a given act of termination by claimant was justified and valid, i.e., to declare that claimant had properly exercised its contractual right to terminate at some point in the past, the arbitral tribunal would have been able to entertain that prayer for relief with a view to deciding whether the termination in question was valid. However – the tribunal continued – the claimant is not making, and has not substantiated, any such claim under this prayer for relief. For the above reasons, the arbitral tribunal found this prayer for relief inadmissible and proceeded to dismiss it.

As a matter of comment, it appears that the tribunal in this case mixed the purpose of the declaration sought. The claimant sought clarity whether the particular breach of the contract entitles him to termination, and the tribunal dealt with the question of correctness of the termination as such, what really did not happen in fact.

On a similar basis, the arbitral tribunal dismissed the relief aimed at declaring the obligations of the respondent if claimant had exercised his right to termination. In this context, the tribunal found that claimant is asking it to pronounce on a hypothetical situation.

A number of other declaratory reliefs dealing with respondent's various breaches were found inadmissible because claimant lacked legal interest with respect to a cause of action for which it was simultaneously seeking monetary relief (damages). The tribunal applied in this case stricter rules of admissibility, relating to subsidiarity principle, however it did not actually cite domestic law.

Finally, in case ICC 2.16 (Austrian *lex contractus* and Swiss *lex arbitri*) the declaration on prospective payment towards the third party, relating to defects of the products resold to such third party, was sought. The arbitrators found the claims admissible without any special analysis of the admissibility prerequisites, characteristic for the litigation practice. The final finding was based on interpretation of the contract, which provided for certain limitation of claims to be raised and in particular of claims for loss of profit.

The autonomous approach was followed in case ICC 2.3, the reasoning for which blends authorities rooted in the Continental and common law traditions. First, the principle that the legal interest belongs to the procedural law area is adopted. In this case, Swiss law was the *lex arbitri*. The arbitral tribunal found that a party requesting declaratory relief had to show his legal or actual interest, having Swiss test as a starting point, which was generally to be assumed in a situation where the legal relationship between the parties is uncertain and this uncertainty may be eliminated through a determination by the tribunal. This uncertainty must be such that the affected party was restricted in its business decisions, resulting in a situation that was unacceptable to that party.[70] The purpose of a declaratory judgement 'is to ensure recognition of a situation of law, once and for all and with binding force as between the parties; so that the legal position thus established cannot again be called in question in so far as the legal effects ensuing therefrom are concerned'.[71] The case at hand dealt with some patent infringements, of which some were the object of a dispute before the state courts while others were not. The respondent argued that, while the patents as such were not in dispute, any declaration concerning them should not be admitted. The tribunal shared the view of the claimant that it was enough that a violation had been threatened or was impeding and that it cannot be excluded that respondent would file further lawsuits with regard to the other patents. This situation is unacceptable for claimant, who asserts that it granted a valid sublicence with regard to all the patents in question. An award in these arbitral proceedings could thus afford certainty to claimant as to whether claimant has a valid right to grant a sublicense with regard to the ten patents in question and whether a third party under such sublicense is entitled to use these patents. Claimant thus had a legal and actual interest in declaratory relief.

The concept of legal and actual interest adopted by the tribunal did not rely on the subsidiarity principle. The tribunal found that availability of specific performance or of an action for performance was not a reason to refuse the granting of declaratory relief. Unless the parties had agreed otherwise, both remedies were available in arbitration proceedings, and declaratory relief was particularly appropriate when the parties wanted a decision on their rights or wished to determine the existence or meaning of a contract.[72] As neither the *lex arbitri* (Swiss law) nor the arbitral procedural rules (ICC Rules) provided otherwise, the possibility of requesting performance did not preclude a request for declaratory relief in this case. A declaration or finding that a contractual obligation had been violated or disregarded often appears as a prerequisite for a performance and damage claim, and there is no reason why an arbitral tribunal should not grant both if the merits of a case support such an adjudication. Here, the arbitration

70. 'Decisions of the Federal Supreme Court of October 30, 1984, BGE 110 II 352, 357' (as cited in the award, case ICC 2.3).
71. The arbitrators referred to the case concerning the Factory at Chorzów, in: 'Publications of the Permanent Court of International Justice (PCIJ), Series A, No 13 (Interpretation of Judgements Nos. 7 and 8 – Judgement of 16 December 1927), p. 20; G. Born, *International.* p. 2482, fn. 327'.
72. 'D.St.J. Sutton, G. Gill and M. Gearing, *Russell on Arbitration*, 24rd ed., 6–109; *see also* G. Born, op. cit. Vol. II, p. 2482, fn. 335' (as cited in the award, case ICC 2.3).

agreement between the parties did not limit the authority of the present arbitral tribunal in this respect and there was, generally, no disadvantage in granting declaratory relief in conjunction with an order for performance. In particular, where the parties have a continuing relationship, declaratory relief has a useful independent function as it may clarify a situation and avoid the risk of disputes over the same issues in the future.

Summing up this case, the arbitral tribunal limited the interest of the parties in obtaining declaration to clarification of uncertain legal position, where such uncertainty impacts the parties' business decisions and is unacceptable to a party and where it can be reasonably hoped that a declaration may dispel such uncertainty. The possibility to claim damages does not eliminate the value of the declaration. Here, the tribunal supported himself with Swiss jurisprudence to define general notion of a legal interest and common law tradition, under which declaration can be followed by the relevant coercive measure.

In case ICC 2.4, where Swiss law was again *lex arbitri*, the findings of the tribunal are marked by a certain inconsistency, but the final solution appears to be autonomous. On the one hand, the arbitral tribunal determined admissibility of declaratory relief in accordance with Swiss law and subjected it to the same test of sufficiency as a request for declaratory relief before state courts.[73] With regard to Swiss state court proceedings, such a legal interest was assumed to exist under Article 88 CCP (i.e., the Swiss Code of Civil Procedure) if: (i) uncertainty exists between the disputant parties with regard to a specific legal relationship that can be clarified by declaratory relief; (ii) the uncertainty is perceived as no longer acceptable for the claimant, for example because it results in a restriction of its economic freedom; and (iii) the uncertainty cannot be resolved by other means, in particular by means of a claim for performance.

The arbitral tribunal showed itself cognizant of new trends towards a more liberal approach to declaratory relief in arbitration, even when the arbitral tribunal is seated in Switzerland.[74] For the purposes of its findings, the tribunal considered the most minimalistic legal interest definition, namely that the declaratory relief requested serves a concrete practical purpose in an actual controversy between the parties, and the claimant must establish that these minimum prerequisites are met. If they are not met, the claim is rejected without prejudice.[75]

This decision, as mentioned earlier, brings some inconsistencies. On the one hand, the tribunal finds that it should apply the procedure of the state courts, without really explaining why this must be so. On the other hand, it finds that it will apply

73. The Arbitral Tribunal referred to: 'B. Berger and F. Kellerhals, *International...* 2nd ed., London 2010, n 1529 F. Wiget, *Fragen der Verfahrensgestaltung vor Gelegenheitsschiedsgerichten nach zürcherischem Zivilprozessrecht*, in: M. Kummer and H.U. Walder (eds), Festschrift zum 70. Geburtstag von Max Guldener, Zürich 1973, p. 367 et seq., p. 370 in particular; Lipschitz, *Weitere Bemerkungen zum Konkordat über die Schiedsgerichtsbarkeit*, SJZ 73 (1977) 59–60, particularly at p. 59.' *See* Annex IV by Nino Sievi *infra*.

74. 'M.E. Schneider, *Non-Monetary...*, p. 29–31; M. Stacher, *Rechtsprechung des Bundesgerichts in Schiedssachen* (2009 und 2010), AJP 2011 p. 125 et seq., at p. 128; M. Stacher, *Das Rechtsschutzinteresse...*, 1124 et seq., at 1132–1133; *see also* D. Akikol, *Die* bundesgerichtliche...,n. 117 (as cited in the award, case ICC 2.4).'

75. 'Bessenichibopp, o.c., note 156, Article 88 N 8' (as cited in the award, case ICC 2.4).

certain minimum requirements, *viz.* existence of a controversy in which a declaration may serve a concrete and useful purpose. If so, it does not really depart from the earlier tribunal's findings, where utility of the declaration is crucial for its granting. In case ICC 2.5, exactly the same line of argument was offered. Interestingly however, the arbitral tribunal stated, that it would admit the requests for declaratory relief to the extent that they underlie and are absorbed in a precise request for monetary relief and the link between the breach and the proven damages is established. This statement stands quite contrary to the subsidiarity principle. The case dealt with the buy-back option and the granted declarations clarified what could be qualified as a buy-back event.

In a similar vein, the arbitrators considered case ICC 2.6 on declaring a breach of contract. Here, the tribunal clearly stated that, while in many domestic civil procedure systems such relief may not be available where the declaration is implicit in the order to pay damages, tribunals hearing international disputes under the rules of a number of organizations, among them the ICC, frequently do grant such relief, provided that the subject matter of the claim and its legal or contractual basis are clearly identifiable. This may assist the parties in their future relationship.[76]

In case ICC 2.7, the arbitral tribunal recalled the ongoing discussion in international arbitration as to the requirements for considering a declaratory relief in arbitration and, in particular, criticizing declaratory actions in arbitration as susceptible to abuse as they may 'encourage Claimants to bring artificial actions to put pressure on Respondents and to gain unfair advantage'.[77] Based on this background, the arbitral tribunal started to examine its authority to grant the declarations, which had a negative character. The arbitrators finally decided to look to the civil procedure rules of *lex arbitri* for inspiration, but not to follow them slavishly, save from the mandatory rules. The local law provided in the typical Germanic way that legal interest is necessary in order to admit declaratory relief and that a declaration serves to ascertain a right or legal relationship. In general, the arbitral tribunal found that both positive and negative declarations are allowed and did not elaborate on the general prerequisites. In the body of the award, however, it is made clear that immediate threat to breach of the contract was one of them. In this case, claimant had made two prayers for negative declaratory relief, i.e., to declare that the conditions of a concession agreement had not been fulfilled and that the penalty requested in the penalty decision was not binding and valid and that therefore, claimant is not obligated to pay this penalty. The arbitral tribunal found that respondent's express and unequivocal statement in the penalty decision that the conditions of the concession agreement were fulfilled and that a failure to comply with the resulting penalty decision may give rise to a right of the

76. The arbitrators relied on: 'N. Blackaby et al., n. 9.61–9.63; for a case where a party to the dispute may have a legitimate interest in obtaining declaratory relief regarding its relationship to a third party (a pattern we find also in these proceedings), cf. Trib. Fédéral (Swiss Federal Supreme Court), 1ère Cour civile, 28 September 2004, A A.S. c. B SpA (with comment FK.) in: F. Knoepfler, *Schweizer Jurisprudence suisse en matière d arbitrage international, Schweizerische Zeitschrift fur Internationale s und Europaisches Recht/Revue suisse de droit international et européen* 2006, 105, 119 et seq.' As concerning the problem of proper identification of the declaration sought, *see* also section §4.03[D] *infra*.

77. 'Cp. P. Dunand and M. Kostytska, *Declaratory Relief...*, p. 1 et seq.' (as cited in the award, case ICC 2.7).

respondent to terminate the concession agreement provided sufficient grounds for an immediate legal interest of claimant to have this legal dispute settled in arbitration. As a result of the penalty decision, claimant had to apply for interlocutory relief before a state court in order to seek judicial protection against respondent's penalty decision. Moreover, the threat to terminate the concession agreement was jeopardizing an important part of claimant's business in the given state so that claimant had a legitimate interest in seeking a determination as to the mutual rights and obligations under concession agreement. For these reasons, the arbitral tribunal held that claimant's declaratory relief is admissible in principle.

Finally, the tribunal admitted the declaratory relief that that claimant is not obligated to pay the penalty as requested in the penalty decision. The arbitral tribunal, however, found that claimant had no legal interest in obtaining a negative declaratory decision on the issue of the penalty decision being not binding and invalid because its legitimate interest in seeking judicial protection against the penalty decision was sufficiently protected by the first declaration sought – that claimant is not obligated to pay the penalty as requested in the penalty decision. Accordingly, the tribunal dismissed this application for relief.

In case ICC 2.8, where Italian law was applicable and the arbitration was seated in Paris, the arbitral tribunal concluded that French law could be applicable to the admissibility of the relief, finding however, that respondent had referred to authorities that do not concern international arbitration, but to proceedings before the French general courts. The tribunal examined independently whether claimant has a legal interest in pursuing its declaratory claims, with the result that it did not follow respondent's arguments. The respondent had submitted that, under French law, the admissibility of a request for declaratory relief depends on two conditions: (i) the claimant must have a legitimate interest to seek relief; and (ii) the request must be sufficiently particularized. Pursuant to Article 122 of the French Code of Civil Procedure, a claim that is not supported by a legitimate interest is inadmissible. Relying on a decision of the Cour d'Appel de Paris, respondent argued that such legitimate interest must be 'personal, direct, arisen and present'. Such a situation exists only when 'the situation in dispute causes [the claimant] a trouble and when the ruling sought would likely put an end to it', and the relief sought must aim at providing the claimant with a practical and identified advantage.

As to the second requirement, respondent submitted that French law does not permit a party to seek a general opinion in respect of a legal or factual situation. Based on these principles, French law only admits declaratory relief in limited circumstances, such as in matters relating to personal status and property rights. In the case of a breach of a contractual obligation, however, the creditor must either seek damages or specific performance.

Respondent concluded that claimant does not have a legitimate interest in the claims aimed at declaring that claimant is not in breach of the shareholders agreement because they are only admissible as defences to respondents' counterclaims. Respondent also challenged claimant's legal interest in claims seeking a declaration that respondent is in breach of the shareholders agreement because he did not make any claim for damages and 'fails to identify its interest in seeking such a general declaration' for any of them, and in particular one additional claim concerning interpretation of the contract.

The tribunal found that claimant has a legitimate interest in seeking a declaration that he has fulfilled his obligations under the parties' agreements and therefore he is not in breach of the SHA and a declaration that respondent has breached its own obligations. In the case of the former claims, this is so in particular in light of the situation that respondent is seeking an award for the damages which, in the opinion of the respondent, have arisen from breaches by claimant. Clearly a declaration that claimant has not breached its obligations arising out of the shareholders agreement or has fulfilled its obligation would improve its factual and, even more so, its legal situation and in particular, in the performance of the shareholders agreement going forward, if he should seek such performance as it avers to intend. Both parties claim breaches, and both certainly have a legal interest in having their differences clarified. There is also a legitimate interest of the claimant seeking a declaration that respondent has breached its own obligation under the shareholders agreement. The parties' obligations under their agreements are closely related to one another. The success of the project depends on their joint cooperation and the fruitful performance of their respective obligations. The consideration of claimant's conduct in the performance of its financing obligation must necessarily take into account the development of the project, as well as its bankability, for which respondent was partially responsible. The consideration of claimant's performance of its obligations related to the project also hinges in part on respondents' own conduct with regards to successfully securing a project. The tribunal, thus, found those claims admissible.

In case ICC 2.9, an arbitration seated in Singapore with UNIDROIT principles adopted as the law applicable to the merits, the tribunal started its analysis of the admissibility of the declaration on wrongful termination of a contract with the comment that, while it has the power to award declaratory relief under section 12(5) of the IAA,[78] such relief is unnecessary if the ruling that the claimant seeks is inherent in any award of damages for termination. That said, the tribunal recognized the usefulness of dealing with the termination issue separately from assessment of any damages only if justification for such a declaration could be found.

The claimant also applied for declarations that the respondent was in breach of the parties' contract. Such declarations were held to be entirely redundant in that they were essentially contained in the part of the award dealing with damages. The findings of the tribunal were formulated independent of any authorities appropriate for the admissibility problem under the *lex arbitri*. However, the principles underlying the subsidiarity rule were observed in this award.

---

78. Section 12(5)(a) of the Singapore International Arbitration Act (Chapter 143 A), (*see* https://sso.agc.gov.sg/Act/IAA1994) provides that, without prejudice to the application of Art. 28 of the Model Law, an arbitral tribunal, in deciding the dispute that is the subject of the arbitral proceedings (*a*) may award any remedy or relief that could have been ordered by the High Court if the dispute had been the subject of civil proceedings in that Court.

In a number of cases the arbitrators do not endeavour to define legal interest themselves or back up their decisions with arguments from the particular jurisprudence or academic writings, simply stating that in certain situations claimant has it or not. In case ICC 2.10, the arbitrators started their deliberations on admissibility of any declaration with the simple statement that the claimant must demonstrate its legal interest in such a declaration and left it at that, not delving into deeper discussion of this issue. In the case at hand, respondent initiated parallel proceedings in the state courts to invalidate the arbitration clause contained in the distribution agreement in question, making for considerable uncertainty. Elimination of this uncertainty was deemed to provide sufficient grounds for the claimant's application seeking a declaration that his termination of the agreement was valid. Claimant thus had a valid legal interest, worthy of protection, in a final award deciding whether the agreement had come to an end or continued to exist. Similarly, in case ICC 2.15 the tribunal, while asked to grant a number of declarations, in general observed in most of the cases, that the claimant did not prove its legal interest (*Feststellungsinteresse/Intérêt à la constatation*) and dismissed such prayers for lack of substantiation of legal interest, without getting into the merits. For clarity sake, it must be noted that none of the parties raised this issue and arbitrators surprisingly did it upon its own initiative. One of the declarations dealt with qualification of the calling of the bank guarantee as a breach of contract. Here the tribunal gave more of the reasoning, stating that such declaration would make sense only in case, when claimant would be automatically entitled to be reimbursed for all excess charges and costs. This in turn would require determination which of such costs would be justified. As such determination was not possible, then the requested declaration 'if justified on the merits, would not be differentiated enough to make such an assessment' and thus claimant has no legal interest in the declaration to be granted. It appears, that in this case the tribunal grounded his findings on the argument, that declaration would not settle the case entirely.

In case ICC 2.18 claimant sought a number of complicated declarations, aiming at interpretation of the agreement pursuant to which Respondent granted claimant and its affiliates a non-exclusive licence to market, use and sell certain products. The arbitral tribunal is dealing precisely with each declaration, dismissing a few based on lack of justified interest or legal interest, which terms are used interchangeably. This lack of interest is manifested, as the given case may be, by three phenomena: by the fact, that respondent does not argue certain allegations or because certain matters were clarified enough earlier in the award, i.e., in another declaration, or because the declaration sought was not precisely or too broadly formulated. In the latter case, the arbitrators elaborated broadly, opposite to others (*see* section §4.04[D]. *infra*).

In addition to the awards identified via a general search, there is one more award which contributes to understanding of the legal interest: case ICC 3.2, with Swiss law as both the law applicable to the merits and *lex arbitri*. The tribunal's analysis started with the point that an arbitral tribunal confronted with declaratory claims must, as a matter of principle, first determine the requirements to be met by such claims or any applicable restrictions on their admissibility, respectively. To this extent, tribunals will, in general, have to decide what law to apply in this regard. However, the arbitral tribunal found that in both cases, i.e., regardless of whether qualified as substantive or procedural issue and, consequently, irrespective of whether assessed under Swiss substantive law or the governing procedural rules, the principle of good faith was applicable and established a minimum standard which any declaratory relief must meet. The good faith test was in fact similar to the test proposed by Leimgruber, as referred to below, were to be fulfilled: (i) the legal position of (one of) the parties to the arbitration was in dispute; (ii) the requested declaration was relevant to resolution of the dispute; and (iii) the declaratory award would serve a practical purpose. Against this background, the arbitral tribunal adopted the opinion that prayers for declaratory relief that merely set out the grounds for justifying other prayers (e.g., for monetary relief or for dismissal of counterclaims) lacked independent significance and were therefore inadmissible. In this case, it is important to note that the tribunal based its identification of declaration prerequisites on autonomous understanding based on good faith factor. This is very important, and such an approach follows the innovative solutions as proposed in legal writings.[79] It is interesting to observe how the tribunal ruling on this case established a link between this factor and the subsidiarity principle, how the declaration on breach of contract, being a premise to awarding damages, would not be seen as an action in good faith. It appears that this could be a matter of utility issue *in extremis*, but not one of good faith as such.

In case ICC 2.11 (Swiss law, Paris), the tribunal stated only that the claimant has a legitimate interest in obtaining a declaration in its favour that the contractual completion time is extended as the project was still ongoing, therefore the final award provided that the claimant was entitled to an extension of time for performance. The tribunal did not elaborate on the notion of interest and did not actually use the phrase 'legal interest'. In case ICC 2.19 the tribunal stated only, that the declaration sought is too general and too unspecific to be granted, without any references to particular provisions or jurisprudence. In case ICC 2.20 (Swiss law as *lex contractus* and *lex arbitri*) the tribunal dealt with multiple declarations relating to proprietary interest of the parties in certain technological information and the content of rights of the parties under the licence agreement. The parties did raise certain arguments relating to the legal interest principle, however tribunal did not really refer to them, swiftly moving into the analyses from the merit perspective. In a few instances only, the tribunal referred to lack of legal interest manifested in lack of substantiation of the imminent danger, that the respondent will represent to anyone in the future that it owns an ownership interest in the technological information instead of speaking of his status as licensee and also that claimant did not suffer any harm in relation to this. The tribunal dismissed another claim due to be too broad and too general.

In case ICC 2.12 (Spanish Law), the tribunal found that the parties, and particularly the respondent, had devoted considerable time and effort to arguing on the additional defences and have asked for **declaratory** relief in relation to these defences. The parties have thus expressed the expectation to obtain a comprehensive declaration on their **legal** rights under the agreement, and it was therefore *just and proper* that these defences be accordingly dealt with as fully as possible.

79. *See* Leimgruber, *supra* n. 3, at fn. 48.

[C] The Local Law Approach

The local/national law, as a direct regulator of the legal interest in arbitration, appeared in merely two cases.

In case ICC 2.13, the arbitral tribunal based its findings only on provisions of the local code of civil procedure and on relevant legal writings, without discussing on what basis local civil procedure rules are applicable to the arbitration. Basing on the legal doctrine and jurisprudence, the tribunal pointed that that legal interest for exclusive declaratory protection in principle does not exist when full legal protection can be achieved through a condemnatory or constitutive claim. Then, in principle, there is no basis for the claimant to require the court to specifically establish what otherwise can and should be established when offering condemnatory or constitutive legal protection. If, however, legal interest in establishing fact has significance which overrides the actual claim, such a declaration is legally justified and is necessary for the protection of other rights or interests, then there is a basis for independent declaratory legal protection. In this case, there were two reliefs sought: a declaration that the share purchase agreement had not been validly terminated and remains in force, and condemnatory relief for restitution of a given number of shares. The tribunal found that the condemnatory claim does not protect all the interests of the claimant, in particular as regards other shares not subject to the pending dispute which could be a subject of expropriation.

Similar findings were presented in case ICC 2.14. Here, a Germanic system of law was applicable as *lex arbitri* and as substantive law. The prayer for relief encompassed a declaration that claimant shall be entitled to full access to documents and information which belong to the claimant and which are in the possession of the respondent foundation. The arbitral tribunal found that, even though it is widely recognized that an arbitral tribunal may grant declaratory relief,[80] neither the local civil procedure code nor the ICC Rules regulate admissibility of declaratory relief in arbitral proceedings. With regard to state court proceedings, the local *lex arbitri* provides that a claim for declaratory relief can only be raised if a claimant can demonstrate a legal interest in doing so. According to judicial authorities of the seat of the arbitration, such legal interest exists only where the matter in dispute can be resolved exclusively by declaratory relief; this is never the case where a claimant could have accomplished the same objective by submitting a request for performance. Accordingly, the necessary legal interest is lacking where the request for declaratory relief is raised together with an entirely overlapping request for performance. Other civil law jurisdictions - such as Austria (228 ACCP) and Switzerland - apply the same restrictions to claims for declaratory relief, and it is, in principle, accepted by legal commentary and the courts, particularly the Swiss Federal Tribunal, that these restrictions also apply if declaratory

80. 'G. Born, *Commercial Arbitration Vol. II*... p. 2480' (as cited in the award, case ICC 2.14).

relief is requested from an arbitral tribunal.[81] Although local courts and legal authorities have yet to address the question of whether the restrictions of local civil procedure codes apply in arbitration, the tribunal ruling on this case considered that the appropriate approach is to apply the principle that the general rules of civil procedure regarding admissibility of declaratory relief apply in arbitral proceedings as well as in state court proceedings. Therefore, also in arbitration, declaratory relief is not available where a party can request performance. In this case, the tribunal found that there is no interest on claimant's part in a declaration dealing with information rights beyond the prayers for specific performance that the tribunal considers admissible. While Austrian legal commentary is not unanimous as to whether such lack of a material, legally or factually protected interest in declaratory relief leads to a dismissal with prejudice or whether the claim must be dismissed without examining the merits of the case (*Nichteintreten*), i.e., without prejudice, the Austrian courts generally hold that a claim for declaratory relief is to be dismissed with prejudice if the requesting party has no protected interest in the declaratory relief.

Following established lines of authority by the Austrian courts, the tribunal ruling on this case found that, due to claimant's lack of interest in a declaration dealing with information rights beyond the prayers that the tribunal considers admissible, and thus capable of being the subject of a request for performance, claimant's request for declaratory relief fails and must be dismissed with prejudice.

[D] Converging Civil and Common Law Elements

When analysing declaratory awards issued by ICC tribunals in the given period, the following conclusion may be drawn. It is an established practice that arbitrators adopt the autonomous approach in establishing principles upon which declaratory relief can be granted and neither adopt domestic procedure directly nor by analogy or subsidarily. Arbitrators are often guided by the principles developed by national sources of law, but such guidance usually a starting point for their own concepts, converging, whether consciously or intuitively, features typical to the two systems of law. This is not to be avoided, because arbitral tribunals very often run quite extensive analyses of the respective authorities rooted in both civil and common law (*see* ICC 2.1). There is a visible impact of the two factors. First, the Swiss sufficiency test, worked out by the Swiss judiciary,[82] is very common starting point for the arbitrators' deliberations. Considering, that Swiss nationals are frequently appointed as arbitrators, this is not surprising. Second, the literature which propagated autonomous approach to legal interest, is important. Especially, M. Schneider declaration that the domestic regulations on legal interest should not be adopted[83] and Leimgruber test of good faith[84] are

81. 'B. Berger and F. Kellerhals, *International...*, 2nd ed. 2010, n 1528 et seq.; for a more liberal angle on this issue, *see* M. E. Schneider, *Non-Monetary...*, p. 26 et seq.' (as cited in the award, case ICC 2.14).
82. *See* Annex IV by Nino Sievi.
83. Schneider, *supra* n. 19, at 30.
84. Leimgruber, *supra* n. 3, at 480–483.

important. The general and a-national understanding of the commercial sense of arbitration as a system of private justice for both parties, and commercial sense of the requested relief, prevails. There were only two cases among the twenty analysed in which the tribunals clearly found domestic restrictions imposed on admissibility of declarations applicable.

The convergence of civil and common law features is visible in two basic dimensions, formal and on the merits.

First, it is significant that arbitrators happily mix the terminology naming proper prerequisites in granting declarations. They use the term 'legal interest' interchangeably with 'legitimate'[85] or 'actual',[86] and 'economic'[87] interest crops up as well. The most popular is the term 'legitimate', which is not surprising as being originated both in Swiss as well as English legal tradition. In a number of examples demonstration of an economic interest only suffices. This propensity to mix is a very interesting manifestation, intuitive or deliberate, of departure from the strict Continental criteria of legal interest.

Second, the formal dimension is related to the question of how the concept of legal interest is treated from the perspective of being a prerequisite or post-requisite element of procedure. Continental legal interest is a prerequisite, a prior condition to granting the declaration. Contrary to that, existence of real interest indicates the limits of the judge's freedom to grant declarations, and to some extent plays a role of 'post-requisites'. Continental judges grant declarations 'only if' legal interest is proven; English judges grant declarations 'unless' there is no real interest in doing so. In other words, a Continental judge asks the question 'can I grant a declaration?' before embarking on analysis whether the content of the declaration is proven. In presented arbitral awards there is a striking example of continental approach in case ICC 2.15 In brief, it was noted that claimant not only did not, but even did not attempt to prove why the tribunal should render the declaratory award, so it should have been dismissed.[88] This case appears to be very rare. Anyway examination of an interest as a prerequisite has been in evidence in a majority of presented case. More English approach was visible in a number of cases, including a vast majority of M&A arbitrations, but also in ICC 2.8, ICC 2.12. or ICC 2.19. It is very interesting to observe that arbitrators hailing from the Continental tradition cannot resist the temptation to evaluate whether any legitimate interest exists as a prerequisite to declaration, even if departing however from the Continental components of the notion of legal interest.

The merit-based dimension of the common/civil law convergence is related to the components of the term 'interest', whether one chooses to designate it as 'legal' or

85. Case ICC 2.1, Case ICC 2.6, Case ICC 2.4, Case ICC 2.8, Case ICC 2.5, Case ICC 2.7, Case ICC 2.11, Case ICC 3.4.
86. Case ICC 2.1, Case ICC 2.3, Case ICC 3.4.
87. Case ICC 2.1.
88. In this case, the tribunal was not consistent in this respect. Among all the declarations, one was refused without examining the preliminary question of whether the claimant had a legal interest, as the tribunal stated explicitly.

otherwise, which endeavour to depart from its local civil law meaning. Most frequently, Swiss procedure is adopted as a point of reference.[89] Accordingly, Swiss law specifies the following features of the legal interest: (i) uncertainty exists between the parties to a dispute with regard to a specific legal relationship, and this uncertainty can be clarified by way of declaratory relief; (ii) the uncertainty is perceived as no longer acceptable for the claimant; and (iii) the uncertainty cannot be resolved by other means, in particular by means of a claim for performance (subsidiarity principle). As provided in Chapter 2, the following elements will supplement the notion of the Germanic legal interest: (iv) the uncertainty relates to the particular right or legal relationship, and not to the facts; (v) the claimant's interest in receiving a declaration is of an objective, and not subjective, character; (vi) the declaration will finally settle the dispute; (vii) in case of a negative declaration, the interests of the parties are properly balanced.

In English law, on the other hand, utility and justice to the parties are the limitations of the judge's discretion to grant declarations. In comparing these two settings, it is visible that justice to the parties is not expressly specified as a component in civil law contexts, save from the negative declarations. Utility, meanwhile, is common to both the Continental and English schools, although there is a different understanding of what, exactly, utility is all about; this is most striking in the strict adoption of the subsidiarity principle or missing value of economic interest in civil law jurisdictions.

The general observations may be made, that arbitral tribunals depart from the Germanic notion of legal interest towards more pragmatic solutions found in common law. The basic legal argument for a departure from the civil meaning of the legal interest by arbitrators is based on the fact that a restricted notion of legal interest is about protecting the courts against being unduly burdened, while in arbitration such public interest does not exist due to financing of the proceedings entirely by the parties. As much has been clearly formulated by Schneider and followed in a number of awards.[90]

Fairness to the parties is not the inherent element of the legal interest tests, save from the postulate to protect the legitimate interests of respondent in case of the negative declaration. In arbitration, it appears that the focus switched from protection of the courts onto the general postulate of the fairness to the parties, as found in English law. In case ICC 2.1, it was ruled that the interest demonstrated before the arbitrators should be legitimate, meaning that a claimant should be required to show that she is in need of legal protection. This is understood quite liberally, being limited by the legitimate interest of respondent who, in his turn, needs to be protected against frivolous or baseless claims. The starting point for the deliberations was proper balance between claimant and respondent. The arbitrators in case ICC 2.12 proceeded in a similar spirit; here, the declaration was granted because it was just and proper to deal with the parties' defences, as the parties had devoted much effort to formulating them. This sounds like almost 'copy paste' from the English judgements.

89. *See* Case ICC 2.4, Case ICC 2.5.
90. Schneider, *supra* n. 19, at 30; VIAC case SCH – 5301 (2014).

While speaking about principles of fairness the principle of good faith has to be discussed. The principle of good faith as a general prerequisite in arbitration is proposed in legal writings such as those of S. Leimgruber.[91] Surprisingly, here all criteria relate to the useful purpose and remain silent about fairness as such, mention of which might reasonably be expected in a discussion of good faith.[92] The full 'good faith' criteria in *verbatim* form were adopted in case ICC 3.2, while the abbreviated test can be found in case ICC 2.3. The arbitrators ruling on the latter held that legal or actual interest is to be presumed in the following situations: the *legal relationship between the parties is uncertain* and *this uncertainty can be eliminated through a determination by the tribunal*. The uncertainty must be such that the affected party finds itself restricted in its business decisions, resulting in a situation that is unacceptable to that party.

In practice, the duopolistic approach - consisting of two mixed criteria only: existence of a dispute or controversy and useful purpose of the given declaration - is generally prevailing. Such a line of thinking is in evidence in cases ICC 2.4 and ICC 2.5, where the arbitral tribunal started its deliberations from the prerequisites used in Swiss civil procedure but finally concluded that, as a minimum, it is required that the declaratory relief requested serves a concrete *practical purpose* in an *actual controversy* between the parties.

The utility approach in its broad sense can be observed in a number of cases. In case ICC 2.7, it was held that an *immediate threat* to breach a contract created a legitimate interest. In case ICC 2.8, utility, in a sense very close to that familiar from common law, was a driving factor, as arbitrators discerned legitimate interest in the fact that a declaration would *improve not only the legal, but also the factual situation*. In case ICC 2.10, although the applicable test is not clearly specified, the criteria are based on considerable uncertainty caused by parallel court proceedings, elimination of which provided sufficient grounds for the claimant's application seeking a declaration

The subsidiarity principle is an important factor throughout the Germanic family of law. As mentioned in the discussion of the Swiss test above, declaratory relief shall not be granted where the uncertainty can be resolved by other means, in particular by means of a claim for performance. There are two versions of this principle. The stricter one results in dismissal of the requested relief in its entirety, while the softer variation denies a separate declaration if such declaration is presumptive to the other relief granted simultaneously.[93] The subsidiarity principle is in general not adopted in

91. As has been raised, Laimgruber defines the principle of good faith in seeking declaratory relief as follows: (i) the legal position of (one of) the parties to the arbitration was in dispute; (ii) the requested declaration was suitable to resolve the dispute; and (iii) the declaratory award would serve a practical purpose.
92. Leimgruber, *supra* n. 3, at 482–483.
93. As a side note, it is difficult to understand such a formalistic approach. If, in the opinion of the arbitrators, the declaration is based on the same cause of action and plays the role of a premise for other relief, there is no reason not to grant a declaration. There is no harm in declaring breach of contract and subsequent damages in lieu of mere damages. If, to the contrary, the declaration introduces separate value, and in particular res judicata effect, the party seeking declaration has an important reason to have his prayer for relief decided separately. Adopting the soft separability principle is a clear manifestation of superiority of dogmatic arrangement of human activities over its common sense.

arbitration. There is clear example in case ICC 2.4, where the tribunal indicated that it is an element of legal interest in Swiss law, but deliberately omitted it in its test of admissibility. In many cases it is not a subject of interest of arbitrators at all.[94] The soft principle of subsidiarity was followed in cases ICC 2.2 and ICC 3.2. The fusion *a rebours* appears in case ICC 2.9 where, basing on Singapore law as common law, the arbitrators adopted the subsidiarity principle in its softer form.[95]

Finally, Germanic systems, save from Swiss law, observe a distinction between economic and legal interests. Without getting mired down in debate whether, potentially, certain economic interests might be seen as having a legal dimension,[96] it should be stated that economic interest, with a reservation of the Swiss jurisdiction, is not sufficient to seek declarations before the state courts. It appears, however, that economic interest should be sufficient in seeking a declaration in arbitration, similar to English law. In case ICC 2.1, as already noted, the arbitral tribunal even uses the term 'actual and economic' interchangeably with 'legitimate interest', granting them a status equal to legal interest in the process of admitting declaratory relief. This line of argument has been also confirmed in Vienna International Arbitration Center (VIAC) case SCH – 5301 (2014).[97] The arbitral tribunal clearly stated that a mere economic interest is usually considered sufficient for a declaratory relief to be admissible.

Further, there is no discussion on the issue of objectivity of the claimant's interest in seeking declaratory relief, whether concerning the existence of the uncertainty or of the impact of such uncertainty on the status or affairs of the claimant. This problem is not in principle a concern for the arbitrators.[98]

As a summary, it might be posited that, in arbitration, the concept of any prerequisites necessary to be demonstrated in order to obtain the declaratory relief is generally not very common, as has been demonstrated by my study of M&A declaratory awards. In many cases, the arbitrators simply answer the questions posed by the parties in the affirmative or negative, not delving into why such a question has been asked. The arbitrators' task is to simply to ascertain that given averment is true or false. In case ICC 1.3, the dispositive part of the ruling corresponded exactly to the order of questions and answers. If, however, arbitrators find it necessary to adopt the concept

94. Tribunals follow the English approach and see no problem in declaring both declaration and coercive measures.
95. S. Leimgruber's stance (*see supra* n. 3, at 486) is that international arbitration should follow the English approach, which does not recognize the subsidiarity principle However, Leimgruber also says that there may be situations in which a declaration is not suitable or sufficient, where respondent admits his obligation but is unable to perform. Then a mere declaration is inadequate, being as it is non-coercive, and the arbitrators should invite the claimant to transform the declaratory relief into a performance remedy. This, however, intervenes too much into the balance of the parties' rights.
96. It is quite difficult to make a clear distinction between economic and legal interest. By definition, the law regulates the entire realm of financial relationships, classifying them as various subjective rights and claims deriving therefrom. In VIAC case SCH-5179 (2011) see the detailed description of the case further in this chapter, the respondent defended his position by alleging that a claimant seeking a declaration on future liability has only an economic interest and not a legal one; this line of argument did not impress the tribunal (*see also* Chapter 5, section §5.06 *infra*).
97. VIAC Selected Arbitral Awards, vol. 1, 2014, C58; A29.
98. On the problem of objectivity and subjectivity please *see* Chapter 2 *infra.*

of interest as a prerequisite to declaratory relief, the autonomous concept of interest decidedly prevails. This concept includes both common law and civil law elements, although it can be named as a converged interest, as has been done in the title of this chapter. This converged interest is definitely closer to the common law real interest, with its flexible and broadly inclusive approach to the utility feature, than to the Continental concept of formalistic legal interest.

§4.04 SPECIFIC ISSUES RELATING TO ADMISSIBILITY OF DECLARATORY RELIEF

[A] Introduction

This final part of this chapter, will be devoted to specific issues raised in the analysed awards relating to admissibility of declaratory relief: declarations on future liability, the procedural or substantial nature of legal interest, the impact of wording on existence of legal interest, validity of *ex officio* authority of the tribunal to determine admissibility of the declaratory relief and, finally, the legal effect of dismissal of the relief for lack of legal interest.

[B] Admissibility of Declarations on Future Liability

The problem of declaring future liability in fact relates to ascertaining liability for future damages, which may arise in connection with actual or future actions. In this respect, it deals with some hypothetical aspects, although in most cases it is not the sort of hypothetical status which cannot be assessed at all for purposes of the declaratory relief, so it should not disqualify an interest in seeking a declaration.[99] There are three potential situations. The first situation assumes declaring appearance of a mere event, in particular breach of contract, which activates legal liability, without deciding what degree of culpability attaches to respondent; in the case of liability based on risk rather than on fault of one degree or another, granting a declaration will be equivalent to declaring liability in principle. This scenario, incidentally, is not a very frequent one in practice. The second situation assumes declaring liability as a principle for future, as of yet unidentified damage/harm. In this case, the declaration relates to ascertaining the damaging event itself and liability of a given party based on the degree of guilt of the party committing a damaging event; it does not define, however, the quantum damage or a causal link, for the simple reason that not all the consequences have materialized yet. It is a useful tool in all situations like breach of confidentiality clauses, non-compete clauses and other contractual covenants. The third situation relates to declaring liability for damage which is defined but which is to transpire in the future. While the harm has not actually occurred yet, ascertaining all the constitutive elements

99. In Germanic jurisdictions there are various limitations in this respect, *see* more Annex III.IV[B] by Beata Gessel-Kalinowska vel Kalisz, Joanna Kisielinska-Garncarek *infra*; Annex I.IV[B] by Ulrich Kopetzki *infra*.

of liability, i.e., the damaging event, the party liable and her degree of guilt, the quantum of damage and a causal link is possible. This kind of declaratory relief is relevant, for example, in cases of tax misrepresentation in the context of share purchase agreements when the tax liability is already known, but is still the object of dispute with the tax authorities and will, as it were, mature once the final tax order/fine is issued.[100]

A declaration of liability in principle based on ascertaining breach of contract appears to create a legitimate interest of the aggrieved party to receive a relevant declaration. In particular, it is true when considering the subsidiarity principle, widely promoted in Germanic system, in cases where a breach and ensuing damage are expected to occur and there is no ready claim for performance as it is premature, so at least a declaration should be available.[101] Such a solution does not require establishment of future facts, as they will be established once the quantum claim materializes. It allows establishment of facts relevant close to the moment when they occur. Waiting until the full damage has occurred will make fact-finding more problematic, bearing in mind memory of the witnesses, to name just one factor. It gives comfort to the claimant to benefit from a *res judicata* effect, with the added advantage of blocking certain pernicious activities of the respondent for the future, especially if combined with cease and decease orders. Finally, depending on the local regulations, the declaration on liability may suspend or interrupt the statute of limitations.

The problem of declaring liability for future loss is not tackled by arbitrators in a uniform fashion, as the examples below show. In case ICC 1.1, for instance – as discussed above – the claim was dismissed. The relief sought encompassed monetary relief at a certain minimum and was accompanied by a further request to declare the general rule of liability for any damages to be incurred in the future. Such a declaration, however, was likewise denied, this on the grounds that, in the opinion of the tribunal, claimant had not substantiated its claim for future losses and the arbitral tribunal found that it cannot (and indeed should not, under Austrian law) award on premises of its own creation. The uncertainty attaching to any future tax liability for the target company's past operations also led the tribunal to conclude that it did not have the tools to effectively decide on any potential future liability in this respect. It is difficult to share this view. The question of insufficient substantiation of the claim is not problematic at all but the statement that the tribunal lacks appropriate tools has no sound footing. The arbitrators in case ICC 2.1, where relief was granted in the situation of damages not realized yet, found that especially in this sort of situation does declaratory relief present a useful tool. In this case, claimant was seeking a declaration

100. This example is a certain simplification seeing as, in many situations, the decision of a tax authority has a confirmatory character and the tax liability arises ex lege simultaneously with the relevant taxable event. In case ICC 1.8, claimants alleged that the accounts of the company acquired based on the SPA included an underestimated tax liability. No final tax decision had been issued yet at that point, but the tribunal, being convinced of the proper tax liability, proceeded to grant damages for misrepresentation.

101. Contrary to this logic, the declaration on liability for future damage is not widely accepted in Germanic tradition due to, once again, lack of legal interest. *See also* case SCH-5179 (2011), as described below.

as to liability for breach of a sale contract. As already recounted above, the goods subject to sale, were further resold by the claimant, and their final buyer claimed, in separate litigation, unsuitability of these goods for their intended use, taking liability to the doorstep of the producer in his capability as producer. The litigation in question was suspended, and claimant was seeking an *in eventu* declaration on respondent's liability for damages to be paid by claimant to the final buyer as a result of the separate litigation. In this context, the arbitrator also considered the argument of prematurity. Respondent argued that claimant had incurred no damage yet and thus has no claim for damages, any such claim being premature and amounting to circumvention of applicable rules. The arbitrator found that, on the contrary, declaratory relief cannot be considered unnecessary especially in a situation where a claim for damages is not possible under the circumstances. Claims for declaratory reliefs are useful tools in particular in a case such as this one, with harm at the very end of a distribution chain threatening as of yet unknown circumstances at other points of that chain.

Both the above decisions were based on Austrian law. In order to make the picture full, additional Austrian case (both *lex arbitri* and *lex contractus*) published by VIAC relating to the future damages is worth mentioning. The dispute in case SCH-5179 (2011) centred on a non-disclosure agreement (NDA). The claimant (buyer) had initiated a process of identifying and acquiring companies complementary to his own business. For this purpose, one of claimant's employees introduced the respondent (seller), who was a natural person, and target company, a company owned by the seller, as a possible acquisition target for the claimant. The parties negotiated the sale and purchase of respondent's shares in the target company. The parties concluded the NDA which, among its other stipulations, provided that neither party should solicit or entice away, directly or indirectly, from the other party or from any entity owned or controlled by the other party any board members, directors or employees. The negotiations were terminated without success. Subsequently, two employees signed employment contracts with companies belonging to the group of companies of the seller. The claimant sought a declaration of liability of respondent for any damages that may be incurred by claimant, directly and/or indirectly, as a consequence of what it saw as poaching of employees by entities directly and/or indirectly controlled or led by respondent, what was combined with a request for a cease and desist order concerning these employees and any other claimants' employees.

The arbitral tribunal analysed, among other things, the understanding of application of the legal interest principle as a prerequisite in this case. According to respondent, claimant did not allege or prove any legal interest required to justify its declaratory claim, its interest being only of economic origin. Also, respondent alleged that claimant had not made any statements on (and let alone proven) the causal connection between the alleged violation of the NDA and any future damage. The arbitral tribunal found this argumentation incorrect. A party must prove its legal interest in order to prevail with a claim for declaratory relief. According to the jurisprudence of the Austrian Supreme Court,[102] as long as there is a possibility that the

102. 'Legal directive ("Rechtssatz") of the Austrian Supreme Court RS0039018' (as cited in the VIAC Case SCH-5179 (2011)).

damaging incident could cause damage in the future, the injured party has a legal interest in a declaratory judgement. Such judgement was duly delivered in the present case: although the claimant had not suffered any harm as at the rendering of the award, it could not be ruled out that it would do so in the future. Thus, the Claimant's legal interest had been established.

The precondition of showing a causal connection had also been fulfilled. According to the Austrian Supreme Court,[103] two steps must be distinguished: step 1 is the causal link between the violation of a contractual obligation and the potentially damaging incident, and step 2 concerns the causal link between the potentially damaging incident and the specific damage in the given case. Only step 1 is to be alleged and proven already in the proceedings on the declaratory judgement, whereas step 2 is only to be dealt with in future proceedings based on an action for performance (compensation). In the present case, the arbitral tribunal considered step 1 to be the causal link between the violation of the non-solicitation clause (i.e., a violation of the contractual obligation) and the retaining of employees (i.e., the potentially injurious incident), whereas step 2 would be the causal link between the employment of employees and the future harm of the claimant (i.e., the concrete future damage). Step 1 was proven in the present case: the causal link between the breach of the non-solicitation clause and the employment constituted the violation itself. Thus, the claimant had established the necessary causal connection.

Therefore, the arbitral tribunal proceeded to find that respondent shall be liable for any harm that may be suffered by claimant (whether directly and/or indirectly) as a consequence of the retaining of employees by any company which is directly and/or indirectly controlled by respondent.

A quite educative case study is presented in the unpublished M&A award in case ICC 3.1[104] (German law, seated in Switzerland). As the circumstances of this case were somewhat unique, they warrant more detailed presentation. In this arbitration, the leading claims were raised by respondent. What is striking in this case is that the declarations sought were based not only on regular causes of action, which appeared prior to the commencement of the proceedings but also on default committed by claimant within the course of the proceedings. The arbitration itself arose out of the share purchase agreement or SPA between the claimant and the respondent. Pursuant to the SPA, the selling side could object to the closing financial statements and adjusted purchase price determination certificate provided by the respondent by sending its notice of objections. The claimant did transmit a notice of objections to respondent, but the parties were unable to reach an agreement on the disputed items of the price adjustment mechanism and submitted their dispute to a neutral auditor. According to the claimant, by its notice of objection, the claimant validly and in due time challenged the respondent's closing financial statements and adjusted purchase price determination certificate, thus, these documents did not become final and binding on the parties

103. 'Austrian Supreme Court's decision 2 Ob 277/08m of October 15, 2009' (as cited in the VIAC Case SCH-5179 (2011)).
104. This award was issued later than 2014, and it was not included in the main body of the analysis; however, it is interesting from the perspective of liability for future events.

and the dispute between the parties was validly referred to a neutral auditor in accordance with the SPA. The claimant brought claims against the respondent for payment of an adjustment to the purchase price under the SPA, as decided by a jointly appointed neutral auditor to whom the parties referred their dispute with respect to the calculation of this adjustment amount.

The respondent did not consider the neutral auditor's opinion as final and binding on the parties, and sought payment of a purchase price adjustment amount calculated on different terms. The respondent also sought damages for various alleged breaches of representations and warranties by the claimant and indemnification for various costs, which the respondent declared as set-off against the claimant's claim.

In the course of the arbitral proceedings, the claimant presented the inventory report to its witness, who was a managing director of respondent's competitor. The report contained confidential information, including lists of the respondent's customers by site and by country and the volume of products supplied to them, placing respondent's competitor in a position to target the respondent's customers. Though the claimant protested that it supplied the managing director of respondent's competitor with a redacted version of the report only, which was disputed by the respondent, the redacted version nonetheless contained sensitive information and confidential business secrets and could have been used to identify the customers.

According to the respondent, by providing the report to a direct competitor, the claimant breached its confidentiality obligations under the SPA. Adherence to procedural rules of the arbitration proceedings or IBA Rules of Evidence did not alter the obligations under the SPA. In any event, claimant had violated 'procedural good faith', which required the parties to an arbitration to refrain from taking steps which aggravate the dispute. In addition to breaching its confidentiality obligations under the SPA, the claimant, by disclosing the report, also breached its non-compete obligations under the SPA. According to the respondent, the managing director of respondent's competitor, after receiving the report, in fact met with several companies which were customers of both respondent's competitor and respondent in order to expand respondent's competitor's business with these customers. Based on the above, respondent filed in the course of the proceedings an additional claim for non-compete and confidentiality violations, which included the declaratory relief.

In this arbitration, then, declarations were sought by both parties,[105] however the tribunal was more focused on respondent's claims. Respondent, in respect of the respondent's purchase price adjustment claim, requested that the tribunal finds that the claimant had failed to submit a notice of objection in accordance with the SPA and that the closing financial statements and the adjusted purchase price determination certificate prepared by the respondent became final and binding upon the parties in accordance with the SPA and, in this connection, orders the claimant to pay to the

105. The claimant was seeking determination that he had a claim for payment from the escrow account in any amount(s) for which respondent had prevented an earlier release from the escrow account by virtue of any claims made by respondent in these proceedings; this was accompanied by other claims, including the claim for payment of the adjusted purchase price and specific performance to hold claimant harmless from any claims of the neutral auditor. All of them were dismissed based on the merits.

respondent the relevant sum as determined by the expert. Both reliefs were granted by the tribunal as requested by the respondent.[106]

In respect of the respondent's claim for non-compete and confidentiality violations, respondent sought a declaration that the claimant was in breach of the SPA, an order that claimant pays liquidated damages and indemnity for the respondent against any damages incurred as a result of the claimant's breach of the SPA; the latter was deemed to be merely declaration.

As concerning confidentiality violations, the arbitral tribunal found that, by providing the unredacted version of the report to a third party, the claimant had breached its confidentiality undertakings.

Adherence to procedural rules of the arbitration proceedings did not excuse a breach of this provision of the SPA. The tribunal therefore declared that the claimant was in breach of the SPA.

The respondent had also sought an order that the claimant indemnify the respondent against any damages incurred as a result of the claimant's breach of the SPA. In its claim for non-compete and confidentiality violations, the respondent noted, 'The Respondent reserves the right to further quantify and amend its claim in this regard and, for the time being, requests declaratory relief only.' Respondent, subsequently, did not amend its respective prayer for relief but upheld its request for a simple declaration. While the claimant argued that, even if the disclosure of the report did constitute a breach of the SPA, no damage could had been incurred, as the report contained only facts already known to managing director of respondent's competitor, the claimant did not object to the respondent's request for a declaration as such, i.e., the claimant did not argue that the respondent would lack the required interest to obtain the declaration sought (*fehlendes Feststellungsinteresse*).

As the tribunal did not accept the claimant's argument that the report contained only facts that were already known to managing director of respondent's competitor, it therefore ordered the claimant to indemnify the respondent against any future damages possibly arising as a result of the claimant's breach of its confidentiality obligations.

Further, the tribunal found that, under the circumstances, the claimant's actions also constituted a breach of the claimant's non-compete undertaking under the SPA.

Though the claimant's primary intention may not have been to actively divert business from respondent to respondent's competitor, the claimant accepted with conditional intent (*dolus eventualis*) that it would negatively affect respondent's position in the market if the second inventory report was disclosed to a managing director of respondent's competitor. The claimant was, at best, careless as to the likely consequences of its actions. The tribunal therefore declared that the claimant is in

106. As a matter of fact, this is another example, that declaration may be combined easily with a coercive measure in arbitration. The relevant part of the dispositive was worded as follows:

> The Tribunal declares that the Claimant failed to submit a Notice of Objection in accordance with [] of the SPA, and that the Closing Date Financial Statements and Adjusted Purchase Price Determination Certificate prepared by the Respondent became final and binding on the Parties in accordance with [] of the SPA; The Claimant is ordered to pay the Respondent EUR [], plus interest at the rate of 10% p.a. from [] up to the date of payment.

breach of the SPA and ordered the claimant to pay to the respondent the contractual penalty.

As to the respondent's request for indemnification against damages incurred as a result of the claimant's breach under the SPA, in its comments on the claimant's response to the respondent's claim for non-compete and confidentiality violations, the respondent stated that it 'is entitled to recover any further losses incurred by its loss of customers. In this regard, the Respondent requests declaratory relief only'. The Arbitral Tribunal found, that under German law, it is accepted that liability to pay damages under section 280(1) of the German Civil Code for future damage can be subject to a declaratory order where there is a possibility that such damage will materialize and the claimant did not object to the respondent's request for a declaration on this ground. The tribunal therefore granted this request, and ordered the claimant to indemnify the respondent against any future damages to be incurred as a result of the claimant's breach of its non-compete obligations.[107]

The above cases demonstrate again that arbitrators tend to follow a more flexible and pragmatic approach than judges in the state courts. The concept of legal interest is deemed broad enough to allow for granting declarations in the sphere of liability for future harm.

[C] Substantive or Procedural

The qualification of a legal interest constituting the prerequisite for declaratory relief in terms of being procedural or substantive is an important factor determining the scope of norms applicable in arbitration. As Schneider rightly points out:

> the procedure before the international arbitral tribunals is governed by the lex arbitri and that the law of civil procedure at the place of arbitration is not applicable neither by analogy nor subsidiarily. Of course, there are rules and principles in civil procedure which can serve as a useful and relevant source of inspiration for international arbitrators. But their application is not automatic and such application should be justified in each case.[108]

Deeper analysis of the nature of legal interest is included in Chapter 2 *supra* and Chapter 5 below, which will tackle this problem from the perspective of the proposed redefinition of the notion of legal interest. Below, I present the way how this problem is dealt with by arbitrators.

In case ICC 2.1, the arbitral provided an exhaustive explanation of the procedural character of legal interest and subsequent autonomous approach to its definition. The tribunal found that legal interest is a matter of procedure and disagreed with the

---

107. The respective part of the dispositive was formulated as follows:

> The Tribunal declares that the Claimant is in breach of [] of the SPA; The Claimant is ordered to indemnify the Respondent against any future damages incurred as a result of the Claimant's breach of [] of the SPA.

108. Schneider, *supra* n. 19, at 30.

respondent who, citing SFC practice, argued that Swiss law on which the parties have agreed as to the merits of their dispute governed the question whether claimant has a legitimate interest to its claims as well. The tribunal confirmed that, indeed, there is a specific decision qualifying claimant's legitimate interest to its claim a matter of substantive law which, therefore, ought to be determined pursuant to the applicable *lex causae*,[109] but it did not subscribe to this view. The arbitrators noted that, as far as can be seen, the SFC's view is quite unique in Continental Europe where, as a general rule, the question whether a claim is supported by a legitimate interest on behalf of claimant is decided, like all other questions related to the admissibility of an action, pursuant to the *lex fori* of the competent court. Indeed, the SFC has shared that view for many decades.

Other arguments in favour the procedural character of legitimate interest as a condition precedent for a given claim concern, predictably, administration of justice and protection of the judiciary against dissipation of its resources.

Also, the question of legitimate interest as a condition precedent to a given claim further concerns the respondent who has an interest not be dragged into legal proceedings which it has not prompted and/or of which the outcome is irrelevant. In that regard too, the *lex fori* of the competent court is better able to decide when a claim is serious enough to have respondent answer it. Finally, the tribunal points out that deciding the admissibility of a claim and, more specifically, the question of legitimate interest on the basis of the *lex causae* leads to quite significant practical problems, particularly in international matters.

According to the contract, the seat of the arbitration was Vienna, so Articles 577–618 of the Austrian CCP applied as *lex arbitri*. Based on this finding, and in accordance with 594 paragraph 1 ACCP, the parties have validly agreed on the ICC Rules to apply to these arbitral proceedings. According to Article 15 paragraph 1 ICC Rules:

> the proceedings before the Arbitral Tribunal shall be governed by these Rules and, where these Rules are silent, by any rules which the Parties or, failing them, the Arbitral Tribunal may settle on, whether or not reference is thereby made to the rules of procedure of a national law to be applied to the arbitration.

Further, the tribunal found that neither the ICC Rules themselves nor the Terms of Reference lay down any provisions as to admissibility of claims for declaratory relief. The tribunal also rejected the respondent's view that the contract (providing for the application of Swiss law), and particularly the proviso 'in every respect', lead to application of 'Swiss procedural law', be it the Swiss Code of Federal Procedural Law (*Bundesgesetz über den Bundeszivilprozess*) or to the general principles of Swiss procedural law. Thus, the tribunal determined that, as none of the ICC Rules, the Terms of Reference or the Supplemental Procedural Rules address the question of claimant's legitimate interest, and as the parties have not, and do not, agree on the principles pursuant to which that question is to be determined, the sole arbitrator shall decide that

109. 'See Decision of the SFC [hereinafter: "SFCD"] 77 II 344, 347; 110 II 352, 353' (as cited in the award, Case ICC 2.1).

question according to the principles which he deems appropriate. Based on this footing, the tribunal made its own autonomous definition of legal interest.

In case ICC 2.3, where Swiss law was applicable as substantive law and as *lex arbitri*, the arbitrators dwelt the developments in the Swiss judicature. Up until then, as they noted, the issue of whether declaratory relief could be granted, if a simultaneous claim for performance arising from the same legal relationship was requested, or was possible, had been dealt with by the courts in Switzerland as a matter of substantive law and in a manner which had excluded relief for a declaratory judgement as an additional remedy. In a more recent decision, the Swiss Federal Supreme Court held that the requirements for declaratory relief as they are applied in court proceedings do not necessarily apply to arbitration proceedings. What with the new Federal Law on Civil Procedure, which treats justified interest as a requirement for declaratory relief as a matter of procedural law, the former judicature – which was based on the assumption that this is a consideration which must be examined under substantive law – no longer applies, with the implication that the subsidiarity principle is no longer valid to arbitration.

In case ICC 2.7, the procedural and substantive approach is quite mixed, to the point that retracing the arbitrators' line of argument on this matter becomes difficult. The arbitral tribunal began by noting that the parties have not agreed any procedural rules on availability of declaratory relief and found that Article 19 ICC-Rules gives the arbitral tribunal broad flexibility and large discretion to settle procedural issues. It then found that, if it qualifies the availability of declaratory relief as a question of admissibility and thus relating to the merits of the dispute, Article 21(1) sentence 2 ICC Rules allows application of the rules of the law which the tribunal determines to be appropriate. Finally, the tribunal found guidance in the procedural rules of the *lex situ arbitri*, but did not follow it directly.

In case ICC 2.8, respondent submitted that, according to the respondent's legal expert, Italian law treats admissibility of declarations as questions of procedure and that, as a result, they must be deemed to be subject to French procedural law (i.e., the law of the seat of the arbitration), even if Italian law is applied as the proper law for resolving the substance of the case. In this case, as mentioned above, the tribunal did not object to such qualification, however it did apply its independent criteria to identify the legal interest of the claimant.

Finally, in case ICC 3.2, the arbitral tribunal found that it was not necessary to take a conclusive position on the questions raised above. If considered as a substantive matter, the requirements for declaratory relief under Swiss substantive law, being the law applicable to the merits of the dispute, would have to be observed here. If considered as a procedural matter, the mandatory provisions of Chapter 12 PILA, the rules contained in the terms of reference, the ICC Rules and any procedural rules determined by the arbitral tribunal would apply. These applicable procedural provisions governing the arbitration did not contain any express rules on declaratory relief. After deliberating substantive versus procedural character of legal interest, the tribunal found, somewhat surprisingly, this qualification as irrelevant, thus avoiding a final opinion on this point. In both cases, i.e., regardless of whether qualified as substantive or procedural issue and, consequently, irrespective of whether assessed under Swiss substantive law or the governing procedural rules, the principle of good faith was applicable and established a minimum standard which any declaratory relief must meet.

It is true for arbitration, as expressed in case ICC 2.1, that in most of Continental Europe the question of legal interest is a matter of procedural law. In addition to the cases referred to above, a similarly clear finding appears in the award in case ICC 2.5. A similar view is indirectly expressed in case ICC 2.8, where the tribunal criticized the respondent's argument that it refers to regulations applicable before the French courts which do not apply before the arbitral tribunal.[110] If not applicable, they cannot belong to the substantive regulations. Even if not expressed directly or indirectly, all cases where the autonomous approach was followed by the arbitrators come down against applicability of domestic regulations, which can happen only in a situation where legal interest is not accounted into the realm of *lex contractus*. As shown above, the number of them is prevailing in the analysed awards. It follows the general tendency of Germanic jurisdictions, and in particular the recent changes in Swiss practice.[111]

[D] The Wording of the Declaration and Possible Interference with the Legal Interest of a Claimant

Formulation of the content of the declaration sought appears to be very important in establishing whether the claimant has a proper legal interest in the given, particular declaration. If the content is too broad or too vague, it might be that the tribunal will find that such a declaration will not serve any useful purpose. This might lead to dismissing the relief sought or, based on the particulars of the case, to granting the declaration in a limited scope only. It has been argued that a declaration which is not properly formulated does not resolve the actual dispute.[112] For the most part, such allegations are to be disregarded. In light of the previous determination that arbitration is a private system of justice funded by the parties concerned, a number of arguments in this respect must fail. If the relief sought is too vague, the claimant may be invited to supplement it unless it interferes with the parties' equality of rights. The most sensitive issue in reformulation of the declaration sought is not to exceed the limits of the claim. In case of pecuniary claims, this task is easy enough. In cases of declarations of a descriptive character, the answers are not always simple.[113] The problem of proper and precise formulation of the relief sought may be rooted not only in legal interest concept but also in particular procedural rules.

In case ICC 2.18 (German *lex contractus*, Swiss *lex arbitri*), the arbitral tribunal based its findings on the ICC Arbitration Rules 1998, and in particular Article 4(3)(c)

110. Similarly, in ICC 12502, the arbitral tribunal denied respondents' argument that the relief sought by claimant, a declaratory award, was inadmissible under French law, noting that respondents relied on French rules of civil procedure, which are not applicable to international arbitrations; *see* Final Award in ICC Case no. 12502, paras 85–86, in XXXIV Yearbook of Commercial, Arbitration 130 (van den Berg ed., 2009).
111. *See* more in section §2.12 *supra*.
112. Leimgruber, *supra* n. 3, at 484–485.
113. *See* Michael J. Mustill & Stewart C. Boyd, *Commercial Arbitration* 390 (1989).

which provides: 'The request shall, inter alia, contain the following information: (c) a statement of the relief sought, including, to the extent possible, an indication of any amount(s) claimed' and Article 18(1)(c), whereby the Terms of Reference 'shall include the following particulars: "a summary of the parties" respective claims and of the relief sought by each party, with an indication to the extent possible of the amount claimed or counterclaimed'. The purpose of these provisions was to force claimant to properly define what it wanted to allow respondent to understand what is at stake, and also to assist in defining and limiting the Arbitral Tribunal's mission. The ICC Rules do not contain any specific provisions as to the degree of precision and determination of relief requested. The Swiss IPL does not contain any such provisions either. It is, however, common ground that a relief requested in an arbitration must be sufficiently clear and precise in order a) to guarantee respondent's right to be heard (Article 182(3) IPL) and b) to make it possible to check whether the arbitral tribunal has decided *extra petita* or *ultra petita* (Article 190(2)(c) IPL). The arbitral tribunal found inappropriate, in cases like the one before that arbitral tribunal, to fix standards that are too rigid or too high since that would make it impossible for an arbitral tribunal to resolve complex issues in ongoing long-term contractual relations. Finally, the Tribunal rightly stated, that a too broad relief requested does not raise any procedural difficulties, as long as respondent understood well enough what the the issues are. An arbitral tribunal can always grant less than what was requested.

The problem of formulation of the declaration to be granted was an issue in a number of cases.

In case ICC 2.4, claimant sought a sweeping declaration of respondent's liability for 'future legal expenses incurred due to the following court proceedings currently pending (...)' between the parties. In this case, claimant – in the opinion of the tribunal – not only failed to establish the required necessity and reasonableness of its past legal expenses (and had his claim for damages in this respect dismissed accordingly), his declaratory claim was also very generic and lacked sufficient specificity. Similarly, also the following prayer, '(...) all present and future damages incurred by Claimant resulting from the breach of fiduciary duties and other possible violations by Respondent of the Memorandum of Understanding', in the opinion of arbitrators, was too broad and could not serve a practical purpose. This case is quite interesting. Here, the claimant based its claims to recover the costs of pending litigation in arbitration proceedings, probably engaging in a shopping exercise as regards the different regimes of costs recovery and finding such recovery before the state courts to be less beneficial to the claimants than before the arbitration tribunal. It appears that the tribunal, by hiding behind the 'too broad' argument (which it in fact was), avoided answering the real question whether such a cost claim is possible in arbitration in principle.

In case ICC 2.17, the declaration holding the respondent to be 'liable on both contractual and tortuous basis for all damages caused to the Claimant pursuant to relevant articles of the Swiss Civil Code (Swiss CC) as well as the Swiss Code of Obligations' as developed in claimant's submissions was dismissed because the claim was too general and too unspecific to be granted.

In case ICC 2.8, the claimant's first prayer for relief was for the tribunal to declare that, under the shareholders agreement, his obligations in respect of the financing of the project were limited to using its commercial best efforts to find project finance lenders available to enter into a project finance facility agreement in order to finance costs of the project to the maximum possible extent. Respondent submitted that, seeing as this is a word-for-word repetition of a respective contractual clause except for the addition of the expression 'limited to', claimant was effectively requesting the tribunal to amend the contract, which the tribunal has no power to do. According to respondent, claimant is free to seek interpretation, but not to add a language to the existing contract or to seek a legal opinion on the nature of the best efforts obligation. In addition, claimant sought a declaration on proper fulfilment of his obligation and breach on the side of respondent. The tribunal found that claimant is far from requesting a general opinion. Rather, because respondent has submitted both before and during this arbitration that claimant had breached its obligations and that respondent has fulfilled its own, which claimant denies, claimant is praying for a determination that would close the controversies and disputes existing between the parties.

In case ICC 2.1, the arbitral tribunal altered the text of the declaration, which it found too excessive and applied in fact the rule *a maiori ad minus*, in the same vein as recommended in above case ICC 2.18. Here, claimant sought from arbitral tribunal 'a declaration that Respondent is obliged to reimburse Claimant for any payments to third party in connection with the goods delivered by Respondent under the Contract'. Taken literally, this prayer for relief not only seeks a declaration holding respondent liable to claimant for breach of the contract as a general matter and for any damages incurred by claimant resulting from claimant's liabilities to a third party and caused by respondent's breach of the contract in particular; rather, claimant sought a declaration holding respondent liable to claimant for any payments made by claimant to a third party in connection with all goods (ever) delivered to respondent under the contract. The tribunal noted that the latter declaration included the two other declarations (liability for breach for contract; liability for liabilities to a third party resulting from such breach), but went far beyond it. While the declarations relating to liability for breach for contract and relating toliability for liabilities to a[third party resulting from such breach were covered by a legitimate interest on behalf of claimant, the overall declaration sought by claimant was not: if granted, it would have heavily undermined respondent's interests and would put respondent at claimant's mercy. Respondent would have to reimburse claimant for all sums which claimant would pay to a third party 'in connection with the goods delivered by Respondent under the Contract', leaving respondent no possibility to contest that claimant's payments to a third party had indeed been caused by respondent's breach of the contract and were justified and reasonable under all relevant circumstances. Taken literally, claimant's prayer for declaratory relief included not only the delivery of the products under the contract in dispute, but any goods delivered to a third party under any purchase order issued pursuant to the contract (which is a frame contract only). Thus, the overall declaration sought by claimant was too broad, too vague and not supported by a legitimate interest. Therefore, the tribunal concluded that claimant had a legitimate interest as to a prayer for relief seeking a declaration which holds respondent liable to claimant for a breach of the contract in general and for all damages incurred by claimant resulting from liabilities to a third party and caused by respondent's breach of the contract in particular. Both of these declarations were contained in claimant's prayer for declaratory relief. Claimant, however, lacked legitimate interest in a declaration holding respondent liable for all sums which claimant would pay to a third party in connection with the goods delivered by respondent under the contract.

A similar situation was observed in case ICC 1.11. In this case, claimant sought two declarations: one that respondent wilfully breached the letter of intent and, two, that he would be entitled to specific performance to consummate the promised transaction. Concerning first declaration, the tribunal found that respondent had breached certain covenants only – the confidentiality obligation, exclusivity obligation and obligation to endeavour to execute a purchase agreement – and, in these respects, formulated a declaration. Opposite solution was adopted in case ICC 2.20 where the claim was dismissed as being too broad and too general. Claimant sought a declaration as to the lack of interest of respondent in certain technology, based on the licence agreement. The tribunal found that declaration encompassed the technology in general and respondent contested only his right to sublicense the technology to third parties.

In terms of formulation of the wording of the relief, there is one interesting decision of the arbitral tribunal which, in fact, transformed the declaratory relief into the constitutive relief that automatically changed the legal position of the parties. In case ICC 3.3 (Romanian law,[114] Paris), the dispute related to exercise of a put option right in a share purchase agreement for the seller to acquire outstanding shares. The claimant exercised the put option by issuing the respective put option notice. The parties could not agree on the number of put option shares and on the put option price. Also, the very put option mechanism applied raised questions as to its legal nature: whether it was in fact a pre-share transfer agreement or a final one.

Claimant elaborated four alternative requests for relief in relation to the put option. In principal relief, the claimant requested that the arbitral tribunal declares that a share purchase agreement was validly made between the claimant and the respondents on the terms (number of shares and price) as specified by claimant and compel payment of the purchase price.

In alternative relief, the claimant requested an award by which a share purchase agreement was deemed concluded between the respondents and the claimant on the specified terms, accompanied by an order to pay the purchase price.

In subsidiary relief, the claimant requested an order merely compelling respondent to pay the sum corresponding to the purchase price as compensation for breach of the obligation assumed under the put option provided for in the agreement.

In final alternative relief, which ended up playing the key role in this case, the claimant requested, should the arbitral tribunal consider that any of the three alternatives above are not correctly calculated and/or should be modified, that the arbitral

114. Under Art. 111 of the Romanian CPC, the interested party may apply for declaration of the existence or non-existence of a right. The courts in Romania are empowered to issue declaratory judgements limited strictly to matters of law; declaratory judgements are not allowed if the benefitting party is entitled to another remedy (i.e., to compensation or injunctive relief); https://uk.practicallaw.thomsonreuters.com/6-502-0226?transitionType=Default&contextData=(sc.Default) (accessed 31 January 2019).

tribunal performs the necessary corrections and issues any decision that it may consider to be just as per the agreement in view of achieving the share transfer from claimant onto respondents corresponding to the put option.

The arbitral tribunal did not elaborate on admissibility of the declarations requested and proceeded directly to the merits of the case. Based on the interpretation of the parties' intent and the wording of the submitted documents, the arbitral tribunal concluded that issue of the put option notice construed an obligation to negotiate the final content of and to execute the share purchase agreement. Also, it established its own interpretation of the formula upon which the number of shares and their price differed from the numbers determined by the claimant in all three alternative declarations sought.

Hence, the arbitral tribunal dismissed the principal relief based on the finding that a put option notice does not constitute the final agreement. In other words, it did not focus on admissibility of the declaration at all, but dismissed the alternative relief based on incorrect calculation of the put option price. It dismissed the subsidiary relief due to the finding that the put option notice constituted only a pre-agreement and that the respective obligations should be enforced in kind. Hence, the request for damages does not provide the proper basis.

In the view of the arbitral tribunal, the final alternative relief as to request was the only basis for assessing claimant's claim. It provided the arbitral tribunal with the power to shape the relief in any way it considers just and fair to achieve the share transfer corresponding to the put option. Having the put option notice in the form of a pre-agreement, the final award of a constitutive nature resulted in a share purchase agreement being executed between the claimant and respondent under the terms as set forth in that award.[115]

There is an important observation to be made here. This manner of going adopted by the tribunal shows that a general request for relief, usually worded along the lines of 'such other relief as the Tribunal may deem just and proper', may afford tribunal more flexibility in reconstruction of a proposed relief into a proper, in the opinion of the tribunal, remedy.

Summing up the above examples, the general conclusion can be drawn that arbitration tribunals approach the wording of the declarations sought rather flexibly, in the spirit of *benigna interpretatio*, aiming at construing a proper remedy based on formulations proposed by the parties. The stance of Leimgruber that the declaration is useless and does not meet the test of good faith if it is too vague or too broad to provide guidance regarding the parties' rights or conduct under a contract[116] must be regarded with great caution. The good faith principle can be considered if the wording of the declaration sought is incomprehensible to the tribunal and the respondent. Otherwise it can be ventured that the limitations need mainly to focus on prohibition to awards ultra petita as otherwise the principle of a maiori ad minus is applied.

115. The wording of the respective part of the dispositive was: 'By issuance of this Final Award, a sale-purchase agreement is deemed to be concluded between Claimant and Respondents at the following terms: [...]'.
116. Leimgruber, *supra* n. 3, at 484.

[E] Legal Interest and *Iura Novit Curia*

For a long time, international arbitration debated the question whether an arbitral tribunal can raise an argument *ex officio* without being submitted by a party if such question will be important for the findings of the tribunal.

In one recent ICC case (unpublished), ICC 3.4 (with Romanian law was both *lex arbitri* and *lex causae*), the claimant sought a declaration that respondent terminated the contract unlawfully, without just reason, i.e., contrary to the contract. Respondent submitted his defences focused on proving validity of the termination notice, but did not raise any argument relating to the lack of admissibility of the relief sought. In these circumstances, the tribunal noted, on its own initiative, that it was widely accepted in international arbitration that an arbitral tribunal may grant declaratory relief[117] however, as with any other claim, a claim for declaratory relief requires the petitioner to demonstrate that it has an actual and legitimate interest.[118] In the tribunal's view, this requirement was not satisfied in the present case. The claimant had not sufficiently explained the reasons why a final decision on the validity of the respondent's termination is required to be made in the present arbitration. There is no apparent actual, much less legitimate interest in obtaining the declaration sought by the claimant, and the claimant did not seek any further relief in relation to the alleged termination without just cause. Since the tribunal did not rule on the issue of the validity of the termination, it therefore concluded that the claimant's claim for declaration should be rejected without prejudice.

This award raises questions as to authority of the tribunal to pose the question of lacking legal interest as a bar to examine declaratory relief in this situation. The case before the Polish court described in Chapter 5 *infra* eloquently shows what unjust consequences can result from raising the legal interest argument *ex officio*. The tribunal did not rely on any obligatory provisions, but on general guidelines arising from writings in international arbitration. This is quite common, as shown in cases cited above. However, contrary to the aforementioned awards, the tribunal applied the concept of legal interest quite strictly, despite not being invoked by any party. Ascertaining validity of a contract or its termination in the situation where the parties dispute such validity and offer a number of arguments to support their contrasting statements construes a legitimate interest for each party to seek a declaration in this respect. There is no doubt that the uncertainty exists as to the existence of a contract, and it is difficult to give reason why a party to the contract would not need to clarify whether or not he is bound by its terms. This appears to be quite clear, and this could in fact be the reason why it was not debated by the claimant at all in the situation that no argument in this respect was submitted by respondent.

Considering the unsolicited legal interest argument as a barrier to grant declarations by arbitrators is not unique. It has been the case in ICC 3.2 and ICC 2.15 as well.

117. 'E.g. G. Born, *International...*, pp. 2480-2483' (as cited in the award, Case ICC 3.4).
118. 'J.F. Poudret and S. Besson, *Comparative...*, para. 572' (as cited in the award, Case ICC 3.4).

This problem is especially important if we consider that most legal experts, as has been presented above, argue against inclusion of stringent criteria construing legal interest.

[F] With or Without Prejudice

While dismissing the declaratory relief, it is quite rare that the tribunal adopts a position whether the dismissal is done with or without prejudice and, if so, what this might mean for the claimant in terms of *res judicata*. If the tribunal does comment on this, it is – in the vast majority of cases – decided to be without prejudice. This is clear enough if it is understood that the decision is given before merits of the case are examined. Dismissal with prejudice has a *res judicata* effect; thus, the case is essentially decided without looking into its merits.

In case ICC 2.4, the arbitral tribunal did not discern the minimum prerequisites for legal interest, namely that the declaratory relief requested serves a concrete practical purpose in an actual controversy between the parties, and rejected the claim without prejudice (*Nichteintreten*), not explaining however the meaning of this.[119] Similar solutions were adopted in cases ICC 2.5, ICC 2.3 and ICC 2.2. In case ICC 2.15, the tribunal explained that the relief is dismissed without prejudice to the claim proper, which claimant might still file before another arbitral tribunal or before a state court.

In case ICC 2.14, the tribunal explained its position more broadly. As the *lex arbitri* belonged to the Germanic system, the tribunal applied Austrian authorities to the problem of dismissal with or without prejudice. They found that Austrian legal commentaries were not unanimous with regard to the question whether lack of a material, legally or factually protected interest in the declaratory relief leads to a dismissal with prejudice, or whether the claim must be dismissed without examining the merits of the case (*Nichteintreten*), i.e., without prejudice. The Austrian courts hold that a claim for declaratory relief is to be dismissed with prejudice if the requesting party has no protected interest in the declaratory relief. Following, then, the lines of authority established in the Austrian courts, the tribunal found that, due to claimant's lack of interest in a declaration dealing with information rights beyond the prayers that the tribunal considers admissible and thus capable of being the subject of a request for performance, claimant's request for declaratory relief failed and was dismissed with prejudice. In this case, the claimant sought a declaration that, in his capacity as a member of a foundation council, he shall be entitled to full access to relevant information. It must be emphasized that, while the merits of the case were not examined, the result is analogical due to qualification of dismissal being with prejudice.

Instead of using the formula typical to common law, tribunals also use a formula in the dispositive section that tribunal dismisses a claim for declaratory relief, without delving into the merits (*see* case ICC 2.1). In ICC 2.15 the tribunal distinguished three

119. 'Bessenichibopp, o.c., note 156, Article 88 N 8' (as cited in the award, Case ICC 2.4).

categories of dismissal of requests for declaratory relief: dismissed for lack of legal interest, dismissed on the merits and dismissed as premature.

§4.05 CONCLUSIONS

Taking a closer look in the realm of arbitration gives the opportunity to find out how arbitrators approach in real practice the problems which raise a number of concerns. Summing up, it must be said at the outset that authority of the tribunal is, as a rule, not challenged and does not give rise to doubts.

In the majority of cases declarations are granted intuitively, without considering any legal prerequisites, including those cases where Germanic law is underlying. Such a finding is confirmed by M&A awards research. The issue of legitimate or legal interest is, for obvious reasons, a matter of concern where Germanic law is the proper law. The notion of the term, however, is marked by both common law and Germanic law features, to where it can be considered a converged one. There is a number of components typical to common law culture: the scope of the declaration includes facts, the dispositive part of the award may include both the declaration and a subsequent coercive measure, no subsidiarity principle is present, and a more liberal approach is to be adopted to declarations of future damages. The basic notion of legal interest includes settling the controversy as a practical purpose limited by protection of legitimate interest of the respondent. This goes in line with the noticeable Swiss evolution of declaratory relief towards pragmatism and liberalization, typical to the common law tradition as well.

Adistinct problem in arbitration, as compared with litigation, is the strict approach to wording of the declaration sought. Too broad, or too vague, formulation of the relief sought might reduce the chances of winning the award if challenged on ultra petita grounds.

CHAPTER 5

The Problem of Redefinition of Legal Interest Concept in Light of the Access to Justice Principles

§5.01 THE NEED FOR REDEFINITION

Introduction. The substance of the norms regulating declaratory relief in the relevant civil procedure codes has hardly changed since their inception, rooted in the theories of the German pandectists who, by definition, tended to keep their distance from the commercial issues of the day. That said, a reservation should certainly be made in the case of the Swiss regulations, in which legal interest was replaced by legitimate interest due to relaxation of the approach adopted in terms of the notion of this prerequisite. With this caveat, legal interest was left as a prerequisite in most of the Germanic systems. The meanings associated with the normative regulations of legal interest were, however, subject to certain changes in the respective jurisdictions, tending towards liberalization of the concept, which did not fully respond to needs of practice. These changes were very important, but they did not affect the very foundations of the matter, and in particular the subsidiarity principle. Moreover, there are legislatures, like those of Hungary or Romania, who have introduced the very concept of subsidiarity into the positive body of law.[1] In order to analyse this problem anew, however, placing it in a new perspective should be in order; dogmatic analysis confined to the strictures of civil procedure will not suffice. The majority debate as pursued at the moment is essentially centred on the character of the subsidiarity principle within the

1. Article 35 of the Romanian CCP, introduced in 2012; in Hungary: Section 172 (3) of the Act CXXX of 2016 on the Code of Civil Procedure (Hungarian CCP). In Germany, the statutory regulations of public procedural law adopted in the 1950s and 1960s also expressly stipulate the subsidiarity principle (*see* § 43 II Verwaltungsgerichtsordnung (VwGO – Code of Administrative Court Procedure) of 21 January 1960 VwGO, 41 II Finanzgerichtsordnung of 6 October 1965 FGO (FGO – Code of Finance Court Procedure).

dichotomy of procedural norms on the one hand and substantive norms on the other – a dispute, incidentally, which is difficult to resolve on the basis of academic debate. The more important issue, one which has not been taken up by the legal doctrine, is that of this legal norm's objective, revolving around the questions of whom, or what, it actually serves, and whom or what it ought to serve: the court, the plaintiff, the defendant, or an idealized conception? Does a claim for declaratory relief serve the plaintiff in utmost realization of her subjective rights, or does it further some other purpose?

On these pages, I propose to localize the issue of legal interest within an access to justice and procedural justice perspective. By adopting this new perspective for study as a complement to purely dogmatic analysis, we afford ourselves material for new conclusions.

The sample case. As a starting point for further analysis, the following case decided by the Polish Supreme Court on 30 October 1990 should be suitable.[2] This case provides a harsh, yet revealing spotlight focusing attention on the injustice which a claimant may face when claiming a declaration in the Germanic tradition. It is sometimes easier to grasp the notions of fairness and fair treatment by considering unfairness and unfair treatment. 'If we focus our attention only on positive virtue, we see it as something flat, without depth or dynamic vigour. We have already seen that justice is a cold virtue. But injustice is something we soon get steamed up about'.[3]The court adopted the common position that admissibility of a claim for establishment by the court whether or not a legal relationship exists is predicated upon existence, or otherwise, of a legal interest in such a declaration. The idea of legal interest, as here until construed in Polish jurisprudence based on Article 189 of the Polish CCP, as typical to all Germanic systems, was that legal interest exists only when the plaintiff, in order to safeguard her legal sphere, may obtain satisfaction by the very fact of establishing that a legal relationship or a right exists (or, alternatively, does not exist) under the given circumstances. The corollary, likewise well-worn in Polish legal usage, is the subsidiarity principle, whereunder no legal interest exists if a claim seeking performance is possible. Yet, as I hope to demonstrate in my analysis of the ruling in this case, application of this interpretation of Article 189 flies in the face of an intuitive understanding of procedural justice. The facts of this case, put in brief, were as follows: in 1979, the parties executed a contract for representation of the principal/investor commissioning construction of a commercial pavilion designed to house various retail and service establishments. The construction was to be completed in 1982. In 1984 the works were still not completed, and the claimant decided to withhold further payments. The plaintiff argued that he had remitted funds as a down payment towards construction of the pavilion contracted, but that the defendant applied such funds towards other construction projects, which resulted in lack of performance of the contract. As a result of this, he ignored a number of successive calls for payment

2. Judgement of 30 October 1990, I CR 649/90, Lex 158145 (Polish Supreme Court); the problem of raising legal interest at the advanced stages of the proceedings may be noticed also elsewhere (cf. as an example, Annex II.III[H] by Alicja Zielińska-Eisen & Tobias Strecker *infra*).
3. John R. Lucas, *On Justice* 4 et seq. (1978).

threatening rescission of the contract if the arrears are not duly cleared. Finally, in a written notice dated 15 July 1988, the defendant notified the plaintiff that he is terminating the contract.

The defendant declined the plaintiff's demand to release the pavilion in its then current state and to account for the costs incurred to bring it to that stage. The plaintiff, in these circumstances, considered rescission by the defendant to be void and, accordingly, adopted the position that the contract continues to bind the parties and sought a declaration that legal relationship instituted by way of the original contract continues to stand.

As a side note, the plaintiff took the alleged culpable delay on the defendant's part as grounds for invoking Article 491 of the Polish CC and stated that, seeing as this statutory provision entitles him – and not the defendant – to either rescind the contract or to demand specific performance, the plaintiff would opt for the latter.

On 30 November 1989, the Voivodship Court in Warsaw dismissed the statement of claim, finding that, by virtue of discontinuing payments for the pavilion's construction in 1984, the plaintiff delayed in performing his obligations pursuant to the contract, leaving the defendant entitled to rescind the contract on the basis of Article 491 of the Polish Civil Code. The plaintiff appealed. In considering the appeal, the Supreme Court did not take any position as to the validity of rescission, finding that the plaintiff lacks legal interest in seeking declaratory relief in that he can readily bring a claim for performance: damages or specific performance, as the case may be. Significantly enough, neither of the parties argued lack of legal interest, so the Supreme Court proceeded to make the relevant finding *ex officio*, surprising both parties.

Considering the case adumbrated above, there is an intuitive feeling that the case was resolved in an unjust manner. There are a few issues which require attention.

First, it should be noted that the court essentially refused to rule on the merits of the case. This case evidently proves that it is difficult to defend the stance, that due to the substantive character of legal interest, the court ruled on merits.[4]As a result, the plaintiff, having nominally proceeded through two instances, remained stuck at his point of departure as regards his substantive claim; he still does not know whether or not the defendant's declared rescission of the contract was effective and, as a result, is largely clueless as regards any future claims on this account. There thus arises the question of what, exactly, prevented the court from ruling on the substance of the entire matter and from settling this not unreasonable dilemma of the plaintiff? While the court did peruse the entire documentation of the case, it still considered itself unable to hand down a definitive ruling in light of the established understanding of the legal interest concept. The court remarked that the plaintiff would have a legal interest only if, faced with a need to safeguard his legal sphere, he could obtain satisfaction by the very fact of establishing that a legal relationship or a right exists, referring to the implied rule that no legal interest exists where there is an alternative claim seeking performance: enforceable damages or a specific performance. In the case at hand, the circumstances adduced by the plaintiff at first instance as well as at appeal indicated

4. *See* §2.12 *in fine*.

that he had several avenues of legal recourse open to him. The Polish Supreme Court wrapped up by stating that the plaintiff had not demonstrated that a declaration confirming existence of a contractual relationship may afford him protection from some other violation of his legal sphere and found the application for declaratory relief inadmissible.

Second, the court engaged in an advisory sort of exercise: it worked out and valuated all possible reliefs which the claimant could seek in the circumstances of the case. In dismissing the relief, the court considered such an outcome to be the most favourable to the plaintiff from among all the others. One could guess, that it was difficult for the claimant at the moment to decide, without further talks to respondent, what would be more practical or possible to exercise – damages or specific performance.[5] The question immediately arises, did the court make this finding based on certain objective or subjective criteria, considering the best interest of the plaintiff or an ideal and abstract one? The Supreme Court justified sending the plaintiff off to pursue another round of litigation by declaring that:

> the need of protecting the plaintiff's legal sphere is more far-reaching than anything which he might hope for from a ruling by this court. Furthermore, pursuing this protection by way of an injunctive relief suit is more straightforward, in that it consummates the demand for establishing existence of a legal relationship, which – in an injunctive relief suit – is addressed by the court as a premise. [translation by author]

In order to arrive at such a conclusion, the court should have compared at least three possible courses of action: undecided, decided to the benefit of the plaintiff, or decided to the benefit of the defendant. The first of these assumes dragging the plaintiff through two instances without winning any closure on the merits, leaving the plaintiff with precious little idea as to the final outcome, only to start afresh, bringing a claim for injunctive relief before another court hearing this claim from the very beginning. The second scenario which should have been considered by the court at least in theory: the court at second instance rules on principle, finding the contract's rescission by the defendant to have been effective, thus closing the matter. The third scenario, finally, would entail the court ruling for the plaintiff, finding defendant's rescission to have been ineffective, whereupon the plaintiff could bring another suit, seeking one or the other injunctive relief. The difference (from scenario one) would be that a court hearing this new claim would be bound by the Supreme Court's finding on principle and, thus, would have its work scaled down for it in that it would only be called upon to elaborate on the details of the specific performance or the quantum of damages, as the case could be. As a side note, the parties could, conceivably, have taken such an outcome as encouragement to settle without further recourse to the courts, negotiating the scope of the performance on their own or through the good offices of a mediator. The court chose the first option, which in no circumstances is the best one from the perspective of subjective interests of the claimant, who was keenly interested in a 'yes'

5. Without being assured, that termination was invalid, the respondent could have had probably denied any discussions or negotiations in this respect.

or 'no' answer. The court did not analyse the subjective interest of the claimant. The decision taken by the court is also not in the best interest of the respondent. There lingers a strong feeling that, if the claimant initiates the proceedings once again to have his case finally settled, as in fact advised by the court, the defendant will be faced again with two proceedings instead of what would most probably have been just one once had the court given its answer to the question posed. If the claimant foregoes lodging his case anew, he will, for all intents and purposes, be denied justice.

Third, this example shows that erecting strong barriers for admissibility of declarations does little to keep the courts from being flooded with cases. Comparing the above three scenarios, the first scenario, as adopted by the court, is only helpful in this regard if the plaintiff reconciles himself to the fact that he was denied having his case decided and does not file the case anew. If, on the other hand, plaintiff again seeks recourse before the courts, this will entail a higher workload for the justice system, as explained above.

Fourth, existence of a legal interest is deemed to be a substantive prerequisite for ruling on a claim based on Article 189 of the Polish Civil Process Code (as in Austria) and, as such, falls to be considered on an *ex officio* basis, whatever the stage of the proceedings. In the above case, no party raised the issue of lacking legal interest. The court, basing its decision on this argument, surprised the parties and accorded an unnecessary advantage to the respondent without asking the parties to make their arguments in this respect.

Finally, while the Supreme Court dismissed the appeal in its entirety, it shied away from ruling on the procedural costs to the benefit of the counterparty, as would normally happen under the common principle 'costs follow the event', justifying this in terms of some general fairness. Such an outcome as to costs is not seen very often, and it is very important, confirming that simple application of the subsidiarity principle was contrary to intuitive interpretation of the right to seek declaration. The reasoning for the Supreme Court decision states that:

> [we have] taken into account the reasons for which the appeal has been dismissed, in particular the fact that the plaintiff has been sent back upon the path of litigation in the quest for injunctive relief, concluding that, seeing as the plaintiff has already shouldered some of the costs entailed in his appeal before this court, considerations of fairness militate against burdening him with further expenditure in general and against enjoining him to reimburse the defendant's legal fees in this appeal in particular. [translation by author]

This amounts to a jarring inconsistency. On the one hand, the defendant has been compelled to retain counsel and, generally, to commit resources to legal proceedings which, given the outcome, were unfounded but, on the other, the court refuses to award to the defendant reimbursement of these costs, and invokes fairness as it does so. This lack of cohesion suggests that even the court itself intuitively harboured some doubts as to this ruling in its ethical aspect, escaping into creative judgement or even subversion, as the case maybe.[6]

---

6. Paul Butler, *When Judges Lie (and When They Should)*, 91 Minn. L. Rev. 1785, 1791 et seq.

The model legal interest. Summing up, the above case shows that the concept of legal interest, and in particular the subsidiarity principle, however strongly rooted in the relevant doctrine and jurisprudence, raise doubts as to their conformity with the modern understanding of procedural justice. Guarantees of 'procedural justice' or of 'due process of law' are meant to maximize the probability of a just result. They deserve to be called 'just' only insofar as we believe that, better than any other procedures, they lead to a just result; they are not just per se.[7] If we find that legal interest as an element of the procedure produces unjust results, then such a procedure is unjust. The above example shows that the procedure undertaken in the specific case did not yield a just result, at least basing on our intuitions as to what is just and what is not. Finding that this one single case was solved in an unjust way does not mean that the entire procedure is unjust. This issue must be tested on more general assumptions and arguments. The below analysis will support the thesis that the concept of legal interest as an element of procedure is dissonant with procedural justice principles and limits access to justice for no good reason, and that redefinition of the concept of legal interest is necessary.

For purposes of this analysis, the following model of legal interest (hereinafter referred as Model Legal Interest) will be tested:

(1) The need of the claimant is of a legal nature and not economic, factual or otherwise.
(2) There is a dispute or controversy between the parties.
(3) The uncertainty relates to the particular right or legal relationship.
(4) The uncertainty is no longer acceptable to the parties.
(5) The claimant's interest in receiving a declaration is of an objective character.
(6) A declaration will finally settle the dispute.
(7) There are no other means to resolve said uncertainty, in particular by means of claim for performance.
(8) In the case of a negative declaratory action, the claimant's interest must further be balanced against the defendant's interest in not having to conduct the proceedings at that point in time.

The judgement cited above will serve for the sake of argument in subsequent chapters, therefore it will be hereinafter referred to as the Sample Judgement.

§5.02 SUBSTANTIVE OR PROCEDURAL JUSTICE

In the course of the dispute as to the nature of the concept of legal interest, it is not finally decided whether it belongs to the substantial or procedural area of law. The problem of qualification of legal interest was explained earlier in Chapter 2.12 *infra*.[8] In

(2007); Jerzy Zajadło, *Sumienie Sędziego*, 79(4) Ruch Prawniczy, Ekonomiczny i Socjologiczny 31, 36 (2017).

7. Wojciech Sadurski, *Social Justice and Legal Justice*, 3 L. & Phil. (1984) 329, 349.

8. *See* also Chapter 4.04 [C].

brief, in Austria, according to prevailing doctrine, legal interest in declaratory relief is deemed to be a procedural requirement.[9] However, according to settled jurisprudence, the courts treat the prerequisites as substantive requirements.[10] Polish doctrine and court practice almost unanimously treat legal interest as a substantive law issue.[11] Swiss law, for certain pragmatic purposes, persisted in qualifying the legal (or, more properly, legitimate) interest as a substantive law feature until 2018, when the Swiss Federal Tribunal finally confirmed the doctrine's position and qualified the interest in declaratory relief as being of a procedural nature.[12] The legal interest in Germany is considered a procedural requirement.[13]

Accordingly, there arises the question whether it is correct to analyse, as proposed here, the question of admissibility based on legal interest from the perspective of procedural justice, or is it better considered in terms of substantive justice principles. It appears that procedural justice criteria should be relevant in this case and that the qualification of the legal interest into one category or another is not so important. The procedure, and in particular civil procedure, can be viewed as a system of norms serving implementation of certain substantive civil rights. In such a context, legal interest plays the role of a prerequisite to granting the declaration, and its lack precludes confirmation of existence or non-existence of a substantive right or legal relationship. In other words, legal interest is a decisive factor for the court's decision whether it can accept the case for adjudication, and not how the court should decide the case. In this meaning, the concept of legal interest is a creature of procedure, acting as a gatekeeper allowing the claimant to receive an answer to the question raised or rejecting such right, and it can be tested against procedural justice criteria.[14] Procedure can be understood also in a broader sense, where actualization of specific subjective rights happens as result of a discourse conducted in accordance with certain procedure. In this way, procedure includes all stages of creation of law, its interpretation and application.[15] For procedure understood in this sense, formal distinctions between

9. Ulrike Frauenberger-Pfeiler, *§ 228* in Hans W. Fasching & Andreas Konecny, *Zivilprozessgesetze Kommentar III/1*, n. 73 (2017).
10. *See* RIS-Justiz RS0039177 and RIS-Justiz RS0039301.
11. Examples: Judgement of 19 March 2015, IV CSK 362/14 (Polish Supreme Court); Judgement of 24 April 2014, III CSK 182/13 (Polish Supreme Court); Judgement of 3 April 2000, I CKN 582/98, (Polish Supreme Court); Judgement of 6 August 2014, I CSK 559/13 (Polish Supreme Court); Andrzej Zieliński, in: Andrzej Zieliński & Kinga Flaga-Gieruszyńska, *Kodeks postępowania cywilnego. Komentarz* 384, *Commentary on § 189 KPC*, 384 n. 1 (Andrzej Zieliński ed., 2017).
12. Decision of 14 March 2018, Case no. 4A_417/2017, BGE 144 III 175, consideration no. 4 (Swiss Federal Tribunal).
13. Ulrich Foerste, in: Hans-Joachim Musielak & Wolfgang Voit, *Zivilprozessordnung: ZPO mit Gerichtsverfas- sungsgesetz, Kommentar, Commentary on § 256 ZPO*, n. 7 (15th ed., 2018).
14. Similarly, Stefan Leimgruber, *Declaratory Relief in International Commercial Arbitration*, 32(3) ASA Bulletin 467, 479 (2014); Karol Weitz, who said that the issue is whether we can hear the case (admissibility) and how we can decide the case (decision on merits). *See* Karol Weitz, *Charakter interesu prawnego jako przesłanka powództwa o ustalenie (art.189 kpc)* in *Sine ira et studio, Księga Jubileuszowa dedykowana Sędziemu Jackowi Gudowskiemu* 656, 666 et seq. (Tadeusz Ereciński, Paweł Grzegorczyk & Karol Weitz eds., 2016).
15. Jerzy Stelmach, Bartosz Brożek & Wojciech Załuski, *Dziesięć wykładów o ekonomii prawa* 87 (2007).

substantive and procedural qualification are likewise irrelevant. This sense of procedure gives further comfort for analysis, because the concept of legal interest must be challenged in more than one dimension: not only in the sphere of its application, but also in the sphere of its creation, giving rise not only to *de lege lata* comments, but also *de lege ferenda* postulates. Due to the very general wording of the provisions of positive law, the concept of legal interest has been shaped by the jurisprudence and academia, so the sphere of creation and application are strongly interconnected.[16] In this sense, the qualification of being substantive or procedural is not important for grasping the real meaning and functioning of the declaratory relief prerequisites.

Such an approach affords freedom from the incessant discussion on the juridical qualification of legal interest as a prerequisite to granting declaration – substantive, or procedural. And the clear-cut, dichotomist division is to some extent artificial, anyway. The substantive versus procedural distinction does not always refer to the essential nature of the institution, swinging from one to the other based on *ad hoc* or interim needs, like in Switzerland. In this country, declaratory relief was classified in a court decision of 1951 as substantive in order to secure access to relief on the same basis in the entire jurisdiction, but this distinction lost its importance in 2010 due to the fact that procedural law ceased to be the individual competence of each canton.[17]

It must be said that the European tendency is in favour of the procedural classification. In Germany, the procedural classification is prevailing, while Austria follows a dual approach: procedural in doctrine and substantive in court practice. In Switzerland, the procedural character was confirmed by the courts in 2018. In Poland, where court practice and jurisprudence almost uniformly favoured substantiveness of declarations, an opposite thesis was recently posited by a prominent Polish processualist, K. Weitz, which may start a new line of jurisprudence.[18]

Qualification of legal interest as a substantive factor may allow avoidance of the question whether functioning of this prerequisite is in fact a serious limitation of access to justice. In Polish jurisprudence, this problem seems to flit by on the margins of a few judgements. If the legal interest constitutes a substantive, and not procedural, premise, the decision of the court is not deemed to be evaluation of formal prerequisites, so therefore it cannot be claimed that the case was not examined on its merits.[19]

Considering the argument presented by W. Sadurski[20] in this respect it is helpful to leave the above dichotomic classification aside. There is not much difference between procedural and substantive justice W. Sadurski, for his part, made the following distinction: substantive justice is the justice of outcome while procedural justice is the justice of process which leads to the outcome. In this light, it becomes convincing enough that the procedure is just as long as it produces a just outcome.

16. It is quite rare that legal interest is defined at the level of statutory law; certain components like the subsidiarity principle appear e.g., in Romania or Hungary. *See supra* n. 1.
17. Stefan Leimgruber, *supra* n. 14, at 469. *See also* Annex IV.III[A] by Nino Sievi *infra*.
18. Karol Weitz, *supra* n. 14, at 673 et seq.
19. Judgement of 19 March 2015, IV CSK 362/14 (Polish Supreme Court); Judgement of 24 April 2014, III CSK 182/13 (Polish Supreme Court).
20. Sadurski, *supra* n. 7, at 329, 346.

Procedural justice is either derived from, and reducible to, substantive justice, or it is not a category of justice (in the strict sense of the word) at all.[21]

This makes the question of classification of legal interest as substantive or procedural less important in the context of testing this concept against principles of fair trial in general.

§5.03 ACCESS TO JUSTICE AND PROCEDURAL JUSTICE PRINCIPLES AS A COGNITIVE PERSPECTIVE

Introduction. Procedural justice does not have one precise, quantitative meaning.[22] First, there are certain intuitive understandings. Such intuitive evaluation was proposed as concerning the Sample Case described at the beginning of this chapter. Such intuitions could be observed in the arbitration awards (as presented in the preceding chapter) which departed from the domestic legal orders, construing understanding of the legal interest based on independent evaluations of what is, in the arbitrators' opinion, the right thing to do. Sadurski stated that just procedure will be such that maximizes the probability of arriving at a just outcome.[23] This rule has found its confirmation in the way of thinking of arbitrators who produced and applied certain procedures which, in their view, tended to produce materially just outcomes. Towards this end, they shunned the legal interest prerequisite altogether or made the requirements much softer.

In the context of civil proceedings, the notion of procedural justice is interrelated with the due process principles. In democratic law and order, civil proceedings should be shaped in accordance with the principles of procedural justice. All these terms, by their very nature, are not strictly defined. Procedural justice may simply mean that certain procedures are shaped in order to achieve the highest probability of issuing the court order in accordance with law and based on genuine evidence.[24] This simple ascertainment, while pleasant to the eye, is very general and does not consider all subtle shades of the realm whose borders are shaped by the material truth (justice) on one hand and formal truth (justice) on the other. It might mean that if we follow the procedural requirements as envisaged in the Model Legal Interest, as established by the court jurisprudence, the result of the Sample Judgement will always be procedurally just as it follows all requirements of Model Legal Interest. The basic question is, however, whether the outcome resulting from such a procedure will, in principle, be

21. He was against pure procedural justice, as presented by John Rawls, *A Theory of Justice* 74–75 (1991), in the sense that pure procedural justice is no justice at all. It is not the case that fair procedure translates into a fair result, but the other way around. *Ibid.*, 348.
22. Considering the subject of this analysis, which is strictly related to the notion of legal interest as a prerequisite to declaratory relief, I do not consider justice in all dimensions relating to what is known after Aristotle, *The Nicomachean Ethics of Aristotle* Bk V 2. 140–144 (Frank. H. Peters transl., 1906) as distributive justice, putting the questions of social justice.
23. Rawls, *supra* n. 21, at 348.
24. Judgement of 21 July 2009, K7/09, OTK ZU 2009/7A/113, 15 (2009) (Polish Constitutional Tribunal).

just. These extremes were reflected in Rawls'[25] ideal concepts of perfect procedural justice, which assumed that a certain procedure can be formed to always achieve a fair outcome if the criterion for what is fair is known as well as pure procedural justice, where it is assumed that fair procedure always leads to a fair result – it is the procedure which dictates the fair result. In reality, we deal with what is called imperfect procedural justice, where a certain procedure aims to produce a fair result, but such result is not guaranteed. Even though the law is dutifully followed, and the proceedings fairly and properly conducted, a wrong outcome may result. It is claimed that the European Union procedures implement the postulate of imperfect procedural justice, not guaranteeing a fair result but increasing the chances of getting as close as possible to the assumed just result.[26] For purposes of further analysis, I will assume that procedural justice means maximizing the probability of producing a just outcome.[27] Putting this question in such general form, it is important to state whether the procedure which limits the right to receive a final judgement by the party maximizes the probability of producing a just outcome? *Prima facie*, the answer is no. Declaratory order, in the logical sense, must simply answer the claimant's question in the affirmative by granting the required declaration or in the negative by dismissing it. It is also possible answer 'don't know' due to lack of sufficient substantiation for a 'yes' or 'no' answer. Then the claim must be dismissed as well. If we understand that just outcome is an answer to the raised question, any ban preventing such an answer will not be just, because the claimant is deprived of an answer.

The question may go deeper, however. Is every question worth answering? And is the answer to such a question a just outcome by itself, and in what circumstances is such a ban justified and acceptable from the perspective of societal norms or the public interest? It thus becomes necessary to test the notion of legal interest against particular components of the procedural justice principle.

Possible components. Procedural justice is the very core of the right to access to justice. The access to justice principle is constructed of four basic entitlements: (i) right of access to the courts *sensu stricte*, meaning a right to commence proceedings; (ii) right to appropriate procedure, shaped in accordance with the procedural justice and transparency principles; (iii) right to obtain a binding court decision in the given case; and (iv) right to have the system of justice properly shaped, including the proper position of the bodies (courts) within the system. The negative element assumes that the legislature will not enact rules which excessively limit access to justice.[28]

Access to justice would be an empty concept in the absence of procedural justice principles.[29] Procedural justice has a number of components. Intuitively any of them,

25. Rawls, *supra* n. 21, at 348.
26. Tomasz Koncewicz, *Sądowa sprawiedliwość proceduralna w prawie europejskim*, XXXV Gdańskie Studia Prawnicze 173, 179 (2016).
27. Sadurski, *supra* n. 7, at 329, 348.
28. Judgement of 21 July 2009, K7/09, OTK ZU 2009/7A/113, 11 (2009) (Polish Constitutional Tribunal); Judgement of 7 September 2014, P 4/04, Dz.U. 2004/204 item 2091,11 (2004) (Polish Constitutional Tribunal); Judgement of 26 February 2008, SK 89/06, Dz.U. 2008/39, item 234, 20 (2008) (Polish Constitutional Tribunal).
29. Judgement of 26 February 2008, SK 89/06, Dz.U. 2008/39, item 234, 20 (2008) (Polish Constitutional Tribunal).

as proposed by any legal writings or judicature, appear obvious enough. It is required that the legislature shapes the procedure in accordance with three basic due process principles.[30] First, the right to be heard assumes opportunity to present one's case and to defend one's position as against the other party, on an equal basis. In this respect, striking a correct balance between adversarial proceedings, evidence preclusion and material truth disclosure as a principle of civil proceedings is important. All subjects of law are treated equally in comparable circumstances. Any inequality must be justified; differentiation is allowed if it serves legitimate purposes, is constitutionally protected and is proportional to the purpose to be achieved.[31]

Second, the right to receive clear justification of the court decision is aimed at avoiding randomness or arbitrariness of the judges. Each court decision should be easy to comprehend by the addressee of such decision.

Finally, the proceedings in which a given party participates must be a part of a predictable and logically coherent system. Solutions undertaken to solve legal problems should be commensurated to the purported goals of a public character (the principle of adequacy) and, on the other hand, should not impose an excessive burden on the party (the principle of proportionality).[32] The law, both legal texts and their established judicial interpretation, should be transparent and easy to comprehend, all along securing all these systemic principles and respecting human rights (the principle of trust).[33]

The above list of components has been established on the basis of judgements of the Polish Constitutional Tribunal, a part of the European democratic system of law. It does not differ from the general approach to the scope of the human rights. Access to justice, or fair trial,[34] belongs to the catalogue of basic human rights as set forth by Articles 6.1[35] and 13 of the European Convention on Human Rights. Core elements of these rights include effective access to a dispute resolution body, the right to fair proceedings and timely resolution of disputes, the right to adequate redress, as well as

---

30. Judgement of 21 July 2009, K7/09, OTK ZU 2009/7A/113, 15 (2009) (Polish Constitutional Tribunal; Judgement of 7 September 2014, P 4/04, Dz.U. 2004/204 item 2091, 11 (2004) (Polish Constitutional Tribunal); Judgement of 26 February 2008, SK 89/06, Dz.U. 2008/39, item 234, 20 (2008) (Polish Constitutional Tribunal).
31. Judgement of 12 January 2010, SK 2/09, OTK ZU 2010/1A/1, 23–24 (2010) (Polish Constitutional Tribunal).
32. Order of 2 December 2010, SK 11/10, 3 (2010) (Polish Constitutional Tribunal).
33. Judgement of 12 January 2010, SK 2/09, OTK ZU 2010/1A/1, 22 (2010) (Polish Constitutional Tribunal).
34. As it appears, access to justice, procedural justice and fair process/due process are strictly interrelated and, for purposes of this study, they can be used to some extent interchangeably. *See also* comments of Galligan on due process and procedural fairness: Denis J. Galligan, *Due Process and Fair Procedures. A Study of Administrative Procedures* 73 (1996).
35. Article 6.1 of the ECHR, first sentence:

    'In the determination of his civil rights and obligations or of any criminal charge against him, everyone is entitled to a fair and public hearing within a reasonable time by an independent and impartial tribunal established by law.'

    Art. 13: 'Everyone whose rights and freedoms as set forth in this Convention are violated shall have an effective remedy before a national authority notwithstanding that the violation has been committed by persons acting in an official capacity'.

the general application of the principles of efficiency and effectiveness to the delivery of justice.[36]

As stated in the European Court of Human Rights (ECHR) decision, the superior axiological assumption of the civil process is fair trial by itself, which includes the right of access to a court and other guarantees laid down by Article 6.1 as regards both the organization and composition of the court and the conduct of the proceedings.[37] Such guarantees include independence and impartiality of the judiciary and fair and public proceedings and procedural equality of parties, including the right to be heard and equality of arms, comprehensive examination and evaluation of the case and securing final determination of the case, binding (upon the parties) implementation of which is secured by the system of justice.[38] Excessive formalism refers to particularly strict interpretations of procedural rules that may deprive applicants of their right of access to a court. This can include strict interpretations of time limits, rules of procedure and evidence. A particularly strict construction of procedural rules by constitutional courts may deprive applicants of their right of access to a court.[39]

Procedural justice imposes on the judge not only the obvious duty of independence and impartiality. The ethos of a judge includes receptiveness, openness and eagerness to construct the proceedings as a coherent unit. The judge must be engaged in the adjudication process.[40]

Access to justice is not meant to protect one party, but to protect both claimant and defendant. Equality of arms is a procedural requirement of fair process.[41]

Optimizing access to justice with other systemic principles. Basic principles of law, procedural justice included, by their very nature are not clearly defined – and, indeed, should not be clearly defined, leaving leeway for their flexible application. R. Dworkin calls 'a principle' a standard, that is to be observed because it is a requirement

36. European Court of Human Rights, *Handbook on European Law Relating to Access to Justice* 17, https://www.echr.coe.int/Documents/Handbook_access_justice_ENG.pdf (accessed 13 January 2019). In European human rights law, the notion of access to justice is enshrined in Arts 6 and 13 of the European Convention on Human Rights (ECHR) and Art. 47 of the EU Charter of Fundamental Rights, which guarantee the right to a fair trial and to an effective remedy, as interpreted by the ECHR and the Court of Justice of the European Union (CJEU), respectively. These rights are also provided for in international instruments, such as Arts 2(3) and 14 of the United Nations (UN) International Covenant on Civil and Political Rights and Arts 8 and 10 of the UN Universal Declaration of Human Rights.
37. Judgement of 21 February 1975 in *Case of Golder v the United Kingdom*, no. 4451/70, Series A no. 18, § 36 (1975) (ECHR).
38. Marcin Walasik, *Analogia w prawie procesowym cywilnym* 7.2.2 (LexisNexis 2013). Judgement of 12 January 2006, *Kehaya and Others v Bulgaria*, nos 47797/99 and 68698/01, (2006) (ECHR).
39. European Court of Human Rights, *Handbook on European Law Relating to Access to Justice* 17, https://www.echr.coe.int/Documents/Handbook_access_justice_ENG.pdf (accessed 13 January 2019).
40. Koncewicz, *supra* n. 26, at 175; Joxerramon R. Bengoetxea, *The Legal Reasoning of the European Court of Justice: Towards a European Jurisprudence* (1993).
41. European Court of Human Rights, *Guide on Article 6 of the European Convention on Human Rights* 58, https://www.echr.coe.int/Documents/Guide_Art_6_ENG.pdf (accessed 13 January 2018). It is interesting to note that, in case of legal interest, the discourse recently developed in the direction of alleged overprotection of the respondent, *see* the Swiss example, Annex IV [III[[D] [2]. by Nino Sievi *infra*.

of justice or fariness or some other dimension of morality.[42] Access to justice as a basic principle of law, however, is not absolute,[43] although any limitations must not restrict or reduce a person's access to justice in such a way, or to such an extent, that the very essence of the right is impaired.[44] Balancing certain principles – always against the background of basis systemic values – is therefore always a necessary exercise while deciding a particular case. Principles, contrary to the norms, are of an ontological character, demanding that something be realized to the highest actually and legally possible degree. Contrariwise, regular norms can be either complied with or not. A conflict of rules can only be resolved by either introducing an exception clause into one rule or by declaring one of the conflicting rules invalid. In a case of conflict of principles, the priority rule might be applied. The principles of a system are not absolute, but only conditional or relative. The task of optimizing is to determine correct conditional priority relations.[45]

Following this vein, access to justice is one of those principles which must be regarded as superior and overarching principle in civil procedure – which, in addition to its own features, is also a forum for alignment of other principles and their optimization.[46] The principles of the democratic state and the principle of legalism provide a basis for the prohibition on interpretations which might narrow its meaning.[47] This means that other principles, such as state security or environmental protection, may not be taken as a reason to deny access to justice, although they may justify certain limitations within the generally accepted margin of discretion of the state

42. Ronald Dworkin, *Taking Rights Seriously*, 22 (1987).
43. Judgement of 21 February 1975 in *Case of Golder v the United Kingdom*, no. 4451/70, Series A no. 18, § 38 (1975) (ECHR).
44. European Court of Human Rights, *Handbook on European Law Relating to Access to Justice* 115, https://www.echr.coe.int/Documents/Handbook_access_justice_ENG.pdf (accessed 13 January 2019); as an example, in *Rosalba Alassini v Telecom Italia SpA*, the case concerned clauses under which an attempt to settle out-of-court was a mandatory condition for certain disputes to be admissible before national courts. The clauses were enacted in the context of transposing Directive 2002/22/EC of the European Parliament and of the Council of 7 March 2002 on universal service and users' rights relating to electronic communications networks and services. The CJEU confirmed that most fundamental rights do not constitute 'unfettered prerogatives' and can be restricted. It referred to ECtHR case law and emphasized that restrictions had to correspond to objectives of general interest. They must not be disproportionate or infringe upon the very substance of the rights guaranteed. The aims of the national provisions at issue – quicker and less expensive dispute settlement, and lightening the burden on the court system – were legitimate, and imposing an out-of-court settlement procedure did not, on the facts, appear disproportionate in relation to the objectives pursued. *See* Judgement of 18 March 2010, *Rosalba Alassini and Others v Telecom Italia SpA and Others,* Joined cases C-317/08 to C-320/08, European Court Reports 2010 I-02213, nn. 63–65 (European Court of Justice).
45. Robert Alexy, *On the Structure of Legal Principles*, 13(3) Ratio Iuris 294, 296–297 (2000).
46. Judgement of 11 March 2003, SK 8/02, Dz. U. 2003/52 item 468, 11 (2003) (Polish Constitutional Tribunal).
47. In Polish Constitution access to justice is expressed in Art. 45 of the Constitution of the Republic of Poland of 2 April 1977 (amended 2009), under which everyone has a right to just and transparent proceedings before independent and impartial courts without undue delay; Art. 77.2 clearly prohibits closing access to justice.

regulator.[48] Within the sphere of legal interest, such features like optimization, effectiveness of the proceedings will require alignment.

Effectiveness of the proceedings is a feature marked by intrinsic internal contradiction in that, on one hand, it enhances access to justice while, on the other hand, it must lead to its limitation. The proceedings should be finished within a reasonable time limit,[49] which requires imposition of certain deadlines on the doings of all the participants, judges and parties alike. Also, bearing in mind limited resources of the justice system, the proceedings should be organized in a manner which takes into account economics, in the sense of reasonably low expenditures. This is a reflection of the general trend to balance the general good and justice at the individual level.[50] This rationale, as pointed out several times earlier, informs introduction of the legal interest prerequisite in the Germanic civil procedure.[51] It was assumed that if no limitation in the form of the legal interest prerequisite was provided, the courts would be flooded with incoming claims. The principle of efficiency, which guarantees speedy and well-organized proceedings, should be valued because justice delayed is justice denied. Bearing in mind that access to justice is the overall guiding principle, only such limitations undertaken in the name of procedural economy should be allowed as are aimed at enhancement of the access to justice itself.

Summary. Summing up the components which are important from the perspective of the evaluation of the legal interest concept, the following should be highlighted. The legal interest as a prerequisite should be clearly founded, easy to comprehend and compliant with the logic of the system in order to be predictable. The notion of the legal concept cannot be restrictive to such a degree as to lead to excessive limitation of access of justice. Any limitations should be adequate to the purported goals of both the entire system of justice and system of civil procedure, including their effectiveness.

§5.04 THE IDEA OF FAIR TREATMENT; NORMATIVE EXPECTATIONS AND INTUITIVE EXPECTATIONS IN LIGHT OF PREDICTABILITY PRINCIPLE

For purposes of this book, the idea of fair treatment of D.J. Galligan[52] is useful to highlight the problem of predictability of the legal interest application in the context of certain intuitions. The central point of procedural fairness is whether a person is given

48. Judgement of 7 September 2014, P 4/04, Dz.U. 2004/204 item 2091, 11–12 (2004) (Polish Constitutional Tribunal).
49. European Convention on Human Rights, Art. 6.1., as amended by Protocols 11 and 14 (4 November 1950), Walasik, *supra* n. 38, at n. 7.2.1 (LexisNexis 2013).
50. Herbert L.A. Hart, *The Concept of Law* 166 (2d ed., 1994).
51. Karl H. Schwab & Gerhard Walter, *Schiedsgerichtsbarkeit* 135 n. 1 (7th ed., 2005); Michael E. Schneider, *Non-Monetary Relief in International Arbitration: Principles and Arbitration Practice* in *Performance as a Remedy: Non-Monetary Relief in International Arbitration* 3, 30 n. 1 (Michael E. Schneider & Joachim Knoll eds., ASA Special Series no. 30, 2011); Richard H. Kreindler, Jan K. Schäfer & Reinmar Wolf, *Schiedsgerichtsbarkeit Kompendium für die Praxis* 222 nn. 759 et seq. (2006); Hans-Joachim Musielak & Wolfgang Voit, *Zivilprozessordnung: ZPO mit Gerichtsverfas-sungsgesetz, Kommentar*, ZPO § 1046 n. 2 (15th ed., 2018).
52. Galligan, *supra* n. 34, at 56–62.

what is due to him or what he is entitled to. As a corollary, to treat someone unfairly is to deny him something that is due to him or that he is entitled to. There follow other issues such as equal treatment or rules governing discretion that are fundamental standards of right treatment in granting or denying dues or entitlements. What is important in the context of this book is the question where such dues and entitlements may come from, and what kind of expectations of participants in the proceedings might be relevant.

Normative expectations. There is a category of normative expectations which are rooted in certain binding and obligatory rules. There might also be other sources of normative expectations, like promises, commitments or even intentions.[53] The idea of community depends on a high level of broadly accepted standards about how people will be dealt with and what entitlements they may expect. The source of normative expectations is basically law, which is deemed to be fair in the sense of normative expectations but could be perceived as unfair in some deeper sense. Then there are cases where treatment according to law cannot be limited only to upholding normative expectations, because the concept of fair and just treatment may be indefensible if it violates some deeper standard of justice. The law is unjust if it is inconsistent with some standards or principles which are more fundamental. Optimization of the conflicting principles of law was dealt with in the previous part. Here, I will focus on certain intuitive expectations and their role in the analysis of the concept of legal interest.

Intuitive expectations. Intuitive expectations maybe be derived from the normative expectations themselves. If we treat normative expectations more broadly, as being the result of not only pure norms and their established interpretations, but also of understandings and assumptions prevailing within the community, it will form the intuitive perception of law. In the case of legal interest, we may assume that practising non-coercive measures lies at the bottom of the social and normative order, and we find that people will intuitively expect that declaratory reliefs will be welcomed as a measure falling into such non-coercive category and expect the adequate interpretation of the notion of legal interest, allowing declaration for the purposes to establish a premise for further proceedings, including negotiation and mediation. Another good example relates to the autonomy of will, a core principle of civil substantive law. If civil procedure is to implement and guarantee the civil substantive legal rights, one may intuitively expect the formulation of the legal interest prerequisite to allow for full implementation of the autonomy of will principle. In this kind of situation, intuitive expectations are a kind of normative expectations, as derived from the general principles of law, which are deemed to be a part of system of law, however contrary to the currently established particular judicial interpretations. This is what I would qualify as a deeper standard of justice.

Intuitive expectations may arise independently of the normative expectations. Intuitionism assumes that there is an irreducible number of primary principles which

53. As an example, if a government prepares a programme to support development of renewable energy and expresses its intentions in this respect, it elicits certain normative expectations of investors, communities, other participants of the community in this connection.

must be weighed against one another by asking which balance, in our considered judgement, is the most equitable.[54] I have qualified the Sample Case judgement based on my individual intuitive standard of justice. International arbitration is an example demonstrating certain collective, as opposed to individual, intuitions. In fact, international arbitration is a testing ground where intuitive expectations not related to normative expectations departing from the domestic requirements can be juxtaposed with the notion of legal interest. As described above, the a-national approach to declaratory relief allowed for defining the legal interest as a prerequisite, based on own experience and intuitions, departing from particular normative regulations and established judicial interpretations. It allowed also to treat this prerequisite as redundant and resign from using it at all. As was demonstrated, such an intuitive approach took us far from the strict Germanic concept of legal interest, albeit inspired by the particular legal orders.

The intuitive expectations of members of society are important if they are regarded as legitimate expectations.[55] It is not possible here to pursue deeper analysis of the interrelationship between the society and the system law, and to what extent social expectations may shape the law and vice versa. One problem, however, needs to be noted – the problem of confidence. The notion of confidence is fundamental since legal processes are social processes, where the goal is to reach a sound practical judgement which can be explained, and which can be seen as rational and reasonable. Confidence is a test whether a reasonable person, entering into the circumstances, will be confident of the result (for the avoidance of doubt: not certain, but confident[56]). Based on cases like the Sample Case, it could be ventured that that there is no such confidence in the case of understanding of legal interest. The question then arises whether such lack of comprehension is only accidental or is part of a bigger problem. The results of the below survey appear to confirm that expectations, both normative and intuitive, are not properly addressed by the system of law in respect of declarations.

Statistical survey. The survey was conducted by the author in 2018 with the aim of analysing data concerning the number of declaratory claims and the ratio between cases accepted and dismissed by the courts.[57] In business cases, the rate of dismissals, both in regional and district courts, was in excess of 80%, while in all business cases in general it was 25% for regional courts and 40% for district courts. In civil cases, the

54. Rawls, *supra* n. 21, at 30.
55. I raise the problem of legitimacy because not always can intuitive expectations of society be treated as legitimate. The role of the normative system can be to influence the system of such intuitive expectations and underlying values.
56. Galligan, *supra* n. 34, at 66.
57. All results of the survey were presented in Beata Gessel-Kalinowska vel Kalisz, *Pojęcia interesu prawnego w powództwie o ustalenie a prawo do sądu – wprowadzenie do dyskusji. Analiza badań statystycznych*, 1 PPH 11, (2009). It was based on data generated by the Ministry of Justice in Poland concerning practice of Polish courts for five consecutive years, i.e., 2013–2015, as concerning cases decided in the given years, with a breakdown into how they were decided. In addition, I have analysed the reasoning of all decisions issued by the appellate courts in one year, i.e., 2016. As concerns the Polish Supreme Court, I have analysed reasoning of judgements issued over the extended period of time of ten years, i.e., 2008–2017, due to the low number of decisions per annum.

difference was slightly smaller. In regional courts, the rate of dismissal of declaratory cases was 76% while in district courts it was 65%. In all civil cases in general, the rate of dismissal was 30% and 35%, respectively. These differences were quite striking; the rate of dismissals of declaratory relief significantly exceeded two-thirds of the cases, while in general this rate amounted to circa one-third. These figures confirm that expectations of claimants were seriously misaligned with expectations of the judicature. Further analysis was intended to answer the question how often the court based its judgement on the admissibility issue, i.e., missing legal interest. Based on extrapolation of the figures achieved in examination of appellate courts and the Supreme Court, it may be assumed that 40% of the cases were dismissed due to missing legal interest.[58] This further means that, in 40% of cases, claimants together with their legal, qualified representatives were not able to properly identify the legal interest in their submissions. This is a high degree of miscomprehension, suggesting that the notion of legal interest is not intuitively perceived by the users in the way expected by the judicature. In this way, the test of confidence and, in turn of predictability, is not fulfilled.

There is a second conclusion flowing from this statistical exercise. If roughly 40% of cases are dismissed for lack of legal interest, it means that all those cases were not examined as to the merits, stopping at the stage of analysis of the prerequisites only. This means that, in all of those cases, the claimant could not exercise fully his right of access to justice. As discussed above, fair trial assumes comprehensive evaluation of the case, securing its final determination. Any limitations of this principle should be adequate and not excessive. A dismissal rate of 40% demonstrates that limitations dictated by strict interpretation of legal interest and aiming to limit frivolous claims are inadequate and excessive. The following observation begs itself. In eight out ten business cases, the declaratory claims are dismissed (in civil cases: seven out ten). It can be assumed further that half of them are dismissed for lack of legal interest. Then, if legal interest could have been disregarded or interpreted not so strictly, the rate of dismissal of declaratory claims would be at the normal level, i.e., closer to the rate of dismissals in the overall number of cases.

Summary. Summing up, intuitive expectations are related to the deeper standard of justice and, as such, must be taken into consideration in shaping the legal interpretations and creating law. Based on a-national cases decided in arbitration and statistical data, it may be ventured that legal interest in its current restrictive shape is not deemed to be intuitively acceptable and understood by the subjects of civil law.

58. For these purposes, I have analysed the reasoning of Appellate Courts, which showed that in some 56% of all 183 published judgements the court denied rights of the claimant by dismissing the appeal of the claimant or, accordingly, taking into account the appeal of the respondent. In 40% of the cases, the court based its decision on finding of lack of legal interest, where half of them related to the subsidiarity principle and only in the remaining 16% there were other reasons taken into consideration.

Analysing the Supreme Court activity, it is difficult to discern one line of judgements as, depending on the year, the number of cases where the court found missing legal interest varies from 73 to 40%. Based on aggregate numbers, i.e., on all 135 examined cases, the results are similar to those for the appellate courts; in half of them, the reason cited was the subsidiarity principle.

§5.05 INHERENT VALUES OF THE CIVIL PROCEDURE

Legal interest and real interest in the light of outcome-related justice. Just outcome is an idea upon which the entire construction of legal proceedings is based. Provided that it is to be debated what just outcome means in concreto, the problem of achieving a just outcome can be dealt with more closely in the context of Rawls' model of pure procedural justice and imperfect procedural justice. The above-described concepts of declaratory relief based on, respectively, legal interest (Chapter 2 *supra*) as adopted in Germanic jurisdictions and real interest (Chapter 3 *supra*) as adopted in UK law represent two distinctive approaches. First, it must be emphasized that, in both systems, the judicature was granted a broad scope of discretion under the respective statutory provisions. The discretion can be characterized as being stronger according to how much guidance can be provided to the judge.[59] In the case of English solutions undertaken in CPR.40.20, the discretion granted was essentially unfettered (i.e., very strong), and in the case of Declaratory Relief Norm it was weaker, as the limitation of legal interest was provided. Yet it should be still be classified as strong due to the fact that the notion of legal interest is very general and discretionary. Within this discretion, the jurisprudence and doctrine produced certain standards which limited the original discretion. Hence, in the Germanic system, the non-related outcome justice model was adopted. This model requires answering the three basic questions of a procedural nature: does the claimant have other equivalent ways of solving his dispute? Does his claim relate to facts or legal rights? Is the need of the claimant of a legal or practical nature? Only then may the court address the merits of the claim. This stage of hearing, which might be the only stage of the proceedings, can be defined as a non-related outcome procedural justice model.

The English proceedings, focused as they are on real interest, tend to be more outcome-related. The basic questions asked by the judge are: Is it just to the parties to grant a declaration? And will a declaration be useful – how will it affect the business or life of the parties?

In the first case, the questions raised are prerequisite to the final outcome, while in the latter case they are post-requisite.

The premises of the discretional decisions of the judge are based on two different foundations: qualification of the needs of a claimant in terms of legal/non-legal in the first case and justice and utility in the latter.

The former model tends visibly towards pure justice; the system assumes that a just outcome will be any outcome produced by the adopted procedure. The latter is focused on what, exactly, a just outcome will be in its substance. The notion of justice is certainly undefined by itself; the judge ascertains what is just on a case-by-case basis. This produces the risk of unpredictability, which is mitigated to some extent by the nature of the precedent system itself. They do not, however, constitute prerequisites which are subject to examination against procedural justice principles. The justice referred to in the English decisions is a criterion of justice as a substantial outcome and

59. Rafał Zakrzewski, *Remedies reclassified* 87 (2005).

not of just procedure, which is instrumental to achieve justice between the parties as a substantial outcome.[60]

Traditional values. The procedures are neither good nor fair independent of values, they must still express a value which can be identified and justified as one which ought to be respected and to which resources ought to be dedicated. Unless it can be demonstrated that a given procedure serves a certain value, such a procedure cannot be connected to fair treatment.[61]

Access to justice in all its multiple components is a basic value in terms of securing fairness which procedure must serve. It is realized as has been mentioned, by a number of instruments which are values in themselves: equality of arms, right to be heard, receiving judgement without undue delay. In this part, the measures aimed at increasing effectiveness of the civil procedure as a potential limitation of due process are considered as well.

The central point of procedural fairness is whether a person is given what is due to him or what he is entitled to, with substantive legal rights always at the foundation and in the background. This coincides with another statement, that the main goal of civil procedure is to implement properly the civil substantive legal relationship and protection of subjective legal rights derived therefrom. Such a formulation of the civil procedure goal is not controversial and viewed as a classic one.[62] Therefore, protection of the substantive legal rights is a second basic value which civil procedure must serve.[63] Interpretation of the respective institutions of civil procedure should be conducted always with a mind to this value. This means, further, that such interpretation should consider the goal and interest of the claimant derived from the principles of the substantive civil law. From the perspective of further analysis, it is important to note that values such as autonomy of the parties in creating their legal relationship, including certain disposal of benefits arising out of the contract, unless limited by the rule of law, must be respected within the civil process.

It is raised in the literature[64] that judicial decisions in individual cases, sorting out individual rights and duties, also have a law-forming value, having impact much beyond the individual case. The public interest was a strong reason to grant declarations in a number of cases in England.[65] This applies, however, not only to common law but also to Continental jurisdictions. The contribution of the courts assumed much greater importance, as manifested in development of European law through the

60. John Thibaut et al., *Procedural Justice as Fairness*, 26 Stan. L. Rev. 1271 (1974); and John Thibaut & Laurens Walker, *A Theory of Procedure*, 66 Calif. L. Rev. 541 (1978), who pursue the idea of procedural justice being instrumental to justice as a substantive outcome.
61. Galligan, *supra* n. 34, at 55–56.
62. Jerzy Jodłowski, in Jerzy Jodłowski et al., *Postępowanie cywilne* 20, 22 (2002). Ianika Tzankova & Martin Gramatikov, *A Critical Note on Two EU Principles: A Proceduralist View on the Draft Common Frame of Reference (DCFR)* in *The Foundations of European Private Law* 421, 424 (Roger Brownsword et al., eds., 2011).
63. More on this topic from the systemic perspective, *see* §5.07 *infra*.
64. Tzankowa & Gramatikov, *supra* n. 62, at 425.
65. *Financial Services Authority v Watkins (t/a Consolidated Land UK)* [2011] EWHC 1976 (Ch), 25–30 (English High Court).

judgements of the Court of Justice of the European Union or the ECHR. This goal is furthered especially in the case of declarations and is, to some extent, underestimated

Evolution of values and goals. Balancing of principles must be viewed also in a certain historical context.[66] Certain values that are important at the given moment of societal development disappear or are subject to alteration at another moment. Civil procedure is one of the elements of the overall system regulating societal relations, so it must be coherent and must not be detrimental to values important from the perspective of the entire system. System of justice must therefore follow the change of values in societal relations.[67]

The same process applies to the proceedings themselves. The virtue of having settled rules of procedure lies in the certainty and stability of their application. The cost, meanwhile, is that procedural rules might over-include in requiring procedures which may not be necessary or under-include by not calling for certain procedures which, in some instances, are needed for fair treatment. Procedural reform is a continuing concern of any legal system, and settled rules need to be re-examined from time to time,[68] especially if the test of confidence is not passed. What, then, does this mean as far as declaratory relief is concerned? English law is an example of evolution of prized values; on the subject of interest here, this occurred basically within seventy years. For a long time, English judges did not consider granting pure declarations in situations where no breach had yet occurred.[69] Knight Bruce V.C. said in 1847 that 'Nakedly to declare a right, without doing or directing anything else relating to the right, does not, I conceive, belong to the functions of this Court.'[70] Come 1919, however, Lord Atkin adopted a completely opposite position, deeming the declaration as 'one of the most valuable contributions that the courts have made to the commercial life of this country'.[71] This shift had to be accomplished through legislative change in order to cut through the established precedent.[72] While appreciating the importance of the relief in question, and inspired by Scottish law, Parliament adopted the Chancery Act of 1850. Preliminary, declaratory relief was used for the purpose of construction of

66. Judgement of 12 July 2001, *Case of Ferrazzini v Italy*, no. 44759/98, ECHR 2001-VII (2001) (ECHR).
67. Galligan, *supra* n. 34, at 15–16.
68. *Ibid*., at 64.
69. For the historical development *see* Lord Woolf & Jeremy Woolf, *Zamir & Woolf: The Declaratory Judgment* 9–36 (4th ed., 2011).
70. *Clough v Ratcliffe* (1847) 1 De G. & S.M.164, 178 (63 E.R. 1016), as cited in Woolf and Woolf, *supra* n. 69, at 9–12.
71. *Spettabile consortio Consortio Veneziano di Armamento e Navigazione v Northumberland Shipbuilding Co, Ltd* (1919) 121L.T. 628, 635 (CA).
72. Interestingly, declaratory relief in US law is similarly regulated by legislative instrument and also in quite comprehensive form. § 2201 Declaratory Judgement Act states that:

> Creation of remedy. In a case of actual controversy, within its jurisdiction [...] upon the filing of an appropriate pleading, may declare the rights and other legal relations of any interested party seeking such declaration, whether or not further relief is or could be sought. Any such declaration shall have the force and effect of a final judgment or decree and shall be reviewable as such. § 2202. Further relief. Further necessary or proper relief based on a declaratory judgment or decree may be granted, after reasonable notice and hearing, against any adverse party whose rights have been determined by such judgment.

any acts of Parliament or of a written instrument or as to the title or evidence of title to any real estate or personal estate. Further amendments broadened the scope of the declarations and lifted other limitations up until the current content of Article 40.20 Civil Procedure Rules (CPR):[73] 'The court may make binding declarations whether or not any other remedy is claimed.' As was explained earlier, the discretion of English judges is now very broad, limited only by the utility of the granted declaration and by fairness to the parties.

Among the Germanic systems, no essential change could be observed save for Switzerland. Swiss law has undergone a significant change. As was described in Chapter 2 *supra*, Swiss law expanded the notion of legal interest into legitimate interest, attempted to enhance its predictability and reformulated the notion of equality and justice as between claimant and respondent.

Modern values. Non-combativeness of measures. Principles and goals of the European system of justice in the sphere of civil procedure have been much changed during the last decades. Providing not only speedier, cheaper, but also less combative mechanisms of resolving disputes within the framework of redefining access to the courts is one of the current social goals to improve access to justice.[74] In this vein, Christopher Hodges predicts that the entire civil justice system may develop similar to the model which has been adopted by the European Commission for consumer collective redress, where encouragement of voluntary settlement is foremost, followed by regulatory assistance, and only then, as a last resort, by judicial procedures.[75] An important goal from this point of view, not specific only to the civil procedure, is enhancing civil society, which puts its faith in mediation and settlement. There are also other reasons why this new approach is attractive: inherent attraction of settling disputes by agreement, the risk of mistaken result in the regular proceedings, and the appealing promise of cheaper and more accessible form of process.[76] Conflict resolution should not be a fight; rather, it should be a 'cooperation experience'.[77]

Non-combativeness of the legal measures is an important value from the perspective of declaratory relief. One of the purposes of the declaration of rights is to clear the field in order to allow for implementation of alternative dispute resolution, such as mediation or negotiation. By clarifying their legal status, the parties may agree on a further mode of conduct in order to not jeopardize their long-term business

73. English Civil Procedure Rules 1998 (SI 1998/3132) as amended by Rule 13 of the Civil Procedure (Amendment) Rules 2001 (SI 2001/256).
74. Richard Susskind, *The End of Lawyers? Rethinking the Nature of Legal Services* 232 (2010).
75. Christopher Hodges, *Public and Private Enforcement: The Practical Implications for Policy Architecture* in *The Foundations of European Private Law* 437, 451 (Roger Brownsword et al., eds., 2011).
76. Galligan, *supra* n. 34, at 41. Alternative dispute resolution has already been recommended, directly or indirectly, in a number of community instruments and proposals. Many of these encourage the Member States to implement ADR, or at least to promote, the introduction and operation of ADR. Please *see* the recent *Statement of the European Law Institute and European Network of Councils for the Judiciary 'The Relationship Between Formal and Informal Justice: the Courts and Alternative Dispute'*, https://www.europeanlawinstitute.eu/fileadmin/user_upload/p_eli/Publications/ADR_Statement.pdf (accessed 13 January 2019).
77. Tzankowa & Gramatikov, *supra* n. 62, at 425.

relationship. Arbitration practice offers good patterns in this regard, with the well-known Aramco case serving as a model in this respect (*see* Chapter 4 *supra*).

Summary. Summing up, for the purposes of the subsequent analysis, the following values of the civil procedure will be considered: (i) the overall principle of access to justice in all its multiple components, (ii) proper implementation of civil substantive rights and its protection and (iii) enhancement of the non-combative legal measures.

§5.06 ARGUMENTS RELATING TO TEXTUAL INTERPRETATION

Lack of statutory definition of legal interest. It is important to note that, in the majority of civil procedure systems employing the concept of legal interest at all, the important features of the legal interest, like its objective character, subsidiarity principle, identification what is legal and what is factual, existence of an actual dispute or controversy as between the parties are not established in positive law, but are a matter of judicial interpretation. Despite the fact that, recently, one may observe in countries such as Romania or Hungary exemptions from this legislative trend, with upgrading of the subsidiarity principle to the rank of statutory regulation, this remains the exception rather than the rule.[78]

Departing from the established conventional interpretation, as discussed earlier in Chapter 2, there is an attempt to focus on semantic interpretation based on pure text of the Declaratory Relief Norm. This text is very concise: claimant may seek declaration of his rights or legal relationship (as the case may be) provided he has a legal interest. Such norm will be further defined as Declaratory Relief Norm.[79] 'Interest' itself can be interpreted as a 'need', and this is how it is frequently construed by legal scholars.[80] This interest is attributable to the claimant and not to any other person because the norm refers to the need of the claimant rather than any other person. This appears to be a decisive factor for granting a declaration where the claimant is not a party to the legal relationship being declared. The claimant cannot base his claim on the needs of any third party; this is a strict limitation. Thus, claimant cannot, for instance, seek declaration of the validity or invalidity of the contract where such validity or invalidity does not have any effect on his sphere of interests. Usually, no impact could be observed where the claimant is not a party to the contract, but this is not always the case. The claimant's rights might, in certain circumstances, be dependent on validity or invalidity of the given third-party contract.[81]

---

78. The fact that the subsidiarity principle is included in the statutory norm does not change the basic findings of this chapter relating to the problem of over-restrictive access to justice, in such a case being more of a *de lege ferenda* than *de lege lata* character.
79. Article 189 Polish CCP, § 256 I of German CCP, § 288 of Austrian CPC and Art. 88 of Swiss CCPC.
80. Tadeusz Rowiński, *Interes prawny w procesie cywilnym i postępowaniu nieprocesowym* 26 (1969); Klaus Reichold, in: Thomas Putzo, *Zivilprozessordnung – Kommentar*, ZPO § 256 no. 13 (38th ed., 2017), who classifies the legal interest ('*rechtliches Intersse*') as a form of the individual need of legal protection ('*Rechtsschutzbedürfnis*').
81. This has been confirmed both in English and Germanic practice, *see* Chapters 2 and 3 *infra* cf. Matthias Jacobs, *Der Gegenstand des Feststellungsverfahrens, Rechtsverhältnis und rechtliches*

The second element which can be derived from the text of the Declaratory Relief Norm it is that the interest of the claimant must be 'legal'. Simultaneously, the norm allows declarations only to the extent that the subject matter is a legal relationship or a right. Reading this together produces a tautology, as it is difficult to imagine having a non-legal interest in terms of establishing legal rights or legal relationship. Legality as an intrinsic element of interest is a logical consequence of the object of the declaration, namely legal rights or relationship, sought by the interested party. These two settings of the term 'legal' demonstrate strong interrelationship between them. This interrelationship is also discernible in courts' reasoning for dismissals, where one and the same situation may give raise to double qualification. In case I Aca 140/10,[82] the court stated that the interest of the claimant in seeking a declaration as to who is authorized to the rights of registration of an industrial design found that the interest of the claimant is factual and not legal, but the court based its reasoning on arguments used by the Supreme Court[83] to support its dismissal of a declaration because there were facts and not legal right to be established, saying nothing about missing factual interest as such.

Economic interest versus legal interest. Focusing first on the notion of legal interest, legal scholars and judges make a distinction between legal interest and interest which is factual, economic or relating to custom. Legal interest should be rooted in and related to a positive norm of law. In general, legal interest is a need which relates to the legal sphere of the claimant. Hence, the purpose of the declaration sought is a distinctive criterion. That said, it must be stated that the legal and economic spheres are not unrelated ones; they will have a lot of elements in common. It is difficult to realize, *prima facie*, how economic claims can, by definition, be disconnected from the underlying juridical creations, forming particular substantive rights and duties. There is a good illustration of this problem in the judgement of the Appellate Court from 21 April 2016.[84] In this case, the claimant sought a declaration that the real estate transfer agreement executed between his debtor and a third party is null and void due to the fact that it was made after claimant had sought a temporal injunction by way of a compulsory mortgage to secure enforcement of his claim against the debtor. Thus, claimant argued, the contract had the sole purpose of harming him. The court found that claimant's interest in a declaration is not of legal, but of the economic character, related only to the impact which execution of the contract might have on the financial situation of the debtor, which in turn was decisive on the possibility to repay the debt. The court stated:

> [d]eclaring invalidity of the disputed contract could be important *merely* for the effectiveness of the requested interim measure and, in the future, for the effectiveness of enforcement of the claimant's proprietary claims. This points to the purely

Interesse bei Rechtsstreitigkeiten vor Zivil- und Arbeitsgerichten, 46–52 (2005), who gives a systematic overview of the established court practice admitting declaratory action with regard to legal relationships with third parties.

82. Judgement of 10 March 2010, I Aca 140/10, Lex 628177 (2010) (Poznań Appellate Court).
83. Judgement of 16 November 1965, I PR 389/65, OSNC 1966/6/100, Lex 12099 (1965) (Polish Supreme Court).
84. Judgement of 21 April 2016, I ACa 894/15, Lex 2152868 (2016) (Warsaw Appellate Court).

economic, and not legal, interest of the claimant. [translation by author, emphasis added]

In this case, the court separated interest from the object of the declaration. The legal relationship, the contract as such, was the object of the declaration. Nevertheless, the interest of the claimant was classified as non-legal and purely economic. It is difficult to agree with such a classification for at least three reasons.

First, the court's way of thinking does not relate at all to the goals of civil procedure associated with implementing and protecting civil substantive rights, as discussed above. The court adopts the position that the court decision would be merely important for the effectiveness of the claimant's rights, which does not constitute legitimate entitlement for the claimant to obtain such a decision. This appears to contradict the general goals of the procedure to protect substantive civil law interests of the aggrieved parties. The interest of the claimant seeking protection for civil rights, regardless of whether it is declaratory relief or claim for performance, is principally of a practical value. The parties to the civil legal relationships, by entering into them, plan to achieve certain practical purposes, and performance of the stipulated duty is aimed at satisfaction of the creditor. The majority of civil law relationships are of a proprietary character, which is clearly practical. But non-proprietary relationships also have their practical underlying goal. Marriage, in and of itself, is not aimed at establishing a legal relationship between the spouses, but everything that marriage means in reality and in practice has special and multidimensional community significance, and marriage as a legal act is an instrument to achieve it. The seller enters into the sale contract in order to receive the purchase price, and the buyer – in order to obtain a title to a thing, defined by the contract. By certain conventional actions, a party intends to achieve a practical goal and not a legal one. It is difficult to imagine what pure legal interest could be intended by the civil law subject to be achieved. If seller claims payment of the purchase price, his interest is undoubtedly economic, which does not detract from its legal dimension, and it impacts the legal sphere, specifically his receivables. In the case at hand, the practical value for the claimant was focused on giving effect to the prospective payment order. There is really not much difference categorially in comparison to claiming payment of the purchase price.

Second, from the perspective of the principles of justice to be done to the parties, the court adopted the stance that the procedure claimed to be just was in fact segregated from the final outcome, allegedly just. It was irrelevant for the court whether the claimant would in fact enforce his receivable, which would be a just outcome of the adopted procedures. Juridical clarity took precedence over substantive justice in this way of thinking. Such a procedure, which does not produce a just outcome (and even is not structured to produce a just outcome) cannot be upheld as just.

Third, there is a need to reflect on the juridical nature of the substantive right as such, which is to some extent fundamental to qualification of what is and what is not a legal interest. There are various substantive rights classified in the theory of private law, including the most distinctive ones like ownership rights and receivables. The ownership right is a certain abstract ideal construct formed by legal relationship. There is an obvious relationship between the owner and the rest of the world, constituting a relationship effective *erga omnes* in and of itself. This relationship cannot be examined at a sensory level. Constitutive to the ownership right is its object, which is sensually perceived; the ownership right may not exist without its underlying material object. In the event of disappearance of this object, the ownership right ceases to exist.[85] This dual nature, both ideal and sensually perceived, of the subjective right is visible in other examples. J. Searle called this phenomenon a realism, stating that for some facts to be institutional – in our case, to be subjective rights – there must be some other facts that are 'brute', this being a consequence of the logical structure of institutional facts.[86] By brute facts, Searle meant things or psycho-physical acts of man. Different entitlements to receive certain assets and behaviours are constituted of a right being an abstract construct and the object at which the right is directed, i.e., behaviours and things. In the case of a monetary receivable, the right is aimed at receiving defined funds. This nature of the subjective right must contribute to the broader understanding of what is meant by legal interest. The assets underlying the given subjective right need to be considered while defining the limits of legal interest as such. In this sense, the meaning of what is 'legal' and what is 'economic' is strictly correlated. One cannot really be considered in separation from the other.

In this case, the court provided, *obiter dicta*, the reasoning which contributed additional arguments in this discourse. It stated that even if the legal interest could be attributed to the claimant, it would be dismissed on its merits.[87] The court compared the claim in question to the *actio pauliana* (fraudulent conveyance claims),[88] which is appropriate in cases where the claimant seeks redress in the context of harmful actions of the debtor. The court considered that *actio pauliana* dictates the limits of the claimant's protection in this sort of matter. The court did not take into account, however, that the interest of the claimant in the *actio pauliana* is similar to the one in the case at hand and that legal nature of the interest of the claimant in *actio pauliana* is not questioned. This last argument shows how the notions of legal and economic interest can become blurred, which may result in over-restrictive limitation to receive the court decision on merits. As noted in Chapter 2 *supra*, the difficulties in separating the economic interest from the legal has led the Swiss to abandon the term 'legal' in this context altogether, and motivated the German jurisprudence to develop a more liberal approach. In Swiss law, the legitimate interest is sufficient if an uncertainty inhibits claimant's economic freedom of decision.[89]

85. *See* Jan Korzonek & Ignacy Rosenblüth, *Kodeks Zobowiązań. Komentarz t.1* 679 (1934); Roman Longchamps de Bérier, *Polskie Prawo cywilne. Zobowiązania* 454 (1999).
86. John R. Searle, *The Construction of Social Reality* 56 (1995).
87. Which, by the way, is much more persuasive than the argument referring to missing legal interest.
88. Article 527 of the Polish CPC.
89. The same argumentation pattern appears in decisions of German court practice as justification for the affirmation of 'legal interest' – e.g., BGH, verdict of 4 July 1962, Case no. V ZR 206/60, published in BGHZ 37, 331.

Factual interest versus legal interest. The interest relating to customs and factual interest as distinct from the legal interest cannot be explored without examination of the object of the declaration, i.e., the right or legal relationship, depending on the respective jurisdiction. Again, the question arises whether interest of the claimant in declaring the legal relationship or legal right can be qualified in any circumstances as non-legal. My thesis is that, if the object of the declaration is legal, then the interest of the claimant is legal as well. If the object of the declaration is factual, the interest of the claimant is factual. If the object of the declaration relates to custom, the interest of the claimant is of custom character as well. If the court is to declare the mere fact that someone has taken a pen and put it to paper, leaving words and sentences, the object of the declaration is the fact, and hence the interest of the claimant is factual. If the claimant further claims that such act of the respondent resulted in a validly signed contract, the object of the declaration is the legal relationship, and hence the interest of the claimant is legal as it relates to the realm of rights and duties. If the court is to declare that the earldom title belongs to the claimant in a jurisdiction where all titles of this sort are rooted in custom only but not in positive rules of law, the interest of the claimant relates to the realm of customs and not of legal rights. I am strongly convinced that claimant has, or does not have, his legal interest as a consequence of the fact that the relief sought is, or is not, directed at declaration of a legal right/legal relationship, and not the other way around.

As has been stated, only a legal relationship or a legal right may be an object of a declaration and therefore facts, perceived as a distinct and opposite ontological category, cannot be declared. In many instances, perception of what is a legal right or legal relationship juxtaposed with facts is too narrow and misleading. Although in German legal literature a few authors advocate the opinion that it should be possible *de lege lata* to apply for a declaratory relief with regard to facts,[90] the court practice in Germany in general has rejected such attempts.[91] Judicial practice in Poland noticed this problem and produced an emergency solution allowing to declare facts, creating directly certain legal relationship or legal rights (*fakty prawotwórcze)*.[92] Examples of such facts include execution of a contract, tortious behaviour, or contribution to incurred loss.[93] While this solution is very useful, allowing for broader application of the declaratory relief, it still emphasizes the contrast between two concepts: facts and legal relationships/legal rights. In order to express relations between facts and legal creations, it is useful to recall the concept of institutional facts, as J. Searle[94] calls them, or conventional acts, as they are referred to by others.[95] There are three basic terms in

90. For an overview on such positions *see* Jacobs, *supra* n. 81, at 44 et seq.
91. *See* BGH, verdict of 3 May 1977, Case no. VI ZR 36/74, published in BGHZ 68, 331, 333. An exception may be a declaratory relief regarding the question, whether a certain person can be considered as inventor, although that is not a merely factual question – *see* BGH, verdict of 24 October 1978, Case no. X ZR 42/76, published in BGHZ 72, 236.
92. Judgement of 17 December 1997, I PKN 434/97, 21 OSNAPiUS, item 627 (1998) (Polish Supreme Court).
93. *See* Annex, III.III by Beata Gessel-Kalinowska vel Kalisz & Joanna Kisielinska-Garncarek *infra.*
94. Searle, *supra* n. 86, at 1–57.
95. Leszek Nowak et al., *Czynności konwencjonalne w prawie,* 33(2) Studia Prawnicze 73 (1972); Stanisław Czepita, *O pojęciu czynności konwencjonalnej i jej odmianach,* (79) 1 Ruch Prawniczy,

Searle's philosophy suited to illustrate also the problem of the identification of the object of declaration: brute facts, social facts and institutional facts.[96] Brute facts, like a mountain, a screwdriver or a piece of paper with the visual attributes of a ten-pound note require no human institutions for their existence. Brute facts may be stated (or declared), but the fact stated must be distinguished from the statement of fact. By collective intentionality of social groups, certain functions can be attributed to the brute facts which transform brute facts into the social facts. The collective imposition of functions can be performed only by virtue of collective agreement in the community. A special subclass of social facts are institutional facts, meaning facts involving human institutions. The fact that the piece of paper is a twenty-dollar bill, bearing certain entitlements for its holder, is an institutional fact. The fact that the sun is 93 million miles from the Earth is a brute fact, the fact that Trump is a president is an institutional fact. Institutional facts may exist only within human institutions, and in particular within a system of constitutive rules. The system of rules creates the possibility of transformation of brute fact into institutional fact by imposing certain functions and meaning on it. Institutional facts are created by the constitutive rules. The application of the constitutive rule introduces new status on a certain brute fact, like rarefying a piece paper into a twenty-dollar bill or the simple raising of a hand into the act of voting. The institutional facts are hierarchically structured; they exist on top of brute physical facts and, as stated above, they are logically dependent on them.

In the realm of civil law theory, institutional facts are understood as conventional acts. Raising one's hand is a brute fact, but if done in a proper setting as prescribed by corporate law rules, it becomes a conventional act called 'voting'. Such brute fact, which includes psycho-physical activity of civil law subjects, is also called in legal science a substratum of the conventional act.[97] If the party identified by the rules of law, in the circumstances identified by the rules of law, undertakes an action identified by the rules of law, such action will cause effects as a conventional act identified in such rules of law. Failing any of the above elements causes such action to be invalid or ineffective.

How does the above deliberation relate to the object of the declaration, namely legal relationship or legal right? In the most common understanding, the legal relationship is a subclass of social relationship[98] regulated by law, thus all comments relating to the institutional facts/conventional acts and interrelationship with its underlying brute facts/substratum of the conventional acts is also applicable thereto as well. Any court decision where such substratum is to be declared as existing or non-existing should be regarded as relating to legal and not factual matters. A similar

Ekonomiczny i Socjologiczny 85 (2017).

96. It is interesting from the declaratory relief terminology perspective that all three ontological phenomena are referred to as facts.

97. Leszek Nowak et al., *supra* n. 95, at 90.

98. Jerzy Ignatowicz, Krzysztof Stefaniuk & Aleksander Wolter, *Prawo cywilne. Zarys części ogólnej* 99 et seq. (1996). Zbigniew Banaszczyk, *Rozdział XII. Stosunek cywilnoprawny* in *System prawa Prywatnego. Prawo cywilne – część ogólna, t.1.* 829, 829 et seq. (Marek Safjan ed., 2007).

structure is applicable to the subjective right per se, as explained above, which – anyway – is created based on a certain legal relationship.[99]

The above approach also explains the status of the facts creating certain rights. There is a whole range of brute facts which are independent of the intent of the parties, and then there are those which are intentionally committed by the parties[100] which cause inception, change or expiration of a legal relationship. Every legal relationship is commenced by any such facts. In light of the above, they belong to the legal relationship directly, and not as applicable in certain situations *mutatis mutandis.*

In the decision of the Polish Supreme Court of 16 November 1965,[101] the court stated that declaring that the claimant submitted properly and on time the objection to the resolution of the Supervisory Board excluding him from the list of cooperative members was a question of facts and not of the legal relationship or legal right. In this case, it appears that the court dealt with the substratum, i.e., the psycho-physical act of delivering the notice, disregarding its transformation into the normative conventional act (institutional fact) upon the norms which provide that a properly and timely filed notice becomes a legally acknowledged objection, which in turn grants certain rights to the claimant, including a right to submit a claim to the court. There should be no question of legality of the claimant's interest, which was, in the long run, aimed at securing his legal status as a member of the cooperative, and in the short run at preserving his right to challenge the decision of the Supervisory Board.

In the above context, many of the decisions in which declarations were dismissed because they were aimed at declaring facts and not rights seem to be incorrect. In VI Aca 1551/15,[102] the claimant sought a declaration that the general assembly of a cooperative is invalid or not existing, as the case maybe, due to false data entered in the records. In this case, the claim was clearly aimed at establishing existence of a whole variety of legal relationships created by the fact of holding a valid or invalid general assembly, and not on establishment of facts constituting the substratum of the given legal act. Similarly, in I PR 389/65,[103] the declaration that respondent is obliged to convene the general assembly was qualified as declaring facts. An interesting matter was raised in the judgement of the Appellate Court in Lodz of 7 December 2016.[104] Here, the claimant sought a declaration relating to correctness of indexes adopted by the court expert in her estimate of the consideration due to claimant for use of his land without contractual basis. The expert opinion was defining the value of the claimant's

99. Banaszczyk, *Ibid.*
100. In the theory of law, this classification is reflected in the division of conventional acts into normative and non-normative acts. The first group is aimed at transformation of the legal situation of the given party, and in civil law systems approximates declarations of intent, and non-normative conventional acts, like notices, declarations of knowledge, which are not aimed at such transformation, *see* Czepita, *supra* n. 95, at 99.
101. Judgement of 16 November 1965, I PR 389/65, OSNC 1966/6/100, LEX 12099 (1965) (Polish Supreme Court).
102. Judgement of 16 September 2016, VI ACa 1551/15 (2016) (Warsaw Appellate Court).
103. Judgement of 16 November 1965, I PR 389/65, OSNC 1966/6/100, Lex 12099 (1965) (Polish Supreme Court).
104. Judgement of 7 December 2016, I ACa 713/16, Lex 2216132 (2016) (Łódź Appellate Court).

receivable. Again, in this case, the court classified the subject matter as a factual and not a legal one.

Summing up the above, the interest of the civil law subjects in declaring their rights or legal relationship in the short run is always legal as long as the declaration sought is aimed at such institutional facts as rights and legal relationship. All facts may be qualified as institutional facts if special function and meaning is attributed to them by legal norms. Such facts will constitute a substratum of a legal relationship or legal right if they are created in a special context, i.e., by an appropriate person, in proper circumstances and in due time, therefore are eligible to be declared. In the long run, interest of the claimant is, by its nature, always not legal because civil law subjects enter into their legal relationships having in mind certain practical – rather than legal – goals. Legal institutions are the instruments to achieve these practical goals. There nonetheless always remains the open question whether such interest can be attributable to the claimant or a third party.

Objectivity as a feature of the legal interest cannot be derived simply from the text of the Declaratory Relief Norm. Quite on the contrary, the understanding of the word 'need', which is undoubtedly the underlying meaning of the term 'interest', assumes a high degree of subjectivity. The Oxford Dictionary differentiates between 'need' and 'desire'. Need means requiring or wanting something because it is essential or very important rather than just desirable. Therefore, need is reasoned while desire need not be reasoned. In a very important point, such want does not have to be objectivized.[105] The 'need' must be treated subjectively, i.e., whether the needed object is necessary from the point of view of claimant and not objectively, in the sense that something should typically be needed by a certain class of claimants in a certain class of situations. In order to achieve such objectivization, special language would be necessary. Such examples can be observed when impartiality and independence of arbitrators is evaluated. An arbitrator may be challenged not when circumstances confirm his partiality or dependence, but when they give rise to justifiable doubts as to his impartiality or independence.[106] This language refers to objectivized criteria and not to the factual mindset of the arbitrator. There is no such language used in the Declaratory Relief Norm. Here, the legislature uses the need (interest) of the claimant, without referring to 'justifiable' need or employing any similar qualificator.

One could say that if a claim refers directly or indirectly to the legal sphere of the claimant, even if legal interest is not attributed to the claimant in the orthodox sense, such attribution must appear at the moment of filing the claim, meaning that as of this moment the appropriate need was identified definitely. This would amount to clear application of subjective theory, which can move the problem to the opposite extreme and render the notion of legal interest meaningless. In each case of filing the claim, the

105. Oxford Dictionaries, https://en.oxforddictionaries.com/definition/need (accessed 31 January 2019).
106. Article 12.2 of the UNCITRAL Model Law on International Commercial Arbitration (1985), with amendments as adopted in 2006, http://www.uncitral.org/pdf/english/texts/arbitration/ml-arb/07-86998_Ebook.pdf (accessed 13 January 2019).

claimant would have legal interest, therefore there would be no point in inserting such a prerequisite.[107]

Objectivity can, as attributed by the court practice and doctrine to the legal interest, refer to the perception of what is deemed to be a controversy/uncertainty between the parties, or whether such controversy is bearable or not by the claimant, as the case may be, whether potential breach constitutes an imminent danger to the claimant. The process of the objectivity/subjectivity test is by definition highly evaluative. In the context of ascertaining what is to be classified as controversy, the respondent may choose to sit mute if approached by the claimant with a certain legal question or to explicitly deny the interpretation of the claimant, or to initiate certain countermeasures against the claimant.[108] The question is, whether it should work as an objective test in this respect: in the eyes of a third party, does only explicit denial count, or is implicit denial (silence) enough? The other possibility is to consider only the situation of the claimant, his state of business affairs, including certain psychological tensions and expectations. Practically, one may not conduct evaluation subject only to objective or only subjective criteria; it is always a matter of degree, of being more or less objective/subjective. Considering purely emotional status of the claimant would lead to acceptance of irrational, even hysterical behaviours, which should not be the case.[109] Nevertheless, there is no argument relating to literal analysis of the term 'interest' for departing in its interpretation from the subjective criteria, which will consider the state of affairs of a particular claimant and his particular needs and put more emphasis to the objective approach. Systemic analysis, as provided below, will contribute more arguments.

Summary. The definition of the legal interest term is not provided by positive provisions of law, but is the product of doctrine and jurisprudence. Textual interpretation provides that restricted interpretation of what is legal and what is non-legal interest (meaning economic, factual, or other) does not rely on coherent criteria. If the scope of the declaration relates to the legal right or legal relationship, the interest should, as a rule, be qualified as legal. The notion of legal right or legal relationship cannot be deprived of its underlying 'brute fact', otherwise coherent application of the legal interest becomes illogical. Finally, textual interpretation also does not provide a basis for indication to what degree the legal interest must be objectivized in order to be sufficient for legal protection. This issue will require more contextual interpretation. All in all, the certain incoherence affecting these three issues leads to marked unpredictability for the subjects of civil law.

107. *See* Annex I.III[C] by Ulrich Kopetzki *infra*.

108. *In Re Clay* [1919] 1 Ch. 66, the claimant sought a declaration that the respondent was entitled to certain sums under the deed of indemnity; the respondent in a letter to the claimant reserved certain such rights but never formulated any request in this respect. The claim was dismissed for lack of controversy. *See also* section §2.15 *supra*.

109. Edward Warzocha, *Ustalenie stosunku prawnego lub prawa w sądowym postępowaniu cywilnym* 50 (1982); stated that the legal interest may neither perceived as purely subjective, shaped by the internal emotions of the party, nor purely objective, independent of them; both of them are interrelated in one notion of legal interest.

§5.07 ARGUMENTS RELATING TO TELEOLOGY AND SYSTEMIC COHERENCE

Introductory remarks. As an introduction to this part of the discussion, the words of Lord Woolf are very meaningful and worth to be reminded:

> The declaration, like any other discretionary remedy, has therefore to be employed with care. [...] But the same can be said of other remedies and there is nothing particular about the nature or the consequence of declaratory relief which calls for extraordinary caution. On the contrary, not being coercive relief, it is less harmful, potentially then other remedies, notably injunctions and specific performance. Extreme caution is both unnecessary and undesirable. On the other hand, care is needed, not only to avoid indiscriminate and unjustified use of declaratory power, but also to prevent declaratory actions from being dismissed and the scope of the remedy being unduly restricted out of extreme caution.[110]

The term 'legal interest' as contained in the Declaratory Relief Norm is a typical general clause, which constitutes a construction element of the relief in question. Similarly, like any other general clause, its designata may change with passage of time, depending on the then-current principles of ethics and historical context.[111] This is an inevitable consequence of the changing values and goals of the system of law in general, including the system of civil procedure. Especially in Central and East European jurisdictions, which have undergone an essential transformation from the socialistic to the liberal-democratic political and economic formation, such change in meaning of moral principles, like contractual justice or equivalence of performance as between the parties, was readily observable, but the labels (terms) remained the same.

The change of approach to the notion of legal interest *prima facie* could be observed in Poland at the level of the Supreme Court. In a number of judgements,[112] the court introduced new interpretation directives, referring to Article 45 of the Polish Constitution and Article 14 of the International Covenant on Civil and Political Rights.[113] It was stated then that legal interest should be interpreted in a flexible way, taking into account the broadly understood right to access to justice in order to secure legal protection in the form of mere declaration of the right or legal relationship, if such declaration is necessary to respond to claimant's actual need. This new guidance, however, did not cause deeper reflection. The only visible result was that claims for declaration of a legal relationship by third parties (if properly substantiated) were

110. Woolf & Woolf, *supra* n. 69, at 130.
111. *See* Chapter 5, section §5.05 *supra*.
112. Judgement of 29 October 2009, III CZP 79/09, 10 Biuletyn SN (2009) (Polish Supreme Court); Decision of 17 December 1993, III CZP 171/93, OSNC 1994/7-8/149 (Polish Supreme Court), Judgement of 1 April 2004, II CK 125/03, Lex 484673 (2004) (Polish Supreme Court); Judgement of 10 July 1997, I CKN 161/97, unpublished (1997) (Polish Supreme Court); Judgement of 20 February 2003, I CKN 58/01, (2003) (Polish Supreme Judgement of 6 October 1998, II CKU 46/98, Lex 35040 (1998) (Polish Supreme Court); Judgement of 31 January 2008, II CSK 378/07, Lex 863958 (2008) (Polish Supreme Court).
113. International Covenant on Civil and Political Rights (ICCPR), Resolution 2200A (XXI) of 16 December 1966, https://www.ohchr.org/en/professionalinterest/pages/ccpr.aspx (accessed 13 January 2019).

allowed,[114] what is similar now to the approach of other Germanic jurisdictions. The problem of access to justice found also its reflection in jurisprudence, however quite surprising in the context of findings of this chapter. The court found that dismissing the claim for lack of legal interest can in no circumstances be qualified as refusal of justice. The legal interest constitutes a substantive, and not procedural, premise, hence the decision of the court is based on evaluation of merits and not the formal prerequisites.[115] Following this line of interpretation, excessive interpretation of legal interest would never be deemed as limitation of access to justice. Hence, the qualification of legal interest as substantive measure may have far reaching consequence, putting an end to the discussion.

The purpose of the Declaratory Relief Norm. Declarations are aimed at resolving disputes as to the existence or non-existence of certain rights or legal relationships, providing legal certainty. One could say that they may play a compensatory role, especially in the case of non-material loss.[116] Negative declarations are valued as a defensive measure.[117] They may facilitate settlement, they may allow for settlement of a dispute at an early stage, thus avoiding compounding of the damage. Above all, it must be emphasized, the overall purpose of declaratory relief is inevitably to give claimant a possibility to seek protection of his subjective rights, shaping his legal sphere, which is rooted in substantive civil law.[118] There is nothing extraordinary in this finding – it holds true for the entire realm of civil procedural law, which does not form a teleologically isolated system. The procedural norms are functionally connected with the system of substantive civil norms, guaranteeing their proper implementation.[119] Also, the Declaratory Relief Norm is directed at confirming subjective rights and corresponding duties and, in this way, to protect the subjects of such rights. Even if the Declaratory Relief Norm were to be embedded in the civil code, it will anyway not lose its function, being a metanorm to other substantive norms. It does not constitute a separate substantive right; it only relates to other rights, creating a protective shield over them. The legal interest is included, simply speaking, as a mechanism activating the possibility to use judges' declarations in a situation of threatened or actual breach of the substantive rights. Or, at least, such function of legal interest *prima facie* should have been ascribed to it.

The Declaratory Relief Norm predicated the competence of the claimant to seek protection on his legal interest. If such prerequisite did not exist in law, it would be

114. Judgement of 20 February 2003, I CKN 58/01, Lex 83830 (2003) (Polish Supreme Court) and Judgement of 27 January 2004, II CK 387/02 (2004) (Polish Supreme Court); Judgement of 1 April 2004, II CSK 125/03, unpublished (2004) (Polish Supreme Court).
115. Judgement of 19 March 2015, IV CSK 362/14 (Polish Supreme Court); Judgement of 24 April 2014, III CSK 182/13 (Polish Supreme Court).
116. *See* Annex IV.IV by Nino Sievi *infra*.
117. *Ibid*.
118. *See* Paul Oberhammer, *Kurzkommentar ZPO, Schweizerische Zivilprozessordnung* Art. 88 n. 6. (Paul Oberhammer, Tanja Domej & Ulrich Haas eds, 2013); Maria Jędrzejewska & Karol Weitz, in *Kodeks postępowania cywilnego. Komentarz. Tom I. Postępowanie rozpoznawcze,* n. 1 (Tadeusz Ereciński ed., 4th ed., 2012). Annex I.III[E] by Ulrich Kopetzki, II.IV[B] by Alicja Zielińska-Eisen & Tobias Strecker *infra*.
119. Jodłowski, *supra* n. 62, at 22. Leo Rosenberg, Karl Heinz Schwab & Peter Gottwald, *Zivilprocessrecht* 3 (18th ed., 2018), *See also* section §5.05 *supra*.

clear that always, when the claimant wishes to confirm his legal situation, he may seek such confirmation. Examples of declaratory relief working without the legal interest prerequisite in the Germanic system will be provided below. For the moment, it is worth noting that the examples of English law and arbitration practice confirm that this is not an unusual situation. The question is, then, what is the purpose of introducing such a limitation. Definitely, the separation of claimants who have legal interest from those whose interest is not legal is aimed at limiting claims which, in the view of the court system, are not important, frivolous or fictitious. Therefore, the purpose of the limitation lies in protection of the courts' interests, in the name of the effectiveness and economics of the system of justice in general. This motive is present in all the literature[120] and should be regarded as a very important guideline to interpreting any limitation of the claimant's rights in a very narrow manner, balancing properly economics versus access to justice in order to not mix opportunism of courts with effective usage of the system of justice resources.

J. Korzonek,[121] while writing on the subsidiarity principle aspect of the legal interest, emphasized that it is absolutely reasonable to expect that claimant, who is authorized to seek more, should seek all at once and not to seek part by part. As much is motivated not only by the processual economy requirements, but by the equally important requirement of protection of respondent, since piecemeal seeking of relief may expose respondent to unnecessary harassment or extra costs. Hence, the court will, as rule, reject declaratory relief without hearing the case on the merits. This stance is not reasoned more precisely, being treated as obvious for this author and many others. Arguments to the contrary are offered throughout this whole chapter. What is important to notice at this stage, is striking unbalance between the parties to the proceedings. The protection is aimed at respondent only. It is important to notice also that in no other type of relief the missing legal interest results in such dismissal of the case. Frivolous claims for performance clearly devoid of merits will be, as a rule, dismissed as such on merits, and not for lack of legal interest, and the costs will be borne by such claimant. Clearly, performance or constitutive claims are not aimed at protection of the respondent to the same degree as it appears in declarations. Potentially there might be exceptions, as described below, but they not change the overall picture.

It is interesting how Swiss law switched its approach to protect respondents' interests in terms of negative declarations. For a long time, in the case of negative declarations, the respondent's right to initiate the proceedings at a time convenient for him was protected. In the recent doctrine and subsequent court decision, meanwhile, it was stated very clearly that the assumption that creditors should benefit from the privilege to choose the time of commencement of proceedings is erroneous and results in unequal treatment of the parties.[122]

The Sample Judgement provides us with an additional motive of using legal interest. The court points to the good of the claimant, for whom the performance claim

120. *See* Chapter 2, section §2.14 *supra*.
121. Korzonek & Rosenblüth, *supra* n. 85, at 640; *see also* Chapter 2, section §2.14 *supra*.
122. Annex IV.III[C][4] by Nino Sievi *infra*.

instead of pure declaration is more convenient. It has been demonstrated that in no circumstances the denial of judgement on merits made by the court due to lack of legal interest at any stage of the proceedings could be beneficial to the claimant. This motive should be definitely considered by claimant at the stage of planning the proceedings. For him, in certain situations, bifurcation of proceedings into two separate ones could be more costly but may bring other benefits. In particular, it may open a conciliatory avenue to closing the dispute. Dismissing an actual declaratory claim for missing legal interest might be detrimental both to the claimant and to the respondent, as both of them will be engaged in subsequent proceedings for performance or give unequal benefit to the respondent in case claimant foregoes pursuing the claim anew.

Declaratory relief within the tripartite system of claims. The declaratory relief (*Feststellungsklagen*) in Germanic tradition is one of the three claims which are owed by a claimant in addition to claim for performance (*Leistungsklagen*) and constitutive claims shaping the legal relationship for the future (*Gestaltungsklagen*). Declaratory relief is a special creature as compared with the two others: it is not coercive, it cannot be the subject of enforcement. Due to its nature, it cannot be subject to the statute of limitations.[123] To some extent, it is similar to the claim for performance, because it does not change the reality. Declaration always forms a part of court reasoning leading to the decision on performance, but it is missing the normative part, ordering the respondent to act in a certain way. Claimant is asking for less compared with a claim for performance. The claimant requests that the court ascertains what perception of reality is proper in terms of a certain legal environment, consisting of facts and conduct, legal norms and contractual stipulations. The nature of the relief is to formulate the logical sentence, valued to be true or false.

The 'interest' being attributed to the given party is the central point of the system of law as such. The purpose of each subjective right is to protect the interest of the authorized subject.[124] The purpose of civil procedure is to protect the implementations of the civil subjective rights. Consequently, in each case legal interest - or legitimate interest, as provided in Swiss law - is necessary for a claim to be legitimate. In Swiss law, similar to the French tradition,[125] this principle is explicitly applicable to all claims, irrespective of the type, as provided in Article 59(2)(a) of the Swiss CCP. In other jurisdictions, namely Austria, Germany and Poland, it is implicitly derived from the system of law.

---

123. This feature might cause certain problems. The example is declaration of nullity of arbitration awards, which could be in certain jurisdictions an object of declarations, circumventing the time limitations to file a claim for award annulment.

124. Rudolf von Jhering, *Geist des römischen Rechts auf den verschiedenen Stufen seiner Entwicklung Band 3, Ausgabe 1* 339 (5th ed.,1906).

125. *See* Art. 31 *Nouveau Code de Procédure Civile*: L'action est ouverte à tous ceux qui ont un intérêt légitime au succès ou au rejet d'une prétention, sous réserve des cas dans lesquels la loi attribue le droit d'agir aux seules personnes qu'elle qualifie pour élever ou combattre une prétention, ou pour défendre un intérêt déterminé. https://www.legifrance.gouv.fr/affichCodeArticle.do?idArticle=LEGIARTI000006410125&cidTexte=LEGITEXT000006070716 (accessed 13 January 2019). Article 17 of the Belgian *Code Judiciaire:L'action ne peut être admise si le demandeur n'a pas qualité et intérêt pour la former'*.

In Germany, the 'legal interest' within the framework of the declaratory action is considered as a specific form of the interest in legal protection ('*Rechtsschutzinteresse*') or need of legal protection (*Rechtsschutzbedürfnis*) required with regard to each type of action,[126] the main difference being that, in other types of action, the requirement of interest in legal protection is not expressly mentioned in the respective statutory provisions. It is claimed that, in all categories of action, the interest of legal protection is a prerequisite of admissibility of the action and serves, primarily, the public interest to protect the organization of jurisprudence from abuse as well as, secondarily, the private interest of the defendant to be protected against abusive claims.[127] It appears in very exceptional situation, in case of an action for performance, if only rarely, that the interest in legal protection may be denied on the basis of subsidiarity considerations, i.e., if the goal of the plaintiff could be achieved in an easier way. Thus, a claim for reimbursement of legal fees can be considered as appropriate, as there is a specific procedure for quantifying the cost of the court proceedings (*Kostenfestsetzungsverfahren*).[128] In some cases, the action for performance is even considered as subsidiary in relation to the declaratory action (or at least the declaratory action is not considered as subsidiary to the action for performance), in particular if there are general obstacles of an enforcement of verdict or it may be assumed that the defendant will comply with a verdict without enforcement.[129] Examples of such 'lifting' of subsidiarity of the declaratory action against the action for performance are claims directed against insolvency receivers, insurance establishments, and generally public legal entities.[130] Such examples, albeit important for understanding the notion of claimant's interest, are of marginal use in practice. To the contrary, in case of declaratory relief, the resigning of the subsidiarity principle is marginal. Thus, simplifyng the matter, it may be submitted that subsidiarity principle is a component of legal interest in declaratory relief only.

Even if legal interest is inherent in claims for performance or shaping the legal relationship, it is mostly assumed to exist while the positive regulations require demonstration of claimant's interest only in the declaratory relief. Leaving aside the doctrinal analysis of the notion of interest of the claimant in all three types of claims,[131] the following issues could be interesting from the procedural justice perspective.

It has already been stated while analysing the values and goals of the system of civil procedure that declaratory relief must be valued equally with other forms of relief. In order to introduce this into the system, the requirement of demonstrating legal interest should be equal to all claims. In order to achieve such equality, the legal or legitimate interest prerequisite should be introduced regarding all the claims, as the

126. Reichold, *supra* n. 80, at n. 13. *See also ibid.*, ZPO § 253 no. 26. Ekkehard Becker-Eberhard, in: Münchener *Kommentar zur Zivilprozessordnung I*, ZPO § 253, n. 11 (5th ed., 2016).
127. Cf. Becker-Eberhard, *supra* n. 126, § 253 at n. 11 and n. 12.
128. *Ibid.*, at § 253 n. 25.
129. *Ibid.*, at § 256 n. 55.
130. *Ibid.*, Jacobs, *supra* n. 81, at 73.
131. *See* in this respect Łukasz Błaszczak, *Znaczenie interesu prawnego w poszukiwaniu ochrony prawnej w procesie cywilnym na przykładzie poszczególnych rodzajów powództw*, in *Ius Est A Iustitia Appellatum Księga Jubileuszowa Dedykowana Profesorowi Tadeuszowi Wiśniewskiemu* (Tadeusz Ereciński et al., ed., WKP 2017).

Swiss system does, or carved out in connection with all three types of claim. The concept that, in performance or constitutive claims, the interest is inherent in the particular substantive rights regulated by the civil code and that, in the case of declaratory relief, it is this legal interest which is a substantive basis for a claim is not convincing. In all three types of claims, including the declaration, the underlying right is regulated by the substantive rules. One cannot declare any right which does not arise out of the specific substantive regulation. Hence, the usual explanation that the concept of legal interest protects the court system against frivolous claims cannot stand in this respect. A contrario, missing legal interest as a prerequisite in other types of claims would suggest that frivolous claims for performance or shaping the legal relationship are allowed and acceptable by the system.

'Frivolous claims' does not necessarily mean that the interest of the party is frivolous, but might be that its formulation is vague or not clear enough to serve as a basis for the declaration. If we agree with this line of argument, it must be admitted that, if *prima facie* a declaration is followed by the request specified in monetary or other specific way, it becomes more real indeed.

The problem of relief being insufficiently specific was presented with arbitration practice as an example[132]. Such matters tend to be handled by arbitrators in quite a flexible way, considering the utility on one hand and *ultra petita* principle on the other. Comparing the three types of claims, it should be noted that the problem of clarity is not necessarily related only to the declarations. Not every performance claim is specified in quantitative terms of money. The same problem of certainty relates to performance claims seeking certain acts by respondent and claims seeking shaping the legal relationship anew, however they are not predicated by proving legal interest ahead of consideration of the merits.

The interest in declaration of subjective right and interest in subjective right per se. The need for subjectivization of the legal interest in terms of understanding the notion of interest in its semantic dimension has been analysed earlier. Now the legal interest will be juxtaposed with the interest in the subjective right per se. It has been emphasized in the literature that legal interest of the claimant must have a clear, objective character. This means that the need to receive the declaration must be objectively legitimate. Consequently, the subsidiarity principle stems from the objective character of the legal interest. If the claimant can have other relief at his disposal, he does not have an objective interest in obtaining a declaration. Further, if the declaration sought does not resolve the dispute entirely, he objectively has no legal interest. The objectivity in this respect does not apply to the given case but to the whole array of problems which constitute, or might constitute, a dispute sensu largo. The problem of objectivity in this respect raises a number of concerns.

As was mentioned earlier, procedures do not exist just for themselves – their role is to guarantee the proper implementation of subjective rights (*subjektives Recht*). In substantive civil law, ascertaining that certain performance on the side of the debtor was delivered correctly, and in particular in accordance with the terms and conditions

132. *See* Chapter 4, section §4.04.[D].

of the given civil law obligation, requires analysis from the perspective of its goal. Satisfaction of the interest of the creditor is the goal of such performance. When implementing his performance, the debtor is obligated to act for the standardized good of the creditor. This good must, of course, be societally accepted, however it is enough to say that only societally accepted goals are considered here. Therefore, the debtor's performance can be deemed properly executed if he acted in accordance with the terms and conditions of the contract, resulting in creditor's interest being fulfilled.[133] It follows from the above that the interest of the creditor, however standardized, still qualifies as a subjective interest. Standardization is necessary for the debtor to assess the legitimate expectations of the creditor in a given relationship.

One of the consequences of the above is the fact that it is the creditor who, as it were, defines and controls the claim. He may claim the entire debt or only a part, if his subjective interest will be secured with such partial settlement. This creditor autonomy rooted in substantive law should be then realized to the largest extent within the civil proceedings, and the concept of legal interest is a restriction of this autonomy. The Germanic concept of legal interest does not protect such interest and, to some extent, is illogical. The procedural norms allow for seeking partial performance, but not for partial declaration. The system does not recognize that the interest of the claimant may focus on non-coercive measure and that it may suffice for his individual needs to have his rights declared. There is a number of arbitration cases which show that such a need is nothing extraordinary. Therefore, analysing legal interest of a party in the context of objective assessment of all the circumstances through the prism of present and prospective future relationships[134] instead of evaluating the present, individual and real needs of the claimant, does not allow full implementation of the subjective civil rights. The same relates to the subsidiarity principle. Application of this principle allows assessment of the claimant's situation in its entirety, with the court assuming the role of a legal advisor, choosing the most effective, in the opinion of the court, way to resolve the entire situation instead of focusing on the particular need of the claimant expressed in his statement of claim.

It is assumed that civil proceedings are aimed at protection and implementation of civil subjective rights, that they should implement to the fullest extent the autonomy of the will of the parties, including the autonomy in finding the way how creditor's interest should be realized, within the limits of contractual stipulations and substantive contractual norms. At the procedural level, this interest can be realized equally by declaratory as well as performance order relief. Interpretation of the term 'legal interest', allowing the judge to decide for the claimant, what is more comfortable and easier from the perspective of protecting claimant's rights, save from exceptional situations, is simply depriving him of this autonomy.

Subjective perception of the existence of controversy. Another vexing question relates to the notion of the term 'controversy' or 'a dispute', located as a foundation of a legal interest. The party has no legal interest in seeking a declaration if there is no

133. Piotr Machnikowski, *Swoboda umów według art. 353 [1] KC, Konstrukcja prawna* 77–78 (2005).
134. Judgement of 22 October 2014, II CSK 687/13 (2014) (Polish Supreme Court); Judgement of 27 January 2004, II CK 387/02 (2004) (Polish Supreme Court).

controversy as between the parties and his case will be dismissed. The perception of what is controversy as between the parties is much dependent on the approach to be adopted in the given case, which may more or less subjective/objective. The 'controversy' criterion is treated differently in declaratory relief as compared with others. In general, the situation in which respondent does not actively defend his position, including preparing submissions and not showing up at hearings, does not mean that there is no dispute between the parties. An even more striking stance is adopted when respondent agrees with the legitimacy of the performance or constitutive claim and the court is faced with the phenomenon of admission of claim. As a rule, admission of a claim by respondent results in final determination of the case by the judge, causing eventual consequences in the decision on costs to be reimbursed to the respondent. There is a prevailing opinion that admission of claim does not mean that there is no dispute between the parties:

> if a claimant was forced to submit a claim to the court against the respondent, it evidences by itself that respondent questioned the claimant's right and his corresponding duty or did not fulfil his duty, without questioning it.[135] [translation by author]

It is striking how meaningful the mere fact of initiation of the proceedings becomes in a performance claim while being completely meaningless in the case of a declaratory claim. There is no good argument militating for such a dual regime. Protection of the system of justice or respondent only in case of one type of claims leads to unjustified differences. If one assumes rationality of a party claiming performance, so that he will not, as a rule, spend money on legal advice and court fees to pursue useless claims, the same assumption surely applies in the case of declaratory claims.

The subsidiarity principle. The objective interpretation of the legal interest prescribes also analysis whether a declaration is the fastest and most efficient way of achieving the assumed goal. The traditional view is that the subsidiarity principle has its roots in a general mistrust against the intentions of the claimant filing a declaratory relief in a situation where a performance relief could be applied for. As the general goal of civil proceedings is the implementation of subjective substantive rights, the fact that the claimant chooses a type of proceedings which is objectively a less effective instrument to achieve this goal indicates that the claimant's intention is not the effective protection of these rights but something else which is not covered by the overall goal of civil proceedings. The claimant's goal itself is also filtered through the exercise of objectivization. It appears that, as analysed by the courts, this problem is reduced to the three types of goals underlying the tripartite classification of claims, with little regard for the rich variety of human motives informing civil law relations.[136]

This way of thinking drove the interpretation of the legal interest to the subsidiarity principle, which is not *expressis verbis* included in a positive norm, being purely interpretational. The mere possibility of seeking performance based on a given cause of action excludes the existence of legal interest to seek only a declaration of right

135. Jerzy Jodłowski, *supra* n. 62, at 38.
136. *See* more earlier in this chapter on purpose of the declaratory relief.

or legal relationship. The subsidiarity principle interpretation has expanded into a general prohibition against seeking a declaration if there exists any other alternative and equivalent (and not superior) relief. Application of the subsidiarity principle leads to a situation where declaratory relief appears to be a remedy less valued than others, and one which is not allowed in cases where a more comprehensive remedy is available. Further, such objectivization accepts arbitrariness of the court, not considering what was already noted about how, teleologically, the claim for declaration and a claim for performance cover different needs and lead to achievement of various goals, with conciliation in the dispute resolution possibly being one of them. This rule deprives the claimant of the choice among the remedies open to the claimant under the law, shifting onto the court full discretion to decide what goals the claimant should pursue, and which procedural way should be undertaken by her. Such a paternalistic approach might have been understandable in the nineteenth century but cannot stand in light of the procedural principle of party-disposition, i.e., one of the guiding principles of modern civil litigation according to which the civil proceedings are regarded as the parties' province. It is the party who should make dispositions in her proceedings, including not only commencement and termination or determination of the matters of facts, but also which route is the most convenient for her. The judge should be finally bound by the parties' motions, especially if they are of a procedural, not substantive nature. The principle of party-disposition is a procedural reflection of the substantive principle of party autonomy and is a part of the general functional correlation between the civil procedure and civil substantive law.[137]

The subsidiarity principle as a component of the legal interest concept escapes the logic of the system of civil procedure also in another way. The traditional understanding of the principle assumes that, if a party may seek performance, i.e., if all elements of the claim are in place, then declaratory relief is forbidden. Objectively, claimant should not be in need of a declaration being granted if he can claim not only declaration, but also fulfilment of the respective act (usually being payment of a receivable). This objectivization of the legal interest pushes its own logic into a systemic trap. If we juxtapose the declaratory claim with the claim for performance in the setting where subsidiarity principle applies, it is clear that the cause of action in performance claim consists of a cause of action in declaratory claim plus a coercive element. In each case where subsidiarity principle is to be applied, the interest of the claimant in granting a declaration is always included in the scope of the interest in granting a performance order. Ergo, if interest in a performance claim is deemed to be legally acceptable, the interest in declaration should be perfectly admissible as well –

137. *See* Principle 10, ALI / UNIDROIT Principles of Transnational Civil Procedure, https://www.unidroit.org/instruments/transnational-civil-procedure (accessed 13 January 2019); Jerzy Jodłowski, *supra* n. 62, at 137; German procedural law doctrine establishes as one of the basic principles the rule of the parties ('*Parteiherrschaft*') consisting in the negotiation or submission principle ('*Verhandlungsgrundsatz*', '*Beibringungsgrundsatz*') meaning that the parties determine the scope of facts being the basis of the court decision and the disposition principle ('*Dispositionsmaxime*' or '*Verfügungsgrundsatz*') meaning that the parties delimit the subject matter of the proceedings.

the claimant is simply asking for less. Applying *argumentum a majori ad minus*, the subsidiarity principle runs against the logic of the system.

Summing up, the subsidiarity principle cannot be derived from the content of the Declaratory Norm and is inconsistent with the basic principles of the civil procedure and civil substantive law, with the result that declarations are a less valuable remedy than the two others. As the Sample Case shows, it results in injustice to both of the parties, as it might cause further trials, meaning more effort and more expenditure to the claimant and respondent unless the claimant foregoes resolution of the case altogether.

The *ex officio* consideration of legal interest prerequisite. The legal interest as a prerequisite is taken into consideration by the court prior to analysis of the case on merits and *ex officio*. It can cause dismissal of the case regardless whether any of the parties raises the issue. The court may dismiss the case based on missing interest at every, even advanced stage of the proceedings. This is a typical feature of this relief in all Germanic jurisdictions.[138] As has been raised in section §2.13 *supra*, Swiss practice adopted the opposite principle under which the courts do not consider missing interest of the claimant unless it is raised by the opponent. It must be emphasized, however, that this pragmatic approach is contrary to the clear regulation of Article 59(2)(a) of the Swiss CCP.

The consequences of the *ex officio* mechanism are observed in the Sample Case and unquestionably may lead to unjust results. There are two issues important in this respect. First, considering legal interest as a ban to consideration of the case on merits without initiative of any of the parties leads to unpredictability of the process, which by itself contravenes procedural justice. The party is surprised by this factor and is not necessarily asked to comment on it.[139] Second, it is a questionable practice in light of the basic precept of giving justice to both parties. In the case of the *ex officio* regime, the respondent is granted a privileged position. Third, the degree of such unpredictability is increased by the fact that the notion of the legal interest is vague and not intuitive. Such factors which are, as a rule, considered by the court *ex officio* like exclusion of the general jurisdiction of the domestic courts, *res judicata*, lis pendens, or lacking legal capacity of the party are much more specific.

In Polish civil procedure, at the appeal level, the basic *criterium divisionis* is whether the given factor relates to the procedure or to the merits of the case.[140] All elements relating to the merits are taken into consideration *ex officio*, a consequence of the old juridical principles *da mihi factum, dabo tibi ius* as well as *facta probantur, iura novit curia*. It follows from this that simple reclassification of legal interest from

138. *See* Chapter 2, section §2.13 *supra*.

139. It must be noted, however, that under German civil procedural law, the court, which would tend to dismiss an action for declaratory relief due to lack of 'legal interest' although the parties have not raised this issue, would be obliged to give notice to such fact to the parties and give them the opportunity to make statements on that issue and adapt their strategy to it – § 139 II German CCP. This obligation of the court, as a rule, would reduce the unpredictability of such dismissals of the claim. Similarly § 182a of the Austrian CCP. *See also* Chapter 2, section §2.13 *supra*.

140. *See* Resolution of seven Judges of the Polish Supreme Court – legal principle of 31 January 2008, III CZP 49/07, OSNC 2008/6/55, Lex 341125 (2008) (Polish Supreme Court).

substantive to a procedural factor amounts to a dramatic change in that all procedural features, save for those causing invalidity of the proceedings, are considered only upon a party's initiative. As can be seen in the Swiss example, such reclassification could be caused by simple pragmatism and not by the very nature of legal interest itself.

There is a number of arguments which might support abandoning the *ex officio* regime in favour of recognition of missing legal interest in declaratory relief, including its unpredictability, unreasonable restrictiveness and lack of cohesion. These are arguments which, in general, support redefinition of the notion of legal interest, or ditching this prerequisite totally, and not only rethinking the limits of court powers. The most persuasive argument, however, relates to lack of legal requirement to demonstrate the legal interest in two other types of claims. If there is no harm in the performance claim and the constitutive claim, the same should apply to the declaratory claim, at least in the area of leaving this to the defensive initiative of respondent, similarly as is done in the case of the objection based on the statute of limitations or jurisdiction of arbitration tribunals. The practice of Swiss courts confirms that such a pragmatic approach is nothing extraordinary.

Quasi declaratory relief. Judicial declaration is a valuable instrument in achieving goals in protection of civil substantive rights. Human creativity has presented alternative solutions which help to achieve similar goals in the event that certain difficulties are encountered, the problems with legal interest indeed. I would call them, in aggregate, 'quasi declaratory reliefs'.

In English law, A. Burrows classifies nominal damages, contemptuous damages and declaratory relief into one group of claims.[141] Nominal damages are in no sense compensatory. Their function is merely to declare that the defendant committed a wrong against the claimant and hence that the claimant's rights have been infringed. Even if the court is satisfied that the claimant did not suffer any harm, it is still entitled to the damages, representing a trivial sum of money, for the defendant's breach of contract or tort actionable per se, i.e., not requiring proof of damage. Such damages are usually at the level of 2–10 pounds. Contemptuous damages are usually awarded in defamation cases, and they reach the lowest of a realm, which is 1 penny. Their function is to admit the alleged wrong of the defendant, but nothing more because of the claimants' own conduct. Such awards amount to a declaration of the claimant's right combined with an admonition of the claimant.

In Germanic jurisdictions, it is accepted practice to claim a small fraction of a monetary claim in order to receive a quasi-declaration of legal rights, which is allowed under positive rules of law[142] or due to general principle of party – disposition in the civil proceedings.[143] This a useful instrument to test the claim at lower costs, due to

141. Andrew Burrows, *Remedies for Torts and Breach of Contract* 489–593 (2009).
142. Article 86 of the Swiss CCP.
143. Judgement of 25 April 2014, II CSK 417/13, Lex 1486970 (2014) (Polish Supreme Court). The German Civil Procedure Code also does not explicitly regulate the action for a partial award ('*Teilklage*'), it is, however, a generally accepted practice – in order to reduce the cost risk – to limit the claim to a part of the alleged claim, and – after obtaining a favourable verdict – to demand additional amounts – cf. Othmar Jauernig & Burkhard Hess, *Zivilprozessrecht* 250 et seq. (30th ed., 2011).

limitation of the value of the claim. If the judgement is positive, then the subsequent, 'full' claim can be filed. What is interesting from the perspective of this discourse, no legal interest is necessary to be proved at the outset of the proceedings, even if the sense of a partial claim is clearly to declare a certain right or a legal relationship.

Awards of a fraction of the main claim are useful as they allow to avoid proving legal interest, what would be impossible in terms of subsidiarity principle. On the contrary, they are subject to the statute of limitations, as any other relief, and do not enjoy the *res judicata* effect. As observed by the authors of the reports included in the annex, this *res judicata* may be observed in subsequent proceedings claiming the rest of the sum, as a practical matter, if no new facts or assertions appear. In Poland, this approach was confirmed by a Supreme Court judgement.[144] Nevertheless, the normative feature of *res judicata* is not available.

Among quasi declaratory awards, different types of preliminary or partial awards can be included.[145] In the case of bifurcated proceedings, their aim is to declare existence of legal rights or legal relationships, and in particular breach of the contract that creates new compensatory rights, before moving to the quantum phase. Systemically, no legal interest is to be attributed to the claimant in this case, as a performance claim by definition enjoys legal interest. If, however, the preliminary or partial ruling denies the claim in principle, it becomes the final ruling in the proceedings, being of a declaratory nature only. The resulting conclusion is that any judgement of the court (save for the bifurcated proceedings) dismissing the claim is of a declaratory nature.

The above examples of quasi declaratory measures indicate the artificiality of delimitation of declaratory relief by the legal interest concept. This is a further argument that legal interest is not an inherent component of a declaratory relief, as concerning its nature, so that it cannot exist without it. Quite on the contrary, it is visibly an extrinsic factor, added to regulate the flow of statements of claim. As the below analysis might show, the economics of the cases demonstrate that this is not really necessary.

Declarations not requiring the legal interest proved. In a number of declarations, the legal interest is not required to be demonstrated at all. Special exclusions are provided by statutory law. In class actions, seeking monetary claims by members of the group can be done by way of declaratory relief. Contrary to the general rules, here the legislature found it expedient to have declarations serve as a mere premise to other proceedings and treated declaration on an equal basis with other remedies.[146]

An interesting concept of incident declaratory relief is provided in German law. The claimant may seek declaration of the legal relationship in the same proceedings in which performance arising from such legal relationship is sought.[147] Therefore, the court may, within a single award, contain both the declaration and the coercive order

144. Resolution of 29 March 1994, III CZP 29/94, Lex 84472 (1994) (Polish Supreme Court).
145. *See* Annex, I.VI by Ulrich Kopetzki; II.9 by Alicja Zielińska-Eisen & Tobias Strecker, IV.V. by Nino Sievi *infra*.
146. Annex III.VI[A] by Beata Gessel-Kalinowska vel Kalisz & Joanna Kisielinska-Garncarek *infra*.
147. Annex II.VI[B] by Alicja Zielińska-Eisen & Tobias Strecker *infra*.

in the dispositive part. The legal interest requirement is not required, as it is subsumed under the performance claim anyway.

In matters relating to labour law, the relevant exceptions aimed at liberalization or exclusion of the legal interest requirement may be provided by statute[148] or by court practice.[149]

One may say that the above examples do not amount to exclusion of the legal interest requirement. Legal interest is mandated in specific provisions of substantive regulations. Nevertheless, in such cases the subsidiarity principle does not apply.[150]

In corporate disputes aimed at declaring validity or invalidity of resolutions, the specified group of claimants, namely members of the corporate bodies, may seek a declaration without proving any prerequisite.[151] Other persons who are qualified as third parties vis a vis the corporate entities are obliged to demonstrate their legal interest. This is a very good example where the concept of 'interest' as a prerequisite to declaration is reasonably grounded. Third parties to the legal relationship being declared inevitably must prove their need to have the declaration granted.

Summary. There has been a number of arguments relating to teleology and systemic incoherence of the legal interest presented above. The declaratory claim, together with the performance claim and the constitutive claim, is one of the three basic claims available to the claimant under civil procedure law. Considering such underlying tenets of the civil procedure as access to justice, protection of the civil substantive rights and support to non-coercive measures, declarations should be treated on an equal basis as compared with the other two, not just as a supplement. Civil procedure, while protecting the civil substantive rights, should secure also full implementation of the autonomy of will principle, as provided by the civil substantive laws. One of the manifestations of this issue should be more leeway to choose the measure which will best serve the needs of the claimant. This, in turn, assumes more thorough understanding of what 'legality' of the interest should mean and more subjective approach to such needs, including what is meant by terms such as 'controversy', 'final settlement of a dispute' or 'endangerment of claimant's legal position'. The subsidiarity principle, by definition, deprives the parties of their right to choose the appropriate protective measure, which is also against the general right of disposition in civil proceedings. The subsidiarity principle combined with possibility of the courts to dismiss the claim *sua sponte* results in lack of predictability and cohesion of the system. Final arguments relate to the examples of the quasi declaratory reliefs and examples of declarations, for which juridical construction does not require proving legal interest at the outset, confirming that legal interest is not an intrinsic component of the declaration whatsoever.

148. Annex I.III[E] by Ulrich Kopetzki *infra*.
149. Annex III.VI[C] by Beata Gessel-Kalinowska vel Kalisz & Joanna Kisielinska-Garncarek *infra*.
150. Annex I.III[E] by Ulrich Kopetzki *infra*.
151. Annex III.VI[B] by Beata Gessel-Kalinowska vel Kalisz & Joanna Kisielinska-Garncarek *infra*; II.VI[C] by Alicja Zielińska-Eisen & Tobias Strecker *infra*, Annex I.III[E] by Ulrich Kopetzki *infra*.

§5.08 BALANCING PROCEDURAL JUSTICE WITH EFFECTIVENESS

Basic principles of law, procedural justice included, by their nature are not, and indeed should not, be clearly defined. This makes for salutary flexibility in their application. Balancing certain principles, having the values of the system of justice as a background, is therefore always a necessary exercise while deciding a particular case.

The principles of law are basic to securing justice in the legal system.[152] Contrary to legal norms, they can be fulfilled in a greater or lesser degree, so collision of principles may appear, in which case priority of the given principle must be assessed. The principles of appropriateness, of necessity and of proportionality are helpful in sorting out appropriate priorities in case fulfilment of one principle leads to non-fulfilment – to put it differently, whenever one principle is only realizable at the cost of another.[153] As has already been stated, access to justice and procedural justice are undoubtedly regarded as superior and overwhelming principles of civil procedure. Procedural justice must be regarded as a metaprinciple which, in addition to its own features, is also a forum for alignment of other principles and their optimization.[154] Introducing certain limitations is compliant with procedural justice if such limitations are caused by the essence and goals of procedural justice itself. On the contrary, while procedural justice is often deemed to be a value by itself, the processual efficiency is not.[155]

So, access to justice cannot be, and never is, unlimited by its nature. Access to justice is access to justice duly shaped. Limitations may be derived from other principles and social values, like ensuring legal security or trust in the system of justice.[156] Therefore, processual economy and efficiency, which enforces certain limitations, have axiological justifications, and are geared at enhancement of the right to access to justice and not its weakening. Enhancement means, generally, rationalization of proceedings by making them more expeditious. One must admit that justice delayed is justice denied. Most of discussions on revision of the civil procedures is concentrated on finding a balance between reducing the excessive length and high costs of the proceedings on one hand and improving the administration of justice on the other.[157] That said, enhancement of effectiveness should not be done at the cost of depriving parties of their rights to have their case decided.

152. Ronald Dworkin, *Taking rights seriously* 22 (1987).
153. Alexy, *supra* n. 45, at 297–298.
154. Judgement of 11 March 2003, SK 8/02, Dz. U. 2003/52 item 468, 11 (2003) (Polish Constitutional Tribunal); Alexy, *supra* n. 45, at 297–298.
155. Judgement of 26 February 2008, SK 89/06, OTK ZU 2008/1A/7 (2008) (Polish Constitutional Tribunal); Judgement of 29 April 2008, SK 11/07, OTK ZU 47/3/A/2008 (2008) (Polish Constitutional Tribunal); Judgement of 1 July 2008, SK 40/07, OTK ZU 101/6/A/2008 (2008) (Polish Constitutional Tribunal); Judgement of 21 July 2009, K. 7/09, OTK ZU 113/7/A/2009 (2009) (Polish Constitutional Tribunal).
156. Judgement of 26 February 2008, SK 89/06, OTK ZU 2008/1A/7 (2008) (Polish Constitutional Tribunal).
157. Tzankova & Gramatikov, *supra* n. 62, at 424.

Any restrictions of the access to justice founded on economy must be carefully examined and narrowly interpreted. Otherwise, it may transgress from procedural rationality towards the opportunism of the judges.[158]

The argument of economy supporting introduction of legal interest with the aim to limit unnecessary claims does not stand up to critical analysis. First, dismissing the claim at the appeal instance, as our Sample Case demonstrates, leads to the initiation of consecutive proceedings, eliminating the economy factor or discouraging the claimant from seeking justice at all. Neither consequence can be accepted.

There is also a question of the economics behind the partial/preliminary judgements in bifurcated proceedings as compared with simple declaratory judgement. It is not necessarily saving time and money by forcing the parties to engage in regular proceedings which, under certain circumstances, might be bifurcated. Saving time and money does not always mean that savings derive from the fact of having one proceeding instead of two. Savings will also be achieved for the parties and for the court alike if they do not have to prepare submissions to be analysed by the court on quantum or other matters which could conveniently be analysed in the subsequent proceedings. This is not always a viable option, but it is a possibility deserving of consideration. The concept of automatic limitation of declaratory claims under the label of legal interest does not reflect on this aspect of processual economy.

No argument has been offered supporting the thesis that liberalization of legal interest criteria, or simply abandoning them, will result in an unreasonably high number of declaratory cases submitted to the court. To the contrary, Polish statistics show that the total number of declaratory claims compared with other claims constitute circa 0.1% in the case of regional courts[159] and circa 0.5% in the case of district courts.[160] Even if one assumes a freezing effect of the restrictive and unpredictable regulations of declaratory relief (absence of which would certainly increase the number of claims), it is difficult to picture a pending flood of cases. As J.R. Searle rightly points out, while rules are codified by the lawyers, most users of the system of justice are unaware of this codification. For this demographic, any liberalization of the criteria might not have any effect, or a negligible effect at most.[161] In certain sectors of business where declarations are highly valued, the increase will be higher than in others.[162]

Reasonableness of the parties must be considered here. It is difficult to assume that the parties will choose this procedural path if they do not have a serious interest in the declaration to be granted. This is, paradoxically, a matter of economy, and not

158. Koncewicz, *supra* n. 26, at 173 et seq.
159. Gessel-Kalinowska vel Kalisz, *supra* n. 57, at 14.
160. *Ibid.*, at 15.
161. Searle, *supra* n. 86, at 128.
162. In my examination of arbitration awards, I have estimated that in M&A cases, circa 16% of cases include declaratory relief, together with other relief or not, *see* Chapter 4 above. This means that, in this business segment, this type of relief is valued and used significantly. On the other hand, in the period of 2010–2014, only twenty cases were identified in which the 'declaratory relief' and 'legal interest' stood together. This does not mean that this is the overall number of declaratory reliefs in the given period of time; there are presumably a great deal of cases, here simply the tribunal did not use the express word 'declaratory' jointly with 'legal interest'.

the legal interest limitation. Nobody will pay twice and proceed twice, doubling her effort, in claiming first a declaration and then, subsequently, performance if her interest is strictly and only in performance.

An interesting observation has been made in respect of the German situation. The validity of the whole protective concept in times of declining numbers of lawsuits could be questioned. In the years 2004 to 2017, the number of newly filed civil actions in Germany has decreased by more than one-third, from 1,938,741 actions in 2004[163] to only 1,244,697 in 2017.[164] Nevertheless, the courts have continued to apply this principle essentially with no alteration.[165]

The putative diluvial effect was also a concern present in United Kingdom when the decision was taken to fully liberate the possibilities for claim declarations under CPR 40.20. In *Midland Land Reclamation v Warren Energy*, the declaration that claimant was entitled to terminate the contract was denied, since if it was granted, it could cause a flood of applications for parties seeking comfort that they were entitled to terminate contracts. This stance was not shared, however, as given the costs of litigation, this concern was unlikely to materialize.[166] The most significant case in this respect is the so-called Arrow declaration.[167] Here, the court held that, while it had no jurisdiction to make any declarations relating to the validity of a certain patent because the patent was never granted in the UK and the court did not have jurisdiction over the foreign designations, it did have jurisdiction to grant declarations in relation to the obviousness of the applicant's own product. This case was evaluated in the subsequent case *Fujifilm v AbbVie*,[168] where the court was not persuaded by respondent that declarations in the Arrow form will open any floodgates. The Arrow decision was of some age by then and had not resulted in many such cases being brought. In *Gouriet v Union of Post Office Workers*, the flood argument was dismissed by the court as 'illusory'.[169] The argument of opening floodgates was raised in the series of cases constituting the *Nokia v InterDigital* litigation saga, likewise with no success.[170]

Summing up, the argument of economic efficiency has been widely used since the moment of introduction of the declaratory relief into the body of the code of civil procedure in Germany in the nineteenth century. There was no persuasive argument to

163. *Statistisches Bundesamt (Destatis), Rechtspflege, Zivilgerichte 2012*, at 13 & 37 (2013).
164. *Statistisches Bundesamt (Destatis), Rechtspflege, Zivilgerichte 2017*, at 13 & 43 (2018).
165. Annex, II.III.[B] by Alicja Zielińska-Eisen & Tobias Strecker *infra*.
166. *Midland Land Reclamation Ltd, Leicestershire CC v Warren Energy Ltd* [1997] ABC.L.R. 01/20 (English High Court), *see* Woolf & Woolf, *supra* n. 69, at 129.
167. **487 Arrow Generics Ltd and Another v Merck & Co Inc* [2007] EWHC 1900 (Pat).
168. *Fujifilm Kyowa Kirin Biologics Company Limited, Samsung Bioepsis UK Limited and Biogen IDEC Limited v AbbVie Biotechnology Limited* [2017] EWHC 395 (Pat), 377 (English High Court), quoting appeal judgement **228 Fujifilm Kyowa Kirin Biologics Co Ltd v AbbVie Biotechnology Ltd* [2017] EWCA Civ 1, 95 (English Court of Appeal).
169. *Gouriet v Union of Post Office Workers* [1978] AC 435, 458 (House of Lords).
170. *Nokia Corp v InterDigital Technology Corp (Application to Set Aside)* [2006] EWCA Civ 1618, 21–22 (English Court of Appeal); *InterDigital Technology Corp v Nokia Corp* [2008] EWHC 504 (Pat), 19–20 (Chancery Division); *Nokia Corp v InterDigital Technology Corp* [2006] EWHC 802 (Pat), 27 (English High Court), *Nokia Corporation v Interdigital Technology Corporation* [2007] EWHC 3077 (Pat), 139 (English High Court).

support it. Quite on the contrary, the statistical data presented above as well as the English law example show that this concern is no longer valid.

§5.09 FINAL CONCLUSIONS

Declaratory relief as a valuable measure. Civil law subjects may have a whole variety of needs, which may be realized in different ways. In substantive civil law, the basic instrument which allows for searching and creating customized solutions in the form of specific legal relationships and creating legal rights is the autonomy of the will of the parties. Civil procedure is created with the goal to protect and guarantee such creativity, provided it is not contrary to the *ius cogens* of the given substantive legal order. There are three basic types of remedies which civil law subjects may use in order to enforce their legal rights: action for performance relief, action for constitutive relief and, finally, action for a declaration. There is no convincing argument for treating one of them, declaratory relief, in a different way than the others. The obvious precept of procedural justice requires treating like cases alike.[171] Declaratory relief is as valuable an instrument as others. The problem is, however, that the needs of the parties which are to be realized in the proceedings aimed at declarations are not perceived by the judiciary as they really are. The parties seek declaratory relief to ascertain their legal positions, to clarify their rights and obligations, and to determine whether they are bound by contracts or other legal instruments. Declaratory awards are meant to enable the parties to settle their disputes early on, quickly and cost-effectively, before they suffer more extensive damage. By clarifying the strengths and weaknesses of the parties' legal positions and establishing legal certainty, declaratory awards may facilitate settlement. In some cases, a declaration of rights and liabilities alone can be a sufficient measure of satisfaction. There is nothing wrong that, in certain cases where purely declaratory relief proves to be insufficient, the winning party may later rely on the declaratory award in seeking monetary or injunctive relief. Common law solutions, as provided in Article 40.20 of the CPR or 2201 of US Declaratory Judgement Act are convincing examples in this respect. Declarations are a useful device where the parties have a continuing relationship and want to resolve what is, in the greater scheme of things, a minor dispute without risking the relationship as a whole by demands for monetary compensation. All these needs are not properly reflected in the current definition of legal interest prerequisite in Germanic legal systems.

'Legal interest' concept in the context of access to justice principle. The aim of the analysis contained herein was to establish whether the concept of legal interest is compliant with the principles which can be derived from the notion of access to justice and procedural justice. The analysis is not easy, and complete clarity is elusive, because both said principles and the concept of legal interest belong to category of constructs which cannot be clearly defined and, therefore, remain dependent on the context of historical, personal and social perceptions. Empirical studies show that individuals are more satisfied with the outcome of the proceedings and are more

171. Hart, *supra* n. 50, at 159 et seq.

willing to obey, if they value the proceedings as fair.[172] There are many ways of interpreting what is 'legal', what is 'interest' and what is 'just'. In the case of the latter, the meaning of what is just was a bit more specified, as it was relating only to one instrument, which is declaratory relief. The starting point for the analysis was the Sample Judgement. A fair result in the Sample Judgement would be a final decision on the merits by the Polish Supreme Court. Dismissing the case must be regarded as denial of access to court. Referring back to Rawls, if one knows what a fair result is, one can construct a fair procedure.

Yet the analysis leads to the conclusion that actual interpretation of the legal interest is too restrictive, not catching the true import of the terms 'legal interest', 'legal right' and 'legal relationship' as objects of declaration. Interest of the parties seeking declaration of legal right or legal relationship is, as a rule, legal, as it is derivative of the object of declaration. On the contrary, the ultimate nature of interest of the parties seeking declarations is always non-legal, because a legal instrument is always a tool for realization of certain non-legal interest. It is also unnecessary to excessively objectivize the notion of legal interest, as this leads to neglecting real needs of the civil law subjects, realization of which is secured by the substantive law. Excessive objectivization of legal interest resulted in introduction of subsidiarity principle, whose artificial nature is alienated from the legitimate needs of the parties. All these factors were aimed at limitation of access to courts, and they do not serve goals other than economy of the proceedings.

Actual interpretation of the legal interest is too vague and too flexible. The notion of legal interest, as opposed to factual or economic interest, is difficult to comprehend because it departs from an ungrounded premise. The example of dual understanding of what is legal and economic in terms of *actio Pauliana* (fraudulent conveyance claims) and relevant declaratory relief[173] is a good example. The same illegibility concerns the problem of proper delimitation of brute facts and facts underlying certain rights or legal relationships. The subsidiarity principle imposes an obligation of weighing different remedies without giving importance to the real needs of the claimant, which ought to be the basic criterion for such evaluation. Without recognition of the relevant needs, the subsidiarity principle is flexible in application.

Actual interpretation of the legal interest concept does not follow the logic of the entire system of civil law, if considering both substantive and procedural laws together and also within the realm of procedure only. As concerns the first dimension, the actual interpretation of legal interest, and in particular the subsidiarity principle, does not allow full implementation of the autonomy of the parties' intent as guaranteed by the substantive law and as reflected anyway in the procedural principle of party-disposition. The regulation of legal principle is also not coherent within the system of legal remedies. This is the only remedy where the legal interest must be demonstrated as a prerequisite; in the case of the two others, legal interest is essentially assumed to exist by the very fact of submission of the claim to the court. It is persuasive that, in each case, legality of interest is derived from the particular regulation of the claimed

172. John Thibault & Laurens Walker, *Procedural Justice: A Psychological Analysis* n. 14 (1975).
173. Section §5.07 *supra*.

right, whether in an action for performance or for declaration. Examples of declaratory reliefs where legal interest is not necessary to be proved demonstrate that this prerequisite is not an intrinsic feature.

On the margin of this analysis, it must be noted that the problem of fairness to the parties so emphasized in English jurisprudence, or the problem of good faith as raised in arbitration, does not receive much attention in Germanic doctrine. It is signalled only while discussing legal interest as a protection of the courts, that it simultaneously may serve as a protection of respondents against unnecessary claims. The Swiss doctrine seems to explore this issue more in depth as compared with other jurisdictions on the occasion of, *inter alia*, negative declarations. The novelty is the Swiss approach to equality of rights of both parties in the case of declarations and not the protection of the respondent only. All in all, the current interpretation of the legal interest leads to abnormal unpredictability, which is compounded by the possibility of considering this prerequisite *ex officio* by the courts.

All these features result in excessive limitation of the civil law subjects' access to justice, as confirmed by statistical data. The arguments explaining such limitation used to be rooted by literature and jurisprudence in the economy of the proceedings and in the desire to prevent a flood of frivolous claims. Yet no persuasive arguments or statistics were offered to support such arguments; quite the opposite, it appears that there is no such risk. Following the bounded rationality paradigm, it must be assumed that parties to the dispute are rational and would make their decision to enter into the proceedings based on assessment of what outcome may be achieved.[174] Opinions supporting legal interest as a barrier against unlimited flow of declaratory requests assume, that the mere possibility to file such a request will be enough for a prospective claimant to do it. Such assumption is wrong. The undertaken behaviour is, as a rule, limited not only by external conditions and constraints, which in this case would be the potential liberty to seek a declaration. The claimant decision will be based also on intrinsic factors resulting from individual processing all available data, including timing, cost and utility of the expected outcome. Entering into two proceedings, one for declaration and one for coercive measure, shall not be conducive to the desired outcome if no good reason supports incurring double costs of legal representation and court fees.

In general, the current interpretation of the term legal interest does not coincide with procedural justice principles in its procedural dimension or on its merits. Procedurally, it may lead to denial of justice, and on merits to contradiction of the generally and intuitively perceived components of legal interest. Legal interest, in this context, must observe the following values: equal protection of both claimant's and respondent's interest, and settlement of disputes in an optimal and non-coercive manner which is economically viable. Economic viability must, however, be considered in a new way. Legal interest interpretation cannot be too restrictive, considering the degree of objectivity and understanding of what is legal and what is non-legal, as

174. Herbert A. Simon, *Models of Bounded Rationality*, vol. 2, 405–406 (1982); William LF Felstiner, Richard L. Abel & Austin Sarat, *The Emergence and Transformation of Disputes: Naming, Blaming, Claiming* 15 Law & Soc'y Rev. 631 (1980–1981).

well as what is deemed to be a declaration of legal relationship and what is just a brute fact. The subsidiarity principle, which provides that an equivalent or better claim is a ban to seeking declaratory relief, runs against such values. Denial of consideration of individual and subjective interest of the claimant in seeking this particular relief and not the other is also against procedural justice. There is also no place for the *ex officio* disqualifying admissibility of the given declaration as against procedural justice. When interpreting given legal norms concerning formal requirements, one must assume that they are introduced with the goal of imposing order, and not to entrapment of the participants in the proceedings.

Redefinition or amendment. Most of the components of the legal interest construing its notion are a product of interpretation. By changing the attitude of the judiciary, the interpretation could be adjusted even without legislative intervention. The above analysis demonstrates an alternative interpretation based on the existing regulation. The Swiss approach could serve as an example. So, *de lege lata*, the following model of legal interest can be construed, as opposed to the Model Legal interest as provided in section 5.01. *infra*:

(1) the character of the interest is legal, as derived from the object of the declaration, and is not contrary by itself to practical needs of the claimant, including the economic one;
(2) there is a dispute or controversy between the parties in the subjective perception by the claimant; any claims deemed unreasonable by the court will result in shifting the costs onto the claimant;
(3) the uncertainty relates to the particular right or legal relationship, including facts upon which the rights or legal relationship is dependent.

Other components of the legal interest, as interpreted by the judiciary and in particular subsidiarity principle, find no basis in the system of law and access to justice principles.

However, this could be insufficient, seeing as the established interpretation is so deeply entrenched among the judges; some manner of intervention might be necessary. If so, what would be the best option – to get rid of the legal interest entirely, or to leave only the term 'interest', without the (confusing, in this context) adjective 'legal'? As a *de lege ferenda* proposal, leaving mere 'interest' as a prerequisite is necessary to distinguish claimants who have an interest in declaration from those who have no interest and are, as Burrows calls them, 'merely interfering busybodies'.[175] The only purpose of the 'interest' as a prerequisite must be a selection of those who have no interest, meaning: ones who seek declaration of the legal relationship, where they are not the party to the given legal relationship and such relationship does not affect their legal status or legal affairs in the broad sense. The interest of all subjects, being a party to the legal relationship must be admitted by definition. The 'legality' of the interest will be secured by the definition of the object of the declaration, being a legal

175. Burrows, *supra* n. 141, at 591.

relationship or a legal right, understood however broadly. The proposed approach, combined with broad understanding of the term 'legal relationship' and abandonment of the subsidiarity principle, will better meet the societal legal and intuitive expectations. The proposed solutions are meant to continue changes in Germanic jurisdictions which, while not very rapid, are generally leading to steady liberalization of the criteria of admissibility of declaratory relief.

Proposed solution will maximize possibility to produce just outcome and will equally serve both claimant and respondent.

Annexes

Reports on Main Features of Declarations in Germanic Jurisdictions

Editor: Beata Gessel-Kalinowska vel Kalisz

ANNEX I

Report on Main Features of Declarations in Austria

Ulrich Kopetzki

Table of Contents

I ORIGINS AND EVOLUTION OF DECLARATORY RELIEFS IN THE AUSTRIAN LEGAL SYSTEM

The Austrian Code of Civil Procedure (Zivilprozessordnung, CCP) of 1895 entered into force in 1898, replacing the Allgemeine Gerichtsordnung of 1781. It was drafted by Franz Klein (1854–1926), whose professed aim was the so-called 'social function' (*Sozialfunktion*) of civil litigation. Contrary to the liberal idea of civil procedure prevailing in the nineteenth century, Klein believed that litigation should not be considered merely as a means of solving individual disputes between private litigants, but as a 'social evil', and hence as a phenomenon that had implications for society as a whole. As such, judicial proceedings should not only serve the interests of the parties, but also the public interest.[1] In drafting the Austrian Code of Civil Procedure, Franz Klein followed in large parts the German Code of Civil Procedure of 1877, which had come into force in 1879.[2] Long passages of the Austrian Code of Civil Procedure are therefore similar, and sometimes even identical, to the provisions in the German Code of Civil Procedure. While Austrian scholars have advocated for an action for declaratory relief long before the enactment of the German Code of Civil Procedure,[3] the relevant provision in the Austrian Code of Civil Procedure establishing declaratory relief (§ 228 Austrian CCP) has been adopted with almost identical wording from the German version (previously § 231, now § 256 German CCP).[4] As such, it has not changed ever since the initial enactment of the Austrian Code of Civil Procedure – its wording is still the same as in the late nineteenth century.

While the interpretation and application of the specific prerequisites for declaratory relief have, over time, been subject to subtle changes and considerable refinement by legal doctrine and jurisprudence, the basic principles of declaratory relief have remained largely undisputed within legal doctrine and unchanged in the courts. Also, there has been no noteworthy debate in academic literature about possible legislative improvements to the action for declaratory relief and its prerequisites. In general, it can be said that there is currently no significant controversy about declaratory relief, its usefulness and its basic requirements as set out in the law and as applied by the courts.[5]

1. *See* Franz Klein, *Zeit- und Geistesströmungen im Prozesse*, in 1 Reden – Vorträge – Aufsätze – Briefe 126–134 (Josef Friedländer & Ottilie Friedländer eds., 1927); Franz Klein & Friedrich Engel, Der Zivilprozess Österreichs, in 3 Das Zivilprozessrecht der Kulturstaaten 186–206 (Adolf Wach & Wilhelm Kisch & Albrecht Mendelssohn Bartholdy & Max Pagenstecher eds., 1927); Andreas Konecny, *Einleitung* margin number 12, in *I Kommentar zu den Zivilprozessgesetzen* (Hans Walter Fasching & Andreas Konecny eds. 3rd ed., 2013).
2. Walter H. Rechberger, *Die Ideen Franz Kleins und ihre Bedeutung für die Entwicklung des Zivilprozessrechts in Europa*, 25 RitsLRev 101, 104 (2008).
3. 2 Joseph Unger, *System des österreichischen allgemeinen Privatrechts* 375 (1859).
4. I/2 Hans Sperl, Lehrbuch der Bürgerlichen Rechtspflege 310 (1928); Georg Petschek, Der österreichische Zivilprozess 247 (1963).
5. But *See*, e.g., Oskar Ballon, *§§ 228 und 236 ZPO*, JBl 1980 323, 326 (arguing that also elements of a legal relation should under certain circumstances be admissible as the subject matter of an action for declaratory relief). Furthermore, see below at Annex I.II and Annex II.VII for a controversy between jurisprudence on the one hand and doctrine on the other hand as to whether the requirements for declaratory relief are to be qualified as substantive or procedural prerequisites.

However, there has been one notable exception to such continuity and lack of controversy. As will be further examined below, Austrian courts have, over time, significantly lowered the requirements for declarations of liability for future damages. While some earlier judgements only granted declarations of liability for future damages when at least some harm had already occurred, the courts now grant such declarations also in cases where no damage has yet occurred and where the occurrence of future harm is merely a possibility. This line of judicial authority has grown in practical importance in the context of a recent series of cases involving private investors suing their banks for damages that they incurred as a consequence of allegedly incorrect investment advice given by those banks. In these cases, the claimants and courts often found themselves unable to assess the damages when the claimants still held the investments. Against this background, the courts often granted declaratory relief, declaring the banks liable for future damages.

II STATUTORY BASIS AND PREREQUISITES FOR DECLARATORY RELIEF

As indicated above, declaratory relief is regulated in § 228 Austrian CCP. It provides that '[o]ne can bring an action for the determination of the existence or non-existence of a legal relation or a right, on the recognition of the authenticity of a document or the determination of its inauthenticity, if the claimant has a legal interest that said legal relation or right or authenticity of a document shall be determined by a judicial decision in the near future'[6] [translation by the author].

Accordingly, two requirements need to be fulfilled in order to successfully bring an action for declaratory relief on the basis of § 228 Austrian CCP: First, the action for declaratory relief needs to be aimed at a declaratory decision regarding the (non-)existence of a legal relation, a right or the authenticity of a document. Second, the claimant needs to have a legal interest in the requested declaration.

Austrian legal doctrine now takes the unanimous view that the action for declaratory relief is a special provision providing legal protection that finds its basis only in procedural law, and that it is thus of procedural nature only.[7] Furthermore, according to doctrine, also the prerequisites stipulated in § 228 Austrian CCP are *procedural* requirements.[8] Accordingly, a lack thereof should lead to a rejection of the claim as inadmissible (*Zurückweisung der Klage mit Beschluss*). However, according to

6. 'Es kann auf Feststellung des Bestehens oder Nichtbestehens eines Rechtsverhältnisses oder Rechtes, auf Anerkennung der Echtheit einer Urkunde oder Feststellung der Unechtheit derselben Klage erhoben werden, wenn der Kläger ein rechtliches Interesse daran hat, dass jenes Rechtsverhältnis oder Recht oder die Urkundenechtheit durch eine gerichtliche Entscheidung alsbald festgestellt werde.'
7. Ulrike Frauenberger-Pfeiler, *§ 228* n. 5, in *III/1 Kommentar zu den Zivilprozessgesetzen* (Hans Walter Fasching & Andreas Konecny eds. 3rd ed., 2017).
8. Frauenberger-Pfeiler, *supra* n. 7, at n. 73.

established jurisprudence, the courts treat the prerequisites as *substantive* requirements.[9] Hence, when determining whether a claimant's action for declaratory relief is well founded, the courts assess whether the prerequisites set out in § 228 Austrian CCP are fulfilled. If a court concludes that this is not the case, it will dismiss the claim with a judgement on the merits (*Abweisung der Klage mit Urteil*).

Against this background, lack of legal interest will lead to the dismissal of the claim on the merits.[10] Furthermore, both according to prevailing doctrine[11] and decided cases,[12] a lack of legal interest is to be considered by the courts ex officio both in proceedings of first instance and in appeal proceedings.

Whether an action constitutes an action for declaratory relief (*Feststellungsklage*), an action for performance (*Leistungsklage*) or an action aimed at creating, changing or abolishing a legal relation (*Rechtsgestaltungsklage*) is not to be assessed by a strict verbatim interpretation of the requested relief, but rather by an analysis of the meaning and overall purpose of the relief sought against the background of the claimant's submissions.[13]

III REQUIREMENT OF LEGAL INTEREST

As indicated above, declaratory relief can only be granted where claimant has a legal interest in the request declaration. As will be further explained below, legal interest is considered to be a special procedural prerequisite for an action for declaratory relief. Primarily for reasons of procedural efficiency, it aims to ensure that declaratory relief is only granted in cases in which claimant has a legitimate interest in the requested declaration. It entails *inter alia* that claimant is only entitled to the requested declaration when it is unable to reach its goal in a simpler or more effective way, e.g., by bringing an action for performance.

[A] The Concept of Interest in Legal Protection under Austrian Law

Austrian procedural law employs the terms *Rechtsschutzinteresse* (interest in legal protection) and *Rechtsschutzbedürfnis* (need for legal protection). These concepts refer to the idea that legal protection shall only be afforded to those who have a legitimate interest acknowledged by the legal system in acquiring the requested measure of legal protection, i.e., a legitimate interest in the proceedings. While the term *Rechtsschutzinteresse* (interest in legal protection) is arguably wider than the term *Rechtsschutzbedürfnis* (need for legal protection), these terms are regularly used interchangeably.[14]

9. *Ibid.*, at n. 74. *See also* RIS-Justiz RS0039177; RIS-Justiz RS0039301 (in the context of legal interest).
10. RIS-Justiz RS0039201; RIS-Justiz RS0038939.
11. Frauenberger-Pfeiler, *supra* n. 7, at n. 73.
12. RIS-Justiz RS0039123.
13. Frauenberger-Pfeiler, *supra* n. 7, at n. 13; RIS-Justiz RS0038879.
14. Konecny *supra* n. 1, at n. 175; Frauenberger-Pfeiler, *supra* n. 7, at n. 79.

According to part of the doctrine, a claimant's need for legal protection is a general prerequisite for granting him legal protection by the courts.[15] However, it is not generally recognized as a general procedural prerequisite (*allgemeine Prozessvoraussetzung*) neither by prevailing doctrine[16] nor by jurisprudence, which is inconsistent on this matter.[17] According to some Austrian case law, a need for legal protection is not a general procedural prerequisite[18] and only necessary where it is specifically required by law.[19] In other cases, a need for legal protection has been considered as a general procedural requirement.[20]

Irrespective whether the need for legal protection qualifies as a general procedural prerequisite, sometimes a need for legal protection is considered as *substantive* requirement for a claim. For example, the courts have qualified claimant's need for legal protection as a substantive requirement of a pre-emptive suit for injunction, i.e., where there was only a danger of a violation of a right.[21] Similarly, the courts have also qualified claimant's need for legal protection as a substantive requirement of suits for injunctions in other circumstances.[22] For example, the courts have deemed such requirement fulfilled – and that a need for legal protection exists – where a claimant seeks an injunction even though an identical preliminary injunction exists already.[23] By contrast, the courts have dismissed a suit for injunction for lack of need for legal protection in a case where claimant was already in possession of an executory title by which it could enforce the requested injunction.[24] Similarly, the courts have dismissed a suit for injunction for lack of need for legal protection in a case where an attorney requested an injunction against someone who provided tenancy agreements on a commercial basis, where the bar association had already obtained an identical injunction against the same respondent and was also already enforcing it.[25]

In addition to, and separate from, any general requirement of an interest in or need for legal protection, the Austrian Code of Civil Procedure does sometimes – partly

15. Hans Dolinar, Marianne Roth & Henriette Duursma-Kepplinger, *Zivilprozessrecht* 117 (15th ed., 2017); Oskar Ballon, Bettina Nunner-Krautgasser & Birgit Schneider, *Einführung in das Zivilprozessrecht* n. 36 (13th ed., 2018).
16. *See* Konecny *supra* n. 1, at n. 177; Walter Rechberger & Daphne-Ariane Simotta, *Zivilprozessrecht* nn. 28–29 (9th ed., 2017).
17. Andreas Geroldinger, *§ 226* n. 14, in *III/1 Kommentar zu den Zivilprozessgesetzen* (Hans Walter Fasching & Andreas Konecny eds. 3rd ed., 2017).
18. *See*, e.g., judgement of 15 November 1993, 3 Ob 505/94 (Austrian Supreme Court); judgement of 23 March 1999, 1 Ob 55/99s (Austrian Supreme Court); judgement of 28 October 1999, 3 Ob 36/99m (Austrian Supreme Court); judgement of 27 May 2002, 8 ObA 285/01x (Austrian Supreme Court). *See also* RIS-Justiz RS0038040.
19. For example judgement of 15 November 1993, 3 Ob 505/94 (Austrian Supreme Court); judgement of 23 March 1999, 1 Ob 55/99s (Austrian Supreme Court). *See also* Geroldinger, *supra* n. 17, at n. 14.
20. RIS-Justiz RS0038062. Cf. also RIS-Justiz RS0038011.
21. RIS-Justiz RS0009357.
22. For example judgement of 17 July 2018, 4 Ob 102/18f (Austrian Supreme Court). *See also* Luitgard Ofner, *§ 81 UrhG* n. 16, in urheber.recht (Guido Kucsko & Christian Handig eds. 2nd ed., 2017).
23. Judgement of 26 June 1990, 4 Ob 93/90 (Austrian Supreme Court).
24. Judgement of 19 September 1995, 4 Ob 69/95 (Austrian Supreme Court). *See also* RIS-Justiz RS0079417; RIS-Justiz RS0037297.
25. Judgement of 19 November 2006, 4 Ob 241/06d (Austrian Supreme Court).

explicitly, partly by implication - require legal interest as a particular procedural prerequisite. Specifically, legal interest is expressly required as a prerequisite for an action for declaratory relief (*Feststellungsklage*, § 228 Austrian CCP) and for a petition for incident declaratory relief (*Zwischenfeststellungsantrag*, §§ 236 and 259(2) Austrian CCP)).[26] The legal interest that is required for an action for declaratory relief is different from any general requirement of an interest in, or need for, legal protection because it finds its express basis in statutory law. Furthermore, the requirement of legal interest is stricter and goes beyond any requirement of an interest in, or need for, legal protection: an interest in, or need for, legal protection would not be lacking in every case in which legal interest is lacking. This is understandable in light of the purpose of legal interest as a prerequisite of declaratory relief as further described below: § 228 Austrian CCP requires special prerequisites for legal protection in light of the merely declaratory and pre-emptive character of actions for declaratory relief.[27] In this context, Austrian legal doctrine considers the requirement of legal interest as a prerequisite for declaratory relief as a particular procedural requirement (*besondere Prozessvoraussetzung*).

[B] Purpose of Legal Interest as a Prerequisite of Declaratory Relief

As indicated above, § 228 Austrian CCP stipulates that the claimant requires a 'legal interest' in the requested declaration. It should be noted at the outset that no statutory definition of 'legal interest' exists and that it has thus been up to the courts and legal doctrine to interpret this requirement of legal interest. Case law and doctrine have been developing the concept of 'legal interest' in a rather casuistic manner, and often with an eye to whether the requested declaration would serve the purpose of legal interest as a prerequisite of declaratory relief. As a starting point to the analysis of the requirement of legal interest, it is therefore helpful to analyse its role and purpose in the civil procedure system.

One of the main purposes of civil proceedings is to resolve a dispute and to create the state required by law.[28] It is a core function of civil proceedings to create legal peace between the parties by clarifying the law for the parties in a binding manner, thus providing a basis for their future (legal) relations.[29] However, the purpose of civil proceedings is not limited to enforcing individual interests, but can also be seen to include the creation of legal peace (*Rechtsfrieden*) and legal certainty in general.[30] Against this background, declaratory relief is generally considered to serve two purposes: first, the purpose of legal protection and the prevention of disputes, and second, the purpose of procedural efficiency.[31]

26. Rechberger & Simotta, *supra* n. 16, at n. 29.
27. Frauenberger-Pfeiler, *supra* n. 7, at n. 80.
28. Konecny *supra* n. 1, at n. 11.
29. *Ibid.*, at n. 17/1.
30. Franz Klein & Friedrich Engel, *supra* n. 1, at 186–204 (1927); Hans Walter Fasching, *Lehrbuch des österreichischen Zivilprozessrechts*, n. 47 (2nd ed., 1990); Konecny *supra* n. 1, at n. 17/1.
31. *See* Fasching, *supra* n. 30, at nn. 1072–1073.

Specifically, declaratory relief serves the purpose of legal protection and of preventing disputes by clarifying the existence of a disputed right or legal relation, thereby preventing future infringement of rights. Specifically, *Fasching* considered that a declaratory judgement supplements the system of repressive legal protection, i.e., a system of dispute resolution in which an enforceable judgement for performance reduces or eliminates the consequences of a violation of a right or seeks to restore a certain legal situation.[32] Such judgement for performance presupposes that a right has already been violated. By allowing for an action for declaratory relief, a claimant may already seek legal protection prior to an actual violation of its rights in order to prevent a future violation of rights by way of a judicial declaration. While § 228 Austrian CCP does not expressly stipulate a necessity of an endangerment of a legal position (as other preventive measures in the field of civil procedure do, such as measures concerning the preservation of evidence or preliminary injunctions), prevailing case law[33] and doctrine[34] consider such requirement to be implicit in the prerequisite of legal interest. If such endangerment exists, a preventive declaratory judgement by a court can help prevent future violation of rights and may thus avoid future court proceedings. That is not to say that declaratory relief may only be sought before a right has been violated – declaratory relief may clarify the legal relation and, in this way, prevent further infringements also in cases where a violation already occurred.

Furthermore, declaratory relief also serves the purpose of procedural efficiency by clarifying the legal situation in cases where the legal order recognizes a legitimate need to clarify disputed legal relations, not only in order to avoid future disputes but also to create a basis for future court decisions.[35] It binds the judge presiding over a subsequent trial: if the subject matter comes up as a preliminary question in a later trial, the judge is obliged to base her decision on this existing ruling.

By contrast, actions for declaratory relief may also lead to procedural *inefficiencies* if they were allowed without limits. Given that a judgement granting declaratory relief does not directly affect a specific right or legal relation, and given that is does not order any performance, the Austrian legislature found it necessary to limit a claimant's entitlement to such judgement for reasons of efficiency. While there is a potentially unlimited number of abstract conflicts, specifically between a person's absolute rights and other legal subjects, legal protection shall only be afforded in the event that an abstract conflict specifically materializes.[36] In that regard, there exists a certain similarity between claims for declaratory relief and actions for an injunction. While there is no express statutory provision requiring legal interest for an action for an injunction, a similar effect is achieved by the requirement developed by case law that

32. Hans Walter Fasching, *§ 228* n. 2, in *III Kommentar zu den Zivilprozessgesetzen* (Hans Walter Fasching & Andreas Konecny eds. 2nd ed., 2004). *See also* Frauenberger-Pfeiler, *supra* n. 7, at n. 2.
33. RIS-Justiz RS0039007; RIS-Justiz RS0039215; RIS-Justiz RS0039096.
34. Frauenberger-Pfeiler, *supra* n. 7, at n. 86.
35. RIS-Justiz RS0037422.
36. *See* judgement of 28 February 1985, 6 Ob 651/83 (Austrian Supreme Court); judgement of 10 May 1990, 6 Ob 549/90 (Austrian Supreme Court); judgement of 22 April 1999, 6 Ob 288/98s (Austrian Supreme Court).

an injunction requires a need for legal protection.[37] Furthermore, legal interest is considered to be lacking in circumstances where other remedies are available (principle of subsidiarity). This also serves the purpose of procedural efficiency, since it would arguably be inefficient to allow an action for declaratory relief where claimant could already bring an action for performance that provides the same or greater legal protection. Historically, the requirement of legal interest was considered necessary in order to avoid abuse of the newly codified action for declaratory relief.[38]

In light of the above, the requirement of legal interest is considered to exist mainly for the public interest in the effective and efficient administration of justice. However, a second purpose can be seen in the respondent's protection from unnecessary and aimless litigation.[39]

[C] Requirement of Legal Interest under § 228 Austrian CCP

As indicated above, in accordance with § 228 Austrian CCP, a claimant is required to have a 'legal interest' in the requested declaration. While the claimant's subjective interest in the requested declaration is manifested by the claimant taking legal action, it is crucial that this subjective interest can be justified by objective factors. As such, the legal relationship or right (or the authenticity of a document) that is the subject matter of an action for declaratory relief must have a direct impact on claimant's legal position.[40] Furthermore, claimant's legal interest must derive from the legal order.[41]

It does not matter, in principle, which area of law affects the claimant's legal status. The legal interest needs not to be derived from private law, it may also have its roots in procedural law, criminal law or public law.[42] Furthermore, the legal interest must derive directly from the disputed right or legal relation. Mere procedural interests, i.e., the desire to gain a procedural advantage, is not sufficient to establish legal interest.[43] By contrast, legal interest has been found to exist where a claimant sought declaratory relief in order to avoid significant future difficulties with regard to showing evidence.[44]

The legal relationship that is subject to a request for declaratory relief must have a direct effect on the claimant's legal position – thus, the request for declaratory relief must be an appropriate means to (i) putting an end to the opponent's interference with

37. *See* above at Annex I. III[A].
38. I *Materialien zu den neuen österreichischen Civilprocessgesetzen* 279 (K.K. Justizministerium ed., 1897); Moritz Sternberg, *Die Feststellungsklage nach der neuen Civilproceßordnung* 6 (1901).
39. *See* Stefan Leimgruber, *Declaratory Relief in International Commercial Arbitration*, 32 ASA Bulletin 467, 481 (2014).
40. Frauenberger-Pfeiler, *supra* n. 7, at n. 82; RIS-Justiz RS0039071.
41. *Ibid.*, at n. 82.
42. *Ibid.*
43. *Ibid.*, at n. 89.
44. Judgement of 17 October 1951, 1 Ob 381/51 (Austrian Supreme Court); judgement of 17 September 1952, 2 Ob 561/52 (Austrian Supreme Court). But cf. judgement of 1 July 1976, 7 Ob 598/76 (Austrian Supreme Court), pursuant to which claims for declaratory relief which aim at avoiding future difficulties with regard to showing evidence are inadmissible.

the claimant's own legal sphere and to (ii) avoiding further legal disputes.[45] In this context, a legal interest has been said to exist when the request for declaratory relief seeks to clarify the entire legal relationship as such in a way that avoids future disputes.[46] However, such a preventive effect can only be corroborated by a request for declaratory relief if there exists a current reason for such a preventive clarification at all.[47] In other words, there must be a specific and current reason which requires a swift court decision to prevent an actual and serious threat of the claimant's legal position.[48] The legal interest in the judicial decision must be current insofar as objective circumstances seem to seriously, concretely (not only presumably) endanger the claimant's legal position.[49] In any event, the declaratory relief must be an appropriate means *in concreto* to eliminate the legal threat for the claimant.[50]

In cases of the so-called 'positive' declaratory relief, legal interest is considered to exist when the existence of the disputed legal relationship is denied by the respondent, causing insecurity and uncertainty; in such cases, it is considered that respondent's denial of the right constitutes a sufficient reason to pre-emptively clarify the legal relation.[51] By contrast, the courts have been known to decide that a claimant lacks legal interest in the requested declaration that respondent is liable for future damages where respondent has admitted (not with merely declaratory, but with constitutive effect) that this is the case.[52]

In the case of the 'negative' declaratory relief, the respondent claims the existence of the disputed legal relationship or right or acts upon it (a situation in which the respondent incorrectly claims that it is entitled to a right and that it intends to act upon it is also described as *Berühmung*).[53] In such cases, legal interest exists if (i) respondent claims the existence of a specific disputed legal relationship or right, (ii) this endangers the claimant's legal position and (iii) the requested declaration is a suitable means to eliminating this danger. The endangerment of claimant's legal position may also be comprised in the fact that claimant is impeded in its freedom of action in legal affairs, or in taking appropriate economic actions.[54]

For example, the courts have ruled that legal interest exists in a case of 'negative' declaratory relief in which respondent claimed that a tenancy agreement between the

45. RIS-Justiz RS0039071.
46. RIS-Justiz RS0038917.
47. RIS-Justiz RS0039071.
48. RIS-Justiz RS0039215.
49. Frauenberger-Pfeiler, *supra* n. 7, at n. 86.
50. Fasching, *supra* n. 30, at n. 1100; Rechberger & Simotta, *supra* n. 16, at n. 606.
51. For example judgement of 29 September 2011, 2 Ob 186/10g (Austrian Supreme Court); judgement of 22 March 2018, 2 Ob 197/17k (Austrian Supreme Court); judgement of 25 April 2018, 2 Ob 18/18p (Austrian Supreme Court). *See also* RIS-Justiz RS0038968; RIS-Justiz RS0039202.
52. Judgement of 4 September 1991, 7 Ob 588/91 (Austrian Supreme Court); judgement of 28 March 1996, 2 Ob 2017/96y (Austrian Supreme Court); judgement of 26 June 1997, 2 Ob 113/97z (Austrian Supreme Court); judgement of 4 September 1997, 2 Ob 100/97p (Austrian Supreme Court).
53. Frauenberger-Pfeiler, *supra* n. 7, at n. 30.
54. RIS-Justiz RS0039096.

parties could not be terminated for a certain period of time.[55] In this case, respondent and claimant's legal predecessor had executed a tenancy agreement concerning the rent of a commercial space. By way of an additional oral agreement, they had also agreed that the tenancy agreement could not be terminated for a period of fifteen years. Claimant acquired the property in question and hence entered into its predecessor's rights and obligations arising out of the tenancy agreement. It was disputed between the parties whether claimant was also bound by the additional oral agreement. Claimant requested a declaration to the contrary, which was granted by the Court of First Instance and overruled by the Court of Appeal. The Austrian Supreme Court confirmed the decision of the Court of First Instance. After analysing the merits of why claimant was not bound by the additional oral agreement, it also found that claimant had a legal interest in the requested declaration. Specifically, the Austrian Supreme Court took the position that claimant intended to terminate the tenancy agreement because it had a personal need for the rented property. Furthermore, the Austrian Supreme Court considered that claimant, if it could terminate the agreement, would have to provide a replacement property to respondent. Given the effort entailed in providing such replacement property, the Austrian Supreme Court concluded that claimant had a legal interest in the requested declaration.

Similarly, the courts have ruled that legal interest exists in a case in which respondent issued to claimant an invoice for advertisements which claimant had never ordered. Claimant requested a declaration that the claim as reflected in such invoice does not exist. The Austrian Supreme Court considered that legal interest exists since claimant is impeded in its freedom of action, given that its economic position would be affected considerably if the alleged claim existed.[56]

By contrast, the courts have deemed legal interest to be lacking in a case where respondent merely claimed to be the owner of a property which, according to the land register, was owned by claimant, when no additional elements substantiated endangerment of claimant's position.[57]

Furthermore, if the respondent infringes the claimant's rights at the factual level only, without claiming the existence of a right to do so, this does not establish a legal interest in a respective negative declaratory relief. In such a case, where there is no disputed legal situation requiring clarification beyond the actual incident in question, the claimant may bring an action for an injunction (*Unterlassungsklage*), which provides greater legal protection than the requested declaration.[58]

For example, the courts have considered that legal interest is lacking in a case in which claimant *inter alia* requested a declaration that respondent is not entitled to fill claimant's basement window shaft with snow and ice.[59] The Austrian Supreme Court considered that respondent did not claim the existence of a corresponding right but that it merely factually infringed claimant's right.

55. Judgement of 8 July 1959, 3 Ob 247/59 (Austrian Supreme Court).
56. Judgement of 16 October 2003, 8 Ob 85/03p (Austrian Supreme Court).
57. Frauenberger-Pfeiler, *supra* n. 7, at n. 30.
58. Judgement of 18 November 2007, 10 Ob 85/07h (Austrian Supreme Court); judgement of 11 November 2013, 7 Ob 176/13b (Austrian Supreme Court).
59. Judgement of 18 November 2007, 10 Ob 85/07h (Austrian Supreme Court).

More generally, as will be addressed below in more detail, legal interest exists only when the claimant is unable to achieve the desired goal (i.e., the prevention of a disadvantage or the enforcement of a right) by other legal means.[60]

Moreover, purely economic interests, piety, reputation or an interest in obtaining information do not suffice to clear the legal interest hurdle, at least not unless a legal provision explicitly protects those interests accordingly.[61]

The distinction between legal interest and economic interest is not always clear-cut. More often than not, economic interest stems from a (disputed or attacked) legal position, and yet this does not render the economic interest as such a protected one. For example, the interest in increased business success, increase in value, increase of own wealth or in a debtor's financial solvency is merely an economic, but not a legal interest.[62]

By contrast, legal interest has been considered to exist if respondent presumes a certain right and, as a consequence, claimant is limited in his freedom to dispose of his assets.[63] For example, in one case the owner of a property requested a declaration that a lease agreement over the property that had been executed between the respondents as lessor and lessee was invalid.[64] The first respondent had been granted a lifelong usufructuary right in the property and the first respondent subsequently entered into a lease agreement for the property with the second and the third respondents. Claimant argued that the lease agreement had been made with the intention to prevent claimant from selling the property for an adequate price, considering that the current owner of the property would automatically enter into the lease agreement with the second and third respondents once the first respondent had died. The Austrian Supreme Court found that claimant had a legal interest in the requested declaration since it was relevant for claimant to know whether the property is encumbered with a lease agreement that would not automatically cease to exist upon expiration of the usufructuary right and that would therefore reduce the market value of the property. Accordingly, in this context of respondent presuming a certain right, the Austrian Supreme Court found that it is sufficient for the establishment of legal interest that the claimant is impeded in its freedom of action in legal affairs or in taking appropriate economic actions (such as sale of the property).[65]

In any event, once legal interest exists, it does not hurt to also have an economic interest; an action for declaratory relief is only impossible in cases where the claimant has nothing but an economic interest.[66]

Legal interest must exist, at the latest, when the oral proceedings of first instance are closed, otherwise the court will consider legal interest to be lacking.[67] It must

60. RIS-Justiz RS0039265.
61. Frauenberger-Pfeiler, *supra* n. 7, at nn. 84–85.
62. *Ibid.*, at n. 84.
63. RIS-Justiz RS0039096; RIS-Justiz RS0038968.
64. Judgement of 5 September 2002, 2 Ob 157/02f (Austrian Supreme Court).
65. *See also* RIS-Justiz RS0038968.
66. RIS-Justiz RS0109286.
67. *See* RIS-Justiz RS0039204; RIS-Justiz RS0039085.

concern the present or, considering the duration of the proceedings, the near future.[68] If the court has doubts regarding the existence of legal interest, it could be debated whether the court could commence investigations ex officio and look for further evidence, or whether it could simply rely on the parties' arguments. Legal doctrine tends to deny an obligation to investigate, as the judge is obligated to point out a need for further evidence to the parties anyway due to judges' general obligation to oversee the proceedings. In any event, it is the claimant carries the burden of proof.[69]

The claimant has to submit at least credible and convincing arguments as to how its claim fulfils the legal prerequisites. The necessary depth and detail of this demonstration depends partly on the subject matter at hand – if the legal interest is evident from the substantive facts of the case, e.g., a claimant's disputed marital status, not much explanation will be needed to show legal interest. If, however, the claimant requests a declaration that a contract between two third parties, who are not involved in the proceedings, is invalid and thus, in some way, impacts his legal standing, more thorough explanation might be necessary.[70]

If legal interest ceases to exist during the proceedings (until oral hearings at first instance are concluded), the court will dismiss the declaratory relief. The benchmark for this cessation of legal interest is considered to be rather high: the judicature demands objective circumstances proving beyond doubt that the threat of the claimant's legal position is eliminated. Whether a respondent's behaviour or statement can also fulfil these requirements can only be assessed on a case-by-case basis, considering the probability of a future dispute.[71]

Since the requirement of legal interest exists mostly for the public interest in the effective administration of justice, it is not subject to the parties' disposition. No acknowledgment, recognizance (*Zugeständnis, Anerkenntnis*), waiver (*Verzicht*) or settlement (*Vergleich*) is available with regard to legal interest.[72] This notwithstanding, the parties can still reach a settlement on the underlying disputed legal relation.

[D] Subsidiarity of Declaratory Relief

In accordance with established jurisprudence and unanimous legal doctrine, the required legal interest for obtaining declaratory relief does not exist where the claimant could reach its aim in a simpler way or if there is an option available that grants more extensive legal protection (principle of subsidiarity). If the court finds that all other legal remedies available would lead to greater procedural efforts or to less legal protection, it will affirm legal interest.[73]

This prerequisite serves the purpose of procedural efficiency, since it requires a claimant who wishes to commence legal proceedings to introduce an action that is

68. RIS-Justiz RS0039263.
69. Frauenberger-Pfeiler, *supra* n. 7, at nn. 126–127.
70. Rechberger & Simotta, *supra* n. 16, at n. 606.
71. Frauenberger-Pfeiler, *supra* n. 7, at n. 131.
72. Rechberger & Simotta, *supra* n. 16, at n. 608.
73. Frauenberger-Pfeiler, *supra* n. 7, at n. 91.

expected to resolve the parties' dispute in an as comprehensive and final manner as possible. An action for performance (*Leistungsklage*)[74] is in principle more suitable to serve this goal than an action for declaratory relief, since an action for declaratory relief usually provides less protection than an action for performance and since only an action for performance may lead to an enforcement title.[75]

An action for declaratory relief is therefore usually subsidiary to a regular action for performance. If the claimant can file an action for performance which would afford the same (or greater) legal protection, then declaratory relief is inadmissible.[76] In particular, it is irrelevant whether the action for performance is an application for an injunction (*Klage auf Unterlassung*) or an action for performance (*Klage auf Leistung*).[77]

However, in order to deny the existence of legal interest in light of a possible action for performance, it must be clear that such action for performance would lead to everything that the claimant could attain with an action for declaratory relief; at the very least, it must be excluded with virtual certainty that claimant could have any additional claims that exceed the scope of protection of the action for performance.[78] The action for declaratory relief is only inadmissible if the possible judgement granting performance will entail everything that a possible judgement granting declaratory relief would entail.[79] For example, legal interest has been found to be lacking in case of a requested declaration that a purchase agreement no longer existed, when claimant could already have brought an action for rescission of the contract.[80]

Notably, it is not always the case that an action for performance will provide greater legal protection than an action for declaratory relief. As will be further explained below, the subject matter of a requested declaration will only be treated as a preliminary question in an action for performance and hence the court's determination of such question will not become res iudicata. Therefore, courts in future proceedings will not be bound by the court's determination of the preliminary question. For example, the courts have concluded that legal interest exists in a situation where the claimant requested a declaration the she validly withdrew from an oral contract by which she agreed to sell a piece of real estate to the respondent. At the same time, claimant had brought an action for eviction, since respondent was currently living on the property. Irrespectively of the incorrect phrasing of the requested declaration (which, again, was aimed at a legal qualification of a fact, namely the

74. The term *Leistungsklage* in the broadest sense includes *Leistungsklagen* in the narrow sense (actions for performance aimed at a specific action by the respondent), *Duldungsklagen* (actions requiring the respondent to tolerate something) and *Unterlassungsklagen* (actions for injunction). Besides this first category, the doctrine discerns two other types of action: *Feststellungsklagen* (actions for declaratory relief) and *Rechtsgestaltungsklagen* (actions aimed at creating, changing or abolishing a legal relationship), *See* Rechberger & Simotta, *supra* n. 16, at nn. 594–614.
75. *See* Frauenberger-Pfeiler, *supra* n. 7, at nn. 110–111.
76. RIS-Justiz RS0038849.
77. *See* Frauenberger-Pfeiler, *supra* n. 7, at n. 111.
78. RIS-Justiz RS0038817; RIS-Justiz RS0038965. *See also* RIS-Justiz RS0039021; RIS-Justiz RS0038849.
79. Frauenberger-Pfeiler, *supra* n. 7, at nn. 110–111; RIS-Justiz RS0038817.
80. Judgement of 8 October 2013, 3 Ob 150/13z (Austrian Supreme Court).

allegedly valid withdrawal from the contract), the Austrian Supreme Court found that the action for eviction was no reason to deny claimant's legal interest in the requested declaration, since the question of whether a purchase agreement existed would only be a preliminary question in the action for eviction.[81]

Notwithstanding the above, a legal interest in the requested declaration may exist in cases where the claimant may bring an action for performance at some point in the future, provided that the requested declaration may finally clarify the legal relations between the parties and avoid future claims for performance.[82] For example, an action for declaratory relief is possible if a contracting party denies the existence of a contractual claim that is not yet due. It is considered that a declaratory judgement that confirms the disputed claim will induce the contracting party to fulfil the claim voluntarily once it becomes due, thereby rendering an action for performance unnecessary.[83]

Similarly, if not all the claims concerned are already due – especially in cases of continuing obligations – a declaratory relief clarifying the entire underlying legal relationship is possible,[84] irrespectively of whether an action for performance would be possible for some claims arising out of the contractual relationship and that have already become due.[85] The same principle applies if claimant merely requests a declaration on liability for future damages even though some damages have already occurred. In such a scenario, the courts have allowed actions for declaratory relief for possible future damages even though claimant could already have brought an action for performance for the damages that have already arisen out of the same incident.[86]

Against such background, it is also possible to combine an action for declaratory relief with an action for performance for those claims that are already due, possibly avoiding future disputes.[87] As will be explained in more detail below, this provides greater legal protection than if claimant were to only pursue those claims that are already due. In such a case, a judge would only implicitly determine the underlying legal relationship as a preliminary question for its ruling on claimant's action for performance, however, the relevance of such determination would be limited to the specific claims pursued in the action for performance.

[E] Exceptions from the Requirement of Existence of Legal Interest

There exist actions for declaratory relief that are based on specific provisions of substantive law (*materiellrechtliche Feststellungsklagen*). It is regularly indicated in Austrian jurisprudence that such actions for declaratory relief do not require the

81. Judgement of 15 May 2013, 3 Ob 21/13d (Austrian Supreme Court).
82. Judgement of 25 September 2001, 1 Ob 186/01m (Austrian Supreme Court). *See also* RIS-Justiz RS0038908.
83. Judgement of 24 April 1977, 2 Ob 585/95 (Austrian Supreme Court).
84. RIS-Justiz RS0038809.
85. RIS-Justiz RS0039110.
86. Judgement of 21 June 2000, 1 Ob 82/00s (Austrian Supreme Court); judgement of 2 August 2000, 2 Ob 187/00i (Austrian Supreme Court).
87. For example RIS-Justiz RS0038944; RIS-Justiz RS0038970.

existence of legal interest.[88] However, it appears that such actions do not actually constitute exceptions to the rule that legal interest is required for any action for declaratory relief. Rather, legal interest is automatically deemed to exist if the requirements laid out in the specific provisions of substantive law are fulfilled. In such cases, it is hence only necessary to assess whether the substantive law requirements are fulfilled – if this is the case, this in itself may demonstrate legal interest.[89] Also, as a consequence of the fact that no separate demonstration of legal interest is required, the question of subsidiarity of declaratory relief does not arise.[90]

Examples for such actions for declaratory relief that are based on specific provisions of substantive law include:

- actions for declaratory relief concerning a shareholder's duty to cooperate pursuant to § 16(1) Austrian Commercial Code;
- actions for declaratory relief concerning the invalidity of a resolution of a general meeting of an AG (*Aktiengesellschaft*) pursuant to § 201 Austrian Stock Corporation Act;
- actions for declaratory relief concerning the invalidity of a contract because of a violation of a statutory prohibition pursuant to § 879(1) Austrian Civil Code (ABGB);[91]
- actions for declaratory relief concerning the existence or non-existence of a servitude pursuant to § 523 ABGB;[92]
- actions for declaratory relief concerning the invalidity of a contract because of lack of capacity pursuant to § 865 ABGB.[93]

Furthermore, there exist exceptions from the principle of subsidiarity in matters of labour law (e.g., matters of § 50(1) Austrian Labour and Social Courts Act (ASGG)). Pursuant to § 54(1) ASGG, declaratory relief is permissible even if the claimant could also file an action for performance (*see also* § 54(5) ASGG).

IV SCOPE OF DECLARATORY RELIEF UNDER AUSTRIAN LAW

As indicated above, § 228 Austrian CCP regulates what matters can be the subject of a declaratory ruling. Specifically, a declaration can concern the existence or non-existence of a legal relation or right. In a point of significant practical importance, Austrian jurisprudence considers liability for future damages to be a legal relationship, so a declaration of such future liability also falls within the scope of declaratory relief. Furthermore, legal relationships with third parties can, in some cases, also be the subject matter of a declaratory relief. Other matters such as facts, legal qualities of facts

88. *See*, e.g., judgement of 9 May 2007, 9 Ob 117/06f (Austrian Supreme Court).
89. Frauenberger-Pfeiler, *supra* n. 7, at nn. 33–35.
90. RIS-Justiz RS0038877.
91. Judgement of 7 February 1989, 5 Ob 508/89 (Austrian Supreme Court); judgement of 28 May 1991, 4 Ob 519/91 (Austrian Supreme Court); judgement of 20 June 2002, 6 Ob 311/01f (Austrian Supreme Court).
92. Judgement of 9 May 2007, 9 Ob 117/06f (Austrian Supreme Court).
93. RIS-Justiz RS0014650.

or legal acts, single elements of legal relationships or abstract legal questions can, in principle, not be the subject matter of a declaratory relief. Finally, it should be noted that there is a statutory exception to the general rule that facts cannot be the subject matter of a declaratory relief: declaratory decisions are also possible as regard the authenticity (or lack thereof) of a document.

[A] Legal Relationship or Right

Declaratory decisions are possible regarding the (non-)existence of a legal relationship or a claimant's right. A legal relationship and a right means the legal connection between people or a person and an object. The terms legal relationship and right are considered essentially equivalent, given that a right may be understood as a subcategory of a legal relationship.[94]

The legal relationship must be part of civil law in the broadest sense.[95] While, as indicated above, a claimant's legal interest may also derive from other areas of the law (e.g., criminal law or public law), a right or legal relationship rooted in such other areas of laws cannot be the subject matter of an action for declaratory relief.[96]

If the existence of a legal relationship depends on a condition, jurisprudence allows declaratory relief under the requirement that only a precisely and clearly defined condition has not yet occurred while the underlying facts of the case are certain.[97]

For example, the Austrian Supreme Court allowed an action for declaratory relief by which a bank requested a declaration against an investor who was liable for capital gains tax the payment of which the tax authority had requested from the bank. The tax authority had compelled the bank to pay a certain amount of capital gains tax on investments owned by the investor, and the bank appealed this decision. While the appeal was still pending, the bank requested a declaration that respondent was liable to compensate the bank for the capital gains tax that it would finally have to pay to the tax authority. Respondent submitted that even if claimant would be ordered to pay additional capital gains tax, respondent would not be obliged to compensate claimant for such payments. While the Court of First Instance granted the requested declaration, the Court of Appeal overturned the decision and dismissed the action for declaratory relief. While the Court of Appeal conceded that, indeed, claimant had a claim for compensation for any such tax payments against respondent, it adopted the position that such claim only existed once claimant actually remitted such payments. Moreover, the Court of Appeal held that the tax authority's ruling was not yet binding and that, accordingly, there existed no payment obligation of claimant vis a vis the tax authority. The Austrian Supreme Court subsequently confirmed the decision of the Court of First Instance, holding that in light of respondent's denial of an obligation to compensate

94. Frauenberger-Pfeiler, *supra* n. 7, at n. 38. *See also* RIS-Justiz RS0039223 (indicating that also single legal consequences of such legal relationship, e.g., claims or receivables, qualify as a legal relationship).
95. Frauenberger-Pfeiler, *supra* n. 7, at n. 47.
96. *Ibid.*, at n. 82. *See also* RIS-Justiz RS0039162; RIS-Justiz RS0039192; RIS-Justiz RS0001477.
97. Frauenberger-Pfeiler, *supra* n. 7, at n. 42; RIS-Justiz RS0047957.

claimant for any future tax payments, claimant had a legal interest to clarify the disputed legal relationship. In that context, the Austrian Supreme Court also noted that if the existence of a legal relationship depends on a clearly defined condition (in this case: the condition of the tax authority dismissing claimant's appeal and ordering claimant to make additional payments), such conditional legal relationship can be the subject matter of an action for declaratory relief.[98]

Furthermore, validity of a contractual provision may also be the subject matter of a declaratory relief. For example, the courts have found that a declaration on the legal validity of an index clause is possible.[99] Similarly, the interpretation of contractual provisions may be the subject matter of a declaratory relief if there is a dispute concerning their interpretation and, in particular, the rights and obligations of a party stipulated therein.[100]

Also the question of the legal qualification of a contract or of specific contractual provisions may be the subject matter of declaratory relief. For example, the courts have granted declaratory relief concerning the question of whether a tenancy agreement qualifies as a lease or sublease agreement. Furthermore, the courts have declared that the contractual provisions in a rental agreement concerning the determination of the lease price were subject to the relevant provisions of tenancy law.[101]

[B] Liability for Future Damages

The obligation to compensate for future harm due to an incident (future liability) can be a subject matter of a declaratory relief. Under Austrian law, it has long been considered necessary to allow declarations of liability for future damages for reasons rooted in the statute of limitations: some earlier court decisions had deemed that the limitation period starts to run with the damaging incident, i.e., even in cases where no damage had yet occurred, provided that such future damage was foreseeable with certainty,[102] or at least likely.[103] The courts do no longer uphold such a view, and the consensus has shifted to where the limitation period only starts to run with the occurrence of actual harm (or, more precisely, with awareness thereof).[104] However, in the case of harm that materializes over a period of time, the limitation period for future damages arising out of the same incident starts to run with the occurrence of the first and initial damage, provided that such further damages are foreseeable. Accordingly, any (foreseeable) future damage arising out of the same incident does not trigger

98. Judgement of 21 April 2005, 6 Ob 237/04b (Austrian Supreme Court).
99. Judgement of 5 June 1974, 1 Ob 58/74 (Austrian Supreme Court); judgement of 24 May 1977, 5 Ob 520/77 (Austrian Supreme Court).
100. Judgement of 11 March 1996, 1 Ob 2018/96p (Austrian Supreme Court); judgement of 23 November 2000, 8 Ob 27/00d (Austrian Supreme Court).
101. *See* Frauenberger-Pfeiler, *supra* n. 7, at n. 46.
102. For example judgement of 30 November 1966, 6 Ob 366/66 (Austrian Supreme Court); judgement of 31 March 1977, 6 Ob 725/76 (Austrian Supreme Court); judgement of 26 February 1992, 9 ObA 21/92 (Austrian Supreme Court).
103. For example judgement of 13 March 1975, 2 Ob 333/74 (Austrian Supreme Court).
104. Raimund Madl, *§ 1489* n. 9, in *ABGB-ON – Kommentar zum Allgemeinen bürgerlichen Gesetzbuch* (Andreas Kletečka & Martin Schauer eds., 2010); RIS-Justiz RS0083144.

separate limitation periods.[105] This corresponds to the now prevailing theory of damage under Austrian law pursuant to which future harm and the first, initial harm are considered to constitute one single unit from the statute of limitations perspective, provided that such future harm is foreseeable (*gemäßigte Einheitstheorie*).

Accordingly, in cases where some damage has already occurred and in which the occurrence of future damage is possible, the aggrieved party must request a declaration of liability for future damage in order to avoid any future damage arising out of the same incident becoming time-barred.[106] Such obligation is only limited in cases where the occurrence of such future damage, even though it could not be excluded with virtual certainty, is unlikely.[107] Similarly, if future damage cannot be foreseen, there is no risk that they may become time-barred.[108] The advantage of this obligation to request a declaration of liability for future damage within the limitation period for the first and initial damage is said to lie in procedural efficiency.[109] If a dispute about damage is pending anyway and if claimant has already brought an action for performance for such damage, it is considered reasonable to require claimant to also request a declaration of liability for future damage.[110] This does not require significant additional procedural efforts on claimant's part. By contrast, it would be unreasonable to require a party that has not yet incurred any damage to commence legal proceedings in order to achieve a declaration of liability for any future damages.[111]

This notwithstanding, according to settled case law, declaratory relief can be granted even if no damage has yet occurred.[112] As indicated above, jurisprudence on this matter tended to be inconsistent and has evolved significantly. While some judgements (only) allowed declaratory relief of liability for future damage if at least some damage had already occurred,[113] it has by now become established that this is not a mandatory requirement. The Austrian Supreme Court has decided that, under certain circumstances, no damage must have already occurred in order to allow a declaration of liability for future damages.[114]

For example, in one case,[115] claimant was the daughter of a woman who had died in a car accident, which had been caused by respondent. Claimant requested that

105. Madl, *supra* n. 104, at n. 9; RIS-Justiz RS0087613.
106. Frauenberger-Pfeiler, *supra* n. 7, at n. 153; RIS-Justiz RS0034286; RIS-Justiz RS0097976; RIS-Justiz RS0087613.
107. Judgement of 19 April 1978, 8 Ob 41/78 (Austrian Supreme Court); judgement of 30 June 1981, 2 Ob 8/81 (Austrian Supreme Court).
108. Judgement of 21 April 2010, 7 Ob 67/10v (Austrian Supreme Court). *See also* Natascha Brandstätter, *Die verjährungsrechtliche Relevanz der Unterscheidung zwischen Primär- und Folgeschäden*, ecolex 2015, 448, 450–452; Natascha Brandstätter, *Die Verjährung nicht vorhersehbarer Folgeschäden*, RdW 2016, 170, 172–174.
109. *See* RIS-Justiz RS0097976.
110. *See* judgement of 19 November 1995, 1 Ob 621/95 (Austrian Supreme Court). *See also* Franz Bydlinski, *Schadensentstehung und Verjährungsbeginn im österreichischen Recht*, in Festschrift für Erich Steffen zum 65. Geburtstag, 65, 82 (Erwin Deutsch & Ernst Klingmüller & Hans Josef Kullmann eds., 1995).
111. *See* Bydlinski, *supra* n. 110, at 65, 82–83.
112. *See* RIS-Justiz RS0038949; RIS-Justiz RS0038865; RIS-Justiz RS0038909.
113. *See* RIS-Justiz RS0040838.
114. *See* Frauenberger-Pfeiler, *supra* n. 7, at n. 56.
115. Judgement of 14 November 1968, 2 Ob 301/68 (Austrian Supreme Court).

respondent be declared liable for any future harm arising out of her mother's death. Claimant was a dependent minor and, as such, entitled to receive child support from her parents. Claimant submitted that she had not yet incurred any damage since her father was financially providing for her. However, claimant argued that she could conceivably incur harm in the event that her father died before she was able to support herself. Claimant submitted that, if such an eventuality occurred, she would not be able to receive any child support from her mother. Claimant relied on § 1327 ABGB, which provides that surviving dependents are entitled to receive compensation for lost subsistence payments and submitted that, in the event of her father's death, she would be entitled to receive such compensation from respondent. The Austrian Supreme Court considered that claimant was entitled to the respective declaration in light of the mere possibility that damage may occur and in light of the risk of future problems relating to the taking of evidence concerning respondent's (sole) responsibility for the accident.[116] Notably, the Austrian Supreme Court framed this situation not primarily as a question of liability for future harm, but as liability for harm the occurrence of which is still subject to a condition precedent.[117]

Furthermore, in a subsequent case,[118] the Austrian Supreme Court ruled that it is not necessary for any damage to have occurred if there was an incident that could easily have led to damage and the lack of actual damage was rather coincidental and if similar incidents that may potentially lead to damage could happen again anytime. In this case, in the course of work on a facade, several damaging incidents had already occurred (building panels came loose), and it was only by lucky chance that did they not cause any damage. However, it was to be expected that such incidents may occur again and that harm may result. The judgement in this case allowed the action for declaratory relief for such future damage on the grounds that it was a coincidence that no damage had yet occurred and that it was likely that future damage would occur. The court considered, among other factors, that the liability for future damages could be declared in cases where such declaration would avoid future disputes. By granting the requested declaration, the court facilitated avoidance of future disputes: such future dispute may have been avoided altogether because respondent may have fixed the facade in order not to actually be held liable for any damage. Furthermore, if the damage did eventually occur, the dispute would be limited since the question of liability had already been determined.

Moreover, in another case,[119] the Austrian Supreme Court granted a declaration of liability for future damages where claimant required a declaration of liability for future damages as a basis for his economic planning. In this case, a child was afflicted with a disability as a consequence of alleged medical malpractice during the child's birth. The father, who was under a legal obligation to support the child, expected to

116. But cf. judgement of 18 February 1971, 2 Ob 27/71 (Austrian Supreme Court) (dismissing an action for declaratory relief in comparable circumstances, finding that the parent's death was not merely a condition precedent for claimant's claim against respondent, but rather a fact that would only create the claim stipulated in § 1327 ABGB).
117. *See also* Frauenberger-Pfeiler, *supra* n. 7, at n. 42.
118. Judgement of 9 March 1983, 1 Ob 544/83 (Austrian Supreme Court).
119. Judgement of 29 April 1997, 1 Ob 2201/96z (Austrian Supreme Court).

incur expenditures for his child in connection with the child's disability. The father requested a declaration that the legal entity that was operating the hospital was liable for any such future damages that the father may incur in the form of expenditures for his child. While the father had not yet made any such expenditures and had thus not yet incurred any damage, the court considered that the father's ability for economic planning was impeded in light of the respondent's denial of any liability for future expenditures. The court considered that the father, in order to assess his financial capabilities, had to know before making any expenditures whether he would be entitled to receive compensation for them afterwards. The background and purpose of this declaratory action was thus quite different than in the other cases described above. Specifically, the declaratory action was aimed at providing the claimant with a decision basis for his economic planning.

In other subsequent cases,[120] the courts granted a declaration for future liability on a general basis when there was a current reason to pre-emptively clarify the legal relationship, which was specifically considered to be the case when the legal relationship appeared at risk because of a significant uncertainty, such as when respondent persistently denies claimant's right.

For example, one case[121] concerned the sale of a real estate property in which the parties had agreed that the seller should be entitled to withdraw from the contract if claimant did not comply with certain terms of payment. Furthermore, the contract stipulated that in, such an event, the buyer would have to pay a penalty corresponding to of 5% of the purchase price and that the seller was also entitled to claim further damages. The buyer failed to secure the necessary funding, and the seller exercised its right to withdraw from the contract. While the buyer offered to pay the contractual penalty, it declined to recognize any liability for future damage, arguing that the parties intended that the contractual penalty would already encompass compensation for any future harm and that no damages could therefore be claimed in addition to the penalty. The seller then sued, requesting *inter alia* a declaration of liability for any future damage that may result from its withdrawal from the contract, arguing that it had not yet been able to sell the property to a third party and that there was a risk that it would eventually only be able to sell the property at a reduced price. The Austrian Supreme Court took the position that it was sufficient that future damage may occur and that it was disputed between the parties whether a correct interpretation of the contract would entitle the seller to recover any such future damage in addition to the contractual penalty. It considered the action for declaratory relief to be admissible because future damage was possible and because the requested declaration would clarify the question of liability in principle. Accordingly, it interpreted the contract and concluded that the contract allowed the seller to recover for any future harm in addition to the contractual

120. For example judgement of 22 April 1999, 6 Ob 288/98s (Austrian Supreme Court); judgement of 22 February 2001, 6 Ob 335/00h (Austrian Supreme Court); judgement of 8 October 2003, 9 Ob 53/03i (Austrian Supreme Court); judgement of 16 June 2004, 7 Ob 120/04d (Austrian Supreme Court).

121. Judgement of 22 February 2001, 6 Ob 335/00h (Austrian Supreme Court).

penalty. In this context, the court confirmed the decision of the Court of First Instance that had declared respondent liable for any future damages.

In light of the above, future liability may now be declared also for at least potentially damaging incidents on a rather general basis.[122] The courts not only allow actions for declaration of future liability when there is a danger of claims becoming time-barred, but also, more generally, when it appears objectively appropriate to clarify certain facts that may be relevant for possible future claims for damages,[123] such as for the prevention of difficulties related to gathering evidence in the future and the clarification of the question of liability on the merits.[124] The mere possibility that future damage may occur is considered sufficient in order to allow an action for declaratory relief.[125] An action for declaratory relief will only be inadmissible when future damage can be excluded with certainty or virtual certainty.[126]

The jurisprudence allowing declarations of liability for future harm has given rise to some criticism in the doctrine since, strictly speaking, liability for future harm does not constitute a legal relationship. It is unanimously accepted that liability for damages would constitute a legal relationship if such liability had materialized on the basis of a cause, unlawful conduct, possibly fault, an existing damage and causality. However, where no damage yet exists, the declaration of liability for future damages can only encompass cause, unlawful behaviour and, where required, fault, but not an existing damage and causality. Accordingly, such declaratory relief would not declare an actual liability, but rather only specific elements of such liability (i.e., the fact that that the injuring party has unlawfully caused the event that may lead to future harm), which would ordinarily not qualify as a legal relationship or right.[127] Also, according to the Austrian Supreme Court, a declaration for liability for future harm can only concern the unlawful conduct itself, but not a specific future damage and causality – it merely declares the respondent's liability for future harm, but it does not declare which specific harm will have to be repaired once such future harm materializes.[128] Hence, even in the case of a declaration for future liability, the claimant will have to prove in a subsequent action for performance whether the claimed damage is covered by the respondent's liability, i.e., in particular whether the damage was caused by the unlawful conduct.

The jurisprudence does not always draw a clear distinction between the objective scope of declaratory relief on the one hand and the existence of legal interest on the other. In some cases, the Austrian Supreme Court specifically found that the existence

122. RIS-Justiz RS0038909.
123. Judgement of 22 November 2007, 8 Ob 73/07d (Austrian Supreme Court); judgement of 25 November 2008, 1 Ob 237/08x (Austrian Supreme Court); judgement of 25 March 2014, 4 Ob 23/14g (Austrian Supreme Court).
124. RIS-Justiz RS0038976.
125. RIS-Justiz RS0038865; RIS-Justiz RS0039018; RIS-Justiz RS0038976.
126. For example judgement of 5 July 2006, 7 Ob 149/06x (Austrian Supreme Court); judgement of 22 November 2011, 17 Ob 29/11f (Austrian Supreme Court); judgement of 28 April 2015, 8 Ob 15/15m (Austrian Supreme Court); judgement of 23 February 2018, 8 Ob 138/17b (Austrian Supreme Court).
127. Frauenberger-Pfeiler, *supra* n. 7, at n. 59.
128. RIS-Justiz RS0038915.

of a liability (for future damage) qualifies as a legal relationship within the meaning of § 228 Austrian CCP.[129] In other cases, the courts addressed the question of whether there can be a declaration of liability for future damage in terms of whether legal interest in such declaration exists.[130] For example, the line of judicial authority that required at least some damage to have occurred by the end of the oral hearing at first instance had it that a lack of such damage would lead to a lack of legal interest in the requested declaration.[131] Similarly, the more recent and established lines of authority that do not uphold such requirement sometimes stipulate that *legal interest* is considered to exist even though no damage has occurred yet.[132] Some judgements even make express reference to the point of view expressed in doctrine that in, cases where no damage has yet occurred, strictly speaking, no *legal relationship* exists, only to then point out that it is nonetheless established case law that *legal interest* is considered to exist in such cases.[133]

The approach that allows an action for declaratory relief where damage has not yet occurred was further defined and has grown in practical importance in a series of cases that involved private investors suing for damages that they incurred as a consequence of allegedly wrongful investment advice from their banks. In these cases, claimants had made investments which they considered to be safe on the basis of their bank's investment advice. When the value of their investments plummeted, they sued their banks, arguing that they had incurred damage as a consequence of their bank's incorrect investment advice on which they had relied upon.

In dealing with these cases, a number of complex legal problems arose, starting with the assessment of damages, specifically when the claimant still held the investments in question. There are essentially two possible views on how to assess the legal situation of investors who had acquired a high-risk, volatile investment as a consequence of incorrect investment advice and who had not yet exited their investment but wanted to claim damages.[134] According to the first view, no (quantifiable) damage has yet occurred because the economic disadvantage only materializes at the end of the assessment period or when the investment is being sold.[135] According to the second view, the legal damage has already occurred at the time of the investment (even though

129. For example judgement of 23 September 1987, 1 Ob 648/87 (Austrian Supreme Court); judgement of 23 May 1989, 5 Ob 550/89 (Austrian Supreme Court); judgement of 22 February 1990, 6 Ob 525/90 (Austrian Supreme Court); judgement of 28 January 2016, 1 Ob 162/15b (Austrian Supreme Court).
130. *See*, e.g., judgement of 3 March 2010, 7 Ob 193/09x (Austrian Supreme Court); judgement of 27 May 2010, 5 Ob 229/09a (Austrian Supreme Court); judgement of 10 September 2014, 7 Ob 91/14d (Austrian Supreme Court).
131. RIS-Justiz RS0040838.
132. For example judgement of 14 July 2005, 6 Ob 295/03f (Austrian Supreme Court); judgement of 10 September 2014, 7Ob91/14d (Austrian Supreme Court).
133. For example judgement of 22 February 2001, 6 Ob 335/00h (Austrian Supreme Court); judgement of 7 June 2006, 9 ObA 87/05t (Austrian Supreme Court); judgement of 21 September 2006, 8 ObA 23/06z (Austrian Supreme Court).
134. *See* Thomas Klicka, *Die Klage auf Feststellung der Haftpflicht bei Anlegerschäden*, ÖJZ 2012, 487, 487–488.
135. RIS-Justiz RS0120784.

it was not yet quantifiable at that time), being comprised in the acquisition of the high-risk investment itself, irrespective of its future price development.[136]

The question of whether some damage had already occurred was important in two aspects. First, it was important for assessing whether a claim for damages may already have become time-barred because the limitation period may have been triggered already by claimant's first awareness of the high-risk nature of the investment, irrespective of whether it still held the investments.[137] Second, it was important for the question of whether an action for declaratory relief would be admissible in light of the principle of subsidiarity and, consequently, for whether an action for declaratory relief would successfully interrupt the limitation period.[138] Specifically, as explained above, in accordance with the principle of subsidiarity an action for declaratory relief is inadmissible in cases where claimant could already bring an action for performance that would provide the same legal protection. However, if the damage is considered to have been incurred already at the time of the acquisition of the investment, the question arises whether a claimant could already bring an action for performance that would provide the same, or greater, legal protection than an action for declaratory relief. If this is the case, an action for declaratory relief would have to be considered inadmissible, would hence not interrupt the limitation period and a claimant's claims for damages would therefore risk becoming time-barred.

Initially, the Austrian Supreme Court followed the view that any (quantifiable) damage would only occur at the end of the assessment period or once the investment was being sold. For example, in one case,[139] the bank's client and subsequent claimant was interested in a safe investment until his retirement in three or four years which would bring higher returns than a savings account. The bank employee, without any detailed explanation, suggested objectively high-risk equity funds and dispelled the concerns of the customer. After less than two years, the price of the investments decreased significantly and the customer brought an action for declaratory relief, requesting that the bank be declared liable for any future losses resulting from the ill-fated investment advice. The Austrian Supreme Court ruled that claimant, who continued to hold the investments, had presently not incurred any damage. While the court acknowledged that therefore, strictly speaking, no legal relationship existed, it considered that there was a current reason for pre-emptively clarifying the legal relationship, given that respondent was denying that the investment advice given was bad and likely to entail future loss. It was due to this denial, and for the avoidance of any future difficulties with respect to taking evidence (considering that claimant was relying also on the witness examination of the bank employee), that the court allowed the action for declaratory relief. The court also noted that the legal situation would be different if claimant had already sold the financial papers, in which case the damage would have occurred already.

136. *See*, e.g., Peter Bydlinski, *Haftung für fehlerhafte Anlageberatung – Schaden und Schadenersatz*, ÖBA 2008, 159, 161; RIS-Justiz RS0129706.
137. *See*, e.g., judgement of 3 November 1997, 7 Ob 253/97z (Austrian Supreme Court).
138. *See* Madl, *supra* n. 104, at n. 15; Frauenberger-Pfeiler, *supra* n. 7, at n. 153.
139. Judgement of 8 October 2003, 9 Ob 53/03i (Austrian Supreme Court).

In another, similar case,[140] the bank's client and eventual claimant bought shares of a third-party equity fund without being advised that this was a high-risk investment and that he could, and should, sell parts of his investments when the prices decreased. Pointing on this allegedly bad advice, the customer sued the bank for damages. The client, who continued to hold all of his investments, quantified the damages by calculating his hypothetical asset value if he had invested in certain low-risk investments, and he proceeded to claim the difference between such amount and the current total value of his investments. The Austrian Supreme Court found that the final damage could not be quantified prior to the sale of the investments and that, therefore, no claim for payment was possible. Furthermore, the Austrian Supreme Court noted that it may also have been possible to grant claimant a claim for restitution in kind (*Naturalrestitution*) if one were to consider that the damage had occurred already when claimant initially acquired the investments. However, claimant had not requested such restitution in kind in the present proceedings. Similarly, the Austrian Supreme Court held that claimant could have brought an action for declaratory relief, which claimant had not done either. Against such background, the Austrian Supreme Court upheld the decision of the Court of Appeal, which had rejected claimant's claim for damages.

As can be seen, the parties and the courts alike have struggled with assessment and quantification of damages. According to the above decisions, no damage – or at least no quantifiable damage – was considered to have been incurred as long as the investors still held the investments in question. Such damage would only occur once they sold their investments. The courts addressed these practical difficulties in quantifying the damages by allowing an action for declaratory relief.

However, this line of jurisprudence which allowed an action for declaratory relief for future damages that would materialize when claimant sold its investments has engendered considerable criticism. While it was possible that no damage would ever occur if the price of the investments recovered again, respondent would be declared liable for any future damage if it occurred. It was pointed out that such declaratory relief would shift the risk of (additional) future price decreases squarely onto the banks; the investors, on the contrary, would be free to choose between an action for declaratory relief (while they still held the investment) and an action for performance (after they had sold). Also, they could bring an action for declaratory relief and then wait and see whether the price would recover again and whether they may even make profits with their high-risk investment. In such a scenario, the investors would retain the chance to make much higher profits than they would ever have made with a low-risk investment while not bearing the risk of any further negative price developments. This would put the investors in a better position than would appear justified to protect their legitimate interests.[141]

Subsequently, the jurisprudence evolved and the Austrian Supreme Court came to cultivate the line that harm consists already in acquisition of the undesired

140. Judgement of 23 February 2006, 8 Ob 123/05d (Austrian Supreme Court).
141. *See*, e.g., Bydlinski, *supra* n. 136, at 161; Florian Linder, *Zur Schadensberechnung und Schadensminderungsobliegenheit bei fehlerhafter Anlageberatung*, ZFR 2006, 104, 105.

investments.[142] Since the damage consists in the deviation from the investor's desired characteristics of the investment (i.e., the investor wanted a safe and low-risk investment and instead bought a volatile high-risk investment), it has been considered to exist irrespectively of whether the price of the investment would increase or decrease in the future.[143] As a consequence, the courts took the position that damage had already occurred also in cases where claimants still held the investments and granted monetary compensation (in the form of the purchase price of the investments minus interest or dividends that the investments had yielded, in principle also taking into account the price development of an hypothetical alternative investment) in exchange for a return of the investments.[144]

In subsequent decisions, the Austrian Supreme Court therefore deemed requests for declaratory relief as inadmissible in cases where claimants still held the investments, taking into account that claimant could already bring an action for performance.[145] In such cases, claimants would only be entitled to declaratory relief when they could show that such action for performance, and hence the return of the investments in exchange for the purchase price, would be impractical (e.g., in a case involving complex financial instruments with multiple contracting parties[146]) or when additional future harm could occur.[147]

Notwithstanding the inadmissibility of an action for declaratory relief when claimant could already bring an action for performance, the Austrian Supreme Court ruled that, in light of the uncertainties surrounding the correct choice of action, also an inadmissible action for declaratory relief would interrupt the limitation period if a corresponding action for performance would only be filed subsequently (i.e., after expiration of the limitation period) and if one of these claims had merits.[148]

142. *See*, e.g., judgement of 10 March 2008, 10 Ob 11/07a (Austrian Supreme Court); judgement of 30 March 2011, 7 Ob 77/10i (Austrian Supreme Court); judgement of 29 September 2011, 1 Ob 85/11y (Austrian Supreme Court); judgement of 27 April 2017, 2 Ob 99/16x (Austrian Supreme Court). *See also* RIS-Justiz RS0129706.
143. *See*, e.g., judgement of 14 September 2011, 6 Ob 9/11h (Austrian Supreme Court); judgement of 24 October 2011, 8 Ob 135/10a (Austrian Supreme Court); judgement of 20 November 2011, 8 Ob 129/10v (Austrian Supreme Court); judgement of 15 March 2012, 6 Ob 28/12d (Austrian Supreme Court).
144. RIS-Justiz RS0129706. While such claim for damages in exchange for transfer of the shares has sometimes been described as a form of restitution in kind, it should be noted that, in fact, claimants are awarded monetary compensation in exchange for transfer of their investments for the purpose of avoiding enrichment to claimants (*see* Christoph Brenn & Petra Leupold, *Feststellungsbegehren versus 'Naturalrestitution'*, EvBl 759, 761 (2012)).
145. *See*, e.g., judgement of 7 July 2008, 6 Ob 103/08b (Austrian Supreme Court); judgement of 11 May 2010, 9 Ob 85/09d (Austrian Supreme Court); judgement of 14 September 2011, 6 Ob 9/11h (Austrian Supreme Court); judgement of 20 November 2011, 8 Ob 129/10v (Austrian Supreme Court); judgement of 15 March 2012, 6 Ob 28/12d (Austrian Supreme Court). *See also* Madl, *supra* n. 104, at n. 15.
146. Judgement of 24 October 2012, 8 Ob 39/12m (Austrian Supreme Court).
147. Judgement of 24 October 2012, 8 Ob 39/12m (Austrian Supreme Court); judgement of 28 August 2013, 6 Ob 53/13g (Austrian Supreme Court). *See also* Madl, *supra* n. 104, at n. 15.
148. Judgement of 28 August 2013, 6 Ob 53/13g (Austrian Supreme Court); judgement of 17 November 2013, 4 Ob 135/13a (Austrian Supreme Court). *See also* Madl, *supra* n. 104, at n. 15.

[C] Legal Relationships vis a vis Third Parties

In principle, a legal relationship can only be subject of a declaratory relief if such legal relationship exists between the parties. However, in some cases declaratory decisions on a legal relationship between a party and a third party, or only between third parties, are also possible. This is only the case when such legal relationship interferes with, and hence has an impact on, the legal status of the claimant.[149] In these cases, the claimant's legal interest must be closely explored, since the decision would usually not have any legal effects for a third party not involved in the proceedings.[150]

For example, courts have granted declaratory relief in a case involving an employer who requested a declaration that an insurance company has to provide insurance protection to one of its employees[151] or in a case involving an owner of a property who requested a declaration that a lease agreement over the property made between the respondents as lessor and lessee was invalid.[152]

[D] Matters That Cannot Be Subject of Declaratory Relief

The following issues *cannot* be subject matter of declaratory relief pursuant to § 228 Austrian CCP.[153]

Facts cannot be the subject matter of declaratory relief, even when they are legally relevant.[154] On that basis, courts have, for example, rejected requests for declarations concerning the question on what date a notice of termination had been delivered,[155] whether a specific resolution had been taken at a general assembly of a limited liability company,[156] and whether respondent has in bad faith prevented the fulfilment of a condition precedent which therefore has to be considered unfulfilled.[157] By contrast, the courts have held that the question of whether someone is a member of an association could be the subject matter of a declaratory relief because someone's membership in an association is a legal relationship.[158] Furthermore, the courts have held that the question whether someone is the author of a specific work can be subject to declaratory relief because authorship legally connects the author with her work and is therefore a legal relationship.[159]

As will be further addressed below, in contrast to the general rule that facts cannot be the subject of declaratory relief, § 228 Austrian CCP expressly stipulates that

149. *Frauenberger-Pfeiler* in *Fasching/Konecny*[3] § 228 n. 64; RIS-Justiz RS0038958.
150. *See* RIS-Justiz RS0039068.
151. Judgement of 25 February 1970, 7 Ob 29/70 (Austrian Supreme Court).
152. Judgement of 5 September 2002, 2 Ob 157/02f (Austrian Supreme Court). *See* above at Annex I.III[B] for further details of the case.
153. *See also* Rechberger & Simotta, *supra* n. 16, at n. 605.
154. Frauenberger-Pfeiler, *supra* n. 7, at n. 68; RIS-Justiz RS0038943.
155. Judgement of 15 July 2013, Rv. I 737/13, GlUNF 6528 (Austrian Supreme Court).
156. Judgement of 21 October 1924, 2 Ob 665/24 (Austrian Supreme Court).
157. Judgement of 4 September 2002, 9 Ob 165/02h (Austrian Supreme Court).
158. For example judgement of 20 January 1993, 3 Ob 567/92. (Austrian Supreme Court) *See also* RIS-Justiz RS0038953.
159. Judgement of 9 November 1997, 4 Ob 311/97g (Austrian Supreme Court).

the authenticity of a document, i.e., the fact that the document indeed originates from the person identified on the document as its author, can be the subject of declaratory relief.[160]

Furthermore, legal qualities of facts or legal acts or single elements of legal relationships cannot be the subject matter of declaratory relief.[161] Thus, declaratory relief cannot be granted on the question whether a specific behaviour qualifies as negligent conduct,[162] whether a specific act was lawful,[163] or whether a specific claim could be offset.[164] However, the courts have allowed a declaration on the question of whether a specific decision by the supervisory board of a limited liability company is null and void[165] or whether a resolution taken by the general assembly amending the charter of an association was valid.[166] Furthermore, as has been described above, established jurisprudence allows declarations of liability for future damages also in cases where no damage has yet occurred – even though, strictly speaking, this amounts to a declaration concerning single elements of a legal relationship only.

Specifically, in one case claimant requested a declaration that the decision of its employer to provide wage slips in electronic form only (rather than also in paper form) was unlawful.[167] The Austrian Supreme Court noted that the action for declaratory relief was aimed at a declaration concerning the legal qualification of an action, i.e., whether providing wage slips in electronic form only was unlawful, which could not be the subject matter of a declaratory relief. The Austrian Supreme Court also considered the possibility of reinterpreting claimant's request in order to give effect to claimant's intended aim of legal protection; however, it concluded that this was only possible in cases where the claimant's prayer for relief had been phrased incorrectly by accident, not by design. In this context, the Austrian Supreme Court noted that, while respondent had pointed out that the requested declaration could not be the subject matter of an action for declaratory relief, claimant insisted on its request and submitted that its request was indeed admissible. Against such background, the Austrian Supreme Court concluded that claimant did not accidentally phrase its request incorrectly, which is why it did not have to analyse the question whether claimant's request could be reinterpreted.[168] For the sake of completeness, it should be noted that claimant received an assessment of its concern nonetheless: while the Court of Appeal dismissed claimant's action for declaratory relief for the reasons set out above it stated *obiter* that, in any event, claimant did not have a right to receive its wage slips in paper form.

160. Frauenberger-Pfeiler, *supra* n. 7, at nn. 49, 70–72.
161. *Ibid.*, at nn. 66–67.
162. RIS-Justiz RS0038857.
163. Judgement of 23 March 2018, 8 ObA 4/18y (Austrian Supreme Court).
164. RIS-Justiz RS0039086.
165. RIS-Justiz RS0038980.
166. RIS-Justiz RS0038953.
167. Judgement of 23 March 2018, 8 ObA 4/18y (Austrian Supreme Court).
168. It should be noted that it is not entirely clear whether the Austrian Supreme Court considered that there would have been a possibility to reinterpret claimant's request successfully; possibly it would have considered a reinterpretation from an action for declaratory relief in an action for performance.

The validity of certain legal acts (*Rechtshandlungen*) cannot be the subject matter of declaratory relief either.[169] This concerns especially statements, notices or declarations which result in legal consequences,[170] such as the termination of an employment contract,[171] a withdrawal from a contract,[172] etc. This is the case because the validity of a certain legal acts is only a preliminary question for the existence or non-existence of the legal relationship.[173]

This notwithstanding, the existence of the legal relationship as such (i.e., whether an employment contract or the lease agreement is currently valid and in effect) can obviously be the subject of declaratory relief. Austrian courts tend to allow such requests concerning the validity of certain legal acts by reinterpreting the request accordingly, i.e., by interpreting a request for a declaration on the validity of a certain legal act as a request for a declaration on the existence or non-existence of the legal relationship that would be affected by the legal act.[174]

For example, in one case claimant requested a declaration that respondent's notice of withdrawal by which respondent purported to withdraw from a contract with claimant was invalid. The court noted that this could not be the subject matter of a declaratory relief. However, the court decided that it could reinterpret claimant's request as a request for a declaration that the respective legal relationship between claimant and respondent continued to exist notwithstanding respondent's purported notice of withdrawal.[175]

Furthermore, in a case concerning the allegedly unlawful termination of the employment contract,[176] the employer had terminated the employment contract with immediate effect, i.e., without regard to the relevant notice periods. Claimant requested both a declaration that (i) the employment relationship continued to exist and that (ii) the employer's termination with immediate effect was invalid. The Austrian Supreme Court ruled that, in principle, even an unlawful immediate termination of the employment contract would validly terminate the contract under Austrian labour law. Accordingly, the Austrian Supreme Court concluded that claimant could only claim its lost earnings until the point in time by which the employment contract could have been validly terminated in compliance with the relevant notice periods. Against such background, the court considered that claimant was not entitled to the requested declaration.

Similarly, in another case concerning allegedly unlawful termination of an employment contract, the employer had terminated the employment contract while the employee was under maternity protection. Claimant requested both a declaration that (i) the employment relationship continued to exist and that (ii) the employer's

169. Frauenberger-Pfeiler, *supra* n. 7, at n. 40. *See also* RIS-Justiz RS0038804.
170. *See* RIS-Justiz RS0039087.
171. Judgement of 27 October 1994, 8 ObA 310/94 (Austrian Supreme Court); judgement of 27 May 2014, 9 ObA 55/14z (Austrian Supreme Court).
172. Judgement of 22 November 1994, 4 Ob 573/94 (Austrian Supreme Court).
173. *See* RIS-Justiz RS0039087.
174. Frauenberger-Pfeiler, *supra* n. 7, at n. 40.
175. Judgement of 22 November 1994, 4 Ob 573/94 (Austrian Supreme Court).
176. Judgement of 22 June 1955, 3 Ob 316/55 (Austrian Supreme Court).

termination was invalid. On the basis of the consideration that the termination was indeed unlawful, the Austrian Supreme Court concluded that claimant had a right in the requested declaration that the employment relationship continued to exist (notably, in this scenario the effect of an unlawful termination was the continued existence of the employment relationship). However, it held the requested declaration that the employer's termination was invalid inadmissible since its subject matter was not the declaration of a right or legal relationship, but the validity of a legal act (i.e., the termination of the contract).[177]

As indicated above, where an employee only requests a declaration that the allegedly unlawful termination of the employment contract was invalid and where it is clear that, in fact, claimant's objective of legal protection is a declaration that the employment relationship continues to exist, the courts may reinterpret such request accordingly and thus grant a declaration that the employment relationship continues to exist.[178]

Moreover, the legal qualification of a legal relationship can, in principle, not be the subject matter of a declaratory relief. However, jurisprudence and legal doctrine take the position that, in some cases, it may be necessary to also allow declarations on the legal qualification of a legal relationship, specifically when they impact on the substance of the disputed legal relationship, i.e., on the parties' rights and obligations.[179] The line between the existence of a legal relationship and the question of its legal qualification can be blurry, and the courts tend to follow a casuistic approach in this regard. The courts have, *inter alia*, allowed declarations on the question of whether a tenancy agreement is subject to specific provisions of tenant protection laws; whether a person qualifies as tenant or subtenant; whether a specific collective labour agreement applies to an employment relationship; whether an employment contract was non-terminable for a specific period of time, etc.[180] By contrast, courts have, *inter alia*, not allowed a declaration concerning the legal reason for someone's acquisition of a property. In one case,[181] claimant brought a principal claim for a declaration that he had acquired a specific property by usucaption and an alternative claim that he had acquired the same property by winning a public auction held under compelled sale. While the Austrian Supreme Court did not have to decide on this specific issue because the matter was referred to the Court of First Instance for the taking of additional evidence, it noted that the legal reason for which claimant acquired the property is merely a preliminary question for what claimant actually wanted, namely a declaration that claimant owns the relevant property (which could be the subject matter of a declaratory relief[182]). The Austrian Supreme Court further noted that the legal reason for claimant's acquisition of the property could not be the subject of declaratory relief and that this consideration, which had not yet been discussed in the proceedings at the

177. Judgement of 15 March 1950, 1 Ob 81/50 (Austrian Supreme Court).
178. RIS-Justiz RS0039010.
179. Frauenberger-Pfeiler, *supra* n. 7, at n. 45; RIS-Justiz RS0038902.
180. *See* Frauenberger-Pfeiler, *supra* n. 7, at nn. 39, 45–46, 48.
181. Judgement of 7 June 2016, 10 Ob 36/16s (Austrian Supreme Court).
182. *See*, e.g., judgement of 21 June 2016, 1 Ob 36/16z (Austrian Supreme Court).

courts of lower instance, would have to be raised with claimant in order to avoid a surprise decision.

Legal relationships which do not exist at the time when the oral proceedings of first instance are closed at the latest cannot be the subject of declaratory relief.[183] For example, it would not be possible to claim nullity of a contract that has not been made yet. By contrast, case law allows declaratory relief concerning the duration of a past employment relationship due to its relevance in social security matters.[184] On the contrary, as indicated above, if a legal relationship depends on some other condition, an action for declaratory relief is possible provided that a precisely and clearly defined condition has not yet occurred while the underlying facts of the case are claimed to be certain.[185]

Furthermore, declarations on legal relationships that are not part of civil law or on rights that are not actionable cannot be the subject of declaratory relief.[186]

In like spirit, abstract legal questions (including abstract questions on statutory law) cannot be the subject matter of declaratory relief.[187] For example, in one case,[188] an employee requested a declaration that her employer would have to observe a notice period of fourteen days before terminating her employment relationship. While the parties had agreed in the contract that the employment relationship could be terminated without any notice period, claimant argued that such clause was unlawful and hence invalid. The Austrian Supreme Court decided that this was merely an abstract legal question that could not be the subject matter of a declaratory relief. In this respect, the Austrian Supreme Court noted that claimant had not even submitted that respondent intended to terminate the employment relationship. Furthermore, the Austrian Supreme Court noted that, in any event, also an unlawful termination in disregard of any applicable notice periods would be effective under Austrian labour law (and may only subsequently entitle claimant to claim for lost earnings), which is why the requested declaration would not have an impact on claimant's specific legal position.

Finally, an action for declaratory relief cannot be a legal remedy against a decision by a court or against the res iudicata effect of a judicial decision.[189]

[E] Authenticity of Documents

As previously indicated, declaratory decisions are possible as regards the authenticity (or lack thereof) of a document. This constitutes an *ex lege* exception from the general rule that facts cannot be the subject matter of a declaratory relief. Also the authenticity of electronic documents can be the subject matter of a declaratory decision.[190]

183. Frauenberger-Pfeiler, *supra* n. 7, at n. 41; RIS-Justiz RS0039178.
184. RIS-Justiz RS0039159.
185. Frauenberger-Pfeiler, *supra* n. 7, at n. 42.
186. *Ibid.*, at n. 47.
187. *Ibid.*, at n. 65. *See also* RIS-Justiz RS0039014; RIS-Justiz RS0038802.
188. Judgement of 16 November 1992, 9 ObA 257/92 (Austrian Supreme Court).
189. Frauenberger-Pfeiler, *supra* n. 7, at n. 10.
190. *Ibid.*, at n. 71.

A document is considered 'authentic' when it indeed originates from the indicated author of the document. Accordingly, the subject matter of the requested declaration is whether the document originates from the person that is indicated as its author. By contrast, the legal validity of the document or the accuracy of information contained therein cannot be the subject matter of declaratory relief.[191]

V THE ISSUE OF RES IUDICATA

If it transpires at the beginning of, or during, pending court proceedings that a legal relationship or right that is disputed between the parties is of preliminary nature (*präjudiziell*) for the decision on the parties' dispute, such preliminary question will usually be addressed in the reasoning of the final judgement. In this way, the resolution will serve as the basis of the decision over the parties' claim. However, as will be explained below, any assessment of the preliminary question will not become res judicata.

An action for performance results in a ruling on the merits of the claim *in concretu*, and only this result becomes res iudicata. The legal effect of res iudicata is limited by the identity of the claim, i.e., if the subject matter of a new claim is identical to the subject matter of a past ruling. The verdict alone is often not sufficient to assess whether the claim is identical. Therefore, the effects of res iudicata do extend to the judgment's reasoning (*Entscheidungsgründe*) insofar as the reasoning serves to interpret and individualize the verdict. This effect is called the 'relative effect of res iudicata of the ratio decidendi' (*relative Rechtskraftwirkung der Entscheidungsgründe*).[192]

That said, with due heed for the above caveat, the effect of res iudicata applies only to the verdict of the ruling and the explicit legal consequences stated therein; it does not apply to the logical prerequisites of the decision or to other logical consequences. In principle, other elements of a judicial decision (the conclusion of facts, the court's legal assessment, determinations of preliminary questions, etc.) do not become res iudicata. Accordingly, if claimant brings an action for performance on the basis of a certain legal relationship, the question of the (non-existence) of such underlying legal relationship is examined as a preliminary question by the court, which – while crucial for the result – does not become res iudicata. If the same legal relationship becomes relevant again in any future proceedings, the judge has to assess the question again as a preliminary question. Accordingly, courts ruling in any future proceedings will have to assess anew both factual and legal preliminary questions that have already been assessed in previous proceedings. In doing so, they may come to different conclusions than the courts in previous proceedings.[193]

Sometimes, however, it may be desirable to resolve the preliminary question not only with effect for the present proceedings, but with res judicata effect for future

191. *Ibid.*, at nn. 71–72.
192. Rechberger & Simotta, *supra* n. 16, at nn. 949–953.
193. Thomas Klicka, *§ 411* n. 68, in *III/2 Kommentar zu den Zivilprozessgesetzen* (Hans Walter Fasching & Andreas Konecny eds. 3rd ed., 2017); RIS-Justiz RS0041572; RIS-Justiz RS0041285; RIS-Justiz RS0102102.

proceedings. In those cases, claimant can introduce an action for declaratory relief or a petition for incident declaratory relief. The result would be a declaratory ruling,[194] in which the legal relationship or right as such becomes the substance of the case and, therefore, the ruling becomes legally binding for other courts in future trials. This is why a legal interest to obtain declaratory relief may exist also in cases in which the claimant may introduce an action for performance, provided that the legal protection afforded to the claimant by a declaratory relief will be greater than the legal protection afforded by an action for performance.

This notwithstanding, it is worth emphasizing that, as far as declaratory rulings go, only the legal relationship or right as such becomes res iudicata. If, for example, claimant obtains a declaratory ruling on liability for future damages, questions of causality or whether any additional damage occurred at all are not covered by the res iudicata effect.

For example, the question of the objective scope of the res judicata effect of a declaratory judgement became relevant in two proceedings in the legal aftermaths of a car accident which had been culpably caused by respondent. In the first proceedings, claimant claimed damages for loss of income for the period between 1 September 1989 through 29 February 1992, arguing that his earning capacity had been diminished as a consequence of his slipped disks, an injury that he alleged was caused by the car accident. Furthermore, he requested a declaration that respondents (i.e., the driver and his insurance company) be liable for any future harm that may arise out of the accident. The court accepted that claimant's slipped disks had been caused by the car accident and, accordingly, partially granted his request for damages for loss of income. Furthermore, the court declared that respondents are liable for all damages that claimant may incur in the future and that are caused by the car accident. In subsequent proceedings, claimant requested additional damages for further loss of income for the period of time between 1 November 1992 and 31 January 1994, arguing that this loss of income was again the consequence of his slipped disks, which were in turn caused by the car accident. The Court of First Instance dismissed the claims, finding that claimant had already been treated for slipped disks prior to the car accident (a fact that had been missed in the first proceedings) and that it could not be established with sufficient certainty that the slipped disks were indeed caused by the car accident. Claimant appealed against the judgement, arguing that the courts in the second proceedings were bound by the court's assessment in the first proceedings that the slipped disks were caused by the car accident. The Austrian Supreme Court dismissed the appeal, finding that the only issue that the courts in the second proceedings could not revisit was the question of whether respondents were liable for harm caused by the car accident.[195] Specifically, the Austrian Supreme Court found that the determination

194. In the case of an action for declaratory relief, i.e., in the first two options, such declaratory ruling may take the form of a *partial* or a *final* judgement (§§ 390, 391(1) and 391(2) Austrian CCP), but not the form of an *interim* judgement (§ 393(2) Austrian CCP). In the case of a petition for incident declaratory relief in accordance with § 236 Austrian CCP, the declaratory ruling could take the form of an interim judgement (§ 393(2) Austrian CCP) or a final judgement (§ 390 Austrian CCP).

195. Judgement of 29 February 1996, 2 Ob 10/96 (Austrian Supreme Court).

that the slipped disks had been caused by the car accident was a mere preliminary question in the first proceedings, which had therefore not become res judicata. The courts in the second proceedings were therefore free to conclude that it had not been proven that the slipped disks were caused by the car accident.

Finally, considering that a court's determination of preliminary questions in an action for performance does not become res iudicata, it is worth noting that claimant may not successfully circumvent any limiting requirements of an action for declaratory relief (such as, in particular, the requirement of legal interest) by introducing an action for performance over only a symbolic amount and by thus implicitly obtaining – in the judgement's reasoning – the court's determination of the underlying legal relationship. In principle, claimant is always free to assert only one out of several claims at a time, or only a portion of a large and divisible claim.[196] For example, a claimant seeking damages in an amount of EUR 1,000 may decide to initiate proceedings in order to only claim a symbolic amount of EUR 1. There may be some strategic procedural considerations militating in favour of such decision, such as exploring what arguments respondent will bring forward, leaving him in a position to make a better informed assessment of the winning chances for the entire claim.

However, as explained above, any decision over such partial claim will only have res iudicata over the amount claimed, irrespective of whether claimant indicated that the claim is only a partial claim.[197] The question of liability is merely a preliminary question which does not become res iudicata. Specifically, if the claimant in the above example subsequently decides to claim the remaining EUR 999 in a second step in separate proceedings, the judge in these proceedings will not be bound by the assessment of the judge in the first proceedings of whether respondent was liable. Accordingly, claiming only a small part of the entire claim entails the risk of contradictory judgments, and therefore does not serve the purpose of (and cannot replace) an action for declaratory relief. Furthermore, it is noteworthy that respondent may be able to avoid such risks of contradictory judgments and of having to defend against a new claim on the basis of the same alleged liability in future proceedings by requesting a declaration that a legal relationship in the form of the alleged liability does not exist, either by way of a counterclaim for negative declaratory relief or by way of a petition for incident declaratory relief.

By contrast, it appears doubtful whether Austrian courts would grant a claimant's request for a petition for incident declaratory relief to the contrary, i.e., a declaration that respondent is liable also for those damages that claimant has not yet claimed, since claimant could already bring an action for performance concerning such claims. According to some scholars[198] and jurisprudence,[199] an incident declaratory relief can also be granted when a claim for performance is already possible.

196. Geroldinger, *supra* n. 17, at n. 24.
197. Klicka, *supra* n. 193, at n. 46. *See also* RIS-Justiz RS0039155; RIS-Justiz RS0041449.
198. Markus Kellner, *Der Zwischenantrag auf Feststellung – Ausgewählte Rechtsfragen zu §§ 236, 259 Abs 2 ZPO*, ÖJZ 2015, 250, 256; Astrid Deixler-Hübner, *§ 236* n. 3, in *III/1 Kommentar zu den Zivilprozessgesetzen* (Hans Walter Fasching & Andreas Konecny eds. 3rd ed., 2017).
199. RIS-Justiz RS0039502. *See also* judgement of 3 December 1985, 5 Ob 97/85 (Austrian Supreme Court).

In contrast to such doctrine and court judgements, the Austrian Supreme Court has held in a recent decision that the principle of subsidiarity applies also in the context of petitions for incident declaratory relief.[200] The case concerned a bank that brought a payment claim arising out of a loan agreement against its client as respondent. Respondent declared set-off with two claims, arguing that he had incurred harm arising out of bad investment advice given by the bank in the context of his acquisition of two different investments. With regard to the second investment, respondent could only claim part of the damage, namely the transactional costs – seeing as he still held the investment, he could not quantify the damage and hence could not declare set-off with a claim over any specific amount of money. While respondent already had a claim for restitution in kind, he could not declare set-off with such claim, since it was not similar in nature to the bank's payment claim. Accordingly, respondent merely declared set-off with his claim for damages in the amount of the transaction costs and introduced a a petition for incident declaratory relief by which he requested a declaration that claimant is liable for any (other) damages arising out of his second investment. While the Court of First Instance granted the requested declaration, the court of second instance rejected the petition for incident declaratory relief, arguing that the question of whether claimant was liable for damages arising out of the second investment would, in any event, be assessed by the court in its decision over the set-off claim and was hence not of preliminary nature for the decision in the present proceedings. While the Austrian Supreme Court did not expressly criticize this (questionable) assessment of the court of second instance, it may ultimately not have been convinced by this reasoning and added that, in any event, respondent lacked the required interest in the declaration sought because it could already bring a separate action for performance, specifically an action for restitution in kind.

Since the Austrian Supreme Court in said judgement did not address the previous jurisprudence in accordance with which the principle of subsidiarity does not apply in the context of a petition for incident declaratory relief, it appears doubtful whether it consciously intended to deviate from said line. Specifically, it does not appear to serve the purpose of procedural efficiency to prohibit a *respondent* from introducing a petition for incident declaratory relief in a situation in which respondent introduces a set-off claim, compelling the courts to assess the claimant's liability in the context of the set-off claim separately and as a preliminary question for claimant's principal claim anyway. Disallowing a petition for incident declaratory relief in such a scenario entails the risk of contradictory judgements when respondent brings an action for restitution in kind in separate proceedings, since the courts will not be bound by the assessment of the preliminary question in the first proceedings.

By contrast, the purpose of procedural efficiency would appear to require a different assessment in a case where the client is the claimant and where the petition for incident declaratory relief would not have been introduced by the respondent (in the context of its set-off claim), but by the claimant (in the context of its principal claim). Imagine a scenario in which the bank client had decided to claim damages only

200. Judgement of 26 June 2014, 6 Ob 86/14m (Austrian Supreme Court). *See also* Kellner, *supra* n. 198.

for the incurred transaction costs while requesting merely a declaration that respondent is liable for all (other) damages arising out of the second investment, even though the client could already have brought an action for performance in the form of a claim for restitution in kind. In such a case, it does not appear justified to treat the request for such declaration differently depending on whether claimant requests the declaration as part of its initial (or amended) prayer for relief or by way of a petition for incident declaratory relief. In both cases, the same procedural efficiency considerations apply – and speak in favour of denying the requested declaration on the basis of the principle of subsidiarity.[201]

In light of the above, it appears that a claimant could not circumvent the prerequisites of an action for declaratory relief (in particular the principle of subsidiarity) by introducing a claim for performance over a part of the claim and subsequently introducing a petition for incident declaratory relief concerning the existence of the underlying legal relationship.

VI SPECIFICS REGARDING THE PETITION FOR INCIDENT DECLARATORY RELIEF (ZWISCHENFESTSTELLUNGSANTRAG) PURSUANT TO §§ 236 AND 259(2) AUSTRIAN CCP

Introducing an action for declaratory relief is not the only means to achieving a binding declaration on a right or legal relationship. Specifically, the parties can introduce a petition for incident declaratory relief pursuant to §§ 236 and 259(2) Austrian CCP in order to obtain a binding determination of a right or a legal relationship. While an action for declaratory relief starts its own procedure, the petition for incident declaratory relief serves the same goal during pending proceedings.

Concerning the question what legal relationship or right can be the subject of a declaration, the same rules apply as for an action for declaratory relief pursuant to § 228 Austrian CCP.[202] Furthermore, it is required that the legal relationship or right is of a preliminary nature for the decision over the present claim currently disputed and that it remains disputed until the decision over the petition for incident declaratory relief (irrespectively of whether it was already disputed before the commencement of the present proceedings or whether it only became disputed during the proceedings).[203]

While the wording of the law in § 236 Austrian CCP does not explicitly require 'legal interest' as a prerequisite, it is still sometimes considered as a prerequisite for a petition for incident declaratory relief. According to prevailing doctrine[204] and case law,[205] legal interest in the requested declaration still must be proven, but in a different form than in the context of an action for declaratory relief. Specifically, the preliminary question does not only have to be of preliminary nature in the present proceedings, but

201. Kellner, *supra* n. 198, at 256.
202. Deixler-Hübner, *supra* n. 198, at n. 4.
203. *Ibid.*, at nn. 6–7.
204. *See*, e.g., Fasching, *supra* n. 30, at n. 1069; Deixler-Hübner, *supra* n. 198, at n. 7.
205. RIS-Justiz RS0039563; RIS-Justiz RS0039600; RIS-Justiz RS0039618; RIS-Justiz RS0039468; RIS-Justiz RS0034336.

also of relevance beyond the present proceedings.[206] This is sometimes considered to be a special form of legal interest.[207] The accumulation of these two requirements (i.e., (i) the preliminary nature for the present proceedings and (ii) the relevance beyond the present proceedings) is considered to replace the requirement of legal interest pursuant to § 228 Austrian CCP.[208] If it were not a mandatory requirement for a petition for incident declaratory relief that the preliminary question at issue is of relevance beyond the present proceedings, this would allow circumvention of the principle of subsidiarity of an action for declaratory relief.[209] If the preliminary question does not have any relevance beyond the present proceedings, there would be no need for an independent ruling since the assessment of the preliminary question would not have any relevance beyond the judgement on the principal claim and it would hence be sufficient to merely address the preliminary question in such judgement's reasoning.[210]

According to doctrine[211] and jurisprudence,[212] when the prerequisites for a petition for incident declaratory relief are not fulfilled, notably when legal interest in the requested declaration is missing, the petition for incident declaratory relief is to be rejected (*Zurückweisung mit Beschluss*).

VII DECLARATORY RELIEF IN THE CONTEXT OF ARBITRATION

The Austrian Code of Civil Procedure includes only one explicit provision dealing with declaratory relief in the context of arbitration, namely § 612 Austrian CCP. Pursuant to § 612 Austrian CCP, a claimant may request a declaratory ruling on whether or not a (national or international) arbitral award exists. Such provision is intended to clarify the legal situation in a case where it is disputed whether an award exists at all, for example when it is disputed whether a particular decision qualifies as an expert determination or as a different decision by an arbitral tribunal, such as a procedural order.[213] § 612 Austrian CCP also requires legal interest when the claimant seeks a declaratory decision by a state court on the question of whether an arbitral award does exist. Unlike an action for the setting aside of an award pursuant to § 611 Austrian CCP, which has to be introduced within three months from notification of the award to claimant, there exists no time limit for an action for declaratory relief pursuant to § 612 Austrian CCP.[214]

206. Deixler-Hübner, *supra* n. 198, at n. 9; RIS-Justiz RS0039563; RIS-Justiz RS0039600; RIS-Justiz RS0039618; RIS-Justiz RS0039468; RIS-Justiz RS0034336.
207. Deixler-Hübner, *supra* n. 198, at nn. 7, 9; judgement of 16 March 1977, 1 Ob 806/76 (Austrian Supreme Court).
208. Judgement of 25 October 1994, 1 Ob 611/94 (Austrian Supreme Court).
209. Deixler-Hübner, *supra* n. 198, at n. 7.
210. Judgement of 16 May 2001, 6 Ob 112/01s (Austrian Supreme Court).
211. Deixler-Hübner, *supra* n. 198, at n. 7.
212. Judgement of 16 May 1991, 6 Ob 547/91 (Austrian Supreme Court); judgement of 3 November 1991, 4 Ob 1/92 (Austrian Supreme Court); judgement of 5 October 1994, 7 Ob 569/94 (Austrian Supreme Court).
213. Christian Hausmaninger, *§ 612* n. 1, in *IV/2 Kommentar zu den Zivilprozessgesetzen* (Hans Walter Fasching & Andreas Konecny eds. 3rd ed., 2016).
214. Hausmaninger, *supra* n. 213, at n. 17.

There exists no express provision allowing for an action for declaratory relief on the question of whether an arbitration agreement exists. The prevailing legal doctrine has it that no action for a declaration that an arbitration agreement exists and that no action for a declaration that the arbitral tribunal lacks jurisdiction is possible.[215]

Furthermore, the Austrian Code of Civil Procedure does not contain any provisions that deal with declarations as a specific form of relief in arbitration. Consequently, national arbitration law does not answer the question what the prerequisites for declaratory rulings in arbitration might be.

As a starting point to the analysis of any such prerequisites under Austrian law, there is the observation that the action for declaratory relief has its basis purely in procedural law, specifically in § 228 Austrian CCP. As such, the prerequisites for declaratory relief as stipulated in § 228 Austrian CCP are not applicable by virtue of Austrian law being the proper law for the merits of the hypothetical arbitration. Similarly, such prerequisites likewise do not apply in an arbitration that is seated in Austria. Since § 228 Austrian CCP is not part of the section in the Civil Procedure Code that governs arbitration, it is not applicable in arbitral proceedings, neither directly nor by analogy. Absent any agreement of the parties do the contrary, principles of domestic civil procedure do not apply in (international) arbitration.[216]

Such a conclusion is in line with the prevailing doctrine, which has it that the action for declaratory relief is rooted in procedural law only and which treats the requirement of legal interest as a special procedural prerequisite (*besondere Prozessvoraussetzung*). As indicated above, contrary to such characterization of the requirement of legal interest by legal doctrine, case law qualifies legal interest as a substantive prerequisite for granting declaratory relief. Specifically, the courts treat the prerequisite of legal interest as a question concerning the substance of the action for declaratory relief, i.e., as a question of whether the action is well founded, as opposed to a special procedural prerequisite (*besondere Prozessvoraussetzung*) that concerns the question of the procedural admissibility of the action.[217]

215. *See* Christian Hausmaninger, *§ 578* n. 19, in *IV/2 Kommentar zu den Zivilprozessgesetzen* (Hans Walter Fasching & Andreas Konecny eds. 3rd ed., 2016) with further references. But *See* Hausmaninger, *ibid.*, at 19–30 (arguing that an action for a declaration that the arbitral tribunal lacks jurisdiction should be possible under certain circumstances).

216. Michael Schneider, *Non-Monetary Relief in International Arbitration: Principles and Arbitration Practice*, in *Performance as a Remedy: Non-Monetary Relief in International Arbitration* 3, 30 (Michael Schneider & Joachim Knoll eds., ASA Special Series 24–25, 2011).

217. *See*, e.g., judgement of 28 March 1912, Rv. II, 274/12, GlUNF 5854 (Austrian Supreme Court) ('materielles Erfordernis der Feststellungsklage'); judgement of 10 January 1933, 2 Ob 6/33 (Austrian Supreme Court) ('für eine den Klägern günstige Sachentscheidung'); judgement of 23 November 2016, 3 Ob 153/16w (Austrian Supreme Court) ('Voraussetzung für die Begründetheit des Feststellungsbegehrens'); judgement of 23 November 2014, 1 Ob 210/14k (Austrian Supreme Court) ('Anspruchsvoraussetzung für die Feststellungsklage'); RIS-Justiz RS0039177 ('Voraussetzung für die Begründetheit des Feststellungsanspruches'); judgement of 31 January 1990, 9 ObA 28/90 (Austrian Supreme Court) ('ein Tatbestandselement des Klagsanspruches'); judgement of 11 November 1997, 7 Ob 312/97a (Austrian Supreme Court) ('ein anspruchsbegründetes Merkmal des Feststellungsanspruchs'); judgement of 15 April 2004, 8 ObA 23/04x (Austrian Supreme Court); judgement of 29 April 2002, 7 Ob 36/02y (Austrian Supreme Court); judgement of 19 November 2001, 7 Ob 310/01s (Austrian Supreme Court) ('Erfolgsvoraussetzung des Feststellungsbegehrens'); judgement of 19 November 2014, 3 Ob 185/14y (Austrian

Given that legal doctrine usually distinguishes between procedural requirements resulting from procedural law as formal requirements (*Prozessvoraussetzungen*) on the one hand and substantive requirements resulting from substantive law as prerequisites for substantive claims (*Erfolgsvoraussetzungen*) on the other,[218] the question could arise whether - according to jurisprudence - the action for declaratory relief or its prerequisites are based in substantive law. However, the courts' distinction between procedural and substantive requirements of an action for declaratory relief does not render the prerequisites for declaratory relief a matter of *substantive law*. When the Austrian Supreme Court refers to a decision on the 'substance' of the action for declaratory relief, it should not be considered to imply that the claim for declaratory relief (or its prerequisites) has its basis in substantive law. Similarly, it should not be considered to blur the boundaries between legal interest and the disputed material legal relationship between the parties.[219] Rather, it appears to consider legal interest as a constituent element (*Tatbestandsmerkmal*) for a purely procedural claim for declaratory relief as rooted in § 228 Austrian CCP, the lack of which should therefore lead to a rejection of the action for declaratory relief (*Abweisung der Klage mit Urteil*).[220]

Accordingly, the prerequisites of legal interest and the limitations concerning the subject matter of declaratory relief are not applicable in arbitration by virtue of application (whether directly or by analogy) of § 228 Austrian CCP. This holds true both for arbitrations that are seated in Austria and for arbitrations in which Austrian substantive law applicable. For the avoidance of doubt, this is not to say that an arbitral tribunal should not require any prerequisites for an action for declaratory relief. The question of what such prerequisites for declaratory relief in arbitration should be is one of the subjects covered in this book.

Supreme Court); judgement of 5 May 2009, 1 Ob 49/09a (Austrian Supreme Court) ('betrifft die inhaltliche Berechtigung des Klagebegehrens.'); judgement of 27 June 2013, 1 Ob 43/13z (Austrian Supreme Court) ('(materielle) Erfolgsvoraussetzung'); judgement of 19 November 2014, 3 Ob 120/14i (Austrian Supreme Court) ('Voraussetzung für die Begründetheit der vorliegenden Feststellungsklage'); judgement of 14 March 2013, 1 Ob 256/12x (Austrian Supreme Court); judgement of 26 January 2011, 1 Ob 176/10d (Austrian Supreme Court) ('Voraussetzung für die Berechtigung eines Feststellungsbegehrens'); judgement of 30 May 2017, 4 Ob 86/17a (Austrian Supreme Court); judgement of 20 March 2015, 9 Ob 6/15w (Austrian Supreme Court); judgement of 20 March 2015, 9 ObA 21/15a (Austrian Supreme Court); judgement of 10 November 2014, 7 Ob 164/14i (Austrian Supreme Court); judgement of 17 September 2014, 4 Ob 76/14a (Austrian Supreme Court); judgement of 4 July 2012, 7 Ob 91/12a (Austrian Supreme Court) ('Voraussetzung für den Feststellungsanspruch').

218. *See* Fasching, *supra* n. 30, at 11–12.

219. *See* Peter Böhm, *Die Lehre vom Rechtsschutzbedürfnis*, JBl 1974, 1, 10–11 (according to whom the Austrian Supreme Court qualifies the claim for declaratory relief as a public law claim ('öffentlich-rechtlicher Anspruch')).

220. But cf. judgement of 28 February 1985, 6 Ob 651/83 (Austrian Supreme Court) and judgement of 29 November 1990, 6 Ob 677/90 (Austrian Supreme Court) (in which the Austrian Supreme Court indicated that if the legal requirements of § 228 Austrian CCP are fulfilled, there is an auxiliary obligation arising out of the legal relation which results in a right that cannot only be the subject matter of an action for declaratory relief but that can also be violated by the other side).

ANNEX II

Report on Main Features of Declarations in Germany

Alicja Zielińska-Eisen & Tobias Strecker

Table of Contents

I THE ORIGINS AND EVOLUTION OF DECLARATORY RELIEF IN THE GERMAN LEGAL SYSTEM

There is no particular single predecessor of the action for declaratory relief in its current form and function in the German legal system. It is said to be rooted in Roman law, which recognized certain preliminary actions, typically concerning declarations of the existence of status, such as marital or class status.[221] These so-called *actiones praeiudiciales* could be filed as independent actions, but regularly served to prepare a second lawsuit.[222]

During medieval times, Germany was split into numerous smaller states that followed a common law approach, influenced by Roman law, canon law and local customs. During this time, the Roman *actiones praeiudiciales* developed to cover a variety of legal relationships, e.g., leases, and their subject matter was not limited to status relationships.[223] In parallel, other actions with a declaratory function emerged, such as an action for 'acknowledgment' of a claim in order to secure it before elapse of the prescription period;[224] or, an action to request, or 'provoke', the counterparty to sue with the aim of settling the dispute conclusively in case there was an imminent risk of violation of rights (*provocatio ex lege diffamari* and *ex lege si condendat*).[225]

The varying and sometimes inconsistent use of these instruments led to a need for codification. Prussia first introduced a type of negative declaratory relief in its general court rules[226] in 1793, which allowed the claimant to state that a claim, purported by the respondent, did not exist.[227] Another provision allowed for a

221. *See* Matthias Jacobs, *Der Gegenstand des Feststellungsverfahrens*, 103–104 (2005).
222. *See Ibid.*, at 104.
223. *See Ibid.*, at 107–108.
224. *Ibid.*, at 106 et seq.
225. *Ibid.*, at 105.
226. *Allgemeine Gerichtsordnung für die Preußischen Staaten.*
227. § 2, 32nd Title of the First Part of the AGO: 'If somebody knows that another alleges to have a claim against him, which he does not want to acknowledge, he is free to appear as claimant

preliminary judgement on the status of heirs, before deciding on the division of an inheritance.[228]

In the nineteenth century, discussions about a uniform solution for the German states began and, after the German Empire was established in 1871, led to works on a first unified code of civil procedure for the entire German territory.[229]

The action for declaratory relief (*Feststellungsklage*) was introduced into the German Civil Procedural Code of 30 January 1877 which entered into force on 1 October 1879 (*Civilprozessordnung*, Former German CCP).[230] Under § 231 Former German CCP, one could claim for a declaration of the existence or non-existence of a legal relationship if one had a legal interest in such declaration by a judge.

Subsequently, § 231 Former German CCP, through the renewed promulgation of the German Civil Procedural Code following amendments introduced in 1898 (*Zivilprozessordnung*, German CCP, otherwise commonly abbreviated as ZPO), became § 256(1) German CCP, and has remained unchanged until today.[231]

The petition for incident, or ancillary, declaratory relief (*Zwischenfeststellungsklage*) was also already incorporated into the Former German CCP. It enabled the parties to seek a declaration on a prejudicial legal relationship in a pending matter when the existence or non-existence of the legal relationship was determinative for the decision in these proceedings. The petition for incident declaratory relief was initially contained in § 253 Former German CCP. Later, in the German CCP of 1898 it became § 280 and eventually, by effect of another amendment in 1977, was included as § 256(2) German CCP. Despite the changes in numbering its wording remains unaltered.[232]

The underlying rationale supporting the introduction of declaratory relief was to equip parties with a remedy that would prevent an infringement of rights through the

---

against the other in the main proceedings himself and to explain the falseness and invalidity of the purported claim.' (Translation by the authors); in German: '*Wenn jemand weiß, daß ein Anderer sich eines gewissen Anspruchs an ihn berühme, welchen er nicht einräumen will, so steht es ihm frei, selbst als Kläger in der Hauptsache wider den selben aufzutreten und die Unrichtigkeit und Ungültigkeit des behaupteten Anspruchs wieder ihn auszuführen.*'

228. § 3, 46th Title of the First Part of the AGO: 'Because, as long as the right to inherit and the quotas of the interested parties are not determined, the division of the estate is not thinkable, these two preliminary questions must be examined and determined first, if the parties are in disagreement about it, following the rules of a general and ordinary lawsuit [...].' (Translation by the authors); in German: '*Da, so lange die Erbrechte und Quoten der Interessenten nicht ausgemacht sind, die Anlegung einer Erbschicht unter ihnen sich nicht denken läßt, so müssen zuvörderst diese beiden Präjudicialfragen, wenn die Parteien darüber uneins sind, nach den Vorschriften des ordentlichen und gewöhnlichen Prozesses erörtert und entschieden werden* [...].'

229. *See* Jacobs, *supra* n. 221, at 114 et seq.

230. Considering its historical development, the declaratory relief is seen as 'a remarkably recent innovation'; Leimgruber, *supra* n. 39, at 469; more specifically with regard to German law *see* Ekkehard Becker-Eberhard in: 1 Thomas Rauscher & Wolfgang Krüger, *Münchener Kommentar zur Zivilprozessordnung mit Gerichtsverfassungsgesetz und Nebengesetzen, Commentary on § 256 German CCP*, n. 3 (5th ed., 2016).

231. *See* Becker-Eberhard, *supra* n. 230, at n. 7.

232. *Ibid.*, at n. 8.

authoritative declaration of one's legal position. In the official justification (*Begründung*) of the draft of the Former German CCP of 29 October 1874, it was explained that, in some cases, it is necessary to declare whether a legal relationship exists even before relying on the material effects of its existence.[233] Only if such a declaration has been made can the parties proceed to determining their conduct without running the risk of serious losses.[234] The legislator acknowledged that the risk of a violation of subjective rights could already be sufficient ground for declaratory relief.[235] Further, it stated that the introduction of the provision on action for declaratory relief makes the remedies *ex lege diffamari* and *ex lege si contendat* superfluous.[236]

From the beginning of this legislative history, the requirement of a legal interest was introduced into the provision on declaratory relief. Already in the justification of the draft of the Former German CCP was it stated that the requirement sufficiently limits the number of claims that might be raised, and that the fear of increase in the number of claims is unfounded.[237]

II THE STATUTORY BASIS AND PREREQUISITES FOR DECLARATORY RELIEF

Under German law, the object of an action for declaratory relief is a legal relationship or the authenticity of a document. The existence or non-existence of a legal relationship or the authenticity of a document can be either asserted by the claimant or counter-claimant (positive or affirmative declaratory relief; *positive Feststellungsklage*), or denied (negative declaratory relief; *negative Feststellungsklage*).[238]

In the traditional view, declaratory relief is a procedural instrument which is aimed at securing 'legal peace' and removing legal uncertainty.[239] A declaratory court ruling, however, is the weakest form of legal protection in terms of efficiency, as it can neither be enforced nor provide for an alteration of the legal situation.[240]

The principal statutory basis for an action for declaratory relief is § 256(1) German CCP (*Feststellungsklage*).[241] It reads as follows:

> To declare the existence or non-existence of a legal relationship, to recognise a document or to establish that it is false, an action may be filed, if the claimant has

233. Carl Hahn, *Die gesammten Materialien zu den Reichs-Justizgesetzen, Zweiter Band: Die gesammten Materialien zur Civilprozeßordnung und dem Einführungsgesetz zu derselben vom 30. Januar 1877, Zweite Abtheilung*, 255 (1881).
234. Hahn, *supra* n. 233, at 255.
235. *See* Jacobs, *supra* n. 221, at 116 with further references.
236. Hahn, *supra* n. 233, at 256.
237. *Ibid.*, at 257.
238. Becker-Eberhard, *supra* n. 230, at n. 9.
239. *Ibid.*, at n. 1.
240. *Ibid.*, at n. 2; Klaus Bacher in: *Volkert Vorwerk & Christian Wolf, Beck'scher Online-Kommentar ZPO, Commentary on § 256 German CCP*, n. 1 (31st ed., 2018).
241. § 256 German CCP is located within Book 2 on the 'Procedural rules for proceedings before the courts of first instance', Chapter 1 on the 'Proceedings before regional courts', and further under the Title 1 on the 'Proceedings until a judgement is issued'.

a legal interest in having the legal relationship or the authenticity or falsity of the document established soon by a judicial ruling.[242]

Further, § 256(2) German CCP introduces an incident declaratory relief (*Zwischenfeststellungsklage*), providing as follows:

> Until the closure of the hearing subsequent to which the judgment will be handed down, the claimant may petition, by extending the claim, and the respondent may petition, by bringing a counterclaim, that a legal relationship which has become disputed during the course of the proceeding be acknowledged by judicial ruling, if the decision on the dispute depends, either wholly or in part, on the existence or non-existence of this legal relationship.[243]

The action for declaratory relief does not only exist in private law, but also in social,[244] administrative[245] and finance matters.[246]

242. Translation by the authors, who have decided to deviate from the English translation provided by the Federal Ministry of Justice and for Consumer Protection, which in particular uses the word 'legitimate interest' instead of 'legal interest'; available at: https://www.gesetze-im-internet.de/englisch_zpo/englisch_zpo.html (accessed 24 January 2019); in German: '*Auf Feststellung des Bestehens oder Nichtbestehens eines Rechtsverhältnisses, auf Anerkennung einer Urkunde oder auf Feststellung ihrer Unechtheit kann Klage erhoben werden, wenn der Kläger ein rechtliches Interesse daran hat, dass das Rechtsverhältnis oder die Echtheit oder Unechtheit der Urkunde durch richterliche Entscheidung alsbald festgestellt werde.*'
243. English translation as provided by the Federal Ministry of Justice and for Consumer Protection, available at: https://www.gesetze-im-internet.de/englisch_zpo/englisch_zpo.html (accessed 24 January 2019), with the adjustment of the parties description ('claimant' instead of 'plaintiff' and 'respondent' instead of 'defendant'); in German: '*Bis zum Schluss derjenigen mündlichen Verhandlung, auf die das Urteil ergeht, kann der Kläger durch Erweiterung des Klageantrags, der Beklagte durch Erhebung einer Widerklage beantragen, dass ein im Laufe des Prozesses streitig gewordenes Rechtsverhältnis, von dessen Bestehen oder Nichtbestehen die Entscheidung des Rechtsstreits ganz oder zum Teil abhängt, durch richterliche Entscheidung festgestellt werde.*'
244. § 55(1) Social Courts Act (*Sozialgerichtsgesetz*, SGG) provides: 'The following can be sought with an action: 1. the declaration of the existence or non-existence of a legal relationship, 2. declaration of which social security insurer is responsible, 3. declaration whether a health disorder or death is the result of an accident at work [...], 4. declaration that an administrative act is null and void, if the claimant has a legitimate interest in its early declaration [...].' (Translation by the authors); in German: '*Mit der Klage kann begehrt werden 1. die Feststellung des Bestehens oder Nichtbestehens eines Rechtsverhältnisses, 2. die Feststellung, welcher Versicherungsträger der Sozialversicherung zuständig ist, 3. die Feststellung, ob eine Gesundheitsstörung oder der Tod die Folge eines Arbeitsunfalls [...] ist, 4. die Feststellung der Nichtigkeit eines Verwaltungsakts, wenn der Kläger ein berechtigtes Interesse an der baldigen Feststellung hat.*'
245. § 43 Administrative Procedure Code (*Verwaltungsgerichtsordnung*, VwGO) provides: 'With an action, the declaration of the existence or non-existence of a legal relationship or the nullity of an administrative act can be sought, if the claimant has a legitimate interest in its early declaration (action for declaratory relief). (2) The declaration cannot be sought, as far as the claimant can pursue its rights by an action for modification of rights or for performance or could have done so. This does not apply if the declaration of the nullity of an administrative act is sought.' (Translation by the authors); in German: '*(1) Durch Klage kann die Feststellung des Bestehens oder Nichtbestehens eines Rechtsverhältnisses oder der Nichtigkeit eines Verwaltungsakts begehrt werden, wenn der Kläger ein berechtigtes Interesse an der baldigen Feststellung hat (Feststellungsklage). (2) Die Feststellung kann nicht begehrt werden, soweit der Kläger seine Rechte durch Gestaltungs- oder Leistungsklage verfolgen kann oder hätte verfolgen können. Dies gilt nicht, wenn die Feststellung der Nichtigkeit eines Verwaltungsakts begehrt wird.*'

In addition to § 256 German CCP, a number of special provisions apply in particular situations, e.g., with regard to the existence of disputed claims in insolvency proceedings,[247] the validity of resolutions of shareholder's general meetings of a German stock corporation, limited liability company or cooperation[248] or the validity of the termination of certain employment contracts.[249] The common trait of these specific types of declaratory relief is that a court usually does not engage in examination of legal interest in the declaration.[250]

III THE CONCEPT OF LEGAL INTEREST UNDER GERMAN LAW

[A] Legal Interest as a Specific Legitimate Interest in Legal Protection

Any court action requires a legitimate interest of the claimant in legal protection (*Rechtsschutzbedürfnis/Rechtsschutzinteresse*).[251] The legitimate interest is generally assumed for most types of actions. Regarding claims for performance, it is usually comprised in the subjective right that is asserted and the respondent's refusal to fulfil the claim.[252] In such cases, the legitimate interest is only missing under special circumstances,[253] e.g., when a claimant is already in possession of an enforceable title for its claim[254] or when the claim is obviously abusive.[255]

For actions for declaratory relief, § 256(1) German CCP explicitly requires a qualified form of such legitimate interest,[256] i.e., a legal interest (*rechtliches Interesse*) in an early declaration by the court (*Feststellungsinteresse*). Courts will examine ex officio in each case whether the claimant has a legal interest in the declaration.[257]

Legal interest is generally present when the claimant's legal position is impaired by a breach or endangered by a legal uncertainty regarding the legal relationship which is to be declared, and if the declaratory relief can eliminate this uncertainty.[258]

246. § 41 Fiscal Procedure Code (*Finanzgerichtsordnung*, FGO) which uses the same wording as § 43 VwGO.
247. §§ 179 et seq. Insolvency Code (*Insolvenzordnung*, InsO); *See also* Annex II. VI[D] *infra.*
248. §§ 241 et seq. Stock Corporation Act (*Aktiengesetz*, AktG); *See also* Annex II.VI[C] *infra.*
249. § 4 Dismissal Protection Act (*Kündigungsschutzgesetz*, KSchG); *See also* Annex II.VI[E] *infra.*
250. *See* Annex II.VI *infra.*
251. BGH, Judgement dated 21 January 1999 – I ZR 135/96, NJW 1999, 1337, 1338; BGH, Judgement dated 14 December 1988 – VIII ZR 31/88, NJW-RR 1989, 263, 264.
252. *See* BGH, Judgement dated 21 September 2017 – I ZR 58/16, GRUR 2017, 1236, n. 37.
253. Klaus Bacher in: *Volkert Vorwerk & Christian Wolf, Beck'scher Online-Kommentar ZPO, Commentary on § 253 German CCP*, n. 28 (31st ed., 2018).
254. Bacher, *supra* n. 253, at n. 29.1.
255. BGH, Court Order dated 26 June 1972 – X ZR 45/69, VersR 1972, 1046.
256. BGH, Judgment dated 19 November 1971 – I ZR 72/70, NJW 1972, 198; Dorothea Assmann, in: *4 Bernhard Wieczorek & Rolf A. Schütze, Zivilprozessordnung und Nebengesetze, Großkommentar, Commentary on § 256 German CCP*, n. 116 (2013); Becker-Eberhard, *supra* n. 230, at n. 37.
257. For exceptions *see* Annex II.VI *infra.*
258. BGH, Judgement dated 13 January 2010 – VIII ZR 351/08, NJW 2010, 1877, 1878; BGH, Judgement dated 27 May 2008 – XI ZR 132/07, NJW-RR 2008, 1495, 1499; BGH, Judgement dated 19 June 1998 – V ZR 43/97, NJW 1998, 3055, 3056; cf. Leo Rosenberg, Karl Heinz Schwab & Peter Gottwald, *Zivilprozessrecht, § 90*, n. 19 (18th ed., 2018).

[B] The Purpose of the Legal Interest as a Prerequisite for Declaratory Relief

The main purpose of the legal interest requirement is to protect the courts from being overburdened with actions for declaratory relief.[259] Whether this is a valid concern is questionable. It assumes that the number of lawsuits would significantly increase without this additional and rather strict prerequisite. It is also doubtful if it is still in keeping with times of declining numbers of lawsuits. In the years 2004 to 2017, the number of newly filed civil actions in Germany has decreased by more than one-third, from 1,938,741 actions in 2004[260] to only 1,244,697 in 2017.[261] Nevertheless, the courts continue to apply this principle essentially with no alteration.

The BGH has adopted the position that this purpose, to ensure effective administration of justice, allows the courts to omit the examination of legal interest and to leave this question open if it is faster or more efficient to dismiss the case on substantive grounds.[262] However, if the court does rule on the question and finds that the claimant lacks legal interest, it has to dismiss the action on procedural grounds.[263] Accordingly, legal interest can be seen as a 'non-qualified', 'conditional' or 'diluted' prerequisite,[264] which is only required in cases of an affirmative judgement on the merits.

It is further argued that the requirement also serves to protect the opposing party from inefficient and frivolous claims.[265]

[C] The Examination of the Legal Interest Ex Officio

The court has to examine the legal interest ex officio in each instance.[266] The parties have no power to agree that it is given, since its purpose is, at least also, to protect the courts. This means that a court of higher instance may find a lack of legal interest, where the previous instances have not.

In a case decided by the BGH, the court clarified that the review of legal interest cannot be limited.[267] Whereas the courts of appeal generally decide on which points they allow for a further appeal on legal grounds (*Revision*), the BGH stated that the review of the legal interest was conducted ex officio and would neither depend on a

259. Reinhard Greger in: *Richard Zöller, Zivilprozessordnung, Commentary on § 265*, n. 7 (32nd ed., 2018); Assmann, *supra* n. 256, at n. 116.
260. Statistisches Bundesamt (Destatis), Rechtspflege, Zivilgerichte 2012, at 13 & 37 (2013).
261. Statistisches Bundesamt (Destatis), Rechtspflege, Zivilgerichte 2017, at 13 & 43 (2018).
262. BGH, Judgement dated 10 December 2007 – II ZR 239 /05, BGHZ 175, 12, 28; cf. also OLG Bremen, Court Order dated 23 April 1986 – 2 W 67/86, MDR 1986, 765.
263. RG, Judgement dated 18 March 1898 – II 358/97, RGZ 41, 369, 371.
264. Assmann, *supra* n. 256, at n. 122 with further references.
265. Assmann, *supra* n. 256, at nn. 116 & 122; Ulrich Foerste in: Hans-Joachim Musielak & Wolfgang Voit, *Zivilprozessordnung: ZPO mit Gerichtsverfassungsgesetz, Kommentar, Commentary on § 256 ZPO*, n. 7 (15th ed., 2018).
266. RG, Judgement dated 14 October 1920 – VI 315/20, RGZ 100, 123, 126; BGH, Judgement dated 8 July 1955 – I ZR 201/53, BGHZ 18, 98, 105 et seq.; BGH, Judgement dated 10 October 2017 – XI ZR 456/16, NJW 2018, 227, 229.
267. BGH, Judgement dated 10 October 2017 – XI ZR 456/16, NJW 2018, 227, 229.

motion of the parties, nor could it be limited by the previous court's decision. In this case the claimant had requested declaratory relief that its loan agreement with the respondent, a bank, had been revoked and was to be rescinded. The second instance had granted the declaratory relief, finding that there was a sufficient legal interest despite the possibility of an action for performance, as the respondent was a bank and therefore it could be expected that it would adhere to the declaratory judgment. It allowed for a review of a substantive legal question but not of its decision on the legal interest. Subsequently, the BGH dismissed the case for a lack of legal interest nevertheless and based its decision on the following reasons: (i) the prerequisite of the legal interest was to be reviewed by the BGH ex officio and notwithstanding any limitations of the appeal court with regards to the further appeal on legal grounds, (ii) the claimant lacked legal interest as it had a reasonable opportunity to bring an action for performance and furthermore (iii) the respondent had expressly stated that it would not comply with the declaratory judgment.[268]

The underlying facts of a dispute however are – as all facts of the dispute – generally at the parties' disposition.[269] The claimant bears the burden of proof as regards demonstrating its legal interest.[270]

[D] The Procedural Nature of the Legal Interest

The requirement of the legal interest, as stipulated by the provision on declaratory relief, is generally considered to be a procedural requirement,[271] and there is little discussion about its nature today.[272]

In the nineteenth century and after the codification of the action for declaratory relief in § 231 Former German CCP, this nature was less clear.[273] For example, Bähr took the view that a legal relationship would not only result in a claim for performance, but also in a claim for acknowledgement and understood the provision as a substantive one.[274] Similarly, Degenkolb found the entitlement to secure one's benefits to be immanent in the subjective right and to emerge where it is endangered.[275] This

268. *Ibid.*
269. Greger, *supra* n. 259, at n. 7; Assmann, *supra* n. 256, at n. 299; Peter Hartmann in: Adolf Baumbach, Wolfgang Lauterbach, Jan Albers & Peter Hartmann, *Zivilprozessordnung: ZPO mit FamFG, GVG und anderen Nebengesetzen, Commentary on § 256 ZPO*, n. 42 (76th ed., 2018).
270. Greger, *supra* n. 259, at n. 7; Assmann, *supra* n. 256, at n. 299; Hartmann, *supra* n. 269, at n. 47; Becker-Eberhard, *supra* n. 230, at n. 73; Foerste, *supra* n. 265, at n. 38.
271. Bacher, *supra* n. 240, at n. 16; Foerste, *supra* n. 265, at n. 7; Becker-Eberhard, *supra* n. 230, at n. 1 (stating that the action for declaratory relief as such is of a procedural nature); Hartmann, *supra* n. 269, at n. 21; Ingo Saenger in: Ingo Saenger, *Zivilprozess: ZPO, Commentary on § 256 German CCP*, n. 1 (7th ed., 2017).
272. Jacobs, *supra* n. 221, at 145.
273. For a historic overview *see* Jacobs, *supra* n. 221, at 123 et seq.
274. Otto Bähr, *Die Anerkennung als Verpflichtungsgrund*, 316 (2nd ed., 1867); *See also* Jacobs, *supra* n. 221, at 124 et seq.
275. Heinrich Degenkolb, *Einlassungszwang und Urteilsnorm: Beiträge zur materiellen Theorie der Klagen insbesondere der Anerkennungsklagen*, 49 (1877).

understanding was in accordance with Savigny's theory that each action was based on a substantive claim.[276]

Eventually, however, a procedural understanding gained the upper hand. It was argued that the declaration sought was not one by the debtor, but one by the court and that the substantive theory could not explain negative declaratory relief which was not based on a subjective right.[277] At first, Wach developed the theory of entitlement to legal protection (*Rechtsschutzanspruch*) which was not the expression of a subjective right but of public nature and primarily directed against the state, in order to protect the claimant's rights, and against the other party only insofar as it had to accept the relief.[278] This was later criticized, since the courts' guarantee of legal protection should not be conditional (*Justizgewährleistungsanspruch*).[279]

Therefore, the still prevailing view is that declaratory relief constitutes a purely procedural institution of its own kind.[280] Occasionally, however, there are calls for a rapprochement to a substantive interpretation.[281]

[E] Subjective Nature of the Legal Interest

The legal interest can be of a subjective, as opposed to objective, nature. It is, for example, sufficient if the parties are in doubt about their legal relationship, even if the court discerns little justification for such doubt. But the uncertainty must be rooted in the legal relationship of the parties, not their doubt as to the applicability and scope of a legal norm.[282] Typical examples are that the respondent has denied or claimed the existence of a legal relationship.

The resulting uncertainty must objectively impair or endanger the claimant's position. Therefore, the respondent's mere announcement to examine a legal relationship does not create a legal interest for the claimant.[283]

In this context, the court needs to undertake a balancing exercise, as illustrated by a recent judgment of the BGH dated 2 October 2018.[284] This case concerned an action by a producer of slug bait for the declaration that it does not make use of the characteristics of a production process patented by a competitor, the respondent, after the latter had filed for independent proceedings for the taking of evidence in this regard. While the Court of First Instance granted the declaratory relief, the Court of Appeal dismissed the action, citing a lack of legal interest. It was considered that the

276. Friedrich Carl von Savigny, *5 System des heutigen Römischen Rechts*, 1 et seq. (1841).
277. Th. Kayser, *Beiträge zur Feststellungsklage*, AcP 70, 455, 460 (1886); *See also* Jacobs, *supra* n. 221, at 127.
278. Adolf Wach, *Der Feststellungsanspruch*, 14 et seq. & 22 et seq. (1889); *See also* Jacobs, *supra* n. 221, at 128 et seq.
279. Jacobs, *supra* n. 221, at 130 et seq. with further references.
280. *Ibid.*, at 131 with further references.
281. *Ibid.*, at 147 et seq.
282. RG, Judgement dated 2 December 1918 – V 282/18, RGZ 94, 227, 234.
283. BGH, Judgement dated 10 October 1991 – IX ZR 38/91, NJW 1992, 436, 438.
284. BGH, Judgement dated 2 October 2018 – X ZR 62/16, GRUR 2019, 110 (prior instance (appeal): OLG Dresden, Judgement dated 31 May 2016 – 14 U 247/15, GRUR-RR 2016, 313).

filing of independent proceedings for the taking of evidence is not sufficient to constitute a legal interest of the claimant in the declaration.

The BGH, while agreeing with the Court of Appeal that the fact of the filing for evidence proceedings and the claims made by the respondent during these proceedings could not be a basis for finding legal interest of the claimant for declaratory relief, still overturned the decision and found that the claimant had a legal interest in the declaration based on the respondent's subsequent allegations that it still had a claim against the claimant. The BGH stated that if the respondent alleges that it has a claim this is sufficient to justify the existence of legal interest on part of the claimant.

[F] Legal Interest versus Economic Interest

The claimant's interest must be of a legal nature. This includes public law relationships insofar as recourse to the civil law courts and not the administrative courts is available.[285] A purely economic interest, a scientific interest or other ideational interests will not suffice.[286] The cases where there is a mere economic interest without a legal interest being simultaneously present are rare; e.g., the hope that a contract of lease is void in order to become the leaseholder itself or the interest of a shareholder in the prosperity of the company have been deemed merely economic interests.[287] Economic interest in having a legal relationship declared to adjust future behaviour, e.g., the exercise of legal rights, accordingly will do.[288] Courts have also found the interest in avoiding future lawsuits sufficient.[289] Impairment of non-material positions can also be sufficient, e.g., the creditworthiness,[290] a person's honour[291] or reputational damage.[292]

When it comes to commercial companies, far-reaching consequences are attached to the status of their directors and officers who represent the company. Thus, the dominant view is that a finding on the status of directors or officers is imbued with legal interest,[293] and that a partner in a partnership generally has a legal interest in determining the ineffectiveness of a shareholders' resolution[294] similar to a claimant seeking a determination to be a shareholder of a German limited liability company (GmbH).[295]

285. Assmann, *supra* n. 256, at n. 26; Becker-Eberhard, *supra* n. 230, at n. 10; Hartmann, *supra* n. 269, at n. 6.
286. Assmann, *supra* n. 256, at n. 120; Becker-Eberhard, *supra* n. 230, at n. 39.
287. Hartmann, *supra* n. 269, at n. 29.
288. BGH, Judgment dated 30 October 2009 – V ZR 253/08, NJW 2010, 534, 535.
289. Assmann, *supra* n. 256, at n. 120.
290. Becker-Eberhard, *supra* n. 230, at n. 37; Herbert Roth in: 3 Friedrich Stein & Martin Jonas, *Kommentar zur Zivilprozessordnung, Commentary on § 256 German CCP*, n. 51 (23rd ed., 2016).
291. BGH, Judgement dated 30 October 2009 – V ZR 253/08, NJW 2010, 534, 535.
292. BGH, Judgement dated 21 September 1987 – II ZR 20/87, NJW-RR 1988, 445.
293. Cf. Assmann, *supra* n. 256, at n. 225.
294. BGH, Judgement dated 9 April 2013 – II ZR 3/12, NZG 2013, 664; Becker-Eberhard, *supra* n. 230, at n. 40.
295. Becker-Eberhard, *supra* n. 230, at n. 40.

[G] The Subsidiarity Principle

There is no general principle of subsidiarity stating that an action for declaratory relief is always inadmissible if a claim for performance is available.[296] Rather, the relationship between the two types of claims is solved when considering the requirement of legal interest.[297] In general, the claimant usually lacks legal interest in declaration if it is possible and reasonable for it to obtain an enforceable judgment. This is justified by reasons of procedural economy, in that it serves to avoid a doublereferral to courts and allows minimization of costs.[298] Accordingly, there is a lack of legal interest in declaration if other remedies provide a simpler and cheaper way to achieve the claimant's objective or if a second lawsuit can be avoided.[299]

This, however, does not always make an action for declaratory relief subsidiary to actions for performance. Despite the possibility to claim for performance, an action for declaratory relief will be admissible due to reasons of procedural economy if the declaration suffices to resolve the dispute sensibly and appropriately.[300] If, for example, a claim concerns past and future obligations, it might be more efficient to render a declaratory judgement on all claims instead of splitting them into different claims.[301] Similarly, the claimant will usually have a legal interest in the declaration if it can be expected that the respondent will defer to the declaratory judgment.[302] The courts usually presume this behaviour if the defendant is, for example, an insurance company[303] or a bank.[304]

The BGH found actions for declaratory relief admissible in situations where the claimant had an interest in a legal relationship exceeding the underlying duty of performance of the contract. For example, in a situation where the tenant is claiming invalidity of the tenancy agreement due to termination or revocation, the landlord has a legal interest in bringing an action for declaration that the tenancy agreement remains valid.[305] In another case the BGH similarly found sufficient legal interest where the claimant sought a declaration that a complex corporate agreement with several staggered duties of performance was valid, without requiring the claimant to file actions for performance of the individual duties of performance when these were due.[306]

296. BGH, Judgement dated 4 June 1996 – VI ZR 123/95, NJW 1996, 2725, 2726; BGH, Judgement dated 9 June 1983 – III ZR 74/82, NJW 1984, 1118, 1119; Becker-Eberhard, *supra* n. 230, at n. 5; Assmann, *supra* n. 256, at n. 190; Klaus Reichold in: Heinz Thomas & Hans Putzo, *Zivilprozessordnung: ZPO, FamFG Verfahren in Familiensachen, EGZPO, GVG, EGGVG, EU-Zivilverfahrensrecht, Commentary on § 256 German CCP*, n. 18 (39th ed., 2018).
297. Becker-Eberhard, *supra* n. 230, at n. 5.
298. Foerste, *supra* n. 265, at n. 12.
299. Bacher, *supra* n. 240, at nn. 26 & 26.1; Becker-Eberhard, *supra* n. 230, at n. 54; Foerste, *supra* n. 265, at n. 12.
300. BGH, Judgement dated 4 June 1996 – VI ZR 123/95, NJW 1996, 2725, 2726; Becker-Eberhard, *supra* n. 230, at n. 55.
301. BGH, Judgement dated 7 May 2008 – XII ZR 69/06, NJW 2008, 2178; BGH, Judgement dated 25 July 2017 – II ZR 235/15, NJW-RR 2017, 1317; Bacher, *supra* n. 240, at n. 26.2.
302. Becker-Eberhard, *supra* n. 230, at n. 55.
303. OLG Braunschweig, Judgement dated 14 October 1993 – 1 U 16/93, NJW-RR 1994, 1447.
304. BGH, Judgement dated 30 May 1995 – XI ZR 78/94, NJW 1995, 2219.
305. BGH, Judgement dated 7 May 2008 – XII ZR 69/06, NJW 2008, 2178.
306. BGH, Judgement dated 25 July 2017 – II ZR 235/15, NJW-RR 2017, 1317.

In the field of unfair competition law, the BGH has held that a claimant seeking the declaration that the respondent is liable for damages for breach of an obligation to cease and desist has sufficient legal interest even where it could determine the damages with the relevant information from the respondent for which it could file an action by stages (§ 254 ZPO) requesting the information as a first stage and damages as a second stage. The BGH held that due to the specific circumstances in matters of unfair competition where, first of all, the scope of the claim for information was very often unclear, the determination of damages regularly requires an expert determination costing time and money. In such cases where there is a higher need of protection against the statute of limitation running out, there is sufficient legal interest for an action for declaratory relief.[307]

Application of the subsidiarity principle, and how it interacts with the legal interest requirement, is exemplified in a BGH judgment dated 4 July 2017.[308] In this case, the claimants sued the respondent, a bank, for a declaration that the consumer loan agreement between the parties had ceased to exist as a result of the claimants' revocation of the agreement. The courts of both instances found the action admissible. The legal interest requirement within the meaning of § 256(1) German CCP was met as the claimants – due to the value of the underlying loan paid out, which would have to be returned along with interest and costs – did not have an expectation that they, on balance, have a claim for payment against the bank after the revocation. The Court of Appeal also indicated that, based on this argumentation, a claim for performance does not take precedence over declaratory action and thereby did not prevent the existence of the legal interest of the claimants.

Notwithstanding the case being so far admissible, the case was dismissed both in the first instance and on appeal based on the argumentation that the respondent had sufficiently informed the claimants on their right of revocation. As such, the declaration of revocation had not been made in due time.

In turn, the BGH determined that the relief sought by the claimants was to be construed as an action for (positive) declaratory relief that the consumer loan agreement was – as a result of the revocation – converted into a relationship of restitution obligations. As such, the case was inadmissible for lack of legal interest. The BGH found that the legal interest was prevented by the rule that claims for performance take precedence and that, in the case at hand, the claimants were to file such claim for restitution of the loan repayment amounts and interest paid until their revocation. The BGH further noted that it was also not likely that even a declaratory judgment in line with claimants' action would finally solve the dispute between the parties and that, therefore, there was no leeway for admitting the claim by way of exception.[309]

307. BGH, Judgement dated 17 May 2001 – I ZR 189/99, GRUR 2001, 1177.
308. BGH, Judgement dated 4 July 2017 – XI ZR 741/16, NJW-RR 2017, 1077 (prior instance – appeal: OLG Frankfurt a. M., Judgement dated 16 November 2016 – 17 U 80/16, BeckRS 2016, 125083).
309. BGH, Judgement dated 4 July 2017 – XI ZR 741/16, NJW-RR 2017, 1077; also referring to BGH, Judgement dated 24 January 2017 – XI ZR 183/15, WM 2017, 766.

[H] The Decisive Point in Time

The legal interest has to be demonstrated at the decisive point in time for the court's decision - generally the last hearing on the facts.[310] If the claimant loses its legal interest during the course of the proceedings, it amends its petition and asks for a declaration of the court that the claim has become pointless during the proceedings and that the respondent shall bear the costs.[311] According to the BGH, the claimant does, however, generally not forfeit its legal interest when an action for performance becomes possible only after an action for declaratory relief has been filed, but can then further pursue its action.[312]

On the contrary, a claimant who has filed an action for negative declaratory relief loses its legal interest once the respondent files an action for performance - either as a separate action or as a counterclaim - and cannot unilaterally withdraw the claim anymore.[313] Generally, in accordance with § 269(1) German CCP, an action cannot be unilaterally withdrawn after commencement of the oral hearing. But German courts have allowed for exceptions in favour of the legal interest when the declaratory relief was almost ripe for a decision and the action for performance was not[314] or when no decision could be expected from the second proceeding.[315]

In a case decided by BGH,[316] after the courts at the first two instances had ruled in favour of the claimant - who was seeking a relief to declare that the respondent did not have a preventive claim with regard to a newspaper's advertisement run by the claimant - the BGH found that the claimant lacked the necessary legal interest.

The BGH took the position that there was no legal interest in the declaration as the respondent's claim for performance; in this case, the claim for preventing the advertisement, which was filed in separate proceedings, took precedence. The BGH based its decision on the subsidiarity principle and, in these specific circumstances, on the circumstances that the declaratory relief in the appeal instance was not ready for a decision at the point in time when in the parallel proceedings brought by the respondent the first hearing was held, and hence the statement of claim could not be withdrawn without the consent of the counterparty (here, the claimant). The BGH

310. Becker-Eberhard, *supra* n. 230, at n. 37.
311. Assmann, *supra* n. 256, at n. 254; regarding costs *see also* Annex II.X *infra*.
312. BGH, Judgement dated 29 June 2011 - VIII ZR 212/08, NJW 2011, 3361; BGH, Judgement dated 4 November 1998 - VIII ZR 248/97, NJW 1999, 639, 640; Assmann, *supra* n. 256, at n. 245; Becker-Eberhard, *supra* n. 230, at n. 60; but *see also* BGH, Judgement dated 31 January 1952 - III ZR 131/51, NJW 1952, 546.
313. BGH, Judgement dated 21 December 2005 - X ZR 17/03, BGHZ 165, 305, 309; BGH, Judgement dated 25 March 1999 - IX ZR 223/97, NJW 1999, 1544, 1546 (counterclaim); *See also* Assmann, *supra* n. 256, at n. 250 with further references; for the question of *lis pendens see* Annex II.VII *infra*.
314. BGH, Judgement dated 3 June 1955 - I ZR 74/54, BGHZ 18, 22, 42; BGH, Judgement dated 28 June 1973 - VII ZR 200/72, NJW 1973, 1500; BGH, Judgement dated 21 December 1989 - IX ZR 234/88, NJW-RR 1990, 1532, 1533; BGH, Judgement dated 21 December 2005 - X ZR 17/03, BGHZ 165, 305, 309; Becker-Eberhard, *supra* n. 230, at n. 66.
315. BGH, Judgement dated 11 December 1996 - VIII ZR 154/95, BGHZ 134, 201, 209; Becker-Eberhard, *supra* n. 230, at n. 66.
316. BGH, Judgement dated 22 January 1987 - I ZR 230/85, NJW 1987, 2680, (prior instance (appeal): OLG Hamm, Judgement dated 24 October 1985 - 4 U 172/85, WRP 1986, 349).

stated that, while it has been held that the requisite legal interest can exceptionally survive even when there is a claim for performance,[317] for this concept to apply the action for declaratory relief must be ready for decision before the parallel claim for performance can no longer be unilaterally withdrawn, i.e., when the first hearing has already been held. It further noted that this also applied at the appeal stage. This consideration is said to be supported by the goal of procedural economy.

IV THE SCOPE OF DECLARATORY RELIEF UNDER GERMAN LAW

[A] A Legal Relationship as the Object of the Declaratory Relief

In accordance with § 256 German CCP, the object of a declaration can only be the existence or non-existence of a legal relationship or the recognition of a document as authentic or false.

[1] Subjective Rights

A legal relationship within the meaning of § 256 German CCP is a legal relationship of a person to another person or to an object.[318] The declaratory relief covers in principle all subjective rights, which include in particular absolute rights such as property and property rights,[319] limited rights in rem,[320] intellectual property rights (copyright, trademark,[321] patent rights[322]), as well as company membership,[323] licensing rights,

317. BGH, Judgement dated 3 June 1955 – I ZR 74/54, BGHZ 18, 22, 42; BGH, Judgement dated 28 June 1973 – VII ZR 200/72, NJW 1973, 1500 with further references.
318. Assmann, *supra* n. 256, at n. 26; Foerste, *supra* n. 265, at n. 2; Bacher, *supra* n. 240, at n. 3; Roth, *supra* n. 290, at n. 21; BGH, Judgement dated 15 October 1956 – III ZR 226/55, BGHZ 22, 43, 47; BGH, Judgement dated 3 May 1983 – VI ZR 79/80, NJW 1984, 1556; BGH, Judgement dated 19 April 2000 – XII ZR 332/97, NJW 2000, 2280, 2281; BGH, Judgement dated 31 May 2000 – XII ZR 41/98, NJW 2000, 2663, 2664; BGH, Judgement dated 7 June 2001 – I ZR 21/99, NJW 2001, 3789; BGH, Judgement dated 16 September 2008 – VI ZR 244/07, NJW 2009, 751; BGH, Judgement dated 7 March 2013 – VII ZR 223/11, NJW 2013, 1744; BGH, Judgement dated 23 April 2013 – II ZR 74/12, BGHZ 197, 162; BGH, Judgement dated 22 January 2015 – VII ZR 353/12, NJW-RR 2015, 398; BGH, Judgement dated 19 November 2014 – VIII ZR 79/14, NJW 2015, 873; Nima Gassemi-Tabar & David Eckner, *Die Feststellungsklage als zulässiges Mittel zur Klärung der (Nicht)Kündbarkeit eines Gewerberaummietvertrages? Oder: Vom Grundverständnis von Gestaltungsrechten*, 14 Neue Zeitschrift für Miet- und Wohnungsrecht (NZM) 869, 870 (2011).
319. BGH, Judgement dated 29 April 1958 – VIII ZR 198/57, NJW 1958, 1293; OLG Saarbrücken, Judgement dated 17 May 2017 – 2 U 72/16, NJW-RR 2017, 1454; OLG Düsseldorf, Judgement dated 16 December 2016 – I-9 U 275/09, BeckRS 2016, 117343; BGH, Judgement dated 28 June 1968 – V ZR 22/65, MDR 1968, 829.
320. BGH, Judgement dated 20 April 2018 – V ZR 106/17, NJW 2018, 3441; BGH, Default Judgement dated 27 March 2015 – V ZR 296/13, NJW-RR 2015, 915.
321. BGH, Judgment dated 6 June 2002 – I ZR 79/00, GRUR 2002, 795 (copyright); BGH, Judgment dated 26 June 2008 – I ZR 290/05, GRUR 2008, 917 (trademark).
322. BGH, Judgement dated 24 October 1978 – X ZR 42/76, NJW 1979, 269 (patent right).
323. BGH, Judgement dated 14 May 1990 – II ZR 125/89, NJW 1990, 2627; BGH, Judgement dated 25 January 2011 – II ZR 122/09, NJW 2011, 1667; BGH, Judgement dated 7 February 2012 – II

contractual relationships such as purchase,[324] rent,[325] lease,[326] loan,[327] insurance[328] – if their effectiveness, existence or duration is uncertain.[329]

[2] Concrete Legal Relationship

The declaratory relief is, emphatically, not an instrument enabling parties to seek a legal opinion from the court as they weigh their options.[330] Therefore it is not admissible to request a declaratory ruling concerning an abstract legal question[331] or a merely intended legal relationship.[332] Yet the distinction between an abstract legal question on the one hand and a legal relationship on the other may become problematic in practice.[333] This is apparent when the court is asked to determine the legal character of an existing contractual relationship, e.g., as either a service or an employment contract.

In a case where the parties disagreed over the qualification of their agreement as either a service or a partnership agreement, while the existence of an agreement was not an issue, the RG held that it was decisive if an imaginary or an existing legal relationship was affected.[334] Since different obligations arise from either a service or a partnership agreement, it deemed the latter to be the case and held the action admissible.[335]

In general, courts have accepted actions for declaratory relief if they were suitable to restore peace between the parties and to prevent further lawsuits.[336] However, if no existing, concrete legal relationship is affected by the interpretation of a legal issue, there will be no legal relationship within the meaning of § 256 German CCP.[337]

ZR 230/09, NZG 2012, 625; BGH, Judgement dated 14 May 1990 – II ZR 125/89, NJW 1990, 2627; BGH, Default Judgement dated 7 April 2008 – II ZR 181/04, NZG 2008, 623.

324. BGH, Judgement dated 23 June 1967 – V ZR 4/66, BeckRS 1967, 31174099.
325. BGH, Judgement dated 18 October 2000 – XII ZR 179/98, NJW 2001, 221; BGH, Judgement dated 24 September 2003 – XII ZR 70/02, NJW 2004, 294.
326. BGH, Judgement dated 13 November 2013 – VIII ZR 257/12, NZI 2014, 177; BGH, Judgement dated 31 May 1989 – VIII ZR 97/88, NJW-RR 1989, 1140.
327. BGH, Judgement dated 27 May 2008 – XI ZR 132/07, NJW-RR 2008, 1495; BGH, Judgement dated 16 May 2017 – XI ZR 586/15, NJW 2017, 2340.
328. BGH, Judgement dated 13 June 1966 – III ZR 258/64, BeckRS 1966, 30397084.
329. BGH, Judgement dated 15 October 1992 – IX ZR 43/92, NJW 1993, 648; BAG, Judgement dated 10 May 2012 – 8 AZR 434/11.
330. Becker-Eberhard, *supra* n. 230, at n. 22.
331. Bacher, *supra* n. 240, at n. 3.
332. Becker-Eberhard, *supra* n. 230, at n. 22.
333. *See* Jacobs, *supra* n. 221, at 38.
334. RG, Judgement dated 27 February 1934 – II 276/33, RGZ 144, 54, 56.
335. RG, Judgement dated 27 February 1934 – II 276/33, RGZ 144, 54, 56 et seq.
336. RG, Judgement dated 27 February 1934 – II 276/33, RGZ 144, 54, 56 et seq.; BGH, Judgement dated 16 December 1999 – III ZR 89/99, NZM 2000, 250; Jacobs holds that a motion to declare that an existing service contract constitutes a labor contract would be inadmissible but could be interpreted as a motion to declare that a labor contract has been executed, Jacobs, *supra* n. 221, at 301.
337. Becker-Eberhard, *supra* n. 230, at n. 23; *See also* District Court Mannheim (*Landgericht*, LG), Judgement dated 29 September 1977 – 4 T 336/76, ZMR 1979, 319, 320.

Framework agreements which relate to future dealings or events that have not occurred yet are therefore insufficient.[338]

As an exception, the German Federal Labour Court (*Bundesarbeitsgericht*, BAG) has, ruled on an abstract legal question by means of incident declaratory relief under § 256(2) German CCP.[339] In the case, two apprentices sued their employer in the retail sector for the difference between their received remuneration and that envisaged in a collective labour agreement. The court rendered an incident declaratory relief on the question of the applicability of the collective labour agreement for the retail sector, noting that such a finding would be exceptional but could avoid future lawsuits.

[3] Current Legal Relationship

The legal relationship must be a current one, not one contingent on uncertain future events. This requirement is, however, not always applied strictly. Courts have found it sufficient that the foundation for a claim has already been established so that it will materialize under a regular course of events with a sufficient degree of likelihood.[340] For example, the Higher Regional Court in Karlsruhe (*Oberlandesgericht*, OLG), decided on an insurer's obligation to cover costs of an orthodontic treatment while the treatment was still in preparation.[341] The distinction is, however, not always clear-cut and has been criticized as inconsistent.[342] The entitlement to a compulsory portion of an inheritance, for example, has regularly been held by the BGH to constitute a current legal relationship, because it would restrict the testator's capacity already while he is still alive.[343] Other inheritance rights, on the contrary, have not been seen as current legal relationships, even when the regular course of events was likely to lead to such an inheritance.[344]

For reasons of procedural economy, courts regularly accept actions for a declaration of the respondent's liability for certain future damages when their amount cannot be calculated yet or if harm has not occurred yet but will likely – or at least possibly[345] – occur under normal circumstances.[346] This avoids the difficulties of establishing the grounds for liability only later, when a damage has materialized.

338. Assmann, *supra* n. 256, at n. 33, Becker-Eberhard, *supra* n. 230, at n. 23.
339. BAG, Judgement dated 25 November 1987 – 4 AZR 361/87, BAGE 56, 357, 360; *See also* Annex II.VI[B] *infra*.
340. *See* Assmann, *supra* n. 256, at nn. 40 et seq. with further references; cf. Bacher, *supra* n. 240, at n. 6; Becker-Eberhard, *supra* n. 230, at n. 32.
341. OLG Karlsruhe, Judgement dated 16 July 1992 – 2 UF 235/91, NJW-RR 1993, 905, 906.
342. Assmann, *supra* n. 256, criticizes, in particular, the respective jurisprudence as inconsistent at nn. 42 et seq.
343. BGH, Judgement dated 14 December 1995 – IX ZR 242/94, NJW 1996, 1062, 1063; BGH, Judgement dated 1 March 1974 – IV ZR 58/72, NJW 1974, 1084, 1085; BGH, Judgement dated 1 October 1958 – V ZR 53/58, BGHZ 28, 177, 178.
344. BGH, Judgement dated 16 May 1962 – IV ZR 215/61, BGHZ 37, 137, 145; Becker-Eberhard, *supra* n. 230, at n. 34; Dieter Leipold in: *11 Franz Jürgen Säcker, Roland Rixecker, Hartmut Oetker & Bettina Limperg, Münchener Kommentar zum Bürgerlichen Gesetzbuch: BGB, Commentary on § 1922*, nn. 171 et seq. (7th ed., 2017).
345. BGH, Judgement dated 21 September 1987 – II ZR 20/87, NJW-RR 1988, 445; BGH, Judgement dated 23 April 1991 – X ZR 77/89, NJW 1991, 2707, 2708; BGH, Judgement dated 17 February

For example, the BGH allowed for declaratory relief stating that an underage child was liable for future damages out of a tort claim under certain circumstances, namely a shift in the monetary situation of all the involved parties leading to the legal ability of the child to pay out damages. It must be noted that in this case, not even all elements for the tort claim on the merits were present at the time the declaratory relief was granted, but the BGH deemed the occurrence of the missing elements sufficiently likely under normal circumstances.[347]

On the contrary, the BGH denied declaratory relief in a case where the likelihood of future damage had not been sufficiently substantiated. In this case, the claimant, as one of several sellers, sought the declaration that the respondent, a notary public, who had notarized a number of property purchase agreements under which the claimant and other sellers had sold a number of plots of lands to different buyers and who had breached his notarial duties in this regard, was liable for future damages to be potentially incurred by the claimant in relation to these agreements while the claimant did not name these buyers in its submissions to the court.[348]

Past legal relationships can be the object of declaratory relief if the claimant has a legal interest in the declaration. This is regularly the case when current rights or obligations result from it.[349]

[4] Elements of a Legal Relationship and Preliminary Questions

Most courts[350] and scholars[351] also hold that elements and preliminary questions concerning legal relationships generally do not fall under § 256(1) German CC.[352] This is because such elements alone do not create a subjective right[353] and such findings would not have a res judicata effect.[354] Accordingly, the non-existence of one of several potential peremptory objections has been deemed insufficient. The OLG Cologne dismissed a claim to declare that the claimant's behaviour during divorce proceedings

1998 – VI ZR 342/96, NJW 1998, 1633; BGH, Judgement dated 16 January 2001 – VI ZR 381/99, NJW 2001, 1431, 1432; BGH, Judgement dated 20 March 2001 – VI ZR 325/99, NJW 2001, 3414, 3415; *See also* Becker-Eberhard, *supra* n. 230, at n. 32, who seems to criticize this jurisprudence as too generous.

346. Bacher, *supra* n. 240, at n. 24.
347. BGH, Judgment dated 26 June 1962 – VI ZR 152/61, MDR 1962, 811.
348. BGH, Judgment dated 15 October 1992 – IX ZR 43/92, NJW 1993, 648, 653.
349. Assmann, *supra* n. 256, at n. 56; Becker-Eberhard, *supra* n. 230, at n. 30; Foerste, *supra* n. 265, at n. 4.
350. The BAG found the declaration on elements admissible if this could settle the dispute in its entirety, BAG, Judgement dated 1 June 1970 – 3 AZR 166/69, DB 1970, 1836, 1837; BAG, Judgement dated 21 April 2010 – 4 AZR 755/08, NJOZ 2010, 1828, 1829.
351. Of a different view: Roth, *supra* n. 290, at n. 27.
352. Becker-Eberhard, *supra* n. 230, at n. 10; *See also* BGH, Judgement dated 3 May 1977 – VI ZR 36/74, BGHZ 68, 331, 332; BGH, Judgement dated 15 October 1956 – III ZR 226/55, BGHZ 22, 43, 48; Assmann, *supra* n. 256, at nn. 37 et seq.; exceptions to this principle include the declaration regarding the authenticity of a document (§ 256(1) German CCP) as well as provisions in the SGG that allow for declarations on certain elements of a legal relationship in social matters (§ 55(1) no. 2 and 3, § 55(2) and § 130(2) SGG).
353. Jacobs, *supra* n. 221, at 297 et seq.
354. *Ibid.*, at 298 et seq.

did not constitute an immoral infliction of harm under § 826 German CCP and exclude potential claims for alimony payment. The court reasoned that this was only one element of the payment claim which depended on further prerequisites in the future. Therefore a declaration could not prevent a future action for performance and was inadmissible.[355] Similarly, the BGH dismissed an action for declaration that the claimant, who had rented out a store which still had to be constructed by the respondent, was not in default. Default was only an element of a legal relationship but not a legal relationship itself, the court held.[356]

As an important exception to this principle, courts regularly agree to render declaratory judgements on default of acceptance together with orders of performance that depend on counter-performance for reasons of efficiency, since this will enable enforcement without further investigations into the counterperformance.[357] For example, if a buyer has declared a contract avoided, its claim for reimbursement of the purchase price would depend on the return of the received goods. In such case, the buyer may ask the court, together with its claim for reimbursement, to declare that the seller is at default in taking repossession of the goods, in order to make its claim enforceable without further assessment.

[5] Partial Legal Relationships

Declarations on partial legal relationships (*Teilrechtsverhältnis*), like certain claims under a contractual relationship, are unproblematic. They constitute a legal relationship in the sense of § 256(1) German CCP.[358]

[6] Procedural Legal Relationships

Declaratory relief is also admissible with regard to procedural legal relationships, when the uncertainty about a procedural legal situation cannot be clarified in pending proceedings.[359] Examples include declarations on the content of an ambiguous judgement when a correction under § 319 German CCP is not possible[360] or of an enforceable settlement agreement.[361]

An example of high practical relevance concerns the case where the reason to adjudicate has been resolved after the action has become pending, e.g., because the respondent has remitted the claimed amount or the goods concerned have been

355. OLG Köln, Judgement dated 14 July 1983 – 25 UF 72/82, FamRZ 1985, 507.
356. BGH, Judgement dated 19 April 2000 – XII ZR 332/97, NJW 2000, 2280, 2281; for more examples *see* Assmann, *supra* n. 256, at n. 37.
357. BGH, Judgement dated 19 April 2000 – XII ZR 332/97, NJW 2000, 2280, 2281; Becker-Eberhard, *supra* n. 230, at n. 26.
358. Jacobs, *supra* n. 221, at 34 et seq.
359. Becker-Eberhard, *supra* n. 230, at n. 17.
360. BGH, Judgement dated 23 September 1976 – VII ZR 14/75, BB 1976, 1433; BGH, Judgement dated 25 September 1972 – VIII ZR 81/71, NJW 1972, 2268 et seq., also clarifying that a correction of the judgement under § 319 German CCP is only possible if the reasoning indicates which decision the court actually wanted to render.
361. BGH, Judgement dated 3 June 1997 – XI ZR 133/96, NJW 1997, 2320, 2321.

destroyed. If the respondent does not join the claimant's motion that the action has become moot, e.g., because it believes that it was unjustified in the first place, the court will from then on treat the action as one for declaratory relief, to find that the initially admissible and justified claim has become moot after the case has become pending.[362] The losing party will then be enjoined to bear the costs of the proceedings. The legal interest of the claimant is generally seen as equivalent to its interest in a favourable decision on costs.[363]

[7] Declaration on Facts

Mere facts cannot be established via declaratory relief, even if they are legally relevant.[364] For example, declaratory relief cannot be sought to determine the question of the untruth of a statement of fact or the illegality of a defamatory statement of facts.[365] Similarly, the BGH has denied availability of declaratory relief for the establishment of the factual basis for the calculation of a claim for the equalization of accrued gains under the matrimonial property regime in a divorce case.[366]

The only exception[367] under § 256(1) German CCP covers fact-finding with regard to the determination of the authenticity of a document, i.e. whether or not the document originates from under the hand of the person identified on it.[368] If the judgment affirms the authenticity, then its legal force excludes any future evidence to the contrary.[369] However, it cannot be ascertained in this process whether the signatory acted within the limits of its authority.[370]

This limitation has occasionally been criticized.[371] For example, in cases of defamatory statements, declaratory relief could serve as the best way to protect the party concerned by declaring falsehood of the statement. The BGH has, however, rejected such attempts to draw conclusions from the substantive law on the procedural requirements of declaratory relief and found the wording of § 256(1) German CCP to clearly exclude declarations on facts.[372]

A special type of declaratory relief introduced in 2018, the model declaratory lawsuit, expressly allows for declarations on facts.[373]

362. This is the prevailing view, cf. BGH, Judgement dated 19 June 2008 – IX ZR 84/07, NJW 2008, 2580.
363. Kai Jaspersen in: Volkert Vorwerk & Christian Wolf, *Beck'scher Online-Kommentar ZPO, Commentary on § 91a*, n. 51 (31st ed., 2018).
364. In detail: BGH, Judgement dated 3 May 1977 – VI ZR 36/74, NJW 1977, 1288, 1289; Becker-Eberhard, *supra* n. 230, at n. 18; Foerste, *supra* n. 265, at n. 2; Greger, *supra* n. 259, at n. 3; Reichold, *supra* n. 296, at n. 10.
365. BGH, Judgement dated 3 May 1977 – VI ZR 36/74, BGHZ 68, 331, 334 et seq.
366. BGH, Judgement dated 11 July 1979 – IV ZR 159/77, NJW 1979, 2099, 2101.
367. Foerste, *supra* n. 265, at n. 6.
368. Greger, *supra* n. 259, at n. 6.
369. RG, Judgement dated 14 May 1935 – III 301/34, RGZ 148, 29, 32.
370. Bacher, *supra* n. 240, at n. 7.
371. For an overview *see* Jacobs, *supra* n. 221, at 43 et seq. as well as BGH, Judgement dated 3 May 1977 – VI ZR 36/74, NJW 1977, 1288, 1290.
372. BGH, Judgement dated 3 May 1977 – VI ZR 36/74, NJW 1977, 1288, 1290 et seq.
373. § 606(1) German CCP; *See also* Annex II.VI[F] *infra.*

[8] Wording of the Petition

§ 253(2) German CCP requires the motion to clearly and exactly state the relief sought. This includes specifying the exact legal relationship which is to be declared to exist or not exist.

In some cases, the classification whether the requested declaration relates to a legal relationship in the sense of § 256(1) German CCP depends on the exact wording of the relief sought. While, for example, a declaration that the termination of an employment contract was not effective may not relate to a legal relationship itself, a declaration that the employment contract still validly exists does.[374] While the courts are generally bound by the parties' petitions (§ 308(1) German CCP, *ne ultra petita*), they are expected to assist the parties in their filing (§ 139(1) German CCP) and held to interpret petitions in accordance with the parties' true intent.[375]

[B] Actions by Third Parties

Courts have regularly affirmed that the legal relationship pursuant to § 256 German CCP is not limited to a legal relationship between the litigants themselves, but extends to relationships between a litigant and a third party[376] or even between third parties.[377] Examples include a claim by a joint-stock company (AG) shareholder, as claimant, for a declaration of invalidity of the closed syndicate agreement by the joint-stock company, or a limited partner against the limited partnership (*Kammergericht* – German Higher Regional Court of Appeal (KG)) on finding the ineffectiveness of the exclusion of another partner from the partnership. This is, of course, only if the claimant is affected in its own rights and has an own legal interest in the declaration vis a vis the respondent.[378]

Nevertheless, the judgement only has *inter partes* effect and does not bind any third party.[379]

This approach has been criticized by legal scholars: despite the procedural nature of declaratory relief, it is aimed to assert substantive rights; and the function of the right

374. Jacobs, *supra* n. 221, at 301.
375. *See also* BGH, Judgement dated 2 July 2007 – II ZR 111/05, NJW 2008, 69, interpreting a motion under 256(2) German CCP as 256(1) German CCP.
376. BGH, Judgement dated 25 February 1982 – II ZR 174/80, BGHZ 83, 122, 125 et seq.; BGH, Judgement dated 8 July 1983 – V ZR 48/82, NJW 1984, 2950; BGH, Judgement dated 23 September 1996 – II ZR 126/95, NJW 1997, 318, 319; BGH, Judgement dated 7 November 1997 – LwZR 1/97, NJW 1998, 229.
377. BGH, Judgement dated 17 May 1977 – VI ZR 174/74, BGHZ 69, 37, 40; BGH, Judgement dated 14 May 1990 – II ZR 125/89, NJW 1990, 2627, 2628.
378. BGH, Judgement dated 16 June 1993 – VIII ZR 222/92, NJW 1993, 2539; Foerste, *supra* n. 265, at n. 5 with further references.
379. BGH, Judgement dated 16 June 1993 – VIII ZR 222/92, NJW 1993, 2539; Becker-Eberhard, *supra* n. 230, at n. 36.

of action (*Prozessführungsbefugnis*) should not be assigned to the legal interest requirement.[380]

A special type of declaratory relief, one which expressly foresees actions being brought by a third party, is the model declaratory lawsuit introduced in 2018 in §§ 606 et seq. German CCP, which allows certain associations to bring an action for declaratory relief against a company in order to assert the rights of consumers.

[C] Declaratory Relief and Limitation Periods

Courts have repeatedly held that an action for positive declaratory relief suspends elapse of the statute of limitations of the subjective right that is to be asserted.[381] Therefore, a claimant usually has a legal interest in a declaratory relief if it is necessary to interrupt the limitation period.[382] On the contrary, a defence against an action for negative declaratory relief has no such effect.[383]

[D] Claims for Payment of Partial Amounts

With regard to claims for a divisible performance, e.g., for payment of a certain sum of money, a claimant can always claim only a fraction without the court assessing its legal interest in such claim.[384] This will, however, not have any effect similar to a declaratory relief as regards the remaining amount of the claim, since the court's decision on the partial claim will have no res judicata effect regarding the remaining part of the claim.[385] A court assessing the remaining part might therefore come to a different finding, even though in practice it will often be guided by the previous court's decision.

In order to achieve a res judicata effect, the party would have to petition for additional declaratory relief under § 256(1) German CCP with regard to the remaining amount. In cases where the declaratory relief is also a basis for the performance claim, no additional legal interest is required under § 256 (2) German CCP. If the court has to decide on the issue anyway in the context of the performance claim, the rationale of the requirement for a particular legal interest becomes void because there is no longer a need for protecting the court or the opponent from frivolous claims.

380. Becker-Eberhard, *supra* n. 230, at n. 36; Greger, *supra* n. 259, at n. 3b; *See also* Assmann, *supra* n. 256, at nn. 109 et seq.
381. BGH, Judgement dated 25 February 2010 - VII ZR 187/08, NJW-RR 2010, 750 with further references; BGH, Judgement dated 25 February 1988 - VII ZR 348/86, NJW 1988, 1380, 1381.
382. Becker-Eberhard, *supra* n. 230, at n. 13; BGH, Judgement dated 25 February 2010 - VII ZR 187/08, NJW-RR 2010, 750.
383. KG, Judgement dated 8 June 1960 - 10 U 414/60, NJW 1961, 33; the BGH left this question open in BGH, Judgement dated 15 December 2009 - XI ZR 110/09, NJW-RR 2010, 640, 641; Becker-Eberhard, *supra* n. 230, at n. 13; for the consequences *see* Annex II.VII *infra*.
384. *See* Annex II.III[A] *supra*.
385. Hans-Joachim Musielak in: Hans-Joachim Musielak & Wolfgang Voit, *Zivilprozessordnung: ZPO mit Gerichtsverfassungsgesetz, Kommentar, Commentary on § 322 German CCP*, n. 67 (15th ed., 2018).

VI EXCEPTIONS FROM THE REQUIREMENT OF LEGAL INTEREST AND SPECIFIC TYPES OF DECLARATORY RELIEF

[A] Preliminary Judgement (§ 304 German CCP)

§ 303 German CCP allows courts to render a preliminary judgement (*Zwischenurteil*) in order to settle procedural disputes upfront. Under § 304 German CCP,[386] courts can issue preliminary judgements also on the liability of a debtor if both the liability as such and the quantum are in dispute. The parties can appeal already on the preliminary judgement. The question of the liability in principle can thus be finally settled before the parties engage in a determination of the amount. It is at the court's discretion whether it renders such a decision, and this discretion cannot be reviewed. The judgement is declaratory in nature. It binds the court in its further determination in these proceedings as well as in further instances. However, the action can still be rejected if the court later finds that the quantum is zero.[387] Therefore the preliminary judgement has, no res judicata effect (*materielle Rechtskraft*) and is not binding beyond these current proceedings.[388] A specific legal interest in a preliminary judgement is not required. The court renders it when it deems this expedient to conduct of the proceedings.

[B] Incident Declaratory Relief (§ 256(2) German CCP)

Pursuant to § 256(2) German CCP, any party can petition for a declaration on the existence or non-existence of a legal relationship if the outcome of a pending case depends on this relationship (*Zwischenfeststellungsklage* or *Inzidentfeststellungsklage*).

The rationale behind the incident, or ancillary, declaratory relief[389] is to enable the parties to obtain a legally binding declaration which has res judicata effect (*materielle Rechtskraft*) regarding the legal relationship that would otherwise not be covered by the dispositive part of a court's decision.[390] In court practice, which has been criticized by some authors[391], the provision is interpreted rather broadly.[392] It is

386. § 304(1) German CCP provides: '(1) If a claim is in dispute regarding both its merits and its amount, the court can make a preliminary decision on the merits. (2) The decision is to be deemed a final judgement for the purpose of appellate remedies; however, the court may order, provided it has declared the claim to be justified and provided that a corresponding application has been made, that oral argument be heard on the claim's amount.' (Translation by the authors); in German: '*(1) Ist ein Anspruch nach Grund und Betrag streitig, so kann das Gericht über den Grund vorab entscheiden. (2) Das Urteil ist in Betreff der Rechtsmittel als Endurteil anzusehen; das Gericht kann jedoch, wenn der Anspruch für begründet erklärt ist, auf Antrag anordnen, dass über den Betrag zu verhandeln sei.*'

387. Saenger, *supra* n. 271, at n. 15.

388. Reichold, *supra* n. 296, § 304, n. 20.

389. The authors have chosen this translation over the sometimes used term 'interim declaratory relief' because the decision is not interim in nature and not made by interim judgement (*Zwischenurteil*); *See also* Annex II.IX *infra*.

390. Becker-Eberhard, *supra* n. 230, at n. 80; Greger, *supra* n. 259, at n. 21.

391. Becker-Eberhard, *supra* n. 230, at n. 86.

aimed at providing a comprehensive dispute resolution, avoiding contradictory rulings and securing procedural economy.[393]

This petition has an ancillary character, as it can be submitted only together with another action or during the course of an ongoing litigation by the claimant or by the respondent as a counterclaim.[394] The subject matter of the petition within the meaning of § 256(2) German CCP is limited to a legal relationship ancillary to the main claim,[395] and the authenticity of a document cannot be declared in such way.[396] The legal relationship is further qualified by its relation to the main claim – the incident declaratory relief is admissible only if determination of the legal relationship is at least in a necessary part prejudicial for the otherwise pending dispute (*Vorgreiflichkeit*).[397] In other words, the court must in any event decide whether the disputed legal relationship exists.[398]

Under § 256(2) German CCP, the petitioner does not need to demonstrate legal interest in obtaining the declaration (*Feststellungsinteresse*).[399] This requirement, which is historically aimed at protecting the courts from unnecessary requests for declaratory relief, is not needed when the court has to decide on the question anyway. But as for any action, the claimant still needs a legitimate interest (*Rechtsschutzbedürfnis* or *Rechtsschutzinteresse*)[400] which is then already given, when the declaration could potentially be relevant beyond the proceeding.[401]

As mentioned above,[402] the courts are held to interpret parties' petitions in accordance with their true intent. Where the legal relationship is not prejudicial, the court can therefore interpret the petition as one under § 256(1) German CCP if it finds that the claimant has a legal interest in the declaration instead.

In 2007, the BGH was called upon to decide on a dispute between a sports club and its rowing division where the latter sought a declaration that the sale of a plot with a clubhouse by the association was invalid.[403] The association brought a counterclaim, requesting the court to find by means of incident declaratory relief that the association was not holding the plot as a fiduciary for the claimant. The court found that such counterclaim was not admissible as incident declaratory relief in accordance with § 256(2) German CCP, as it lacked the required element of prejudiciality, since this

392. *Ibid.*, at nn. 81, 84 & 86.
393. *See* Becker-Eberhard, *supra* n. 230, at nn. 81, 84 & 86; Wolfgang Voit in: Hans-Joachim Musielak & Wolfgang Voit, *Zivilprozessordnung: ZPO mit Gerichtsverfassungsgesetz, Kommentar, Commentary on § 1046 German CCP*, n. 39 (15th ed., 2018).
394. Becker-Eberhard, *supra* n. 230, at n. 80; Voit, *supra* n. 393, at n. 40.
395. Bacher, *supra* n. 240, at n. 39; Becker-Eberhard, *supra* n. 230, at n. 41.
396. Becker-Eberhard, *supra* n. 230, at nn. 80, 84.
397. *Ibid.*, at nn. 80, 85.
398. BGH, Judgement dated 23 April 2013 – II ZR 74/12, BGHZ 197, 162; BGH, Judgement dated 23 April 2013 – II ZR 74/12, NJW-RR 2013, 873; BGH, Judgement dated 2 July 2007 – II ZR 111/05, NJW 2008, 69; also BGH, Judgement dated 17 June 1994 – V ZR 34/92, NJW-RR 1994, 1272 et seq.
399. Bacher, *supra* n. 240, at n. 39; Becker-Eberhard, *supra* n. 230, at n. 80.
400. *See* Annex II.III[A] *supra*.
401. BGH, Judgement dated 5 May 2011 – VII ZR 179/10, NJW 2011, 2195, 2196; BGH, Judgement dated 21 February 1992 – V ZR 273/90, NJW 1992, 1897; Greger, *supra* n. 259, at n. 25.
402. *See* Annex II.IV[A] *supra*.
403. BGH, Judgement dated 2 July 2007 – II ZR 111/05, NJW 2008, 69 et seq.

determination was irrelevant to the decision of the main claim.[404] Nonetheless, the court found that the respondent had a legal interest in the declaration and that the counterclaim was admissible as an action for declaratory relief under § 256(1) German CCP.[405]

In the context of § 256(2) German CCP, the BAG has even done without a concrete legal relationship and allowed for a declaration on an abstract legal question by means of incident declaratory relief. In a case before the court, two apprentices sued their employer in the retail sector for the difference between their received remuneration and that envisaged in a collective labour agreement. The court rendered an incident declaratory relief on the question of the applicability of the collective labour agreement for the retail sector, noting that such a finding would be exceptional but could avoid future lawsuits.[406]

The petition may also be made in the alternative, for example in the event that the main claim is dismissed.[407] This is illustrated by a case where the claimant sued for payment of remuneration for construction services based on a notarized agreement concerning sale of a plot of land to the respondent with the obligation to build a house and a garage on that plot. Outside of the notarized agreement, the parties had agreed that, instead of the garage, the claimant shall build another bathroom at no extra cost. The respondent defended itself by relying on the agreement outside of the notarized agreement, which led the claimant to petition for incident declaratory relief in the alternative, in the event that its main claim for payment was dismissed, to find that the notarized agreement is void for lack of the legally required form for the whole agreement. The court found that, indeed, a petition for incident declaratory relief can also be brought in the alternative.[408] Furthermore, the court stated that, in order for the necessary element of prejudiciality to exist, it suffices that the existence or non-existence of the disputed legal relationship may have relevance for the parties in the future in excess of the current main dispute, as the rationale informing § 256(2) German CCP is to provide the possibility to have such existence or non-existence of a legal relationship decided with binding legal effect.[409]

[C] Invalidity of Shareholder's Resolutions (§ 249 AktG)

Another exemption from the legal interest requirement is instituted in the German Stock Corporation Act of 6 September 1965 (*Aktiengesetz*, AktG).

The AktG in § 249 introduces a specific kind of action aimed at declaring the invalidity of resolutions of shareholder's general meetings of a German stock corporation (*Aktiengesellschaft*, AG). It is also applicable with regard to German limited

404. *Ibid.*
405. The association had a legal interest in the determination if it was indeed obligated to hold the plot of land as a fiduciary or in trust as the claimants where claiming to have such property rights in the plot of land; BGH, Judgement dated 2 July 2007 – II ZR 111/05, NJW 2008, 69.
406. BAG, Judgement dated 25 November 1987 – 4 AZR 361/87, BAGE 56, 357.
407. Bacher, *supra* n. 240, at n. 39; Becker-Eberhard, *supra* n. 230, at n. 88.
408. BGH, Judgement dated 21 February 1992 – V ZR 273/90, NJW 1992, 1897.
409. *Ibid.*

liability companies (GmbH)[410] and cooperatives (*Genossenschaft*).[411] The primary statutory grounds for nullity are listed in § 241 AktG and cover, in particular, situations that a resolution adopted by the general meeting shall be null and void if it was adopted by a general meeting that was inadmissibly convened,[412] if it has not been recorded by a notary public,[413] if it is irreconcilable with the nature of the stock corporation or if it violates regulations exclusively or primarily instituted for the protection of the company's creditors or that otherwise serve the public interest, or – finally – if its provisions are contrary to public policy.

In such cases, § 256 German CCP is not applicable, with the practical effect that the prerequisite of legal interest shall not be examined by the court.[414] This considerable facilitation applies, however, only to the range of entities mentioned expressly in § 249(1) sentence 1 of the AktG, including the shareholders, management board and its members, and the members of the supervisory board, who are entitled to bring a declaratory action under this special provision. Their legal interest is justified by their membership (shareholder) or by status as corporate bodies (management and supervisory board).[415]

If an entity outside of the group listed in this AktG provision endeavours to invalidate a resolution, § 256 German CCP and, as a consequence, the requirement of legal interest is applicable.[416] It is accepted that such persons should be allowed to apply for declaration of invalidity of a general meeting resolution. However, in such cases, the specific legal interest should be answered in the affirmative only in exceptional circumstances, e.g., if the claimant was dismissed from a position on the body of the company by the disputed general meeting resolution.[417]

The specific provision on the declaration of a resolution's invalidity was not introduced with regard to resolutions of other bodies of the company, i.e., resolutions of the management board, supervisory board or audit committee. Resolutions by these bodies may be subject to declaratory relief based on § 256 German CCP.

[D] Insolvency Proceedings

If, after the insolvency of a party, the insolvency administrator or another creditor disputes a claim, a creditor can file an action for declaratory relief under §§ 179 et seq.

410. BGH, Judgement dated 25 April 1966 – II ZR 80/65, NJW 1966, 1458; OLG Koblenz, Judgement dated 17 November 2005 - 6 U 577/05, NZG 2006, 270, 271; OLG Hamburg, Judgement dated 31 May 1995 - 11 U 183/94, NJW-RR 1996, 1065.
411. BGH, Judgement dated 23 February 1978 – II ZR 37/77, BGHZ 70, 384, 388.
412. § 121 AktG.
413. § 130 AktG.
414. BGH, Judgement dated 25 February 1965 – II ZR 287/63, BGHZ 43, 261.
415. Carsten Schäfer, in: 4 Wulf Goette, Mathias Habersack & Susanne Kalss, *Münchener Kommentar zum Aktiengesetz, Commentary on § 249*, n. 4a (4th ed., 2016); Lutz Englisch, in: Wolfgang Hölters, *Aktiengesetz, Commentary on § 249*, n. 3 (3rd ed., 2017).
416. BGH, Judgement dated 25 April 1966 – II ZR 80/65, NJW 1966, 1458; OLG Hamburg, Judgement dated 31 May 1995 – 11 U 183/94, NJW-RR 1996, 1065; OLG Naumburg, Judgement dated 6 February 1997 – 7 U 236/96, NZA-RR 1997, 177.
417. BGH, Judgement dated 25 April 1966 – II ZR 80/65, NJW 1966, 1458.

Insolvency Code (*Insolvenzordnung*, InsO) in order to have the validity of the claim established. The claimant does not have to prove a particular legal interest in the declaration, it follows from the circumstance that a disputed claim can otherwise not be registered in the insolvency schedule and the claimant may lose its claim.

[E] Dismissal Protection (§ 4 KSchG)

§ 4 Dismissal Protection Act (*Kündigungsschutzgesetz*, KSchG) allows for dismissal protection by way of a judgement, declaring that the employment relationship was not terminated or amended by a specific termination notice or notice of amendment.[418] The claimant's legal interest in the declaration is comprised in the uncertainty as to the validity of the termination or amendment and the goal to prevent an insufficient termination or amendment from becoming valid after three weeks, according to § 7 KSchG.[419] No further legal interest is required.[420] This, however, will not be the case if the employer did not declare the termination, unless it is unclear if a declaration had to be understood that way.[421]

The provision applies to all employment relationships.[422] The declaration under § 4 KSchG only covers the specific termination notice or notice of amendment referred to by the claimant. In practice, therefore, such an action is often combined with an action for declaratory relief under the general provisions of § 256(1) German CCP in order to have the court declare that the employment relationship has also not been terminated or amended by other means and still exists.[423] For this second action, the general requirements, including legal interest, have to be fulfilled.[424]

[F] Model Declaratory Lawsuits (§§ 606 et seq. German CCP)

Since 1 November 2018, §§ 606 et seq. German CCP allow for a model declaratory lawsuit. The introduction of these provisions is regarded by some as aiming to unburden the courts from the numerous lawsuits engendered to the Volkswagen emissions scandal[425] also known as Dieselgate. They allow certain associations to bring an action for a declaration on factual or legal requirements for claims or legal

418. § 4 KSchG, in German: '*Will ein Arbeitnehmer geltend machen, dass eine Kündigung sozial ungerechtfertigt oder aus anderen Gründen rechtsunwirksam ist, so muss er innerhalb von drei Wochen nach Zugang der schriftlichen Kündigung Klage beim Arbeitsgericht auf Feststellung erheben, dass das Arbeitsverhältnis durch die Kündigung nicht aufgelöst ist. Im Falle des § 2 ist die Klage auf Feststellung zu erheben, daß die Änderung der Arbeitsbedingungen sozial ungerechtfertigt oder aus anderen Gründen rechtsunwirksam ist.* [...].'
419. *See* Curt Wolfgang Hergenröder in: 11 Franz Jürgen Säcker, Roland Rixecker, Hartmut Oetker & Bettina Limperg, *Münchener Kommentar zum Bürgerlichen Gesetzbuch: BGB, Commentary on § 4 KSchG*, n. 35 (7th ed., 2016).
420. Hergenröder, *supra* n. 419, n. 35.
421. BAG, Judgement dated 22 May 1980 – 2 AZR 613/78, BeckRS 2009, 67100.
422. *See* Hergenröder, *supra* n. 419, nn. 2 et seq.
423. *See* Heinrich Kiel in: Rudi Müller-Glöge, Ulrich Preis & Ingrid Schmidt, *Erfurter Kommentar zum Arbeitsrecht, § 4 KSchG*, n. 36 (19th ed., 2019).
424. Kiel, *supra* n. 423, at nn. 37–39.
425. Erich Waclawik, *Die Musterfeststellungsklage*, NJW 2018, 2921, 2922.

relationships.[426] The action can be brought against businesses and is binding for consumers who have registered accordingly.[427] It requires a specific form of legitimate interest (*Rechtsschutzbedürfnis* or *Rechtsschutzinteresse*); according to § 606(3) no. 2 German CCP, the claims or legal relationships of at least ten consumers have to be affected by the requested declaration.[428] Additionally, fifty consumers have to register for the claim within two months,[429] failing which the action becomes inadmissible.[430] A further legal interest in the declaration (*besonderes Feststellungsinteresse*) is not required.[431]

[G] Rejection of Claims

In substance, all court decisions dismissing an action for performance or for amendment of a legal relationship are of declaratory nature, as they declare that the claimant's subjective right does not exist.[432] A specific legal interest of the defending party is, of course, not required but is the counterpart to the claimant's legitimate interest.[433]

VII LIS PENDENS

According to § 261(1) and (3) no. 1 German CCP, after a lawsuit has become pending (*rechtshängig*), another lawsuit concerning the same subject matter cannot be filed unless the former case is dismissed. In the German understanding, the subject matter of the dispute is defined by its two elements, the petition and the submitted facts.[434] This means that a second action is only barred by a previous one if both of these elements correspond.

Therefore, if a purported debtor first files for negative declaratory relief, declaring that the alleged claim does not exist, then this does not bar the creditor's later claim for performance.[435] This is because the petition for performance is understood to entail and to go beyond that of a mere declaration.[436] In order to avoid conflicting findings, courts hold that, with the subsequent action for performance, the action for declaratory relief loses its legal interest once the later action cannot be unilaterally withdrawn.[437]

426. § 606(1) German CCP.
427. § 613 German CCP.
428. Lutz in: Volkert Vorwerk & Christian Wolf, *Beck'scher Online-Kommentar ZPO, Commentary on § 606 German CCP*, n. 46 (31st ed., 2018).
429. § 606(3) no. 3 German CCP.
430. Lutz, *supra* n. 428, at n. 49.
431. *Ibid.*, at n. 46.
432. Assmann, *supra* n. 256, at n. 4; *See also* OLG Hamburg, Judgement dated 11 September 1985 - 15 WF 168/85, BeckRS 2009, 87156.
433. *See also* Annex II. III[A] *supra*.
434. This is the almost unanimous view; *See* Becker-Eberhard, *supra* n. 230, at n. 32.
435. Foerste, *supra* n. 265, at n. 16.
436. BGH, Judgement dated 7 July 1994 - I ZR 30/92, NJW 1994, 3107, 3108; Saenger, *supra* n. 271, at n. 22.
437. BGH, Judgement dated 11 December 1996 - VIII ZR 154/95, NJW 1997, 870; Christoph Thole, *Aktuelle Entwicklungen bei der negativen Feststellungsklage*, 66 NJW 1192, 1194 (2013); *see also* Annex II.III[G] and Annex II.III[H] *supra*.

This approach has rightfully been criticized by scholars,[438] since it does not prevent conflicting findings or promote efficiency - and, in fact, may invite opportunistic shenanigans. After the action for declaratory relief has been withdrawn, the court will nevertheless have to render at least a summary decision in order to decide on the costs, while the second court will have to decide on the same question again.[439] Since the action for performance is even deemed possible after a first instance judgement has been rendered on the declaratory relief,[440] the creditor can await this outcome before filing for another first instance judgement on his action for performance.[441] Some authors have therefore suggested that the proceedings regarding the action for performance should be suspended until a decision on the declaratory relief has been rendered if a first instance decision has already been rendered or is imminent.[442]

According to the Higher Regional Court of Appeal in Berlin (KG), an action for negative declaratory relief also does not bar a subsequent action for positive declaratory relief regarding the same legal relationship because the latter may suspend limitation periods whereas the defence against a negative action could not.[443] As for the subsequent action for performance, the claimant then loses its legal interest in the negative action.[444]

In the converse constellation, an action for performance entails a petition for a declaration of the existence of a claim and therefore bars a later action for negative declaratory relief.[445]

The picture is different for actions for negative declaratory relief that fall under the Brussels-Ia-regulation.[446] Under Article 29(1) Brussels-Ia, when 'proceedings involving the same cause of action and between the same parties' are brought before a second court, it must stay the proceedings. This provision has to be interpreted autonomously, and the ECJ sees the same cause of action given when both actions are at the core identical. This it deems to be the case for an action for performance and its neglecting action for negative declaratory relief. Therefore, other than in a purely German context, an action for negative declaratory relief filed in one country bars an action for performance in another[447] and presumably also positive declaratory relief on the same issue.

438. Thole, *supra* n. 437 at 1194; *see* Assmann, *supra* n. 256, at n. 255 with further references.
439. Assmann, *supra* n. 256, at n. 255 with further references.
440. BGH, Judgement dated 21 December 2005 - X ZR 17/03, BGHZ 165, 305, 309 et seq.
441. Assmann, *supra* n. 256, at n. 256.
442. *See* Assmann, *supra* n. 256, at nn. 255 et seq. with further references.
443. KG, Judgement dated 8 June 1960 - 10 U 414/60, NJW 1961, 33; the BGH left this question open in BGH, Judgement dated 15 December 2009 - XI ZR 110/09, NJW-RR 2010, 640, 641.
444. Foerste, *supra* n. 265, at n. 17.
445. Becker-Eberhard, *supra* n. 230, at n. 66.
446. For a comparison *see* Thole, *supra* n. 437, at 1192.
447. *Tatry*, Slg. 1994, I-5439, 5475 et seq. (ECJ).

VIII RES JUDICATA EFFECT

Generally, the operative part of a judgment in an action for declaratory relief determines the extent of the legal effects.[448] Only if the operative part alone is not sufficient to fully account for the legal effects is it possible to look at the statement of facts, the reason for decision and the submissions by the parties.[449] Once a judgment becomes legally enforceable, the parties will be precluded from disputing the findings of the court on grounds that they could have brought forward before the closing of the last hearing on the facts.[450]

Furthermore, under § 325(1) German CCP a judgment that has entered into force takes effect for and against the parties to the dispute and the persons who have become successors in title of the parties after the matter has become pending.[451]

If the claimant sought to prove the existence of a legal relationship by an action for positive declaratory relief (*positive Feststellungsklage*) and the court rejects it as unfounded, this will entail a declaration that the legal relationship does not exist.[452]

A subsequent claim for performance by the claimant would be dismissed as unfounded (*unbegründet*) and not merely inadmissible (*unzulässig*).[453] The claim would be admissible due to the different subject matters of the claims and unfounded because the court would have to assume the non-existence of the legal relationship due to the judgment in the action for declaratory relief.[454]

If a negative action for declaratory relief (*negative Feststellungsklage*) is successful on its merits, the legal relationship between the parties will likewise be deemed not to exist.[455] However, if such a claim is rejected as unfounded, this will have the same effect as a positive action for declaratory relief, i.e., that the legal relationship is deemed to exist.[456]

448. Musielak, *supra* n. 385, at n. 57.
449. BGH, Judgement dated 14.02.2008 – I ZR 135/05, NJW 2008, 2716; Musielak, *supra* n. 385, at n. 57.
450. Musielak, *supra* n. 385, at n. 57.
451. In German: '*(1) Das rechtskräftige Urteil wirkt für und gegen die Parteien und die Personen, die nach dem Eintritt der Rechtshängigkeit Rechtsnachfolger der Parteien geworden sind oder den Besitz der in Streit befangenen Sache in solcher Weise erlangt haben, dass eine der Parteien oder ihr Rechtsnachfolger mittelbarer Besitzer geworden ist.*'
452. BGH, Judgement dated 1 December 1993 – VIII ZR 41/93, NJW 1994, 657, 659; Musielak, *supra* n. 385, at n. 58.
453. BGH, Judgement dated 29 September 1989 – V ZR 326/87, NJW 1989, 392, 394; Musielak, *supra* n. 385, at n. 58.
454. Musielak, *supra* n. 385, at n. 58.
455. *Ibid.*, at n. 59.
456. BGH; Judgement dated 17 February 1983 – III ZR 184/81, NJW 1983, 2032, 2033; Musielak, *supra* n. 385, at n. 59.

IX DECLARATORY RELIEF AS INTERIM RELIEF

The German CCP does not foresee declaratory relief as interim relief (*Feststellungsverfügung*).[457] Nonetheless, courts have occasionally issued such rulings.[458] Under § 256(1) German CCP, they are confined to establishing the existence or non-existence of a legal relationship, as for example the preliminary invalidity of a resolution of the supervisory board of a stock corporation (AG) due to lack of information to the employees' representative members of the supervisory board[459] or the preliminary determination of the shareholder status of a shareholder of a limited liability company (GmbH) after the wrongful redemption of its shares.[460] Such relief has furthermore been used to preliminarily establish that no employment relationship exists, so that a football player can be entered on a transfer list of the German *Bundesliga*.[461]

X COSTS

Court fees and statutory attorney's fees[462] generally depend on the value of the dispute, which corresponds to the economic value of the claim to the claimant. According to § 3 German CCP,[463] the court has discretion in its determination. It may even estimate the value of the claim.[464] For claims for declaratory relief, courts regularly deduct approximately 20% of the value, depending on the circumstances of the case.[465] Where an economic value cannot be determined, the courts have used the figure of EUR 5,000 as an anchor for the estimate.[466]

457. The German CCP only mentions interim measures to secure a claim (§ 935 German CCP) or to preliminarily regulate a relationship (§ 940 German CCP). In addition, the courts have already recognized preliminary measures for performance in certain cases.
458. *See* Jacobs, *supra* n. 221, at 93.
459. OLG Hannover, Judgement dated 27 June 1989 – 7 O 214/89, ZIP 1989, 1330.
460. OLG Rostock, Court Order dated 15 January 1997 – 6 U 167/96, GmbHR 1997, 449 (while denying an injunction to block the effects of a public auction of the shares due to the invalidity of the redemption of the shares of the shareholder concerned).
461. Regional Labor Court in Berlin (*Landesarbeitsgericht*, LAG), Judgement dated 31 August 2000 – 10 Sa 1728/00, NZA 2001, 53, 54 et seq.
462. The statutory attorney's fees represent the minimum amount which attorneys must, in principle, charge for their services in court litigation as well as the maximum amount that the winning party may claim as reimbursement for their fees from an unsuccessful opponent (§ 91(1) German CCP).
463. § 3 German CCP applies to the assessment of the amount in dispute for purposes of establishing the jurisdiction, by reference it also applies to determination of the amount in dispute to calculate the court fees (§ 48(1) 2 Courts' Fees Act, *Gerichtskostengesetz*, GKG) and attorney's fees (§ 23(1) Attorneys' Fees Act, Rechtsanwaltsvergütungsgesetz, RVG).
464. *See* Rainer Hüßtege in: Heinz Thomas & Hans Putzo, *Zivilprozessordnung: ZPO, FamFG Verfahren in Familiensachen, EGZPO, GVG, EGGVG, EU-Zivilverfahrensrecht, Commentary on § 3 German CCP*, n. 2 (39th ed., 2018).
465. Kurt Herget in: Richard Zöller, *Zivilprozessordnung, Commentary on § 265*, n. 7 (32nd ed., 2018).
466. § 23(3) RVG defines EUR 5,000 (EUR 4,000 before 1 August 2013) as reference point for the amount in dispute for the determination of attorney's fees. The courts have used this reference also to estimate the value of a claim for other purposes; *See* BGH, Court Order dated 17 November 2015 – II ZB 8/14, BeckRS 2015, 20307, n. 13; BGH Court Order dated 5 November

A deduction of 20% of the amount in dispute does not necessarily mean that court or attorney's fees suddenly become 20% cheaper. The cost effect will depend on additional factors, e.g., if the deducted amount falls in another tier of costs. Additionally, the costs are not proportional to the amount in dispute. Therefore, a deduction of 20% of the amount in dispute will often lead to a cost reduction of only 10%–15%, while in some cases it could be 0%.[467]

XI DECLARATORY RELIEF IN ARBITRATION SEATED IN GERMANY

The German Arbitration Law is found in the tenth book of the German CCP in §§ 1025 et seq. and, since its revision, effective 1 January 1998, is a close adaption of the UNCITRAL Model Law on International Commercial Arbitration. Therefore it is not surprising that, as in most jurisdictions,[468] there is no express reference to the declaratory powers of arbitrators in the German Arbitration Law itself.[469]

It is said that 'commentators and legal practice pay little attention to the question'[470] because 'to a German, the declaratory function of the judiciary is the most natural thing in the world'.[471] It is therefore uncontested that arbitral tribunals seated in Germany have the power to grant declaratory relief.[472] However, what appears to be an open issue is whether the legal interest prerequisite for declaratory relief, as known before the state courts, applies in any way also in arbitration where the German Arbitration Law is the *lex arbitri*.

As § 256(1) German CCP is generally considered a procedural regulation,[473] there seems to be little concern, as known for instance under Swiss law,[474] as to whether the requirements for declaratory relief are to be categorized as a matter of procedure or as a substantive law issue. Therefore this question is usually discussed in the context of the applicable procedural rules.

2013 – II ZR 220/11, BeckRS 2013, 20402, n. 1; BGH, Court Order dated 14 June 2010 – II ZB 20/09, NJW-RR 2010, 1582, n. 9.

467. For example, the fees for a claim over EUR 4,000 fall in the same tier as for a claim over EUR 3,200; *See* attachment 2 GKG and attachment 2 RVG.
468. *See* Leimgruber, *supra* n. 39, at 475; one noteable exception is section 48(3) of the English Arbitration Act 1996.
469. Only § 1040(3) German CCP mentions the possibility for the tribunal to render a declaratory decision which is however limited to the determination of its own jurisdiction and does not extend to the subject matter of the dispute, *see* Stefan Rützel, Gerhard Wegen & Stephan Wilske, *Commercial Dispute Resolution in Germany: Litigation Arbitration Mediation*, at 145 (2005).
470. Leimgruber, *supra* n. 39, at 475.
471. Peter Schlosser, *Right and Remedy in Common Law Arbitration and in German Arbitration Law*, 4 Journal of International Arbitration, 27 (1987).
472. *See* Richard Kreindler, Jan Schäfer & Reinmar Wolff, *Schiedsgerichtsbarkeit – Kompendium für die Praxis*, 222 (2006); Leimgruber, *supra* n. 39, at 474–477; Joachim Münch in: 3 Wolfgang Krüger & Thomas Rauscher, *Münchener Kommentar zur Zivilprozessordnung mit Gerichtsverfassungsgesetz und Nebengesetzen, Commentary on § 1046 German CCP*, n. 5 (5th ed., 2017); Karl Heinz Schwab & Gerhard Walter, *Schiedsgerichtsbarkeit* at 135 (7th ed., C.H.Beck 2005); Voit, *supra* n. 393, at n. 2.
473. *See* Annex II.III[D] *supra*.
474. *See* Annex IV.III[A] *infra*.

Save for fundamental principles and mandatory provisions, § 1042(3) German CCP allows the parties to determine the procedure themselves, which is often done by reference to a set of arbitration rules. But parties' agreements rarely go into such detail as to list prerequisites for declaratory relief.[475] Similarly, arbitration rules usually lack guidance on this issue.[476] The question is then whether arbitrators should apply or be guided by the rules of civil procedure for state courts.

At the outset, there is general consensus that the *lex arbitri*, i.e., the tenth Book of the German CCP, exclusively governs the arbitral proceeding and that the rules of civil procedure as applicable in state courts do not apply in arbitration.[477]

The non-applicability of the requirements under § 256 German CCP find support in literature,[478] and the courts have also confirmed it.

Already in 1920, under the old arbitration law,[479] the former German Supreme Court - the RG - had to decide on a dispute between the buyer and the seller of two band saws.[480] The parties had agreed to refer disputes about the existence of defects to arbitration and the tribunal seized had found that the saws were indeed defective but that it had no jurisdiction to rule on any amounts due. When the buyer confronted the state court with its claim for payment, the court had to decide if the arbitral award had to be treated as a preliminary judgement[481] or as a declaratory relief, since only the latter could prolong the limitation period of six months to thirty years. Eventually, the RG held that in order to make this determination, it would be irrelevant if the claimant has had a legal interest in a declaration as required by § 256 German CCP, since the arbitral tribunal enjoyed considerable freedom in determining its procedure.[482] It qualified the award as granting declaratory relief.

475. *See* Leimgruber, *supra* n. 39, at 477.
476. *Ibid*; Patric Dunand & Maria Kostytska, Declaratory Relief in International Arbitration, 29 Journal of International Arbitration, Issue 1, 4.
477. Klaus Peter Berger, *Herausforderungen für die (deutsche) Schiedsgerichtsbarkeit*, SchiedsVZ 2009, 289, 294; Karl-Heinz Böckstiegel, Stefan Michael Kröll & Patricia Nacimiento, *Germany as a Place for International and Domestic Arbitrations: General Overview* in *Arbitration in Germany: The Model Law in Practice* 9 (Patricia Nacimiento, Stefan Michael Kröll & Karl-Heinz Böckstiegel eds. 2nd ed., 2015); Joachim Münch in: 3 Wolfgang Krüger & Thomas Rauscher, *Münchener Kommentar zur Zivilprozessordnung mit Gerichtsverfassungsgesetz und Nebengesetzen, Commentary on § 1025 German CCP*, at n. 13 (5th ed., 2017); Stefan Rützel, Gerhard Wegen & Stephan Wilske, *supra* n. 469, at 129 et seq.; Nathalie Voser, Dorothee Schramm & Florian Haugeneder, *Schiedsverfahren und anwendbares Recht*, in Hellwig Torggler, Florian Mohs, Friederike Schäfer, Venus Valentina Wong (eds), *Handbuch Schiedsgerichtsbarkeit: Deutschland – Österreich – Schweiz* at 249 et seq. (2nd ed., 2017); *see also* Gerhard Wagner, *Commentary on the German Arbitration Law*, in *Arbitration in Germany: The Model Law in Practice* 63 (Patricia Nacimiento, Stefan Michael Kröll & Karl-Heinz Böckstiegel eds. 2nd ed., 2015).
478. Kreindler, Schäfer & Wolff, *supra* n. 472, at 222, n. 759; Voit, *supra* n. 393, n. 2; *See also* Schneider, *supra* n. 216, at 30.
479. The German Arbitration law remained largely unchanged from 1879 until 1998 and already contained many of the key principles found in modern arbitration laws, for a summary on its history *see* Karl-Heinz Böckstiegel, Stefan Michael Kröll, Patricia Nacimiento, *supra* n. 477, at. 4.
480. RGZ 100, 118.
481. *See* Annex II.VI[A] *supra*.
482. RGZ 100, 118, 121, in German: '*freie[...] Stellung [...] für die Gestaltung seines Verfahrens.*'

In 1976, the BGH rendered a similar decision in a dispute between a lessor and the lessee of a gas station.[483] The parties had agreed that in case of specific changes of the consumer price index, the parties had to readjust the rent accordingly, as far as it was reasonable. When such changes occurred, the parties got into a dispute over the adjustment which was referred to arbitration. The arbitral tribunal rejected the lessor's claim for outstanding rent as unreasonable but granted the lessee's counterclaim for a declaration that under the agreement the rent could not be raised above the index. The lessor requested the court to annul the award under § 1041 no. 1 German CCP in its pre-1998 version, which allowed for annulment if the award was the result of an inadmissible procedure. One of the reasons brought forward was that the lessee had lacked legal interest in the declaration by the tribunal, as required under § 256(1) German CCP. Without further reasoning, the BGH held that in arbitration, declaratory relief was not subject to the requirements of § 256 German CCP but that an economic interest, which was given in this case, was sufficient. The court did not annul the award.

This only shows that courts have accepted declaratory awards absent the legal interest requirement of § 256(1) German CCP. It is, however, very likely that courts would equally accept awards dismissing such actions as inadmissible, since none of the grounds for annulment, listed in § 1059(2) German CCP,[484] may be fulfilled. The question, to which extend arbitrators should be guided in their discretion by the requirements of § 256(1) German CCP therefore has to be decided in the light of its goal and purpose.

As mentioned above, the primary purpose of the legal interest requirement for declaratory relief is, to protect state courts from being overburdened by inefficient, useless or even frivolous actions.[485] As has been held by several scholars, this rationale does not apply to arbitration: unlike state courts, arbitrators do not provide a scarce public resource that needs to be protected from being overstrained.[486] Quite to the contrary, there is no shortage of arbitrators willing to take up new cases, and the costs of arbitration burden the parties, not the public.[487] At the same time, tribunals should not limit the parties' access to justice without good justification.[488] It has therefore been said that in arbitration the restrictions regarding declaratory relief should not apply.[489]

However, another reason, mentioned for the limiting requirements of § 256 German CCP, is to protect the opposing party from being dragged into unnecessary court proceedings.[490] This concern may be equally valid in arbitration. It has therefore

483. BGH, Judgement dated 10 June 1976 – III ZR 71/74, WM 1976, 910.
484. This provision widely resembles Art. 34 UNCITRAL Model Law on International Commercial Arbitration, which in turn reflects the grounds for refusal of enforcement listed in Art. V of the New York Convention on the Recognition and Enforcement of Foreign Arbitral Awards.
485. *See* Annex II.III[B] *supra*.
486. Karl Heinz Schwab & Gerhard Walter, *supra* n. 472, at n. 135; Kreindler, Schäfer & Wolff, *supra* n. 472, at 222; Voit, *supra* n. 393, at n. 2.
487. Schneider, *supra* n. 216, at 30.
488. Kreindler, Schäfer & Wolff, *supra* n. 472, at 222, n. 759; Daniel Girsberger & Nathalie Voser, International Arbitration: Comparative and Swiss Perspective, 293 (3rd ed., 2016).
489. Kreindler, Schäfer & Wolff, *supra* n. 472, at 222; Schneider, *supra* n. 216, at 30.
490. Schwab & Walter, *supra* n. 472, at 135.

been held, that tribunals should not disregard the prerequisite of legal interest completely but instead lower the requirements so that an economic interest is sufficient.[491]

In view of the authors, arbitrators should not be too restrictive about admitting actions for declaratory relief. In general, any legitimate interest of the claimant should be sufficient. It should be deemed missing in case of pointless or abusive actions.[492] Questions of subsidiarity, e.g., when a claimant could potentially avoid a second arbitration by bringing an action for performance instead of declaratory relief, are better addressed by allocating the costs of the arbitration accordingly.[493] This solution offers the desired flexibility to which arbitration aspires.

491. *Ibid*; Kreindler, Schäfer & Wolff, *supra* n. 472, at 222; Voit, *supra* n. 393, at n. 2.
492. Schneider, *supra* n. 216, at 31: principle of abuse of rights should be used to deal with declaratory actions without serious justification.
493. Schneider, *supra* n. 216, at 31.

ANNEX III

Report on Main Features of Declarations in Poland

Beata Gessel-Kalinowska vel Kalisz & Joanna Kisielińska-Garncarek

Table of Contents

I ORIGINS AND EVOLUTION OF DECLARATORY RELIEFS IN THE POLISH LEGAL SYSTEM

The history of modern civil procedure in Poland was determined by three main systemic transformations occurring due to changing political circumstances in the twentieth century.[494] The first transformation occurred when Poland regained her independence in 1918. Work on Polish civil procedure began promptly in November 1919, employing the comparative method and drawing certain inspirations from modern European legal systems in order to create the former Polish CCP dated 29 November 1930[495] (the 'Polish FCCP'). The whole concept of declaratory reliefs under the Polish FCCP was based mainly on the German institution of *Feststellungsklage.*[496] Article 3 of the Polish FCCP stated that anyone may seek judicial protection while preventing violation of his right and, at the same time, while having legal interest in establishment of a legal relationship or right. Therefore, at that point in time, declaratory relief was deemed mainly a precautionary procedural measure.[497] Jurisprudence of the time expressly emphasized that declaratory action was admissible solely if it was necessary to prevent violation of rights that might occur in the future.[498] At the same time, such threat of violation must have been considered as serious.[499] Consequently, declaratory action was unacceptable if the right had already been violated in the past, thus providing basis for a more far-reaching claim resulting from such violation.[500] If a receivable had been due, the claimant was, as a rule, entitled solely to action of a broader scope, e.g., for payment of the respective amount.[501] For instance, claimants used to request declaration of an obligation to remedy harm which might occur in the future as a result of specified tortious behaviour.[502] The legal interest – another prerequisite of declaratory reliefs – was defined as the necessity to secure the benefit consisting in protection of claimant's rights from violation in the future.[503]

The second transformation took place after WWII, when Poland found itself under the political influence of the Union of Soviet Socialist Republics. The legal system

494. Anna Stawarska-Rippel, *Trzy transformacje w procedurze cywilnej w Polsce w XX wieku. Wzorce rozwiązań*, 11 Zeszyty Prawnicze UKSW 353, 353 et seq. (2011); cf. Beata Gessel-Kalinowska vel Kalisz, *Mixing Legal Systems in Europe; the Role of Common Law Transplants (Polish Law Example)*, 4 ERPL 789, 789 et seq. (2017).
495. Wacław Miszewski, *Polski kodeks postępowania cywilnego a procedura cywilna rosyjska*, 11 RPEiS 111, 111 (1931); Gessel-Kalinowska vel Kalisz, *supra* n. 494, at 792.
496. Włodzimierz Werhanowski, *Znaczenie interesu prawnego w procesie cywilnym* 29–30 (1908); cf. Franciszek Ksawery Fierich, *Postępowanie przed sądami okręgowemi* in *Polska procedura cywilna. Projekty referentów z uzasadnieniem. Komisja Kodyfikacyjna R.P., Sekcja postępowania cywilnego*, 328 (1928).
497. Edmund Wengerek, *Powództwo o ustalenie*, 21 RPiE 1, 1–33 (1959).
498. Judgement of 2 December 1937, C I 3290/36, Official Compilation 1938, item 525 (Polish Supreme Court).
499. Judgement of 14 January 1938, C II 1716/37, Official Compilation 1938, item 470 (Polish Supreme Court).
500. Judgement of 29 April 1949, Wa C 12/49, 2 Nowe Prawo (1946) (Polish Supreme Court).
501. Jan Hroboni, *Stosunek wzajemny powództwa o ustalenie i powództwa o świadczenie*, 21–22 PPC 642 (1934).
502. Wengerek, *supra* n. 497, at 7.
503. Zygmunt Hahn, *Interes prawny w skardze o ustalenie*, 23 PPC, 705, 705–706 (1935).

of interwar Poland, including provisions of the Polish FCCP, did not square with the principles of the new Polish polity.[504] The idea was now to remodel civil procedure so as to accommodate the new socialist reality in which the conflation of official and investigative powers made for a certain repressiveness.[505] The new Code of Civil Procedure, remaining in force until today, was adopted as late as in November 1964 (the 'Polish CCP').[506] From the very beginning, it included a provision allowing a claimant with legal interest to file a claim for declaratory relief. In accordance with Article 189 of the Polish CCP, providing the statutory basis for declaratory awards, the claimant may apply to the court for establishment of the existence or non-existence of a legal relationship or a right if he has legal interest in doing so, without any further prerequisites. It is evident at first sight that the Polish legislature abandoned the concept that declaratory relief might be given solely in order to protect a right which had not been violated at the moment of bringing the claim[507] or that it should serve as preventive measure.[508] Therefore, the possibilities for obtaining a declarations were, prima facie, considerably extended. However, the newly introduced wording of Article 189 opened heated discussions regarding the definition of legal interest (section III *infra*), the legal nature of the aforementioned provision (section II *infra*) and the scope of subsidiarity rule (section III[B] *infra*).

The third transformation came about soon after 1989. It would appear that the existing system of law should have been revised to eliminate the rules and principles characteristic for the socialist legal system.[509] However, when it comes to declaratory reliefs and the notion of 'legal interest', the wording of the Polish CCP as well as interpretation thereof have both remained largely unchanged. Therefore, in building the definition of legal interest under Polish law, we may refer to debates pursued among legal scholars in the early 1960s and even earlier – some views and ideas presented on the basis of Article 3 of the Polish FCCP might still serve as a good point of reference, with due heed for intervening adjustments of the procedural law. The liberalization of social and economic processes in Poland post-1989 has not influenced the concept of declaratory reliefs to any significant extent. Quite on the contrary, in some aspects, views expressed in the jurisprudence seem to become stricter with the passage of time, certainly as regards the scope of the subsidiarity principle.

II STATUTORY BASIS AND PREREQUISITES FOR DECLARATORY RELIEFS

As already indicated, the current statutory basis for declaratory reliefs is included in Article 189 of the Polish CCP. In line with the aforementioned provision: 'the claimant

504. Stawarska-Rippel, *supra* n. 494, at 362.
505. Gessel-Kalinowska vel Kalisz, *supra* n. 494, at 802.
506. The Act – Code of Civil Procedure dated 17 November 1964, Journal of Laws of the Republic of Poland no. 43, item 296, with subsequent amendments.
507. Maria Jędrzejewska & Karol Weitz, *Kodeks postępowania cywilnego. Komentarz. Tom II. Poste powanie rozpoznawcze* (Tadeusz Ereciński ed.), 82 et seq. (2016).
508. Judgement of 14 July 1972, III CRN 607/71, 4 OSNCP, item 64 (1973) (Polish Supreme Court).
509. Stawarska-Rippel, *supra* n. 494, at 368.

may apply to the court to establish the existence or non-existence of a legal relationship or a right if he has legal interest in doing so'. This relatively laconic regulation sets forth the main prerequisite of declaratory relief, i.e., the claimant's legal interest. Only upon establishment of existence of legal interest in obtaining a specific declaration may the court proceed to substantively assessing correctness of the claimant's statements regarding existence or non-existence of the legal relationship or right.[510] In other words, legal interest is a prerequisite for admissibility of declaratory relief[511] to be assessed by the court in the first order of sequence, and lack thereof shall lead to dismissal of the claim without any reference to the main application set out in the statement of claim.

The specific wording of Article 189 of the Polish CCP indicating the prerequisites upon the existence of which declaratory relief might be awarded raises the question of the legal character of the aforementioned provision.

This issue, however, is not regarded as controversial or, at any rate, has not been deemed to warrant deeper discussion in Polish legal doctrine and jurisprudence. According to the prevailing (practically unanimous) view, this regulation is of a substantive nature, the fact that it has been embedded within the procedural law notwithstanding.[512] As other provisions of Polish civil law do not give sufficient grounds to formulate the claim for declaratory relief, Article 189 of the Polish CCP constitutes a substantive source of the right to apply for a declaration.[513] Furthermore, existence of legal interest shall be deemed as a substantive condition of declaratory relief.[514] Therefore, it cannot be treated solely as a formal aspect of the declaratory claim which would lead to rejection of statement of claim.[515] Quite on the contrary, lack of legal interest leads, as a rule, to dismissal of the claim.[516] Admissibility of a request for declaratory relief, i.e., the existence of claimant's legal interest, is examined by the court at the very beginning of the proceedings ex officio, even if the respondent

510. Bronisław Czech, *Kodeks postępowania cywilnego. Tom I. Komentarz. Art. 1–366* (Kazimierz Piasecki & Andrzej Marciniak eds.) 851 (2016); judgement of 13 September 2007, III CSK 123/07, 1–2 OSG, item 12 (2009) (Polish Supreme Court).

511. Judgement of 27 June 2001, II CKN 898/00 (Polish Supreme Court).

512. Judgement of 3 April 2000, I CKN 582/98 (Polish Supreme Court); judgement of 6 August 2014, I CSK 559/13 (Polish Supreme Court); judgement of 19 March 2015, IV CSK 362/14 (Polish Supreme Court); Andrzej Zieliński, *Kodeks postępowania cywilnego. Komentarz* (Andrzej Zieliński & Kinga Flaga-Gieruszyńska eds.), 392–393 (2017); Czech, *supra* n. 510, at 851.

513. Judgement of 17 November 2000, V CKN 221/00 (Polish Supreme Court).

514. Judgement of 22 November 2002, IV CKN 1519/00 (Polish Supreme Court); Elwira Marszałkowska-Krześ, *Przesłanki materialnoprawne powództwa o ustalenie istnienia bądź nieistnienia uchwały wspólników w spółce z o.o.*, 9 PPH 28, 28–29 (1998).

515. Certain proposals *de lege ferenda* enabling rejection of the claim in a situation of lack of legal interest were recently fielded among Polish scholars (cf. Łukasz Błaszczak, *Znaczenie interesu prawnego w poszukiwaniu ochrony prawnej w procesie cywilnym na przykładzie poszczególnych rodzajów powództw* in *Ius est a iustitia appellatum: księga jubileuszowa dedykowana Profesorowi Tadeuszowi Wiśniewskiemu* (Michał Tomalak ed.) 35, 79–80 (2017). However, introduction of such a procedural solution would require amendment of the Polish CCP.

516. Judgement of 3 April 2000, I CKN 582/98 (Polish Supreme Court); judgement of 24 April 2014, III CSK 182/13 (Polish Supreme Court); Jerzy Jodłowski, *Postępowanie cywilne*, 76(Jerzy Jodłowski & Władysław Siedlecki eds., 2016).

does not raise a plea in this regard. This point of view is well established in jurisprudence[517] as well as in legal doctrine.[518]

Recently, a contrary (although isolated) view was expressed in legal doctrine, supporting the theory according to which legal basis for declaratory reliefs is of a procedural character and cannot be regarded as a substantive provision.[519] It is indicated that legal interest, serving as a prerequisite for declaratory relief, is in fact not the subject matter of the relevant civil proceedings (it is not the substance of the case). Quite on the contrary, the subject matter relates solely to existence or non-existence of a legal relationship or a right indicated in the statement of claim as well as the factual circumstances invoked in this regard. Legal interest is relevant solely from the perspective of the claim's admissibility. Furthermore, Article 189 of the Polish CCP regulates the procedural relation between the claimant and the court (i.e., the competence of the court to render a specific type of award), and not the civil substantive relationship between the respective parties of the dispute.[520] The procedural nature of legal interest might also stem from:

- the rationale of introducing this concept into the Polish legal system, which is to reduce the number of unnecessary, and sometimes irrational, claims brought before the courts;[521] as well as
- the subsidiarity principle emphasized in the jurisprudence, implying the necessity to assess whether the claimant has another procedural possibility to safeguard his rights (*see* item 3(B) *infra*).[522]

III CONCEPT OF LEGAL INTEREST UNDER POLISH LAW

Notwithstanding the nature (substantive or procedural) of Article 189 of the Polish CCP, certain efforts should be made in order to define the notion of legal interest, being as it is an indubitably central aspect of the declaratory relief system. As already indicated, neither Article 189 of the Polish CCP nor other provisions of Polish civil law include such a definition. Therefore, the legislature leaves the field in this regard open to doctrine and to the judiciary. Although it is commonly stated that legal interest shall

517. Judgement of 22 November 2002, IV CKN 1519/00 (Polish Supreme Court); judgement of 6 February 2015, II CSK 325/14 (Polish Supreme Court).
518. Czech, *supra* n. 510, at 865.
519. Karol Weitz, *Charakter interesu prawnego jako przesłanka powództwa o ustalenie (art.189 k.p.c.)* in: *Sine ira et studio, Księga Jubileuszowa dedykowana Sędziemu Jackowi Gudowskiemu* 656, 656 et seq. (Tadeusz Ereciński & Paweł Grzegorczyk & Karol Weitz eds., Wolters Kluwer 2016). Cf. Henryk Trammer, *O właściwe miejsce dla 'czystych' norm materialnego prawa cywilno-jurysdykcyjnego (na marginesie prac nad kodyfikacją prawa cywilnego)*, 1–2 Przegląd Notarialny 20, 20 et seq. (1949).
520. Weitz, *supra* n. 519, at 673.
521. Judgement of 22 August 2016, III C 430/16 (District Court in Warsaw).
522. Beata Gessel-Kalinowska vel Kalisz, *Pojęcie interesu prawnego w powództwie o ustalenie a prawo do sądu – wprowadzenie do dyskusji. Analiza badań statystycznych*, 1 PPH 2019, 11, 18.

be assessed individually, on a case-by-case basis,[523] such statements as may be gleaned from the legal doctrine and from case law are basically uniform and of a general nature.

There is a common understanding among scholars as to the main features of legal interest under Polish law. Namely, the legal interest is very frequently perceived as the legal need to obtain the declaratory relief of specified content,[524] arising out of the legal situation of the claimant.[525] In other words, legal interest stems from the claimant's uncertainty as to his legal position and/or law.[526] Some scholars also identify legal interest with a lasting threat to claimant's rights which deserve a certain level of protection.[527] Summing up the above-mentioned definitions expressed in the Polish law context, it might be concluded that legal interest involves the claimant's need to secure certainty as to a specific legal relationship or right.[528] Legal interest exists when the effect of a declaratory award will afford protection of the claimant's rights, i.e., it will either definitely put an end to an existing dispute or prevent such a dispute from arising in the future.[529] The claim provided for in Article 189 does not enable the court to establish a legal norm by effectuating definitive interpretation of the statutory provision defining claimant's rights and duties,[530] but it may serve as a basis for defining the substance of the contractual norm.[531]

As a point of difference from Article 3 of the Polish FCCP, declaratory relief currently does not serve as a precautionary procedural measure, and it may be successfully sought even if rights of the claimant had already been violated.[532] Another significant difference to the previous procedural provision is that there does not have to be a threat (especially a serious threat, as emphasized previously) to claimant's rights - mere uncertainty of rights suffices in order to effectively bring a claim for declaration.[533]

523. Ireneusz Kunicki in: *Kodeks postępowania cywilnego. Komentarz* (Agnieszka Góra-Błaszczykowska ed.) 628, 630 (2016).
524. Tadeusz Rowiński, *Interes prawny w procesie cywilnym i w postępowaniu nieprocesowym*, 26 (1971).
525. Cf. Edward Warzocha, *Ustalenie stosunku prawnego lub prawa w sądowym postępowaniu cywilnym*, 48 (1982); judgement of 25 January 1995, III CZP 179/94 (Polish Supreme Court) along with commentary by Elżbieta Budna, 4 Radca Prawny 111, 111 et seq. (1995).
526. Wengerek, *supra* n. 497, at 14.
527. Jan Klimkowicz, *Glosa do orzeczenia SN z dnia 13 kwietnia 1965 r, II CR 266/64*, 7–8 OSPIKA, item 166 (1966).
528. Kunicki, *supra* n. 523, at 630; Przemysław Telenga in *Kodeks postępowania cywilnego. Tom I. Komentarz do art. 1-729* (Andrzej Jakubecki ed.) 358–359 (2017).
529. Elwira Marszałkowska-Krześ, *Kodeks postępowania cywilnego. Komentarz* (Legal Infromation System Legalis) (2018).
530. Zieliński, *supra* n. 512, at 392.
531. For example, the lessee will have a legal interest in definition of the terms of the lease relationship. Judgement of 14 December 1998, III CKN 78/98 (Polish Supreme Court). Cf. Małgorzata Manowska, *Kodeks postępowania cywilnego. Komentarz. Tom I. Art. 1-505[38]* 553 (2015).
532. Jędrzejewska & Weitz, *supra* n. 507, at 97–98.
533. Judgement of 14 July 1972, III CRN 607/71, 4 OSNCP, item 64 (1973) (Polish Supreme Court). In this judgement, the Supreme Court points out that a state of threat to claimant's rights does not have to exist in order to bring the declaratory claim – the claimant's uncertainty as to its legal position is perfectly sufficient for this purpose.

For instance, in the judgement of the Court of Appeal in Warsaw dated 29 December 2016 (VI ACa 1087/15), the claimant requested the declaration of invalidity of the housing cooperation's resolution in the part stating that: 'if the premises are not inhabited, the maintenance costs shall be calculated in such a way as the premises were inhabited by one person'. It was argued by the Court of First Instance that there is no legal interest on the side of the claimant in obtaining declaration since his premises were subject to a lease agreement. Therefore, the cited part of the resolution did not pertain to his legal situation existing at the moment of initiating the proceedings. This line of reasoning was rejected by the Court of Appeal, which pointed out that examination of existence of legal interest cannot be simply reduced to assessment of current factual background of the case (in these proceedings: to assessment whether the premises are currently inhabited or not). The claimant is entitled to obtain a certain declaration removing the state of his legal uncertainty if such declaration might have an influence on hypothetical situations in the future. In this meaning, declaratory action is of a preventive nature.

These days, the Polish courts often emphasize that the notion of legal interest should be regarded broadly – as a need for establishing certainty with regard to existence of a legal relationship or right in order to provide the claimant with full legal protection encompassing all possible effects that already exist or may arise in the future. The approach taken by the courts towards legal interest should always take into account the claimant's access to justice.[534] A claimant seeking declaratory relief should not be refused without legitimate grounds – bearing this in mind, legal interest must be assessed flexibly, with due regard to claimant's access to the courts, and reasonably adapted to the factual circumstances of each case through teleological interpretation of Article 189 of the Polish CCP.[535] The standards reflected in the Polish Constitution (especially in Article 45, stating that everyone shall have the right to a fair and public hearing of his case, without undue delay, before a competent, impartial and independent court) as well as in acts of international law (including Article 14 of the International Covenant on Civil and Political Rights) shall be duly observed while assessing the existence of legal interest.[536]

The necessity to assure proper access to the court was expressly invoked in the judgement of the Polish Supreme Court dated 8 February 2013 (IV CSK 306/12).[537] On the contrary, within the same decision, the Supreme Court stated that the legal protection based on Article 189 of the Polish CCP might be granted solely when the claimant is not able to obtain equivalent protection in any other proceedings. Therefore, it might be concluded that even due regard to the claimant's access to the court does not soften the rather strict approach to the subsidiarity principle, which will be covered in detail in section [B] *infra*.

534. Judgement of Supreme Court dated 1 April 2004, II CK 125/03.
535. Jędrzejewska & Weitz, *supra* n. 507, at 98; judgement of 27 January 2004, II CK 387/02 (Polish Supreme Court); judgement of 8 February 2013, IV CSK 306/12, 10 Biuletyn SN (2014) (Polish Supreme Court); judgement of 22 October 2014, II CSK 687/13 (Polish Supreme Court).
536. Judgement of 29 October 2009, III CZP 79/09, 10 Biuletyn SN (2009) (Polish Supreme Court).
537. 10 Biuletyn SN (2014). Cf. judgement of 22 October 2014, II CSK 687/13 (Polish Supreme Court); judgement of 20 February 2003, I CKN 58/01 (Polish Supreme Court).

It should be emphasized that legal interest, as a prerequisite for granting claimant's motion, is envisaged also in other provisions of Polish civil procedure. For instance, in line with Article 730^1 paragraph 1 of the Polish CCP, security or injunction may be sought by any party or participant in proceedings if he substantiates his claim and legal interest in having the security or injunction granted. A legal interest in having the security or injunction granted exists where the absence of security or injunction would prevent or significantly hinder the enforcement of a judgement issued in the case or would otherwise prevent or significantly hinder the achievement of the objective of proceedings in the case. Furthermore, the concept of legal interest is applicable to the institution of securing evidence. According to Article 310 of the Polish CCP, evidence may be preserved on a motion before proceedings are commenced or ex officio in the course of proceedings where there are reasonable grounds to believe that the taking of such evidence will be prevented or significantly obstructed or where it is otherwise necessary to determine the current status quo. Although this provision does not expressly entail the requirement of legal interest, it is indicated by scholars that lack of legal interest in preservation of evidence shall lead to dismissal of the respective motion.[538]

[A] Objective Nature of Legal Interest: Legal versus Factual Interest

The mere fact that an interest in obtaining declaratory relief is described as 'legal' indirectly implies another feature of this concept – its objectivity.[539]

Legal interest, defined as a need to obtain a court decision in order to remove the uncertainty of a right or legal relationship, should have an objective character.[540] This general statement, closely related to the so-called subsidiarity principle, merits in-depth analysis in that lack of this element may lead to dismissal of the declaratory claim under Polish law.

Objectivity of legal interest in obtaining a declaration means that this prerequisite may not be assessed from the perspective of claimant's subjective beliefs and needs.[541] It is an interest perceived as deserving protection by the legislature and objectively justified in light of the law. The objective element, in the context of declaratory reliefs, refers to the necessity of securing an award settling the uncertainty of a legal relationship or a right.[542] In this context, judges often refer to 'reasonable assessment of the situation', separated from the claimant's personal feelings about the need for a declaratory award.[543] In other words, it is the average person's sense of reasonableness that shall be taken into account, and not the position of the particular claimant. If claimant's subjective beliefs were the factor deciding upon the admissibility of claim,

538. Joanna Misztal-Konecka, *Kodeks postępowania cywilnego. Tom I. Komentarz. Art. 1–366* (Kazmierz Piasecki & Andrzej Marciniak eds.) 840 (2016).
539. Rowiński, *supra* n. 524, at 20–22; Wengerek, *supra* n. 497, at 14; judgement of 26 March 2014, V CSK 239/13 (Polish Supreme Court).
540. Wengerek, *supra* n. 497, at 14.
541. Rowiński, *supra* n. 524, at 20.
542. *Ibid.*, at 26.
543. Judgement of 1 December 1983, I PRN 189/83 (Polish Supreme Court).

we would presumably be left with a situation where the claimant always has a legal interest when requesting a declaration and resolution of the dispute,[544] thus voiding the admissibility prerequisite's legal and practical importance.

To venture an example, the claimant will not be deemed to have objective legal interest in bringing a claim which would initiate fictitious proceedings - even if such action might be beneficial for him for some personal reasons in the given factual circumstances. Additionally, claimant's legal interest cannot be assessed as objective if the proceedings would lead to inconsistency with rules of societal coexistence, binding legal provisions or with the legitimate aim of civil proceedings.[545]

The objective legal interest is also sometimes presented as the opposite of factual interest in securing the court's declaration.[546] Factual interest obtains when the claimant, although interested in settling the case, cannot invoke any provisions of substantive law supporting the need to obtain declaratory relief.[547] By its very nature, factual interest also has a subjective character, based as it is on claimant's personal needs and beliefs, without any reflection in legal provisions.

The differentiation between legal and factual interests in the context of declaratory reliefs was elaborated in the judgement of Court of Appeal in Warsaw dated 16 March 2017 (VI ACa 2018/15). In the factual background of the case, the claimant aimed at obtaining declaration of non-existence of several resolutions adopted by the extraordinary general meeting of shareholders. The aforesaid resolutions included mainly appointment of the President of the management board as well as appointment of the company's proxy. The claimant raised that his legal interest is connected with the necessity to clarify whether the company is represented by duly authorized persons. As the claimant intended to collect his debts from the company, he wanted to make sure that his future dealings will be conducted with lawfully appointed persons. Additionally, in the claimant's view, the company was not properly represented in a number of civil and criminal proceedings pending with company's involvement. The courts of first and second instance concluded that there is no legal interest justifying declaratory relief in the case at hand. Questioning the proper representation of the company by the claimant, despite the respective entries into the National Court Register, might be assessed solely as the factual interest in obtaining declaratory relief. Even if the declaratory award were issued in the requested form, the claimant would not be entitled to question the entries made in the National Court Register. Moreover, legal interest cannot be identified in terms of intent to deprive persons of the possibility to act in pending criminal or civil proceedings (in which appropriate authorities will examine, among other issues, also the company's representation).

Objectivity of legal interest excludes also the possibility of requesting establishment of rights or legal relationships which will arise in the future.[548] This issue was

544. Rowiński, *supra* n. 524, at 183–184.
545. Cf. Władysław Siedlecki, *Fikcyjny process cywilny*, 2 PiP 212, 225 (1955); judgement of 20 December 1979, III PR 78/79 (Polish Supreme Court).
546. Aleksandra Wilczyńska, *Interes prawny i jego granice w postępowaniu cywilnym*, 9–10 Palestra 31, 33 (2010).
547. Wilczyńska, *supra* n. 546, at 32.
548. Judgement of 12 October 2017, IV CSK 712/16 (Polish Supreme Court).

elaborated upon by the Polish Supreme Court in its judgement dated 12 October 2017 (IV CSK 712/16). In the factual background of the case, the claimant requested the court to determine that he is entitled to acquire real estate from a municipal authority at a 95% discount on the basis of the Property Management Act and a resolution of the city council. The Supreme Court observed that the claimant's right to a discount cannot be established at this relatively early stage when the possibility of purchasing the immovable property is not certain from the legal point of view - additional prerequisites must be fulfilled in order to make such acquisition legitimate. Specifically, the real estate was not classified as held for sale on the basis of an order of the city mayor, which was indispensable in light of applicable law. The declaration claim was therefore, at least, premature, and the claimant's need to remove uncertainty as to his legal position was not objective. The necessity to remove legal uncertainty should stem from the claimant's current legal situation - a hypothetical right which may, or may not, arise in the future does not justify a declaratory claim.

An example of a broad approach to the concept of the legal interest in jurisprudence is presented in the Polish Supreme Court judgement dated 5 February 2009 (I CSK 332/08), in which it was held that legal interest on the part of the claimant is not excluded by virtue of the fact that the receivables in question have become barred through operation of the statute of limitations. The Supreme Court adopted the standpoint that, in these circumstances, the claim as such has not expired, only the debtor can now successfully evade payment unless he waives his right to invoke the statute of limitations (Article 117 § 2 of the Polish Civil Code). In this context, it is emphasized that assessment of the legal interest ought not go so far as to have the court declare lack of legal interest merely by virtue of the fact that, if a declaratory award is given, it may not have further practical effect.[549]

It is also well established under Polish law that, whenever the claimant might benefit from a claim for performance (more far-reaching than declaratory relief), objectively he has no legal interest in obtaining a declaration.[550] Such a conclusion gives rise to the so-called subsidiarity principle widely known in Continental jurisdictions, stemming from the general concept of legal interest as interpreted in the Germanic tradition.

[B] Subsidiarity Principle

Declaratory relief appears to be, by definition, a remedy less valued than others, and one which is not allowed in cases where a more comprehensive remedy is available. As a rule, under Polish law, the mere possibility of seeking performance based on a given cause of action excludes the existence of legal interest to seek only a declaration of right or legal relationship. This rule is referred to as the subsidiarity principle, and it does not allow for any discretionary choice among the remedies open to the claimant.[551] A lack

549. Judgement of 13 September 2007, III CSK 123/07, 1–2 OSG, item 12 (2009) (Polish Supreme Court).
550. Czech, *supra* n. 510, at 853.
551. Jędrzejewska & Weitz, *supra* n. 507, at 99–100; Kunicki *supra* n. 523, at 630.

of legal interest is connected with the fact that a declaration would constitute solely one of the prerequisites to grant a claim for performance, e.g., claim for payment.[552] In other words, in such a situation, claim for declaration loses its autonomous and independent character[553] in that the claimant is able to obtain fuller protection by means of other remedies.[554]

One of the arguments in favour of striking out declarations in a case where a claim for performance (as a more far-reaching claim) is available is that the courts should not be overloaded with frivolous litigation.[555] Furthermore, the defendant should not incur more time and costs by answering in two proceedings instead of one. As an example, in a damages case, where two proceedings – one on the merits, and one seeking quantum – could be available, the first one without the second one would not be allowed.

The subsidiarity principle was recognized under Polish law as soon as the concept of legal interest was introduced as a prerequisite for declaratory relief. However, analysis of judicial authorities leads to the conclusion that the approach towards its application is becoming stricter with the passage of time. The courts not only distinguish civil claims more far-reaching than declaration, but also refer to other remedies available to the claimant – in non-contentious or administrative proceedings.[556] In other words, according to current Polish jurisprudence, the claimant has legal interest in obtaining a declaration only if declaratory relief is the only possible remedy in his legal position.[557] There is no legal interest whatsoever where the claimant has at his disposal any other relevant alternative way to protect his rights, even if this alternative is not actually better, but merely equally protective in the eyes of the court. It does not matter whether the claimant foregoes the other possibilities or not.[558]

Such an approach of the courts leads to the conclusion that, before initiating court proceedings, the claimant should: (i) conduct a full analysis of the legal remedies available in his legal position; and (ii) consider whether one of these remedies is objectively at least an equivalent of declaratory relief. If the claimant does not find an alternative, but the court discerns such an alternative after the statement of claim has been submitted, the declaratory claim will be dismissed in its entirety. One may conclude that Polish law always gives priority to actions other than declarations. The declaration cannot serve as a first step for a subsequent claim for an injunction.

A typical example of application of subsidiarity principle is an interrelation between declaratory claim and claim for payment. The judgement of Court of Appeal in Łódź dated 9 September 2016 (I ACa 270/16) might be recalled in this regard. The

552. Zieliński, *supra* n. 512, at 390; Manowska, *supra* n. 531, at 552; judgement of 19 October 1959, 4 CR 537/58 (Polish Supreme Court).
553. Czech, *supra* n. 510, at 853.
554. Judgement of 15 May 2013, II CSK 727/12 (Polish Supreme Court).
555. Judgement of 22 August 2016, III C 430/16 (District Court in Warsaw).
556. Judgement of 22 November 2002, IV CKN 1519/00 (Polish Supreme Court).
557. Judgement of 9 February 2012, III CSK 181/11, 7–8 OSNC, item 101 (2012) (Polish Supreme Court); judgement of 24 May 2017, III CSK 155/16 (Polish Supreme Court).
558. Judgement of 24 April 2014, III CSK 182/13 (Polish Supreme Court).

claimant requested the court to declare that he had effectively withdrawn from the agreement for sale of real estate, pointing out that he would be entitled to certain pecuniary claims in connection with this withdrawal (including, *inter alia*, reimbursement of purchase price). In the court's opinion, the declaratory relief would not definitely settle a dispute between the parties or prevent the occurrence of such dispute in the future. Quite contrarily, the declaration on withdrawal's effectiveness would certainly provoke initiation of payment proceedings in the future. In other words, decision regarding effectiveness of withdrawal constitutes the prerequisite of claim for payment.

Another practical example of subsidiarity principle might be given by reference to the judgement of Supreme Court dated 8 February 2013 (IV CSK 306/12). In the factual background of the case, the claimant was seeking for declaration that investment expenditures had been incurred by him, as the perpetual usufructuary, in a certain amount. The Supreme Court held that the claimant had been able to obtain legal protection by way of administrative proceedings. Namely, the expenditures incurred by perpetual usufructuary might be counted against the annual fee for perpetual usufruct in a special procedure regarding adjustment of this fee. It appears that the possibility to achieve claimant's goal in administrative proceedings automatically rules out the existence of legal interest on the basis of Article 189 of the Polish CCP.

The more far-reaching claim, excluding the possibility to effectively submit request for declaration, might be also rooted in the Act on Land and Mortgage Registers and Mortgages, as invoked in the judgement of Supreme Court dated 7 March 2013 (IV CSK 469/12). The claimant – a housing cooperative – requested the declaration of invalidity of the lease agreement as well as the agreement on establishment of a separate ownership of premises. The respondent's rights to premises were entered in the real estate register. In the claimant's view, the invalidity resulted from the fact that the respondent was not a member of housing cooperative and respective resolutions of cooperative's supervisory board had not been adopted properly. In line with the Supreme Court's reasoning, the lack of legal interest in this case was connected with existence of the claim to eliminate discrepancies between the content of mortgage register and actual legal state of the real estate, which is a more comprehensive claim.

Irrespectively of the foregoing, in a case where more than one effect may result from a declaration awarded by the court, the declaratory claim shall be held admissible. Thus, the subsidiarity principle deeply rooted in Polish law notwithstanding, the Supreme Court recognizes situations in which it is admissible to request a declaration despite the existing claim for performance. Such a configuration is interestingly illustrated in the judgement of the Supreme Court dated 2 July 2015 (V CSK 640/14).[559]

The factual background of this case is connected with a lease agreement between the parties to the proceedings concerning part of a building to be used as a hotel. The tenant initiated proceedings by requesting, on the basis of Article 189 of the Polish CCP, a declaration of nullity of the lease agreement. Subsequently, the landlord brought an action for payment of rent arrears for a period of more than two years. In the

559. Cf. judgement of 11 September 1953, I C 581/53, 3 OSNCK 3, item 65 (1954) (Polish Supreme Court).

proceedings for payment, invalidity of the lease agreement was also averred by the tenant as an argument for dismissal of the claim. Therefore, in declaratory proceedings, the court faced a problem whether the claimant had legal interest in obtaining declaratory relief in the light of pending payment proceedings.

The Polish Supreme Court, ruling on the facts described above, confirmed that legal interest shall be perceived as an objective need either to protect the rights of the claimant or to eliminate the uncertainty as to the existence of a legal relationship or a right. As a rule, the possibility to bring a more far-reaching claim and, accordingly, to obtain fuller protection excludes the possibility of recourse to declaratory relief.[560] This principle remains applicable also in a situation where a certain issue which might be the subject of declaratory relief (e.g., invalidity of an agreement) is raised within payment proceedings initiated against an entity/person interested in obtaining declaration of a specific content. In such a case, all the issues might be resolved within one dispute. However, certain exceptions in this regard might occur. The claimant will not lose legal interest in the meaning of Article 189 of the Polish CCP if the potential award rendered in the proceedings initiated by a claim for performance does not fully remove uncertainty with regard to the legal position.[561] In other words, the claimant has a legal interest in obtaining declaratory relief despite the existing claim for performance (to be brought by or against him) if the legal relationship gives rise to other, more far-reaching consequences which cannot be settled in proceedings for performance. In such a case, only declaratory relief might give effective and full protection to the claimant.

Referring to the factual circumstances of case V CSK 640/14, the Polish Supreme Court held that there are many rights and obligations of the claimant stemming from the lease agreement, including *inter alia* an obligation to pay rent, to take care of the building, to perform ongoing repairs or to pay damages in the event of improper performance of the contract. Therefore, the possibility to invoke invalidity of the contract in proceedings for payment does not provide the claimant with the full protection of its legal interest. Even if the claimant's position is vindicated by the court in the dispute regarding payment of arrears, such judgement is not binding for other courts deciding on potential further cases arising out of the contract in the future (Article 365 of the Polish CCP). Therefore, the judgement given in the proceedings for payment does not cover the claimant's legal interest to such an extent as declaratory relief – pending payment proceedings do not exclude the possibility of obtaining a declaration. Summing up, it should be concluded that the subsidiarity principle excludes the possibility of seeking declaratory relief if the claimant has at its disposal a more far-reaching claim for performance, and not when the claimant is sued for one of the possible benefits that might stem from the contract. The award given in payment

560. Cf. judgement of 19 February 2002, IV CKN 769/00, 1 OSNC, item 13 (2003); judgement of 30 November 2005, III CK 277/05 (Polish Supreme Court); judgement of 29 March 2012, I CSK 325/11 (Polish Supreme Court); judgement of 15 May 2013, III CSK 254/12 (Polish Supreme Court).

561. Cf. judgement of 8 March 2001, I CKN 1111/00 (Polish Supreme Court); judgement of 27 January 2004, II CK 387/02 (Polish Supreme Court); judgement of 21 March 2006, V CSK 188/05 (Polish Supreme Court).

proceedings would not prevent potential disputes arising from the same contract in the future.

[C] Purpose of Legal Interest as a Prerequisite of Declaratory Relief

Article 189 of the Polish CCP has a twofold purpose. First, it enables protection of certain rights of the claimant and requesting that the court declare existence or non-existence of a legal relationship or right. Second, this possibility is considerably limited by the necessity to establish the legal interest in obtaining a declaration. Therefore, a question arises as to the reasons why such a prerequisite was introduced into the Polish CCP. It might be assumed that legal interest serves as a specific safeguard against frivolous and fictitious lawsuits which might be brought, and which might unduly burden the courts, if not for the legal interest admissibility prerequisite. Consequently, limitation of the possibility to apply for declarations was introduced, bearing in mind the procedural economy rules as well as the necessity to protect the court from declaratory proceedings backlogs.

In the jurisprudence, one may find assertions such as this by the District Court in Warsaw: 'The aim of this limitation [of possibility to obtain declaratory relief – author's note] is that the necessity of settling contentious issues by the courts should concern solely these situations in which it is indispensable for providing legal protection.'[562] This motive was observed even in the context of the previous Polish FCCP regulations. It was stated that a person with a claim broader in scope declaratory should act rationally and initiate more far-reaching proceedings instead of prosecuting separate cases in a piecemeal fashion. The interests of both the court (in the first place) as well as of the respondent (forced to bear the procedural costs of numerous cases) was duly observed.[563]

In light of the above, there should be no doubt that the main aim of legal interest is to reduce the number of entities entitled to obtain declaratory relief. Although this rationale behind the content of Article 189 of the Polish CCP is perfectly understandable, it cannot lead to restrictions of the right to a fair trial – which, of course, is a constitutionally protected right.

[D] Legal Interest versus Economic Interest

Legal interest is constantly subject to varied considerations in the Polish jurisprudence. In this connection, one can observe an interesting distinction between 'legal' and 'economic' or 'commercial' interest in obtaining a declaratory award.[564]

On the one hand, it is emphasized by legal scholars that the notion of legal interest (being as it is a substantial restriction of the possibility to obtain a declaratory award) shall be perceived relatively broadly. To wit, it should encompass interests of

562. Judgement of 22 August 2016, III C 430/16 (District Court in Warsaw).
563. Jan Korzonek, *Powództwo o ustalenie według projektu K.P.C.*, 11 Głos Sądownictwa 635, 640 (1930).
564. *See*, e.g., judgement of 23 December 2014, I ACa 441/14 (Court of Appeal in Szczecin).

both a proprietary and a non-proprietary nature[565] (including, for instance, protection of personal interests[566] or belonging to a particular gender group[567]). This means that the claimant's request for a declaration might concern legal relationships or rights of this twofold character. An example of an economic interest that might be protected by way of declaratory relief can be given with reference to the judgement of the Court of Appeal in Białystok dated 14 July 2016 (I ACa 49/16). The declaration of invalidity of a donation agreement was sought by the claimants since only one daughter of the donator received a real property on the basis of the contract. The issue was of particular importance from the perspective of claimants' future succession rights, which might have had a narrower scope if the agreement remained valid. In other words, disposal of real estate made by the donator violated economic rights of the claimant, with significant impact on their legal position. An interest of a commercial nature was deemed to be an undoubted 'legal interest' within the meaning of Article 189 of the Polish CCP.

On the other hand, the courts sometimes dismiss applications for declaratory relief due to the purely economic character of interest attributable to the claimant. For instance, it was held by the Court of Appeal in Warsaw that striving for realization of claimant's purely economic interest excludes the possibility to issue a declaratory judgement since Article 189 of the Polish CCP cannot simply lead to protection of claimant's commercial position.[568] Due to this, a company was held not to have legal interest in requesting a declaration of invalidity of a framework contract regarding currency transactions, since it had been already terminated in the past and did not cause any legal effects for the future. Even if the claimant did have certain pecuniary claims arising out of transactions conducted on the basis of the contract in the past, it could demonstrate only an economic (and not legal) interest in obtaining a declaration. At the same time, the court explained that the contract's termination implies effects for the future but does not eliminate the consequences of actions undertaken before service of the termination notice.

This view expressed by the Court of Appeal might be assessed as controversial. The court expressly confirmed that certain receivables on the side of the claimant might have arisen before the contract's termination. Due to this fact, the declaration of invalidity (which would have an ex tunc effect) had crucial significance for assessment of potential claims, even ones of a pecuniary nature. The need for declaration of non-existence of a legal relationship between the parties pertains undoubtedly to the legal position of the claimant and should be duly observed by the court. The claimant should have a right to seek a judgement which would remove its uncertainty as to the contractual legal relationship.

The purely economic interest of the claimant was the reason for dismissing the declaratory claim by the Court of Appeal in Warsaw also in the judgement dated 21

565. Zieliński, *supra* n. 512, at 392; Czech, *supra* n. 510, at 852; Kunicki, *supra* n. 523, at 630; Jędrzejewska & Weitz, *supra* n. 507, at 102; judgement of 20 December 1967, III CZP 84/67, 12 OSP, item 262 (1968); judgement of 14 July 2016, I ACa 49/16 (Court of Appeal in Białystok).
566. Stefan Grzybowski, *Ochrona dóbr osobistych* 129 (1957).
567. Judgement of 22 March 1991, III CRN 28/91 (Polish Supreme Court).
568. Judgement of 30 October 2013, I ACa 692/13 (Court of Appeal in Warsaw).

April 2016 (I ACa 894/15). The claimant company sought declaration of invalidity of a sale contract executed with respect to real estate between two companies while the claimant was the creditor of one of them. In the claimant's view, his debtor had transferred the assets which, normally, could and would be applied towards satisfaction of creditor's receivables. In other words, the agreement made to the creditor's detriment should be declared invalid. Without assessing the intentions of the debtor's legal actions, the Court of Appeal decided that the inveighed sale agreement did not have a direct impact on the claimant's legal sphere. Execution of the contract could not have created a state of legal uncertainty on the side of the claimant, who did not have any rights connected with the real estate and perceived his legal interest solely in the context of securing debtor's assets and possible satisfaction of the claim in the future. Given the factual background of this case, Claimant's legal interest had an economic dimension only.

Similar conclusions were drawn by the Court of Appeal in Gdańsk in the judgement dated 13 August 2013 (I ACa 353/13).[569] In this case, the claimant was seeking a declaration of invalidity of a resolution of the worker cooperative's board concerning admission of certain persons as members of the cooperative. According to claimant's assertions, his legal interest was directly connected to the fact that the resolution's adoption was aimed at throwing obstacles in the cooperative's liquidation process. Additionally, the claimant was a member – and president, no less – of the cooperative's management board and, as a result of the resolution changing the personal composition of the cooperative, the claimant stood to lose entitlement to a percentage share in the cooperative. The interest in obtaining a declaration thus defined was perceived by the Court of Appeal solely as a 'factual' and 'economic' one, not giving entitlement to declaratory relief on the basis of Article 189 of the Polish CCP.

The position presented by the Polish courts, denying claimant's right to effectively apply for declaration due to purely 'economic' nature of its interest, is not unanimous. Moreover, it is sometimes argued that existence of legal interest with regard to economic rights cannot be excluded even if such rights have not yet become effective.[570]

IV SCOPE OF DECLARATORY RELIEFS UNDER POLISH LAW

If, at the initial stage of civil proceedings, the court decides that the claimant has a legal interest in obtaining a declaration, all factual circumstances and legal reasoning invoked in the statement of claim should be assessed. Following the outcome of evidentiary proceedings, the court will decide whether claimant's request to declare the existence or non-existence of a legal relationship or right is justified.

569. Cf. judgement of 31 May 2016, I ACa 1025/15 (Court of Appeal in Szczecin).
570. Judgement of 5 December 2002, I PKN 629/01, 11 OSNAPiUS, item 194 (2004) (Polish Supreme Court); judgement of 2 June 2006, I PK 250/05, 1-12 OSNP, item 156 (2007) (Polish Supreme Court).

[A] Subject Matter of Declaratory Reliefs

It appears prima facie that the necessity of proving existence of legal interest in declaratory proceedings implies that only legal relationships or rights might be subject to a declaration. Although these notions seem to be interrelated, Article 189 of the Polish CCP expressly indicates that the claim might aim solely at obtaining declaration of existence or non-existence of legal relationship or right. For these purposes, legal relationships should be understood as relationships of obligation/contractual relationships of different kind regulated by the Polish Civil Code as well as other legislation. The notion of rights shall be construed as referring to subjective rights of an absolute character, including property rights, personal rights as well as intangible property rights.[571]

It is inadmissible to request the court to declare on facts, factual backgrounds of the case or on characteristics of things even if they impact, to some extent, on the claimant's legal position.[572] In light of the above, the courts refuse to issue declaratory reliefs with regard to issues such as: date of birth,[573] cancellation of a will,[574] the fact that an appeal against a general meeting had been submitted,[575] occurrence of an accident at work,[576] capitalization rate and other facts taken into account in expert opinion[577] as well as possession of certain documents by national institutions.[578] Furthermore, the declaratory proceedings cannot be initiated and conducted solely in order to obtain evidence for the purpose of other proceedings.[579]

It should be noted, however, that there exists a special category combining facts and legal relationships, so-called law-creating facts, which might constitute the subject of declaration if, as a result, such declaration leads to establishment of a legal relationship or right.[580] For instance, it is admissible for the court to declare that a successor is unworthy to inherit (Article 929 of the Polish Civil Code)[581] since such a declaration will directly lead to establishment of a group of persons entitled to inherit. The courts would also be entitled to declare e.g., the fact of a contract's execution,

571. Warzocha, *supra* n. 525, at 71–72.
572. Władysław Siedlecki, *Zarys postępowania cywilnego* 148 (1968); judgement of 5 October 1982, III CRN 244/82 (Polish Supreme Court); judgement of 22 May 1953, I C 26/53, 12 PiP 905 (1953) (Polish Supreme Court).
573. Judgement of 17 April 1951, C 530/50, 1 OSN, item 39 (1952) (Polish Supreme Court).
574. Judgement of 21 September 1965, II CR 265/65, 11 OSP, item 243 (1966) (Polish Supreme Court).
575. Judgement of 11 November 1965, I PR 389/65, 6 OSNCP, item 100 (1966) (Polish Supreme Court).
576. Judgement of 13 June 1973, I PR 156/73, 11 OSNCP, item 206 (1973) (Polish Supreme Court).
577. Judgement of 7 December 2016, I ACa 713/16 (Court of Appeal in Łódź).
578. Judgement of 17 December 1997, I PKN 434/97, 21 OSNAPiUS, item 627 (1998) (Polish Supreme Court).
579. Judgement of 23 February 1999, I PKN 597/98, 8 OSNC 8, item 301 (2000) (Polish Supreme Court).
580. Judgement of 8 October 1952, C 1544/52, 8–9 PiP 369 (1943) (Polish Supreme Court); judgement of 11 September 1953, I C 581/53, 3 OSNCK, item 65 (1954) (Polish Supreme Court).
581. Judgement of 26 February 1968, III CZP 101/67, 12 OSNPC, item 203 (1968) (Polish Supreme Court).

tortious behaviour or contribution to incurred loss.[582] All these factual circumstances imply per se an impact on the respective legal positions of the parties. For instance, the mere fact that a contract was effectively made entitles the parties to bring claims in the event of improper performance or non-performance thereof. Similarly, a partner has legal interest in requesting the declaration that agreement of civil partnership was effectively terminated at a specific date – such declaration aims de facto at establishment of existence or non-existence of legal relationship or right.[583]

The borderline between the category of mere facts and law-creating facts can be hard to define by claimants seeking legal protection. For instance, in the factual background of the case VI ACa 1551/15 decided by the Court of Appeal in Warsaw on 16 September 2016, declaratory relief was sought with regard to non-existence of the management board and supervisory board of a cooperative as well as non-existence of decisions adopted by these cooperative bodies. However, it was held by the Court of Appeal that the submitted claim was aimed solely at declaration of facts. Even if the declaration was granted by the court in the form requested by the claimant, the relief would not lead to determination of any right or legal relationship.

[B] Declaration of Future Harm under Polish Law

The scope and admissibility of declaratory reliefs under Polish law is related to an interesting issue of possibility to declare liability for damage that might arise in the future and that does not exist at the moment of giving the judgement. One may imagine a situation when the claimant's intention is to safeguard his legal position for the future. For instance, the claimant might seek a judgement declaring that the legal liability of his opponent will arise always when certain prerequisites are met – if harm occurs in certain circumstances, liability shall be borne to a given extent.

Any generalization in this regard would be improper due to the far-reaching differentiation of principles of liability for damages, encompassing both tortious and contractual liability in their various kinds.

There are three potential situations in which the problem of declaring future liability might occur. The first situation assumes declaring appearance of a mere event, in particular breach of contract, which activates legal liability, without deciding what degree of culpability attaches to the respondent. The second situation might pertain to declaring liability in principle for a future, as of yet unquantified amount of damage/harm. The award given in such a case ascertains the damaging event itself and liability of a given party based on the degree of culpability of the party committing such damaging event; it does not define, however, the quantum damage or any causal link (since not all the consequences have materialized yet). The third situation relates to declaring liability for harm which is defined but which is to transpire in the future. While the harm has not actually occurred yet, ascertainment of certain constitutive

582. Warzocha, *supra* n. 525, at 73.
583. Judgement of 15 November 2000, I ACa 947/00 (Court of Appeal in Katowice).

elements of liability, i.e., the damaging event, the party liable and her degree of guilt, or a causal link, is already possible.

Despite the varied possible configurations of cases involving declaration of future damage as well as possible usefulness of this tool, this issue is raised by Polish doctrine and jurisprudence in one aspect only - that of personal harm subject to certain modifications in the future. No in-depth consideration has been conducted e.g., with regard to material damage arising out of contractual liability.

Utmost significance attaches to the judgement adopted by seven judges of the Polish Supreme Court on 17 April 1970 (III PZP 34/69[584]). In this case, it was held that, in proceedings concerning harm resulting from bodily harm, issue of an order for payment does not exclude establishment of the defendant's liability for loss stemming from the same occurrence/tortious conduct that might arise in the future. The view expressed by the Supreme Court is closely related to the specific nature of harm resulting from physical injuries and the likelihood that it may become aggravated in the future.[585] It secures the interests of the injured party who decides to seek some financial award (e.g., disability benefits) in the future, as it is often impossible to readily foresee all the future consequences and health impact of injuries. The Supreme Court emphasized also the necessity to construe the notion of legal interest in a flexible manner. The above-mentioned considerations were not referenced to future material damage - Polish jurisprudence remains silent in this regard.

[C] Admissibility of Declaratory Claims Brought by Third Parties

The effectiveness of the declaratory reliefs system depends *inter alia* on the circle of persons/entities entitled to bring a claim for declaration. It is of the utmost importance that, under Polish law, a declaratory claim might be submitted by a third person, one not bound by the legal relationship or right subject to the declaratory proceedings.[586] For instance, an adoptive parent might claim for establishment of descendants of an adopted person even though the case would not interfere with her/his personal rights,[587] or a child from a first marriage is entitled to claim for annulment of a bigamous marriage.[588] This impliedly means that legal interest goes, in some ways, beyond the legal relationship or right to be established in declaratory proceedings. However, the declaratory relief must have a certain impact on the legal position of such third party (in particular, on the legal relationship between such third party and one of the parties to the proceedings).[589]

In the factual background of the Supreme Court's judgement dated 30 October 2008 (II CSK 233/08), the claimant requested a declaration of invalidity of a sale

584. Cf.: Alfred Ohanowicz, *Glosa do uchwały z dnia 17 kwietnia 1970 r., III PZP 34/69*, 10 OSP 419, 419 et seq. (1971).
585. Adam Szpunar, *Ustalenie odpowiedzialności za szkodę przyszłą*, 5 Palestra 7, 13 (1973).
586. Judgement of 27 January 2011, I CSK 237/10 (Polish Supreme Court); judgement of 21 March 2013, II CSK 406/12 (Polish Supreme Court).
587. Judgement of 20 April 1962, 1 CR 1069/60, 6 OSNCP, item 132 (1963) (Polish Supreme Court).
588. Judgement of 3 February 1970, II CR 517/69, 2 OSN 2, item 26 (1971) (Polish Supreme Court).
589. Judgement of 24 April 2015, II CSK 438/14 (Polish Supreme Court).

contract pertaining to perpetual usufruct title in a property and the buildings sited thereon. The contract had been executed between respondents (a commercial entity and Polish municipality) as a result of tender proceedings. The claimant essentially defined his legal interest in terms of the possibility to participate in tender proceedings once again. On this set of facts, the Supreme Court made two important observations. First, the existence of legal interest in obtaining a declaration cannot be simply eliminated by the fact that the claimant is not a party to the legal relationship subject to declaratory proceedings. Second, the state of uncertainty existed in the legal sphere of the claimant – it concerned the issue whether the real estate had been actually transferred from the municipality's assets. The declaration would successfully remove this doubt on the side of the claimant.[590]

The issue of 'third-party declarations' might also be illustrated by the factual circumstances constituting the basis for the judgement by the Polish Supreme Court dated 24 April 2015 (II CSK 438/14). The claimant, a member of the management board of company X, asked the court to declare that a sale agreement executed between the company and its contractor was null and void due to lack of requisite consent of the general meeting. In the claimant's view, his legal interest was connected with the fact that the declaratory award would exclude the risk of claimant's liability for execution of the contract by the company without the approval required under Polish law. The Supreme Court expressly stated that, theoretically, a member of the management board might be entitled to join in such proceedings, even as a third party, concerning the contractual relationship arising out of a sale agreement. However, in the facts of this specific case, none of the legal provisions invoked in the statement of claim justified existence of legal interest of the management board member. Even if the court did declare invalidity of the sales contract, the claimant would not be released from potential liability in his capacity as member of the management board.

Another example is presented in the judgement of the Polish Supreme Court dated 2 February 2017 (I CSK 558/16). The claimant, a tenant of premises, asked for a declaration that the sale agreement made between his landlord and a third party had been null and void. Claimant's legal interest was directly connected to the fact that, following the execution of the agreement, the third party increased the rent and, as a next step, filed a request for tenant's eviction from the said premises. In the view of the Court of Appeal, legal interest did not exist in the case at hand – the claimant was merely a tenant of the premises and, therefore, from claimant's perspective, it was of no relevance who was the owner of the real property. This line of reasoning did not convince the Supreme Court, which held that declaratory relief issued in the factual circumstances of the case might have a certain impact on claimant's rights under the tenancy agreement even if the claimant has no property rights in the real estate.

Similar conclusions might be drawn also with regard to the respondent's side in declaratory proceedings – the statement of claim may be brought not only against parties involved in the legal relationships or rights subject to declaration. However, the claimant must have legal interest in a declaration made with regard to these

590. Cf. judgement of 27 January 2004, II CK 387/02 (Polish Supreme Court).

persons/entities. A person not linked to the subject of the declaratory proceedings in any way cannot be effectively sued in such a case. Some connection to the object of the proceedings is clearly needed, a claimant may not charge about suing just anybody - he must identify an entity with a legal interest in the outcome which has a specific tie to the right or legal relationship in question.[591] For instance, a notary public cannot act as respondent in proceedings for declaration of nullity of a notarial deed drawn up before such notary.[592]

This is because, in the context of proceedings for declaratory relief, the claimant must demonstrate that it has a legal interest in bringing a suit against the specific defendant and that his defendant poses at least a potential risk to claimant's legally protected interests, and also that the effect of the declaratory award - once final - will afford protection for the claimant. Such protection may be comprised either in definitive settlement of an ongoing dispute or in preventive obviation of such a dispute in the future, i.e., objective elimination of the grounds for dispute .[593]

V LEGAL MEASURES SIMILAR TO DECLARATORY RELIEFS

[A] Declaratory Reliefs versus Preliminary Awards

Another important issue in the context of declarations under Polish law pertains to the relation between declaratory reliefs and preliminary judgements. The legal framework for preliminary awards is provided by Article 318 paragraph 1 of the Polish CCP: 'If the court decides that the basis of claim is justified, it may render a preliminary judgement as to the basis only. With respect to the disputed amount of claim, the court may order the hearing to be continued or adjourned.'

It follows from the language of this statutory provision that, in a preliminary judgement, the court may decide on existence of claimant's right or legal relationship.[594] Such preliminary award can only be positive/affirmative (favourable for the claimant), constituting a decision of declaratory nature.[595] If the claimant's right or legal relationship was deemed by the court not to exist, the whole claim must be dismissed, without rendering a preliminary decision.

It follows from the above that the claimant might bring a claim for a certain action (e.g., a claim for payment) and, at the first stage of the proceedings, obtain an equivalent of declaratory relief in the form of a preliminary judgement. The claimant does not need to demonstrate the existence of legal interest in obtaining such

591. Judgement of 25 January 1995, III CZP 176/94, 5 OSNC, item 74 (1995) (Polish Supreme Court); judgement of 25 January 1995, III CZP 179/94, 5 OSNC, item 76 (1995) (Polish Supreme Court); judgement of 15 March 1995, III CZP 28/95 (Polish Supreme Court).
592. Judgement of 30 May 2000, IV CKN 36/00, 12 OSNC 12, item 223 (2000) (Polish Supreme Court).
593. Judgement of 18 June 2009, II CSK 33/09, OSNC-ZD no. B, item 47 (2010) (Polish Supreme Court).
594. Judgement of 13 January 2005, IV CK 446/04 (Polish Supreme Court).
595. Agnieszka Góra-Błaszczykowska & Bartosz Karolczyk & Kazimierz Lubiński, *Czynności decyzyjne* in *System Prawa Procesowego Cywilnego. Tom II. Część II. Postępowanie procesowe przed sądem pierwszej instancji* 643 (Tadeusz Ereciński & Tadeusz Wiśniewski eds., 2016).

preliminary award, as it is a part of the performance or constitutive claim, where demonstration of a legal interest is not necessary. This action is, however, undertaken at the sole discretion of the court – it is not available to the claimant as a matter of course.

On the contrary, the binding effect of preliminary awards is relatively narrow. First, a preliminary award is binding solely with regard to the claim (as to its scope and amount) brought in the proceedings in which preliminary judgement is given. Any subsequent change of the claim renders the preliminary judgement obsolete to the extent that any alteration interferes with the content of preliminary judgement.[596] Second, if the claimant withdraws the statement of claim after the preliminary judgement is rendered and becomes final, this decision does not become invalid or unenforceable. However, the proceedings should be terminated in line with Article 355 § 1 of the Polish CCP. If, afterwards, the claimant brings a claim referring in its scope to the final preliminary judgement, this preliminary judgement cannot serve as basis for a decision in other proceedings (separate declaratory relief).[597] In other words, the courts are not bound by preliminary judgements in other proceedings. The opposite solution would lead to circumvention of the basic rules regarding declaratory reliefs and of the legal interest prerequisite.[598]

[B] Declaratory Reliefs versus Claims for Payment of a Symbolic Amount

Theoretically, a claimant seeking declaratory relief may also claim for payment of a symbolic amount (such as 1% of his entire claim). In such a case, the existence of legal interest on claimant's side will not be subject to the court's assessment, and the claimant – if successful – will have the benefit of an award prejudging both the principle of liability as well as part of the claim's amount.

Claiming only part of the amount due is a course of action which is always open to the claimant in line with principle of disposition, one of the cornerstones of Polish civil procedure.[599] When such a motion is submitted, the court is bound by the scope of proceedings delineated in the statement of claim (Article 321 § 1 of the Polish CCP). It is entirely up to the claimant which claims, and what amounts, shall be subject to civil proceedings.[600] In the judgement of 25 April 2014 (II CSK 417/13), the Supreme Court expressly stated that Polish procedural law, as a rule, does not prevent claimant

596. Jacek Gudowski in: *Kodeks postępowania cywilnego. Komentarz. Tom II. Postępowanie rozpoznawcze*, 496 (Tadeusz Ereciński ed.) (2016).
597. Kazimierz Piasecki, *Wyrok pierwszej instancji w procesie cywilnym* 348 (1981); Agnieszka Góra-Błaszczykowska, Bartosz Karolczyk & Kazimierz Lubiński, *supra* n. 595, at 648.
598. Cf. judgement of 20 October 1970, II CR 190/70, 6 OSNCP, item 106 (1971) (Polish Supreme Court); judgement of 5 June 1991, III CZP 43/91, 1 OSNCP, item 12 (1992) (Polish Supreme Court); judgement of 6 June 1997, II CKN 201/97, 11 Biuletyn SN 11 (1997) (Polish Supreme Court); judgement of 8 June 1998, I CKN 636/97, 1 OSNC, item 14 (1999) (Polish Supreme Court).
599. Judgement of 15 May 1937, III C 781/35 (Polish Supreme Court).
600. Judgement of Supreme Court dated 22 October 2015, IV CSK 766/14; judgement od Supreme Court dated 25 April 2014, II CSK 417/13.

from fragmentation of claims. Any part of the claim may be freely submitted for the court's consideration. Only in exceptional circumstances does the Polish legislature provide for mechanisms preventing such actions, as in the case of simplified procedure (Article 505^3 paragraph 3 of the Polish CCP).

This possibility of issuing an award pertaining to a small percentage of the claim only raises questions as to res iudicata effect of such decision.

[C] Res Iudicata Issue

In accordance with Article 366 of the Polish CCP, a final and non-revisable judgement shall have the force of res iudicata only insofar as it relates to the subject matter of determination with respect to the cause of action, and only between the same parties. And Article 365 paragraph 1 of the Polish CCP provides: 'A final and non-revisable decision shall be binding not only on the parties and the court which rendered the decision, but also on other courts, state and public administration authorities and other persons in the instances provided for by the law.' More thorough analysis of these two legal concepts, res iudicata and binding effect of court awards, would depart far beyond the scope of this study.

However, in the context of claims for payment of symbolic amounts, the judgement of the Supreme Court of 29 March 1994 (III CZP 29/94) should be noted as a first point of reference. The Supreme Court held that: 'In a suit for the further part of the claim arising from the same legal relationship – that proceeding beyond the finally recognized portion – the court may not, given unchanged circumstances, rule differently as to the principle of the respondent's liability [translation by author].' This dictum, which may be construed as opening wide possibilities for absconding the duty to demonstrate the existence of legal interest in order to obtain a decision prejudging the principle of liability, has been strongly criticized in Polish legal doctrine.[601] It was indicated that, due to the full application of the disposition principle in Polish civil procedure, a judgement regarding only part of the claim cannot be binding upon the court deciding on the remaining part of that same claim.[602] In particular, legal assessment regarding the principle of liability should not have such a binding effect,[603] and a claimant submitting parts of its claim in several separate proceedings should bear all the consequences implied in this strategy, including the risk of ending up with two contradictory judgements.

Current Polish jurisprudence is not unanimous in this regard, as illustrated by two Supreme Court judgements from 2016. In the judgement of 7 April 2016 (III CSK 276/15), it was held that, in proceedings involving only a part of the claim, the decision regarding the principle of liability is not binding upon other courts. On the contrary, in

601. Paweł Grzegorczyk, *Przedmiotowy zakres prawomocności materialnej wyroku w procesie częściowym* in *Aurea Praxis Aurea Theoria. Księga pamiątkowa ku czci Profesora Tadeusza Erecińskiego* (Jacek Gudowski, Karol Weitz eds. 185, 185–224 (2011).
602. Cf. Marcin Dziurda, *Wyrok w procesie częściowym a prawomocność materialna*, 23 MoP 1266, 1267 (2018).
603. Dziurda, *supra* n. 602 at 1267–1268.

its judgement of 4 November 2016 (I CSK 736/15), the Supreme Court indicated that the court deciding on further parts of the claim is bound by the previous decision in the scope regarding the principle of respondent's liability.

VI EXCEPTIONS FROM THE REQUIREMENT TO DEMONSTRATE EXISTENCE OF LEGAL INTEREST

Albeit the concept of legal interest is inseparably linked with the institution of declaratory relief, in some instances the legislature has deliberately waived this general prerequisite for admissibility. In some exceptional circumstances, it is possible under Polish law to obtain declaratory relief despite lack of legal interest on the side of the claimant.

[A] Declaratory Reliefs in Collective Proceedings

First, such a solution was adopted by the Polish legislature in the Act on Pursuing Claims in Collective Proceedings dated 17 December 2009 (the 'Act on Collective Proceedings').[604] In accordance with Article 2(3) of this statute, in cases of pecuniary claims, the claim might be limited solely to a request for declaration of defendant's liability for a certain occurrence or occurrences, without rendering a decision as to the amount of the claim. It is expressly stated that, in such proceedings, the claimant is not obligated to prove the existence of legal interest on his side.

This exceptional regulation was introduced to the Polish legal system (which, as a general rule, requires the existence of legal interest in declaratory disputes) due to the specific nature of collective proceedings. The need for a declaratory award might arise if the circumstances attributable to the members of the group are differentiated to such an extent that unification of the amounts claimed is not possible.[605] In such cases, declaratory relief shall serve as a prejudgement, relevant from the perspective of individual payment proceedings to be initiated by each member of the group in the future.[606]

Article 2(3) of the Act on Collective Proceedings constitutes *lex specialis* vis a vis Article 189 of the Polish CCP – it creates a specific form of declaratory award in the Polish legal system.[607] As legal interest does not have to be demonstrated, the subsidiarity principle is likewise not applicable in collective proceedings. Therefore, a declaratory award might be issued even if a more far-reaching claim is available to the claimant. This was probably the main aim of introducing the regulation under which

604. 7 Journal of Laws of the Republic of Poland, item 44 (2010), with subsequent amendments.
605. Explanatory Memorandum to the Act on Pursuing Claims in Collective Proceedings of 17 December 2009, 4, available at: http://orka.sejm.gov.pl/Druki6ka.nsf/0/0E73993108750163C125758A004227CB/$file/1829.pdf (accessed 13 January 2019).
606. Due to this fact, declaratory reliefs in collective proceedings are more justified and reasonable in factual circumstances concerning e.g., construction disasters than in cases involving a variety of individual factors.
607. Małgorzata Sieradzka, *Dochodzenie roszczeń w postępowaniu grupowym. Komentarz,* 120 (2018).

the claimant is released from the legal interest test. After obtaining a declaration, individuals will be able to sue the defendant for payment of damages in a specific amount. The Explanatory Memorandum to the Act on Pursuing Claims in Collective Proceedings expressly states that 'demonstration of legal interest is redundant since the members of the group always desire to have a possibility to pursue their individual payment claims'.[608]

It is, however, of utmost importance that declaratory claims in collective proceedings may be brought only in the case of pecuniary claims.[609] If non-pecuniary claims are subject to collective proceedings, Article 189 of the Polish CCP will then be applicable to any declaration, and the claimant will be obligated to prove the existence of legal interest on his side.[610] Moreover, the wording of Article 2(3) implies that a collective declaratory claim might pertain only to positive declarations regarding liability of the respondent. It does not encompass a situation in which a declaratory claim is aimed at establishing the existence of other legal relationships (e.g., legal effects in the field of property law) or declaring the non-existence of respondent's liability.[611] In such cases, only Article 189 of the Polish CCP (regarding the requirement of demonstrating legal interest) might be used as a legal basis for declaratory relief. The above leads to the conclusion that the claimant is released from the obligation to prove legal interest in a relatively small range of cases only.

Similar to proceedings pending on the basis of Article 189 of the Polish CCP, a declaration issued in collective proceedings cannot pertain to the factual background or facts of the case.

[B] Declaratory Reliefs under the Commercial Companies Code

The second exemption from the general requirement of demonstrating legal interest is instituted in the Polish Commercial Companies Code (the '**CCC**') dated 15 September 2000,[612] which introduces a specific kind of proceedings aimed at declaring invalidity of resolutions of shareholders meetings of both limited liability companies (Article 252 of the CCC) as well as joint-stock companies (Article 425 of the CCC). A limited group of entities (encompassing *inter alia* the management board, supervisory board, individual members of the aforesaid bodies, shareholders who voted against the given resolution and demanded that their objection be put on the record, and shareholders who were unduly prevented from participating in the meeting of shareholders) is entitled to apply to the courts for declaration of a resolution's invalidity in proceedings initiated against the company.

608. Explanatory Memorandum to the Act on Pursuing Claims in Collective Proceedings of 17 December 2009, 4, available at: http://orka.sejm.gov.pl/Druki6ka.nsf/0/0E73993108750163C125758A004227CB/$file/1829.pdf (accessed 13 January 2019).
609. Tomasz Jaworski in *Ustawa o dochodzeniu roszczeń w postępowaniu grupowym. Komentarz* 124 (Tomasz Jaworski & Patrick Radzimierski eds., 2010).
610. Jaworski, *supra* n. 609, at 124.
611. *Ibid.*, at 126.
612. Journal of Laws of the Republic of Poland, item 1577 (2017).

In each of the above-mentioned cases, Article 189 of the Polish CCP is not applicable, with the practical effect that the prerequisite of legal interest shall not be examined by the court.[613] This far-reaching facilitation applies, however, only to the range of persons/bodies mentioned expressly in the CCC who, a priori, are entitled to bring a declaratory claim. Their legal position is justified either by their post/function (e.g., on the management board or supervisory board) or by factual circumstances connected with adoption of the resolution (e.g., their objection against the content of the challenged resolution).

If an entity outside the group listed in this CCC provision endeavours to invalidate a resolution, Article 189 of the Polish CCP and, as a consequence, the prerequisite of legal interest shall be applicable.[614] However, the view that persons not mentioned in the Polish CCP should be allowed to apply for declaration of invalidity of a shareholders meeting resolution is not unanimous. Some authors observe that such a possibility should be excluded, bearing in mind *inter alia* the necessity to protect certainty of commercial dealing.[615]

Furthermore, a resolution might be held invalid by the court only if it contravenes Polish law and when the claim is brought before the court within the deadline set forth in the CCP, expiring at the end of six months from receipt of notice of the resolution, not later, however, than after three years of the resolution's adoption.

Finally, it should be emphasized that the specific regulation pertaining to declaration of a resolution's invalidity was not introduced in the Polish CCP with regard to resolutions of other bodies of the company, i.e., resolutions of the management board, supervisory board or audit committee. Resolutions by these bodies might be subject to declaratory proceedings only based on Article 189 of the Polish CCP;[616] as a consequence, the claimant would be obligated to demonstrate the existence of legal interest on his side.

[C] Declaratory Reliefs in Employee Relations

Reduced requirements with regard to existence of legal interest in obtaining declaratory relief and subsidiarity principle might be observed in the area of employment law.

For instance, in the judgement dated 10 April 2014 (II PK 179/13) regarding declaration that the parties are bound by an employment contract for an indefinite

613. Judgement of 1 March 2007, III CZP 94/06, 7–8 OSNC, item 95 (2007 (Polish Supreme Court); cf. judgement of 19 January 2016, VI ACa 777/15 (Court of Appeal in Warsaw); judgement of 20 January 2016, I ACa 1042/15 (Court of Appeal in Szczecin). Cf. Janusz Szwaja in *Kodeks spółek handlowych. Komentarz. Tom III* (Stanisław Sołtysiński, Andrzej Szajkowski, Andrzej Szumański, Janusz Szwaja eds.) 1325, 1334–1335 (2008).
614. Mateusz Rodzynkiewicz, *Kodeks spółek handlowych. Komentarz*, 583–585 (2018).
615. Marcin Chomiuk in: *Kodeks spółek handlowych. Komentarz*, 1053 (Zbigniew Jara ed., 2018); Andrzej Koch, *Charakter sankcji wobec sprzecznych z prawem uchwał spółek kapitałowych*, 2 PPH 4, 4 et seq. (2007). Cf. view expressed by Janusz Szwaja, *supra* n. 613, at 1334–1335.
616. Judgement of 18 September 2013, III CZP 13/13, 3 OSNC, item 23 (2014). Cf. Józef Frąckowiak in *Kodeks spółek handlowych. Tom II. Komentarz do art. 151-300* (Andrzej Kidyba, Józef Frąckowiak, Katarzyna Kopaczyńska-Pieczniak, Marek Michalski, Alekdander Witosz) 686–687 (2018).

term, the Supreme Court held expressly that: '(...) the mere possibility to bring a more far-reaching claim (in this case the Supreme Court referred to a claim for admission to work – author's note) does not exclude the existence of claimant's legal interest to obtain declaration on existence of legal relationship or right, if such declaration assures the protection of claimant's rights in a broader extent'. Adoption of an opposite approach would be assessed as contravening the main aim of declaratory relief, i.e., provision of effective legal protection within the broad concept of access to justice.[617]

Another interesting decision was handed down by the Supreme Court on 19 May 2016 (I PK 264/10). In the view expressed by the Supreme Court, the prerequisite of legal interest shall be construed in a flexible manner, bearing in mind the necessity to conduct purposive interpretation of this notion, the factual circumstances of each individual case, claimant's access to the courts as well as the issue whether the party might obtain full protection by bringing a more far-reaching claim.

VII DECLARATORY RELIEFS IN ARBITRATION

There is no extended discussion among Polish scholars on special features of proceedings for rendering declaratory awards in arbitration. This might be due to the fact that Article 189 of the Polish CCP is deemed (almost unanimously) to be a provision of substantive nature, which shall be applicable to cases resolved on the basis of Polish substantive law.

However, a view expressed by Tadeusz Ereciński and Karol Weitz shall be indicated at this point. According to the aforementioned authors, the prerequisite of existence of legal interest does not have to be fulfilled while taking declaratory action in arbitration proceedings. Quite the opposite, economic interest in obtaining declaration is perceived as sufficient, following opinions expressed by German legal doctrine.[618] The arguments supporting this line of reasoning were neither developed nor followed by other scholars.

617. Cf. Kazimierz Piasecki, *Postępowanie sporne rozpoznawcze,* 150 et seq. (2004).
618. Tadeusz Ereciński, Karol Weitz, *Sąd arbitrażowy,* 301 (2008) referring to Jens-Peter Lachmann, *Handbuch für Schiedsgerichtspraxis,* 359 (2008).

ANNEX IV

Report on Main Features of Declarations in Switzerland

Nino Sievi

Table of Contents

I ORIGINS AND EVOLUTION OF DECLARATORY RELIEFS IN THE SWISS LEGAL SYSTEM

Already most of the old cantonal codes of civil procedure contained a specific provision dealing with declaratory actions.[619] For example, § 92 of the 1913 Zurich Code of Civil Procedure[620] and later § 59 of the 1976 Zurich Code of Civil Procedure[621] provided that actions regarding the determination of existence or non-existence of a legal relationship or the authenticity or inauthenticity of a document would only be entertained if there was a specific legal interest and in the declaration. These provisions, as in other cantonal codes of civil procedure, were evidently inspired by § 256 of the 1877/1889 German Code of Civil Procedure.[622]

In addition, certain federal laws, such as the Federal Act on Debt Enforcement and Bankruptcy (Swiss FDEB)[623] or the Swiss CC,[624] foresaw (and still foresee) specific actions for declaratory relief. For example, Article 29(1) of the Swiss CC provides for the right of seeking a declaration that one's right to their name be confirmed.

Later on, the Swiss Federal Tribunal has held that, also outside of these Federal Acts, Swiss federal law foresees a general declaratory action.[625] The Swiss Federal Tribunal reasoned that federal private law had to ensure its uniform enforcement.[626] Thus, the availability of declaratory actions – a way of enforcing private law – had to

619. Cf. Oskar Vogel & Karl Spühler, *Grundriss des Zivilprozessrechts und des internationalen Zivilprozessrechts der Schweiz*, § 7 n. 20 (2012); Alexander Sieben, *Feststellungsklagen nach eidgenössischem und kantonalem Recht*, 24–26 (1948). For an analysis of earlier history of declaratory actions, cf. Bernhard Bodmer, *Die allgemeine Feststellungsklage im schweizerischen Privatrecht*, 5–7 (1984).

620. 'Auf Klagen betreffend Feststellung des Bestehens oder Nichtbestehens eines Rechtsverhältnisses oder der Echtheit oder Unechtheit einer Urkunde wird nur eingetreten, wenn ein rechtliches Interesse an der Feststellung besteht.'

621. *Ibid.*, https://www.zh.ch/internet/de/rechtliche_grundlagen/gesetze/erlass.html?Open&Ordnr=271,13.06.1976,,059 (accessed 4 December 2018).

622. Bodmer, *supra* n. 619, at 23–24. However, the interpretation of these provisions developed differently compared to Germany. In particular, the term 'legal interest' was given a wider meaning also covering factual and economic interests, cf. *Id.*, at 83–85.

623. (30 March 1911), SR 281.1, https://www.admin.ch/opc/en/classified-compilation/19110009/index.html (accessed 4 December 2018).

624. (10 December 1907), SR 210, https://www.admin.ch/opc/en/classified-compilation/19070042/index.html (accessed 4 December 2018).

625. Decision of the Swiss Federal Tribunal dated 30 October 1984, published in BGE 110 II 352.

626. Decision of the Swiss Federal Tribunal dated 30 October 1984, published in BGE 110 II 352, consideration no. 1: 'La questione della ricevibilità dell'azione di mero accertamento è, in linea di massima, una questione di procedura e, di conseguenza, una questione disciplinata dal legislatore cantonale. Un'eccezione a questa regola è fatta soltanto quando il diritto federale prevede in singoli casi, espressamente o implicitamente, un azione di mero accertamento: in questi singoli casi, una siffatta azione è proponibile in virtù del diritto federale, senza riguardo a quello processuale cantonale che la ignor.' Cf. also decision of the Swiss Federal Tribunal dated 1 July 1993, published in BGE 119 II 368, consideration no. 2.a.

be regulated on a federal rather than cantonal level. Accordingly, the admissibility of declaratory actions was deemed to be governed by Swiss federal law. The cantonal codes of civil procedure had henceforth no material effect anymore in relation to declaratory actions.[627]

In line with this decision, a specific provision on declaratory actions was included in the Swiss CCP,[628] which replaced all cantonal codes of civil procedure in 2011.

II STATUTORY BASIS AND PREREQUISITES FOR DECLARATORY RELIEFS

The statutory basis for declaratory actions is to be found in the Swiss CCP. Article 88 of the Swiss CCP provides as follows:

> By filing an action for a declaratory judgment, the plaintiff demands that the court establish that a right or legal relationship exists or does not exist.

The admissibility of such actions depends, among other, on the claimant having an interest in its claim. In Swiss civil procedural law, every court examines ex officio whether a claimant has a legitimate interest in the requested relief (*Rechtsschutzinteresse*).[629] If a claimant lacks such interest, a Swiss court will deem the claim inadmissible and dismiss the claim (without prejudice). The existence of such legitimate interest is generally presumed for actions of performance or money.[630]

In the context of declaratory actions, the courts require that the claimant has a legitimate interest in the requested declaratory relief (*Feststellungsinteresse*). Contrary to claims for performance or money, such interest is not presumed and requires a detailed examination in every individual case. The interest is usually of legal nature, the main objective being to deal with a legal dispute. However, the interest may also be of factual nature, in particular the interest can be based on purely economic considerations.[631] For example, a claimant might be looking at further investment activities, but due to an asserted claim by a third party is unable to do so.[632] In such case, the true purpose of an action seeking a declaration that the third party does not have a claim is to free up the necessitated funds for the planned investment.

While the existence of a legitimate interest in the requested relief does generally not cause any issues if the relief is directed at the payment of a sum of money or the

627. Alexander Markus, *Berner Kommentar, Schweizerische Zivilprozessordnung*, Art. 88 n. 1 (Andreas Güngerich ed, 2012).
628. (19 December 2008), SR 272, https://www.admin.ch/opc/en/classified-compilation/20061121/index.html (accessed 4 December 2018).
629. Cf. Art. 59(2)(a) of the Swiss CCP.
630. Cf. decision of the Swiss Federal Tribunal dated 26 May 2003, Case no. 4C.7/2003, consideration no. 5.
631. Decision of the Swiss Federal Tribunal dated 11 March 2009, Case no. 4A_548/2008, published in BGE 135 III 378, consideration no. 2.2; decision of the Swiss Federal Tribunal dated 3 February 2005, Case no. 4C.335/2004, published in BGE 131 III 319, consideration no. 3.5; decision of the Swiss Federal Tribunal dated 7 March 1994, published in BGE 120 II 20, consideration no. 3.a.
632. Markus, *supra* n. 627, at Art. 88 n. 9.

performance of a specific act, the examination of whether a claimant has sufficient interest in the requested declaratory relief (*Feststellungsinteresse*) often gives rise to controversies. In recent times, there have been some developments in the Swiss Federal Tribunal's case law in this regard. The Swiss Federal Tribunal has eased the access to negative declaratory actions in the context of debt enforcement proceedings.[633] Furthermore, in 2018, it has abandoned its long-standing practice inhibiting negative declaratory actions in the context of forum running. Overall, the attitude towards declaratory actions seems to become less restrictive.[634]

III CONCEPT OF LEGITIMATE INTEREST UNDER SWISS LAW

As previously explained, a declaratory action requires the claimant to demonstrate sufficient interest in the requested declaratory relief (*Feststellungsinteresse*). The courts examine whether such interest exists in every case, as it forms a condition for the admissibility of the action.

[A] Nature of the Interest in Declaratory Relief

For a long time, it was highly disputed whether the interest in a declaratory relief is of substantive or procedural nature.[635]

Before the entering into force of the Swiss CCP, the Swiss Federal Tribunal has held consistently that the interest in a declaratory relief was of substantive nature.[636] This stance could be mainly explained by the Swiss Federal Tribunal's objective of ensuring that the access to a declaratory action was regulated on a federal level.[637] At the time, civil procedure was not regulated at a federal law, rather each canton had its own code of civil procedure. Thus, for the Swiss Federal Tribunal to attain its objective, it had to qualify the interest in a declaratory relief as a matter of substantive law, which was governed on a federal level.

In doctrine, the majority argued for the interest in declaratory relief to form part of procedural law. On the one hand, dogmatic arguments were put forth based on the

633. Decision of the Swiss Federal Tribunal dated 16 January 2015, Case no. 4A_414/2014, published in BGE 141 III 68.
634. Cf. decision of the Swiss Federal Tribunal dated 14 March 2018, Case no. 4A_417/2017, published in BGE 144 III 175.
635. For a detailed analysis, cf. Nino Sievi, *Die negativen Feststellungsklagen des schweizerischen Rechts im Anwendungsbereich des Lugano-Übereinkommens*, nn. 43 et seq. (2017).
636. Decision of the Swiss Federal Tribunal dated 30 October 1984, published in BGE 110 II 352, consideration no. 1; decision of the Swiss Federal Tribunal dated 26 September 1997, published in BGE 123 III 414, consideration no. 7.b; decision of the Swiss Federal Tribunal dated 21 February 2003, Case no. 4C.370/2002, published in BGE 129 III 295, consideration no. 2; decision of the Swiss Federal Tribunal dated 3 February 2005, Case no. 4C.335/2004, published in BGE 131 III 319, consideration no. 3.5.
637. Cf. Marco Stacher, *Das Rechtsschutzinteresse im internationalen Verhältnis*, Allgemeine Juristische Praxis, 1124, 1125 (2007); Flavia Weber, *Die Feststellungsklage nach der Schweizerischen Zivilprozessordnung*, n. 56 (2013); Sievi, *supra* n. 635, at nn. 28 et seq.

concept of actionability (*Klagbarkeit* or *Klagerecht*).[638] On the other hand, and more pragmatically, the Swiss CCP's explicit reference to the prerequisite of an interest in the requested relief was taken as an indication that this interest is of procedural nature.[639]

The Swiss Federal Tribunal, even before the entering into force of the Swiss CCP, started to leave the question of the interest's nature open again.[640] In 2018, the Swiss Federal Tribunal finally confirmed the doctrine's position and qualified the interest in a declaratory relief as being of procedural nature stressing that as a condition of admissibility it formed part of procedural law.[641]

[B] Purpose of the Legitimate Interest Test

The purpose of the legitimate interest test is to ensure that the courts are not burdened with unnecessary claims.[642] As such, the test has the function of a filter.[643] The courts shall only admit declaratory actions which, if granted, do have the potential to improve the claimant's position. Such improvement would, for example, be missing if a claimant seeks a declaration concerning an issue that is completely undisputed among the involved parties.

[C] Standard Test for Sufficient Interest in a Declaratory Relief

The Swiss Federal Tribunal generally follows a standard test, in order to determine whether a claimant has sufficient interest in a requested declaratory relief. However, sufficient interest can also exist outside of this standard test.[644]

Pursuant to the standard test,[645] a declaratory action is admissible if (i) there is an uncertainty, (ii) whose continuation is no longer bearable to the claimant and (iii) provided that there is no other relief available to the claimant. Additionally, (iv) in case of a negative declaratory action, the claimant's interest must further be balanced against the defendant's (i.e., the creditor's) interest in not having to conduct the proceedings at that point in time.

---

638. Stacher, *supra* n. 637, at 1126–1128; Sievi, *supra* n. 635, at nn. 46 et seq.
639. Marc Weber, *Basler Kommentar, ZPO*, Art. 88 n. 3 (Karl Spühler, Luca Tenchio & Dominik Infanger eds, 2017); Weber, *supra* n. 637, at nn. 60–61; Daniel Füllemann, *Schweizerische Zivilprozessordnung, Kommentar*, Art. 88 n. 24 (Alexander Brunner, Dominik Gasser & Ivo Schwander eds, 2016), Felix Dasser, *Feststellungsinteresse in internationalen Verhältnissen*, Jusletter, n. 23 (29 September 2003).
640. Cf. e.g., decision of the Swiss Federal Tribunal dated 13 March 2007, Case no. 4C.318/2006, published in BGE 133 III 282, consideration no. 3.4.
641. Decision of the Swiss Federal Tribunal dated 14 March 2018, Case no. 4A_417/2017, published in BGE 144 III 175, consideration no. 4.
642. Dasser, *supra* n. 639, at n. 17; Stacher, *supra* n. 637, at 1129; Bodmer, *supra* n. 619, at 76; Ulrich Haas & Piotr Wojtowicz, *Neuerungen bei der Feststellungsklage nach Schweizer Recht*, Zeitschrift für Zivilprozess International, 301, 302 (2014); Sievi, *supra* n. 635, at n. 55.
643. Paul Oberhammer, *Kurzkommentar ZPO, Schweizerische Zivilprozessordnung*, Art. 88 n. 10 (Paul Oberhammer, Tanja Domej & Ulrich Haas eds, 2013); Weber, *supra* n. 637, at n. 51.
644. Cf. *infra* Annex IV.III[D].
645. Cf. e.g., decision of the Swiss Federal Tribunal dated 30 June 2010, Case no. 4A_170/2010, published in BGE 136 III 523, consideration no. 5.

[1] Uncertainty

Above all, there must be an uncertainty, which a declaratory judgment would resolve.[646] The uncertainty stems from the parties' lacking agreement as to a specific right or legal relationship.[647] In other words, there must be a disagreement between the involved parties. Such disagreement is usually evidenced by the parties' assertions or protests.[648] Examples of such uncertainties are the disputed validity of a termination notice, a dispute whether certain acts are violation a non-compete clause or an asserted (but not yet initiated) claim for money.[649]

[2] No Longer Bearable to the Claimant

The continuation of the uncertainty must be unbearable to the claimant. This subjective requirement is composed of two elements. On the one hand, the uncertainty must have such an effect on the claimant that it inhibits his economic freedom of decision (*wirtschaftliche Bewegungs- und Entscheidungsfreiheit*).[650] On the other hand, the uncertainty must not have a foreseeable end in the near future.

An uncertainty inhibits a party's economic freedom of decision for example because it forces the inhibited party to make provisions in its balance sheet for an asserted claim against it.[651] Equally, an asserted claim can hinder a party's investment activities as there is uncertainty in relation to the available funds on a long-term basis.[652] In addition, also the effect of an asserted right or claim in the public sphere must be considered. For example, an asserted debt can influence a party's credit rating as well as trustworthiness.[653]

However, a party's economic freedom of decision is not considered inhibited if the dispute only concerns a moderate amount.[654] The courts shall not be burdened with proceedings that are of no real importance to a claimant. Thus, resolution of the uncertainty put to the court with a declaratory action must potentially have a positive

646. Cf. e.g., decision of the Swiss Federal Tribunal dated 30 June 2010, Case no. 4A_170/2010, published in BGE 136 III 523, consideration no. 5: 'wenn die Rechtsbeziehungen der Parteien ungewiss sind und die Ungewissheit durch die richterliche Feststellung beseitigt werden kann …'.
647. Weber, *supra* n. 637, at n. 140; Weber, *supra* n. 639, at Art. 88 n. 13; Oberhammer, *supra* n. 643, at Art. 88 n. 13.
648. Bodmer, *supra* n. 619, at 89; Oberhammer, *supra* n. 643, at Art. 88 n. 13.
649. Cf. Markus, *supra* n. 627, at Art. 88 n. 20.
650. Cf. decision of the Swiss Federal Tribunal dated 11 March 2009, Case no. 4A_548/2008, published in BGE 135 III 378, consideration no. 2.2: 'il faut au contraire que l'on ne puisse pas exiger de la partie demanderesse qu'elle tolère plus longtemps le maintien de cette incertitude, parce que celle-ci l'entrave dans sa liberté de décision.'
651. Cf. e.g., decision of the Swiss Federal Tribunal dated 14 May 2008; Case no. 4A_530/2007, consideration no. 2.2.
652. Cf. e.g., decision of the Zurich High Court dated 18 March 2003, Case no. NE020044, consideration no. 2.
653. Cf. Sievi, *supra* n. 635, at n. 65. Also cf. *infra* Annex IV.III[D][1].
654. Decision of the Swiss Federal Tribunal dated 7 March 1994, published in BGE 120 II 20, consideration no. 3.c.

impact on the claimant. This impact is generally inexistent or at least not significant enough in cases concerning low amounts of money.

Which amount is required in a specific case for a declaratory action to be admissible depends on the individual characteristics of the claimant.[655] The amount having an impact on a specific claimant will depend on the financial background of this party. The threshold for a private individual is lower than for a global bank. Courts have held amounts of CHF 14,000,[656] CHF 37,900[657] or CHF 77,000[658] to be sufficient for private individuals, but not CHF 2,000[659] or CHF 376.30.[660] On the contrary, the Zurich Commercial Court has dismissed a negative declaratory action concerning an asserted claim for CHF 10.6 million brought by a bank with a balance sheet total of CHF 1 billion.[661]

In doctrine, it is argued that the threshold should be set at a low level, in order to ensure that access to justice is not denied.[662] In case of doubt, a court shall assume that the continuation of the uncertainty does inhibit a party's economic freedom of decision. Some scholars even argue – in contrast to the Swiss Federal Tribunal's case law – that any amount is sufficient, as the claimant's will to have an uncertainty (no matter the amount) resolved provides the required interest in the relief.[663]

While the Swiss Federal Tribunal has continued to require that the amount at issue be substantial, it has also recognized that the requirement can lead to unsatisfying results in the context of enforcement proceedings under the Swiss FDEB. Therefore, it has recently changed its practice for declaratory actions that stand in direct connection to ongoing enforcement proceedings.[664] However, this change of practice does not affect declaratory actions outside of enforcement proceedings, as the decision of the Swiss Federal Tribunal was based on the specific characteristics and consequences of enforcement proceedings under the Swiss FDEB.[665]

The *second element* of the unbearableness requirement relates to the foreseeable duration of the uncertainty. If the uncertainty will anyway be resolved in the near future, a claimant does not have sufficient interest in a declaratory relief.[666]

655. Sievi, *supra* n. 635, at n. 66.
656. Decision of the Swiss Federal Tribunal dated 7 March 1994, published in BGE 120 II 20.
657. Decision of the Zurich Commercial Court dated 12 June 2007, published in Blätter für Zürcherische Rechtsprechung (ZR) 2007, at 299.
658. Decision of the Swiss Federal Tribunal dated 7 March 1994, published in BGE 120 II 20.
659. Decision of the Swiss Federal Tribunal dated 21 November 2005, Case no. 4P.239/2005.
660. Decision of the Swiss Federal Tribunal dated 14 May 2008, Case no. 4A_530/2007, consideration no. 2.2.
661. Decision of Zurich Commercial Court dated 27 August 1993, published in Blätter für Zürcherische Rechtsprechung (ZR) 1994, at 94.
662. Isaak Meier, *Schweizerisches Zivilprozessrecht – eine kritische Darstellung aus der Sicht von Praxis und Lehre*, 212 (2010); Füllemann, *supra* n. 639, at Art. 88 n. 10; Sievi, *supra* n. 635, at n. 73.
663. Oberhammer, *supra* n. 643, at Art. 88 n. 16; Weber, *supra* n. 637, at nn. 175 et seq.
664. Decision of the Swiss Federal Tribunal dated 16 January 2015, Case no. 4A_414/2014, published in BGE 141 III 68, cf. *infra* Annex IV.III[D][1].
665. Sievi, *supra* n. 635, at n. 79. Also cf. *infra* Annex IV.III[D][1].
666. Cf. e.g., decision of the Swiss Federal Tribunal dated 3 February 2005, Case no. 4C.335/2004, published in BGE 131 III 319, consideration no. 3.5.

This is of particular relevance for negative declaratory actions. If the creditor is about to initiate legal proceedings themselves, the uncertainty will anyway soon be resolved. Accordingly, the Swiss Federal Tribunal has held that a negative declaratory action is not admissible if the initiation of a claim for performance or money is imminent.[667] In particular, the Swiss Federal Tribunal has held that a claimant's interest in having a dispute heard by a specific court was not sufficient to justify a negative declaratory action – thereby barring any attempts of forum running.[668] The court argued rather pragmatically (and unreasoned) that the claimant's interest had to exist independent of a specific court and that admitting such practices of forum running would inevitably lead to further burdensome work for the court. However, this line of argument has been abandoned (at least) for international cases.[669]

When exactly the initiation of a claim must be considered imminent is not entirely clear from the Swiss Federal Tribunal's case law. The cases to be decided by the Swiss Federal Tribunal concerned rather extreme cases, in which the creditor had already initiated conciliation proceedings[670] or had announced the initiation of a claim in the coming weeks.[671] In doctrine, it is argued that the criteria for assuming imminence of a claim should be handled rather restrictively focussing on the mentioned cases of the Swiss Federal Tribunal.[672] Thus, a claim is to be considered imminent if a creditor announces explicitly or implicitly their plan to initiate a claim within the next weeks.

However, when a claim for performance or money is imminent, the courts should dispense with the standard test altogether.[673] After all, the main purpose of the sufficient interest test is to prevent the courts from being burdened with unnecessary and useless proceedings. However, when a claim is imminent, it is already evident that the courts will be burdened with handling the dispute existing between the parties.

Instead of relying on the legitimate interest test, courts should in such cases rather examine whether the party initiating a declaratory action has a legitimate

667. Cf. e.g., decision of the Swiss Federal Tribunal dated 26 September 1997, published in BGE 123 III 414, consideration no. 7.b; decision of the Swiss Federal Tribunal dated 3 April 1995, Case no. 4C.400/1994, consideration no. 2.a.
668. Decision of the Swiss Federal Tribunal dated 3 February 2005, Case no. 4C.335/2004, published in BGE 131 III 319, consideration no. 3.5: 'Da das Feststellungsinteresse unabhängig vom Gerichtsstand vorliegen muss, kann es nicht durch das Interesse an einem bestimmten Gerichtsstand ersetzt werden. Ansonsten würde die vom Gesetzgeber getroffene Regelung der Gerichtsstände umgangen bzw. ausser Kraft gesetzt. Zudem würde die Zulassung des "forum running" dazu führen, dass die Parteien möglichst schnell und ohne vorherige Ankündigung zu den ihnen genehmen Gerichten "rennen" und klagen müssten, um ihren Gerichtsstand zu sichern. Dies wäre nicht sachgerecht, da damit aussergerichtliche Vergleichsverhandlungen oder einvernehmliche Streitlösungsverfahren gefährdet und die Gerichte mit unnötigen parallelen Verfahren belastet würden.'
669. Cf. *infra* Annex IV.III[D][2].
670. Decision of the Swiss Federal Tribunal, dated 6 July 2007, Case no. 4A_143/2007.
671. Decision of the High Court of the Canton of Thurgau dated 22 March 2004, published in Rechenschaftsbericht des Obergerichts des Kantons Thurgau an den grossen Rat (RBOG) 2004, at 128 (later forming the object of the appeal in the decision of the Swiss Federal Tribunal dated 3 February 2005, Case no. 4C.335/2004, published in BGE 131 III 319).
672. Füllemann, *supra* n. 639, at Art. 88 n. 23; Sievi, *supra* n. 635, at nn. 88 et seq.
673. Cf. Sievi, *supra* n. 635, at n. 91.

interest in having a claim dealt with by the particular court seized. Recently, the Swiss Federal Tribunal has followed this approach in the context of forum running in an international setting and abandoned its earlier practice.[674]

[3] No Other Remedy Providing Equivalent Relief (Subsidiarity Principle)

A declaratory action is generally considered a subsidiary remedy. It is only admissible if neither a claim for performance or money[675] nor an action for modification of the legal relationship[676] are available to the claimant.[677] For example, a claim requesting a declaration that A owes B the amount of CHF 100,000 is generally inadmissible, as A could sue for payment of the amount.

Essentially, the subsidiarity principle shall prevent a claimant from preparing its claim for money by first conducting proceedings for a declaration that the defendant is liable and only later claiming the actual money.[678] This separation of the proceedings is considered unnecessary and not compatible with the general principle of procedural efficiency.[679]

However, if the damages have not yet occurred or are still growing, a claim for money is simply not yet possible. Accordingly, a request for declaration that a defendant is liable for future damages stemming from its unlawful actions is considered admissible if for considerable time the damages will not be determinable.[680]

The Swiss Federal Tribunal has, furthermore, acknowledged that there are other scenarios in which declaratory relief might be sought not just in preparation of a later

674. Decision of the Swiss Federal Tribunal dated 14 March 2018, Case no. 4A_417/2017, published in BGE 144 III 175. For details on the case, cf. *infra* Annex IV.III[D][2].
675. Cf. Art. 84 of the Swiss CCP.
676. Cf. Art. 87 of the Swiss CCP.
677. Cf. e.g., decision of the Swiss Federal Tribunal dated 11 March 2009, Case no. 4A_548/2008, published in BGE 135 III 378; decision of the Swiss Federal Tribunal dated 20 December 1996, published in BGE 123 III 49; decision of the Swiss Federal Tribunal dated 1 July 1993, published in BGE 119 II 368.
678. Cf. Weber, *supra* n. 637, at n. 207.
679. Decision of the Swiss Federal Tribunal dated 20 December 1996, published in BGE 123 III 49; Urs Schenker, *Schweizerische Zivilprozessordnung*, Art. 88 n. 8 (Baker & McKenzie ed, 2010); Adrian Staehelin, Daniel Staehelin & Pascal Grolimund, *Zivilprozessrecht – Unter Einbezug des Anwaltsrechts und des internationalen Zivilprozessrechts*, § 14 n. 25 (2013).
680. Decision of the Swiss Federal Tribunal dated 20 December 1996, published in BGE 123 III 49, consideration no. 1; decision of the Swiss Federal Tribunal dated 2 July 1992, published in BGE 118 II 254, consideration no. 1. Cf. Oberhammer, *supra* n. 643, at Art. 88 n. 6; Füllemann, *supra* n. 639, at Art. 88 n. 13.

claim for money or performance.[681] However, such scenarios would only exist in exceptional circumstances.[682]

In doctrine, the Swiss Federal Tribunal's approach is criticized. Already, Bodmer stated that declaratory actions do obviously not only have the function of preparing a later claim for performance or money.[683] Accordingly, the conception of a declaratory action as subsidiary remedy should be dropped. If a declaratory action was actually used as mere preparation for a later claim for money or performance, the required interest would still lack – not because of a general subsidiarity of declaratory actions, but rather because the interest of pursuing a procedurally inefficient route is not worthy of protection.[684]

Going even further, Bessenich and Bopp argue that a declaratory action must be admissible, even if its sole purpose is the preparation of a later claim for performance or money.[685] They point out that it is the claimant's autonomy to choose how to proceed in order to enforce its rights. A limitation of this autonomy is not warranted. However, Weber rightfully replies that inefficient proceedings do not solely concern the claimant, but also cause impediments to a defendant and the courts.[686] Thus, a declaratory action as mere preparation for a later claim for money or performance is inadmissible, unless such claim is not yet possible (e.g., future damages).

Overall, the majority of doctrine argues that the general concept of subsidiarity should be dropped. Nonetheless, procedurally inefficient choices of a claimant are not supposed to be granted protection.

[4] Additional Prerequisite for Negative Declaratory Actions: Balancing with Interests of the Defendant

When assessing the admissibility of a negative declaratory action, the courts will balance the interest of the claimant – i.e., presumptive debtor – with the interest of the defendant – i.e., presumptive creditor.[687]

681. Decision of the Swiss Federal Tribunal dated 18 November 1971, published in BGE 97 II 371, consideration no. 2: 'Auch bei Möglichkeit einer Leistungsklage kann aber ein selbständiges Interesse an gerichtlicher Feststellung bestehen. So verhält es sich z.B., wenn es darum geht, nicht nur die fällige Leistung zu erhalten, sondern die Gültigkeit des ihr zugrunde liegenden Rechtsverhältnisses auch für dessen künftige Abwicklung feststellen zu lassen.' Also cf. Weber, *supra* n. 637, at n. 210, with further references.

682. Cf. e.g., decision of the Swiss Federal Tribunal dated 11 March 2009, Case no. 4A_548/2008, published in BGE 135 III 378, consideration no. 2.4: 'Seules des circonstances tout à fait exceptionnelles pourraient faire apparaître un intérêt suffisant à entrer en matière sur l'action en constatation de droit.'

683. Bodmer, *supra* n. 619, at 86–87.

684. Weber, *supra* n. 637, at nn. 218 et seq.; Stacher, *supra* n. 637, at 1130.

685. Balthasar Bessenich & Lukas Bopp, *Kommentar zur Schweizerischen Zivilprozessordnung*, Art. 88 n. 12 (Thomas Sutter-Somm, Franz Hasenböhler & Christoph Leuenberger eds, 2016).

686. Weber, *supra* n. 637, at n. 220.

687. Cf. e.g., Decision of the Swiss Federal Tribunal dated 15 December 2005, Case no. 5C.264/2004, published in BGE 132 III 277, consideration no. 4.2; decision of the Swiss Federal Tribunal dated 3 February 2005, Case no. 4C.335/200, published in BGE 131 III 319, consideration no. 3.5; decision of the Swiss Federal Tribunal dated 16 January 2015, Case no. 4A_414/2014, consideration no. 2.3.

The debtor's interest lies in the resolution of an uncertainty. By contrast, the creditor has an interest in choosing the timing of the commencement of the proceedings themselves. A negative declaratory action might force a creditor to conduct proceedings at an inopportune time. This can be particularly harmful to creditors, since they bear the burden of proof for their claim.[688] In view of this, the Swiss Federal Tribunal gives particular weight to evidentiary issues of a creditor when approaching the balancing of interests.[689] However, where such evidentiary issues do not exist, the balance of interest is usually decided in the debtor's favour. A strong indication for the lack of evidentiary issues are previous threats of legal actions issued by a creditor, as such threats lead to the assumption that the creditor is ready to pursue its claim in court.[690]

In doctrine, this additional requirement for negative declaratory actions faces strong criticism.[691] Above all, Oberhammer puts forth that the consideration of the creditor's interest stems from the erroneous assumption that the creditor has the privilege of choosing the time of commencement of proceedings.[692] This is not acceptable, as the principles of the burden of proof apply equally to both parties. Thus, the initiation of proceedings can also cause a debtor to face significant evidentiary issues.[693] In essence, attribution of the privilege to determine the timing of proceedings to the creditor results in unequal treatment of the parties. In addition, potential evidentiary issues of a creditor can also be addressed by a court when managing the proceedings (e.g., provide for longer deadlines or a stay of the proceedings) and do thus not justify denying the debtor access to a court.

The Swiss Federal Tribunal has noted this criticism in a recent decision.[694] In the case in question, it then, however, left the question open whether it would continue to apply this additional requirement. Hence, it is unclear whether the interests of the creditor will in the future still be taken into consideration when deciding on the admissibility of a negative declaratory action.

688. Decision of the Swiss Federal Tribunal dated 3 February 2005, Case no. 4C.335/200, published in BGE 131 III 319, consideration no. 3.5: 'Wer auf Feststellung klagt, dass eine Forderung nicht besteht, zwingt damit den beklagten Gläubiger zu vorzeitiger Prozessführung. Damit wird die Regel durchbrochen, dass grundsätzlich der Gläubiger und nicht der Schuldner den Zeitpunkt für die Geltendmachung eines Anspruches bestimmt. Der vorzeitige Prozess kann den Gläubiger benachteiligen, wenn er zur Beweisführung gezwungen wird, bevor er dazu bereit und in der Lage ist.'

689. Decision of the Swiss Federal Tribunal dated 7 March 1994, published in BGE 120 II 20, consideration no. 3.a; decision of the Swiss Federal Tribunal dated 30 October 1984; published in BGE 110 II 352, consideration no. 1.b.

690. Decision of the Swiss Federal Tribunal dated 11 August 2004, Case no. 4C.192/2004, consideration no. 2.2.

691. Oberhammer, *supra* n. 643, at Art. 88 nn. 26 et seq.; Weber, *supra* n. 637, at nn. 195 et seq.; Meier, *supra* n. 662, at 213; Füllemann, *supra* n. 639, at Art. 88 n. 16; Bessenich & Bopp, *supra* n. 685, at Art. 88 n. 10; Sievi, *supra* n. 635, at n. 115.

692. Oberhammer, *supra* n. 643, at Art. 88 n. 28.

693. Sievi, *supra* n. 635, at n. 114.

694. Decision of the Swiss Federal Tribunal dated 14 March 2018, Case no. 4A_417/2017, published in BGE 144 III 175, consideration 5.2.2. For details on the case, cf. *infra* Annex IV.III[D][2].

[D] Sufficient Interest Outside of the Standard Test

The Swiss Federal Tribunal indicated various times that a declaratory action may still be admissible under certain circumstances, even if it fails the above-described standard test.[695] Such circumstances have, in particular, been found to exist in the context of debt enforcement proceedings and forum running situations.

In addition, certain Federal Acts explicitly provide for specific declaratory actions. For such declaratory actions, sufficient interest in the declaratory relief is assumed to exist if the conditions of the specific legal provision are fulfilled.

[1] Negative Declaratory Action in Reaction to a Payment Order

Where a creditor has initiated enforcement proceedings and filed a payment request (*Betreibungsbegehren*) against a debtor with the debt enforcement office, said office will issue a payment order (*Zahlungsbefehl*) and serve it upon the debtor.[696] The debtor has ten days to object against the payment order (*Rechtsvorschlag*).[697] If the debtor does so, the creditor must initiate court proceedings, in order to continue with the enforcement proceedings.[698]

All payment orders issued against a debtor are listed in a debt registry (*Betreibungsregister*). This registry can be accessed by third parties who demonstrate sufficient interest. They can assess a certain person's creditworthiness and solvency by checking the payment orders issued against the person in question during the last five years.[699] For example, it is common for a Swiss landlord to request to see an excerpt of the debt registry before letting an apartment to someone.

When a creditor, however, does not pursue their claim after the debtor has objected to the payment order, the entry in the registry persists, thus tainting the debtor's credit rating. Until 1 January 2019, the Swiss FDEB did not provide the debtor with a specific remedy to have the entry removed in such cases.[700] The debtor could only file a general negative declaratory action under Article 88 of the Swiss CCP requesting the declaration that the claim put forth with the payment order does not exist. Once such declaratory judgment was obtained, the debtor could have the entry removed from the registry.

The Swiss Federal Tribunal has for a long time applied its standard test to this specific scenario.[701] This meant, in particular, that the payment order had to concern

695. Cf. decision of the Swiss Federal Tribunal dated 30 June 2010, Case no. 4A_170/2010, published in BGE 136 III 523, consideration no. 5; decision of the Swiss Federal Tribunal dated 3 February 2005; Case no. 4C.335/2004, published in BGE 131 III 319, consideration no. 3.5.
696. Article 69 of the FDEB.
697. Article 74 of the FDEB.
698. Articles 79 et seq. of the FDEB.
699. Article 8a of the FDEB.
700. Cf. Sievi, *supra* n. 635, at n. 127, with further references to decisions of the Swiss Federal Tribunal.
701. Cf. decision of the Swiss Federal Tribunal dated 16 February 1999, published in BGE 125 III 149, consideration no. 3.d; decision of the Swiss Federal Tribunal dated 25 July 2002, Case no. 7B.97/2002, published in BGE 128 III 334.

an amount significant enough to be considered to hinder the debtor's economic decision freedom. In view of the potential impact of just a single entry in the registry on a person's credit rating, this practice was heavily criticized in doctrine.[702]

In 2016, the Swiss Federal Tribunal reacted to this criticism and changed its former practice ruling that the admissibility of a negative declaratory action in reaction to a non-pursued payment order was not dependent on the amount being substantial.[703] It explained that the listing of the payment order in the registry had significant consequences for the person in question. Accordingly, any person faced with a non-pursued payment order is presumed to have sufficient interest in requesting a judicial declaration that the debt in question does not exist.[704] An exception solely applies where the payment order was issued for the sole purpose of interrupting prescription and the debtor had previously refused to sign a corresponding waiver.

As of 1 January 2019, the situation of non-pursued payment orders is specifically addressed in the Swiss FDEB. Pursuant to Article 8(3)(a) of the Swiss FDEB, one can apply that an entry in the debt registry will not be made visible to third parties if a creditor fails to initiate a claim within three months after the payment order has been issued. Further, under Article 85a of the Swiss FDEB, a debtor is explicitly granted the option to initiate a negative declaratory action in reaction to a non-pursued payment order.[705]

These new provisions of the Swiss FDEB will render the previous case law on negative declaratory actions in reaction to a payment order obsolete. A debtor wishing to clean his debt registry has the remedy of Article 8(3)(a) of the Swiss FDEB at their hands. If a debtor wishes to, nonetheless, pursue a negative declaratory action before a court, they can rely on Article 85a of the Swiss FDEB.

[2] Negative Declaratory Actions in Forum Running Situations

In particular, in an international setting, it is not uncommon for parties to try and have the dispute heard at their preferred venue (so-called forum shopping). In the European judicial area, the rules on *lis pendens* have led to a race to the courthouse between

702. Weber, *supra* n. 637, at n. 201; André Equey & Reto Vonzun, *Mittel und Wege zur Beseitigung der negativen Auswirkungen des Betreibungsregistereintrags grundloser Betreibungen, unter besonderer Berücksichtigung der Klage auf Aufhebung der Betreibung nach Art. 85 SchKG*, Allgemeine Juristische Praxis, 1337, 1345 (2011); Florian Chaudet & Peter Schauffelberger, *Le droit de consultation du registre de poursuites en relation avec l'inscription de poursuites frappés d'opposition non levée; quelques voeux et quelques pistes en faveur du poursuivi concernant l'Art. 8 LP*, 317, 321 (Juan Carlos Landrove ed, *De lege negotiorum, études autour du droit des affaires en l'honneur du professeur François Chaudet*, 2009).

703. Decision of the Swiss Federal Tribunal dated 16 January 2015, Case no. 4A_414/2014, published in BGE 141 III 68.

704. Decision of the Swiss Federal Tribunal dated 16 January 2015, Case no. 4A_414/2014, published in BGE 141 III 68, consideration no. 2.7: 'das schützenswerte Interesse an der Feststellung des Nichtbestands der Forderung grundsätzlich zu bejahen, sobald diese in Betreibung gesetzt wurde, ohne dass der Feststellungskläger konkret nachweisen muss, dass er wegen der Betreibung in seiner wirtschaftlichen Bewegungsfreiheit empfindlich beeinträchtigt wird.'

705. Cf. *infra* Annex IV.III[D][3]&[4].

prospective claimants and defendants - the latter usually filing a negative declaratory action.[706] The person to file their claim first blocks the dispute for any other court in the European judicial area.[707] Thus, the fastest party can choose the venue for a particular claim. This phenomenon is generally referred to as forum running.

The Swiss Federal Tribunal has consistently denied that a claimant had sufficient interest in securing a specific court for proceedings.[708] Also, in application of the standard test, it has deemed a negative declaratory action to be inadmissible if made in a forum running situation.[709] In such situation, the claim for money or performance of the creditor is imminent. Thus, the Swiss Federal Tribunal held that the continuation of the uncertainty was not unbearable, since the uncertainty was soon to be resolved by the creditor's imminent claim for money or performance. Hence, it was deemed bearable for the debtor to await the initiation of the claim for money or performance by the creditor.

This practice was heavily criticized in doctrine.[710] Above all, it was argued that there was evidently an interest in having one's case heard by a specific court, as evidenced by the very existence of forum running.[711] Furthermore, leaving the choice of the forum to one party only - i.e., the creditor - was deemed incompatible with the principle of equality of arms.[712] In addition, given that in a forum running situation a court will anyway soon be burdened with the case in question, the general purpose of the interest test - preventing courts from being burdened with unnecessary work - does not apply.[713] Accordingly, courts should abandon the standard test in such situation and solely assess whether a party has sufficient interest in a particular forum.

The Swiss Federal Tribunal has reacted to this criticism and changed its long-standing practice in 2018.[714] In said case, the Swiss Federal Tribunal had to decide a case, in which the claimant had initiated a negative declaratory action in Switzerland. The purpose of this claim was to prevent the counterparty, which was asserting a claim based on competition law, from starting proceedings in England. While the Swiss Federal Tribunal did not make any statements on the specific effects of the Lugano

706. Cf. decision of the Swiss Federal Tribunal dated 30 June 2010, Case no. 4A_170/2010, published in BGE 136 III 523; Gion Jegher, *Mit schweizerischer negativer Feststellungsklage ins europäische Forum Running - Gedanken anlässlich BGE 123 III 414*, Zeitschrift für Schweizer Recht, 31 (1999).
707. Cf. Art. 27 of the Lugano Convention and Art. 29 of the EU Regulation no. 1215/2012.
708. Decision of the Swiss Federal Tribunal dated 3 February 2005, Case no. 4C.335/2004, published in BGE 131 III 319, consideration no. 3.5.
709. Cf. e.g., decision of the Swiss Federal Tribunal dated 26 September 1997, published in BGE 123 III 414, consideration no. 7.b; decision of the Swiss Federal Tribunal dated 3 April 1995, Case no. 4C.400/1994, consideration no. 2.a.
710. Ivo Schwander & Daniel Füllemann, *Anmerkung zu BGE 136 III 523*, Allgemeine Juristische Praxis, 1243 (2011); Füllemann, *supra* n. 639, at Art. 88 n. 26; Sievi, *supra* n. 635, at nn. 645 et seq.
711. Sievi, *supra* n. 635, at n. 94; Füllemann, *supra* n. 639, at Art. 88 n. 26.
712. This argument is of particular relevance for cases falling within the scope of application of the Lugano Convention, cf. Felix Dasser, *Lugano-Übereinkommen (LugÜ)*, Art. 27 nn. 52 et seq. (Felix Dasser & Paul Oberhammer eds, 2011); Sievi, *supra* n. 635, at nn. 615 et seq.
713. Sievi, *supra* n. 635, at n. 91.
714. Decision of the Swiss Federal Tribunal dated 14 March 2018, Case no. 4A_417/2017, published in BGE 144 III 175.

Convention on the legitimate interest test, it held that, in an international case, a party's interest in a certain forum was sufficient to deem a (negative) declaratory action admissible.[715]

Thus, the Swiss Federal Tribunal now recognizes that a party being in a forum running situation has sufficient interest in securing the forum of its choice for the imminent dispute. Strikingly, it did not apply the standard interest test to reach this conclusion. Rather, it disregarded the standard test and determined the existence of sufficient interest in the forum independent from the standard test. Thus, it assumed the forum running situation to be of a special nature justifying the disapplication of the standard test.[716]

This recent case demonstrates a liberalization of Swiss law's stance on the admissibility of (negative) declaratory actions in an international context. Nonetheless, a few questions remained open, such as when exactly a forum running situation exists. The Swiss Federal Tribunal has emphasized various times in its decision the significance of the creditor's claim being imminent.[717] However, it has not strictly defined when it considers such claim to be 'imminent'. Thus, some uncertainty remains.

[3] Declaratory Actions Explicitly Provided for by Federal Acts

Several Federal Acts contain specific provisions foreseeing the possibility of a declaratory action. The standard test for sufficient interest does generally not apply to these declaratory actions. Rather, the conditions for admissibility of such actions are deduced from the wording of the specific provisions. If the relevant conditions are met, the claimant is deemed to have a special interest (*besonderes Feststellungsinteresse*) liberating him from the standard interest test.[718]

[4] Declaratory Actions of the Swiss FDEB

The Swiss FDEB foresees two negative declaratory actions in relation to the inexistence of a debt for which enforcement is sought.[719] Both are directed at having the inexistence of a debt established, for which enforcement proceedings have been

715. Decision of the Swiss Federal Tribunal dated 14 March 2018, Case no. 4A_417/2017, published in BGE 144 III 175, consideration no. 5.4: 'Zusammenfassend ist festzustellen, dass jedenfalls im internationalen Verhältnis das Interesse einer Partei, bei einem bevorstehenden Gerichtsverfahren einen ihr genehmen Gerichtsstand zu sichern, als genügendes Feststellungsinteresse zu qualifizieren ist.'
716. Cf. Decision of the Swiss Federal Tribunal dated 14 March 2018, Case no. 4A_417/2017, published in BGE 144 III 175, consideration no. 5.3.2: 'Das tatsächliche Interesse, einen Prozess in diesem und nicht in jenem Staat zu führen, und damit daran, eine negative Feststellungsklage in der Schweiz erheben zu können, kann erheblich sein, allein wegen der unterschiedlichen Verfahrensrechte, der unterschiedlichen Verfahrenssprache, Dauer und Kosten der Verfahren etc.'
717. Decision of the Swiss Federal Tribunal dated 14 March 2018, Case no. 4A_417/2017, published in BGE 144 III 175, consideration nos 5.3.2, 5.3.3 and 5.4.
718. Füllemann, *supra* n. 639, at Art. 88 n. 14; Oberhammer, *supra* n. 643, at Art. 88 n. 3a.
719. Articles 83(2) and 85a of the Swiss FDEB.

commenced, and at bringing the enforcement proceedings to a halt. The main point of distinction lies in the previous enforcement steps undertaken by the creditor.

Pursuant to Article 83(2) of the Swiss FDEB, a debtor whose opposition against the debt enforcement (*Rechtsvorschlag*) has been provisionally lifted by the court (*provisorische Rechtsöffnung*) may launch a negative declaratory action (in these circumstances called *Aberkennungsklage*) within twenty days of the court judgement. If the debtor fails to file such action within the indicated time limit, the creditor may request the continuation of the debt enforcement and the debt enforcement office will move forward to seizing the debtor's assets.[720] The sufficient interest in such case is deduced from the judgment provisionally lifting the debtor's opposition against the enforcement proceedings and the ongoing enforcement proceedings. Thus, the debtor must only demonstrate the existence of such judgment, that his claim is filed within the indicated deadline and that the creditor has not withdrawn the enforcement proceedings.[721]

The other declaratory action is provided for in Article 85a of the FDEB. Pursuant to said provision, a debtor may file a negative declaratory action against any creditor who has initiated debt enforcement proceedings against them.[722] The only prerequisite for there to be sufficient interest is thus the existence of ongoing debt enforcement proceedings.[723]

Evidently, there is a significant overlap between Article 83(3) and Article 85a of the FDEB. In fact, Article 83(2) of the FDEB constitutes the more special claim, which a debtor will always choose if its conditions are met. The main advantage of this claim is the mandatory stop to the enforcement proceedings.[724] A creditor will not be able to request continuation of the enforcement proceedings until the court has decided on the negative declaratory action. In contrast, a negative declaratory action under Article 85a of the FEDB only stops ongoing enforcement proceedings if a court deems the negative declaratory action to have high chances of success.[725]

720. Cf. Arts 83(3) and 88 of the Swiss FDEB.
721. Dominik Vock & Danièle Müller, *SchKG-Klagen nach der Schweizerischen ZPO*, 142 (2012); Alfred Syz, *Aberkennungsklagen und Aberkennungsprozess gemäss Art. 83 Abs. 2 SchKG*, 19 (1972); Adrian Staehelin, *Basler Kommentar, Bundesgesetz über Schuldbetreibung und Konkurs I*, Art. 83 n. 17 (Adrian Staehelin, Thomas Bauer & Daniel Staehelin eds, 2010).
722. The old version of Art. 85a of the Swiss FDEB (in force until 31 December 2018) further required that the debt enforcement proceedings not be blocked by the debtor's opposition to the enforcement proceedings. This additional prerequisite severely limited the practical relevance of this claim.
723. Karl Spühler & Lucas Tenchio, *Feststellungsklagen gemäss Art. 85a Abs. 1 SchKG nach gültig erhobenem Rechtsvorschlag?*, Allgemeine Juristische Praxis, 1241, 1242 (1999); Bernhard Bodmer & Jan Bangert, *Basler Kommentar, Bundesgesetz über Schuldbetreibung und Konkurs I*, Art. 85a nn. 4 and 6 (Adrian Staehelin, Thomas Bauer & Daniel Staehelin eds, 2010).
724. Cf. Art. 83(3) of the Swiss FDEB.
725. Article 85a(2) of the Swiss FDEB.

[5] Declaratory Actions in Relation to the Establishment of the Personality Infringements and Violations of the Federal Act of Unfair Competition

Article 28a(1)(3) of the Swiss CC provides that a person may ask the court to make a declaration that an infringement of their personality is unlawful if it continues to have an offensive effect. This action is frequently combined with an application to have the judgment published.[726]

The provision requires that the claimant is still affected by the personality infringement.[727] The duration for which a person is affected after the end of an infringement depends on the individual circumstances and the nature as well as intensity of the infringement.[728] In particular, the amount of time which has passed since the infringement can be an indication whether the infringement still affects the claimant.

Similarly, Article 9(1)(c) of the Federal Act on Unfair Competition[729] provides for a declaratory action in order to have someone's act declared to be unlawful, i.e., that a specific action was 'unfair' and has violated the provisions of the Federal Act on Unfair Competition. The admissibility of the action depends on the offensive effect to continue.[730]

The purpose of both declaratory actions is not to resolve an uncertainty between the parties. The actions are directed at addressing the negative effects of the infringements. It is the interest in having these negative effects dealt with that builds the underlying interest of these claims.

[6] Declaratory Actions under the Federal Act on Patents for Inventions

The Federal Act on Patents for Inventions[731] (Swiss Patents Act) foresees two different kinds of declaratory actions. On the one hand, a party may apply to a court to have the patent declared null.[732] On the other hand, any person demonstrating an interest may bring an action to obtain a declaratory judgment on the existence or non-existence of a circumstance or legal relationship governed by the Patents Act, such as the validity of a particular patent or that a person has not violated a particular patent.[733]

726. Cf. Art. 28(2) of the Swiss Civil Code.
727. Weber, *supra* n. 637, at nn. 345 et seq.
728. Decision of the Swiss Federal Tribunal dated 14 December 1965, published in BGE 91 II 401.
729. (19 December 1986), SR 241, https://www.admin.ch/opc/de/classified-compilation/19860391/ (accessed on 4 December 2018).
730. Decision of the Swiss Federal Tribunal dated 8 July 1997, published in BGE 123 III 354, consideration no. 1.b: 'Mit anderen Worten setzt die Feststellungsklage gemäss Art. 28a Abs. 1 Ziff. 3 ZGB und Art. 9 Abs. 1 lit. c UWG voraus, dass der Kläger ein schutzwürdiges Interesse an der Beseitigung eines fortbestehenden Störungszustandes geltend machen kann.'
731. (25 June 1954), SR 232.14, https://www.admin.ch/opc/en/classified-compilation/19540108/index.html (accessed 4 December 2018).
732. Articles 26 et seq. of the Swiss Patents Act.
733. Article 74 of the Swiss Patents Act.

Both actions, even though specifically foreseen in a federal act, must satisfy the standard interest test as foreseen under Article 88 of the Swiss CCP.[734] This can be explained by the fact that the declaratory actions of the Patents Act seek to address an uncertainty, e.g., is a particular patent void. In contrast, the declaratory actions of the other Federal Acts outlined above seek to address another impediment of the claimant, e.g., threat of debt enforcement or continuing negative impacts of an infringement.

[E] Consequences of Lacking Interest

If a claimant lacks the required legitimate interest, a condition for the admissibility of the claim (*Prozessvoraussetzung*) remains missing.[735] Accordingly, a court will dismiss the claim (without prejudice).[736] The claimant will in such circumstances usually be qualified as the succumbing party and thus be burdened with the costs of the proceedings (including a compensation for the other party's attorneys' fees).[737]

Even though a claimant might be able to demonstrate a sufficient legitimate interest when initiating a declaratory action, such interest may disappear throughout the course of the proceedings. For example, a claimant requesting the declaration of a debt that is not yet due, might lose the legitimate interest in the requested relief because the debt falls due during the proceedings and thus opens up the possibility of a claim for money.[738] The subsequent disappearance of the legitimate interest must lead to a dismissal (without prejudice) of the claim, as the interest – same as all conditions for admissibility of a claim – must exist at the time when judgment is rendered.[739]

Importantly, a court will examine ex officio whether a specific claim fulfils all conditions of admissibility.[740] Thus, a court will verify whether a claimant has a sufficient interest in the requested relief, even if the defendant does not put forth any objections in this regard. Strikingly, even a second instance court can address this question *sua sponte*.[741] Thus, a second instance court could find that a claimant lacks the required interest in the requested relief, although neither the opposing party nor the first instance court have brought up this issue.[742]

734. Decision of the Swiss Federal Tribunal dated 24 January 1990, published in BGE 116 II 196, consideration no. 1.b.
735. Article 59(2)(a) of the Swiss CCP.
736. Article 59(1) of the Swiss CCP
737. Cf. Art. 106(1) of the Swiss CCP.
738. For further examples, cf. Weber, *supra* n. 637, at n. 104.
739. Decision of the Swiss Federal Tribunal dated 4 September 2013, Case no. 4A_256/2013, consideration no. 2.2: 'Par ailleurs, l'intérêt à la constatation doit exister au moment du jugement.' However, the exact form of such decision is controversial, cf. Sievi, *supra* n. 635, at n. 123.
740. Article 60 of the Swiss CCP.
741. Article 310 of the Swiss CCP. Cf. Kurt Blickenstorfer, *Schweizerische Zivilprozessordnung, Kommentar*, at Art. 310 n. 6 (Alexander Brunner, Dominik Gasser & Ivo Schwander eds, 2016); Martin Sterchi, *Berner Kommentar, Schweizerische Zivilprozessordnung*, at Art. 310 n. 4 (Andreas Güngerich ed, 2012).
742. However, it is rather unlikely that a second instance court would do so. While it does have the power to address legal issues *sua sponte*, courts have already declared that it is generally the

IV SCOPE OF DECLARATORY RELIEFS UNDER SWISS LAW

Pursuant to the wording of Article 88 Swiss CCP, the object of a declaratory action consists in the establishment that a right or legal relationship exists (so-called positive declaratory action) or does not exist (so-called negative declaratory action).

The terms 'right' and 'legal relationship' in the sense of Article 88 Swiss CCP must be interpreted widely.[743] 'Rights' covers not objective, but subjective rights, which give a person an individual claim.[744] 'Legal relationships', on the contrary, are legal relations arising out of a concrete set of facts between a multitude of people or between a person and an object.[745]

A declaratory action must thus concern the existence, content or extent of rights and obligations. However, the action must relate to a specific right or legal relationship. General, abstract or hypothetical questions of law may not form the object of a declaratory action.[746] Equally, declaratory actions may not merely concern the (non-) existence of facts, including the question of authenticity of a document.[747] Disputed facts, which might be relevant to a dispute between parties, can form the object of an action for precautionary taking of evidence.[748] Such action enables a party to have evidence taken before initiation of full proceedings. For example, if a seller and a buyer are in dispute about whether the purchased good is fit for purpose, an action for a declaration that the good is (not) fit for purpose will not be admissible, but an action for precautionary taking of evidence (e.g., appointment of an expert to examine and report on the status of the purchased good) could be.

Furthermore, a declaratory action solely concerning a preliminary question (e.g., whether a contracting party had the required mental capacity to enter into the contractual relationship) or single elements of a legal relationship are not admissible.[749] However, an exception is made for the establishment of specific acts' unlawfulness.[750] For example, violation of a politician's personality rights in a newspaper article was held to be best responded to with a declaration of the unlawfulness

appellant's duty to address the flaws of the first instance court judgment, cf. e.g., decision of the Zurich High Court dated 21 May 2014, Case no. LB140028, consideration no. 3.

743. Decision of the Swiss Federal Tribunal dated 26 May 2003, Case no. 4C.7/2003, consideration no. 5: 'Leur objet est habituellement de faire constater, selon le droit fédéral, l'existence ou l'inexistence – actuelle et prétendue – d'un "rapport de droit" (cf. Art. 25 PCF), notion qui doit être interprétée très largement.'
744. Bodmer, *supra* n. 619, at 55 et seq.; Weber, *supra* n. 637, at n. 26 (mentioning the example of whether someone is the rightful owner of an object).
745. Decision of the Swiss Federal Tribunal dated 19 November 1954, published in BGE 80 II 362, consideration no. 3.
746. Decision of the Swiss Federal Tribunal dated 19 July 1996, published in BGE 122 III 279, consideration no. 3.a. Also cf. decision of the Swiss Federal Tribunal dated 14 May 2008, Case no. 4A_530/2007, consideration no. 2.3.
747. Report on the preliminary draft of the Swiss CCP of June 2003, at 44, https://www.bj.admin.ch/dam/data/bj/staat/gesetzgebung/archiv/zivilprozessrecht/vn-ber-d.pdf (accessed on 4 December 2018). Cf. Weber, *supra* n. 637, at Art. 88 nn. 5–6; Meier, *supra* n. 662, at 210.
748. Cf. Art. 158(1)(b) of the Swiss CCP.
749. Weber, *supra* n. 637, at Art. 88 n. 6; Oberhammer, *supra* n. 643, at Art. 88 n. 6.
750. Decision of the Swiss Federal Tribunal dated 23 September 2004, Case no. 5C.167/2003, published in BGE 131 III 26, consideration no. 12.2.2; decision of the Swiss Federal Tribunal

of the relevant statements (in combination with publication of the declaratory judgment), as such relief would be more appropriate for addressing the violation of honour suffered by the politician.[751]

As just explained, a declaratory action does not seek to change a legal relationship – as a claim for payment or performance does –, but to establish the existence or non-existence of a legal relationship.[752] Its purpose is thus to create legal certainty about the current status of rights and legal relationships. Resolving disputes about the existence of rights and legal relationships preventively ensures legal peace and does thus ultimately serve the enforcement of substantive private law.[753]

In addition, certain scholars ascribe a declaratory action a compensatory nature where a claimant seeks the declaration that certain behaviour of the defendant was unlawful. The judicial declaration shall ease the non-material suffering of the claimant.[754] For example, a violation of honour is usually responded to by a declaration of the relevant act's unlawfulness, rather than awarding a certain amount of money as compensation.[755] Such function is further increased if such action is combined with a request for publication of the judgment, as it seeks to liberate the claimant from the negative effects of the defendant's behaviour also on a public level.

A negative declaratory action does, in addition, also serve the anticipated defence against an asserted claim. The debtor is not required to await the initiation of the claim by the creditor, but can start proceedings itself. In this regard, declaratory actions form part of the procedural equality of parties.[756]

V LEGAL MEASURES SIMILAR TO DECLARATORY RELIEFS

There are two instruments in Swiss civil procedural law that potentially carry a declaratory element despite the absence of a declaratory action. On the one hand, a partial claim will lead to a judgment having a factually (although not legally binding) declaratory effect in relation to the full claim. On the other hand, a court has the power to limit the proceedings to specific questions and render an interim judgment on this question. This enables a court to give a preliminary and declaratory ruling on the existence of a right or a legal relationship.

The first instrument is enshrined in Article 86 of the Swiss CCP. A claimant can choose to only file a partial claim, i.e., only sue for part of the asserted claim. This approach is often used to test a claim while keeping the costs of the proceedings limited

dated 20 July 2001, published in BGE 127 III 481, consideration no. 1.b. However, it is unclear whether such exception must also be made for the establishment of specific acts' lawfulness, cf. Sievi, *supra* n. 635, at nn. 36–37.

751. Decision of the Swiss Federal Tribunal dated 23 September 2004, Case no. 5C.167/2003, published in BGE 131 III 26, consideration no. 12.2.2.
752. Cf. Füllemann, *supra* n. 639, at Art. 88 n. 1.
753. Cf. Oberhammer, *supra* n. 643, at Art. 88 n. 7; Weber, *supra* n. 637, at n. 9.
754. Oberhammer, *supra* n. 643, at Art. 88 n. 6.
755. Cf. Decision of the Swiss Federal Tribunal dated 23 September 2004, Case no. 5C.167/2003, published in BGE 131 III 26, consideration no. 12.2.2.
756. Cf. Gerhard Walter & Tanja Domej, *Internationales Zivilprozessrecht der Schweiz*, 552 (2012); Jegher, *supra* n. 706, at 44.

due to the lower amount in dispute.[757] If a claimant is successful with its partial claim, it will then in subsequent, new, separate proceedings sue for the remainder of the asserted claim.

However, while the judgment on the partial claim gives an indication as to the merits of the full claim, it does not contain any binding declaration in this regard. The judgment does only have res judicata effect in relation to the part actually claimed for.[758] In new subsequent proceedings, a claimant will have to resubmit all the evidence on which he has based the partial claim and the court will administer it anew. The court will do so independent from the findings of the court which has previously ruled on the partial claim.

Nonetheless, the judgment on the partial claim, will in the subsequent proceedings - if submitted - usually carry significant weight.[759] In some instances, in particular when no new arguments or facts are put forth in the subsequent proceedings, one could even ascribe a factual declaratory effect to the judgment on the partial claim.

As to the second instrument, pursuant to Articles 125(a) and 237 of the Swiss CCP, a court has the power to limit the proceedings to a specific issue and render an interim judgment (*Zwischenentscheid*) on this issue. A court can order such limitation of the proceedings *sua sponte* or upon an application by a party.[760]

Accordingly, proceedings may be limited to the question of (non-) existence of a right or a legal relationship.[761] An interim judgment on this issue will naturally be declaratory in nature. Hence, any claim for money can be broken up into a first declaratory judgment on the (non-) existence of the debt. However, the interim judgment will only have binding effect on the court that has rendered it; the judgment does not have res judicata effect.[762]

VI RES JUDICATA EFFECT OF A DECLARATORY JUDGMENT

If a court grants a positive declaratory action, the relevant right or legal relationship is established. In turn, if such action is rejected, the court establishes the non-existence of such right or legal relationship. The court's declarations have res judicata effect for the mentioned establishments.[763] Thus, if in a later claim the (non-) existence of the right

757. Bessenich & Bopp, *supra* n. 685, at Art. 86 n. 6. However, a defendant has the possibility to respond with a counterclaim suing for a declaration that there is no claim at all (decision of the Swiss Federal Tribunal dated 13 June 2017, Case no. 4A_576/2016, published in BGE 143 III 506). By doing so, a defendant makes the full alleged claim the object of the proceedings.
758. Bessenich & Bopp, *supra* n. 685, at Art. 86 n. 10; Füllemann, *supra* n. 639, at Art. 86 n. 9.
759. Weber, *supra* n. 637, at Art. 86 n. 14.
760. Article 124(1) of the Swiss CCP.
761. Cf. decision of the Swiss Federal Tribunal dated 6 October 2006, Case no. 4C.197/2006, published in BGE 132 III 785, consideration no. 3.2. Cf also Markus Kriech, *Schweizerische Zivilprozessordnung, Kommentar*, Art. 237 n. 4 (Alexander Brunner, Dominik Gasser & Ivo Schwander eds, 2016).
762. Decision of the Swiss Federal Tribunal dated 3 April 2002, Case no. 4P.282/2001, published in BGE 128 III 191. Also cf. Daniel Staehelin, *Kommentar zur Schweizerischen Zivilprozessordnung*, Art. 237 n. 14 (Thomas Sutter-Somm, Franz Hasenböhler & Christoph Leuenberger eds, 2016).
763. Füllemann, *supra* n. 639, at Art. 88 n. 27; Weber, *supra* n. 637, at n. 126.

or legal relationship becomes an issue again, reference must simply be made to the declaratory judgment. A court is precluded from ruling again on the (non-) existence of this right or legal relationship.

The res judicata effect of a judgment rejecting a negative declaratory action is less clear. Generally, the rejection of declaring the non-existence of a right or legal relationship is considered to establish the existence of such right or legal relationship.[764] In terms of an asserted debt, this means that the existence of the debt is established, but not its amount.[765] However, the last point is disputed among scholars.[766]

In any case, a declaratory judgment cannot serve as basis for enforcement proceedings. Its content is purely declaratory and does not contain any order of performance (*Leistungsbefehl*). Thus, before initiating any enforcement proceedings, a party would have to initiate new court proceedings seeking an order of performance which could then form the basis of enforcement proceedings.[767] However, it is argued by some scholars that a direct connection to a specific payment order could be sufficient to dispense with the lack of an order of performance in the judgment.[768]

764. Cf. decision of the Swiss Federal Tribunal dated 27 February 2009, Case no. 4A_32/2009, consideration no. 1; Weber, *supra* n. 637, at Art. 88 n. 27; Markus, *supra* n. 627, at Art. 88 n. 59.
765. Füllemann, *supra* n. 639, at Art. 88 n. 27; Oberhammer, *supra* n. 643, at Art. 88 n. 30; Weber, *supra* n. 637, at n. 326. The Swiss Federal Tribunal, however, makes an exception to this and also considers the amount to be established if the negative declaratory action took the form of an *Aberkennungsklage* in the sense of Art. 83(2) of the Swiss FDEB, *See* decision of the Swiss Federal Tribunal dated 28 April 1998, published in BGE 124 III 656, consideration no. 5.4. Scholars also argue that the same would have to apply if the negative declaratory action, although not made under Art. 83(2) of the Swiss FDEB, takes direct reference to a specific payment order in pending enforcement proceedings, cf. Tarkan Göksu, *Negative Feststellungsklage: ausgewählte Aspekte und neuere Entwicklung*, Zeitschrift für Zivilprozess- und Zwangsvollstreckungsrecht, at 191 (2009).
766. Cf. Meier, *supra* n. 662, at 214; Sievi, *supra* n. 635, at n. 229.
767. Füllemann, *supra* n. 639, at Art. 88 n. 27; Sievi, *supra* n. 635, at n. 231.
768. Göksu, *supra* n. 765, at 191.

Bibliography

Menno Aden, *Internationale Handelsschiedsgerichtsbarkeit* (2d ed., 2003).

Diana Akikol, D*ie bundesgerichtliche Rechtsprechung zur Schiedsgerichtsbarkeit im Jahr 2010,* 8 Jusletter 1, 23 (August 2011).

Neil Andrews, *English Civil Justice and Remedies* (2007).

Aristotle, *The Nicomachean Ethics of Aristotle Bk V 2.* (Frank. H. Peters transl., 1906).

Dorothea Assmann in: *4 Bernhard Wieczorek and Rolf A. Schütze, Zivilprozessordnung und Nebengesetze, Großkommentar, Commentary on § 256 German CCP* (2013).

Klaus Bacher in: *Volkert Vorwerk and Christian Wolf, Beck'scher Online-Kommentar ZPO, Commentary on § 253 German CCP* (31st ed., 2018).

Klaus Bacher in: *Volkert Vorwerk and Christian Wolf, Beck'scher Online-Kommentar ZPO, Commentary on § 256 German CCP* (31st ed., 2018).

Otto Bähr, *Die Anerkennung als Verpflichtungsgrund* (2nd ed., 1867).

Oskar Ballon, *§§ 228 und 236 ZPO,* JBl 1980 323 et seqq.

Oskar J. Ballon, Bettina Nunner-Krautgasser and Birgit Schneider, *Einführung in das Zivilprozessrecht* (13th ed., 2018).

Zbigniew Banaszczyk, *Rozdział XII. Stosunek cywilnoprawny in System prawa Prywatnego. Prawo cywilne – część ogólna,* t.1. (Marek Safjan ed., 2007).

Ekkehard Becker-Eberhard in: *1 Thomas Rauscher and Wolfgang Krüger, Münchener Kommentar zur Zivilprozessordnung mit Gerichtsverfassungsgesetz und Nebengesetzen, Commentary on § 256 German CCP* (5th ed., 2016).

Józef Bekerman, *Powództwa o ustalenie stosunku prawnego,* 47 Gazeta Sądowa Warszawska 428 (1923).

Bernhard Berger and Franz Kellerhals, *International and Domestic Arbitration in Switzerland* (2d ed., 2010).

Klaus Peter Berger, *Herausforderungen für die (deutsche) Schiedsgerichtsbarkeit,* SchiedsVZ (2009).

Klaus Peter Berger, *International Economic Arbitration* (1993).

Balthasar Bessenich and Lukas Bopp, *Kommentar zur Schweizerischen Zivilprozessordnung* (Thomas Sutter-Somm, Franz Hasenböhler and Christoph Leuenberger eds, 2016).

Nigel Blackaby et al., *Redfern and Hunter on International Arbitration* (5th ed., 2009).

Kurt Blickenstorfer, *Schweizerische Zivilprozessordnung, Kommentar* (Alexander Brunner, Dominik Gasser and Ivo Schwander eds, 2016).

Łukasz Błaszczak, *Znaczenie interesu prawnego w poszukiwaniu ochrony prawnej w procesie cywilnym na przykładzie poszczególnych rodzajów powództw* in *Ius est a iustitia appellatum: księga jubileuszowa dedykowana Profesorowi Tadeuszowi Wiśniewskiemu* (Michał Tomalak ed., 2017).

Bernhard Bodmer, *Die allgemeine Feststellungsklage im schweizerischen Privatrecht* (1984).

Bernhard Bodmer and Jan Bangert, *Basler Kommentar, Bundesgesetz über Schuldbetreibung und Konkurs I* (Adrian Staehelin, Thomas Bauer and Daniel Staehelin eds, 2010).

Peter Böhm, *Die Lehre vom Rechtsschutzbedürfnis*, JBl 1974.

Gary Born, *International Commercial Arbitration* (2d ed., 2014).

Natascha Brandstätter, *Die Verjährung nicht vorhersehbarer Folgeschäden*, RdW 2016.

Natascha Brandstätter, *Die verjährungsrechtliche Relevanz der Unterscheidung zwischen Primär- und Folgeschäden*, ecolex 2015, 448 et seqq.

Christoph Brenn and Petra Leupold, *Feststellungsbegehren versus 'Naturalrestitution'*, EvBl (2012).

Andrew Burrows, *Remedies for Torts and Breaches of Contract* (3rd ed., 2004).

Andrew Burrows, *Remedies for Torts and Breach of Contract* (2009).

Paul Butler, *When Judges Lie (and When They Should)*, 91 Minn. L. Rev. 1785 (2007).

Franz Bydlinski, *Schadensentstehung und Verjährungsbeginn im österreichischen Recht*, in Festschrift für Erich Steffen zum 65. Geburtstag (Erwin Deutsch and Ernst Klingmüller and Hans Josef Kullmann eds., 1995).

Peter Bydlinski, *Haftung für fehlerhafte Anlageberatung – Schaden und Schadenersatz*, ÖBA 2008, 159 et seqq.

John Cartwright, *Contract Law. An Introduction to the English Law of Contract for the Civil Lawyer* (2nd ed., 2013).

Florian Chaudet and Peter Schauffelberger, *Le droit de consultation du registre de poursuites en relation avec l'inscription de poursuites frappés d'opposition non levée; quelques voeux et quelques pistes en faveur du poursuivi concernant l'Art. 8 LP*, 317 (Juan Carlos Landrove ed, *De lege negotiorum, études autour du droit des affaires en l'honneur du professeur François Chaudet*, 2009).

Marcin Chomiuk in: *Kodeks spółek handlowych. Komentarz* 1053 (Zbigniew Jara ed., 2018).

Wayne Covell and Keith Lupton, *Principles of Remedies* (4th ed., 2008).

Bronisław Czech, *Kodeks postępowania cywilnego. Tom I. Komentarz. Art. 1–366* (Kazimierz Piasecki and Andrzej Marciniak eds., 2016).

Felix Dasser, *Feststellungsinteresse in internationalen Verhältnissen*, Jusletter (29 September 2003).

Felix Dasser, *Lugano-Übereinkommen (LugÜ)* (Felix Dasser and Paul Oberhammer eds, 2011).

Heinrich Degenkolb, *Einlassungszwang und Urteilsnorm: Beiträge zur materiellen Theorie der Klagen insbesondere der Anerkennungsklagen* (1877).

Astrid Deixler-Hübner, *§ 236*, in *III/1 Kommentar zu den Zivilprozessgesetzen* (Hans W. Fasching and Andreas Konecny eds. 3rd ed., 2017).

Hans Dolinar, Marianne Roth and Duursma-Kepplinger H, *Zivilprozessrecht* 117 (15th ed., 2017).

Patric Dunand and Maria Kostytska, *Declaratory Relief in International Arbitration*, 29 Journal of International Arbitration 1 (2012).

Ronald Dworkin and Ronald Dworkin, *Taking Rights Seriously* (1987).

Marcin Dziurda, *Wyrok w procesie częściowym a prawomocność materialna*, 23 MoP 1266 (2018).

Tadeusz Ereciński and Karol Weitz, *Sąd arbitrażowy* (2008).

Lutz Englisch in: *Wolfgang Hölters, Aktiengesetz*, Commentary on § 249 (3rd ed., 2017).

André Equey and Reto Vonzun, *Mittel und Wege zur Beseitigung der negativen Auswirkungen des Betreibungsregistereintrags grundloser Betreibungen, unter besonderer Berücksichtigung der Klage auf Aufhebung der Betreibung nach Art. 85 SchKG*, Allgemeine Juristische Praxis, 1337 (2011).

Hans W. Fasching, *Lehrbuch des österreichischen Zivilprozessrechts* (2nd ed., 1990).

Hans W. Fasching, *§ 228*, in *III Kommentar zu den Zivilprozessgesetzen* (Hans W Fasching and Andreas Konecny eds. 2nd ed., 2004).

William L.F. Felstiner, Richard L. Abel and Austin Sarat, *The Emergence and Transformation of Disputes: Naming, Blaming, Claiming* 15 Law & Soc'y Rev. 631 (1980–1981).

Franciszek Ksawery Fierich, *Postępowanie przed sądami okręgowemi in Polska procedura cywilna. Projekty referentów z uzasadnieniem. Komisja Kodyfikacyjna R.P., Sekcja postępowania cywilnego* (1928).

Ulrich Foerste in: *Hans-Joachim Musielak and Wolfgang Voit, Zivilprozessordnung: ZPO mit Gerichtsverfassungsgesetz, Kommentar, Commentary on § 256 ZPO* (15th ed., 2018).

Nicholas H.D. Foster, *Comparative Commercial Law: Rules or Context?* in *Comparative Law. A Handbook* 263 (Esin Örücü and David Nelken eds., 2007).

Ulrike Frauenberger-Pfeiler, *§ 228*, in *III/1 Kommentar zu den Zivilprozessgesetzen* (Hans W Fasching and Andreas Konecny eds. 3rd ed., 2017).

Daniel Füllemann, *Schweizerische Zivilprozessordnung, Kommentar* (Alexander Brunner, Dominik Gasser and Ivo Schwander eds, 2016).

Denis J. Galligan, *Due Process and Fair Procedures. A Study of Administrative Procedures* 73 (1996).

Nima Gassemi-Tabar and David Eckner, *Die Feststellungsklage als zulässiges Mittel zur Klärung der (Nicht)Kündbarkeit eines Gewerberaummietvertrages? Oder: Vom Grundverständnis von Gestaltungsrechten, 14 Neue Zeitschrift für Miet- und Wohnungsrecht* (NZM) (2011).

Andreas Geroldinger, *§ 226*, in *III/1 Kommentar zu den Zivilprozessgesetzen* (Hans W. Fasching and Andreas Konecny eds. 3rd ed., 2017).

Beata Gessel-Kalinowska vel Kalisz, *Mixing Legal Systems in Europe; the Role of Common Law Transplants (Polish Law Example)*, 4 ERPL 789 (2017).

Beata Gessel-Kalinowska vel Kalisz, *Pojęcie interesu prawnego w powództwie o ustalenie a prawo do sądu – wprowadzenie do dyskusji. Analiza badań statystycznych*, 1 PPH 11 (2019).

Daniel Girsberger and Nathalie Voser, *International Arbitration: Comparative and Swiss Perspective* (3rd ed., 2016).

Tarkan Göksu, *Negative Feststellungsklage: ausgewählte Aspekte und neuere Entwicklung*, Zeitschrift für Zivilprozess- und Zwangsvollstreckungsrecht, 191 (2009).

Agnieszka Góra-Błaszczykowska and Bartosz Karolczyk and Kazimierz Lubiński, *Czynności decyzyjne in System Prawa Procesowego Cywilnego. Tom II. Część II. Postępowanie procesowe przed sądem pierwszej instancji* (Tadeusz Ereciński and Tadeusz Wiśniewski eds., 2016).

Reinhard Greger in: *Richard Zöller, Zivilprozessordnung, Commentary on § 265* (32nd ed., 2018).

Paweł Grzegorczyk, *Przedmiotowy zakres prawomocności materialnej wyroku w procesie częściowym* in *Aurea Praxis Aurea Theoria. Księga pamiątkowa ku czci Profesora Tadeusza Erecińskiego* 185 (Jacek Gudowski, Karol Weitz eds., 2011).

Stefan Grzybowski, *Ochrona dóbr osobistych* (1957).

Jacek Gudowski in: *Kodeks postępowania cywilnego. Komentarz. Tom II. Postępowanie rozpoznawcze* 496 (Tadeusz Ereciński ed., 2016).

Ulrich Haas and Piotr Wojtowicz, *Neuerungen bei der Feststellungsklage nach Schweizer Recht*, Zeitschrift für Zivilprozess International, 301 (2014).

Carl Hahn, *Die gesammten Materialien zu den Reichs-Justizgesetzen, Zweiter Band: Die gesammten Materialien zur Civilprozeßordnung und dem Einführungsgesetz zu derselben vom 30. Januar 1877, Zweite Abtheilung* (1881).

Zygmunt Hahn, *Interes prawny w skardze o ustalenie*, 23 PPC 705 (1935).

Peter Hartmann in: *Adolf Baumbach, Wolfgang Lauterbach, Jan Albers and Peter Hartmann, Zivilprozessordnung: ZPO mit FamFG, GVG und anderen Nebengesetzen, Commentary on § 256 ZPO* (76th ed., 2018).

Christian Hausmaninger, *§ 578*, in *IV/2 Kommentar zu den Zivilprozessgesetzen* (Hans W Fasching and Andreas Konecny eds. 3rd ed., 2016).

Christian Hausmaninger, *§ 612*, in *IV/2 Kommentar zu den Zivilprozessgesetzen* (Hans W Fasching and Andreas Konecny eds. 3rd ed., 2016).

Philipp Heck, *Gesetzesauslegung und Interessenjurisprudenz*, in 112 *Archiv für die civilistische Praxis* (AcP) 6 (1914).

Günter Henn, *Schiedsverfahrensrecht: Handbuch für die Praxis* (3d ed., 2000).

Curt Wolfgang Hergenröder in: *11 Franz Jürgen Säcker, Roland Rixecker, Hartmut Oetker and Bettina Limperg, Münchener Kommentar zum Bürgerlichen Gesetzbuch: BGB, Commentary on § 4 KSchG* (7th ed., 2016).

Kurt Herget in: *Richard Zöller, Zivilprozessordnung, Commentary on § 265* (32nd ed., 2018).

Christopher Hodges, *Public and Private Enforcement: The Practical Implications for Policy Architecture* in *The Foundations of European Private Law* 437 (eds. Roger Brownsword et al., 2011).

Jan Hroboni, *Stosunek wzajemny powództwa o ustalenie i powództwa o świadczenie*, 21–22 PPC 642 (1934).

Rainer Hüßtege in: Heinz Thomas and Hans Putzo, *Zivilprozessordnung: ZPO, FamFG Verfahren in Familiensachen*, EGZPO, GVG, EGGVG, EU-Zivilverfahrensrecht, Commentary on § 3 German CCP (39th ed., 2018).

Jerzy Ignatowicz, Krzysztof Stefaniuk and Aleksander Wolter, *Prawo cywilne. Zarys części ogólnej 99* et seq. (1996).

Matthias Jacobs, *Der Gegenstand des Feststellungsverfahrens* (2005).

Sigvard Jarvin, *Non-Pecuniary Remedies: The Practice of Declaratory Relief and Specific Performance in International Commercial Arbitration*, in *Contemporary Issues in International Arbitration and Mediation – The Fordham Papers* 167 (Arthur W. Rovine ed., 2007).

Kai Jaspersen in: *Volkert Vorwerk and Christian Wolf, Beck'scher Online-Kommentar ZPO, Commentary on § 91a* (31st ed., 2018).

Tomasz Jaworski in: *Ustawa o dochodzeniu roszczeń w postępowaniu grupowym. Komentarz* (Tomasz Jaworski and Patrick Radzimierski eds., 2010).

Gion Jegher, *Mit schweizerischer negativer Feststellungsklage ins europäische Forum Running – Gedanken anlässlich BGE 123 III 414*, Zeitschrift für Schweizer Recht, 31 (1999).

Maria Jędrzejewska and Karol Weitz, *Kodeks postępowania cywilnego. Komentarz. Tom II. Postępowanie rozpoznawcze* (Tadeusz Ereciński ed., 2016).

Maria Jędrzejewska and Karol Weitz, *in Kodeks postępowania cywilnego. Komentarz. Tom I. Postępowanie rozpoznawcze* (Tadeusz Ereciński ed., 4th ed., LexisNexis 2012).

Jerzy Jodłowski, in Jerzy Jodłowski et al., *Postępowanie cywilne* 20 (2002).

Jerzy Jodłowski, *Postępowanie cywilne* (Jerzy Jodłowski and Władysław Siedlecki eds., 2016).

K.K. Justizministerium (ed.), I *Materialien zu den neuen österreichischen Civilprocessgesetzen* 279 (1897).

Th. Kayser, *Beiträge zur Feststellungsklage*, AcP 70 (1886).

Markus Kellner, *Der Zwischenantrag auf Feststellung – Ausgewählte Rechtsfragen zu §§ 236, 259 Abs 2 ZPO*, ÖJZ 2015, 250 et seqq.

Heinrich Kiel in: Rudi Müller-Glöge, Ulrich Preis and Ingrid Schmidt, *Erfurter Kommentar zum Arbeitsrecht, § 4 KSchG* (19th ed., 2019).

Franz Klein and Friedrich Engel, Der Zivilprozess Österreichs, in 3 Das Zivilprozessrecht der Kulturstaaten (Adolf Wach and Wilhelm Kisch and Albrecht Mendelssohn Bartholdy and Max Pagenstecher eds., 1927).

Franz Klein, *Zeit- und Geistesströmungen im Prozesse*, in 1 Reden – Vorträge – Aufsätze – Briefe (Josef Friedländer and Ottilie Friedländer eds., 1927).

Franz Klein and Friedrich Engel, Der Zivilprozess Österreichs, in 3 Das Zivilprozessrecht der Kulturstaaten (Adolf Wach and Wilhelm Kisch and Albrecht Mendelssohn Bartholdy and Max Pagenstecher eds., 1927).

Thomas Klicka, *Die Klage auf Feststellung der Haftpflicht bei Anlegerschäden*, ÖJZ 2012, 487 et seqq.

Thomas Klicka, *§ 411*, in *III/2 Kommentar zu den Zivilprozessgesetzen* (Hans W. Fasching and Andreas Konecny eds. 3rd ed., 2017).

Jan Klimkowicz, *Glosa do orzeczenia SN z dnia 13 kwietnia 1965 r, II CR 266/64*, 7–8 OSPIKA, item 166 (1966).

Andrzej Koch, *Charakter sankcji wobec sprzecznych z prawem uchwał spółek kapitałowych*, 2 PPH 4 (2007).

Georg E. Kodek and Peter G. Mayr, *Zivilprozessrecht* (4th ed., 2018).

Tomasz Koncewicz, *Sądowa sprawiedliwość proceduralna w prawie europejskim, XXXV Gdańskie Studia Prawnicze 173* (2016).

Andreas Konecny, *Einleitung*, in *I Kommentar zu den Zivilprozessgesetzen* (Hans W Fasching and Andreas Konency eds. 3rd ed., 2013).

Jan Korzonek, *Powództwo o ustalenie według projektu K.P.C.*, 11 Głos Sądownictwa 635 (1930).

Jan Korzonek and Ignacy Rosenblüth, *Kodeks Zobowiązań. Komentarz t.1* (1934).

Richard Kreindler, Jan Schäfer and Reinmar Wolff, *Schiedsgerichtsbarkeit – Kompendium für die Praxis* (2006).

Markus Kriech, *Schweizerische Zivilprozessordnung, Kommentar* (Alexander Brunner, Dominik Gasser and Ivo Schwander eds, 2016).

Ireneusz Kunicki in *Kodeks postępowania cywilnego. Komentarz* 628 (Agnieszka Góra-Błaszczykowska ed., 2016).

Jens-Peter Lachmann, *Handbuch für die Schiedsgerichtspraxis* (3d ed., 2008).

Ian Langford, *Fair Trial: The History of an Idea*, 8 (1) Journal of Human Rights 37 (2009).

Karl Larenz, *Methodenlehre der Rechtswissenschaft* (6th ed.,1991).

Frederick H. Lawson, *Remedies of English law* (2nd ed., 1980).

Stefan Leimgruber, *Declaratory Relief in International Commercial Arbitration, 32(3) ASA Bulletin* 467 (2014).

Dieter Leipold in: *11 Franz Jürgen Säcker, Roland Rixecker, Hartmut Oetker and Bettina Limperg, Münchener Kommentar zum Bürgerlichen Gesetzbuch: BGB, Commentary on § 1922* (7th ed., 2017).

Julian D.M. Lew, Loukas A. Mistelis and Stefan Kröll, *Comparative International Commercial Arbitration* (2003).

I. D. Lifschitz, *Weitere Bemerkungen zum Konkordat über die Schiedsgerichtsbarkeit*, 73 SJZ 59 (1977).

Florian Linder, *Zur Schadensberechnung und Schadensminderungsobliegenheit bei fehlerhafter Anlageberatung*, ZFR 2006, 104 et seqq.

Roman Longchamps de Bérier, *Polskie Prawo cywilne. Zobowiązania* (1999).

John R. Lucas, *On Justice* (1978).

Raimund Lutz in: *Volkert Vorwerk and Christian Wolf, Beck'scher Online-Kommentar ZPO, Commentary on § 606 German CCP* (31st ed., 2018).

Piotr Machnikowski, *Swoboda umów według art. 353 1 KC, Konstrukcja prawna* 77(2005).

Raimund Madl, *§ 1489*, in ABGB-ON – Kommentar zum Allgemeinen bürgerlichen Gesetzbuch (Andreas Kletečka and Martin Schauer eds., 2010).

Małgorzata Manowska, *Kodeks postępowania cywilnego. Komentarz. Tom I. Art. 1–505[38]* (2015).

Alexander Markus, *Berner Kommentar, Schweizerische Zivilprozessordnung* (Andreas Güngerich ed, 2012).

Elwira Marszałkowska-Krześ, *Kodeks postępowania cywilnego. Komentarz* (Legalis 2018).

Elwira Marszałkowska-Krześ, *Przesłanki materialnoprawne powództwa o ustalenie istnienia bądź nieistnienia uchwały wspólników w spółce z o.o.*, 9 PPH 28 (1998).

Francesca Mazza, *International Chamber of Commerce (ICC)* in *Performance as a Remedy: Non-Monetary Relief in International Arbitration* 141 (Michael E. Schneider and Joachim Knoll eds., ASA Special Series No. 30, 2011).

Isaak Meier, *Schweizerisches Zivilprozessrecht – eine kritische Darstellung aus der Sicht von Praxis und Lehre* (2010).

Wacław Miszewski, *Polski kodeks postępowania cywilnego a procedura cywilna rosyjska*, 11 RPEiS 111 (1931).

Joanna Misztal-Konecka, *Kodeks postępowania cywilnego. Tom I. Komentarz. Art. 1–366* (Kazimierz Piasecki and Andrzej Marciniak eds., 2016).

Joachim Münch in: *3 Wolfgang Krüger and Thomas Rauscher, Münchener Kommentar zur Zivilprozessordnung mit Gerichtsverfassungsgesetz und Nebengesetzen, Commentary on § 1025 German CCP* (5th ed., 2017).

Joachim Münch in: 3 Wolfgang Krüger and Thomas Rauscher, Münchener Kommentar zur Zivilprozessordnung mit Gerichtsverfassungsgesetz und Nebengesetzen, Commentary on § 1046 German CCP (5th ed., 2017).

David R. Muñoz, *The Power of Arbitrators to Make Pro-Futuro Orders*, in *Performance as a Remedy: Non-Monetary Relief in International Arbitration* 87 (Michael E. Schneider and Joachim Knoll eds., ASA Special Series No. 30, 2011).

Hans-Joachim Musielak in: Hans-Joachim Musielak and Wolfgang Voit, Zivilprozessordnung: ZPO mit Gerichtsverfassungsgesetz, Kommentar, Commentary on § 322 German CCP (15th ed., 2018).

Hans-Joachim Musielak and Wolfgang Voit, Zivilprozessordnung: *ZPO mit Gerichtsverfas-sungsgesetz, Kommentar*, ZPO § 1046 nb. 2 (15th ed., 2018).

Patricia Nacimiento, Stefan Michael Kröll and Karl-Heinz Böckstiegel (eds.) *Arbitration in Germany: The Model Law in Practice* (2nd ed., Kluwer 2015).

Leszek Nowak et al., *Czynności konwencjonalne w prawie*, 33(2) Studia Prawnicze (1972).

Paul Oberhammer, *Kurzkommentar ZPO, Schweizerische Zivilprozessordnung* (Paul Oberhammer, Tanja Domej and Ulrich Haas eds, 2013).

Alfred Ohanowicz, *Glosa do uchwały z dnia 17 kwietnia 1970 r., III PZP 34/69*, 10 OSP 419 (1971).

Ofner L, *§ 81 UrhG*, in urheber.recht (G Kucsko and C Handig eds. 2nd ed., 2017).

Georg Petschek, *Der österreichische Zivilprozess* (1963).

Kazimierz Piasecki, *Postępowanie sporne rozpoznawcze* (2004).

Kazimierz Piasecki, *Wyrok pierwszej instancji w procesie cywilnym* (1981).

Jean-François Poudret and Sébastien Besson, *Comparative Law of International Arbitration* (2d ed., 2007).

John Rawls, *A Theory of Justice* (1991).

Walter Rechberger and Daphe –Ariane Simotta, *Zivilprozessrecht* (9th ed., 2017).

Walter H. Rechberger, *Die Ideen Franz Kleins und ihre Bedeutung für die Entwicklung des Zivilprozessrechts in Europa*, 25 RitsLRev 101 et seqq. (2008).

Alan Redfern and Martin Hunter, *Law and Practice of International Commercial Arbitration* (3rd ed., 1999).

Klaus Reichold in: Heinz Thomas and Hans Putzo, *Zivilprozessordnung: ZPO, FamFG Verfahren in Familiensachen, EGZPO, GVG, EGGVG, EU-Zivilverfahrensrecht, Commentary on § 256 German CCP* (39th ed., 2018).

Mateusz Rodzynkiewicz, *Kodeks spółek handlowych. Komentarz* (2018).

Leo Rosenberg, Karl Heinz Schwab and Peter Gottwald, *Zivilprozessrecht* (18th ed., 2018).

Herbert Roth in: 3 Friedrich Stein and Martin Jonas, *Kommentar zur Zivilprozessordnung, Commentary on § 256 German CCP* (23rd ed., 2016).

Tadeusz Rowiński, *Interes prawny w procesie cywilnym i w postępowaniu nieprocesowym* (1971).

Thomas Rüede and Reimer Hadenfeldt, *Schweizerisches Schiedsgerichtsrecht* (2d ed., 1993).

Stefan Rützel, Gerhard Wegen and Stephan Wilske, *Commercial Dispute Resolution in Germany: Litigation Arbitration Mediation* (2005).

Wojciech Sadurski, *Social Justice and Legal Justice*, 3 L. and Phil. (1984).

Ingo Saenger in: Ingo Saenger, *Zivilprozess: ZPO, Commentary on § 256 German CCP*, n. 1 (7th ed., 2017).

Carsten Schäfer in: 4 Wulf Goette, Mathias Habersack and Susanne Kalss, Münchener *Kommentar zum Aktiengesetz, Commentary on § 249* (4th ed., 2016).

Urs Schenker, *Schweizerische Zivilprozessordnung* (Baker and McKenzie ed, 2010).

Peter Schlosser, *Right and Remedy in Common Law Arbitration and in German Arbitration Law*, 4 Journal of International Arbitration (1987).

Michael E. Schneider, *Non-Monetary Relief in International Arbitration: Principles and Arbitration Practice*, in Performance as a Remedy: Non-Monetary Relief in International Arbitration: Asa Special Series 24–25 3 et seqq. (Michael E. Schneider and Joachim Knoll eds., 2011).

Michael E. Schneider, *Non-Monetary Relief in International Arbitration: Principles and Arbitration Practice* in *Performance as a Remedy: Non-Monetary Relief in International Arbitration* 3 (Michael E. Schneider and Joachim Knoll eds., ASA Special Series No. 30, 2011).

Christoph Schreuer, *Non-Pecuniary Remedies in ICSID Arbitration*, 20 Arbitration International 324 (2004).

Rolf A. Schütze, Dieter Tscherning and Walter Wais, *Handbuch des Schiedsverfahres* (2d ed., 1990).

Rolf A. Schütze, Dieter Tscherning and Walter Wais, *Handbuch des Schiedsverfahrens: Praxis der deutschen und internationalen Schiedsgerichtsbarkeit* (2d ed., 1990).

Karl Heinz Schwab and Gerhard Walter, Schiedsgerichtsbarkeit (7th ed., C.H.Beck 2005).

Ivo Schwander and Daniel Füllemann, *Anmerkung zu BGE 136 III 523*, Allgemeine Juristische Praxis, 1243 (2011).

John R. Searle, *The Construction of Social Reality* (1995).

Alexander Sieben, *Feststellungsklagen nach eidgenössischem und kantonalem Recht* (1948).
Władysław Siedlecki, *Fikcyjny process cywilny*, 2 PiP 212 (1955).
Władysław Siedlecki, *Zarys postępowania cywilnego* (1968).
Małgorzata Sieradzka, *Dochodzenie roszczeń w postępowaniu grupowym. Komentarz* (2018).
Herbert A. Simon, *Models of Bounded Rationality* (1982).
Nino Sievi, *Die negativen Feststellungsklagen des schweizerischen Rechts im Anwendungsbereich des Lugano-Übereinkommens* (2017).
Han Sperl, *I/2 Lehrbuch der Bürgerlichen Rechtspflege* (1928).
Karl Spühler and Lucas Tenchio, *Feststellungsklagen gemäss Art. 85a Abs. 1 SchKG nach gültig erhobenem Rechtsvorschlag?*, Allgemeine Juristische Praxis, 1241 (1999).
Marco Stacher, *Das Rechtsschutzinteresse im internationalen Verhältnis*, Allgemeine Juristische Praxis, 1124 (2007).
Marco Stacher, *Rechtsprechung des Bundesgerichts in Schiedssachen (2009 und 2010)*, 1 AJP/JPA 125 (2011).
Adrian Staehelin, Daniel Staehelin and Pascal Grolimund, *Zivilprozessrecht – Unter Einbezug des Anwaltsrechts und des internationalen Zivilprozessrechts* (2013).
Adrian Staehelin, *Basler Kommentar, Bundesgesetz über Schuldbetreibung und Konkurs I* (Adrian Staehelin, Thomas Bauer and Daniel Staehelin eds, 2010).
Daniel Staehelin, *Kommentar zur Schweizerischen Zivilprozessordnung* (Thomas Sutter-Somm, Franz Hasenböhler and Christoph Leuenberger eds, 2016).
Anna Stawarska-Rippel, *Trzy transformacje w procedurze cywilnej w Polsce w XX wieku. Wzorce rozwiązań*, 11 Zeszyty Prawnicze UKSW 353 (2011).
Jerzy Stelmach, Bartosz Brożek and Wojciech Załuski, *Dziesięć wykładów o ekonomii prawa* (2007).
Martin Sterchi, *Berner Kommentar, Schweizerische Zivilprozessordnung* (Andreas Güngerich ed, 2012).
Moriz Sternberg, *Die Feststellungsklage nach der neuen Civilproceßordnung* 6 (1901).
Richard Suskind, *The End of Lawyers? Rethinking the Nature of Legal Services* (2010).
David St.J. Sutton, Judith Gill and Matthew Gearing, *Russell on Arbitration* (24rd ed., 2015).
Alfred Syz, *Aberkennungsklagen und Aberkennungsprozess gemäss Art. 83 Abs. 2 SchKG* (1972).
Adam Szpunar, *Ustalenie odpowiedzialności za szkodę przyszłą*, 5 Palestra 7 (1973).
William Tabb and Elaine Shoben, *Remedies in a Nutshell* (2005).
Przemysław Telenga in *Kodeks postępowania cywilnego. Tom I. Komentarz do art. 1-729* 358 (Andrzej Jakubecki ed., 2017).
John Thibault and Laurens Walker, *Procedural Justice: A Psychological Analysis* (1975).
John Thibaut et al., *Procedural Justice as Fairness*, 26 Stan. L. Rev. (1974).
John Thibaut and Laurens Walker, *A Theory of Procedure*, 66 Calif. L. Rev. (1978).
Christoph Thole, *Aktuelle Entwicklungen bei der negativen Feststellungsklage*, 66 NJW (2013).
Michael J. Tilbury, *Civil Remedies, Vol I Remedies in Particular Contexts* (1990).

Henryk Trammer, *O właściwe miejsce dla 'czystych' norm materialnego prawa cywilno-jurysdykcyjnego (na marginesie prac nad kodyfikacją prawa cywilnego)*, 1–2 Przegląd Notarialny 20 (1949).

Ianika Tzankova and Martin Gramatikov, *A Critical Note on Two EU Principles: A Proceduralist View on the Draft Common Frame of Reference (DCFR)* in *The Foundations of European Private Law* 421 (eds. Roger Brownsword et al., 2011).

Joseph Unger, 2 *System des österreichischen allgemeinen Privatrechts* (1859).

Dominik Vock and Danièle Müller, *SchKG-Klagen nach der Schweizerischen ZPO* (2012).

Oskar Vogel and Karl Spühler, *Grundriss des Zivilprozessrechts und des internationalen Zivilprozessrechts der Schweiz* (2012).

Wolfgang Voit in: Hans-Joachim Musielak and Wolfgang Voit, *Zivilprozessordnung: ZPO mit Gerichtsverfassungsgesetz, Kommentar, Commentary on § 1046 German CCP* (15th ed., 2018).

Rudolf von Ihering, *Geist des römischen Rechts auf den verschiedenen Stufen seiner Entwicklung* (1906).

Rudolf von Ihering, *Scherz und Ernst in der Jurisprudenz* (1884).

Friedrich Carl von Savigny, *5 System des heutigen Römischen Rechts* (1841).

Frederich C. von Savigny, *System des heutigen Römischen Rechts* (8th ed., 1849).

Nathalie Voser, Dorothee Schramm and Florian Haugeneder, *Schiedsverfahren und anwendbares Recht*, in Hellwig Torggler, Florian Mohs, Friederike Schäfer, Venus Valentina Wong (eds), *Handbuch Schiedsgerichtsbarkeit: Deutschland – Österreich – Schweiz* (2nd ed., 2017).

Adolf Wach, *Der Feststellungsanspruch* (1889).

Erich Waclawik, *Die Musterfeststellungsklage*, NJW 2018.

Jeffrey Waincymer, *Procedure and Evidence in International Arbitration* (2012).

Marcin Walasik, *Analogia w prawie procesowym cywilnym* 7.2.1 (LexisNexis 2013).

Gerhard Walter and Tanja Domej, *Internationales Zivilprozessrecht der Schweiz* (2012).

Edward Warzocha, *Ustalenie stosunku prawnego lub prawa w sądowym postępowaniu cywilnym* (1982).

Flavia Weber, *Die Feststellungsklage nach der Schweizerischen Zivilprozessordnung* (2013).

Marc Weber, *Basler Kommentar, ZPO* (Karl Spühler, Luca Tenchio and Dominik Infanger eds, 2017).

Karol Weitz, *Charakter interesu prawnego jako przesłanka powództwa o ustalenie (art.189 k.p.c.)* in *Sine ira et studio, Księga Jubileuszowa dedykowana Sędziemu Jackowi Gudowskiemu* 656 (Tadeusz Ereciński and Paweł Grzegorczyk and Karol Weitz eds., Wolters Kluwer 2016).

Edmund Wengerek, *Powództwo o ustalenie*, 21 RPiE 1 (1959).

Felix Wiget, *Fragen der Verfahrensgestaltung vor Gelegenheitsschiedsgerichten nach zürcherischem Zivilprozessrecht*, in *Festschrift zum 70. Geburtstag von Max Guldener* 370 (Max Kummer and Hans U. Walder eds., 1973).

Włodzimierz Werhanowski, *Znaczenie interesu prawnego w procesie cywilnym* (1908).

Aleksandra Wilczyńska, *Interes prawny i jego granice w postępowaniu cywilnym*, 9–10 Palestra 31 (2010).

Lord Woolf and Jeremy Woolf, *Zamir and Woolf: The Declaratory Judgment* (4th ed., 2011).

Jerzy Zajadło, *Sumienie Sędziego*, 79 (4) Ruch Prawniczy, Ekonomiczny i Socjologiczny 31 (2017).

Rafał Zakrzewski, *Declaratory Relief in Litigation and Arbitration in England and Wales*, 1–2 AER 12 (2017).

Rafał Zakrzewski, *Remedies Reclassified* (2005).

Andrzej Zieliński, *Kodeks postępowania cywilnego. Komentarz* (Andrzej Zieliński and Kinga Flaga-Gieruszyńska eds., 2017).

Andrzej Zieliński, in: *Andrzej Zieliński and Kinga Flaga-Gieruszyńska, Kodeks postępowania cywilnego. Komentarz 384, Commentary on § 189 KPC* (Andrzej Zieliński ed., 2017).

Konrad Zweigert and Hein Kötz, *Introduction to Comparative Law* (2011).

White Book 2018, item 40.20.2; Westlaw UK, Commentary last updated 27 November 2017.

Table of Cases

Austria

Austrian Supreme Court

England

English Courts of Appeal

Nokia Corp v InterDigital Technology Corp (Application to Set Aside) [2006] EWCA Civ 1618 (English Court of Appeal)., 39, 43, 69, 176

Re Trident Fashions plc Re The Insolvency Act 1986 Exeter City Council v Bairstow and others [2006] EWCA Civ 203 (English Court of Appeal)., 39, 60

Point Solutions Ltd v Focus Business Solutions Ltd [2007] EWCA Civ 14 (English Court of Appeal)., 39

The Office of Fair Trading v Foxtons Ltd [2009] EWCA Civ 288 ((English Supreme Court of Judicature Court of Appeal)., 64

Rolls-Royce Plc v Unite the Union [2010] 1 WLR 318 (English Court of Appeal)., 40, 42, 48, 52, 65

Milebush Properties Ltd v Tameside MBC [2011] EWCA Civ 270 (English Court of Appeal)., 39, 64, 69

Football Association Premier League Ltd v QC Leisure [2012] EWCA Civ 1708 (English Court of Appeal)., 39

Howden North America Inc & Anor v ACE European Group Ltd & Ors., [2012] EWCA Civ 1624 (English Court of Appeal)., 58, 60

House of Lords

Russian Commercial and Industrial Bank v British Bank for Foreign Trade Ltd. [1921] 2 A.C. 438 (House of Lords), 41

Vine v National Dock Labour Board [1957] A.C. 488 (House of Lords), 41

In Gouriet's case [1978] AC 435, 501 (House of Lords), 64

Meadows Indemnity Co Ltd v Insurance Corporation of Ireland Pld and the International Commercial Bank Plc [1989] 2 Lloyd's Rept 298 (English Supreme Court of Judicature Court of Appeal)., 64

In re F [1990] 2 AC 1 (House of Lords), 39, 40, 54

Chartbrook Limited v Persimmon Homes Limited [2009] UKHL 38 (House of Lords), 85

Toropdar v D, [2009] EWHC 567 (QB); [2010] Lloyd's Rep. I.R. 358 (House of Lords), 39

English High Courts

Lewis v Green [1905] 2 Ch. 340, 61, 62

Patten v Burke Publishing Co Ltd [1991] 1 WLR 541 (Ch), 47, 50, 60, 69

Midland Land Reclamation Ltd, Leicestershire CC v Warren Energy Ltd [1997] ABC.L.R. 01/20 (English High Court), 176

Financial Services Authority v Rourke [2002] C.P. Rep.14 (English High Court), 40, 43, 47, 51, 54, 66, 68

Judgement of 28 February 2005 *Toneylogo Limited v Totem Communications Limited, British Telecommunications Group Plc*, unreported, Westlaw UK, (2005) (English High Court), 40

JP Morgan Europe Ltd v Primacom Management GmbH [2005] EWHC 2426 (Comm) (English High Court), 51

Point Solutions Ltd v Focus Business Solutions Ltd [2005] EWHC 3096 (English High Court), 56

English Family Courts

English Commercial Courts

Chancery Division

EU

European Court of Human Rights

Germany

German Federal Labour Court

German Federal Supreme Court

German Higher Regional Court of Appeal

German District Courts

German Higher Regional Courts

Supreme Court of the German Reich

RG Judgement of 27 September 1883, case no. IV 229/83, RGZ 10, 368 (Supreme Court of the German Reich), 17
RG Judgement of 18 March 1898 II 358/97, RGZ 41, 369 (Supreme Court of the German Reich), 229
RG Judgement of 02 December 1918 V 282/18, RGZ 94, 227 (Supreme Court of the German Reich), 231
RG Judgement of 14 October 1920 VI 315/20, RGZ 100, 123 (Supreme Court of the German Reich), 230
RG Judgement of 27 February 1934 II 276/33, RGZ 144, 54 (Supreme Court of the German Reich), 237, 238
RG Judgement of 14 May 1935 III 301/34, RGZ 148, 29 (Supreme Court of the German Reich), 242

Poland

Polish Constitutional Tribunal

Judgement of 26 February 2008, SK 89/06, Dz.U. 2008/39, item 234, 20 (2008) (Polish Constitutional Tribunal), 141
Judgement of 26 February 2008, SK 89/06, OTK ZU 2008/1A/7 (2008) (Polish Constitutional Tribunal), 174
Judgement of 29 April 2008, SK 11/07, OTK ZU 47/3/A/2008 (2008) (Polish Constitutional Tribunal), 174
Judgement of 1 July 2008, SK 40/07, OTK ZU 101/6/A/2008 (2008) (Polish Constitutional Tribunal), 174
Judgement of 21 July 2009, K7/09, OTK ZU 2009/7A/113, 15 (2009) (Polish Constitutional Tribunal), 139, 141
Judgement of 7 September 2014, P 4/04, Dz.U. 2004/204 item 2091 (2004) (Polish Constitutional Tribunal), 140, 141, 144

Polish Supreme Court

Judgement of 15 May 1937, III C 781/35 (Polish Supreme Court), 278
Judgement of 2 December 1937, C I 3290/36, Official Compilation 1938, item 525 (Polish Supreme Court), 258
Judgement of 14 January 1938, C II 1716/37, Official Compilation 1938, item 470 (Polish Supreme Court), 258
Judgement of 29 April 1949, Wa C 12/49, 2 Nowe Prawo (1946) (Polish Supreme Court), 258
Judgement of 17 April 1951, C 530/50, 1 OSN, item 39 (1952) (Polish Supreme Court), 273
Judgement of 22 May 1953, I C 26/53, 12 PiP 905 (1953) (Polish Supreme Court), 273
Judgement of 11 September 1953, I C 581/53, 3 OSNCK 3, item 65 (1954) (Polish Supreme Court), 268, 273
Judgement of 19 October 1959, 4 CR 537/58 (Polish Supreme Court), 267

Polish Appellate Courts

Polish District Courts

Switzerland

Swiss Federal Tribunal

Swiss Cantonal Courts

Arbitration Courts

ICC

ICDS

VIAC

Other/Ad hoc

Table of Legislation and Statutes

Austria

English

Germany

Poland

Polish Code of Civil Procedure dated 29 November 1930 (the 'Polish FCCP'), 258
Polish Commercial Companies Code (the 'CCC') dated 15 September 2000, 281w
The Act – Code of Civil Procedure dated 17 November 1964, Journal of Laws of the Republic of Poland no. 43, item 296, with subsequent amendments, 259
The Act on Pursuing Claims in Collective Proceedings dated 17 December 2009 (the 'Act on Collective Proceedings'), 280

Romania

Romanian Code of Civil Procedure, 131

Singapore

Singapore International Arbitration Act s. 12(5) (2012), 5, 75

Switzerland

Swiss Civil Code, 10 December 1907, SR 210, https://www.admin. ch/opc/en/classified-compilation/19070042/index.html (accessed 4 Dec. 2018)., 286
Federal Act on Debt Enforcement and Bankruptcy, 30 March 1911, SR 281.1, https://www.admin. ch/opc/en/classified-compilation/19110009/index.html (accessed 4 Dec. 2018)., 286
Federal Act on Patents for Inventions, 25 June 1954, SR 232.14, https://www.admin. ch/opc/en/classified-compilation/19540108/index.html (accessed 4 Dec. 2018)., 301
Federal Act on Unfair Competition, 19 December 1986, SR 241, https://www.admin. ch/opc/de/classified-compilation/19860391/ (accessed on 4 Dec. 2018)., 301
Federal Code of Civil Procedure, 19 December 2008, SR 272, https://www.admin. ch/opc/en/classified-compilation/20061121/index.html (accessed 4 Dec. 2018)., 14, 287
1913 Zurich Code of Civil Procedure.
1976 Zurich Code of Civil Procedure, https://www.zh.ch/internet/de/rechtliche_grundlagen/gesetze/erlass.html?Open&Ordnr=271,13.06.1976,059 (accessed 4 Dec. 2018), 286

Turkey

Turkish Code of Civil Procedure (Hukuk Muhakemeleri Kanunu) Act No. 6100 dated 12.01.2011, 92

USA

28 U.S. Code Chapter 151 – Declaratory Judgements, https://www.gpo.gov/fdsys/pkg/USCODE-2009-title28/pdf/USCODE-2009-title28-partVI-chap151-sec2201.pdf (accessed 31 Jan. 2019, 2)

International Instruments

Legal Principles Developed by the Austrian Supreme Court

Index

1. Moshe Hirsch, *The Arbitration Mechanism of the International Center for the Settlement of Investment Disputes*, 1993 (ISBN 07-923-1993-1).
2. Aida B. Avanessian, *Iran-United States Claims Tribunal in Action*, 1993 (ISBN 18-533-3902-4).
3. Isaak I. Dore, *The UNCITRAL Framework for Arbitration in Contemporary Perspective*, 1993 (ISBN 18-533-3573-8).
4. Vesna Lazić, *Insolvency Proceedings and Commercial Arbitration*, 1998 (ISBN 90-411-1115-8).
5. Joachim Frick, *Arbitration in Complex International Contracts*, 2001 (ISBN 90-411-1662-1).
6. Katherine Lynch, *The Forces of Economic Globalization: Challenges to the Regime of International Commercial Arbitration*, 2003 (ISBN 90-411-1994-9).
7. Christoph Liebscher, *The Healthy Award: Challenge in International Commercial Arbitration*, 2003 (ISBN 90-411-2011-4).
8. Hamid G. Gharavi, *The International Effectiveness of the Annulment of an Arbitral Award*, 2003 (ISBN 90-411-1717-2).
9. Abdulhay Sayed, *Corruption in International Trade and Commercial Arbitration*, 2004 (ISBN 90-411-2236-2).
10. Gabrielle Kaufmann-Kohler & Thomas Schultz, *Online Dispute Resolution: Challenges for Contemporary Justice*, 2004 (ISBN 90-411-2318-0).
11. Christopher R. Drahozal & Richard W. Naimark (eds), *Towards a Science of International Arbitration: Collected Empirical Research*, 2005 (ISBN 90-411-2322-9).
12. Ali Yeşilirmak, *Provisional Measures in International Commercial Arbitration*, 2005 (ISBN 90-411-2353-9).
13. Christian Bühring-Uhle, *Arbitration and Mediation in International Business*, second revised edition, 2006 (ISBN 978-9-041-12256-8).
14. Bernard Hanotiau, *Complex Arbitrations: Multiparty, Multicontract, Multiissue and Class Actions*, 2006 (ISBN 978-9-041-12442-5).
15. Loukas A. Mistelis & Julian D.M. Lew (eds), *Pervasive Problems in International Arbitration*, 2006 (ISBN 978-9-041-12450-0).
16. Julian D.M. Lew & Loukas A. Mistelis (eds), *Arbitration Insights – Twenty Years of the Annual Lecture of the School of International Arbitration, Sponsored by Freshfields Bruckhaus Deringer*, 2006 (ISBN 978-9-041-12606-1).
17. Mark Kantor, *Valuation for Arbitration: Compensation Standards, Valuation Methods and Expert Evidence*, 2008 (ISBN 978-9-041-12735-8).
18. Christoph Brunner, *Force Majeure and Hardship under General Contract Principles: Exemption for Non-Performance in International Arbitration*, 2009 (ISBN 978-90-411-2792-1).

19. Loukas A. Mistelis & Stavros L. Brekoulakis (eds), *Arbitrability: International & Comparative Perspectives,* 2009 (ISBN 978-90-411-2730-3).
20. Sam Luttrell, *Bias Challenges in International Commercial Arbitration: The Need for a 'Real Danger' Test,* 2009 (ISBN 978-90-411-3191-1).
21. Monique Sasson, *Substantive Law in Investment Treaty Arbitration: The Unsettled Relationship Between International Law and Municipal Law,* Second Edition, 2017 (ISBN 978-90-411-6103-1).
22. Ileana M. Smeureanu, *Confidentiality in International Commercial Arbitration,* 2011 (ISBN 978-90-411-3226-0).
23. Won Kidane, *China-Africa Dispute Settlement: The Law, Economics and Culture of Arbitration,* 2011 (ISBN 978-90-411-3674-9).
24. Karel Daele, *Challenge and Disqualification of Arbitrators in International Arbitration,* 2012 (ISBN 978-90-411-3799-9).
25. Crina Baltag, *The Energy Charter Treaty: The Notion of Investor,* 2012 (ISBN 978-90-411-3428-8).
26. Alexandra Diehl, *The Core Standard of International Investment Protection: Fair and Equitable Treatment,* 2012 (ISBN 978-90-411-3869-9).
27. Manuel Indlekofer, *International Arbitration and the Permanent Court of Arbitration,* 2013 (ISBN 978-90-411-4766-0).
28. Günther J. Horvath & Stephan Wilske (eds), *Guerrilla Tactics in International Arbitration,* 2013 (ISBN 978-90-411-4002-9).
29. Albert Badia, *Piercing the Veil of State Enterprises in International Arbitration,* 2014 (ISBN 978-90-411-5162-9).
30. Nadja Erk, *Parallel Proceedings in International Arbitration: A Comparative European Perspective,* 2014 (ISBN 978-90-411-5264-0).
31. Simon Vorburger, *International Arbitration and Cross-Border Insolvency: Comparative Perspectives,* 2014 (ISBN 978-90-411-5419-4).
32. Ahmad Ali Ghouri, *Interaction and Conflict of Treaties in Investment Arbitration,* 2015 (ISBN 978-90-411-5417-0).
33. Reto Marghitola, *Document Production in International Arbitration,* 2015 (ISBN 978-90-411-5159-9).
34. Alfonso Gómez-Acebo, *Party-Appointed Arbitrators in International Commercial Arbitration,* 2016 (ISBN 978-90-411-6671-5).
35. Jonas von Goeler, *Third-Party Funding in International Arbitration and Its Impact on Procedure,* 2016 (ISBN 978-90-411-5015-8).
36. Dean Lewis, *The Interpretation and Uniformity of the UNCITRAL Model Law on International Commercial Arbitration: Focusing on Australia, Hong Kong and Singapore,* 2016 (ISBN 978-90-411-6700-2).
37. Stavros Brekoulakis, Julian D.M. Lew & Loukas Mistelis (eds), *The Evolution and Future of International Arbitration,* 2016 (ISBN 978-90-411-7004-0).
38. Rémy Gerbay, *The Functions of Arbitral Institutions,* 2016 (ISBN 978-90-411-6217-5).

39. Maximilian Clasmeier, *Arbitral Awards as Investments: Treaty Interpretation and the Dynamics of International Investment Law*, 2017 (ISBN 978-90-411-8357-6).
40. Tony Cole (ed.), *The Roles of Psychology in International Arbitration*, 2017 (ISBN 978-90-411-5921-2).
41. Pietro Ferrario, *The Adaptation of Long-Term Gas Sale Agreements by Arbitrators*, 2017 (ISBN 978-90-411-8232-6).
42. Jacob B. van de Velden, *Finality in Litigation: The Law and Practice of Preclusion – Res Judicata (Merger and Estoppel), Abuse of Process and Recognition of Foreign Judgments*, 2017 (ISBN 978-90-411-8342-2).
43. Dolores Bentolila, *Arbitrators as Lawmakers*, 2017 (ISBN 978-90-411-8354-5).
44. Giacomo Marchisio, *The Notion of Award in International Commercial Arbitration: A Comparative Analysis of French Law, English Law, and the UNCITRAL Model Law*, 2017 (ISBN 978-90-411-8391-0).
45. Csaba Kovács, *Attribution in International Investment Law*, 2018 (ISBN 978-90-411-9675-0).
46. Mary Mitsi, *The Decision-Making Process of Investor-State Arbitration Tribunals*, 2019 (ISBN 978-90-411-9600-2).
47. Ahmet Cemil Yıldırım, *Interpretation of Contracts in Comparative and Uniform Law*, 2019 (ISBN 978-94-035-1130-6).
48. Beata Gessel-Kalinowska vel Kalisz, *The Legal, Real and Converged Interest in Declaratory Relief*, 2019 (ISBN 978-94-035-1244-0).

www.ingramcontent.com/pod-product-compliance
Lightning Source LLC
LaVergne TN
LVHW020644300926
849161LV00004B/812
* 9 7 8 9 4 0 3 5 1 2 4 4 0 *